Two postcard views of Kovel. Left, *A Krambude (old style restaurant),"* c.1910. Right, *"Kowel on the Turiya,"* 1917. Public domain, courtesy of Ellen Stepak. During the first World War, German soldiers stationed here sent home postcards like these. Not in original book.

Kowel; Testimony and Memorial Book of Our Destroyed Community (Kovel, Ukraine)

Translation of
Kowel; sefer edut ve-zikaron le-kehilatenu she-ala aleha ha-koret

Original Book Edited by:
Eliezer Leoni-Zopperfin

Originally published in Tel Aviv, 1957

A Publication of JewishGen, INC
Edmond J. Safra Plaza, 36 Battery Place, New York, NY 10280
646.494.5972 | info@JewishGen.org | www.jewishgen.org

©JewishGen, Inc. 2021. All Rights Reserved
An affiliate of New York's Museum of Jewish Heritage – A Living Memorial to the Holocaust

Kowel; Testimony and Memorial Book of Our Destroyed Community (Kovel, Ukraine)
Translation of *Kowel; sefer edut ve-zikaron le-kehilatenu she-ala aleha ha-koret*

Copyright © 2021 by JewishGen, INC All rights reserved.
First Printing: December 2021, Tevet 5782

Editor of Original Yizkor Book: Eliezer Leoni-Zopperfin
Project Coordinator: Bruce Drake
Layout and Name Indexing: Jonathan Wind
Reproduction of Photographs: Sondra Ettlinger
Cover Design: Nina Schwartz, Impulse Graphics

This book may not be reproduced, in whole or in part, including illustrations in any form (beyond that copying permitted by Sections 107 and 108 of the U.S. Copyright Law and except by reviewers for public press), without written permission from the publisher.

JewishGen INC. is not responsible for inaccuracies or omissions in the original work and makes no representations regarding the accuracy of this translation. Digital images of the original book's contents can be seen online at the New York Public Library website or the Yiddish Book Center website.

Printed in the United States of America by Lightning Source, Inc.

Library of Congress Control Number (LCCN): 2021950883

ISBN: 978-1-954176-27-0 (hard cover: 376 pages, alk. paper)

About JewishGen.org

JewishGen, an affiliate of the Museum of Jewish Heritage - A Living Memorial to the Holocaust, serves as the global home for Jewish genealogy.

Featuring unparalleled access to 30+ million records, it offers unique search tools, along with opportunities for researchers to connect with others who share similar interests. Award winning resources such as the Family Finder, Discussion Groups, and ViewMate, are relied upon by thousands each day.

In addition, JewishGen's extensive informational, educational and historical offerings, such as the Jewish Communities Database, Yizkor Book translations, InfoFiles, Family Tree of the Jewish People, and KehilaLinks, provide critical insights, first-hand accounts, and context about Jewish communal and familial life throughout the world.

Offered as a free resource, JewishGen.org has facilitated thousands of family connections and success stories, and is currently engaged in an intensive expansion effort that will bring many more records, tools, and resources to its collections.

Please visit https://www.jewishgen.org/ to learn more.

Executive Director: Avraham Groll

About the JewishGen Yizkor Book Project

Yizkor Books (Memorial Books) were traditionally written to memorialize the names of departed family and martyrs during holiday services in the synagogue (a practice that still exists in many synagogues today).

Over the centuries, as a result of countless persecutions and horrific atrocities committed against the Jews, Yizkor Books (Sefer Zikaron in Hebrew) were expanded to include more historical information, such as biographical sketches of famous personalities and descriptions of daily town life.

Following the Holocaust, the idea of remembrance and learning took on an urgent and crucial importance. Survivors of the Holocaust sought out other surviving residents of their former towns to memorialize and document the names and way of life of those who were ruthlessly murdered by the Nazis. These remembrances were documented in Yizkor Books, hundreds of which were published in the first decades after the Holocaust.

Most of these books were published privately, or through landsmanshaftn (social organizations comprised of members originating from the same European town or region) that still existed, and were often distributed free of charge. Sadly, the languages used to document these crucial histories and links to our past, Yiddish and Hebrew, are no longer commonly understood by a significant percentage of Jews today. As a result, JewishGen has undertaken the sacred responsibility of translating these books into English so that the culture and way of life of these communities will be preserved and transmitted to future generations.

In 1986, a group of farsighted JewishGenners started a project to pool their efforts together in groups based upon their ancestors from each town and donate money to get the Yizkor books of their ancestral towns translated into English. As the translated material became available, it was made accessible for free at www.JewishGen.org/Yizkor. Hardcover copies can be purchased by visiting www.JewishGen.org/Press (see below).

It is our hope that the translation of these books into English (and other languages) will assist the countless Jewish family researchers who are so desperately seeking to forge a connection with their heritage.

Director of JewishGen Yizkor Book Project: Lance Ackerfeld

About the JewishGen Press

JewishGen Press (formerly the Yizkor Books-in-Print Project) is the publishing division of JewishGen.org, and provides a venue for the publication of non-fiction books pertaining to Jewish genealogy, history, culture, and heritage.

In addition to the Yizkor Book category, publications in the Other Non-Fiction category include Shoah memoirs and research, genealogical research, collections of genealogical and historical materials, biographies, diaries and letters, studies of Jewish experience and cultural life in the past, academic theses, and other books of interest to the Jewish community.

Please visit https://www.jewishgen.org/press/ to learn more.

Director of JewishGen Press: Joel Alpert
Managing Editor - Jessica Feinstein
Publications Manager - Susan Rosin

Notes to the Reader

The images in the original book were reproduced from photographs from the time of the first edition. These reproductions were already of poor quality, being pre-war and at least 30 or more years old. As a result the images in the book are not very good and the best achievable.

A reader can view the original scans of the book on the websites listed below.

The original book can be seen online at the New York Public Library site:

https://digitalcollections.nypl.org/items/4617c3d0-7a72-0133-3b5f-00505686d14e

or

at the Yiddish Book Center web site:

https://www.yiddishbookcenter.org/collections/yizkor-books/yzk-nybc314210/leoni-tsuperfain-eli-ezer-kovel

To obtain a list of all Shoah victims from Kovel, Ukraine, the reader should access the Yad Vashem web site listed below; one can also search for specific family names using family name option. These lists are continually updated by Yad Vashem, so it is worthwhile to periodically search these lists.

There is more valuable information (including the Pages of Testimony, etc.) available on this website: http://yvng.yadvashem.org

A list of all books available from JewishGen Press along with prices is available at: https://www.jewishgen.org/press/

Acknowledgements

I'd like to thank JewishGen's Lance Ackerfeld who helped get me started in this project and my translators: Amy Samin who did a lot of the early work, and especially Ala Gamulka who volunteered to help finish it to honor her husband's Kovel roots.

I'd also like to dedicate the book to my Kimmel family ancestors who made their home in Kovel before their descendants emigrated to New York City.

Bruce Drake

Credits for Book Cover

Front cover:
The canal, 1916, postcard. Public domain, courtesy of Ellen Stepak. During the first World War, German soldiers stationed in Kovel sent home postcards like this one.

Golda Zwick, c.1935. Courtesy of Chaim Zwick. From a larger family portrait.

Sara and Abraham Wolk in front of their house, c.1935. Courtesy of Silvia Wolk.

Back cover:
Top: *Chaim Dov Fine (Fajntich), left, and an unknown associate on Warszawska Street, October 20, 1934.* Courtesy of Phyllis Fien.

Bttom: *18-year-old Shlomo Zwick (standing, center left) with Zionist pioneer training group at a building project in Kovel, c.1925.* Courtesy of Haim Zwick.

GeoPolitical Information

Kovel, Ukraine is located at 51°13' N 24°43' E 259 miles WNW of Kyyiv

	Town	District	Province	Country
Before WWI (c. 1900):	Kovel	Kovel	Volhynia	Russian Empire
Between the wars (c. 1930):	Kowel	Kowel	Wołyń	Poland
After WWII (c. 1950):	Kovel'			Soviet Union
Today (c. 2000):	Kovel'			Ukraine

Alternate Names for the Town:

Kovel [Ukr, Rus, Yid], Kowel [Pol], Kovla, Kovle

Nearby Jewish Communities:

Turiysk 11 miles SW
Milyanovichi 12 miles WSW
Nesukhoyezhe 12 miles NNE
Ozeryany 14 miles SSE
Cheremoshno 15 miles ENE
Kupychiv 15 miles S
Holoby 16 miles SE
Dolsk 16 miles WSW
Lukov 17 miles W
Melnytsya 17 miles ESE
Povorsk 18 miles E
Datyn' 21 miles N
Hulivka 22 miles E
Stobykhva 24 miles ENE
Kiselin 25 miles S
Ozyutichi 25 miles S
Troyanivka 26 miles ENE
Dubechne 28 miles NW
Kashivka 28 miles E
Hradysk 29 miles ENE
Sokol 29 miles ESE
Lyuboml 30 miles W
Volodymyr Volynskyy 30 miles SSW

Jewish Population: 8,521 in 1900

Map of Ukraine with **Kovel** indicated

TABLE OF CONTENTS

Article	Author	Page
The Holy and the Pure: God Will Avenge Their Blood	Devorah GOLDHABER	3
The People of the Book	Zvi RESNICK	4
Testimony for the Generations	Eliezer LEONI	5

The Early Days of the City - Its Character and Essence

Article	Author	Page
A History of the Jews of Kovel	Dr. Rephael MAHLER	8
In the Shadow of the City's Early Days	Eliezer LEONI	18
The Character of Kovel	Yaacov TEITELKAR	22
About Kovel and Its Jews	L. HAZAN	24
The Inhabitants of Kovel	Baruch BORK	26

Memories, Folklore and Way of Life

Article	Author	Page
Sketches of Sights and Characters	Yosef ARICHA	29
In the Cycles of the City	Dr. Reuven BEN-SHEM	39
About Kovel, City of My Birth	Rabbi Dr. Michael GREIBER	46
Kovel	Moshe FISHMAN	54
Memories of a Hebrew Teacher in Kovel	Yaacov KOBRINSKI	56
These I Will Remember…	Itzhak MARGALIT	58
In Memory of Our City, Kovel	Hertzl GOLDBERG	61
From the Recent and Distant Past	Moshe BATAR	62
The Kovel Forest	Yaacov TEITELKAR	64
Kovel during the First World War	Baruch BARROK	66
Memories of the Bund in Our City	Yehuda MILLER	71
Folklore		75

Education, Literature and Theater

Article	Author	Page
From the Poorly Educated to the Hebrew Gymnasia	Eliezer LEONI	82
Talmud-Torah	Yaakov TEITLEKER	101
Jewish Educational Institutions	Dr. Mordechai LEIBERSON	104
Founding of the Primary Schools and the Hebrew Gymnasia	A.M. WEISBROT	107
Herzliah School and Tarbut Gymnasia	Tzvi TANNENBAUM	109

About the Kindergartens of Kovel	Chaya HOTMAN (BECKER)	111
The Hebrew Kindergarten of Kovel	Hava SEHR-WERBA	112
The Jewish-Polish Gymnasia	Dr. Yaacov HASIS	113
The Poet Kalman Liss	L. ELITZAKI	115
Kalman Ben-Zion Liss	Esther LISS-CHAIM	119
Kovl (Kovel) (poem)	Kalman LISS	120
Yona Rosenfeld	Yohanan TWERSKI	122
Yosef Avrekh	Yaacov TEITELKAR	128
From the Writings of Yosef Avrekh		131
Kalman Gutenboim, z"l	Yitzhak OGEN	132
Prominence	Yosef AVREKH	134
In Memory of Yosef Borak, Z"L	Yaacov KOBRINSKY	136
About the Kovel Voice and Its Editor	S. BAMA	138
The Art of Theater in Our City	Yaacov TEITELKAR	139
The Mission of the Habimah Studio in Kovel and its Goal	S. KALONIMUS	145

Torah and Hasidism

Images of Torah Scholars	Yekhezkel GOLDBERG	148
The Center for Torah Study Named for Shlomo Projenski, z"l	Rabbi Shmuel-Yosef WERBA	152
The Great Synagogue, Its Cantors and Poets	Yitzhak WALDMAN	154
The Elder of Neskhiz and His Descendants	Eliezer LEONI	156

The Zionist Movement and Zionist Youth Movements

Dawn of the Zionist Movement in Town	Eliezer LEONI	161
Zionist Activity Before the Balfour Declaration	Avraham–Meir WEISBROT	166
The Poaley Zion Movement in Kovel	Aharon WERBA	172
From the Dawn of the Hechalutz in Kovel	Shlomo HERI, Moshe WEISBROT & Shamai FRANKPOVITCH	175
The Halutz in Kovel	Aharon WERBA	176
The First Training Division in Kovel	Yitzhak MARGALIT	179
About The Halutz During Its Low Point	David PERLMUTTER	181
The Scouts Organization in Kovel	Eliezer (Lusia) HODOROV	182
History Of The Scouts Movement In Kovel	Eliyahu MENDEL	185
Hashomer Hatzair	Aharon LEVY, Mordechai BLORIE	187
Some Thoughts on the Hashomer Hatzair Club	Mordechai MELAMED	192
From the Seniors Group to the Hashomer Hatzair Club	David PERLMUTTER	194
Hachalutz Hatzair	Aryeh RABINER	196

Institutions, Movements and Organizations

Municipal Institutions	A.M. WEISBROT	203
On the Taz Institution in Kovel	Sonia MARGALIT	204
The Orphanage	Yaacov TEITELKAR	207
The Ort School	Baruch BORK	212
Medical Institutions and the Physicians of Kovel	Dr. Mordechai LEIBERSON	213
The Founding of Bikur Cholim and the New Hospital	Eliezer LEONI	215
The Lives of Kovel's Laborers	Mordechai HINIZON	216
The Clubhouse Named For Y.L. Peretz	A. DOARI (POTCHTER)	217
Righteous Lodging	Yaacov TEITELKAR	218
Institutions, Groups and Gathering Places	Meir ROSENBLATT	220
The Orphanage From Within	M. OLITZKI	224
The Founding of the ORT School and Its Development	Avraham GALAZ	226
The Carpenters Association	Hertz LEVIN	227
The Home for the Aged in Kovel	Meir ROSENBLATT	229

On the Eve of the Holocaust

A Sketch of the City of Kovel	Yehoshua (Shaike) GOLDSTEIN	232
The Last Meeting	Baruch AVIVI	232
Kovel – My Home	Meir BEN-MICHAEL	233
My Trip to Kovel in the Year 1939	Dr. Y. GLICKSMAN	236
"Anusim" on the Eve of the Holocaust	Yaacov KOBRINSKI	238
Jewish Life in Kovel Under The Soviet Rule	Yehoshua FRANKFORT	239
Under Soviet rule, in captivity and return to Kovel	Monia GALPERIN	243
The Refugees' Kitchen	Zalman PORAN (PROSSMAN)	246
Kindergartens in Kovel under the Soviet Regime	Freida ROSENBLATT-BUCHWALD	247
The Crumbling of the Economic and Cultural Systems	Leuba GALMAN-GOLDBERG	250

The Destruction of Kovel

Cry For Mourning	Rabbi Yehuda, son of Kalonymus	252
Woe for this Beauty that is Rotting in the Earth	Eliezer LEONO-TZUFRIFIN	252
Thus the City was Destroyed	Ben–Zion SHER	255
The Entrance of the Germans into the City	Dora ROPHE-GOODIS	276
As an Aryan in the Kovel Ghetto	Ephraim FISHMAN	278
In the Jaws of Death	Asher PERES	281
I Lived With Mentey	Aharon WEINER	283
The Gleanings of Genocide	Sima PANTORIN-REICHSTOL	287
Thanks to a Righteous Woman in Sodom	Sarah BRONSHTEYN-GEVERTZMAN	288
In the Maw of the Lion	Rivka SHTERN-GOLDSHTEYN	290

My Escape from the Ghetto	Lola FRIEDMAN-INGBER	293
I Struggled With Death…	Sima PANTORIN-REICHSTOL	295
How was I saved from Destruction?	Miriam GOLDSTEIN	298

Kovel in Its Destruction

Glorified and Sanctified	Yaacov TEITLEKER	301
The Bells Rang	Pinhas DRORI	301
Writings on the Wall	Shlomo PERLMUTTER	302
Notes in Hebrew by Our Loved Ones		304
Notes in Yiddish by Our Loved Ones		306
Notes in Polish by Our Loved Ones		312
Remember What Amalek Did to Thee	Pinhas PANTORIN	317
What I Saw and Heard During the City's Liberation	Dr. Yakov HASIS	321
From the Scene of Destruction	Dr. Mordechai LEIBERSON	324
On the Rubble	Moshe GOODIS	327
In Memory of the Beitar Club in Kovel	Yerachmiel WIRNIK	328
Deep Pits, Red Clay	Sh. HALKIN	331

They Fell on Guard Duty

Devorah Baran, God will avenge her blood		334
Luba Lederhandle, God will avenge her blood		335
Leah Fish, God will avenge her blood		336
Sheindel Schwartz, God will avenge her blood		337
Yechiel Sheinbaum, God will avenge his blood		338
From the Activities of the Kovel Expatriates Organization in Israel	Tzvi RESNICK	340
Dr. Avraham Gorali z"l	Editorial Staff	343

Necrology 345

Name Index 349

Kowel; Testimony and Memorial Book of Our Destroyed Community
(Kovel, Ukraine)

51°13' / 24°43'

Translation of
Kowel; sefer edut ve-zikaron le-kehilatenu she-ala aleha ha-koret

Edited by: Eliezer Leoni-Zopperfin

Published in Tel Aviv 1957

Acknowledgments

Project Coordinator:

Bruce Drake

Our sincere appreciation to the Israeli Organization of the Jews of Kovel and its Surroundings for permission to put this material on the JewishGen web site.

This is a translation from: *Kowel; sefer edut ve-zikaron le-kehilatenu she-ala aleha ha-koret* (Kowel; testimony and memorial book of our destroyed community), ed. Eliezer Leoni-Zopperfin, Tel Aviv 1957

Note: The original book can be seen online at the NY Public Library site: Kowel

This material is made available by JewishGen, Inc. and the Yizkor Book Project for the purpose of fulfilling our mission of disseminating information about the Holocaust and destroyed Jewish communities. This material may not be copied, sold or bartered without JewishGen, Inc.'s permission. Rights may be reserved by the copyright holder.

JewishGen, Inc. makes no representations regarding the accuracy of the translation. The reader may wish to refer to the original material for verification.
JewishGen is not responsible for inaccuracies or omissions in the original work and cannot rewrite or edit the text to correct inaccuracies and/or omissions.
Our mission is to produce a translation of the original work and we cannot verify the accuracy of statements or alter facts cited.

[Page 3]

The Holy and the Pure

God Will Avenge Their Blood

[Page 5]

The People of the Book

By Zvi Resnick (Secretary of the Organization)

Translated by Ala Gamulka

After two years of constant and hard work we were successful. We created a memorial for our holy community of Kovel.

We brought back the splendor, the beauty, the nobility for which our home town was so well–known. We did not spare any effort and we did all we could to collect and edit the material for memorializing our town.

The idea to publish the Kovel Memorial Book was born as the battles of the World War II died down. It was after Hitler was defeated. There was no doubt then that the end had come for the Jews of Kovel, as we had feared.

Previous Executive committees of the Organization had dealt with the publication of the book. These were our comrades Eliahu Mendel, Pinhas Drori, Baruch Avivi, Yeshayahu Avrech and the late Dr. Avraham Gorali, z"l.

Two years ago, the Executive Committee invited our friend Eliezer Leoni–Tsuperfein to become the editor of the book. His enthusiasm and diligence must be recognized. He infused wind into our sails, invested his literary talents and his invaluable experience. Night became day as he collected material, put it together and prepared it for publishing. He met with Holocaust survivors, wrote their stories in proper Hebrew and smoothly edited everything. He proofread every page and checked every letter for accuracy. He treated even small errors seriously and made sure the exterior of the book matched its content. It is thanks to him that the skeleton of the book received a body and became a reality.

Our editor wanted the book to be successful and he recognized the heavy task with which he was entrusted. For that reason, he sought counsel from our illustrious teachers and Rabbis: M. Fishman (principal of Herzliah School in Kovel), Z. Ariel–Leibovitch (principal of the Bialik School in Tel Aviv), Y. Rotman–Netaneli and Dr. R. Ben–Shem (principals of Sokolov–Laor School in Jaffa), Yaakov Kobrinsky (principal of Klomel School in Kovel) and Mr. Yaakov Teitleker, a veteran teacher from Kovel. He listened to their intelligent advice and their remarks are reflected in the pages of this book.

The members of the Book committee must be recognized for their dedication: teacher Tuvia Veisbrott; the founder and director of the Hebrew studio "Habima" in Kovel, our friend Shalom Kolonymus–Klonitsky; our friends Luba Goldberg and Eliahu Mendel listened to the editor's reading of the material. He heard their comments and he directed his work accordingly.

[Page 6]

The members of the Association who should be congratulated are: Luba Goldberg, Bluma Shapiro, David Blitt, Sima Pentorin, Noah Bein, Leah Fidel, Tuvia Fried and Tzvi Resnik. They participated in all the committee meetings and checked the content. They also made corrections when necessary. They did not spare any effort and dedicated their time and involvement. They also worked hard to collect funds and they realised the dream that previous committees had begun.

It is our pleasant duty to mention the financial assistance given to us by the Ministry of Education and Culture of the State of Israel– still headed then by the late David Remez. It is thanks to the former secretary of the Ministry, our friend Yeshayahu Avrech that all this happened.

A special thank you to our fellow townswoman, Mrs. Gutchia (nee Rubenstein) and her husband Mr. Boris Goldstein (Honduras), Mr. Verba (Uruguay), Haim Vinter and Yaakov Flederman (Argentina), Mr. Greenberg (Mexico), Mr. Meir Rosenblatt (France) and to the organization of former residents in Argentina. They all contributed considerable sums towards the publication of the book.

A heart–felt thank you to all our former townspeople living in Israel and abroad who helped the editor in many ways to ensure publications. Also, those who, with great difficulty, wrote their memoirs for the book.

Our special thank you to the libraries and the individuals who assisted in the collection of historical material: Mr. Lachover (Barzilay library), Mr. Ungerfeld and Mr. Rogoff (Beit Bialik library in Tel Aviv), Mr. Lavi (Shaarey Zion library in Tel Aviv), Mr. I.

Pogrebinsky (Beit Achad Ha'am in Tel Aviv), Rabbi Margaliot (Rambam library in Tel Aviv) and Mr. Morgenstern from Tel Aviv who allowed the editor to use his rich private library.

Last, but not least, our thanks to the respected historian Dr. Raphael Mahler who wrote the history of our town and saved, from oblivion, important material for the historiography of Kovel.

The book must belong in every single home of our former residents because in it are embedded the town and the souls of its Jews. The book breathes the air of our fathers, mothers and all those dear to us. They were all taken from us with such cruelty.

[Page 7]

Testimony for the Generations

By Eliezer Leoni

Translated by Ala Gamulka

Such a sad melody emanates from these pages. It is the voice of the blood of our fathers and mothers, brothers and sisters, wives and children that is shouting to us.

The book was sculpted by hands that were cut, legs that were severed, eyes that were torn out, hearts that stopped beating. The song is over and the violins are silenced– all because of the blood that flowed like water.

[Page 8]

It is not a secular book. These are pages of prayer. Everything in them, every letter, is washed in tears. The book was formed by these tears. It is a book of lamentations, of mourning the destruction of our town.

We were unable to list names of all our dear ones who were victims due to lack of space. However, they are all etched in the scrolls of our memory. This is a collection of the precious souls of our beloved townspeople and it is found deep in our hearts and that of the entire nation.

These scrolls are arteries through which streams the blood of the sainted, pure angelic children of Kovel. They were slaughtered and burned. It is also the blood of our holy souls. The hearts of all those who were so dear to us and left us forever are beating in these scrolls.

This book is a permanent memorial to the soul of our town. It will never be forgotten. The embers of our town will remain until the coming of the Messiah. The book will be handed over to our descendants and to all coming generations as a memento of our town.

The book reflects only a fraction of the cultural and moral wealth with which our town was blessed. There was a large Jewish community in Kovel. It was honest, good, and God–fearing. This wonderful community was filled with strong sources of life. It is difficult to describe their depth and breadth. Even if our days are filled with rivers of ink and our heavens and earth are complete with scrolls, our people would all be authors– it would not be enough to fully describe the town. Our sorrow and despair are so deep because the treasures of humanity that were destroyed are endless.

Our violin is weak and not sufficient to mourn our great destruction. In the Temple there was a special musical instrument, called a rake, and it produced one hundred songs. Perhaps this magical instrument could have been used to accompany our deep sorrow.

Our literature is rich in lamentations. It begins with David's mourning of Saul and continues to our times when many more have been written. These dirges reach heights of human genius, but they cannot describe the horrors that occurred in our time. Our horrors were outside the normal laws of man and nature. We are waiting for an outstanding poet who can aptly describe what happened. It will be someone who will use special, noble language to write about our terrible losses.

Our dear victims are waiting for a Jewish Homer, and perhaps even someone superior to him.

For Future Generations; Children Will Be Born and They Will Tell Their Children

Psalms 78:6

[Page 9]

This will be someone who will author the great ballad that will shake the world.

The great destruction of our days has created a background for the growth of legends, similar to the legends in the Talmud. In our book there are chapters about the destruction which should be placed together with the legends in the Talmud about the razing of the Temple. I must say that these legends are even more frightening than those of the Talmud.

The completion of the book is now a gravestone for a great community that is no longer here. The sun has set on our town. Our dear people are gone. Everything is now covered in ashes–. There are now sandhills where our homes stood and lives are snuffed out. All signs of life are erased. Trees that had grown for centuries are cut down and the shadows of death are hanging over the ruins. Our town had existed for over five hundred years.

All the families of Kovel that had lived and rejoiced together are now gone, destroyed. The nests with their birds and goslings are ruined. The world continues as before. The stars in heaven are still shining. The fields of Kovel are still producing and blossoming. The birds are singing, the streams are flowing slowly. At night there are still boats with riders. However, the voices have changed. We no longer hear the sounds of our young men and women. Our children do not sing magnificent songs. The bones of our youth are rotting in the cemetery on the other side of the river. Young hearts have stopped beating and young people no longer eye the blue sky as they sing. Our laughter and happiness are snuffed out forever.

The roads of Kovel are in mourning. The atmosphere is filled with sadness and sorrow for the beautiful people that were felled by the murderers. There is no God in this place. The heavenly spirit has been exiled together with its Jews. Gone and destroyed are the numerous houses of learning that were full of this exalted essence. The Torah scrolls are burned and have disappeared with their letters.

Where are our dear mothers who loved us so much, who did not take care of their health and who sacrificed themselves for our sake? Is there really not even one left? Not even one that turned to stone when viewing the terrible slaughter, the killing of children, big and small? Is her stony figure not standing in the market or in the cemetery or any other corner of the ruined town? Are her frozen eyes not shedding a river of tears?

[Page 10]

She cries about her children, all the children of our town and the tears sting and continue to flow. They do not stop– just like Zacharias' blood that boils and flows. These tears will flow forever because there is no comforting her. Who will give her back her children? Who will elate her with the sounds of her frolicking young children?

In these times of sadness and of unity with our town and her saintly victims, we hear from afar loud sounds. These are the sounds of the waves of tears of this unfortunate mother. Our tears mix with hers. The number of letters in this book is equivalent to the number of tears that I shed when I understood the extent of the Holocaust. Who knows if we will ever really understand it. There has never been such sorrow as ours. Who can understand the despair of these mothers whose children were slaughtered in front of their eyes? Who can understand the pain of the brides whose grooms were murdered near them? Who can fathom the hurt of the fathers whose blood was mixed with that of their children?

In these scrolls we built a new holy gravestone and we will thus fulfill the commandment of "you will elevate my bones from here". We raised the spiritual bones of our dear ones and we have placed them in the pantheon of our nation. The bones will be in the shadows of the heroes, those killed for the sake of their religion. It begins with Rabbi Akiba and Rav Hanania Ben–Tardyon who were garroted with irons. With each passing of the garrottes they would say:" The flint will be intact".

The names of our fellow townspeople are listed in the memorial book of the Creator and each one of our dear ones has been stamped there. Their names will shine like the stars in the sky and will be embroidered in the shield of Israel and its redeemer.

The day we publish the book is difficult and terrible. On this day we bring into our homes the box of ashes of all the Jews of Kovel. We remember all those who are no longer with us– those who were taken like sacrificial lambs to the cemetery and all others. Their souls are shaking and hovering. On every page there are groups of gentle and innocent souls who did not live and were not redeemed. Our hearts are full of mourning over them. Our tears are flowing. May their souls rise and their names be sanctified!

[Page 13]

The Early Days of the City - Its Character and Essence

A History of the Jews of Kovel[*]

By Dr. Raphael Mahler

Translated by Amy Samin

The Jewish community in Kovel is as old as the city itself. The village Kavele[1] on the banks of the Tura has been known since the fourteenth century as a transition point on the way from Lithuania to Ruthenia.

In the year 1518 Prince Vasil Mikhailovitch Sanguszko, lord of the village of Kavele, received permission from King Sigismund I to establish a city which would benefit from the Magdeburg Law[2] and which would be settled by Poles, Ruthenians, Jews, Armenians and Tartars.

Regarding the legal situation of the Jews of Kovel under the leadership of Prince Sanguszko, it is known that they were required to pay a variety of taxes. In 1536, Kovel became the property of Queen Bona when she traded her estate in Volhynia to Prince Sanguszko. That same year, Queen Bona approved the Magdeburg Rights for the citizens of the city, and ordered the Jews to inspect and reinforce the walls and gates of the city just as did all of the other citizens of the city.

During the same period Kovel, like the Volhynia region itself, belonged to Lithuania, but in 1569 it was annexed to the Kingdom of Poland[3].

In 1540, the Jews of Kovel suffered, as did the other Jewish communities in Lithuania, when baptized Jews accused them of performing circumcisions on Christian children.

[Page 14]

The property taxes on the Jews were quite burdensome, until they were reduced by Queen Bona. In 1547 Queen Bona granted to the Jews of Kovel, as part of the Piotrków district, certain privileges which dealt with property taxes. By the order of that proclamation of rights, the Jews of Kovel were freed from the burden of the taxes they had paid during the reign of Sanguszko, excluding the payment of a golden florin[4] for large houses and a half-golden florin for small houses. The same proclamation granted to the Jews of Kovel the same rights as all of the other citizens of the city.

The right to buy and sell merchandise in the marketplace was given special emphasis. On the other hand, the Jews were expected to assume the same obligations towards the city as all of the citizens; and the starosta (regional governor) of Kovel in those times, Franciszek Peltshevski, was required to refrain from preventing the settlement of more Jews in Kovel, and to ensure that the Jews enjoyed the same rights as the other residents of the city.

This generosity on the part of the queen can be easily explained if we recall that at that time Jews were known to be excellent merchants, and their trade reached all the way to the Tartars in Otshakov.

Two indisputable facts prove that the Jews of Kovel were organized into their own community. In the proclamation of rights of 1547 mentioned above, the house of the rabbi specifically was exempt from property tax, and this was borne out on the tombstones in the cemetery of Kovel in the second half of the sixteenth century.

The specific order given by the queen to the starosta of Kovel allowed Jews from outside of the city to move to Kovel, which proved that the Jewish community of Kovel continued to grow. This is supported by the fact that in the sixteenth century the Jews of Kovel paid 45 golden florins "pobór" tax (property tax).[5]

In 1565 King Sigismund Augustus gave Kovel as a gift to Prince Andrei Kurbski, who had fled Moscow in fear of the Czar Ivan the Terrible. This gift ended up paying for itself when Prince Kurbski, together with the division of émigrés from Moscow, took control of a region during the Polish War with Ivan the Terrible.

These changes in the government were disadvantageous to the Jews of Kovel, whose fates depended on the benevolence or cruelty of the landowner. While from time to time Kurbski would come to the Jews of Kovel with arbitrary demands for money, in 1569 his cruelty reached its zenith.

[Page 15]

One Sabbath day in July 1569, under orders from Prince Kurbski, Ivan Kelemet, one of his agents, closed all of the Jewish houses, as well as the synagogue. A number of Jews, as it turned out some of the wealthier Jews of the city, namely Yuska Shmoilovich, Avram Yakovovich and Bogdana[6], wife of Aharon, were put into a dungeon filled with water located under the castle of Kovel. Ivan Kelemet fabricated a story based on a flimsy pretext to justify his evil actions. He claimed that those who were imprisoned owed money to the baptized Jew Lavrin and other citizens of Kovel.

The Jewish community at Vladimir, under which the Jews of Kovel were subject, appealed to the deputy starosta of Kovel in a formal complaint regarding these cruel acts. An agent of the king sent the beadle to the castle, but he was prevented from entering. As he stood outside the castle he could hear the shouts and cries of those imprisoned in the dungeon. The beadle confirmed that the homes of the Jews were closed and sealed. In response to the complaints of the Jews of Kovel, Ivan Kelemet replied that he was merely acting under the orders of Prince Kurbski, who had the authority to judge his Jewish subjects, even unto the penalty of death.

The matter eventually reached the Sejm of Lublin in 1569. King Sigismund Augustus, who judged the matter at that sitting of the Sejm, ordered the immediate release of the imprisoned Jews, giving as his reason that they were his subjects and that only he, the king, had the authority to deprive them of their legal rights.

Ivan Kelemet responded by saying that he was only obligated to obey the orders of his liege Kurbski, and not those of the king. In order to prove this bizarre claim, he went so far as to order the Jews who still remained in the city to leave Kovel. A few days later he came to his senses and released the Jews from the prison; they were covered in blood. He also ordered the removal of the seals on the synagogue and the Jewish homes.

We do not have specific information about the lives of the Jews of Kovel under the remainder of evil reign of Prince Kurbski, but it is possible to assume that their suffering continued. In fact, in the same year, 1569, after Kurbski had been forced to do the bidding of the king and reopen the homes of the Jews, he threatened to take revenge on them in the fullness of time. A few years after the events described, the nobles who had the ear of the king continued to make complaints against the wild behavior of Kurbski.

In the year 1583 Andrei Kurbski died. In 1590 Kovel and the surrounding estates were confiscated from Kurbski's widow by a ruling of the government court, and were turned over to the king. Thus ended the forlorn period of the lives of the Jews of Kovel under the governance of the villain.

[Page 16]

However, one cannot conclude that from then on, the lives of the Jews of Kovel were those of calm, serenity and self-governance; and that a quiet new era of building and development followed.

The civil war between Christians and Jews that had begun with the founding of the city of Kovel was renewed with a fury. The war continued until the third partition of Poland in 1795, when the Volhynia passed into the governance of the Russians. This war was stopped a few times by peace treaties signed by the warring parties, or by order of the king's councils.

As early as 1556, the people of Kovel appealed to Queen Bona to restrict the Jews of the city to living only in the street of the Jews. The Jews did not even enjoy the privilege they had been granted by the queen's son the year before which promised them freedom to live and work anywhere in the city, and which had first been granted them as early as 1547.

The queen ruled that the Jews must leave their homes that were not located on the Jewish street, but she also ordered any Christians who owned homes in the Jewish street to leave and to sell their homes. This is a typical example of *privilegium de non tolerandus christianis* (the right to non-tolerance of Christians), a right that was given to Jews in all of the places where their own right to settle was shrinking to specific Jewish streets or Jewish quarters, such as Kracow, Kazimierz, Posen, and most of the cities in Lithuania. Thus we have before us an example of an indecisive and inconsistent policy implemented by the rulers of Poland in the dispute between the Jews and the urbanites of the sixteenth century.

Mostly, it was the urbanites whose claims were met, because their needs were taken into consideration more than those of the Jews and because they had the connection of religion and faith with those in power. However, often the decrees against the Jews would, a short time later, be cancelled and their previous rights restored either because it was advantageous to the government treasury to do so, or thanks to the gifts which the Jews would present to the king. As it turned out, the order of Queen Bona of 1556 was never put into action, because in 1569 King Sigismund Augustus approved for the second time the rights he had previously given to the Jews of Kovel in 1547.

However, the ruling of the king did not resolve the conflict between the Christian urbanites of Kovel and the Jews of the city regarding the freedom to reside and do business in the city. Indeed, it achieved the opposite, adding new reasons for friction between the two sides. The more the Jewish settlement in Kovel grew, the problem of the participation of the Jews in the city's taxes, which were meant to cover the city's growing expenses, became more serious.

A compromise was reached at the start of the seventeenth century in the matter of the dwelling rights of the Jews, according to the ruling of "Adon Radomski" which apparently reached the heart of the matter in the guise of the agent of the king.

[Page 17]

That ruling, which was made by the starosta of Kovel at that time, Crown-Chancellor Sajnesni Kriski and stamped with the seal of the city council of Kovel, granted Jews the right to live and buy homes in the marketplace, in the streets around the marketplace, and anywhere else in the city. In 1614 a formal agreement was signed by both sides, which discussed potential points of dispute at length.

The rulings of the agreement were as follows: the citizens formally promised not to plot against the dwelling rights of the Jews and would not limit their rights to purchase houses in the marketplace, in the surrounding streets, or "anywhere else in the city" but rather would "leave them in peace forever." In addition, the participation of the Jews in the taxes of the city was settled. From time to time military writs reached the city, and it was agreed that the Christians would bear two-thirds of the economic expenses of the army, and the Jews one third. Three administrators, two Christians and one Jew, would be elected to handle these financial matters. Owners of stores and small shops (*kramnice y kletki*) were all to pay, without exception, twelve Lithuanian groszy per year. The same rule applied to salt stores. "The bakers" and other merchants would pay six groszy a year. The breweries, breweries of sweet beer, and taverns "those that are located next to the dam and those located in the same yard" would pay eight groszy a year. The places for stalls in the marketplace would be rented to Christians and Jews alike for the amount of six groszy a year. The income from poll taxes, taxes on pedestrian crossings on bridges, and the tax on the municipal beeswax refinery (*woskoboynia*) were required to be paid through leasing, two years for Christians and one year for Jews, with equal leasing conditions. Expenditure of that income would be decided upon jointly by Christians and Jews. "Municipal improvements" and "times of municipal financial depression" were two reasons to require from each household, Christian and Jewish, three groszy per year, and sometimes even twice a year; however, this was required to be agreed to, from time to time, by both the city council and the Jewish community together.

The final ruling determined that, at the time of the election of a new member of the city council the retiring member of the council must present an accounting of all expenses and income of the city; this accounting was to be presented in the presence of the Jew whom the Christians (in other words, the city council) deemed to be trustworthy.

Only one copy remains of this document, written in Polish and dated 1660. It reaffirms the previous rulings. In this approval it unequivocally states that the agreement of 1614 was written simultaneously in three "writs" with commentary in three different languages: Polish, Yoni (in other words, Russian) and Hebrew. On the part of the city, the document was signed by the regional judge, Ostapsky Samnovitch, the mayor Herich Mitzniv[7], three council members, five city elders(scabini, ławniki) and five representatives of the common man (pospolity człowiek).

[Page 18]

From the side of the Jews, the following people signed in their own names and on behalf of the whole Jewish community: Avraham (Awruszko) Ben-Aharon, Rabbi Gedalia (Rebigdala) Ben-Mordechai, Kopel Yechimovitch (Ben-Haim) and Moshe Ben-Hazagag (Szklarzewicz)[8] who were considered elders (leaders) of their community.

The agreement that was signed between the city council and the Jewish community in Kovel does not only cover the provision of equal rights of commerce and the burden of taxes for the Jews. The ordinance that most characterized the agreement was the provision allowing the Jewish community to participate in the inspection of the municipal income and expenses. It is not difficult to assume what motivated the city council to make this concession to the Jews. In the same agreement it is mentioned that the equality of the taxes for stores and small shops was made in consideration of the fact that the situation in Kovel was not as sound as that of Brisk (Brest). It is possible to conclude that the Christian citizens of Kowel had come to realize that confining the progress of Jews in commerce was damaging to the city and weakening its position in its competition with Brest.

However, even after the formal agreement of 1614, any peace that existed between the two sides did not last long. The Christian citizens preferred competing against the Jews over the city's competition with Brest. As early as 1616, King Sigismund III sent a committee to Kovel to investigate complaints the urbanite Christians had made against the Jews. The urbanites complained that the Jews had purchased every Christian home and tavern, and excluded them from farming the taxes imposed by the Sejm, and also from farming private taxes. Regarding the matter of performing free work for the city, they falsely accused the Jews of being unwilling to bear the burden of inspecting the city's walls and claimed they were shirking their duty of defending the city. In 1619 a ruling was passed in the matter of the tax farming of the Jews, according to which the official tax collector was required to transfer the taxes to the state treasury, and not to the Jews who farmed this income.

All of the disputes that broke out between the Christian urbanites and the Jews until that time had mostly been concerned with the question of Jewish commerce, although in those days a war broke out between the artisans of Kovel and the Jewish artisans. In 1618 the tailors and furriers obtained a privilege from King Sigismund III, which mainly discussed the problem of the Jewish artisans.

[Page 19]

The king decreed that the Jewish tailors and furriers were subordinate to the Christian artisan guilds and must make the same payments into the treasuries of the guilds that applied to the Christian artisans. As a guarantee that the Jews would, indeed, fulfill their obligation they were required to pay thirty-two Lithuanian groszy for the benefit of the Kovel fort and the same amount to the account of the artisan guild.

It is possible to think, theoretically, that all was well and good, that there was nothing in the king's words to impose an injustice on the Jewish artisans, and that it was composed of good intentions – to impose equal obligations on both Jews and Christians, especially if we note that in certain cities, restrictions were placed on the Jewish artisans' ability to sell the crafts they made, or they were denied the right to work at all. In the sixteenth century, for example, tailors and leatherworkers of Lvov were forbidden from selling their wares at fairs. In Vilna, Jewish tailors were only allowed to sell their products to other Jews. In Lublin, Jewish tailors and furriers were forbidden from selling their goods in the city or its suburbs at all, except during fairs.

In truth, the privilege granted in the year 1618 to the tailors and furriers of Kovel did not provide any preferential rights to the Jewish artisans. In fact, the opposite was true: the intent was a decree against the Jews. The privilege did not deal with the status of the Jewish artisans as part of the guilds, but rather with their obligations alone. The Jewish tailors and furriers were not given any right to express an opinion or vote in the guilds. They didn't enjoy any rights of guild members, but in spite of that were required to make the same payments to the guild treasury that the Christian artisans were required to pay. In addition, it must be taken into account that Jewish artisans, as it turned out, had also organized their own guilds, as is known from the records of these cities: Krakow, Lvov, Posen, Przemycel, Lutsk, Berdychiv, and others. It is therefore possible to understand the size of the burden borne by the Jewish artisans. They were obligated to pay twice; once to the Jewish guilds, and once to the Christian guilds from which they derived no benefit.

The atrocities that took place in the lives of Jews during the uprising of Chmielnicki, the events known as the Pogroms of '48, did not pass over the Jewish community of Kovel. From the complaint presented by the Catholic priest of Kovel to the court in the fortress of Ludmir in 1650, we learn that in 1648 the *schismatikos*[9] drowned in the river all Jews and Catholics who were unable to flee the city.

[Page 20]

It is therefore not surprising that in the year 1651 the Jewish settlement in Kovel numbered only twenty houses.

It wasn't long before the Jewish settlement in Kovel had once again reached its previous situation. In 1660, the agreement between the city council and the Jewish community which had been signed in 1614 was renewed. Those who signed the renewal on behalf of the Jewish community were Rabbi Gedalia Ben-Mordechai, the head of the community, who had also signed the original agreement dated 1614, Moshe Ben-Avraham[10] and Yaacov Ben-Eliakim.

In 1661, a government asset assessor (losterator) arrived in Kovel; the 1614 agreement had been renewed prior to his arrival. However, a new restriction was added: both sides were required to honor all of the rulings of the agreement, with a penalty at a rate of 10,000 Lithuanian groszy (shak). This penalty would apply to whichever side lobbied the king to cancel the agreement and grant a new privilege. While ostensibly this punishment was added to the agreement by the assessor with the intent that it be applied equally to both sides, in actuality it was directed at the Christian urbanites, who had sent countless delegations to the king to complain about the Jews.

The royal assessor approved the rights mentioned above that were given to the artisan guilds of the tailors and furriers in 1618. However, he limited the rights of the Jewish artisans with the explanation that those rights applied only to artisans who were long-standing residents of Kovel. On the other hand, in the event that the Jews of the nearby towns and villages should be so impudent as to engage in the occupations of tailor or furrier, or to buy the products of such tailors and furriers, the Christian guilds would have the right to confiscate those products. "Foreign Jews" (from outside the city) who were caught committing this "crime" would be fined two Lithuanian groszy paid to the king's fort, and two more groszy paid to the treasury of the artisan guilds.

From the documents that were generated by the visit of the assessor, we learn of the malicious accusations made by the Kovel priest, Stanislaw Kocherski regarding the Jewish community of Kovel which revealed the legal and economic situation of the Jewish community and its legal and economic enslavement by the Church.

The main reason for the dispute between the Church and the Jewish community in Kovel was the matter of Jewish payments for the benefit of the Church. This dispute broke out for the first time in the days of the previous priest, Mikolai Malkovski, who demanded that the Jews of Kovel make an annual payment of one golden florin per household and the shoulder (łopatki) cut of a slaughtered animal.

[Page 21]

The collection of such payments was not a new idea in Poland in those days.[11]

King Jan Casimir, to whom both sides presented their petitions, first obligated the Jews in his ruling of 1659 to pay those taxes to the priest. The Jews appealed this ruling based on previous rights and written proofs that clearly verified that the priest had no basis for his demands. As a result, the king ordered the clerk of Kovel, Stephan Chernitzski, to release the Jews from the execution of the aforementioned ruling, as long as the dispute would not be brought to court again. However, in spite of the king's ruling, the new priest Stanislaw Kocherski continued to demand that each Jewish household make the monetary payment as well as the portion of meat. In addition, relying on a decision made by the king in 1659, he demanded other payments, such as candle wax for Good Friday, pins and nails for the needs of the church, and incense. The Jews, however, refused to make those payments, so the priest Kocherski falsely accused them of new crimes, and thereby found the way to take his revenge on them.

Previously, during the time of the priest Malkovski, the Jews had begun construction of a synagogue on the square between the Uniate churches[12] and the Catholic Church. The priest did everything in his power to interfere with the synagogue, relying on the laws of the Church and the state. Immediately after the death of the priest Malkovski, the Jews took advantage of the lack of a new priest and completed the construction of the synagogue. Immediately after receiving his appointment, the new priest Kocherski approached the deputy starosta, demanding the synagogue be closed based on the claim that the synagogue building was taller than the other churches around it, and also claiming that the Jews prayed too loudly and that the noise and shouting could be heard from far away.

The deputy starosta replied that if the priest should close and seal the synagogue, he would not only reopen it, but he would kill any person (emissaries of the priest) he found next to the synagogue. In spite of those specific threats, the priest sealed the synagogue. The Jews of Kovel appealed to the king's assessors, who immediately reopened the synagogue. However, after the assessors had left the city, the priest had the synagogue sealed once again.

In 1661, when the king's assessor came again to Kovel, the two sides submitted their positions.

[Page 22]

In addition to the sins previously mentioned, the priest found new transgressions. The false accusations he reported to the assessor included the complaint that the Jews engaged in commerce in the streets during Christian holy days, and that they forced their Christian women servants to work on holy days.

The Jews absolutely denied the claims of the priest. Regarding the payment of taxes to the Church, the Jews relied on the king's decision which had annulled the earlier ruling until a new trial had taken place. Regarding the synagogue, the Jews testified that their previous synagogue had been taller than the one currently being built. In addition, they stated that it was a lie that they made noise while praying. Furthermore, the Jews said that they did refrain from commerce on Christian holy days, and that they did not employ Christian servants at all.

After hearing the claims of both sides, the king's representative immediately reopened the synagogue and warned the priest to show more moderation and patience regarding all of his complaints against the Jews, until such time as the king made a new ruling. Meanwhile, the priest was instructed to leave the Jews alone.

The complaints of both sides and the response of the Jewish community to the false complaints of the priest (Remanifestatio) were registered at the fortress office (notary) and assumed to be material for legal re-clarification.

In spite of all this, the dispute between the priest and the Jewish community in Kovel was not resolved. Similarly to the situation in other large Jewish communities in Poland, the burden of obligations on the Jews of Kovel in the seventeenth century was heavy. The role of the Jews in money lending changed completely compared to the Middle Ages, when the Jews were the most important money lending source in the country. Now, in the seventeenth century, the Jewish communities borrowed money themselves from the nobles, the priesthood or the orders of monks and nuns, in order to pay their regular taxes (poll tax), and the special taxes which they owed to the King's treasury. Not just the communities, but the provincial organizations and the autonomous central organization of the Jews, the Council of Four Lands, sank deeper and deeper in debt; the interest alone accumulated into enormous amounts.

The community of Kovel had a longstanding debt to the local church of 700 golden florins. The priest Malkovski, predecessor of the priest Kovalski, whose dispute with the community was over his complaint about the Jew's payment to the Church, had surely intended to pressure the Jews by falsely accusing them while forcing them to pay the debt. However, the Jews managed to obtain a five year extension on their debt in the trial at the fortress of Ludmir. Incidentally, it was decided that the Jews must pay interest in the amount of 70 gold florins per year.[13]

[Page 23]

The new priest, Kovalski, was not satisfied, knowing that the Jews were paying only the interest on the debt; he insisted that they also pay off the debt itself. The assessor, who went to Kovel in 1661, ruled according to the previous judgment that the Jews must pay only the interest for five years, and only after that time would the priest be entitled to take the Jews to court to settle the debt.

A few dozen years later, in 1710, we learn of a renewed dispute between the city council and the Jews. The head of the Kovel region determined that the Jews must pay one-third of all of the taxes and municipal fees. From this document, it can also be proven that the Jews of Kovel managed a wide area of commerce, both in and outside of the country. In order to avoid paying taxes and fees, many Jews would settle in the suburbs outside the city walls so that the laws of the city would not apply to them.

The political and legal status of the Jews of Kovel was decided in the seventeenth century by the privilege of King Władysław IV, which was approved in 1650 by King Jan Casimir.

As we mentioned, Volhynia was annexed in 1569 to the Kingdom of Poland. In spite of that, the legal situation of the Jews of Volhynia and especially the Jewish jurisdictional area did not change, and remained as it had been in Lithuania. The main difference between the Jews of the Kingdom of Poland and those of Lithuania was in the area of judicial organizations related to proceedings between Christians and Jews in cases where the Jew was the defendant. In such a case, in the Kingdom of Poland the dispute was brought before a Jewish court, under the authority of the voivode (palatine), deputy palatine, or a "special Jewish judge" (Sędźia żydowski), a Christian, and with the participation of the Jewish judges (assessors). In Lithuania, this authority was given in such cases to the starosta or his deputy. The privilege given to the Jews of Kovel in 1650 granted them the right to be judged before Jewish judges (przed doctorami swemi). Disputes between Jews and the urbanites of Kovel in which the Jew was the defendant were required to be discussed on appeal before the deputy starosta of Kovel with the participation of one of the Jewish elders. Regarding the first level of hearings, nothing was mentioned about the privilege in such matters. It turned out that the Jewish court would also discuss matters between Jews and urbanites if the Jew was the defendant.

The privilege also determined that the Jewish synagogue would remain in place. It is possible to assume that the square was located between the Uniate Churches and the Catholic Church, according to what we recall from the dispute between the Jews and the priest. In the same privilege it is mentioned that the Jewish ritual bath (mikveh) was located "on the river bank" behind the dams (za grobelkami) on the way to Milanovac. As was customary in those days, the synagogue and the cemetery were exempt from the burden of municipal taxes, taxes for the king, and the tax for the benefit of the king's fortress. The privilege also released the Jews of Kovel from the obligation to give the shoulder portion (łopatki) of the slaughtered animal to the king.

[Page 24]

The development of the Jewish settlement in Kovel into a well-populated community can be attributed to the fact that Kovel had the right to representation in the autonomous institutions of the Jews of Volhynia.

As it is known, the autonomous institutions of Volhynia were structured differently from the rest of the institutions in the area. In the rest of the provinces in the Kingdom of Poland, the autonomous Jewish institution was divided into three levels: community, provincial community, and the Council of the Four Lands. In Volhynia, the autonomous institutions were structured on four levels; small communities were not directly subordinate to the provincial committee, but instead to larger communities which were the only ones represented on the Volhynia provincial committee. At the beginning, there were only four such large communities: Ostróg, Kremenetz, Lutsk, and Ludmir (Volodymyr-Volynskyi). In the seventeenth century, before Kovel had a representative on the provincial committee, it was subordinate to the Ludmir community. By the end of the seventeenth century, Kovel was separate from Ludmir and rose to the level of a central autonomous community. At the convention of the provincial community of Volhynia in the town of Horokhiv, Kovel is mentioned as a community independent of Ludmir. Kovel was already an independent community and collected taxes from smaller communities such as Kamin-Kashyrskyi, Wyżwa and Michnowce. From the report of the king's commissar who was sent to the convention of the provincial committee we learn that Kovel was not involved in any disputes with its subordinate communities, and therefore sent no delegates to the convention of the provincial committee (the provincial committee was convened in order to settle disputes between large and small communities). Only in a document from the year 1730 was mention made of a dispute over the poll tax that arose between Kovel and Wyżwa, which succeeded in releasing itself for a brief time from the authority of the community of Kovel. However, in 1732 the town of Wyżwa appeared in a document about tax division as a part of the Kovel province. In 1726, and also in 1739, the town Nezkizh (Niesuchojeże) appeared as subordinate to the Kovel community.

The signatures of the elders and rabbis of Kovel appear on the Jewish poll tax list of the Kovel region in the eighteenth century. In 1720, at the convention of the provincial council in Berestechko, the following representatives signed their names: "Rabbi Itzhak Ashkenazi son of the rebbe of Kovel, and Shlomo Zalman (son of my master and father), our teacher and rebbe Rabbi Yehoshua of blessed memory."

Both of them came "on the orders of the leaders of the holy Kovel community." The third signatory was "Nachman son of my beloved father Moshe the righteous of blessed memory." In 1724 "Aryeh Leib son of the genius and rebbe our teacher and rebbe Rabbi Yehoshua of Kovel the righteous of blessed memory" also signed the document concerning the division of the poll tax (Dyspartyment). He signed his name as the son of the rabbi, although it is fair to assume that he was, himself, a rabbi. In 1730, the name of the same Leib, son of Yehoshua, appeared. In 1735 the following people signed the document regarding the division of the poll tax:

[Page 25]

"The holy Yechiel Michal may God hear him, of the holy community of Kovel and its environs[14] and Yonah son of our master and father, our teacher and rebbe Avraham Halevi of Kobla".

In the year 1737 the following names appeared in the official copy of the poll tax list: Abram Matysowicz, Zús Rabinowicz[15] Wolfowicz.

The size of the Jewish community of Kovel in the eighteenth century was not known until the year 1765, when a census was taken of the Jewish population of Poland. Up until 1765, we did not have any tax lists except for the Jews of Kovel and the surrounding area. According to the survey (losterchia) that took place in 1661, the Jews of Kovel paid:

Fort tax:	urbanite Jews	– 400	golden florins	Christians	– 321	golden florins
Forest tax (gajowe)	"	– 70	"	"	– 23	" "
Land tax (prętowe)[16]	"	-17.75	"	"	– 30	" "
Total		487.75			374	

We may learn from this that, aside from the land tax which was lower, the Jewish urbanites paid higher taxes than did the Christian urbanites. One cannot conclude from this that the Jewish population outnumbered the Christians, but rather that the tax burden was heavier on the Jews.

In the year 1725 the Jewish community of Kovel alone (including villages) paid a poll tax of 1,000 golden florins; in 1726 – 1,448 golden florins, and in 1738 – 1,555. From the entire Kovel region (the city of Kovel and the surrounding towns and villages), the amounts of Jewish poll tax were recorded as follows:

In the year	1719	2,100	golden florins
"	1723	1,847	"
"	1724	1,482	"
"	1728	1,000	"
"	1729	820	"
"	1733	720	"
"	1739	1,650	"

As is shown on the list, the amount of poll tax paid by the central community in Kovel and its environs decreased. This could have been the result of the impoverishment of the Jews of this area, and the Council of the Four Lands and also the provincial committee of Volhynia took this into consideration and granted them a suitable tax break

[Page 26]

However, there is another obvious explanation: starting in 1730 and through 1738 Kovel ceased to appear on the tax rolls for the Jewish Kovel region. This proves that Kovel paid the Jewish poll tax separately, and that the Jewish community in Kovel left the sub-province of the Kovel region. Such instances of the deterioration of the Jewish provincial institutions increased throughout the eighteenth century. The most common pattern was that the central community of the province would separate and leave the smaller communities to their own devices as a smaller province. In 1764 as is known, the central autonomous institutions of the Jews (the Council of the Four Lands, the provincial committees) were revoked. Henceforth, the poll taxes were collected directly from the communities, according to population – two golden florins per person. In connection with this, by the end of 1764 and the beginning of 1765, a census of the Jewish population of all of Poland (the Polish-Lithuanian Commonwealth) was created.

This census revealed the following numbers: the Kovel community included (not including the city of Kovel itself) the following towns: Michnowce, Wyżwa, Milanowicze, and fifty villages.

The number of Jewish souls in all of the Kovel communities one year of age[17] and older during that same year reached 1,516; the number in the city of Kovel alone reached 827 souls. In the town of Wyżwa 168 Jewish souls were registered; in Michnowce the number was 18 and in Milanowicze 10. In the fifty villages of the Kovel community there were 493 Jewish souls; in other words, an average of ten Jewish souls in each village.

The 827 Jewish souls in the city of Kovel comprised 187 Jewish families; of those 137 were homeowners and the remaining fifty were tenants. The number of homeowners is, without a doubt, larger than the number of Jewish homes; in Kovel, as in other towns, the Jewish "homeowners" were found to be living in homes which they rented from their Christian owners. Indeed, for the year 1784 we know of only 94 Jewish households in Kovel.

Unfortunately, the census did not indicate the professions of those counted; it is therefore difficult for us to draw any conclusions about the economic situation of the Jews of Kovel in those days. However, the index to the census sheds a certain amount of light on the social situation of those counted. Of the 827 souls, 209 of them were mentioned in a separate section as being "abjectly poor amongst the Jews of Kovel" (samo ubóstwo w m. Kowla). Of the 137 Jewish homeowners, 37 were included in the same paragraph; of the fifty tenants, 24. Altogether that is 61 Jewish families.

[Page 27]

The truth is that the number of the poor was substantially larger than what was listed in the census, and it turns out that a decisive majority of the Jewish population of Kovel was poor, as was the case in other cities.

The census list was prepared, as is known, in the following manner: the rabbi, an elder, the beadle, and the Christian "revizor" went to every house and listed all who lived there. The section regarding the "abjectly poor" was not based on professions, but rather on a topographical basis. This section marked specific neighborhoods which were known by the name "abjectly poor." The deciding evidence for that topographical factor was clear to the census takers; in the preparation of this section they provided the following fact: the professions of "vintner," which was applied to the bartender in a tavern, and waiters[18] appear four times in the section for the "abjectly poor." However, those professions also appear twice in the section that includes the remainder of the Jews. The only musician who is listed in the index was a man named Wolf the Musician, who could in no way be considered an extremely rich man; he did not appear in the section for the "abjectly poor," but rather in the section applied to other Jews.

Although in the census professions and occupations were not specified, we still find names of eight home owners who employed workers, or artisans. Of them, three were artists who each employed one assistant and five who employed two assistants, altogether thirteen assistants. There is no doubt that this number is random, and that the number of assistants was actually significantly higher. In the census there appeared a list of 29 servants; four were male, and 25 female. Usually only one female servant was employed; only in two cases do we find families which employed two Jewish female servants, and in once instance three female servants who worked in the home of Rabbi Damta.

One resident, a tenant named Lazer ben Todrus (Leysor Tordusowicz), was without a doubt and according to all indications, the richest Jew in the city. We can learn this from the number of servants he employed: two male and two female servants. Of the 27 grooms and sons who received the financial assistance mentioned above, the rabbi alone supported three married sons, while the rest of the home owners each supported only one.

The name of the rabbi who signed the index of the census was Yekutiel ben Yosef (Kisiel Josyfowicz). The city elder who signed was "Avigdor, our beloved father, the honorable rebbe and teacher, Sender of blessed memory, the monthly leader of Kovel (Syndorowicz Kwartalny[19] Wigdor Kowelski)."

[Page 28]

The third member of the team of census takers was the beadle: "Yehuda-Leib son of rebbe Moshe Shemesh of the holy community of Kovel" (in Polish, Leybe Moskowicz Szkolnik).

The census of 1789 teaches us that at that time there were in Kovel 150 Christian households and 94 Jewish households. Eighteen of the Jewish households were listed as "inns" (domy zaiezdne) and 76 as "small houses." The Jews paid "tax" to the King at a rate of 1,080 golden florins, that is, for the defense of the city. In addition to that they contributed various offerings of slaughtered beef which were calculated thusly: 30 golden florins instead of the shoulder piece (łopatki) of the animal and ten blocks of candle wax worth 12 golden florins each; altogether 120 florins. It is astounding that the "piece from the back" was included, because in the seventeenth century King Władysław IV had granted a privilege to the Jews explicitly exempting them from this tax.

It is likely that this can be explained by the fact that in 1744 the Jewish synagogue burned down and all of the privileges and certificates were destroyed. There is no doubt that this was the same synagogue that the Jews built in 1660 "on the square between the Catholic church and the Uniate churches"; the same synagogue which so troubled the mind of the priest Kovalski.

The Jewish community of Kovel understood very well the significance of the loss of the privileges; immediately after the fire, in 1745, they had inscribed in the court records in the Ludmir fort a "public statement" which claimed that together with the synagogue all of the old privileges and subsequent confirmations thereto were lost.

In the Jewish book census which was taken in 1776 in order to determine a stamp tax for books, 759 Hebrew (and Yiddish) books were registered in Kovel; in the nearby villages of the Kovel community 141 Jewish books were found.

In 1795, the year of the third partition of Poland, Kovel like the entire Volhynia region, came under Russian governance.

In 1799 eleven Jews were registered in Kovel as merchants; no Christians were listed under that occupation. There were also listed 1,308 Christian urbanites and 811 Jewish urbanites. In the year 1847 the entire Kovel community numbered 2,647 souls. In 1897 the population count in Kovel was 17,697 residents; of those, 8,521 were Jews. According to the census taken in 1921, the population of Kovel numbered 20,818 residents, and of those 12,758 were Jews.

[Page 29]

That same census determined that in Kovel there were 317 Jewish industrial enterprises (factories and workshops) which employed 654 people. Of them, 110 employed laborers. Of the people employed by the 317 Jewish factories were listed 311 homeowners, 47 of their family members, 288 Jewish workers (277 men and 11 women) and eight non-Jewish employees.

The factories branched out into the following areas: the clothing industry – 309 people; leatherworkers – 60 people; food industry - 58 people; building – 49 people; graphics – 3 people; cleaning – 54 people. Only a few people were employed in the remaining areas of industry.

Sources and Literature About Kovel

Regesty i nadpisy I. II; Russko jewr. Archiw I, II, III; Baliński-Lipinski: "Starożytna Polska" II; Berszadskij: "Litowskije jewreje" 349 – 50; Władymirskij-Budanow: "Kijewskaja Staryna" 1888, I 22. Lustracja Wołynia z lat 1661, 1789 (Archiwum Skarbowe w Warszawe, Oddz. XLVI); "Dyspartymenta pogłównego żydowskiego". Taryfa pogłównego żyd. powiatu Włodżimierskiego z r. 1765 (A.G. Oddz. 65 A. Nr. 2. 23, A.G. Oddz. 65 B. Nr 18.) Akta poborowego (Arch. Skarbu Oddz. I Nr. 62). The Jewish Industrialist – Ventures in Poland 1921 (Materials of Dushyant County). Jewrejskaja Encykłopedia IX.

*	The original name of the article: *Tzu Der Geschichte Fun Yidden in Kovel*, printed in the journal <u>Landkantnisch</u>, Number 1, Warsaw 1933. Translated into Hebrew by Eliezer Leoni.
1	Even today, the town is called Kavele in Yiddish. In addition, the rabbis and leaders of Kovel in the 18th century sign the name of the city using its ancient name of Kovli.
2	German settlers in Poland in the Middle Ages received the right to self-government, similar to the law of the city of Magdeburg in Saxony. That law included the right to choose a mayor, who was given the title "judge" (advocatus, from which the Polish word wójt is derived), the right to choose a city council of twelve members, the right to a trial in financial and personal disputes in the city's own autonomous courthouse, and the right to pass laws regarding the legal internal business of the city. The Magdeburg Law was adopted in many cases in cities where the citizens were not Germans but were, rather, Poles, Ukrainians, et cetera.
3	The Kingdom of Poland was the name given to the portion of the Polish Commonwealth which was ruled by a governor who was crowned king, as opposed to the Eastern portion – Lithuania, where the governor was called Grand Duke.
4	The price of the golden florin in the first half of the sixteenth century was 45 cents. The standard golden florin was 30 cents.
5	"Pobór" – this was the name of the property tax, which was imposed occasionally on all of the residents of the kingdom according to the decision of the Sejm.
6	Slavic names for Jewish women, such as the name Bogdana, are still found today; for example Zelta, Cherna, et cetera.
7	The wójt was at this time, first and foremost, a judge, the chairman of the court of city elders (ławniki). For this reason, even today villagers call the wójt by the name judge. The actual mayor and chairman of the city council was called burghermeister (burmistrz).
8	Among the representatives of the "common man" on the side of the city were mentioned two leatherworkers. It is likely that Moshe Ben-Hazagag was not a leader, because he was listed as a representative of the "common man" on the side of the Jewish community.
9	*Schismatikos* means separatists in Greek (from the Greek root schizein, to separate). The separatists were Greek Orthodox, "praboslavs" (translator's comment).
10	According to all indications, this is the same Moshe Ben-Avraham - Mosko Abrahamowicz – son of the community leader Avraham Ben-Aharon (Awruszko Aronowicz) whose name is signed on the agreement dated 1614. The title of community leader would usually pass as an inheritance from father to son.

11 In the 17th century, the Jews in Hrubieszów would make payments to the priest in taxes and "gifts" as follows: for St. Jacob's Day, 20 florins; for Christmas and Easter, 2 pounds of pepper, one pound of ginger, one pound of cumin, two units of cloves, two units of turmeric, one unit of nutmeg and three pounds of sugar crystal.

12 The "Unio Catholica" was the union of the Christians from the East with the Roman Catholic Church. They recognized the example of the Roman Catholic Church, and in particular acknowledged the pre-eminence of the Pope (translator's note).

13 As we can see, the Church charged 10% interest on the debt.

14 The letter "hay" in the Hebrew translation was omitted in order to avoid taking the name of the Lord in vain.

15 Rabinowicz was not at that time the family name; rather it was as it sounds: son of the rabbi.

16 Land tax, or prętowe: tax for the measurement of the division of land.

17 The Jews were required to pay a poll tax on each person one year and older. Therefore, the census takers did not include Jewish infants (younger than one year).
The social situation of those categorized as "paupers" is revealed by the fact that amongst them only two fathers-in-law are listed as providing financial support to their sons-in-law; while in the category of "affluent" 25 sons and sons-in-law are listed as receiving support.

18 For comparison, see my article "Hebrew-Yiddish Documents of the Divisions in Poland in the 18th Century." YIVO Journal, 1932.

19 In ancient Poland, each and every year three to five elders were chosen who would take turns filling that role every quarter year or every month. For this reason, the elder was called the "monthly leader" (or, in Polish: Kwartalny).

[Page 30]

In the Shadow of the City's Early Days

by Eliezer Leoni

Translated by Amy Samin

1. The Old Cemetery

In *HaMelitz* from the year 5653, 9 February 1893, we read: "Exactly when our Jewish brethren came to live and set down roots in this city is not known to any of its residents; the old registries that perhaps could have provided some information are not here, because in the large and terrible fire that befell the city thirty-six years ago (in 1857), in which all of the houses and synagogues were destroyed, the records burned as well."

"In our estimation, Jews settled in this area approximately 500 years ago. Although there is no direct evidence of this, there is the evidence of graves and remnants of ancient tombstones in the cemetery. To this day, there are ancient tombstones in the Ancient Cemetery (there are three cemeteries here: the New, the Old, and the Ancient), some at least three hundred years old, and doubtless what was intended to be a monument simply collapsed into a heap of ruins under the weight of the years. It could be that they were first put there at the time the first Jews arrived in the area."

The Old Cemetery is practically the only one from which it is possible to learn the nature and the essence of the city. Its reputation is engraved in Paleolithic, ancient tombstones. Accumulated and buried in those unhewn stones is the first information about the generations of authors and wise men who lived in our city.

And though, in the year 1857, a horrible fire consumed the city and all of its historical records – the registry of the *Chevra Kadisha* and some of the earliest tombstones still remain.

In the registry from the year 5482 (1722), we read a brief description of the early days of the city. The historian of the *Chevra Kadisha* writes: "The city of Kovel is an ancient one, surrounded by the cities in the Volyn region, where some of the earliest great rabbis, brilliant Jews, settled - the heads of *yeshivas* of that generation. The greatest genius of his generation, Rabbi Yitzhak, son of the brilliant Rabbi Natan (son of the rebbe) Shimshon Shapira, was the head of the yeshiva in the holy community of Kovel sometime around 1577; also the brilliant rabbi, the great, the Hassid, our teacher the rabbi Yehuda Yudel, author of the book <u>Kol Yehuda</u> was head of the rabbinical court in the city and the great genius, the wonder of the generation, our teacher the rabbi Yosef Yaski (the head of the rabbinical court and master of the *yeshiva*, author of the book *Yesod Yosef* was one of his sons, the four cedars he planted in Israel, Cedars of Lebanon, great Torah scholars. To our great sorrow, the tombstones of his sons have been lost from the cemetery, for it was the custom in the city at that time to make the tombstones from wood."

[Page 31]

From this brief historical review we learn upon which foundation stones the Jewish community of the city was based: rabbis, great scholars, the wonders of the generation, wise men, the authors of books, and the greatest of them all was the head of the yeshiva, Rav Shimshon Shapira, who lived 379 years ago. But that rabbi was not the, the creator of the spiritual world of our city. There were great, wise men who came before him, but their names have been lost because it was not the custom to leave carved records; rather they created tombstones from wood and the passage of time brought about their destruction.

Heplio-lithography, that is, the etching of words onto ancient tombstones is itself of interest, because by such means we can learn the wording on tombstones from past generations. Its most essential value and importance is that it allows us to reconstruct the spiritual portrait of the city in its first centuries of existence.

We provide here the text from several ancient tombstones from the Old Cemetery whose importance lies in the things they can teach us about the history of our city.

"Here Lies / Rabbi Shmuel, return in peace / A judge of Israel who knows every hidden sign / A priceless gem, our teacher the rabbi [unknown] and our Sages the brilliant / Hasid the exalted Shmuel, son of the rabbi, the great tamarisk, our teacher the rabbi Mordechai Margalit / Whose soul ascended in purification to Heaven on 1 Elul 5494. / May his soul be bound in the bonds of everlasting peace."
This rabbi, who was in all likelihood the son of the famous Rabbi Margalit, died in the year 1733, that is to say, 223 years ago.

[Page 32]

"Here Lies / He who went to his eternal rest / The honorable rabbi, the great light, the well-known Yeshiah / Baharab, the great tamarisk, our teacher the rabbi of blessed memory / Was gathered to his Maker and returned his soul to God / on Sunday 10 Sivan 5484 / Today his soul will be bound up in the bonds of eternal life / In the shadow of God he will await the arrival…"
The words engraved on this tombstone stop with the word "arrival" because the remainder is buried in the ground. This rabbi died in 1723, that is to say, 233 years ago.
"Here Lies / The wife and devout rebbetzin / M. Yenta, daughter of our teacher the rabbi Shneor / Feibush. She died on 12 Kislev 5506 / and her modest daughter Mrs. Leah / daughter of Shimon died on the day…"
The remainder is erased, and it is only possible to learn that the name of the rabbi was Shimon. This rabbi's wife, the daughter of Rabbi Shneor-Feibush, died in 1745, that is, 211 years ago.
"In the year 5372 / Here rests Aharon son of our teacher the rabbi / Rav Yitzhak of blessed memory 7 Nisan / this month will be a sign for you / called the first of the months of the year / buried a Hasid, leader and head of Dorot-Olam…"
The remainder is sunken into the earth. According to this tombstone, it appears that he was one of the employers of that era. It is impossible to identify his place of birth because the tombstone is sunken in to the ground. This tombstone is from the year 1611, that is, 345 years ago.

[Page 33]

"Here Lies / a yeshiva rabbi / We mourn the beauty which is rotting in the earth. / Our wonderful teacher the rabbi Yehuda Leib son of the rabbi and teacher Aharon / his soul is in the garden of peace."
This tombstone had also sunk halfway into the earth in 1900, and it was impossible to copy everything that was etched there. The tombstone is from 1748, or 208 years ago.
"Here Lies / Miriam who died and was buried / daughter of the righteous judge, our teacher Chaim HaLevy of blessed memory / 12 Nisan 5588."
This tombstone stood by the *shteibel*, and next to it more tombstones were found. By all signs, there were quite a few graves there. This tombstone is from 1827, 129 years ago.

These tombstones confirm the tradition of the city elders, because in the earlier generations the city was populated by wise men and brilliant scholars, who were known collectively as the Wise Men of Kovel. The city of Kovel was a metropolis of Torah and wisdom. Those who served as its rabbis were exalted scholars.

The great preacher of blessed memory, Rabbi Avraham of Turiysk, author of the book *Magen Avraham* (Shield of Abraham), praised those geniuses lavishly, and said, "In the two old cemeteries of Kovel one may discern a Sanhedrin, for in their dust are concealed and held the wise, the sagacious, and the brilliant."

Even if we assume that the Magid from Turiysk was speaking of a small Sanhedrin, one that had only twenty-three members, and not a Great Sanhedrin with seventy-one, the righteous man's words prove that the city was filled with wise men and authors.

[Page 34]

2. The Transition from Town to City

In the year 1847 there were 2,647 Jews in Kovel. Fifty years later, in 1897, that number had grown to 8,521; in other words, during that period the Jewish population of Kovel more than trebled in size.

In *HaMelitz* from 1893, Heinech Geller writes that in that year the number of residents of the city was fifteen thousand, and most of them were Jews. Geller's testimony is authentic and there is no reason to doubt his credibility; based on that we can say that in a half-century's time the city's Jewish population increased more than five-fold.

What caused this growth? Just as with the soul of man, whose purpose cannot be fully investigated, also in the material world, in economics, unknown factors operate which cannot be deciphered. Even if we do not know the processes which brought about this rapid growth in the number of the city's Jews, there is one economic factor which is known completely and for a certainty, the laying of the second railroad line in Russia during those years.

From the time the tracks were laid, the city threw off its old form and reinvented itself. Almost magically, wide, paved roads began appearing in the city, including the beautiful Beit HaNetivot Street, along which the houses were built in the new style. Next to the old city, whose aging houses were decaying and whose streets were small and narrow, there arose a fresh new city on the sands full of energy and beauty. Alongside the new houses and streets there arose a new Jewish settlement in the city, brimming with life.

This metamorphosis, this major change in the character of the city, came about thanks to the actions of an exceptional man of many achievements – Yaacov-Aharon Entin of blessed memory, who was the contractor for the railroad.

Entin settled in Kovel more than one hundred and twenty years ago. He was originally from the city of Romaniv in the Mohilov Region, near the city of Lyady. He was a Chabadnik, an enthusiastic follower of Rabbi Menachem-Mendel, author of the *Tzemach Tzedek* and the grandson of Rabbi Shneur-Zalman, the founder of the Chabad movement of Hasidism.

Entin had a friendly relationship with the prince Korsakov-Dondukov of Romaniv, and thanks to his recommendation the railroad tracks were given over to him.

Before he received the job, Entin traveled to see the *Tzemach Tzedek* [Righteous Scion] and receive his blessing. The rabbi blessed him, and added that a great future good would come to the Jews of the city because of the railroad line and help would come from the heavens.

[Page 35]

Reb Yaacov Entin of Blessed Memory

    Entin was a grand, wealthy man whose worth was about half a million rubles. As an intelligent student, he knew well the saying, "If I am only for myself, what am I?" He therefore invested much of his wealth in large building projects, in order to provide income and occupation to the Jewish laborers in the city. That was the stimulation, the galvanizing force, which drove him to build the 30 large barracks for the "Kovelski folk." The laborers who worked on those projects were mostly Jews. Not for nothing did the workshop owners weep, saying, "Who will provide us with work if Reb Yaacov-Aharon is gone?"

    On 29 Tevet 5658, in the magazine *HaTzfirah*, Heinech Geller described this man thusly: "The deceased was an elder and the pride of the community, always the first to give in every matter of charity, God-fearing and honest as any man.

[Page 36]

    His heart was as wide as an open hall, and he improved the lot of many paupers, providing them with an escape from their poverty. His home was always open to the poor and those going through difficult times, and they were treated like family. He never ate bread alone, without inviting someone in need to share his meal. No matter how great his wealth, his heart was never proud, and he was humble; he always gave a warm reception to any poor person who asked for his help. He paid for the weddings of many impoverished orphans, and he never sent widows away empty-handed, always taking care of their financial needs and their peace of mind."

    "The deceased loved his people with all of his heart and soul, and the holy land was his heart's desire; he always yearned to settle there. Every year, he sent a great deal of money to every charitable institution in Eretz Yisrael. He was concerned about the Hebrew laborers, ensuring they had a place to earn their livelihood, and was heavily invested in building without any benefit to himself, but rather only for the purpose of providing work for the Hebrew laborers."
    Entin died on 17 Tevet 5658 (1898) at the age of 77. Merchants left their shops, and laborers were absent from their work, in order to attend his funeral. The stores were closed, and the teachers left their *cheders* and all as one man came to pay their last respects to the deceased. No one, not even the city elders, had ever seen such a funeral.

    Entin lived on Old Vakzalna Street. He built a synagogue in his yard which was called the *Beit Midrash* of Entin. His wife, Nechama Entin, was exceptional in the generosity of her heart and her concern for impoverished *yeshiva* students. For that purpose, she built a *yeshiva* with her own money, a wonderful house of prayer; all expenses were paid for from her own pocket. That house of study was the only one of its kind in the city.

[Page 36]

Character of Kovel

By Yaacov Teitelkar

(from the Way of Life of Kovel)

Translated by Amy Samin

The city of Kovel – widespread was its renown. A son of Kovel who traveled abroad and was asked about his origins would be absolutely certain to elicit a joyful reaction: "Ah, Kovel! I know it, I know it… Indeed, I have been there…" Not because Kovel was an important strategic and commercial crossroads near the main Warsaw – Lublin – Kiev road, needed by one and all. Kovel was close to the heart of every Jew, the city was like a mother of the Jewish people, a campus devoted to the purity of tradition and the original popular-national Jewish way of life. There was no movement towards an imitation of the corrupt "goyish" culture… The mother tongue ruled in the home, on the street, in society, and no Jewish child heard "goyish" except from the mouth of the Sabbath goy who came, wearing a thick *sarmiga*, to serve the Jews on *Shabbat* by extinguishing the candles in the candelabra, filling the samovar, and gulping down the first cup of cholent with a slice of bread …and on the eve of Yom Kippur, affixing the wax candles in their holders in the synagogue and replacing them when they melted away from the heat.

[Page 37]

Or they would hear the foreign tongue on market day, when the farmers from the nearby villages would gather, blocking the streets of the city with their carts loaded with wood and merchandise. The Jewish peddlers and the housewives would walk between the wagons, inspecting the chickens and scouting out goods, handling everything as if they'd already bought it. The farmers leave their womenfolk sitting in the wagons and go off to wander through the marketplace and stopping to peddle their wares in the stores. Seven merchants grab hold of one "goy," crying "Listen!" and begin describing their merchandise in a language that is half goyish and half Yiddish. There is no doubt that the goyim learned a little Yiddish, and dressed up their own language with a bit of the language of the Jews, ending up speaking "goyyiddish."

Nevertheless, the Jews of Kovel never caught on to Yiddishism. When the waves of the revolutionary anti-tsarist movement arrived – at the start of the 20th century – on the shores of Kovel, there was a whole new spirit. The youth of Kovel began to prepare vigorously for the struggle against the tsar, and the workers began to organize for the class struggle with the bourgeoisie. When the political parties aligned with socialism, Yiddishism and anti-Zionism began their activity; all of that movement resembled nothing more than foam on the waves, and there was no fundamental change in the everyday activity of Kovel. The Yiddish school, which had been founded by the Bundists as a counter-weight to the schools founded on the *Tarbut* system and to the *Talmud Torah,* couldn't compete and was closed. Most of the workers – the tailors, the shoe makers, and the carpenters who were caught up in the socialist idea of this world, and who prepared for the class struggle in order to improve the economic situation of the proletariat, did not stop considering themselves completely faithful sons of Israel, and continued to visit the house of study morning and evening and to listen to the proletarian speaker, the excitable Yosman –whose words were as pearls of wisdom, and whose harsh remarks preached of the world to come, kosher Judaism, and national loyalty. And when the time came to select a school for their sons, they did not hesitate to choose the *Talmud Torah* and the *Tarbut* school…And so the contribution of the Kovel youth to the Zionist pioneer movement and the rising tide of aliyah to the homeland was enormous.

Independent pioneering kibbutz cells were founded. Even the frailest of youths, pupils of the schools and the Hebrew gymnasia, girded their loins, took up saws and axes in their hands and set out for "preparation"… to the astonishment of their parents, who did not understand this "insanity" of their sons: why did they want to compete with the goyim, "hewers of wood, bearers of water," to ruin themselves with hard work, with the shameful toil of a day laborer, at a time when, thank God, nothing was lacking in the home. A few even sailed to a foreign land, suffering shortages and overcoming all kinds of obstacles and difficulties, waging the "war" against their parents, and preparing themselves with self-sacrifice for the building of the homeland.

[Page 38]

Nothing changed during the days of the First World War, nor the days of the occupation of Kovel by the Germans of Wilhelm, who did not prevent commercial and economic negotiations with the Jews, in order to take advantage of their initiative and talent for supplying provisions for their army. For their part, the Jews did not refrain from taking advantage of the rights given to them by the commandants and the highly-placed clerks with respect to their trades and professions (from whence arose the fatal confidence during the days of World War II that, once again, during the occupation by Hitler, things would not be so bad for them; for this reason most of the Jews of Kovel were unwilling to leave the city…). Also for this reason, they accepted the bad conditions, since they weren't too awful. For example, the Germans were distressed by the annoying problems of hygiene and cleanliness. For this reason, the Wilhelmian Germans were unwilling to allow the mountains of refuse and garbage outside the crowded wooden houses in the lanes of the "city," and nor the filth in the streets that had been the norm, nor yet on the lack of public restrooms. They began a program of public repairs and cleaning, and the goyim – the *yekkim*[slang for Germans] – never quite understood that the Jew, whose entire being was occupied with matters on a completely otherworldly level, did not have time for such mundane matters. Not only that, according to their habits and in their own special way, they began to investigate the internal matters of the Jews, to pass laws, give instructions and make lists of things the Jews were told to do, with fixed dates for bathing and laundering, and specific instructions for the use of candlesticks for the Sabbath candles in order to prevent fires. In spite of their efforts, none of the Jews followed their orders, for they only obeyed the instructions they received from God.

The Germans had less work to do in the Zand quarter (so called because it was built upon sandy ground) of Kovel which, not only from a topographical but also cultural-social standpoint, represented the center of advancement in the city. As opposed to the crowded wooden houses of the "city" there were stone houses, arranged along paved roads with clean sidewalks, including many of the city's public institutions: the old and new stations; the "Niebieski" Prospect (the new "Vokzalni" Street) – the romantic promenade for the young couples of the city; cinema houses; the newly-repaired bathhouse,; the Projenski synagogue for the "aristocracy" of the city, and the synagogue of the Zand – the center of religious, cultural-commercial life, the center for ritual objects of the Jews of "the sands" at the service and under the management of the famous beadle-mohel Reb Pinchas; the luxury shops with their modern showcase windows, the printing houses, the post office, and the *magistrat* [municipality]. When the Germans left the city in 1919, it was possible to find signs of renovations and decorations in the German style next to the houses of the Zand, and woven huts of German design, which the Jews of the Zand chose to imitate. Almost nothing remains now of the German influence in the city… The proud Poles who inherited the place of the Germans in World War I, and were the lords of the land when they took control of the eastern Ukraine, imposed their own culture on the occupied population, spreading a net of systematized assimilation by means of the creation of a chain of elementary schools at which in the beginning attendance was optional but later became mandatory.

[Page 39]

There were more than a few parents who preferred the practical value of "be a man outside and a Jew at home," who sent their sons and daughters to the Polish schools, and the Polish language began to take root in Jewish neighborhoods, becoming a symbol of the "bon ton" (cultured, well-educated high society). However, the despotic Poles could not defeat the determination of the Jews of Kovel to continue to maintain their traditional, nationalist lifestyle, even when the anti-Semitic Polish government refused to provide support for their educational institutions. Instead, the Jews themselves contributed the funds from their own pockets for two *Tarbut* schools – the *Herzliya* School in Zand and the school named after Dr. Klomel in the "city." Not only that, they did not rest until they had, with their own power, established an original Hebrew gymnasia in a splendid building in the center of town, where hundreds of faithful and devoted pioneers were educated in the idea of independence and statehood in their homeland.

Neither were the Jewish youths frightened by the new Polish decrees, which worsened daily and forbade Jewish nationalism. They established cells and training *kibbutzim* [collective farms] for work and *aliyah* [moving to Eretz Yisrael] and overcame the lack of accessibility and the limitations, taking to the streets of the city every year with spectacular ceremonies in celebration of Jewish holidays and demonstrating their strong desire to preserve the continuance of Jewish history and tradition.

In the last years before World War II and the victimization of a people, the Polish rulers became more and more harsh, forbidding all nationalist activity and celebratory public ceremonies, but they were no match for the stratagems of the youth against the worsening restrictions of the government. Their strength never lessened, and their resolve never weakened.

The Jews did not change their attitude during the start of World War II, when the Polish government was destroyed and was subordinated to the Soviet rule. It was difficult for the Jews of Kovel to withstand the deep cracks in the wall of their nationalism made by the Bolsheviks, with their fundamental and revolutionary economic, cultural and national differences. Some of the changes included the destruction of private commerce, the closure of the *Tarbut* schools and the *Talmud Torah*, and the establishment of communist schools in their place, and the sabotage thereby inflicted by the government on the way of life of the Jews, harming the soul of the Jewish child to the sorrow of the nationalists, the requirements of the cooperatives and their organization, which dissuaded the Jewish laborer from observing the Sabbath and celebrating his holidays by overworking him. All of this depressed and subdued the Jew's spirit, and perhaps because of this it is possible to see why the Jews of Kovel refused to leave the city at the onset of hostilities between the Germans and the Russians, when they were given the opportunity to flee to the Soviet Union, with the sword of Hitler hanging over their heads...

[Page 40]

Normally, the Jews accepted the Russian Bolsheviks, seeing them as rescuers from the threat of the German-Polish war, from the atrocities of the constant bombings and the fear of hooligans in the intervening days between the collapse of Poland and the expected German victory. Since during that time the Russians did not impose the rules of the communist government, the Jew was able to live in peace, and private commerce was able to operate together with the government cooperatives. The Jew knew how to manage, to go his own way in the tremendous national Bolshevist stream, which bathed them in comfortable waters in the midst of the Jewish nationalist-populist way of life of the Jews of Kovel and they lacked for nothing. That is, until the German – Soviet war broke out and the Soviets rushed to leave the city, leaving the Jews in the maw of the insane, ravaging Nazi beast and their lives were consumed. May their memories be blessed forever!

About Kovel and Its Jews

by L. Hazan

Translated by Amy Samin

It is heartbreaking to recall the many Jewish communities of Eastern Europe that were destroyed and lost in the deluge of blood.

The heart breaks many times over for the Jewish community that you once knew and where you once spent days and years, where you lived with people in joy and sorrow, at work and at rest, with hopes and aspirations. Together with them you longed for your homeland, with them you laid the foundation for building a people in our land, creating a culture, and reviving the language; but they were not able to see this dream come to life, because of the hand that was sent to destroy, which cut off their lives and brought them an agonizing death, while their eyes searched for help that did not come: perhaps someone will save us. But rescue did not come; dark despair covered everything, bringing with it horrible death.

How much Torah and wisdom, how much activity and thought, initiative and industriousness, how much Jewish intelligence and Jewish kindheartedness and feeling and devotion, how much vitality and spiritual and corporeal beauty were lost and will never return. Those who survived the Holocaust, the likes of which had never before been seen, ponder with broken hearts filled with anger, "How could it have happened? How could the pure have fallen? How could such an abomination have taken place so openly, and the heavens were indifferent, and the Throne of God didn't shake and collapse?

[Page 41]

Kovel, Kovel, the city and home of Jewish Volhynia...

Forests and swamps shared the vast plain that sprawled over hundreds of kilometers. Not mountains nor hills, but one plateau, and among the forests and the swamps, towns large and small populated by Jews, and among them Kovel, the "big city."

There were days, long ago, when the God-fearing Jews of Kovel wandered the plain, strong of faith and virtuous, spending time in the courtyards of the righteous, gathered together as a flock, requesting protection from danger. Calamity, the evil impulse, disease – where else could the Jews find protection, if not in the shade of such righteous ones?

Jews would sit and stand in their stores, waiting for shoppers, discussing matters relating to the house of study, criticizing the rabbi and the cantor, and complaining about the difficult times that had befallen them.

The border in those days was the river, and it was as if it had always told the city, "To here and no further!" and so the city gathered into itself, its streets and alleys, the marketplace and the shops, the houses of study and the cemetery. On the other side of the river were sand dunes, fields and gardens, and all other things with which no Jew had any contact.

But when the railroad tracks were laid and on the other side of the river a large train station was built from which trains set out for all parts of the country, their cars filled with lumber, linen, and leather, and arrived bringing all kinds of merchandise, the city began spreading out towards the railroad station. The Jews passed the watery border, built homes, warehouses and shops on the sands, and made a comfortable life there. But Jews cannot live without a house of study; so on the sands were built new houses of study and the sounds of prayer and Torah and filled the air.

*

Time passed and the seasons changed, and the Enlightenment spread out into every area, and the winds of change blew through the Jewish streets. In its heart, the Diaspora began to tire of exile and the longing for far-off Eretz Yisrael took hold, transforming into real activity. The Jews of Kovel were among the first in Poland to form strong ties with the ancient homeland of the people. Those who were experts in constructing on foreign sands thought about building a home on the sands of the shores of the Mediterranean Sea. They sent their sons to nationalist-pioneering youth movements which operated on behalf of the land, the sounds of the Hebrew language were heard in homes and on the streets, and Hebrew schools were founded, the crown jewel of which was the Hebrew *Gymnasia*.

Altogether, there were six or seven *gymnasias* in Poland, and one was in Kovel! Not for nothing did that happen, nor did random fate have a hand in the selection of that city as the home for one of the Hebrew buildings in a foreign country.

[Page 42]

The groundwork had been done, the desire was strong, and feelings were deep, all of which provided the strength to do battle with the state educational authorities, which regarded Hebrew educational institutions with a disapproving eye, opposed their establishment and harassed them as much as they were able. It was those things that gave the strength to overcome the internal obstacles and inhibitions, the lack of funds and support required for a high school, which had many expenses, and with empty hands but full hearts those involved did many great and wondrous things, producing class after class of young men and women, who were talented and prepared to go and build Eretz Yisrael and to live and renew the culture.

We, whose luck spared us the Holocaust, allowing us instead to sit and watch the building of Eretz Yisrael, know very well the part Kovel had in that building. That praiseworthy combination of vivacious Jews rooted in the past with education and common sense was useful for understanding the real, future needs of the people for a safe landing on the promised shores.

Bitter destiny brought a cruel end to that work; many of Kovel's Jews never arrived on that shore. Pioneers of spirit and pioneers of deed no longer come from Kovel to Eretz Yisrael. The bloodbath that drowned the community left no remnants; the heart breaks for the dear Jews who were lost and for Eretz Yisrael, which was denied a vital force for its revival.

*

And if we are speaking about the Jews of Kovel it is impossible to refrain from mentioning, in pain and in sorrow, the principal of the Hebrew gymnasia, Yosef Avrekh, may God avenge his blood. Ill-fated due to a physical disability, he was a devoted educator who also worked for the public good together with his friend, the afore-mentioned Asher Frankfort, in many different activities.

Those two were always the first to take action, and they were also the first to be touched by the unclean hands of the ravening German beasts that extinguished their souls, and after them the Holocaust came to the entire splendid Jewish community of the city of Kovel, one among the many Jewish communities, near and far.

*

[Page 43]

Who will count the number of the good Jews of the city, and of the many faithful people, of the innocent children and the pure mothers, of the young men and women, for whom we had such great hopes, and our hope was lost? Who will give us recompense?

My heart, my heart is with you, Jewish Kovel, and with the other Jewish cities in Eastern Europe, that were destroyed and no longer exist.

Is there comfort? Is there reparation for their blood?

Inhabitants of Kovel

By Baruch Bork

Translated by Amy Samin

The population of Kovel was made up of Jews, Ukrainians, and Poles. Until the resurrection of Poland, the number of Poles was so tiny that even a child could count their number. In commemoration of their names: the priest Shovelski (a friend to the Jews), the pharmacists Prejmovski, Eismond, Friedrichson, and a number of workshop owners.

The small, paltry church stood empty, even on Sundays. It only filled on the holiday of Christmas, when the Polish landowners from the surrounding area would come to pray.

With the outbreak of World War I and the establishment of the Polish government in the city, there were radical changes in the composition of the city's population. When the Russians had left the city in 1915, many Russians and Ukrainians left with them and Kovel had become in essence a city of Jews. With the German occupation of the city, Poles began to appear, and with the establishment of the country of Poland the city was flooded, literally, with Poles. Even so, the Jews remained the majority, with the Poles coming after. Ukrainians made up a small minority.

The Poles and the Ukrainians lived on the outskirts of the city, and the Jews in the center. The entire center of town was free of Christians. In the center of town were the government buildings and the municipal institutions. The treasury office, the offices of the regional governor, the health maintenance organization, insurance offices, city management, fire station, the P.K.O. Bank, the post office and the Sejmik. There were also a few Russian and Polish doctors and a few pharmacies.

Close to the outbreak of World War II, when on the Polish street the slogan "birds of a feather flock together" (*swój do swego*), which carried anti-Semitic undertones at that time, was the order of the day, a couple of Polish department stores opened in the Zand [so called because it was built on sandy ground] quarter of the city.

The relationships between the Jews and their Christian neighbors were normal; it's even possibly to say friendly, aside from the Andeki youth who were openly anti-Semitic and gathered in the engineering school (*miernicza szkoła*).

[Page 44]

In that school was raised and educated the hangman of the Jews of Kovel, Artur Schultz may his memory be cursed, who served as an officer in the Gestapo and was the person in charge of the *aktia* [roundup of the Jews for transport to death camps]. With the increase in the number of Poles in the city, the small, paltry church barely had room for its worshippers, so the Poles, together with the priest Prolet Snervarovski (who was, by the way, a good friend to the Jews) applied for permission to build a large, splendid church in the Zand quarter.

In the 1920s there were clashes between the Jewish youth of the city and the Polish youth which reached such serious dimensions as to involve crimes literally on the scale of pogroms. Only thanks to the intervention of the priest Prolet Snervarovski with the *starosta* [elected leader] Kovichi and the commander of the foot soldiers of Battalion 50 which was stationed in Gorky, were the Jews of Kovel saved from calamity. Indeed, with every threat that posed a danger to the Jews of the city, the priest used his authority to nullify the decree.

Most of the Polish population was made up of laborers and clerks, though most of the educated Poles would advance to other positions. Almost all of them belonged to the P.P.S. [Polish Socialist Party] and the N.P.R., such that the Andeki Party with OSAN did not have a large influence on the life of the city.

The majority of the Jewish population was religious. The fathers belonged to *Agudah* and *Mizrahi*. Those who did not hold political views were simply Chassids – of Trisk, Kotsk, Lubavitch, Stolin, Karlin, Neschiz, Steppen, and Radzin. Even most of the artisans and workshop owners of the older generation were religious. I remember a story people would tell about a man, a ladies' tailor, named Itchi Previn, who before his death instructed his family to put his worktable, at which he had toiled for 60 years, into his grave with him. When the Messiah came, the table would testify that he had never taken the leftover scraps of fabric for his own use.

It seems to me, that if someone were looking for one of the world's *lamed vavnikim* [36 righteous men], he could be assured of finding him amongst the workshop owners of Kovel.

The younger generation was freer in their activity, and mostly concentrated in the Zionist movements: General Zionists, *Hitachdut*, *Poale Zion* Left, *Hechalutz*, *Hechalutz Hazair*, *Hashomer Hazair*, *Beitar*, *Gordonia* and *HaOved*. A not insignificant number belonged to the Bund, and only a handful joined the communist party. Nevertheless, all of them, except for the communists, prayed in the synagogue on the Sabbath and it is hardly necessary to mention that they were quite devoted in their prayers during the Days of Awe.

The youths who, while at their clubs, released themselves from the burden of the *mitzvot* [religious commandments] would, upon their return home, behave like kosher, God-fearing Jews. Only here and there could you find a family whose son walked about bareheaded, but those cases were quite rare. The majority of the Jews of the city ended their lives in the framework of religion and tradition.

[Page 47]

Memories, Folklore and Way of Life

Sketches of Sights and Characters

by Yosef Aricha

Translated by Amy Samin

1. In the Still of the Night

Sometimes in the still of the night, as I sit alone on the veranda, serene after the nuisances of the day and the tumult of the city, surrounded by the murmurings of the night and the sparkle of the stars, suddenly scenes from my youth appear before me. They burst forth in an ambush and compel me to commune with them in the silence, demanding my complete attention; for those who created them amidst the joys of life are no longer, they have been slain. The sights are merely isolated scenes, glimmers of lost souls in the heavens: they are drawn before my eyes filled with pleasant memories, saturated with the radiance of the past and the charm of youth. It was the time of adolescence, the springtime of life, engraved upon my heart and absorbed into my essence, a yearning for all that is good, and beautiful, and noble. And there was I, one of the youths of Kovel, sculpting my character, dreaming dreams and spinning daydreams, experiencing first love. It was the first soul-stirring experience, filled with longing and tenderness, pleasant and sweet, when disappointment chases sleep from the eye; all of the first misgivings on the brink of adolescence.

Only in the still of the night do they come, all of those dear characters who did not complete the circle of their lives because of the cruel fate that no one, not us nor our fathers, could have imagined in all of its terror. There is in that communion with those sights and characters a sort of kindling of a memorial candle, as a sign of remembrance, for we cannot forget. The sacred obligation is to share that collection of memories, even if only a few strands of the web of life that was burned beyond recognition, to hoard the scattered embers of the fire of life that once illuminated and warmed.

The city that long ago was once aflutter and bustling with life and movement rises and stands before my eyes. I walk those streets, wandering amongst the ruins, revisiting the once-dear places, encountering my young friends who were not granted salvation, the charming girls, the affluent households, the extended families, relatives, merchants, artisans, the well-educated and the common folk, all of the representatives of the various strata of society which together made up the people of the Diaspora of Poland. I see many of them going about their tasks, busy in their professions, in the stores and the workshops, in wealth and in poverty. I recall various events, in both humorous and unhappy circumstances, and characters who, each and every one of them, could be used as the subject of a fascinating story; but this time, only general things or a very few incidents flow from my pen to paper.

I was a lad of thirteen when I came, together with all of my family; refugees of the war in 1919, uprooted from the city of my birth, Olevsk in the Ukraine, seeking a haven in Kovel in the Volhynia. We had left behind us our abandoned property, childhood memories and a wonderful town which we had left after the pogroms and to which we would never return.

[Page 48]

I knew that Kovel was only one stage in our passage; I had already made the conscious decision that the only path leading away from the bleeding land was immigration to Eretz Yisrael, an escape and the ultimate refuge. Kovel provided me with a place to prepare, and I was not distracted from that purpose; six years later I fulfilled my dream. Those six years of my youth were most invigorating, and they inspire my imagination as I pen these lines.

2. The River and the Bridge

Whenever I give a passing thought to Kovel, there appears before my imagination the inclined bridge above the river which divided the town into two main parts. First there was an old wooden bridge which rested on thick, tightly-fitted and interwoven wooden

The concrete bridge above the Tura

beams, beautiful but moldy and half-rotten; and later, a concrete bridge which was built by an enormous Russian engineer who, as well as he knew how to diligently supervise the pouring of the concrete – work which I followed closely for it was new to me and of great interest – was also diligent in gulping down liquor. I enjoyed listening to the ripe Russian and the wealth of curses he used, which definitely kept my attention and apparently also that of his workers, if one can judge by the pleasure they showed, with smirks and winks directed equally at the cursed and the curser. He was, however, an expert at building bridges and the one he built in Kovel was a fine one.

[Page 49]

Always, when I would make the ascent to the city – or as it was called, "the sand dunes" – or on my return, I would stop in the middle of the bridge and lean against the railing, delaying my progress while I filled my gaze with the flowing water which carried in its current signs of distant places; the refuse of beaches and settlements, the isolated boat in the hands of either a fisherman or a pleasure sailor, a laundress busy with her washing, and far off, at the bend of the river, nude bathers diving into the river from a slightly steep beach, a place known for the occurrence of drownings every year yet which drew with a magical pull the best swimmers to try their strength in a fervor of swimming and diving, while the most daring of them would show off their skill by jumping from a tall tree on the other bank.

I was drawn to the bridge also in the winter, when the river was frozen and covered with a dusting of snow. The snow would be cleared to the banks on either side, to allow the skaters to show off their wondrous tricks. Among them was my younger brother, who would draw the eye like few others could, with his agility and flexibility as he passed by, flying like an arrow sent from a bow, his silver skates close to his shoes scratching the ice with his easy movements. Many people would crowd the bridge, amazed at the sight, the girls coveting him with their eyes.

The bridge and the river… it was actually one of the smaller rivers, the Tura River. I never investigated its origins nor the twists and turns of its currents, where it strayed amongst the thick reeds on the far horizon, twisting like a brook with arms here and there, rivulets which formed an isolated island where trees grew sparsely, and joined together joining together in a wide spill on one side of the bridge. On the other side, the Tura gathered itself into one channel, deeper and more permanent, the water kissing the left bank on which were crowded the older, moldering houses of the city, the cramped lanes and yards, fenced and leveled, disordered, bustling with life and crowded with humanity. From the sawmill came the grating sounds of the saws, a never-ending whine, with the sounds of the sledgehammers and the bellows blended into the clamor. Sounds of life, and of labor; while on the other side of the river it seemed the city was significantly farther away, as if it had always reclined amongst the wide, grassy meadows, spreading into the distant horizon to the green iron bridge which bore the railroad tracks. Those widespread meadows were used for grazing cows and goats, for games, for youth movement gatherings, and especially for soccer matches.

Another arm of the river encircled the city with narrow, filthy channels that ran toward Trisk and Brisk, two long streets with one-story houses, some paltry and tumbledown, others new and substantial, well-kept, flooded with the scents of the gardens and fields which gave them the appearance of a village; for here the big city had not yet taken over with its straight lines and crowded conditions. Also on this arm of the river were wooden bridges which lacked the tumult of life that could be found on the part of the river that went through the center of town.

[Page 50]

3. On a Summer's Morning

Another happy coincidence that particularly raised the importance of that area in my eyes was that we lived for a number of years in the Stock family house on the banks of the river. In order to prevent the erosion of the land of the yard, which faced the river, wooden girders were thrust into the banks, a kind of shield against floodwaters, and also used as a pier for two or three boats which were bound together by chains. One of those boats was for our use, that is, for myself and my two brothers. On the other side of the river stood the large two-story walled house of old Varba, which housed first the Herzliya Hebrew school, then later the Hebrew gymnasia; the two institutions in which I received my education. On summer days I would walk to school over the bridge, while in the winter I would take an even shorter route; I would walk across the river on the ice.

Sometimes early on a summer's morning I would rise, and if on the same day the schedule included the subject of mathematics or algebra, something to which I was not partial, I would drop my knapsack into the boat, sit in the rear seat and, taking up the single oar would, with difficulty, paddle against the current, all the while straining my eyes to be sure no teacher was by any chance watching me, until I would disappear from view into the thicket of reeds upriver.

And there, far from the city, I would continue paddling, with great effort, against the current, more than a little tired from the effort of using only one oar, now paddling on one side, and then on the other, to a place where the beach curved slightly, and there I would tarry, giving myself a brief rest. There I would sense the rustling of the reeds, hear the twittering of the nearby birds, and my eyes would follow the colorful butterflies that glittered in the sunshine. After a short respite, I would continue my tour upriver, trying as hard as I could to make progress, taking pleasure in the knowledge that my reward would come upon my return down river, flowing easily with the current. Then, I would simply use the oar occasionally to steer, as the boat glided pleasurably and easily along on the water, and I would know why all the effort going up had been worthwhile.

Upon my return, there was little point in going to school even though the hour of mathematics class had passed. Instead, I would spend the remainder of the day lying supine in the field, my mind occupied with many thoughts. Two days later, however, when the teacher called me to the board and my failure to solve the exercise was obvious to all of my classmates, the teacher would send me back to my seat, saying, "It's no wonder! The time that you should have spent studying was instead wasted in boats on the river." He used the plural, boats, but to me the hours of pleasure spent in that single boat on a summer's morning are something I remember until today.

[Page 51]

4. The Hebrew Gymnasia

At that time, a daring experiment was made to found a Hebrew gymnasia in Kovel, although there already were other Hebrew gymnasia in Poland. Asher Frankfort (may God avenge his blood), its energetic founder and director, did not hesitate in the face of difficulties and his courage was boundless. In spite of all the uncertainties he founded the gymnasia, assembled a team of enthusiastic teachers, gathered students from educated homes who spoke the language, and within a short period of time the gymnasia became an important source and supporter of culture in the public life of Kovel. Also in this city, all of the Jewish political parties were reflected as in a looking glass in all of their different tendencies, the nationalistic and those in opposition, with which Poland was blessed in abundance when it first regained its independence.

I was among the first students of the gymnasia. I don't know if my head was more preoccupied with soccer and sport in general than studies, but I do know that in this institution I came to understand my obligation to the values of the past, our language and literature, and I enjoyed the influence of a few excellent teachers, men of soul and vision, who planted within us a longing for our origins. Two of them I meet still today with great fondness; they are Z. Ariel and Dr. Yaacov Nataneli. The first well understood the spirit of a disorganized student like myself; he was a man graced with the understanding of a great pedagogue, who was not strict about every detail, and who could see into the hearts of his students. The second knew how to instill in me a fondness for Hebrew literature, its poetry, and the relationship of the values of beauty and esthetics. He praised my compositions highly and was very welcoming to me. My first writing was published in "Mashtelah L'Sofrim Tzirim" ("Nursery for Young Writers"), which A. Lovoshitzki referenced in the margins of the "Kochav" ("Star"), a monthly literature magazine for youth, which was published in Warsaw and Lódz. In those days in Kovel I dreamed of becoming a Hebrew-language writer, and my collected works included stories, essays and legends.

I have especially good memories of the teacher Joseph Avrekh (may God avenge his blood), a man of soul and fervor in his conversation and his lessons, a dear man who did not find salvation and go to the Holy Land. After his death, a legend grew surrounding his behavior, that of honorable steadfastness and bravery against the Nazis. While on the verge of death he hurled into the faces of those beasts everything he held in his heart, and with a prophet's rage predicted that they would not escape from punishment; he told them these things while filled with fear as he awaited his execution.

[Page 52]

He continued talking until a filthy hand shoved a gun in his face. I also remember well the music teacher Feinstein, (may God avenge his blood) thanks to whom we learned Hebrew music and songs. And there was a teacher of Polish and German who would come to teach us from Lvov, a very cultured and polite woman who experienced for the first time the renewal of Hebrew culture, which was foreign to her. Later, teachers Dr. Ben-Shem and Hazan came, each with his own expertise, fostering education and enlightenment; other teachers came, as well. Each one was diligent in his profession, though equipped with textbooks which lacked more than they provided, and were superficial and imprecise.

The gymnasia was crowded with students whose language was Hebrew, from Kovel and the surrounding area; the children of towns and villages, boys and girls who thronged to experience the flavor of the Hebrew ambiance. The gymnasia was a fortress for the proponents of Hebrew culture, who saw it as both a victory and an achievement. Receptions were held there in connection with the Jewish holidays and important dates in the genesis of national revival. Live performances were given in Hebrew, which demonstrated great ability, and created a unique atmosphere effervescent with the collaboration of teachers and students. They were a great source of pride for the adults, parents and community leaders, when they came to witness the wonder and excitement of the Hebrew revival which paved the way for an even more daring fulfillment in the near future, and brought together members of the national movement.

Later, after I had left Kovel and moved to Eretz Yisrael and had learned how the gymnasia had prospered, the principal Dr. Frankfort came as an emissary; we helped him construct a building especially for the gymnasia. I remember that when he held in his hands the journal "Davar," wherein I had published an article of appreciation about the gentleman, his life's work and the purpose of his visit, his eyes sparkled with joy and his face wore a rosy blush. When he embraced me with great affection and patted my shoulders, he brought back old memories when he said, "Do you remember when I used to shout 'Stop! Stop! Stop!'?"

Of course I remembered. At the public receptions held at the gymnasia, gymnastics were part of the program. The receptions were held in the same auditorium that was used for gymnastics lessons and there were rings and a trapeze suspended from the ceiling. Without boasting, I can safely say that in this area of my studies I was indeed outstanding. When I performed my acrobatic feats on the trapeze and the rings, Dr. Frankfort would fear I was about to fall – God forbid - from the equipment, tumble to the ground, and shatter my bones. He would jump up from his seat filled with trepidation, and shout with all of his strength, as he attempted to save me from calamity, "Stop! Stop! Stop!" He would return to his seat and relax only when he saw me standing once again on the stage, still alive and in one piece, pale from exertion and wearing an expression of victory on my face.

Oy! Those evening receptions…At one of them, I had in my pocket a big bar of chocolate which I had bought before-hand to give to a girl I thought pretty, but by the time I could rescue her from the circle of boys that surrounded her, and found in my heart the courage to walk with her outside, arm in arm, the chocolate bar in my pocket had turned into a warm puddle.

[Page 53]

5. Youthful Mischief

The locations of our games and entertainments would vary from place to place, according to need and circumstances; we met frequently at the sports field, went swimming in the river, arranged bicycle races, attended the silent movies or entertainment houses, and we even gathered on the lane where the great synagogue was located. On holidays, or the eve of Simchat Torah, we would encounter one another there; young men and women would flirt outside, with much joking and frivolous behavior, then we would enter the synagogue and, for a scant hour, behave circumspectly.

The great synagogue was an enormous building, built at the front of burnt red bricks which darkened with the passage of time, with the façade looking out into the gloomy lane. It was quite solid, and covered with a design of protuberances and projections. At the corners pillars rose up from solid bases. In the upper windows there were large stars of David. Inside, it looked different; it was swathed in the brilliance of many radiant lamps, tinted and magnificent. I see the synagogue full of people, and its front courtyard teeming with humanity. Also before my eyes are the gatherings of the young men and their mischief. This night, there is to be a gathering of the people, with a speech by a famous man from Warsaw, the capital, who will discuss the elections of the Polish Sejm. He is a famous Zionist, a jealous protector of Hebrew language and culture. At the entrance are guards wearing the ribbons of the Maccabi movement, who refuse to allow us, the youth, to enter.

One young man, nimble and daring, began to plan an invasion of the synagogue. His group of friends was right behind him, ready for action. He led them around to the back of the synagogue, stopping by the faded old wooden fence. He peeked through the cracks at the door through which the worshippers would exit to the yard. He pointed to the upper portion of the door, where there was fixed a piece of glass, intended to bring in some light to the darkness inside. He turned to his friends:

"First we need to shatter the glass, and then break in," he said.
"But who will break the glass?" wondered one of the youths, the one with the crossed eyes, while looking from side to side to see if anyone was listening to him.
"Definitely not you!" said Menachem, the leader of the group, mockingly. As he spoke, he bent down, picked up a stone and threw it at the opening in the door with perfect aim.

[Page 54]

We could hear the tinkling of the glass as it shattered into bits, and immediately afterwards the voice of Menachem:

"Friends! Bend down and cover your heads." His friends obeyed him, throwing themselves face down onto the dry and dusty earth while holding their breaths, except for Menachem who kneeled down and peeked into the yard through the crack

"What do you hear?" asked someone.
"Complete silence."
"Maybe they went out to ambush us?"
Menachem listened very carefully, and then calmed his friends:
"No. I think that those inside didn't even hear the glass break, because it's very noisy in there, and the door to the sanctuary is always kept closed. Very soon we'll begin to climb."

Just to be sure, he waited another few minutes. Once he was certain there was no danger, he was the first to jump up and with great agility threw himself over the fence. His friends were quick to follow. In the yard they found an old wooden plank, which they took and placed at an angle leading up to the small aperture in the door as a sort of ladder. The daring and nimble Menachem went first, clearing away the pieces of broken glass still clinging to the window frame and sticking his head through to peer around inside. All was darkness, compressed and unpleasant, filled with the musty smell of mildew. The young man listened very carefully for a moment, to assure himself that all was well, then quickly slid his legs down. He hung by his fingertips for a moment, clinging to the door above, let go and slid down straight into a barrel filled with the water that had been used by worshippers for the ritual washing of hands, which stood in front of the door.

This was a nasty shock for Menachem. He was submerged in the cold and murky water up to his thighs, but he kept quiet and didn't let a sound escape his lips, for an idea was already forming in his mind. He carefully climbed out of the barrel, looked up towards the opening and saw the face of one of his friends who was preparing to follow him. He quietly told him:

"Come straight down, quickly…"

The youth slid swiftly down, straight into the barrel. He broke out in moist goose bumps, and prepared to let out a shout, but Menachem quickly covered his mouth with his hand, while whispering in his ear:

"Don't yell, you fool! They'll all jump into the barrel…"

[Page 55]

The two stood, wet and dripping and called to the third to follow them:

"Come down, quickly!"

He also jumped straight into the barrel. They slapped their hands over his mouth, while comforting him with the same whispered words, then calling to the fourth:

"Come down, quickly!"

"Just like that, my dears" whispered the jubilant Menachem, "straight into the barrel, whoops!"
"You villains! Why didn't you tell me?" said one youth.

Menachem laughed, "Why didn't we tell him?...Do you think that this lovely dunking was waiting only for us?"
"But how will I go home?" asked the one who complained.
"How?" mocked Menachem. "On foot."

The rest burst into laughter, which only added to the youth's wrath.

"You're mocking me, you thief!"
"What did you say?"
The youth was silent.
"What did you say?"
"I said what I said."
"Oh, yeah? I'll show you…!" and Menachem raised his hand and slapped the youth on the cheek.
"You hit me?" he shouted, angry and insulted. He jumped onto Menachem, fists flying. One of the youths quickly tried to separate the two combatants; but Menachem, secure in his strength, called out to him in the heat of battle:

"Let me go, and I'll teach him the story of Balak!"

The two youths grappled in the darkness; locked together in combat they rolled around on the floor, the heavy sounds of punches and the ringing of slaps filling the room. After only a few minutes, Menachem sat astride the other, pounding on him in a rage. He only released him when the youth's howls and wails became so irritating and strident that they seemed likely to summon people to discover their source. Menachem got up off him and threw himself to the door, where he shot back the bolt and burst outside, accompanied by his friends, inflamed, sweaty and satisfied. He had proved his prowess in fighting.

"You really taught him a lesson!" said one of the youths.
"I could take on three more like him!"
Suddenly, Menachem turned to one of the others and said,

[Page 56]

"Tell me, is the scratch on my face quite large?" He stopped next to a light so the one he questioned could get a good look.

The youth looked, took hold of Menachem's chin and tilted his face up.

"A fair-sized scratch. All the way across the cheek."
"That pig!" complained Menachem. "He scratches with his nails just like a girl!"

The scratch worried him quite a bit and spoiled his mood. Clothes would dry out, but the scratch – what of that? It couldn't be wiped from the face…It was a shameful mark of disgrace engraved upon his face by his rival, and his mother would demand to know the meaning of it. His friend tried to calm him:

"No matter, in another two or three days the scratch will be gone completely."
"Yes, but how can I go home?"
"How?" teased one of his friends, paying him back. "On foot!"

6. A Fair Division

Near our home on the river was the house of Kaploshnick. Even now I don't know if that was a nickname or his real name. Unlike his name, Kaploshnick (hat maker) sold rather than made hats. He had a fine house, and a tidy shop with a picture window, quite splendid. He had two sons, and since he was a widower, his sons kept house for him while he ran the business by himself; behaving honorably toward the women and treating everyone with respect.

His two sons rarely left the house, keeping busy with whatever it was that they did there. Their father was not a tall man, yet was still taller than they. He was known for his conversation and his occupation, his measured gait and his polite manners, which inspired respect. He was a smooth sort of elderly man, with his head of snowy white hair and his meticulous manner of dressing. In the winter he wore clothing from a fine quality black woven cloth; and in summer, a lightweight white cloth. He wore glossy patent leather shoes upon his feet. His tie was always impeccably arranged, and his collar shiny; in his entirety he was an example of cleanliness, precision and neatness. He was known as a well-organized, polite man, who always spoke pleasantly, yet he had a commanding presence; he had a strong personality and imposed his will on others. He was far from being an idle old man; not in his own eyes, nor in the eyes of the ladies.

One day he set the whole town talking about something he had done, something that was difficult to understand but yet was accepted with good spirit and enjoyment, as a sort of pleasurable joke. On a trip to Warsaw he met there M.G., also of Kovel, and who also operated a shop that sold hats. The two businessmen from Kovel went together to purchase a large quantity of bonnets in a variety of styles. In order to save on shipping costs, the two decided to have all of the hats sent together in one crate to Kaploshnick's address. When he returned from the city and received the package, Kaploshnick told his friend to come and pick up his half of the hats.

[Page 57]

For some reason, the fellow did not come. Two days later, Kaploshnick again told him to come, but still he didn't respond. After a few more days, Kaploshnick sent one of his sons to M.G. with yet another message to come and take his hats; this time there was also a warning, for Kaploshnick's patience was at an end. He waited after that announcement was delivered, but – worse luck – the man still did not come. This infuriated Kaploshnick, who saw it as an insult to his honor. He did not send any further messages, but he invited two of his Jewish neighbors to come to his shop, and told them:

"Do you see this crate? There are hats and bonnets inside that my friend, the merchant M.G. and I purchased together, each paying for his portion. The merchandise belongs half to him and half to me. I have invited him three times to come and pick up his portion, but he has not come. You will be my witnesses, because I am going to divide up all of this merchandise into two equal lots while you watch. I will not give preference to myself, nor will I short-change his portion."

And so, in the presence of the two witnesses, the old man grasped hold of a pair of scissors and sat down with restraint on a chair close to the crate, which he opened and from which he removed one of one style of hat, and another from a different style. With great care and gravity, he cut each hat in two. One piece he laid down on his right, for himself, and the other on his left side for the merchant who did not come. When he had finished his work, he called for a porter and sent the half on the left to its owner. The town was agog!

He was seen two days later, walking outside near his shop, elegantly dressed as was his wont, a serious expression of deep thought engraved upon his face. He approached people and greeted them without a single sign of levity. Clearly, he did not see his actions as amusing or a joke, for someone who believes in order and discipline expects others to treat him as he treats them.

7. The Scouts Organization

A particular source of pride was the Scouts organization founded by Baden-Powell. At its head stood Lucia Hodorov (now ship's captain Eliezer Hadrav) who, even as a young man, showed great talent for action and a fine skill for organization. He used to give enthusiastic and inspiring speeches in formal Russian. My friends and I wrote him a letter, because we thought that it wasn't right for the head of a Jewish organization such as that to give speeches in Russian. We considered it an insult to our national feeling. Lucia accepted our assertion. At his next public appearance, he spoke in Yiddish, and a short while later he succeeded in learning Hebrew and began making speeches in that language. From the beginning it was an exceptional educational organization run in the spirit of Baden-Powell; later, national nuances with an orientation towards developing our values was added.

It is to Lucia Hodorov's credit that the youth of Kovel were bound together in a unified group. His counselors imparted to the youth the genesis of self-knowledge and a recognition of the uniqueness of our national values.

[Page 58]

Hodorov organized parties for the youth which included singing, acting, reciting and gymnastics (in which my younger brother Yoelik and I would climb to the top of a living pyramid), trips on Lag B'Omer, formations, and field trips – we presented an impressive appearance. And for us, it meant the first meetings with girls, going walking on moonlit nights, and romance, the flavor of which will always remain in our memories. It is appropriate to also mention the movement Hashomer Hatzair, which was a competitor to the Scouts organization. This rivalry frequently set the town abuzz with many ideological arguments over differences in purpose and character. There were cases of "defection" from one group to the other, and more than once parents were forced to intervene when the fiery discussions moved beyond their narrow focus and became issues involving the public and its leaders. In other words, among the youth there was quite a bit of agitation.

9. Firefighters

I remember the pride with which we would anticipate the parade of the firefighters of Kovel. Leading the company, following the sounds of its orchestra, the Jewish captain Brandes would march or ride upon his horse, wearing a shiny copper hat and with a pistol strapped to his thigh. A proper company of men, wearing copper hats and equipped with firefighting tools, marched after him in an orderly and regimented fashion. Bringing up the rear were wagons equipped with water barrels and the red fire extinguishing equipment. The firefighting unit was an entirely Jewish organization, all volunteers, who were amazingly skilled in putting out the fires, both real and fabricated, which broke out in Kovel almost every day.

The firefighters proved to be a talented, extremely disciplined organization, nearly military in its fine, well-organized performances of duty. The public appreciated their fine appearance during parades and holidays, which caused the Christians of the city to view the Jews with more respect. The sounds of the orchestra's music raised our spirits and we reveled in every display of Jewish bravery, and in every hint of order and discipline customary in a civilized nation. We took those things to be glimmers of freedom and a felt desire to show others that these were not merely simple firefighters, but sons of a minority that, if left undisturbed in their organizations, could create institutions no less marvelous than those of their neighbors, brave in spirit and strong in body.

10. Sports Organizations

There were also sports organizations, whose soccer teams made a name for them in the area. The commissioner of the Maccabi team borrowed me from Kadima as a goalie because I had a reputation for being an excellent goal keeper in spite of my youth.

[Page 59]

I took part in all of the important competitions that took place between various towns against teams made up of citizens or soldiers in the army, which came to play in our city, and I traveled with the Maccabi team to Luts'k, Rivne, Brest, Ludmir, Lublin and other towns. These soccer competitions always turned into events in the city, drawing many spectators, and if it should happen that the two teams represented two peoples, such as Jews or Poles, there was often a great deal of expectation and apprehension over the results. Just as a loss would spoil the mood of the supporters of one team, a victory would raise the spirits of the winners. Often the military orchestra from the army base at Gorky would play. The atmosphere was usually celebratory, and the well-to-do people of the city would be amongst the spectators. Although there was no lack of incidents between the players, or outbursts of anti-Semitism from the proud Polish players when a loss would cause them to lose control of themselves, usually the competitions were carried out in a sportsmanlike atmosphere and the officiating was, more often than not, objective. We established ties of friendship with the players from the other Jewish teams, and it should be pointed out that there were many excellent athletes who could have been part of national teams. From time to time the ranks of our team would thin out, because many players left Kovel; some moved to the Holy Land, others emigrated to Argentina or other places. I myself moved to Eretz Yisrael in 1925, the year I reached my peak as a soccer player. In the farewell parties given in my honor by my friends and the sports organizations, I received, among other things, three silver tokens engraved with the figure of an athlete standing in a goal, of varying designs. In my wanderings those tokens were lost, but the memory of them is engraved upon my heart, and if I close my eyes for a moment, I see the soccer field and my young friends (as they were then!) running on it, healthy and refreshed, abundantly joyful and full of life.

A significant portion of the youth of Kovel was educated in the gymnasia that was part of the heritage of the Russian government, under the direction of Klara Davidovna, an educated and energetic woman. With the transfer of government to the Poles, the curriculum of the gymnasia was transferred to a Polish system of study. She understood that in keeping with the times, it was in her interest to support the national Jewish spirit that existed in Kovel. She dedicated hours to the study of the Hebrew language, Hebrew literature, and Jewish history. During the receptions she organized, one could hear coming from the stage Hebrew songs and scenes from national theater productions. The students of that gymnasia had a sports organization by the name Legia. Some of the youth who participated were assimilated Jews who, over the course of time, were caught up in the current of nationalism, and a few of them moved to Eretz Yisrael. There was also a sports organization for nationalist youth, which was called Bar Kochba, as well as one from the Hebrew gymnasia, which was called Kadima.

[Page 60]

11. Kadima

Whenever I think about Kadima and my friends from that time, my heart swells with feeling. A few of the members of Kadima moved to Eretz Yisrael; a clear and understandable result after much advanced planning. The desire to fulfill that aspiration was always with us, first and last. Among the first to go were Uri Alpert, the first president of Kadima, and myself, also a former president of Kadima. I went with my older brother Moshe. After us came Shlomo Cantor, Yitzhak Finkelstein, the Vikus brothers, Flanzman, Erlich and Meir Segal z"l, and others. Those who hesitated and did not go to Eretz Yisrael, for one reason or another, perished.

Kadima was a national organization in the fullest sense of the word. Its rules were written in Hebrew, and even on the playing field it was possible to hear Hebrew coming from the mouths of its members. This did not prevent the members of Kadima from joining other organizations such as the Scouts or Hashomer Hatzair. A few joined the Hechalutz (Pioneer) organization and went to work in the training quarries in Klosova. Only after training at the kibbutz (collective settlement) in Klosova could members, according to a set order, receive permission to move to Eretz Yisrael. My older brother and I were able to jump to the head of the line thanks to an immigration license we were sent by one of the farmers in Rehovot. This farmer had pleasant memories of my father, whom he had known when, in 1914, he moved to Eretz Yisrael and was housed in the home of the farmer's father in Rehovot.

The matter of moving to Eretz Yisrael occupied most of the time of the young members of Kadima. I had arguments with some of the members who, for some reason, delayed completing the required training. In my heart I believed that if they did not immigrate soon, it was doubtful they would do so later on. Even now, my heart aches for two of them, those who were my very best friends. One of them was Yaacov Segal, smart and handsome; he was my best friend, the person I could share secrets with and talk to about anything; the other was Baruch Toib, who was level-headed, knowledgeable, and pleasant company. Even though he and I once courted the same girl, there existed between us true friendship and understanding. I know that they were both active in cultural and public life, for they were possessed of special qualities and wonderful personalities. But when the time came to immigrate – they missed their opportunity.

12. The Muscovite Shoemaker

We called him the Muscovite shoemaker because he always used to tell us stories about the city of Moscow. He was tall, bony and strong, with a face like a young man, with his dreams written there. He lived in a basement in the lane near our house, and we often had disputes with him over the newspapers, weeklies, and magazines that we would always buy before the Sabbath, and which he would "steal" from us. It turned out that he read incessantly, and was always thirsty for anything he could lay hands on to read that was written in Yiddish, which was his only language.

[Page 61]

[Page 62]

I used to visit him frequently, mainly because my shoes were constantly in need of repair and I would exploit them, with patch upon patch, repairs to the heels and soles, until they were tattered beyond repair. I was a regular visitor of the Muscovite shoemaker, because he didn't keep his word, and I would have to urge him on. I will admit, I found him fascinating. First of all, he sang, and beautifully, while he worked. He frequently sang folk songs by Avraham Reizel and others. They were songs that touched the heart, about young seamstresses shriveled by poverty, about the difficult days of workers, the simple people and the bitter-hearted, and about revolutionaries who had been sent to Siberia.

Mostly, the songs were about Moscow and Siberia. Those were the subjects that he would most often discuss. He told me of the walls of the Kremlin, of the huge bell and the tremendous cannon, which were truly king-sized; of the revolutionaries working underground, and the assassins of tyrannical kings and governors. He described magnificent adventures as if he himself had planned and performed them. He also spoke of his own imprisonment, how he stood trial and was sent to the wilderness of Siberia, and how under the influence of Gershoni, who escaped his prison in a barrel of cabbage, he too was able to escape and return to Kovel. He would speak of these things with a natural charm, filled with a great many details and dramatic incidents. His wife was a tender, delicate blond who I always saw sitting in the corner, her pregnancy near full term, smiling a gentle smile and nodding her head while she listened, as if to stories created in the imagination of one of her children. Later, the meaning behind her mysterious smile became clear to me; I learned that the shoemaker had never been to Moscow, had never been arrested and had certainly never been to Siberia. In fact, he had never left the confines of Kovel. All of his stories were the fruits of his imagination and his extensive reading of newspapers, which provided him with abundant material. In spite of that, his character was not damaged in my eyes, for I knew him to be a man who, living in poverty in his narrow basement, could create for himself a world full of experiences in order to escape his humdrum life. He was able to fill the lack in his life with his rich imagination, which took flight to Moscow and the wilderness of Siberia.

Kadima group, 1923. Courtesy of Anna Didrikh Arsenieva and the Israeli Organization of the Jews of Kovel and Its Surroundings.
Standing, left to right: Benyamin Kaminski, Levenberg, Ben-Zion Soinyuch, Shmuel Vikus, Shlomo Cantor, Meir Segal, Feivel Erlich, Benyamin Mekaveh, Yitzhak Finkelstein.
Seated, left to right: Faculty advisor Semen Didrikh, Yoelik Dolgin (editor), Baruch Toib, author Yosef Aricha (president of Kadima), Avraham Flanzman, Avraham Waldman, Shbedyuk.
Seated on the ground, left to right: Shmuel Goz, Yaacov Becker, Izik Zafran. This photo was replaced using another print from the same negative.

13. Not Completely Finished

I have committed to paper only a tiny portion of my collection of memories, some scenes and character sketches. Due to a lack of time I did not write more, and what I have written was done in haste. There are still many things in my heart of which I have not spoken, and my eyes still wander the streets and lanes of Kovel as I recall the dealings I had with those who I encountered on my way, and through a veil of fog (or tears…) I see the dear and beloved, whose flame of life was cruelly extinguished by the Satan of our generation.

[Page 63]

The stories that survived of what occurred among those imprisoned in the synagogue, the words they wrote in blood on the walls before setting off on their final journey to a mass grave outside of town, sentence us to return and rekindle their memories. May these few pages be as memorial candles.

[Page 63]

In the Cycles of the City

by Dr. Reuven Ben-Shem

Translated by Amy Samin

1. A Lamentation for Kovel

I knew you Kovel, I knew you, loved you, engraved you on my brain and in the depths of my soul for you are, and were, deserving of that, Kovel.

I knew you from both sides of the bridge, the Zands and the city. I knew your streets, teeming always with Jews - men, women and children, workers and students, merchants and artisans, wearing weekday clothing and immersed in the practical business of living and economics, and then again adorned in Sabbath clothing with their souls shining from their eyes, examining the world of the Holy One, Blessed be He, and the world of the *goyim*.

I knew your youth, Kovel, the dear, pleasant Jewish youth who loved and dreamed, who yearned and dreamed, worked and expected, prepared for a life of exile on one hand and the release from slavery on the other.

And now you are gone, Kovel, now your name has been erased from the map of the Jewish people, that which lived and is no longer in Poland, and the Jews in their everyday clothes and their Sabbath finery no longer can be found in you, almost all of them were cut down. My heart, my heart goes out to you, dear beloved city, I lament you: "Woe for the beauty that is rotting in the soil!"

The Jews who fought and hoped are no longer in Kovel, those who expected salvation, who mourned - deep in their hearts, in the darkness of night and in the darkness of their lives - the lament of Israel; Jews who dragged their lives from one abyss to another, while deep in their hearts they carried the eternal hope, the great expectation of Israel Saba: the day will come, the day of emancipation, and the herald will call out freedom to the life-long slaves of the *goyim* – freedom for the Jewish people.

Today, no one waits any longer in Kovel, for there are no more to wait…no more Jews. Jewish Kovel is dead; it is dead and will never rise again. Only memories of what was familiar, known, and bound close with ties of love within them will bring Kovel to life, and they will carry it deep in their hearts because there is no freedom from that bitter memory.

[Page 64]

Foreigner and resident was I, Kovel. I spent months within your walls, months of work and creativity, immersed in the lively Jewish way of life that brought pleasure and satisfaction.

The year was 5684 [1924]. Polish and Jewish Kovel had barely managed to lick the bleeding wounds the war had inflicted, leaving the city in the ruins which served as living testimony to the German-Russian-Austrian-Polish-Bolshevist-Ukrainian explosions which fell time and again from the skies of Kovel upon the city.

Like her neighbors, Kovel passed from hand to hand, from a defeated enemy to a victorious enemy. The defeated took out their rage, and the victors celebrated their success, by spilling Jewish blood. Jews were massacred with the departure of the Ukrainians and slaughtered upon the arrival of the Poles. When the Germans left, the Ukrainians took over the massacre, and in a sort of Bolshevist *Had Gadya* they were replaced by the Poles – the legionnaires of Pilsudski and of Heller – and the Jewish blood flowed.

Between killings, from defeat to victory, the Jews of Kovel continued, with their vibrant Jewish strength that is so unique to our people, in their work and their labor, the work of Israel Saba. They did not give up, and with the dawn they would hurry to pray at the Great Synagogue, one of the smaller synagogues, or in one of the *shtiebels* [small houses of prayer] in the city and the Zands. Even late into the night, the sounds of prayers for salvation did not cease in the homes of the Jews. Although it may tarry, every Jew would wait for its arrival. Such prayers were constantly on the lips of the Jews, in the *cheders*, and the schools, where they would study, cry, sigh, and dream – dream of the great day of emancipation. Reality forced hundreds of Jewish youth to the *goyish* forces, where dozens of them died on the front lines on foreign soil.

Although in 5684 the Jews were still licking their wounds, and the blood spilled from the ruptured veins of the Jewish public was still fresh and had not yet dried, they still returned to a full life. There were two Jewish *gymnasias* in the city, in one of which the language of instruction was Hebrew, and the sounds of the Hebrew youth could be heard signifying a revival, and also an arrival yet to come.

2. The Hebrew *Gymnasia*

In the Hebrew *Tarbut gymnasia*, I wore three hats, for I was a teacher of Latin, Polish, and history. I discovered three things there which only Jews in the Diaspora were capable of bearing without harming or being hurt by them:

    a. A Jewish-nationalist teachers' group in which every heart, every soul, contained the same cry, the same longing, the same dream: Zion and emancipation. This group was under the control and instructions of the Polish governing body, which was hostile to the Jewish people and which harassed their way of life, their culture, their aspirations and dreams.

[Page 65]

    b. A curriculum which was designed to inculcate in the hearts of the pupils a love for the Polish homeland, its past and its future. We were required to implant in the hearts of the Jewish youth a love for the Polish people, admiration for the rulers of Poland, its aristocracy and its despots, in a program which included learning Polish songs and reciting Polish poetry and the works of its authors, with no choice in my instruction. "The spirit of the youth is the property of our nation," claimed the Polish supervisor, demanding the Polish soul of the Hebrew youth. The *Tarbut Gymnasia* fulfilled its obligations precisely, but from the opposite direction – from west to east, towards Jerusalem and its soul.

    c. And finally, the rending of the soul of the Jewish way of life in the Diaspora: the tear within. They stood camp against camp, Jews against themselves. The assimilated were on one side, the nationalists on the other, and communists in the middle, in the arteries of the people. Suspicion and instability placed obstacles and stumbling blocks, bad-mouthing and all of the other side effects that occur in nature in the miserable fight for existence and the search for a spiritual handhold under uncertain circumstances.

The principal, Asher Frankfort, may his blood be avenged, brought me into my position and then lay in wait behind the door, listening to see what would be my fate. Would the students be disruptive, ready to swallow me alive like a fox according to the obligation of every student in the world (and Jewish children were not exempt from this custom) of testing the new teacher, of learning what he is made of, and discovering what they could get away with?

My first morning passed successfully. I was called to the principal, and he presented me with his advice and fatherly instructions. Frankfort was the initiator, the founder of the institution, the organizer, the person in charge in the eyes of the public, and the official principal of the *gymnasia*. He was filled with anxiety over the fate of his life's work. Jewish cleverness and Hebrew tradition merged in him in his struggle with destiny. He fought with the Polish *kortor* [inspector] he struggled with the parents who preferred to send their children to the schools with "rights," he strove to eradicate from the hearts of the students the negative attitude they had regarding the value of Hebrew and the Hebrew teachers, and he fought with himself, that the moth of desperation and the mosquito of doubt wouldn't consume him from within.

And I was absorbed into the staff of teachers.

The winter struck with full force. The bitter cold held the universe in its frosty arms with an iron grip. The snow squeaked underfoot, and the chill of the wind sent sharp needles into us and we, the teachers of the *Tarbut* school, warmed ourselves at the hot stove of the gymnasia.

[Page 66]

The head of the warm-up review was Leibovitz[1] with his witty jokes and his sharp insights, radiating cleverness, Israel Saba and his eternal dream.

His sidekick and some-time assistant, and frequently his scholarly opponent, was my friend Yaacov Netaneli-Rothman[2] who had a reputation as a lyricist and was an expert in the *Torah* of Israel on the one hand and the wisdom of the *goyim* on the other.

During this period *HaTzfirah* published his series entitled "*Higionut*" [Common Sense], and around the stove each and every word was dissected, and armed with our paltry knowledge we argued over every definition and every sentence. We raised doubts about everything, doubts to annoy him, doubts about the existence of what he had written in one of his articles, the doubt of common sense – like seasoning on food. Then the well-springs of his knowledge bubbled forth, and he flooded us with idioms, simple explanations, interpretations, and justifications from near and far.

Our friend Dr. Hollander, lawyer, history teacher, stood apart. His knowledge of Hebrew was not in direct proportion to his knowledge of history; his contributions to the discussion were limited to corrections of historical dates and ensuring that the facts were accurately stated. He was knowledgeable of all of the dates of the teachers' meetings, salaries and similar facts.

Angry and withdrawn sometimes, and with occasional outpourings, pacing in the small room that was used as the teacher's lounge, was my dear close friend Yosef Avrech, may his blood be avenged. He possessed a wealth of knowledge about the history of Israel and the *Talmud*. He sharpened his teeth with restrained anger and wrath that made his eyes blaze, and he tormented himself. He chastised not only us but especially the Diaspora, our poor living conditions, and the shame of the Diaspora which was exposed and revealed to all.

Our conversations might include a serious matter in the *Talmud*, or the words of the *Rambam*, an explanatory note (commentary) of the *Rabad* [Rebbe Avraham Ben David], and the adjutants of the *Rambam*, all of which found in him their knight and judge, one who fought their battles, who prosecuted their offenses and sought their repair.

And in his excitement, the man brought evidence from the *Rif* [Rebbe Itzhak Alfasi], from *Tosefot*, from Bialik, and from Yehuda Leib Gordon, all in one basket. I looked deeply into his eyes, and it seemed to me that a holy fire was burning in them, not to be extinguished. I felt in every fiber of my soul that that severe fire was fashioned from one skin, one material, one foundation, inquiring, "All of my days I have been disappointed – now that it comes to me I cannot fulfill it?"

And from far off, also in spirit, were the other teachers. The teacher Pip (Latin, Polish), the teacher Zidenzeig (drawing), the teacher Feinstein may his blood be avenged (music) – the staff of Hebrew teachers in the Hebrew *gymnasia* on Polish soil in a Volhynian winter.

[Page 67]

The bell would ring, and we would flinch as if bitten by a snake, leaving our places and going to the classrooms. The stove was abandoned, and the fire brought into the classrooms, where the process of squeezing Jewish knowledge while within a ghetto created by the *goyim*, or goyish knowledge with a Jewish spice, into the heads of the Jewish pupils would begin.

The students of the *Tarbut gymnasia* in Kovel were fortunate in that the hearts of their teachers beat, as did those of the pupils, in a rhythm of grief and longing, in a yearning aspiration, hidden and bubbling deeply and intensely.

3. The Domain of *Hashomer Hazair*

Before noon I was a teacher; after noon my time, energy, and experience were devoted to *Hashomer Hazair*.

When I arrived in Kovel, I discovered a chapter that was meager and neglected, one that was in the process of crumbling away. Its biggest competitor was *Shomer* Trumpeldor which, under the direction of Lusia Hodorov, was as an omen for *Hashomer Hazair*, and the chapter and its spirit were diminished. The parade of the Trumpeldors -

Dr. Ben-Shem in the company of the older group in Hashomer Hazair

[Page 68]

their uniforms, their songs, their leaders, and especially their customs, and their venerated leader-commander Hodorov - attracted the youth to their ranks. When I arrived in Kovel, *Hashomer Hazair* was in decline. Only one step stood between it and extinction.

These were my virtues:

  a. A reputation as a leader and organizer of youth
  b. Membership in the highest ranks of *Hashomer Hazair*
  c. A teacher with a doctorate in philospohy
  d. An exciting speaker
  e. A faithful observer of religious ritual and belief in the ways of *Hashomer Hazair*

When I left Kovel, the chapter there of *Hashomer Hazair* was one of the largest and most important (both in quality and quantity), the best organized and most beautiful in Poland. As successful as I was with the chapter of *Hashomer Hazair* in Grodno, such was my success in Kovel.

All of my time, thoughts, actions, feelings and aspirations were focused on my labors on behalf of the movement. I performed many practical acts of kindness, from early in the morning until late at night. My room was the headquarters, a beehive of activity, filled for hours with action and instruction. All of my books, visits, meetings, words, and plans were devoted to one thing: *Hashomer Hazair*.

The chapter grew to a marvelous size. Students from the *Tarbut* school, in their desire to become endeared to me, joined the ranks of the movement. The students of the Karla Davidova *gymnasia* envied them, and they too joined the chapter. And whenever I set out in my *Hashomer Hazair* uniform, wearing my boots and Baden-Powell hat and with a walking stick in hand, the youth would stare at me and run to join our ranks. In *Hashomer Hazair* we inspired intense longing for Israel, the ritual of work, a love of singing, respect for society, demand for change, and aspirations for action.

And when every night wonderful songs burst forth from lungs and hearts, the parents of Kovel would stand in a column of surprise with tears in their eyes. They would wait for hours for their sons and daughters to return from the chapter.

Twice I was asked by the secret police to come and discuss my group. I remembered well the stories of the young men who were suspected of communism, and who were cruelly tortured (blows with a doorknob in the ribs, under the lungs in the area of the liver, pressure on the fingernails, suffocation, freezing of the feet and so forth) in the interrogation rooms of the same secret police. I went to those interviews with an agitated, pounding heart. I was warned and sent home with a characteristically polite Polish accompaniment. The authorities of the school (the *kortorion*, the inspectorate), began to take an interest in me, arguing about Zionism, society, youth, and loyalty.

[Page 69]

The Lag B'Omer parade of Hashomer Hazair in 5690 [1930]

[Page 70]

In praise of the Jewish youth, I will say that while the *gymnasia* students would dance the *Hora* all night at the chapter, they took upon themselves the burden of the strictest of discipline during their classes in the day time.

4. Kovel Nights

On *Simchat Torah* I went out, accompanied by the heads of the regiments and groups of *Hashomer Hazair*, to watch the Trisk Rebbe (of the famous family of sages from Trisk) dance. In the heat of a fire not of the world of judgment, with books of *Torah* in their hands, the Chasids danced, their faces impassioned, their eyes closing and opening, their legs pumping up and down. Carried on the wings of eagles, dancing, becoming excited, as if day and exile, sin and sleep did not exist. There was only the leap heavenward towards the unseen, but soon to be known, infinity. They skipped, jumped, rose up, passed over, hopped, and lifted their legs in an incomprehensible dancing experience, on and on until the watchers were short of breath. The hearts of the dancers beat like cuckoo clocks, their hearts shaking heavily, a dance over the chasm of forgetfulness, the chasm of memory, to the pinnacle of creation, the peak of the *Temirin*, a dance of joy, joy in the *Torah*, joy in forgetfulness, in revival, in desperation, without pride.

The Holy Rebbe Lula,
may his righteous memory be blessed

[Page 71]

All around us, in great numbers were many pleasant Jews of Volhynia. I knew them. They were a mixture of Jews, a geo-political-topo-ethnographical mixture. Volhynia, near the border of Russia, Poland near Lithuania, Melorussia, and Belorussia absorbed the blood and life from them all. The Jews of Volhynia did not have in them the cold logic of Lithuanian common sense, nor leniency of opinion, nor the vulturine character of the Poles. Rather, the Jew of Volhynia had within him the enthusiasm for a mixture of longing for the Ukrainian plains, and a yearning for Belorussia and for Lithuanian insight as well. And above all, simplicity; simplicity within a multiplicity of idioms, the simplicity of the steppes and the Ukrainian plain. And the eyes of those watching the dancing blazed, enjoyed and moaned, enjoyed and nodded.

And the rebbe stepped out to dance. The Chasids stepped aside for him, leaving space in the middle of the dance floor. The rebbe closed his eyes, lifting his head, swaying back and forth, thrusting his fingers into his broad sash, adjusting the hat on his head, stepping past the table and past the crowd, and into a dervish-like dance, mysterious, wild, and enthusiastic, the likes of which I had never seen.

The Chasids around him applauded, sang and hummed, sighed and prayed, and the rebbe danced. Half an hour passed, then an hour, and the dance continued without ceasing, neither becoming greater or less. The rhythm was frozen. The world was frozen; life itself was frozen. It was as if the life-giving sun was inside the Kovel rebbe's synagogue and with it the Chasids and the observers.

Walking and jumping, jumping and spinning, spinning and hopping, hopping and skipping, skipping and making a half-bow, without speaking a word and without changing expression. Only the face of the rebbe was burning, blazing, illuminated.

I was jealous, so jealous, of the power of the idea, the force of which was strong enough to warm not only one heart, but the hearts of many.

The winter nights continued. With various kinds of sports activities, I enriched the paltry life of the Diaspora and enriched and roused the youth and myself.

Every Sabbath Eve I went out with the heads of the regiments and groups for a nighttime trek. The unhappy parents objected, and wouldn't change their attitude even knowing that I, the teacher, accompanied them. The number of trips increased, and so did the number of participants. The frost and the cold put the world and the houses of the *goy* villagers in the area surrounding Kovel to sleep. Lights were extinguished, dogs barked, and Jewish youth trekked through the fields of Poland – Volhynia, walking, taking in the sights, searching, longing, dreaming, learning to strengthen body and soul, learning to wait, to aspire, and to achieve.

On one of the nights, I swore in all of the graduates with the *Hashomer Hazair* pledge. After I had commanded them all to seclusion in the darkness, at a distance of a one kilometer radius, those who returned had made a steadfast decision to remain in *Hashomer Hazair* for the rest of their lives. And in the darkness of a Polish night, opposite the villages of vast Volhynia, accompanied by the bites of Ukrainian dogs, in foreign fields and secret forests, the Jewish youth swore eternal devotion to their far-off homeland and to a life of work in a sincere social manner.

[Page 72]

Group of members of Hashomer Hazair from Regiment B in the year 1927

Other nights, I would take them out for field games. In the darkness the members of *Hashomer Hazair* would crawl, moan, and lie down, becoming familiar with the scent of the earth and the sweat of their fellows, the scent of the sweat of fear, and the taste of search and wandering.

And bonfires erupted in the night, lighting dark fields and restless hearts. And also in the cold and darkness we journeyed together on sleds far from the agitation and tumult of the city, to the heart of the surrounding nature; slapped by the strong wind we rode at a gallop, and the youth kept up with us.

I left behind hundreds of youth with saddened hearts, clutching a photo of me dressed in my *Hashomer Hazair* uniform close to their hearts with the real love and fondness of friendship, when I left Kovel. I took with me the best of my memories and part of my dream.

And Kovel was destroyed, as were her Jews – the young men and women, the teachers, the leaders, an entire dear and sacred community; a community where dreams of salvation were spun and the urge for a life of freedom was woven.

It died and will not rise again. The ministers of the nation will not extinguish its candle; it will be passed on to light the darkness of the land of dreams, the land which the heart of the Jews and youth of Kovel, in moments of death and strangulation, embraced and kissed in their souls.

Notes:

1. Today the principal of the government school named for Haim Nachman Bialik of blessed memory, in Tel Aviv and the author of textbooks.
2. One of the directors of the *gymnasia* Sokolov Leor in Tel Aviv-Jaffa, poet and author.

[Pages 73-85]

About Kovel, City of My Birth
Memoirs and Notes

By Dr. Michael Greiber

Translated by Amy Samin

From the Depths of the Past

Within the darkness of the clouds, which in our time darkened the skies of Eastern Europe, there sometimes broke through shining, glowing rays. They rise up and intensify into streams of memories of exemplary Jewish life. Innocent and modest, quiet and honest in Kovel; this was *Kavele*, the city of my birth.

Similar to the lives of most of the Jews in the cities and towns of Russia, Volhynia, Lithuania, and Poland, the life was, in many ways, and in particular from a moral standpoint, one of altruism and mutual aid, the complete opposite of the lives of the Christians in those countries.

I remember Kovel from the earliest part of my childhood, during the 5660's, or the start of the twentieth century in their numbers in memory of Jesus, which were soaked with Jewish blood, from Kishinev to the massacres of the murderous Hitler, may his name and memory be erased.

An ancient record existed in Kovel and was preserved by the *Chevrah Kadisha* [burial society] there. The writer Ansky Rapaport visited Kovel and became very interested in the place. In the old cemetery on Matisov Street (near the center of town in those days), there remain unbroken tombstones carved nearly four hundred years ago. The Jewish community of Kovel has existed for more than four hundred years, but until 1758 it was subordinate to Ludmir; only then did its dependence on the other city cease according to the decision of the Polish government. Even in those days the merchants of Kovel ran large businesses, and had trade connections with merchants in the Tartar city of Ochkov. In the days of the edicts of 1648 and 1649 Kovel was also destroyed. Its Jewish citizens were killed, and only about 20 families remained. The Jews of Kovel rebuilt the city fairly quickly, and resumed commerce activities. On the third of March 1666 at the Jaroslaw fair, the leaders of the Jewish communities signed a financial commitment to the treasurer of King Jan Casimir and the first to sign was Yisrael ben Shmuel of Kovel.

In 1687, the record of the Council of the Four Lands tells of the presence at the Jaroslaw fair of those leaders, eighteen in number, and the fourth to sign was Rabbi Haim bar Moshe Meshulam from Kovel.

In 1690, in Jaroslaw, the sixth to sign according to the order among the fourteen Jewish leaders was Yehoshua Segel of Kovel.

In 1697, the record of the Council of the Four Lands regulations for printers was signed by Rabbi Yeshayahu bar Natan-Neta of Krakow, previously of Jaroslaw, and later of Kovel.

[Page 74]

In 1700 Rabbi Naftali-Hertz Ashkenazi, rabbi of the holy community of Kovel, was registered, and in 1701 on the 27th of the first Adar of 5461 it was written in the community record of Tiktin: "Our rabbi and teacher Rabbi Naftali-Hertz bar Yisrael (Ashkenazi) was named chief justice of the rabbinical court and teacher in the holy community of Kovel. After a year, he was appointed chief justice of the rabbinical court in Lvov - and the list is long.

In the book in praise of the Baal Shem Tov, edited by Horodsky (Dvir Publishers, Tel Aviv), on page 160 it is written: "And by the way, I will write that I heard from the Rabbi Yechiel, chief justice of the rabbinical court in the holy community of Kovel, etc."

The name of Kovel was well-known amongst the greatest Jewish authors. Also Y.L. Peretz wanted to glorify it in his story *Mishnat Chasidim*; in the groom's speech it is written: "And the exalted court in the holy community of Kovel showed astuteness and there is no higher."

Thus many generations ago there were great, glorious and well-known rabbis in Kovel up to the great Rabbi Meshli Pinsker who was, in fact, the last rabbi in Kovel. After his death more than fifty years ago, the people of Kovel did not receive a new rabbi because there were three or four judges and a teacher of Jewish law. Just a short time before the outbreak of World War II (1939) and the destruction of Kovel; upon the death of the judge Rabbi Shaul Grebitzer may his righteous memory be blessed, a place opened up, and they brought over the Trisk Hasids (most of whom were from Kovel), for many years the neighbor of our rabbi and teacher Rabbi Yaacov-Arieh of Trisk, the son of the Magid of Trisk. The decision was made in the community council led by the businessman Moshe-Aaron Perl may G-d avenge his blood, to select as the city's rabbi the son-in-law of the Trisker rabbi, Rabbi Nahum-Moshe, may G-d avenge his blood.

Kovel's Jews

The Jews of Kovel (it is possible to say without exception) were exceptional in their purity of hearts, pleasantness, and love of their fellow Jews. I never saw a Jew of Kovel raise a hand against another Jew. In spite of that, I was an eyewitness at a very early age to how the Jews of Kovel defended one another with no distinctions, in a case of suspicion of an injury done by a goy.

It was enough that a Jewish child of about 7 years old would burst into a home or shop, shouting: "I saw a goy chasing after a Jew" and immediately, in the blink of an eye, a group of dozens of Jewish youths would gather to judge the goy who would dare to attack Jews. I saw a young Jew, about 17 years old, a shop assistant (if my memory serves me, his name was Sushnaski, son of the Jew Izboyzchik) who attacked a group of Russian soldiers with a corporal at their head, for insulting a Jewish woman who sold pottery in the marketplace, threatening to treat her as if they were in Kishinev. That corporal was taken to the hospital smashed to pieces. His friends nursed their injuries for a long time, and only through the intervention of many *goyim* on that market day were the Jews stopped and taken to the police. From there, understandably, they were freed because of a bribe.

[Page 75] [Page 76]

The Jews of Kovel in the street, at home, and in the synagogue, were always ready to help any Jew in need with a generous hand, and all the more so foreign Jewish soldiers in the area. Since Kovel was so close to the border, there were always many battalions of regular soldiers, cavalry, and artillery corps around. In the spring and summer, on the days when the Russian army performed maneuvers, they were joined by many regiments from other places. There were always many Jewish soldiers, and every resident found it necessary, at every opportunity, to invite one or more soldiers to his home for a meal, all the more so for Shabbat or a special day.

Sometimes, if a Jewish soldier refused to be parted from his friends, the homeowner would with a wide smile include all of the soldier's friends in the invitation to a meal.

In about 1909 a proper and excellent restaurant for soldiers was organized, serving meals on holidays in the *Talmud Torah* building, first in the old building on Malovalodimirski Street and later on in the new building opposite Pirogov's *Gymnasia* which was besmirched in the days of the Nazis.

The public kitchen for Jews in the army

I recall one time, on the first of the intermediate days of Passover in the morning, they suddenly announced that a great many Jewish soldiers had arrived and were in need of proper food for the holiday. Immediately, youth of every stripe - from students of the *Gymnasia* to apprenticed workers, daughters of good families and housemaids, and with great enthusiasm baked, within just a few hours, *matzahs* and everything that was required, in the *matzah* factory of Monish Roizen of blessed memory.

There were many charitable organizations in Kovel, both official and unofficial: *Moshav Zkenim*, *Bikur Cholim* (apart from the well-known Jewish hospital), *Laynat Tzedek*, *Malbish Arumim* (providing, in particular to the students of the Talmud Torah, food, suits for holidays, and shoes), *Beit Yetumim* (orphanage), and *Gmilut Chesed*. All of those organizations existed thanks to the regular monthly donations made by the Jews of Kovel, and each one of those organizations had a regular collector of donations. (When I visited for the last time in 1934, I found ten such public organizations, not counting *Gmilut Chesed* funds and unofficial organizations).

I remember in 1914 at the outbreak of World War I when the expulsion of the Jews of Galicia by the Cossacks began, the first refugees came to Kovel in six freight cars that stopped by the old train station. Within just a few hours the cars will filled with food, clothing, and household objects, and they added - of course - traveling expenses.

And another example of the generous hearts of the Jews of Kovel: on his way to Constantinople [Istanbul], as an emissary of the management of the World Zionists to publish a Zionist newspaper, Jabotinsky of blessed memory was delayed for a day and a night in Kovel, without anyone knowing of his arrival or his departure.

[Page 77]

He discovered two Zionist activists who knew the purpose of his journey and at his request he received eight hundred rubles in cash (an astonishing sum in those days). The money was given with the personal guarantee of my father, Reb Moshe-Haim Greiber, may G-d avenge his blood, who was one of the board of directors of the Mutual Credit Bank, which was later covered by donations at the end of the year at the time of the dividend payment of the stocks in the Jewish Colonial Bank.

I also remember one time when Judge Shik became gravely ill and needed a dangerous operation by a famous professor in Warsaw who demanded an enormous sum. A delegation of movers and shakers, with the attorney Appelboim of blessed memory at their head, insisted that the head of the *Gmilut Chesed*, Motil Fishbein of blessed memory, provide the entire sum required from the coffers of the *Gmilut Chesed*. Fishbein was against the idea, saying, "We cannot empty the entire fund for the sake of one person in need, even if he is a very important man."

On the morning of the Sabbath, before the reading of the Torah, Appelboim and his friends appeared on the stage of the Great Synagogue and in an impassioned speech he appealed for the aid of those assembled to put pressure on the *gabbai*, Fishbein.

In a heart-wrenching cry Fishbein explained his reasons, protesting, "We cannot sacrifice an entire city of poor Jews and peddlers, who need the *Gmilut Chesed* for their survival. I will contribute 50 rubles from my own personal funds." The gathering supported Fishbein's position unanimously, promising to raise the necessary funds, G-d willing, after the end of the Sabbath. And so it happened.

Those leaders and the generosity of the Jews of Kovel did not cease even after World War I. Kovel raised an exceptional sum in aid of the Jews of Russia in 1922 (delivery of food packages) as well as in fundraising campaigns for the *Keren Hayesod* [United Jewish Appeal] (as was declared with great enthusiasm by the head of the *Keren Hayesod*, Mr. Leib Yaffe, may G-d avenge his blood).

The Origins of Zionism in Kovel

The Jews of Kovel (like the Jews of Volhynia in general) excelled at having a warm Jewish heart and strong nationalist feelings, extraordinarily so.

During the time of the *Hibat Zion* movement and the *Odisay* Committee, they used to go to the various houses of prayer in Kovel (which, taken together with all of the synagogues numbered more than twenty) in an organized fundraising appeal on the eve of Yom Kippur in support of the settlement of *Eretz Yisrael*. In the statements printed by the *Odisay* Committee, one can find all of the details, including the names of the wheeler-dealers.

This close tie with *Eretz Yisrael* existed thanks to several families, who would continuously receive greetings and letters from their elderly parents in Jerusalem (such as those that, Moshe-Haim Greiber, may his blood be avenged, received from his father Reb Eliezer in Jerusalem, and the Kastelnesky family from their mother in the Holy City).

[Page 78]

Delegations from Tiberius and Jerusalem would regularly visit Kovel in the winter, in order to empty the collection boxes in the name of Rabbi Meir, Master of the Miracle, in order to receive the donations in cash given with a generous hand as was the custom of the Jews of Kovel.

After the First [Zionist] Congress, a Zionist committee was founded in Kovel which was headed by physicians Dr. Perlman and Dr. Feinstein, the dentist Dr. Lipshitz (the son-in-law of Yisrael Hanich), Reb Moshe-Haim Greiber, Yisrael Projneski, and the assistant pharmacist Porer (from Eismont's pharmacy).

The first Zionist gathering in Kovel took place on 2 April 1898. A committee was elected, and it was decided to send a representative to the Congress. On 15 August 1898, Dr. Feinstein left Kovel as the representative to the Second Congress. Dr. Feinstein wrote the following words in his journal in the Russian language: "Here I am, suffering from melancholy and oppression; it seems to me that Zionism will be my cure."

On 24 August 1898 a public gathering took place in the big house of study (in the Sands). More than 800 people took part in the gathering, according to the testimony of Dr. Feinstein and other eyewitnesses. Dr. Feinstein, who was the speaker, provided a detailed report of the Second Congress. At the time, Dr. Feinstein wrote in his journal that in his opinion, he personally suffered a complete failure.

After that, Dr. Feinstein focused his attention principally on the matter of the construction of a Jewish hospital. On 23 May of the same year, the government permitted the use of 10,000 rubles cash of the meat tax funds for the hospital building. That autumn, the foundation was laid but from the beginning there were disputes with the contractor Projneski.

In January of 1900 there was a stock distribution enterprise in Kovel for shares in the Jewish Colonial Bank of London. It goes without saying that the members of the Zionist committee and their friends among the merchants of Kovel were among the first to sign up for the shares. That same month, Dr. Feinstein wrote that he had saved 40 rubles for "a rainy day" and he used them to buy four shares in the bank.

After the Fourth Zionist Congress, there was a decline in Zionist activity in Kovel. The *Intelligensia* group was disbanded. Dr. Feinstein publically announced the transfer of all of his matters to Dr. Perlman.

On the 1st of October 1900 the Jewish hospital building in Kovel was completed. Dr. Feinstein still continued, for a certain time, his activities on behalf of the committee members mentioned above, until the 1st of January 1901. At that time he withdrew from Zionist activity, and continued his work at the hospital. In the report he delivered at the time, it says that "70% of the signing fees on the bank stocks had already been collected in cash, in other words four thousand three hundred and ninety one rubles." Dr. Feinstein of blessed memory transferred his four shares to the Zionist Committee in Kovel.

[Page 79]

At that time and for the next few years there was a big decline in Zionist feeling in Kovel, especially among the elderly with Dr. Feinstein as their leader. In his journal entry dated 24 September 1903 Dr. Feinstein writes: "Since Kishinev, Homel, and just before the matter of Uganda instead of Palestine which was, still, very far away from us, we had no choice but to return to the urgent matter of assimilation."

However, Dr. Feinstein was mistaken. Although Dr. Perlman and Dr. Lipshitz left Kovel, there still remained other devoted Zionists and go-getters in Kovel (among them, Yisrael Projneski, Moshe-Haim Greiber, Yehuda Hite, Yaakov Bork and a new star who had come from Projny, Mendel Kosovski of blessed memory).

After a while there appeared in Kovel young forces. According to custom in Czarist Russia, educated young people who were suspected of nationalist activities were sent into forced exile in far-off parishes (especially after the assassination of Pinchas Dashbasky of blessed memory. He traveled from Kovel to Petersburg for this purpose. The Russian Interior Minister Palva, gave this order in a special and secret dispatch sent to the ministers of the shire). Several enthusiastic students from Kiev, Odessa and other places arrived in Kovel. I remember Luitzki and Zalichneko and a few of their friends. Expatriate students like that were almost always equipped with a letter of recommendation for my late father. In cases like that, they made sure, first of all, to provide the guest with a source of income, in other words, teaching one or two private lessons, from which he would be able to earn a decent living. I, myself, studied with the two I have mentioned, one after the other. Most of the time those two young men were dedicated to the public, especially the youth.

After a few years a group developed for the young "intelligentsia." They recruited to their number the student, Asher Frankfort, may his blood be avenged. Hefet's two sons joined, as did a few other youths from nearby towns.

The distribution of the Zionist shekel and also the organizations that supported the *Keren Kayemet L'Israel* (emptying the collection boxes, collecting donations on the eve of Yom Kippur, and on Purim) was well-organized and the money would be sent regularly to Odessa, to the main committee run by Ussiskin of blessed memory. Kovel was famous, in a good way, among the Zionist leaders in Russia; therefore various speakers, lecturers, and emissaries would frequently come to visit. In most cases, the speeches were delivered to limited groups on Saturday nights in the house of study of Projneski of blessed memory. Only rarely were the speeches made in the auditorium of the theater or the cinema, with announcements and ticket sales. The first Zionist speech I heard was on a Sabbath afternoon by a Zionist preacher (I believe it was Rabbi Nissenboim of blessed memory).

[Page 80]

The speeches of Moshe Kleinman of blessed memory (later the editor of the Zionist *HaOlam*) I heard in my childhood on Saturday nights in the synagogue of Projneski. The first lecture I heard in the auditorium of the Expert Cinema was given by Haim Greenberg of blessed memory. Also present at that lecture was the student Asher Frankfort, who was the organizer as well as the ticket seller and usher at the entrance to the auditorium; he founded the Hebrew *Gymnasia* in Kovel.

There was another very important public Jewish center in Kovel which was very active in aiding the Jewish residents of the place, both materially and spiritually. At that time, there were five official banks in Kovel: a) a branch of the government bank; b) a branch of the Commercial and Industrial Bank of Russia; c) the First Mutual Credit Bank; d) the privately-owned Weintraub-Lobzovsky bank; and e) the Second Mutual Credit Society Bank, led by Brish Rabinrazon of blessed memory. The First Mutual Credit Bank was the Jewish commercial and labor center of Kovel, and also a center for matters relating to Zionism.

Zionist and nationalist activists were employed at the bank, like Heft, Yehosha Leiberman, Yosef Burstein (a product of the yeshiva in Novoharodek and a person of high morals), the genius Yosef Valular of blessed memory, and others.

Kovel was also one of the first cities to send students to the Herzliya *Gymnasia* in Tel Aviv, including attorney Yaacov Eisen. From Kovel, one of the most praiseworthy teachers of the previous generation, Turkanitch of blessed memory, moved to Eretz Yisrael. Also Dr. Avraham Kastelnesky of blessed memory left Kovel; he went on to become a special advisor on economic matters of Eretz Yisrael at the Jewish Agency in London.

Nationalist-Zionist publications such as *Resevit, Yebreiskiya Jashan*, and the publications of the K.K.L. in Yiddish) were used as proof against the strong spiritual outburst which swept over the Jewish youth of Kovel during that confusing time, after the Russo-Japanese war and the failure of the Russian Revolution, when the Jewish youth were helpless and oppressed. During that confusing time that feeling was expressed in Bershadsky's <u>Aimless</u>, two essays by Ahad Ha'am, and Brener's admiration for Jesus.

In Odessa at that time a group of Jewish youth - graduates of the *gymnasia* - changed their religion and as a group took to the streets of the city. But the Jewish youth of Kovel attempted every experience, and Jewish defense existed in Kovel during that period, which may have been the reason there were no pogroms against Jews there, nor any injury to their property.

[Page 81]

Spiritual Life in Kovel (Before World War I)

Education in Kovel was of interest to each and every individual and to the community as a whole. On almost every street, large or small, there were small religious elementary schools (*cheders*) headed by experienced and expert teachers.

As I recall, there was one teacher of young children just starting their schooling, known as the *Melamed* (teacher) of Leibishov, who taught for generations, dealing in the sacred work for more than fifty years, and in whose school there were always 40 - 50 students.

Out of the great love and respect I had for him, I would create a memorial to him, if it were not for the fact that I can't remember his first name. He was a pedagogue of the highest order, and it is difficult to find another example of his success in teaching and the influence he had on those tender, refreshing and lively children.

Of all the teachers I had, until I left the *cheder* at the age of 11, his marvelous and patriarchal example remains with me, the glory of a first teacher, the grand old man with his long, meticulously trimmed white beard, the marvelous figure of the *Melamed* of Leibishov.

In many of the houses of study and synagogues in Kovel teachers sat during the week, teaching babies from the *Beit Raban* in the side rooms of the houses of study.

In addition to those, there were modern schools and cheders founded by the Jewish enlightenment movement in Kovel. In particular was the influence of the municipal school (as it was called, because there were two, not one, completely separate - one for girls only and one for boys only). The boys and girls from the two schools would meet only once a year, at the graduation ceremony at the end of the school year. Parents of the graduating students were also invited to the ceremony.

All subjects were taught at the municipal school, in the Russian language of course. The school was a very good one, and there were only three preparatory classes and two departments.

Graduates of the second department, the last one, were proficient in the Russian language, grammar and mathematics, and also some history, geography, and biology. They were offered positions as bank clerks in the government-run bank (*kaznatsheistva*), in the post office and in any government office as well as in privately-run department stores.

Those who wanted to continue their studies were readily accepted into the third department of the gymnasia, but the best students would study a little German during the summer months and were accepted, following an examination, directly into the fourth department of the Czarist *gymnasia*.

[Page 82]

School teachers under the directorship of Mr. Weinberg in 1916

From right to left: Beryl Rozin (Hebrew), Solomia Perlmutter (Polish), Yania Grau-Kramer (Polish) Frenrich (school supervisor), Raya Pomeranz (Polish and German), Sara Blumfeld-Tzelvich (Hebrew and drawing), Mr. Weinberg (school principal)

A school called *Talmud Torah* was established for poor children. Once a year they received new suits of clothing for Passover, shoes and a little food. The teachers of the *Talmud Torah* were Lekach, the educator Mesalonim, Lushchik, and two named Sander.

The modern and organized schools were: a) the cheder founded by the enlightenment movement, *Maskil el Dal*, which was supported by the *Mefitze Haskalah* organization in Russia; b) the private school run by the educator Geller of blessed memory (one of the veteran teachers and an experienced writer for the Hebrew newspaper); c) the school for girls run by Dr. Shershbeski, and the very well-run school for girls of Slotzker, the first person in Kovel to introduce the method of teaching Hebrew in Hebrew and used for that purpose the textbooks of Krinsk: First Review, and Spoken Hebrew; and d) the school named for Weinberg.

There were two *gymnasia*, one for girls run by Dr. Firogov, may his name and memory be erased, and a municipal *gymnasia* for boys. In the girls' *gymnasia* the vast majority of the pupils were Jews. The ministry of public education in Russia cancelled, before the outbreak of World War I, all of the limitations on the education of Jewish girls in the high schools, but severely limited the education of Jewish boys, saying they could only make up 10% of each class.

[Page 83] [Page 84]

In the municipal *gymnasia* for boys it was understood that, because of the draconian restrictions, the number of Jewish boys in each class was miniscule, 3 to 4. Many of those who wanted to provide their sons with a high school education were persuaded to send them to other cities. In many of the houses of prayer and houses of study, individual Jews sat and studied Torah, and in the evenings and on weekdays were paid to teach the community *Ein Yaacov*, *Chaye Adam*, and the weekly Torah portion.

There was also a *yeshiva* in Kovel, which for some unknown reason never became well-known. In the side rooms next to the *Leinat Tzedek* house of prayer, there was a Hebrew library which was run by volunteers. That library would regularly receive almost every new Hebrew book that appeared in Warsaw. Textbooks of all kinds in foreign languages were provided by the bookstores of Ashkenazi and

Mendel of blessed memory. At Ashkenazi's shop they would also stock textbooks in Hebrew and grammar. Gittlin's new bookstore in Kovel was the first to carry Hebrew dictionaries, literature, poetry, and research books. He was the first to disseminate in Kovel the small Hebrew Dictionary of Ben Yehuda, and Grazovsky-Kloizner's pocket dictionary, the writings of Smolanskin, Mapo, Yehuda Steinberg, and Bialik.

Yisrael-Moshe Bess of blessed memory distributed religious texts and ritual articles, but he had several official competitors with bookstores, and some not-so-official competitors (book peddlers who wandered to the houses of study and synagogues selling their wares).

In Kovel one would often meet authors, rabbis, or educated men who had come with detailed lists of book-lovers in their hands, and they would approach them and offer their books.

In 1913 the first weekly newspaper in the Russian language, called *Chayei Kovel* (Life in Kovel) appeared in Kovel. The editors and publishers were students from the city, guided by editors such as the student Levitzky and his friends.

Once, the principal of the Hebrew *gymnasia* for boys, Sositzki, found himself insulted in the feuilleton by the editor, in which the principal Sositzki was described as extremely difficult and strict, who terrorized everyone around him. The court accepted Sositzki's lawsuit and found the editor guilty of willfully causing insult and sentenced him to six months in jail. The editor appealed the sentence. The trial was quite costly and in the end the newspaper went out of business.

At about the same time the poet Zissa Weinfer left Kovel and wandered to the United States and Yosef-Haim Zagorodsky who was one of the regular writers for the newspaper Moment in Warsaw.

[Page 85]

In Kovel there appeared a significant number of almost every Yiddish newspaper published in Warsaw, as well as *HaTzfirah*, the Russian weekly newspaper *Niva*, and the business newspaper *Yediot HaBursa* (Stock Market News). Every week the *Niva* would publish installments of books by the great Russian writers such as Dostoyevsky, Pismesky, Gershin, Goncharov and others. The youth in particular would read these stories voraciously.

Also the children's newspapers *HaShachar* [The Dawn] and *Ben HaShachar* [Son of the Dawn] of Krinsky, and the weekly children's newspaper of the boys from the Bilubavitch *yeshiva*, *HaAch*, [Brother] had subscribers in large numbers in Kovel. There were also a few subscribers to the children's weekly *HaChaver* [The Friend] which appeared in Riga and was published by the teacher Mansovitch.

There were also Zionist youth groups in Kovel that would gather occasionally for debates on Zionism or to listen to a visiting lecturer. They would meet in private homes, mostly on side streets outside the city. There was also in Kovel an organization for boys of bar mitzvah age. They made a rule that they must speak amongst themselves only in Hebrew, and they made up games in Hebrew, such as a word game with two letters, and riddles.

The Jews of Kovel always excelled at generosity and a willingness to give and to contribute to all in need. After the death of Professor Mendelstem of blessed memory in Kiev in 1912, there began a heated dispute in the newspaper between the initiators of the idea to found a Hebrew university in his name in Jerusalem, between Dr. Hindes and Dr. Bendarsky, and their fierce opponent Hillel Tzeitlin, may God avenge his blood, Kovel responded by organizing a dispute between the Zionists on the same subject, and one hundred rubles (à princely sum in those days) were collected on the spot for the university fund.

The second graduating class of the Russian gymnasia in 1921

In the first row, fourth from the right: the principal Mrs. Clara Davidovna-Erlich

[Page 85]

Kovel

By Moshe Fishman

Translated by Amy Samin

From a distance of thirty years' time you come to my mind, sometimes clearly, other times blurred and foggy, but always accompanied by a pleasant sensation, as if one has touched something beautiful and dear.

When in 1922 I was asked by the *Tarbut* representative from Kovel to take on the management of the Herzliya Elementary School I was hesitant to accept the proposal. Kovel is a regional city in the province of Volyn (Volhynia), of which I had heard that it had plenty of flour, but no *Torah*; and I, a student of Lithuania who preferred the spiritual to the physical, didn't believe that in Kovel I would find any kind of meaningful cultural activity.

[Page 86]

After I accepted the position and came to Kovel, I wondered whether my work at the school would bring me any satisfaction. However, after I had been in the city a little while, I was quickly convinced that religion isn't everything. In that small town I discovered a settlement of Jews, lively and vivacious, with a vigorous nationalist modern culture of broad scope. I did not check to see if people were studying the Mishna or *Ayn-Yaacov*, learning *Torah* together in the synagogues between *mincha* and *ma'ariv*. Nor did I check whether there were ten idlers sitting in the synagogue studying *Torah*. But it gladdened my heart in the mornings to see the wonderful sight of the children and grown youths and toddlers, all thronging to the *Tarbut* schools: the Hebrew gymnasia, the Herzliya elementary school, and the kindergartens.

In the evenings one can hear voices singing, the tumult of arguments as the young people left the youth clubs. Next to the Zionist club there was always movement: people entering and leaving, all the while continuing their discussions on nationalist subjects. The language of Hebrew was frequently heard in the mouths of the youth as they went on their way to the schools or the clubs.

[Page 87]

The Herzliya School made a place for itself among all of the other institutions. The name itself says it all, and together with its students it had a special spirit of happiness and national pride. The school was founded about fifteen years after the death of the great visionary, and his spirit still sweeps through the Jewish community and fills the heart with hope and faith. In addition, that period of time in Poland was particularly stormy. The Jewish minority was waging a persistent war for its rights as citizens and as a people, under the brave leadership of Yitzhak Greenboim, the representative to the Polish Sejm. The Jewish people of Poland held their heads high and made plain their desire for a substantial change in their lives.

Then the *Hechalutz* movement was created, and many groups of young people, men and women, joined in many cities and towns, and they prepared themselves for life in Eretz Yisrael. They set their hands to all sorts of physical work, and also studied Hebrew and gathered knowledge about Eretz Yisrael.

The students of the Herzliya School with Their Teachers

The teachers sitting in the third row, from right to left: Zev Tzernitchki (today Lieutenant Colonel Tzur), Dr. Abba Shafroch-Poysner, unknown, the principal Mr. Moshe Fishman, unknown, Haim Hochberg, Shimon Feinstein.

The Jews were proud of their nationalist organizations and their expansion to other cities. I knew personally the group of people who were in charge of the all of the cultural and Zionist activity. Their involvement in those matters was complete and total. The first of the group was Yitzhak Gitlis, may his blood be avenged. The cultural work was sacred to him, and he was involved in it even while at work in his shop. I remember fondly his wife Sarah, who never stood in the way of his public service.

I also remember the remaining activists, the pharmacists Finkelstein and Goldstein, and others who were enthusiastic and devoted to the cultural work in their hearts and souls. There were also great founders who sent their sons to the Hebrew schools and did not pursue the lure of the Polish gymnasia. When the Hebrew educational institutions would host celebrations in the city, those people considered themselves the guests of honor. The educational institutions were not just the glory and splendor of the city of Kovel and the decisive force in its spiritual character; they were also greenhouses for raising the builders of the homeland in *Eretz Yisrael*.

[Page 88]

Memories of a Hebrew Teacher in Kovel
in memory of Benny Mahmadi Zev, God rest his soul

By Yaacov Kobrinski

Translated by Amy Samin

A.

Preparation for the Start of a New Academic Year

Quite a lot of preparation went on in the Jewish schools of Kovel prior to the start of a new academic year. Two elementary schools, a preschool, a full *gymnasia*; altogether 23 – 24 classes with 850 – 900 pupils. This was the affiliation with the *Tarbut* movement in the city. Aside from that, there was the library and the night school. Every institution at that time was chock full of problems. Not like the government schools, which had programs, a division of labor among the teachers, textbooks, etc., readymade data from the authorities…The Hebrew teachers were left with ample room for initiative and independent decision–making. We devoted many meetings to clarifying fundamental questions about Jewish education, to intense soul searching, and to criticizing our mistakes. Oh, how we debated our special difficulties, such as: imposing the Hebrew language, the relationship between the school and the various youth movements, Hebrew–language textbooks, inculcating an atmosphere of *Eretz Yisrael*.

In addition to this, the directors and secretaries were immersed in financial matters and tired disputes with parents over the tuition. There were multiple needs, and sometimes we would demand, aside from the clearing of previous debts, also additional funds, just like the Rebbe of Drežnik, at the time when many parents were asking for a discount. The severe cases would go before the full committee of *Tarbut* and first and foremost, its dear chairman, Moshe Pearl, may his memory be blessed, who was a masterful persuader and whose influence was great in all circles of the Jewish population.

The parents were not tempted by the possibility of educating their sons in Polish public schools without tuition fees, preferring to continue bearing the burden of the payments; just "don't make the boys into *goyim*."

Praises to the Jews of Kovel, may their memories be blessed, who were weighted down by financial difficulties, impoverished due to the discriminatory policies of the Polish government, and who despite everything carried on their backs the entire network of schools with no help from the municipal budget or the government. They saved even unto the slice of bread from their mouths and quite simply proved their loyalty to the values of the eternal People!

Meanwhile, the children began bringing home the products of their school: new songs in Hebrew, folktales, bible stories, news from the Land of Israel, and at that time there was held the first project of the Jewish National Fund: the delivery of *Rosh Hashanah* greetings, and the parents saw the fruits of their labors and their hearts swelled.

[Page 89]

B.

The Chanukah Reception at the School

The traditional celebration of Chanukah was the biggest party of the Hebrew School.

Almost immediately after Sukkot we went into action, devoting weeks to searching for material and processing it, to multiple rehearsals, and to technical preparations. On the evening, children and their parents gathered in the school building. All of the furniture was moved into one room at the end of the building, and the rest of the rooms were completely emptied and used as dressing rooms for the participants in the show. Children and adults, far more than the capacity of the small auditorium, pushed their way inside. But everyone happily accepted the crowded conditions. The holiday atmosphere, enhanced by the special clothing of the children, was reflected abundantly in their faces and shone brightly from their eyes. Everyone was busy and the pride was enormous. Nothing need be said about those who participated in the show and in the choir –they appeared on the stage! But there was plenty of work for others: some were busy helping the younger actors get dressed, others were used as ushers in the auditorium – they were in charge of putting JNF stickers onto the clothing of the guests and solicited them to place a donation in the Blue Box; and then there were those who had the most enviable job – pulling the ropes to raise and lower the curtain.

And the curtain rose… The candle lighting was accompanied by the choir. The conductor – who was the veteran singing teacher Shimon Feinstein, may his blood be avenged, who played a big part in developing the musical talent of his pupils. After the religious tunes (*These Lights*, *Maoz Tzur*) they performed some new songs which had been composed in Eretz Yisrael. The curtain went up again, and on the stage were the toddlers of the group – the preparatory students. Exclamations were heard from all sides at the sight of the beautiful costumes (mostly, of course, from paper) and the scenery – the handiwork of their teacher Pnina Goldsblatt z"l. They presented a children's tale, staged with songs and dances, and including such personages as dwarves, birds, flowers, the moon, snow, a forest. This adorable performance received wild applause.

Then it was the turn of the students of the upper classes to present performances with nationalist content and real suspense. One skit brought to the stage the outbreak of the rebellion of the Maccabees in *Kfar Modi'in*, and the second was set in biblical times and told the story of Elijah the Prophet, with emphasis on two exciting moments: his rebuke of the villainous act of the Jezreelite Naboth ("you have killed and also taken possession?!"), and his dispute with the priests of Baal. The great power of such performances was that they illustrated the chain of the generations and our struggle for existence in a comprehensive and convincing way.

[Page 90]

And in conclusion, a staging of the story by Sholem Aleichem, "Chanukah Money", which provided several pupils with a good sense of humor – who were also the known "pranksters" – with the opportunity to show off their talents in a constructive manner. Then the singing of "*Hatikva*" and the ceremony was concluded. The crowd began to leave without haste. The parents parted from the teachers with a friendly handshake and expressions of thanks and recognition.

Indeed, it was universally agreed that it had been worthwhile to invest such a great effort, because an event such as this was the highlight of the educational work.

C.

The *Gymnasia* Building Named after H.N. Bialik

Whenever we would walk along the street past the Polish schools, a sigh would inadvertently break loose from our hearts. They had wonderful, spacious buildings, while our schools were housed in the worst possible conditions. For the *Herzliya* School, a house was purchased from its owner, although on the two floors there was very little space, small rooms with no corridor – a total area of 280 square meters for 350 pupils!

The school named after Dr. Klomel was located in a rented house, old and ramshackle, on the verge of collapsing. In the apartment of the *Gymnasia* there were only two classrooms that were more or less suitable, without even the most elementary conditions for laboratories, no hygienic arrangements, not even a yard of any kind.

Until the principal of the *Gymnasia*, Asher Frankel may his blood be avenged, who was born in Kovel and was one of the most senior of the teachers and *Tarbut* activists, took it upon himself – or more correctly, threw himself into the vortex – to make it his goal to establish an improved home for the *Gymnasia*.

It was a daring idea; there were those who said "crazy". The main problem was "where can the money be found?" – there was no answer but one: the principal of the *Gymnasia* and the members of the *Tarbut* board set out with the "red kerchief" and began collecting donations – and not the customary donations of a few gold coins, but fifty and upwards.

It was necessary to use every possible means: personal influence, taking advantage of various connections, harassing stubborn refusers with dozens of visits, saying words of solicitation and sometimes also difficult things, fighting and even gaining haters – and over the course of a year they collected seventy thousand gold coins, a fantastical sum for the Jews of Kovel, among whom there were no wealthy folk.

[Page 91]

Aside from collecting donations, there was a lot of work to be done directly related to the construction of the building, which rested entirely on the shoulders of Principal Frankfurt: purchasing a plot of land, drafting a blueprint of the building, and gaining approval from the municipality and from the Board of Governors – and it was precisely there that the focus was on minutiae, with the intention of putting up obstacles to the progress of the project. Then there was overseeing the construction of the building, purchasing the building materials, partially with promissory notes, and then worrying about repaying the notes, in order to once again be eligible for credit…

Only once they had reached the end of construction and the interior finishing work was it discovered that there was not a penny left, and there was nowhere else to go for more money, and so, in 1934 Mr. Frankfurt decided to visit *Eretz Yisrael* and the immigrants from Kovel there and try to change the natural order of the world: instead of delivering donations from the Diaspora to the Land of Israel, to move them this time in the opposite direction. The idea was initiated, and Mr. Frankfort brought back more than twenty thousand gold pieces, and a short time later the beautiful building stood proudly on its hill.

Although only about 50% of the plan was constructed, there was plenty of space for six classrooms and the most important auxiliary rooms, a large physics and chemistry laboratory, a magnificent auditorium, wide, light–drenched corridors, and in addition a playground worthy of the name. A pleasant feeling encompassed me every time I visited this place, and I enjoyed the integration of "the beauty of Japheth in the tents of Shem".

But it lasted only two years. I remember: in 1940 I came there for a meeting of Soviet teachers; at that time it was a Ukrainian high school. I was curious to see the plaque honoring those who had a part in the construction of the building, and I looked for it in the familiar place near the entrance. I didn't find it. It was gone.

[Page 92]

These I Will Remember…

By Itzhak Margalit

Translated by Selwyn Rose

A. The Enchantment of the Town

After many nights of wandering hither and thither the family arrived at Kovel. It seemed as though we had come out of the darkness and into the light.

I was enchanted by the railroad station, enthralled by it as if by the Almighty.

My father (Z"L) saw that I was impressed and said to me: "After the First World War the Germans sent engineers to build railroad stations in Russia. These stations were built to a uniform plan because they were intended to act as recognizable strategic signposts when next the German army invades Russia."

And indeed, in the Second World War the German officers made straight for these iconic landmarks.

It was 2:00 o'clock in the morning. The town was wrapped in darkness. By chance there was a carriage with a fine–looking horse harnessed to it adorned with fine reins. The driver, a fat Jewish man, courteously offered his services. As the carriage proceeded along the cobble–stoned road the clickety-clack of the horses' hooves together with the wheels of the carriage noisily shattered the silence of the night.

[Page 93]

The town seemed peaceful, quiet – as if the hand of time had not touched it, as if the terrors of war had not yet arrived here. And indeed the town suffered less during the Holocaust than many other towns. There was a legend in the town that the Rabbi (May his memory be for a blessing), from Niesuchojeże (Nezkizh) – blessed the town wishing that no hater of Israel will ever conquer it and never bring upon it sadness. And indeed the blessing of this pure righteous man endured.

The magnificent Kovel railroad station

We arrive at a bridge. The carriage stops and the wagon–master gives us a bit of a history lesson: "The town," says he, "is not one but two: the new and the old."

It is wrapped in a blanket of mystery and antiquity. I feel somewhat as if pages of history are unrolling before me. I am encircled by an atmosphere of an ancient, ancient town.

I was intoxicated by the enchantment of the town that appeared before my eyes as if it were a legend. The carriage arrived at the Dresden Hotel and we went in.

We assuaged our hunger and quenched our thirst. We had warm and pleasant beds and after so much wandering around I had the comforting feeling that at last we had reached a safe haven.

B. Rabbi Velvele's Dance

The evening darkens. The autumn winds are blowing and playing their music. The Jewish community hurries from three different directions Maciejow Street, Brest Street (Brest–Litowsker Street) and Apczyczena(?) Street, by way of the old cemetery.

Men, women and children congregated in the synagogue of Rabbi Velvele Twerski. When the congregation finished the evening prayer they commenced the ceremony of "*Hakefot*"[1] Rabbi Velvele is invited to carry the Scroll. The old man takes the Scroll in his hands, covers his head with his prayer–shawl and shows his disciples just exactly what "Rejoicing of the Law" really means.

The old man starts dancing and continues with determination until he can no more. For more than an hour but Rabbi Velvele shows no sign of fatigue and no indication of tiring. He becomes bereft and naked of all earthly reality and corporeality, floating, as it were, on worlds far above. He is physically connected with nothing – but nothing – of the material world. He becomes transfigured into a spiritual abstract entity. He is entirely integrated into the Being of the Holy One Blessed be He. Rabbi Velvele is elevated in the eyes of his disciples to a being not of this world. Fear of the Almighty fills their hearts. Fear of the Rabbi shows on their faces. And Rabbi Velvele dances on and on until at last exhaustion conquers him. His disciples ask each other in amazement: "What can we say about Rabbi Velele's dance?"

As if "on the wings of eagles"[2] the story of the Rabbi's dance spreads speedily throughout the town. One's heart bursts into joyous song, the furrows of care on the faces of the Jews disappear, everyone is joyful; on every street there is only exultant joy and happiness. As evening turns into night wonderful music is heard. Everyone is singing and sweetness continues to flow from the dancing of Rabbi Velvele. The following day, "*Simchat Torah*", the Rejoicing of the Giving of the Law, we wait near the stadium for Rabbi Shmuel Mendel (Z"L), (the father of Eli Mendel). Rabbi Shmuel was one of the faithful disciples of Rabbi Velvele, and leaves the synagogue of the Rabbi singing and dancing the length of Brest Street, coming to the stadium and crossing the fields to his home on Kolyava Street.

[Page 94]

We young Jewish lads were captivated by the singing and dancing of Rabbi Shmuel Mendel and joined in, together with him.

Rabbi Velvele! Rabbi Velvele! How could you have fallen into the clutches of the rogues and thugs? Your mouth has uttered majestic words of Torah and gladdened the heart with wonderful melodies – how did your mouth and words become as ashes!

C. The *Heder* of Rabbi Shaye of Trojanówka

Thus is the portrait of Rabbi Yehoshua of Trojanówka engraved upon my memory or, as we called him, "Shaye Trojanówka": a tall Jew, white–bearded, resembling somewhat a sort of "*Zaken Aharon*"[3] in the flesh, with watery eyes and spectacles perched upon his nose secured on one side by a cord looped around his ear. The skin of his fingers was cracked and a strong smell of snuff came emanating from them.

And what did the "*Heder*" look like? Simply a building tottering on the brink of collapse, its walls sunken into the ground with the windows level with the ground. And inside? Two frail benches, a table and a bed. In the adjoining room – the Rabbanit's bed, a closet and the kitchen. Rabbi Shaye Trojanówka didn't consider teaching simply a "spade to dig with"[4] in order to make a living but as a divine and heavenly elevated mission. The acquisition of *Torah* by the youth of Israel was his salary. His reputation was thereby established as an honest and fair teacher.

When we arrived from Russia the first concern of my father (Z"L) was to ensure I was not lacking in, or bereft of *Torah* – he sent me to Rabbi Shaye Trojanówka. However I didn't stay there for long. It was like this: a boy pinched me under the table. I reacted, stood up and slapped him. The Rabbi struck me on the hand with a stick. I snatched the stick from his hand and ran round the table, out through the window and home.

I refused to continue learning in the *Heder* of Rabbi Shaye Trojanówka. Strangely, in spite of the respect due to him, he swallowed his pride and came to my father trying to persuade him to return me to the *Heder*.

My father understood my feelings and declined to do so instead, because of his concern for my Torah studies, it was suggested that Rabbi Shaye Trojanówka will come to our house and teach me from 6 in the morning until 8 – the hour I must leave for school.

This episode demonstrates clearly the stature of Rabbi Shaye Trojanówka. He feared I would stray from the paths of *Torah* study and begin to follow unsatisfactory topics and cultures; he therefore had no concern for his rightful honor and self–respect and came daily to our home to teach me – and all this to ensure a Jewish lad didn't neglect *Torah* study.

[Page 95]

D. An episode in the life of Mr. Frankfurt (May G–d avenge his blood)

Mr. Frankfurt was an excellent mathematician but at the time of the founding of the gymnasium "*Tarbut*" he was not sufficiently fluent as a Hebrew speaker to be formally engaged. With that as a background there arose some linguistic "misunderstandings" and one of these I will now relate:

During the first days of the gymnasium, there was not sufficient revenue to employ a full–time secretary. Frankfurt took on a member of his department who had excellent handwriting, Levi Schwartz, and employed him as a secretary.

On one occasion, Schwartz presented Frankfurt with a letter he had prepared and began to leave. Frankfurt took the letter, looked through it and not understanding something called out to Schwartz, "Go away!" (instead of "Come here!"). Schwartz understood he was being dismissed and continued on his way back to his department while Frankfurt continued to shout, "Go away!" Scared into reaction, Schwartz began to run down the stairs with Frankfurt pursuing him; Schwartz runs and Frankfurt runs after him with his "Go away, I said!" Full of emotion, Mr. Frankfurt went into the teachers' room to tell them all of what had happened and said in his incorrect Hebrew: "He ran away and I ran after him." When Frankfurt saw the smiles on the faces of the others, he realized his mistake and from that moment knew well the difference between "Come here," and "Go away."

Translator's notes:

1. "*Hakefot*" means literally 'encircling' and here refers to the ceremony of removing all the Torah scrolls from the Holy Ark and parading them round the synagogue (and sometimes out in the street) in a joyful manner, celebrating the festival of "the Giving of the Law". By tradition the process continues until all the male members have carried one of the scrolls and participated.
2. Taken from Exodus XIX; 4.
3. "Zaken Aharon". Novella and elucidations on the Torah by Rabbi Ahron Yosef Koretz of Zablotów, Galicia and New York. Printed in Krakow, 1930
4. A phrase taken from "Ethics of the Fathers" Chap. 4: 7 suggesting that using of Torah for earthly matters, such making a living, is profane.

In Memory of Our City, Kovel

By Hertzl Goldberg

Translated by Amy Samin

I close my eyes in order to bring forth memories of our beloved city, Kovel. Great is the distance from then until now, nearly thirty years have passed since we, the children of the *Tarbut* School, joined *Hehalutz Hazair* [a youth movement, literally Young Pioneer].

Many events occurred during those tempestuous times. Our city was erased from the face of the earth, and multitudes of our dear ones were destroyed Of all of our dreams and memories, only one remains, a pile of bones at the far edge of the city; there lies our cherished past.

We left behind in our city the years of our childhood and youth, the home of father and mother, grandfather and grandmother, uncles and aunts, grandchildren and great-grandchildren: the beloved, winding river, the slopes of the bridge, so pleasing to us all, the chapter of *Hehalutz Hazair*, *Freiheit*, the vibrant and rousing pioneering movement; years of work and tireless dedication by volunteers, young and old, on behalf of the movement and not in order to receive a reward.

I recall the Hebrew language, spoken freely, which was like a miracle to me, Tabenkin [Yitzhak Tabenkin, a Zionist activist] who visited Kovel.

[Page 96]

I remember the many Hebrew schools throughout the city. I recall Fabrichna Street, when the movement was just coming into being, and the first Klosova people returned with approval for immigration to the Land of Israel, who were the first swallows of the fifth *aliyah* [immigration of Jews to the Land of Israel]. In my mind's eye I can see the large, expansive auditorium on Lotzka Street, which was always filled with hundreds of youth from all stations of life, who strived to make *aliyah*. Those multitudes waited with bated breath for their opportunity to immigrate. And although the gates of the homeland were locked against us, no one gave up hope, and for many years they participated in preparation groups.

I also remember the summer colonies in the villages, in the bosom of nature surrounding the city, and the emissaries from the Holy Land who appeared there like angels from heaven, proclaiming their message day and night. There isn't enough paper to recount the way of life in our city in those days.

And all of that was destroyed in those tempestuous times. Our entire past, all of our loved ones, can be found in a hill of ash, on the edge of our far-off town. Great is our pain and our sorrow.

From the Recent and Distant Past

By Moshe Batar

Translated by Amy Samin

In 1924 we moved from our apartment in Kovel Vatoroy to Toshovsky Street. My father of blessed memory was a Trisk Hasid, and I was raised in the atmosphere of the Trisk synagogue.

The Trisk shtiebel was notable for a certain liberality. Strict attention was not paid to the saying of prayers; in the corridors, conversations were held on matters of global politics, Zionism and the Jewish people.

There we found Jews who understood our spirits, who joined us in a variety of pranks on the eve of Simchat Torah and other holidays.

Reuven Tzavik of blessed memory stands before me with his broad smile; he spoke the same language as the young people. He would give this one a pinch, and another he would honor with a slap on the back.

I remember Joseph Papa of blessed memory with his silken kapote, who on Sabbaths and holidays would read from the Torah with trills and special melodies while swaying to and fro.

And who does not recall Ephraim Rabiner of blessed memory? With his devotion to prayer that infused every fiber of his being, and who took note of every guest in the synagogue, approaching them during a break in the prayers, and arranging places for them to stay. Everyone listened to Reb Ephraim. Such respect and affection we had for that Jew, who spared no effort in arranging hospitality in the homes of the Jews for the many guests and soldiers who appeared in the city on the eve of holidays.

[Page 97]

And who does not remember the prayers of Shlomo Mendel of blessed memory during the Days of Awe? His "I'm a poor devil!" His conversations with the Master of the Universe. It was an experience you would never forget.

Within the walls of the Trisker shtiebel important Zionist activity was carried out. That activity was especially felt on the eve of Yom Kippur. Yoseph Tzavik and the son of Yoseph Papa organized the Zionist fundraising. All of the streams of Zionism were housed in that synagogue. Of particular note was one of the Jabotinsky Hasids, Yoseph Gelman, son of the ritual slaughterer Asher Gelman of blessed memory, who was proficient in the Talmud and equally knowledgeable of each and every article written by his rabbi, Jabotinsky.

I recall the lecture given by Mr. Itzhak Greenboim in Kovel on the subject of "Zionism and the Situation of the Jews in Poland." Joseph Gelman of blessed memory interrupted and heckled him, "And what about Jabotinsky's statements in his article?" At the time, Jabotinsky had written an article in the daily press saying that England had misappropriated its role and was not fulfilling the Mandate, and that we must deliver the Mandate to the Polish government which was interested in Jewish migration.

Greenboim answered Gelman by saying that after a speech made by Trotsky at the time of the Revolution, many had been willing to walk through fire, but many had disagreed with the things he had said, and repudiated them. "And therefore young man, that which is sacred in your eyes is not sacred to me."

When I become engrossed in the past and bring to mind how vigorous life was, with a youth that was gripped with and devoted to lofty ideals but in the end was lost, my heart is filled with sorrow. Alas for its loss.

From those days I can also recall a conversation I had with Rabbi Valula, may his righteous memory be blessed. What happened was this: with great sorrow we remember our dear parents, many of whom rent their clothing and sat *shiva* for their sons and daughters who underwent training and decided to make *aliyah* to the Holy Land. My own mother, God rest her soul, prostrated herself on the grave of my father of blessed memory, in order to convince me not to move to the Holy Land.

I knew that my mother believed in Rabbi Valula with every fiber of her being, so I said we should ask the rabbi for his advice, and whatever he suggested I would do.

We went to see the rabbi in the afternoon. Rabbi Valula sat on his wide chair, with his shtreimel on his head. The rabbi presented me with a variety of evidence in support of the promise the Holy One Blessed be He required of the people of Israel: do not speed the end[1]: "'Unless the Lord builds the house, they who build it labor in vain: unless the Lord keeps the city, the watchman stays awake in vain.' (Psalms 127:1) You, the pioneers, will not bring glory with the path you have chosen, because it does not come from God."

The rabbi came at me with passages from Psalms, and I answered him with verses from Hillel: "If I am not for myself, who will be for me?" Not for nothing did I study at the yeshiva of Rabbi Yagodnik of blessed memory.

[Page 98]

In the end, I asked my mother to step out of the room for a moment, and when we were alone I said to the rabbi, "I didn't come here to listen to *Halacha* on if it is permitted to make *aliyah* to Eretz Yisrael. It is decided, and no passages, from the first to the last, can change it. But, holy rabbi, you must understand my spirit; if you do not agree, you are - God forbid - likely to lose a Jewish soul." The rabbi gazed at me with astonished and embarrassed eyes. He called my mother into the room and gave his blessing to my *aliyah* to Eretz Yisrael.

Before I left, I went out for one last look at the city before leaving it forever. My heart trembled and shook within me. Here I had grown up and put down roots. It was difficult parting from those beloved Jews, the Jews of Kovel. But I was comforted in my heart that we would see one another again one day in Eretz Yisrael. I wandered down Toshovsky, Luchka, and Zorek Streets, glancing across the city park where we had woven so many dreams on moonlit nights.

The train began moving, extracting me by force like a tree pulled up from its roots. I didn't imagine, no Jew of Kovel could have imagined, that the sword of Damocles was suspended above their heads, that a bloodbath was about to wash over them and sweep everything away, and that the marvelous community of the Jews of Kovel was about to be cut down by an unbearable slaughter the likes of which our people had never before seen, even in the very darkest of times in our history.

Translator's note:

    1. By making *aliyah*, the Jews would be hastening the arrival of the Messiah, since it is believed that the Messiah will come when all of the Jews have returned to Eretz Yisrael.

[Page 98]

The Kovel Forest
(A brief glimpse of the town)

by Yacov Teitelkar

Translated by Amy Samin

Dedicated to my saintly and pure daughter
Raizele, G-d rest her soul

Dense forest. Abundant shade. Fertile ground of establishment and settlement of generations. Flowing with life, the rooted life of Israel Saba. Drenched in golden sunshine and dewy with precious moonbeams, fruitful and thriving. Each and every tree with its juicy roots, fertile and saturated, on its splendors, its fronds, and its bustling tendrils. And worlds upon worlds emerged and struggled and yearned. And stars put on a show, shining and twinkling overhead… embroidering and swallowing eternity - the eternity of Israel will not lie…

Here is the giant oak. Spreading through the forest, and his dimension and height is Moshe Pearl. A Jewish man inside and out. He came from the town of Trisk Forest and made his world in the city of Kovel - a world of national action.

[Page 99]

A typical Jew in appearance and in the purity of his soul. Devoted to his people with all of his soul and might. A faithful and active Zionist. He was the head of the Zionist movement in Kovel. At the same time, he was involved in meeting the needs of the public with faith and a wellspring of energy that came in a constant outpouring from his heart. He was dedicated to creating a fund to revive the failed popular savings and loan in Kovel; he was its leader and it improved. He became the community leader of Kovel and its president. He worked in cooperation with the office of the Polish municipality, directing it to act in ways that would help his overlooked and disadvantaged brothers. An expert bookkeeper, he would find the extremes and extract from the complexity of the Polish magistrate, creating situations that benefitted Hebrew education and culture and by some miracle, fund them.

He devoted himself to Hebrew education in Kovel, and was involved in the local *Tarbut* chapter, serving as its leader. He was one of the leading figures in the construction of a marvelous building for the first Hebrew *Gymnasia* in Kovel, Tarbut-based and including all of the latest refinements, from bottom to top, and he did so with complete simplicity and love, sincere humility and great modesty. A strong man. When asked about his colleague, his impoverished brother, he would bend down towards his questioner like a reed and speak to him in the words of his people and answer with his soul and his gallant heart.

Here is the olive tree, the sprig and the giant. Giving its fruit and oil to all around it. Yossel Shochat, "Borjui". A haberdashery merchant, and one of the powerful community elders in the city, he was well-respected and capable. A modest and humble man who studied in the *yeshiva*. A "*yeshiva*" boy" who became one of the town's most successful merchants. There wasn't a single educational or charitable organization working on behalf of society in Kovel that did not receive direct aid from Yossel Shochat - the father of charity in the city. He had a gentle and pleasant appearance, and spoke in a quiet and measured tone. His laugh and his gaze were modest. He was pleasant to everyone and shrank from receiving honors. He was occupied with his business but there was never a day on which he set aside the bible, and there was never an occurrence on which you would not find him at home, hunched over the *Gemara* and swimming through the sea of the *Talmud*.

Here is the ancient date palm - old man Appelboim. He came from far away. A lawyer. All his life he kept his distance from Judaism and its institutions; in his old age he returned to his origins and devoted himself to the abandoned and dilapidated orphanage. With his own money he rebuilt the roof of the temporary orphanage, and from there he went on to find a permanent home for the orphans of Kovel, becoming the faithful and devoted grandfather in heart and soul. An exalted elder. He spoke and behaved ponderously and continued to visit the orphanage until the day of his death, concerned for their needs and caring for his pupils, fostering their joy in his old age.

In the city and in the garden of orphans there blossomed a sturdy birch -

[Page 100]

Rayzah - the soul of the orphanage who sacrificed herself for the sake of the orphans, giving them the most precious thing of all: a mother. A maiden from a wealthy family, she left her home and the family wealth and put all of her desires and priorities into the adoption of the orphans and their freedom from the status of orphan. She served as an exemplary savior to the orphans, to the amazement of all who came to the city of Kovel. She began her activities in the latter days of the First World War, after the bloody trip of Blech-Balkovitz, Petliora and their gang in the villages of Volhynia leaving behind them a harvest filled with bereavement and loss, and many widows and orphans among the Jewish residents, who were in need of sponsorship and aid from the big city of Kovel. Rayzah was not satisfied with social philanthropy, she saw herself and her personal mission as returning to the orphan that which he had lost, the warm atmosphere of family, maternal love and warmth… she worried over them as a mother would, she guided them and watched over them. She pondered and plotted day and night how she could improve their situation, how she could make their lives sweeter and more pleasant. She rented private apartments for them (before the orphanage was built by Appelboim) offering them the possibility of independent lives that did not depend on their fellow man. There were none among the people of means, whether those with a generous hand or those whose hand was closed tight, who did not know Rayzah and have enough of her … and Rayzah was not concerned for her honor and did not pay attention to personal insult, caring only that "her boys" had what they needed.

Modest, tall, with a slow, smug smile, she would sometimes voice her concern and her resentment to her intimate friends about the rigidity and stubbornness of the orphanage's board members, the Friends of Honor who looked only at the eyes of the orphans, but not at their hearts.

Here also is the "father" of the orphans of Kovel, Asher Erlich, partner in the work of Rayzah and her assistant, who sacrificed no less than she on behalf of the orphans, his students, friends and the well-spring of his life. The official secretary of the orphanage, he managed and guided them, restrained them, accompanied them and protected them wherever they went. He was a Communist in his outlook, and he worked in comfortable and easy partnership with the Zionists (most of them on the board of the orphanage). He kept himself separate from the wealth of political parties, and all of his educational work was not a teaching of fundamentals, but was first and foremost human-Jewish. Short of stature, steadfast and strong, his most noticeable feature was his level-headedness and his emotional equilibrium, his taking a stand and his lack of hesitation in everyday life and in not so normal life, all of which influenced his students/friends, the orphans.

And here is the glorious citrus, with his majestic appearance and noble spirit - the young rabbi of Kovel, Rabbi Nachum Misheli, a well-versed Torah scholar and educated as well. Educated in every way, the scent of progress emanated from him, noticeable from a distance. He was involved in health issues. He pronounced opinions and observations.

[Page 101]

An enthusiastic lecturer he could always be found at the municipal synagogue where the Torah content was intertwined by golden threads to nationalism and popular Zionism. He called out to and awakened the Jews of Kovel to awake and become acclimatized / integrated to the fundamentals of Judaism and its traditions, to remain strong in the face of persecution, boycott and economic distress caused by the conservative, anti-Semitic Polish government, and to place their hope and safety in the hands of the Creator.

And here is the willow, the tree that is planted by flowing water - the beadle of the house of study in the Sands (Zamdiker Beit Midrash) - Pinchas the Beadle and the *mohel* [ritual circumciser] in one. He was the accepted expert of the physicians, who ushered thousands of Jews into the covenant of our father Abraham, and the doctors of the city trusted him and asked for his advice. He was the beadle of the house of study and in fact was responsible for all of the sacred, religious and social work. A faithful shepherd and counselor to the people in every matter of religion and proper behavior, a mediator between them and the Master of the Universe - portly, weak and short of breath, he never knew fatigue. Involved in the commonplace, but his eyes and head were always in the clouds.

And here is the most populist, basic type - unique unto himself, the painter Yosman. A common man, a proletarian worker. There was not a single workers' society, organization or public institution in which he did not appear as a lecturer - warrior who spoke his piece and would not be silenced, his bell-like voice would explode in the ears even from a distance, demanding the proper rights of the workers. At the same time, he was also an excellent preacher, fittingly standing on the *bima* [dais] in the house of study before a large audience and between the *mincha* [afternoon] and *maariv* [evening] prayers and lecturing. He would illuminate all who listened on the Torah and good deeds, while integrating that with exhortations to awakening a sense of nationalism and a Zionist mission - a return to Zion, the redemption and rebuilding of the Land of Israel. And on the dark winter nights, he would sit before the open books of the *Gemara* and recite before the "world" a chapter of the *Mishnah* and *Ayin Yaacov*.

And here is the handsome tree, juicy and sweet-smelling, the quick-witted Jew, pleasant and comfortable, involved with all of the people of the city, the secretary of the *Tarbut* and the Jewish *gymnasia* - Yaacov Kopchick, whose face never showed sadness and who was always smiling and hospitable. And he generated smiles and a welcoming feeling in all who saw and heard his mirth and his witty and lush chorus, and his Jewish wisdom that was peppered with wit. There is no doubt that even during the *action* during which he and his brother were taken to be slaughtered, he smiled and acted the smart aleck in order to make his fellow victims smile, to make the bitterness of death a bit more pleasant and sweeter for himself and for others, with his peace of mind and his caustic and ridiculing jokes about their fate and death itself…

And here… here… thousands of blossoming trees in the city of Kovel, creating fruit and offering up their sweet scents, struck down by the angel of life, rooted, blossoming and growing, enjoying the brilliance of the sun and creating enjoyment in those around them, struck down in the depths of their roots, and sending their branches skywards.

[Page 102]

Parents and their progeny, worlds and their longing for the future, suffering their burden and weaving the life story of an ancient nation, its traditions and experiences, its trials and its joys.

And here - the tender buds, the innocent boys and girls, delicate and honest, fair and beloved, refreshing, spring-like, full of youthful vigor. With the pleasant faces of the boys and girls, with the beauty of their bright eyes. With the end of their dream, their tender souls and their pure confidence in the world of the Holy One, Blessed be He… with the scent of their blossoms and the whisper of their shoots, in their joy and happiness, and the magic of their songs, the youthful songs and the lives rising up and sprouting within the shady forest of Kovel…

And all of those were wiped out, ripped out by their roots by a murderous hand, surrounded, mechanized and scheduled by a cruel criminal, wicked and satanic … for all eternity.

Kovel during the First World War

By Baruch Barrok

Translated by Selwyn Rose

It is summer 1914. The information about a general mobilization spreads like lightning.

War has been declared! In the streets groups of people met, stood around. Posters appeared on nearly every wall, that whoever held in their possession a red card was obliged to report within twenty–four hours to the town's military officer.

Unimaginable panic arose. The following day one could already see women with tear–stained faces accompanying their husbands and parents their sons, on what was to be for many of them their last journey.

Within a few days one saw in the town farm wagons arriving from the Front (the Front was about 50 kilometers from the town near Volodymyr (Ludmir)), with the first wounded. Their bandages were stained red and soaked with blood from their injuries – they were the first victims of the confrontation between the Russian and Austrian armies.

People congregated in the streets to look at the terrible sight. The women were wringing their hands and sobbing bitterly. But in time they became used to the sight of the spilled blood.

Day and night heavy forces hurried to the front – artillery, cavalry and infantry. Behind them came long convoys of wagons, all moving in the direction of Ludmir.

Shock and horror struck the Jewish community on hearing that Michael, the son of Rabbi Shaye of Kirshina was killed not far from Ludmir. He was the first victim sacrificed by the Jewish community. The cries of the family reached the heavens and split the skies. The victim became the topic of conversation of the worshippers in all the synagogues and Study–Houses of town.

[Page 103]

Many in town decided to leave; everyone who had relatives in the nearby towns and villages packed their belongings took their children and toddlers and left, some to Melnytsya (Melnitza) and some to Nesukhoyezhe (Nezkizh) and some to Kamen–Kashirskiy, to Stobykhivka and other places.

The safest place was considered to be Lubieszów (?) (Liubeshiv?), near Kamen–Kashirskiy.

The strategic "specialists" among us saw in their astrological signs that no danger would encompass the town so the rich people of town went there; but they were to be disappointed because after very short period the village, together with nearly all other "safe" places in the vicinity were obliterated and wiped off the map.

Life in town continued along normal paths. New banknotes appeared in town, shiny and sparkling just out of the mint. The large silver Ruble was almost never seen. To whatever the Jewish people turned their hand – they made money. The trade in salt, in matches and kerosene was very popular. Those engaged in that business prospered to the degree that in the *Heder* of my Rabbi all sorts of strange people appeared. Out of the hearing of the children he was called all sorts of nicknames from the world of commerce such as "dealer" "bargainer" "genie", etc. In the *Heder* children whispered among themselves that the Cossacks hanged the Galician Rabbis by their long side–locks on trees and exiled many of them to Siberia.

Religious women appeared in town carrying wicker–work baskets of various shapes and sizes, passing from house to house collecting whatever they could: bread, underwear, foodstuff, clothing both warm and light – to fight the hunger among the convoys of soldiers camped at the railroad station.

From time to time a known face from Kovel appeared among the soldiers. Whoever left the hospital with "release papers" or a rehabilitation pass for a month or two, became part of the town.

The war entered Kovel stealthily and silently. Life continued on peacefully the Front was far from the town. Suddenly the Jewish population of Kovel was happy: "Przemyśl has been liberated!" Soldiers hugged and kissed each other in the street. But it was the "calm before the storm". Only a few months later they started to evacuate the town. Many of the Christian residents had already left town and now the Jews were leaving – the rich and those who could do so among them.

In town the civil administration stayed on. A volunteer police–force was formed that was comprised only of Jews. At their head stood Dowzhinski (a Christian), the Fire–Chief with Gorberg(?) as his deputy.

The evening before the German entry into town Jews living on the edges of town evacuated their homes and concentrated in the center. This was because our Jewish "strategists" stated that the battles would take place at the approaches to the town and not reach the center. But one has to take into account an additional factor of greater importance: the houses in the suburbs had been empty for some time, evacuated by their Christian residents who had fled to the center of Russia. The Jewish people were concerned that the retreating Russian army and the Cossacks will run wild and loot whatever they can lay their hands on.

[Page 104]

Even so, Jews in the center of town were also apprehensive about living alone, each one in his own house and collected together in groups crammed into the same house. Every night they sat and discussed politics. The Jewish residents became divided into two opposing camps: pro–Russian on one side and pro–German on the other. The pro–Russians strategy stated that leaving town temporarily was the thing to do and that they would return quickly. And the proof was that the Russians were advancing towards Berlin.

In spite of these strategic considerations – the Germans entered Kovel. A representative of the pro–German party went to welcome them. He was met by a large, over–weight German and greeted him peaceably.

The German asked where he might get some bread, butter and eggs. The Jew stood there struck dumb not understanding German. The German then became very angry, attacked the unfortunate Jewish man, knocking him to the ground and with one blow knocking out three teeth. The pro–German lay there on the ground covered in blood while the pro–Russians looked on from their look–out place laughing.

Lying on his bed, covered in a plethora of dressings and bandages, he consoled himself with the thought that that one incident didn't speak generally of all Germans. Indeed that German was evil but the good ones will yet come. And indeed they did – in June 1941.

With the entry of the Germans and the Austrians the serene order of life in town became disturbed. All businesses were closed down and many of them didn't open again until the entry of the Poles on 24th December 1918.

As the Germans entered town, so Jewish trade came out into the open. There were a large number of sellers of bread and rolls and the Austrian soldiers fell upon them like locusts. Large store–houses together with the bakeries emptied out quickly and sales by the suppliers dried up, unable to cope with the large demand. The same occurred with the distributors of tobacco and cigarettes. The soldiers bought everything.

Nevertheless the "prosperity" in town didn't last long. The stocks of flour got used up. The flour–mill burnt down and a second one also broke down. Similar woes and breakdowns occurred with the tobacco and chocolate production. Moscow, Kiev and Bardichev, the suppliers of these items were over the other side of the Front. The sources of essential items and livelihood lessened.

An atmosphere of orphaned isolation enfolded the Jewish community. The town emptied of its politicians and there was no one to turn to in times of woe.

On the other hand contacts began with the conquering army. A period of requisitioning and confiscation began. Everything was taken: copper cooking utensils, mangles and even locks and door–handles, live–stock, horses, furniture, apartments and even the Study–Houses.

[Page 105]

The Committee of Public Hygiene and Sanitation

[Page 106]

Then came edicts concerning forced labor. People were stopped in the street, taken from their homes, brought down from the attics and brought up from cellars. All the people were taken for work: Austrians, Germans and Polish Legionnaires. These last were shot and killed immediately and two Jewish men: a wagon–driver the father of five small children – and a builder from Ludmir Street.

The town is divided into two areas. The old, historic town is in the hands of the Germans and the "Sands"[1] in the hands of the Austrians. Life in the "Sands" was a paradise compared to that in the "old town" where there were strict curfews from 9 in the evening until 6 in the morning. Whoever was caught on the streets during curfew hours was imprisoned for 10 days or fined 30 Marks. Whoever was found for a second time spent a month inside or a payment of 100 Marks and who yet again was caught was hanged by the hands and would stay so for at least an hour or more – all depending on the whim of the military commander Meyer.

With the stabilization of the regime the voluntary police force was disbanded and a permanent force was created in its place, comprised mainly from the civilian police–force. The police commander in the "Sands" was Rabainker(?) and his assistant Sh. Axelrod. Neither of them were residents of Kovel. The police commander in the old town was M. Danziger. There was also a Sanitary Commission and among the committee's responsibilities was the town cleanliness. At its head, if my memory is correct – Ruper(?).

I recall an episode connected with one of the policemen from those days. He was called Dodier. Dodier's "elevated" rank was so "exalted" that even his porter's–like shoulders were ashamed of him. Until the Germans and Austrians arrived he was like the dirt beneath the feet of the fire–men. Now his hour had come; he was "elevated" to the rank of policeman and he was mobilized into the police force with the power to abduct Jews for forced labor.

It happened one day as he was walking on the street he saw one of the officers of the Great Synagogue, Brish Rabinrazon – a Jewish man about fifty years of age. Dodier approached him. With all his many "accomplishments" he was "favored" with yet one more: he stammered. Brish Rabinrazon asked him: "Dodier, at my age I'm going to sweep the streets?" in reply to Dodier's demand. In his stuttering way Dodier replied, "I r–r–r–run t–t–t–to the s–s–s–street?" meaning: "What! You want me to go and sweep the streets?"

In time there were changes and even improvements in the working arrangements. Two Works Committees were formed one in the old town and one in the "Sands". All males between the ages of 18–55 were obliged to register and present themselves to a medical board for evaluation. Whoever received grade 'A' was fit for all types of hard physical labor, grade 'B' for light work and 'C' was considered unfit and discharged. Men who received grade 'AA' were in addition forbidden to leave town. The committees were in touch with the military commander in town and supplied the workers in alphabetical order. Thus it worked out that everyone was called about once every 5–6 weeks. Of course it all depended on the numbers of workers required at any time by the commander. It was also possible to pay "ransom" and those who could afford to do so sent a willing replacement for money.

[Page 107]

In the autumn of 1915 the situation was more or less normal. The less fortunate, poor people managed to acquire a little food that they collected from the fields and gardens that had been abandoned by their owners. They collected potatoes, cabbage, beets and other vegetables and other produce. By something of a miracle, the windmill on Brisk Street did its share and worked energetically on the grain brought by the poor people to be ground. The same thing happened in the "Sands". There, the grain was milled by the small mills of Shimon Zokner and Stolier because the flour–mill of Berl Amernic had been commandeered by the army.

The mayor in those days was Mr. Mendel Kosovsky (Z"L) who was one of the founders of the Zionist organization in town and one of the most–liked among the leading citizens. It was his blessed intervention that caused the shops to be reopened where the sale of all sorts of foodstuffs was by food vouchers. Nevertheless although the portions were small and insufficient hunger was kept at bay and no one died of the hunger. The Jews of Kovel revived and everyone began to think of ways and means of finding sustenance for himself. Many coffee bars opened in town. Wherever one turned one saw large signs reading "*Kiddush Levana*[2]": "Coffee bar". In the windows was written "Tea with rum", beer, muffins, etc. Later on kiosks appeared full of good things like pocket–knives, post–cards, mirrors and haberdashery. All the goods carried some kind of patriotic message, for example; when taking a mirror in the hand four "heads" were drawn on the glass. In the center a portrait of Wilhelm II, to the right Franz–Josef, to the left, the Turkish Sultan and even the Bulgarian King was represented. On the knife–blades was etched "God – Punish England!" The haberdashery items were brought by the Jewish traders of Kovel from Lvov and even Vienna. At first the goods were brought by wagon and afterwards by train.

In order to transport the goods from afar by wagon, a few traders formed "partnerships" and co–operated with each other and thus all the good that came into town were concentrated in the hands of six or seven "members" like Avraham–Yankel Gzebmacher, and the "company" of Moshe Notie and the Frishbergs." In the "Sands" the "Company" of Daf(?)–Mirski and Goshko and the Company of Suzanna and Reznik. Every "Company" was composed of perhaps 8–10 "members".

During the initial period the companies were illegal and unauthorized. The journey by wagon was long, hard and exhausting lasting some weeks. When the railroad came into use the journey became significantly easier but it became necessary to obtain special permits and that depended on the mood of the town's commander and not everyone was lucky.

[Page 108]

Spring 1916. The town was in turmoil. Whispers here and there said that the Austrians are leaving Kovel. It was the evening before the festival of *Shavuot* and Brusilov pierced the Front to the south west, recaptured Lutsk and was closing in on Kovel. And indeed the Austrian army was beginning to evacuate the town. But suddenly the German army transferred forces from other Fronts, obstructing the Russian advance and even forcing the Russian army back as far as the River Stokhid, just about 30 kilometers from Kovel. The Germans stabilized their Front there until the end of 1918 until the revolution in Germany put an end to the conquests of Wilhelm's Germany.

The "secure and safe places" to which many of the Jewish people fled were virtually wiped of the face of the earth following the bloody wars that raged there and in the surroundings. Thus was the fate also of Melnytsya (Melnitza), Stobykhivka Manevychi (Manevych), Tschartorisk(?) and all the towns on the banks of the Stokhid. The people left behind them all that they had and returned to town in the clothes they stood in and bereft of all belongings.

It was clear from the outset that the returnees would not increase the food supplies in town. People were seen wandering the streets with inflated stomachs. The sad situation forced the city notables, at their head Doctor Feinstein and Mendel Kosovsky (Z"L), to open soup–kitchens and distribute meals to the needy. But notwithstanding their concerned attention the population was stricken with hunger.

Epidemics began to spread throughout the town – typhus killed many. Not a day passed without a victim being claimed. The Red Cross wagons had no rest or respite.

After the sick were removed the sanitary police arrived immediately with a large steam–driven appliance steaming all the articles in the house and thoroughly cleansing the house itself, marking the house on the outside with the letter "F" (free of lice), encircled the house with barbed wire and hung a notice saying: "Caution – Typhoid fever!"

Later an order was given that everyone's identity–card must carry an additional 'disinfected' certificate.

At the end of the Succoth festival in 1916 a number of wagons, accompanied by police suddenly arrived at the home for the homeless and the police began to evacuate all the residents. Terrible cries of distress from the unfortunate people filled the air but nobody heeded them. They were loaded on to the wagons and transported to the railroad station and exiled to the depths of Poland – Kielce, Radom and other places. Many of them never made it back to Kovel.

The horrible sight returned for us again to witness in January 1917. The cold winter was intense – but "orders are orders!" The people must be sent: little children and old men, bare–foot, hungry and abandoned – the lottery fell upon everyone. Who the initiator of this "*Aktzia*" I know not to this day. In general 1917 was the hardest year for the Jews of Kovel.

[Page 109]

In the months of February–March 1918, when we were at the last reserves of our strength a miracle occurred as if a magic wand had been waved. The information spread that a peace delegation headed by Trotsky had arrived at Brest–Litowsk. And then the treaty flew away with the embittered response of Trotsky: "No peace, no war."

The situation changed. With the speed of lightning, the news spread in town that Moshe Danziger had obtained a travel document allowing him to cross the border. It was "the first swallow of spring" that arrived in town from far away Russia.

After a while the streets filled with convoys of horses, both young and old, horses of residents and horses belonging to the military, with their long flowing tails and manes. It was heart–warming. Although it was a strange warmth, as if of mourning, so close to the heart. The town was perfumed from the scent of the Ukrainian fertile fields. It was silent information that a new era, a new reality is in the offing – a life of physical health, a life of sustenance, a life of peace and serenity. The summer brought an end to the ripped–apart families; the fathers returned to their families, the parents to their children and the children to their parents.

And indeed – just days before Passover – the first "summer 'swallow'" from the far reaches – one of the Enoch family members returned to town; I forget his name.

With his coming the town clearly felt the war was over. As summer progressed all the Jewish folk who had fled the town, returned, as well as to the surrounding area with its towns and villages, where they had sought refuge during the war

Very slowly the town recovered, the wounds healed over and again life resumed its course.

Translator's notes:

1. A quote from JewishGen's "Kehila Links": "The River Turija flowed through the town. Kovel was divided into three quarters. On one side of the river there was the Old Town, called Zand [in Yiddish], or Sand, as it had been built on sandy ground."
2. The prayer recited for the New Moon each month, presumably used here simply as a trade–name by the shop.

Memories of the Bund in Our City

by Yehuda Miller

Translated by Ala Gamulka

A. The first plant nursery of Jewish socialism in Kovel

In 1902, my older brother Issar returned from Odessa. He came together with his friend "Leibel the Brisker". My brother was a Hebrew teacher and Leibel taught Russian.

[Page 110]

My brother Issar had socialist leanings and belonged to the "Bund". His purpose in coming to town was to plant the idea of socialism in Kovel. He rented a three-room apartment and opened in it a Hebrew school. Externally, it was a Hebrew school where Hebrew and Russian were taught. However, at night, the school became a clubhouse- a meeting place for Jewish socialist youth in Kovel. The beginning of the Bund came with the opening of the school in 1904. The seed of socialism was sown in the earth of Kovel.

In the evenings and the nights there were many discussions of problems of the Jewish, socialist world. The Bund in Kovel was fortunate to have many important visitors such as Vladimir Madam and Litvak. Madam lectured in Russian on the topic "Mensheviks and Bolshevism". After the lecture there were stormy debates until early in the morning.

There were also debates between the Bund and Socialist Zionists. I remember the bitter argument about this topic in 1907 in the house of Kharon. The Bund was represented by one of its greats, called "David" and Shloimke Kharon was the Socialist Zionist's.

The Kharon house stood near the flour mill belonging to Aramernik. About 100 people attended. The debate was harsh- till death do us part. "David" had great rhetorical skills and overcame Shloimke. Shloimke's face was heated, but when he calmed down he was able to tell his rival: You beat me, but you did not change the world view of the social Zionists. In the annals of Jewish history can be found the final sentence of the Bund, but the Zionist ideal will survive forever. We have no place in the Diaspora. We must return to our homeland and to fight there for socialism in our own land.

Isaac Miller, Z"l, founder of the Bund in Kovel

[Page 111]

Among the first to join the Bund I remember Yehiel, son of Itche-Meir, the sexton of the old house synagogue in town, the son of Rabbi Goldschmidt, Ben-Zion Kendal, Shmulik the carpenter, Shike, the cantor's son, Nutta the painter and Moshe Sheifelt (his father was called Sheifelt and owned a coffee shop in a basement on Ludmir street).

At a later time, many working youth joined the Bund. The university students Adela Gurberg and Mania Rudman showed interest in the Bund movement. Yuliya Licht and Boria Appelbaum participated in Bund activities.

B. The Union of Jewish Workers and the First Strike

Mendel Moher Seforim said: "Artisans were debased among the Jews just as were the Jews among the nations ("In Those Days, Ch. 12). Truly, the Jewish worker was looked down upon and had to labor from dawn to midnight.

At the dawn of the twentieth century the following factories could be found:

1. Textile plants belonging to Avraham Tzupefein and Moshe-Shlomo Dundik and his brother
2. Flour mills of Armernik and Goldberg
3. Brewery of Shkolnik
4. Brick factories of Efrati, Segal and Bakhover
5. Tannery of Yosef-Nute Goldstein
6. Kartoflik- women's tailor
7. Khayat - men's tailor
8. Isaac-Leib - building contractor
9. Wineries, among them one owned by Moshe Gurberg
10. Furniture factory of Shimon Kirzhner

There were also, in town, painting contractors who worked for the government, 2-3 carpentries and a sawmill.

In small plants there were 2-3 workers who toiled for little pay until midnight. The salary barely covered their needs.

In 1905 large homes were being built in town. In Kovel there were no professional builders and they had to be brought from Brest-Litovsk.

[Page 112]

These builders were Jewish and they taught us how to build. There were also houses built without plaster and there, Russian laborers were the experts.

In those days I began to learn the building profession and I belonged to a union. I felt, on my body, what it meant to be a laborer. Working conditions were almost unbearable. We worked 12 hours a day, from 6 am to 6 pm. We began to think about improving our working conditions and we realised our only solution was a strike. We gathered all the Russian laborers and we spoke to them. We demanded the lowering of the day to 9 hours. The employers refused to even listen to us. One fine day a general strike was announced- in all sections of the construction industry. After a long and hard struggle, the employers gave in to our demands and we began to work 9 hours a day.

The strike made a great impression in our town. Those who worked 2 to 3 people in a plant woke up and demanded their rights. We began to gather them and in a short time we had 400 workers. They were organized according to their specialties: locksmiths, carpenters, construction workers, plasterers and painters.

We rented an apartment on Yuridika street. We placed a coffee shop in front, but we gathered the workers twice a week. In addition to union business we also organized a large educational campaign.

I must admit a historical fact. Before the Bund came to town, not one Jewish worker had ever read a newspaper or a secular book. A few read "Hamelitz", but the majority had no idea of a newspaper. Our first educational session consisted of bringing newspapers to town. Propaganda material arrived from Geneva to Berdichev. Kovel was then part of the Berdichev region. From there the material was sent to Rovno and from Rovno to Kovel.

In addition to written material there was also an oral education. From time to time lecturers and leaders came to Kovel from Zhitomir and Berdichev. During their visits they would smuggle in newspapers, leaflets and books.

C. Self-Defence Organization

During the Russo-Japanese war Kovel served as a transit station and we were afraid that the reservists who passed through on their way to the front would attack us. We were prepared for what was coming and we organized our self defence. There were members of the Bund and the Socialist Zionists in the command group.

Many of the wealthier residents fled the town. Among them was Hillel Goldberg, the owner of the flour mill. The self-defence group took over his house. The house stood in the center of town. Since serious pogroms were expected in Kovel there were additional defencemen from Brest-Litovsk, Berdichev, Rovno and Lutsk that joined us.

[Page 113]

We collected money and we bought weapons. We had some revolvers from earlier days. We divided the town into several zones and each sector had experienced defence people. I served as a link and brought reports to the central command in the Goldberg house.

We were tense for six weeks and expected the worst, but to our delight nothing happened. The weapons remained and we wondered where to place them.

At that time there was a rabbi in Kovel sent by Rabbi Brik. His secretary was Moshe Segal, my friend. We managed to hide the weapons in the rabbi's cellar. The Rabbi had no knowledge of this. One day Moshe Segal came to tell me that the weapons had to be removed because government inspectors were due to check the Rabbi's cellar.

At the time construction was started on armories in Gorky. Our friends from Brest Litovsk were employed there. We put the weapons in packages- 10 revolvers per package- and we hid them temporarily in Gorky.

We searched for a permanent hiding place. The owner of the forest in Ziliny, Moshe Weintraub, was a member of the Bund in spite of his wealth. We spoke to him and he allowed us to hide the weapons in a space in the forest.

D. The year 1905 in town

The events in town in 1905 caused my arrest and also that of other members of the Bund. These events had to do with demonstrations that we had planned after the Gafon parade which had ended in the loss of life among the workers.

The Bloody Ninth of January created waves of demonstrations in the socialist world. In Russian towns there were parades and protest meetings against the cruel rule of the Tsar. The Bund in Kovel decided also to organize a demonstration. The committee included the university student Grisha from central Bund. We stayed up an entire night and prepared a detailed programme for the parade. All workers in town knew about the coming demonstration. In the morning we went outside and found a great upheaval in town. There were dozens of soldiers in the streets. I told Grisha to give me his Browning and I began to run home through the fields in order to hide it together with propaganda material he carried.

On the way I had to pass by homes of non-Jews. They knew what was going on and of my involvement. They caught me and brought me to the soldiers. I was arrested in the yard of the sawmill. The clerk Shia Epels was there and saw me being arrested.

[Page 114]

The soldier who had arrested me was riding a horse and he tied me to him with a belt. He brought me to the main road and handed me over to two guards. They took me to the chief of police who was residing in Perlmutter's house.

More prisoners were brought in. Among them were the son of Yosef Neta Goldstein, Perlmutter's son, Yosef the carpenter and Schwartzblat. Comrade Lindenbaum from Lubomil was also with us. There were seven of us in jail. In the evening we were moved to the prison. On the second day of our arrest our friends were able to contact us and to bring us food. Comrades Hinda Kirshner, Sonia Goldstein and Batya Goren bribed the assistant to the director of the prison and he allowed them to bring us party literature. He also gave us news of the world.

The "sin" of owning secret literature was punishable by exile to Siberia. In those days it was an enticing location because many important Socialist leaders had been sent there. Some members were keen on being sent to Siberia for that reason. It was a badge of honor.

I recall an interesting episode from my stay in prison. In those days there was, in Kovel, a government doctor of Tatar extraction. He was one of the Righteous among the nations. When he heard about our arrests he came to our cell wearing a long black coat. Inside he had sweets for us. "I am your secret friend"- he would tell us. In order to comfort us he would announce that the Tsar's days were numbered.

I began to prepare myself for the interrogation and I decided to admit that I belonged to the Bund- let whatever will be will be. After three months a high-ranking police officer came from Kiev and he and the prosecutor, an officer from the prison, began the interrogation. Their arrival was known in town and many people came to the entrance of the prison to wait for the results of the interrogation.

I was first to be questioned. The first question was asking me if I was a member of the movement. I decided to give a positive answer. When the prosecutor asked me the name of the movement I replied- Construction workers movement. This reply surprised the prosecutor. He whispered to the officer: "Whom did you arrest? He does not even know what the movement Is." I enjoyed this doubt and the prosecutor ordered my release until the trial. Lindenbaum was confused in his answers, was found guilty and was sentenced to a prison term of a year and a half. Prison conditions were dire and when he was released he was sick with tuberculosis. I never saw him again.

[Page 115]

Folklore

Translated by Amy Samin

A Time to Laugh
(Ecclesiastes 3: 4)

Eyal – El

One of the elderly teachers would say to his wife on Friday: "Sarah, my wife, give me a biscuit "*mit shmeerachatz*" (with spread)." He was afraid to say the word "*eyal*" (oil) because the word sounded like "El" (Elohim, one of the names of God).

(told by Yechezkel Goldberg)

Tzom – Tzum

Rabbi Avraham Szoferfin of blessed memory was one of the wealthy men of the city, but he also possessed a pleasant voice, and he would pray before the Holy Ark during the *musaf* prayers, obviously not in order to receive a reward. When he prayed during the Days of Awe and reached the prayer "*Teshuvah, tefilah* and *tezdakah*" which meant *Teshuvah* (repentance) – *tzom* (fast); *tefilah* (prayer) – *kol* (voice); *tzedakah* (charity or righteousness) – *mammon* (money), the worshippers would instruct: "don't read *tzom*, but *tzum – kol – mammon*." In other words, it is not enough that the leader of the prayers must have a pleasant voice, he must also be rich.

(told by Yechezkel Goldberg)

The Funny Story of Rabbi Yechiel Vagsholl, may God avenge his blood

On the eve of the Sabbath Rabbi Yechiel Vagsholl, may God avenge his blood, would say, "Now, I am happy with my portions; it is forbidden to hold and count money and I am as the rich men." When the Sabbath was over, he would say, "Woe is me. Now it is permitted to hold and count money…"

(told by Yechezkel Goldberg)

The Right Answer

Rabbi Yechiel Vagsholl, may God avenge his blood, was in competition with the Holy One, blessed be He – he would make matches. He would come to visit us on Simchat Torah and the second holiday of Passover. He once told us this anecdote: a young man was matched to a young lady from Lusk.

[Page 116]

It was agreed that the bridegroom and the bride would meet halfway, in other words, in Rozyszcze. The man we're speaking of, who had never before seen the young lady, approached her. His first question was, "How are you?" The young lady understood right away with whom she was dealing and put him in his place: "I spent my money for nothing."

(told by A. Lowny)

Three Hundred and Ten Immersions

When Berele, the son-in-law of Eidel of Matsiov, would go to the mikveh, he would immerse himself a great many times. Once, they asked him, "Berele, why do you immerse yourself so many times?" He replied, "I immerse myself three hundred and ten times for the three hundred and ten worlds. With each immersion, I repair a world."

(told by Yechezkel Goldberg)

The Story of Leib the Gravedigger

My father of blessed memory told me this story: According to Jewish law, it is forbidden to leave an open grave. Once, someone of the Efrat family died. Leib the gravedigger was ordered to dig a grave. Leib dug the grave, but the funeral party accompanying the dead was delayed. What did Leib do? He climbed into the grave, stretched out, and waited for the dead.

Late at night the funeral party arrived at the cemetery. They shouted: "Leib! Leib!" There was no answer. The group approached the place where the grave should be, and as they drew near the open grave, Leib climbed out of it, giving up his place to the dead.

(told by Monya Galperin)

Rabbi – Not a Year

In the tractate Irobin it is written: "The rabbi didn't review – Rabbi Hyeh [from the word chayim, "life"], how does he know?" Rabbi Hyeh was the student of Judah Hanasi. If the rabbi does not review the *halacha* (law), how will his student learn? Based on that saying, a play on words was created: A rabbi would come once a year to our city, to visit his disciples. One time, the rabbi came in the middle of the year. One of his disciples was surprised, and said, "Rabbi – not a year," in other words, it hasn't been a year since the last visit. The rabbi answered, "What, Rabbi Hyeh? If I don't come twice a year, how will I live?"

(told by Yechezkel Goldberg)

[Page 117]

"Love your neighbor as yourself"

"Don't seek revenge nor hold a grudge against your own people." "Love your neighbor as yourself." How is it possible to love your enemy? To not hold a grudge nor seek revenge against him? Think of yourself as one part of a body, or part of a greater whole. Can one part of the body take revenge against another?

(told by Haim Avrekh z"l)

Question and Answer

How is it possible that a small boy can control one hundred bulls; that they all listen to him? The answer: Because each of the bulls thinks that the other ninety-nine bulls and the boy are chasing him.

(told by Pinchas Winfeld (Hotchles) z"l)

The Interpretation Died

A rabbi is teaching his pupil from the *Chumash*: "And Sarah died in Kiryat Arba." He read and explained, "*Vetamat* (died) – *Iz geshterbin.*" Sarah – Sarah… He stands and asks, "Who is dead?" The student: "*Vetamat* is dead." The rabbi hits him. "Goy! The interpretation of '*vetamat*' is 'dead'!" The pupil cries, then repeats obediently, "The interpretation is dead."

(told by Zusia Kanter of blessed memory)

The Equine Cantors

Some Jews with Zionist leanings prayed in the House of Study named for Projenski. They were suspected of short-changing in the planting and were told to find another place to pray. Not far away was the barn of Moshe Dondik, who had two horses. They built a division inside the barn, and there they established the synagogue of the Zionists. The manager was Mr. Goldstein, may God avenge his blood, from Hadrogoria.

On the even of Kol Nidre as the cantor was praying, the horses began to neigh, drowning out the voice of the cantor.

The worshippers shouted, "Moshe Dondik, what is this?" Moshe Dondik said to them, "Why are you shouting? Considering the miniscule rent you're paying me, you want I should bring Sirota [Gershon Sirota, known as the Jewish Caruso] to sing? For that rent, the horses are good enough cantors for you."

(told by Rabbi Shmuel-Yosef Werbe)

[Page 118]

The Clean-Handed Tailor

There was in our town a ladies' tailor, Itchi Previn. They tell the story that, before his death he instructed his family to put his worktable, at which he had toiled for 60 years, into his grave with him. When the Messiah came and the dead arose, the table would testify before the King of Kings that he had never kept for himself the scraps; that is, he had never taken the leftover pieces of fabric that remained after sewing the clothing, without the owner's knowledge.

(told by Baruch Bork)

Response to a Pest

Yaacov Kuptshik, may God avenge his blood, was quick-witted and bright. Once, a large group of students walked with him in the direction of the school. A spiteful fellow passed by and said to him, "Kuptshik, you have lived to see your own well-attended funeral."

"On the contrary," replied Kuptshik, "we're arranging yours."

(told by A. Lowny)

Kuptshik Yearns for a Jewish State

Once, during prayers, Kuptshik said, "I long to see a Jewish state." When he saw that the worshippers did not react with enthusiasm to his words, he smiled and said, "If we put a *minyan* (ten men) into the synagogue, and make a lot of noise, go outside and see how much noise there could be in a place where a few million Jews gathered together."

(told by A. Lowny)

V'yichlu is Dead

I heard the following anecdote from my brother Yaacov, may God avenge his blood: Once there was a young man who had trouble reciting the *Kiddush* (blessing over the wine). Whenever he tried to bless the wine, the words were garbled in his mouth.

His father figured out a stratagem to solve the problem: he decided to give all of the "goyim" his son had befriended nicknames from the *Kiddush*. One was called "*V'yichlu*", another "*Hashamayim*" and so on. Sure enough, the stratagem worked and soon he had memorized all the words of the *Kiddush*.

The one day the goy with the nickname *V'yichlu* died. On the eve of the next Sabbath, the son rose to bless the wine, saying, "*Hashamayim v'ha'aretz v'kol tzavam.*" And where is "*V'yichlu*?" asked the father. "*V'yichlu* is dead," replied the son.

(told by A. Lowny)

[Page 119]

How do the Dead Live?

Mr. Frankfort said once to Kuptshik, may God avenge his blood: "Do you know something, Kuptshik? We, the teachers, are the only ones who are forbidden to strike, as it is written: 'You may not take a child from the house of his teacher, even to build the Holy Temple.'"

Kuptshik smiled and said in a pleasant voice, "A father and son went for a walk, and they reached the cemetery. The son asked his father, 'Father, how do the dead live?' The father was confused by the question and answered, 'The dead, my dear son, make their living from the tombstones upon their backs.' The son asked, 'How is it possible to make a living from a tombstone?' '*Aza panim heven zie taka'a*' the father answered."

Frankfort understood the thinly-veiled hint, smiled, and did not say a word.

(told by A. Lowny)

Peretz, the Water Carrier

Peretz was ill-fated (it shouldn't happen to us): he was missing something in his head. He made his living bringing water to the homes of the Jews in the Zand. He was well-known by reputation in the Jewish community and the goyish community.

When the time came for him to serve in the army, Peretzele went and reported in, to fulfill his duty as a citizen. The doctors knew who this new "recruit" was. The chief doctor approached him, patted him on the shoulder and told him, "You, Peretzele, will make a fine soldier." Peretzele saluted him just like a proper soldier should and replied, "No, I won't, Doctor – I'm crazy!"

(told by David Blitt)

Hilniu

"Hil" was a happy Jew, a pauper, who had the nickname "Hilniu the Crazy." But he was a seer. He could tell on which day the holiday of Passover would fall, on which day Shavuot, all of the Jewish holidays. When people met him on the street and asked him, "Hilniu, on which day five years from now will the holiday of Sukkot fall?" he would answer on the spot, and there was no cause to doubt his response.

When a *brit* [*brit milah*, ritual circumcision] was arranged, the respected women of Kovel would come to him and would prepare refreshments for the guests at the public expense.

When he was asked once, "What do you do, Hilniu?" he replied, "Hil does a *brit* and the public pays."

(told by David Blitt)

[Page 120]

Rabbi Ozer Shadchan's Theory of Relativity

Who says that only Kalman Guttenboim understood Einstein's Theory of Relativity? When Guttenboim was still in diapers, Rabbi Ozer was already giving lectures on the subject. One story goes like this: Once Rabbi Ozer went to a young man of Kovel and said to him, "Yankel, I have for you a lovely and demure bride, really beautiful."

The two of them went to the young lady's house. The young man looked at his intended and saw that she was far from beauty and close to ugly. When the young lady went to the kitchen to prepare refreshments for her guests, Yankel asked the matchmaker, "Rabbi Ozer, this is your beauty?" Rabbi Ozer replied, "Everything in the world is relative. Compared to my wife, this bride is extremely beautiful."

(told by David Blitt)

Another Story About Rabbi Ozer

Rabbi Ozer never saw much success. The bridegrooms he tried to match were stubborn. Once he suggested a match to one of the young men. Rabbi Ozer was sure that this time the match would be successful.

The next day, Rabbi Ozer encountered the young man and asked him, "*Nu*? How did it go?" The young man understood subtlety, and replied, "I went to see the young lady, and I did like the story of Esau, as it is told in *parashat Toldot* [a portion from the *Torah*] 'and he did eat and drink, and rose up, and went his way…'"

(told by David Blitt)

Going Out to Welcome Borochov

Once there were days of inflation in the *Hehalutz* movement. Young ladies who came of age and did not have a bridegroom decided to join *Hehalutz* and move to *Eretz Yisrael*.

Obviously, their interest in the matters of the work movement was very slight, as the following story illustrates: every academic year, we had a tradition of honoring the memory of Borochov. On the Friday afternoon, I saw a group of girls heading towards the train station. "What's the hurry?" I asked. Surprised that I did not know, they answered me, "We are going to welcome Borochov…"

(told by Arieh Rabiner)

Beer for Passover

This is the tale of a Jew from a village who, two weeks before Passover, came to see a respected rabbi in the town to ask for his approval of a beer that was kosher for Passover. The Jew explained to the rabbi that he alone prepared the beer, and he did not trust any mother's son in matters of *kashrut* for Passover. He had purchased all new equipment, casks, barrels and so on; he watched closely over the barley, with the utmost of care, just like *matzah shmurah*.

[Page 121]

The rabbi explained to him that there was no possible way to make beer kosher for Passover, for any barley that soaked in water for more than 18 minutes began to be leavened.

The Jew was unconvinced and said, "Really? If I tell the rabbi that everything is brand new and watched over with the utmost care, with no room for doubt, as a matter of fact, the rabbi should come and see for himself and explain how this could be *hametz* [not kosher for Passover]?"

And so the argument went on with no end in sight, until the beer maker got an idea, and said, "If the honorable rabbi will show me a clear ruling that my beer is *hametz*, I will accept it."

The rabbi stood before the Jewish beer maker, opened the *siddur* [prayer book], and read to him, "…who has sanctified us with His commandments and decreed beer [in reality, 'bi'ur' or 'the removal of'] *hametz*." And when the Jew saw the law specified in the holy prayer book, he conceded the argument.

(told by Rabbi Dr. Michael Grayver)

A Story about Moshke the Porter

This is a story about Moshke the porter of blessed memory, who was famous for his quick-wittedness and his devotion to all Jews. One day, a merchant who was well-known in the city approached him in the marketplace, and proposed that he deliver a small crate of merchandise in his wagon. It was the kind of merchandise that there was a need to whisper about it in front of others; saccharine, which required the supervision of the tax officials and the secret police. Moshke and the merchant agreed that he would wait for him outside the city on the road leading to Brisk.

The merchant went to the appointed place, and Moshke prepared to travel with the cart-load of merchandise. After only a few moments, there appeared a detective and some policemen. They stopped Moshke and his wagon and took them to the commander of the police in that quarter. They began to interrogate Moshke about the owner of the forbidden merchandise, and he played innocent: "How on earth would I know?"

After a few hours, the regional commander of the police himself began to interrogate the prisoner: "How can this be? A man gave you merchandise and you don't know who he is or what he is?" "Mr. Police Commander, sir," answered Moshke patiently, "does it seem reasonable to you that when a traveler comes to me, I should demand that he identify himself and show me his passport? Mr. Commander! Your policemen, you should pardon my saying, did not behave wisely here. They should have listened secretly to learn more of this matter; I would have told them to stand to the side, close by me, so that I could point out the merchant to them. However, they – those geniuses – didn't do that. They caught and arrested me. Obviously much will be made of this in the city. And who, but a gullible person, would behave that way?"

[Page 122]

The regional commander of the police burst out laughing, called to his subordinates, and pointed to Moshke, saying, "This simple Jew has more sense in his little finger than all of you put together, you blockheads." He then turned to Moshke and said, "I see that you are very quick-witted. I will give you back your crate and you will travel in your wagon back to your place in the market and wait there until the owner of the merchandise appears."

Moshke agreed to this proposal and returned in his wagon to his place in the market, followed at some distance by the policemen. Delighted with his jest, Moshke climbed up on his wagon and taking up the reins waved them in the air, calling out in a loud voice for a long hour, "Hey! Jewish reb, owner of this merchandise! Come and journey with me!" All those sitting and standing about in the market roared with laughter, as they saw Moshke winking broadly to the detectives, who were trying to hide.

(told by Rabbi Dr. Michael Grayver)

[Page 123]

Character from Folklore: The chimney sweep of Kovel and his dog, for once, standing at attention

[Page 127]

Education, Literature and Theater

From the Poorly Educated to the Hebrew Gymnasia
[History of Hebrew Education in Kovel]

by Eliezer Leoni

Translated by Ala Gamulka

At the end of the 19th century there was an important change in the educational field in town. Inside the walls of the ancient town fresh winds were blowing. These came from Greater Russia.

We were witnesses to a double process: at one end religion was strengthened and became a haven while at the other end secularization appeared – bringing in new spiritual trends. There was now an interest in Eretz Israel.

The Trisk Hassidism was then at its height and it aspired to spread in all parts of Volyn and even further. The Grand Maggid sent his son Rabbi Yaakov–LIbeniu to conquer Kovel and to attract souls to Trisk Hassidism. On the banks of the Turia River stood an enclosure, a fortress full of erroneous ideas, that intended to envelop the town in the teachings of the grandson of the one from Chernobyl. In his court there were Kabbalists, delusional writers of amulets, ascetics, separatists, postponers of the end and believers in redemption.

These visionaries found a ripe ground. The town was shrouded in poverty, Life was not good economically for the Jews. As usual, when there is nothing in this world, man begins to dream of the next world.

However, in spite of the fact that this was a time of longing for the mysterious and the unknown, there was an opposing current. This was a humanistic current. It was an era on the eve of Zionism and the Bund in town. It was a time of the awakening of the population to life and creativity. There was now a rift among the people of Kovel. New forces appeared, rising from a slumber of a few hundred years. There were people walking around town with "heretic" books in their arms. They announced the revival in our town. Economics and agriculture became the new topics. Religious education lost its hegemony. A group of young educated people appeared and they demanded a change of values and a new approach to education. They demanded a secular education and the introduction of sciences and Zionist ideology.

This was a struggle between two opposing ideologies and it caused a schism– social and philosophical.

The result of this ideological struggle was the founding of the secular school "The Poorly Educated".

[Page 128]

These educated young people were "helped" by external sources. In 1893 there was a terrible plague in town and there were many victims. As a result, orphans remained without parents and education.

This group of educated young people was influenced by the Movement of the People (Grodnaya Volya). They decided to educated the people out of goodness and not for commendation.

These young people had been educated in the Russian liberal literature and were greatly influenced by two leaders– Petreyev and Tchernishevskiy. The latter had penned a tractate on art in which he stated that life is wonderful. He saw education as a preparation of man for real life. There was nothing superior to it.

This belief was the motto of "The Poorly Educated"– educate the poor children of Kovel to a practical and creative life and a trade.

It was not only ideas that created the school. There was also an economic reason. The dire economic depression within the Jewish community of Kovel at the end of the 19th century led to this ideology.

Many generations had previously earned their living by owning pubs and restaurants. In 1896 a new law was announced prohibiting licenses for these establishments in small towns. Only large cities were given permits.

Thousands of Jews in Kovel were placed in terrible economic straits as a result. This led to the thinking that Jews had to be prepared for other occupations in order to earn a living.

In an issue of Hamelits (1896) Lipsky called on the Jews of Kovel to abandon spiritual ideas and to work in agriculture and as craftsmen. He offered to publicize this idea and to send teachers to train the youth in productive occupations.

The large number of miserable orphans were part of the first classes in the "The Poorly Educated" school. Its name means exactly that– to educate the poor.

This school was the preparatory ground for the network of Hebrew schools that were later created in town. They became famous in the entire area. This school was the nursery, the first seeds for the wonderful Hebrew educational institutions to come.

The curriculum in "The Poorly Educated" included Hebrew language and grammar, Russian language and grammar, Torah with Rashi interpretation, Prophets with simple explanations, arithmetic, geography, Calligraphy and Ethics.

[Page 129]

The teachers were: M. Shainin–mathematics; Gershonovitz, Zvi Efrat and Binyamin Gurfinkel–Jewish studies; Binyamin Yudkovitz, principal, taught Russian; Boymel and M. Efrat–calligraphy.

Among the rest of the staff we should mention Fidut, son–in–law of the "kilkiever Rabbi" who lived in the House of Learning on the sands; Lipsky who was well–known for his writings in "Hamelits"; as well as Zvi Hazan and Heinich Geller.

The school was under the authority of The Poorly Educated which was headed by M. Brik, Zalman Kharon and Pessach Roizen. Rabbi Brik's wife –who died young at the age of 34– was one of the most enthusiastic supporters of the school and worked tirelessly for the benefit of the poor students.

The school was opened in August 1893. It started in dire circumstances, in a narrow room with rickety benches and desks. There were eight poor boys, but they represented the saying: "Watch out for poor children because Torah will emanate from them". These boys did well in their studies and they were well–known in the community for their achievements. One of these boys was celebrated by all of us. He was Asher Frankfurt who is the principal of the Hebrew Gymnasia. Frankfurt was one of these poor boys. Another student was Isser Miller, founder of the Bund in our town.

The school grew and a year later had forty students. The school was moved from the narrow and dark room to the House of Learning of Sender Kuznits (Sender the Musician). It was situated behind the house of the Krasavitza (Beauty) near the army barracks.

In 1894, the young women belonging to Daughters of Zion established a society called Malbish Arumim (Clothes for the Poor). The purpose of this society was to provide clothing and shoes to the students of the school. Daughters of Zion put on, from time to time, parties for the purpose of raising funds for the school.

It is important to note that these children were truly poor and were even provided with food by the school. The school also received support from other sources. There was an amateur theater in town. This troupe presented play reading evenings in three languages– Russian, Yiddish and Hebrew. All income was dedicated to supporting the school.

One time a famous singer of those days came to town. He was G. Yosilov from KIdenov. The Kol Zion Society asked him to give a benefit concert for the students of From the Poorly Educated. Yosilov graciously accepted and he thrilled listeners with the song "On the Ruins of Zion" by Dolitsky. The income was so large that it permitted the school to expand.

[Page 130]

During the first five years of its existence, 1893–1898, there were 187 students. 73 completed their studies and 42 left before the end of their studies. Most of the students were apprenticed to different craftsmen– printers, photographers and commerce. Fifty of the graduates were able to earn a living from these occupations.

On 17.08.1898, there was a gala evening organized by the From the Poorly Educated society. To mark five years of the school's existence, Dr. Perlman, one of the outstanding intellectuals in town, opened the festivities. He spoke warmly of the value of the school and the great usefulness it brought to the poor people in town. He also praised the new atmosphere in Jewish education in town. He praised the founders 8212 – D. Gershonovitz, D. Efrat, I. Liberman and Ma'ze. The principal of the school, Yudkovitz spoke about the history of the school from day one. He described the spirit of rapprochement and the dedication which spurred on the teaching staff and the educators. They were doing this holy work as volunteers and because they were devoted to the children of town.

When principal Yudkovitz died there was a serious crisis in the school. The organizing committee met to discuss the next step. A. Kastelansky proposed to transfer the running of the school to the Zionists under Kol Zion Society. His proposal was accepted and after a Zionist administration took over the school blossomed even more.

In those days there was no co–education. There were young girls from poor homes who were unschooled. This was a serious problem. A few young women who were well–educated and who came from respected families in town, decided to establish a special school for these girls. The originators of this idea were the sisters Shinkar, members of a veteran family in town. One of them–Anna– later married the famous Pinhas Dashevsky.

The school was founded in 1900. It was actually the first trade school in town. The curriculum included the study of the Hebrew language, calligraphy, arithmetic and Russian language. The teachers were volunteers. There was great emphasis on the acquisition of a trade.

During the initial year the girls advanced in sewing and embroidery. At the end of year there was an exhibition showcasing the work of the students. In the exhibition were pillows embroidered in various colors, kerchiefs woven with great artistry, beautiful blouses, children's coats made of wool and linen, small tablecloths embroidered with flowers as well as toys.

[Page 131]

The girls earned money by sewing shirts for "Clothing for the Poor Society. In the first year of the school they earned 5 rubles.

The girls progressed well in the study of Hebrew and at the final gala at the end of the first year they charmed the audience with their Hebrew songs, well–pronounced.

The school had two classes– upper and lower. In the upper group there were 28 students and in the lower– 22.

Herzliah School, Its teachers and students

There were two principles which governed the establishment of Herzliah School. One was the amazing mix of teachers and educators, well–respected, who came to town from different places to teach Jewish values and science to the children of town. The other was the great hunger for learning, the thirst for knowledge that characterized the youth of Kovel.

Mr. Masievich, z"l,
the first principal of Herzliah School

In the Talmud there is a story about Rav Hanina and Rav Haya who were quarreling. What should be done that Torah study would not be forgotten in Israel? Rav Haya said: "I will go sow flax, I will fashion snares and I will catch turtles. I will feed the meat to the orphans and use the hide to make scrolls. I will write the five Books of the Torah on them. I will then go to a city where there are no teachers for the young and I will read the Chumash to the children. I will then teach these children the six books of the Mishnah. This is how I will ensure that Torah will not be forgotten in Israel".

[Page 132]

The teachers of Herzliah School were imbued with the same dedication that Rav Haya had envisioned. They, too, came to our town to give their knowledge and to make certain that Torah was not forgotten by the children of the town.

On the other hand of the coin, these teachers found students who were prepared to learn from their masters. Even, according to the elderly Hillel, on Shabbat.

The publication "Tslilim" (Sounds) was issued by the students in the year 1924. In it, we read an essay titled "What Does School Mean to Us?". It reflects the amazing yearning of the children of Kovel for the acquisition of knowledge and perfection. We read, among the rest:" School is like a live fountain of water where everyone who drinks from it is revived. It is the source where we acquire Torah and wisdom. It gives us everything we need in our lifetime and it opens our eyes to see straight. Without this school we would be like a flock without a shepherd, fumbling un the dark. School fulfills the needs of the students. Without school we would be ignorant. School opens the gate and leads us from darkness to light. It directs us on the proper path and moves us confidently to the larger world".

Important educational work was performed in this school. However, the staff did not depend on oral Torah only. In 1924 it was decided to publish a journal dedicated to the issues of education and hygiene.

The plan was not accomplished for various reasons. However, the outline that was done in writing shows us the serious intentions of the teachers.

The editor of the journal, principal Moshe Fishman, writes in the introduction: "In these pages that are written for your consideration, we posed the following goal: to help, you, the parents to decipher the educational problems of your children.

Who among you is not worried about the future of your children? Who among you does not desire for his child to be educated and refined, healthy and well–mannered? Jewish fathers and mothers always sacrifice a great deal to make his child happy. Your intentions are good and necessary, but you do not always know the correct path for achieving your goal.

In every culture and nation there are those who are educated and who are thinkers and who achieve great successes in the educational field. There are always publications for simple folks, but this is not our case. We are poor in pedagogical literature.

[Page 133]

Our times bring serious problems in education and we are listening for solutions. We want our children to stay abreast of societal development.

We, the teachers of your children, will attempt, from time to time, to solve some questions that pertain to the education and the health of your children."

[Page 134]

The school administration even gave an opinion on the inclusion of theatre arts and the occupations connected to them, such as, singing and dance.

A drama society was organized in the school under Sh. Klonitsky. Excellent plays were produced. I recall Purim 1924 when" The Pocket Knife" by Shalom Aleichem was presented in the Express theatre. It was very successful and the audience was highly impressed. A year or two later the play "The Tax Collector" by Peretz was performed, starring the student Yerachmiel Rovner.

There was also a choir in the school and it was conducted by Sh. Feinstein. It was of high artistic quality.

Tslilim

Written by students of Herzliah School

Ah Sinful nation, a people laden with iniquity… Isaiah, I;4
On right – ISAIAH
Bottom left – illustrated by Yitzhak Atlas
Student fifth grade

    The school was truly public. Its students were poor– children of laborers and middle– class parents. They became the core of the pioneering youth movements, especially "The Young Pioneer" (Hechalutz Hatzair). Almost all its counsellors came from Herzliah School. The enthusiasm we had for studying Bible and Revival poetry was also directed towards Plekhanov, "History of Materialism" by Lange and "The Call to Socialism" by Landver.

    Today, when I look back at this turbulent and interesting part of my life, I ask myself: where was our inner meaning? On what where we nurtured? I reply: Denial and belief were intertwined in us. The jump to the ideology of the world of socialism was too sudden and too quick. We did not entirely abandon true belief, but we did not reach denial. We said "Hang on to this and do not leave that". We created a kind of match between the Kotzker and Neskhizher courts and Marx and Plekhanov. We belonged to both sides. We were somewhere between a house of learning and denial.

We read socialist literature and we argued day and night: What is the role of the past in our education? Is it change, destruction or integration? Secrecy and discovery were unequal. Some of us were fervent materialists and Marxist dialectic served as a holy example not to be doubted. Others were iconoclasts who went further and fed calves to foreign deeds. However, inside, we were true believers with deep religious sentiment. On Yom Kippur and especially during Kol Nidre we feared the day of judgement as did our parents. Even the extremists among us followed all the laws. We felt that the laws of materialism were a bit heavy.

At first, we were caught in the world of changing values. The library of the small synagogue with its antiquated scrolls and yellow pages, with Midrash Raba and Ein Yaakov, seemed to us archaic.

[Page 135]

Herzliah School in the first years of its existence

[Page 136]

It was obsolete. We were stuck between the movement and the House of Learning. The Hora swept us, but the prayer of Unetaneh Tokef touched our hearts. This was because the prayer leader evoked memories of generations of suffering Jews.

In time there was a balance between these two extremes. We understood that Ein Yaakov does not contradict Marx. It is possible to be a rabid socialist and still be immersed in Talmudic issues. We did not reach this conclusion easily. There were many struggles and endless discussions. This is what happened to many of the students at Herzliah school. There was a great upheaval in their lives on their road to socialism.

From the students to the teachers. We really liked Mr. Chaim Hochberg, z"l. He was truly knowledgeable in all parts of the Torah. He was a talented man, full of deep knowledge, but, first and foremost, he was a good friend to the students.

Hochberg did not frighten us. He obtained our respect with his pleasant ways and his gentle character.

Whenever he was absent from our classes we were quite sad because we loved him. We were attached to him with admiration and love.

Hochberg used to invite some of his students to his house for discussions about literature and language. I remember that these conversations included the influence of the Bible on Shakespeare.

We were young and we did not always absorb everything. However, when we were older these conversations encouraged us to study Shakespeare. We then realized how deep and wonderful had been our cherished teacher's discussions.

In addition to these attributes, Hochberg was also a great mimic. He could imitate many personalities at Hanukah and Purim parties. Especially amusing was his mimicry of a certain butcher that he knew in his childhood.

I was once fortunate to hear him speak about the origins of the name Kovel. I do not recall the circumstances, but Hochberg came up with the theory that it was a Hebrew name. He said that Kovel is mentioned in the Bible (Ezekiel, 26;9)– "And he shall set his engines of war against thy walls…" The meaning of the phrase is an instrument that can break down walls. The legend that the name of our town came from Koval– blacksmith proved his point. In olden times the blacksmiths of our nation used to fashion arms. (Samuel I, 13;19) "Now there was no smith found throughout all the land of Israel; for the Philistines said, Lest the Hebrews make them swords or spears". Of course, this was a Jewish genius having fun with the Torah.

[Page 137]

Hochberg was the best of the Russo–Polish Jewry. In him one saw popular warmth together with an advanced education. He was the pride of the school.

He was born in Sokolov, Podolia, in 1895 and he received a strict religious education. Even at a young age he went from yeshiva to yeshiva and he was famous for his genius. However, he felt that his place in the House of Learning was too narrow. He then began to read secular books, on his own. Without the guidance of any teachers he obtained an encompassing European schooling and he was known as an outstanding teacher. He arrived in Kovel at the end of 1924., brought by Zev Tchernitsky.

Haim Hochberg, z"l

They were relatives. Tchernitsky's mother and Hochberg"s mother were sisters. Tchernitsky taught in a Hebrew school in Smititsh. Its principal was M. Fishman. When the latter was invited to Kovel to become the principal of Herzliah School, he brought first Tchernitsky and then, Hochberg.

We were quite depressed when we learned of his illness. We believed he was only sick and that he would recuperate. No one thought of the possibility that one day our beloved teacher was on his deathbed. I visited him one day and Hochberg was sorry that he was attached to his bed, totally inert. During our conversation he told me a Hassidic tale with a moral. It was said that one of the great Hassidim stood on a bridge on Christmas Day. He saw that a cross was being cut in the frozen waters. One of his followers passed by and was worried: What does our Rabbi have to do with this filth?

[Page 138]

The Tzaddik replied: My child, my child, go and see. The moving water is a symbol of purity, but when it freezes it becomes a source of impurity. This is also how man lives. Movement, enthusiasm and dancing purify and clean man's soul. Hochberg finished with a touch of sadness: I feel as if the forces of impurity are sticking to me because the wells of life and happiness are now frozen.

Hochberg saw that I was very sad and he felt that I, and not he, deserved pity. In order to distract me from my sad thoughts he told me a story from his student days. He heard that, living near the town where he was studying, there was a Jew. He was over 100 years old., but he was still alive. Hochberg went to visit this wonder of nature, this Methuselah and he was invited in. Hochberg saw an old man sitting at the table, maybe 80 or 90 years old, reading a volume of Gmara. He asked his host: who is this old man? The Metuselah replied– this is my son! Hochberg told this story with great humor and we both laughed. We were overcome by a fit of laughter. I left him comforted and hopeful.

I remember a rainy Friday night. I came home from a visit in the "Hechalutz" branches in Lyudmil and Matseyev. On the way I stopped at a newsstand and I noticed a large headline in Koveler Shtime (Kovel Voice), announcing the death of Haim Hochberg. I felt something dying inside of me. It was as if I were paralysed – everything was frozen. The letters were flying like embers. Hochberg is gone? He was so young, so fresh, so full of life, only 35 years old. Death overtook him for eternity? An important part of our lives has been taken away. He was a leader in Jewish education in town.

The rain fell and the town was enveloped in sadness. A dear great person had been called up to heaven. I had heard from Hochberg the following:" Anyone beloved by God dies young". His death confirmed this saying.

In our school there were two more teachers whom we followed– thirsty for their wisdom and their teaching. They were Zalman Ariel–Leibovitz and Yaakov Kobrinsky, may they have long and good lives.

Leibovitz was connected to an unforgettable episode in our school life. Leibovitz taught in the Hebrew high school in the mornings. In the afternoons he taught Jewish subjects and science in Herzliah school. I remember his first lesson. He told the story of Archimedes who ran in the streets yelling "Eureka! I found it!". The story was told with great skill and we were all quite impressed. We sat with our mouths open. We saw, from the first moment, that this was an outstanding educator.

We loved Yaakov Kobrinsky for a different reason. He had a healthy humor and he never stopped smiling at his own jokes.

[Page 139] [Page 140]

Kobrinsky taught Hebrew, geography and science. He knew how to give life to these subjects by infusing his teaching with jokes and anecdotes. When one of the girls asked him: "What is the purpose of tears?", he replied: "In order to cry". After he amused us he explained well that tears are necessary for the cleansing of the eye.

He followed the methods of Rabbi Meir. "When Rabbi Meir taught a chapter, he would do one third halacha, one third legends and one third proverbs". Mr. Kobrinsky always put legends and proverbs before halacha. He had the soul of Breslev. He followed the philosophy of Breslev that a happy man always succeeds and that sadness brings failure. I am certain that this philosophy allowed him to overcome the terrible, inhumane suffering that he endured. He was able to overcome and remain healthy in body and soul.

The First graduating class of Herzliah School in Kovel 1927

I loved his conversations outside the classroom during breaks between classes. This mainly also occurred at Hanukah and Purim parties. I well remember some of them that reflect his epicurean character. During geography class he spoke about earthquakes and reasons for their happening, but he had not yet given a scientific explanation. He told us the story by Yehuda Steinberg "From the Bathhouse": Haim Sofer and Hirsh–Yekil Melamed came out of the bathhouse on a Friday evening and they were discussing world events. Have you not heard– Hirsh–Yekil stopped walking and asked– about the previously unheard–of earthquake? He continues: "The newspapers say that all this is because of a volcano!" Haim Sofer controlled himself, but finally he roared: "Is it not enough that you are not a learned person, but you are coarse and simple. Do you not know what is an earthquake? It is written â€˜one who looks at the earth will shake". You tell me stories about a creature called a volcano." Mr. Kobrinsky took Haim Sofer's side and defended the Biblical point of view that an earthquake is founded on theology and not science. They felt that even evil events come from a higher being. Using folklore Mr. Kobrinsky opened our eyes to the world of research.

Mr. Kobrinsky was uncomfortable with the idea of "wearing a head covering". It was an insult to say that someone is "wearing a hat" (i.e. he is observant). When one of the students mentioned that it is a proper expression, as stated in the Torah: "And Abraham rose up early in the morning and saddled his ass" (Genesis, 22:3)– saddled= put on a head covering. Mr. Kobrinsky replied that this was the issue– there was a head to be covered…

Among the praiseworthy teaching staff of Herzliah School, the personality of the principal, Mr. Moshe Fishman, really stands out. He is here in the Israel with us. Mr. Fishman was one of the leaders in Jewish education in our town. The first principal was, actually, Mr. Manievitch, but during Mr. Fishman's time the school reached very high standards. Thanks to his energy and amazing talents the school became a nursery. In it, our amazing youth, the precious saplings, grew and became the pillars of Zionist education and we saw the rejuvenation of the Hebrew language and the organization of youth movements in our town. The Hebrew Gymnasia was the result of this growth. It is difficult to imagine the establishment of the Hebrew Gymnasia without the basis given at Herzliah. The hard work of Mr. Fishman and his staff produced this great human product– the cherished students.

Mr. Fishman was very strict. His students feared him, but sometimes he relaxed and was able to joke. When he once asked a student to come and the latter moved slowly, he said: "You have appeared from your place"!

He once asked one of the students to find a quotation from the Bible, but he had difficulty in finding it. Mr. Fishman then told us the following anecdote: A woman came to the rabbi and asked a question about kashrut. The rabbi went to his book shelf, took out a book, studied it and then said:" It is kosher!" The woman was in doubt and said: What is special about this? Anyone can take a book, study it and declare a ruling. The rabbi replied:" You are correct. However, you need to know where it is written".

One day, one of the girls asked a philosophical –metaphysical question. Mr. Fishman, an experienced educator, knew that the mind of a girl in Grade Six is not sophisticated enough to understand such deep matters. He told the following story: He, Mr. Fishman, once served as an inspector for "Tarbut". He went to one of the schools and heard a lesson in zoology. A girl asked: If we have to protect animals, who allowed us to kill them for food? Even Maimonides, as her father told her, allowed this. The teacher was embarrassed and Mr. Fishman came to his rescue by saying: I feel a strong wind coming from the window near the ceiling. Perhaps you can ask this student to close it and then you will answer her question. The poor girl tried hard to close the window and she sat down ashamed. Then Mr. Fishman asked a tall student to close the window. The student got up, raised his arm and easily closed the window with one motion. Is it not magic? ended Mr. Fishman.

[Page 142]

The girl calmed down and did not look for the answer from the teacher. She understood that she is not mature enough to understand these matters.

This story shows the genius of Mr. Fishman as an educator and his deep understand of educational issues.

The most important part of Mr. Fishman's philosophy was to educate students to behave tactfully and in good taste. We would call this diplomacy. Two people can say the same thing, but one is rude and the other pleasant. We forgive the second one, but not the first one. As usual, Mr. Fishman had a story about the father who was angry with his son who had ordered him as follows:" Father, send me money!" A friend said the son should have asked: "Father, send me money". It is exactly the same words, but politeness is essential.

Once I was sitting in the Neskhizher House of Learning. It was where I attended prayers on week days, Shabbat and holidays. I took down an old book from a shelf. It happened to be Midrash Tankhuma. In it I found that Mr. Fishman's stories were not new but came out of the writings of our sages. R. Levi stated that both Abraham and Job said the same thing, but Job was afflicted while Abraham was rewarded". Job 22;9 states "This is one thing, therefore I said it. He destroys the perfect and the wicked". Abraham was clever said (Genesis 18:23) – "Wilt thou also destroy the righteous with the wicked?" They both actually uttered the same thing–that God eliminates the righteous with the wicked, but Abraham was a "gentleman" and was polite. This was one of the most important lessons Mr. Fishman tried to instill in us, the students of Herzliah.

Mr. Fishman worked to develop literary talents among his students. He established, for that purpose, the "Inclusive Notebook" in which the best pieces of writing were published. This "Notebook" served as the basis for the collection "Tslilim" (Sounds) which was published in 1924. The editor was Mr. Fishman. When we read this collection these days, we are astonished at the beautiful Hebrew style used by the students. This offering by the students of Herzliah demonstrates how Hebrew education was excellent and how hard the students worked on their own development.

Mr. Fishman did not believe in overdoing the amount of reading. He used to say:" Read a little and learn a lot. Learning is the basis for a person's enlightenment." He awakened in us the desire to learn, to reflect and to study. As the basis for our philosophical advancement, our principal brought us to the works of Achad Ha'am. For us Achad Ha'am was the ultimate source for Jewish wisdom. His works were a hidden well, a closed garden, but whoever could solve the secrets of his deep intelligence was a superior person. Mr. Fishman opened for us the gates to Achad Ha'am. He straightened the rocky road and we were able to continue along a proper road. We were quite comfortable with all the deep articles such as "Resurrection of the Spirit", "Moshe" and "Body and Soul".

[Page 143]

The entire school reacted when we heard that Achad Ha'am had died in 1927. There was a memorial assembly in the Great Synagogue and Mr. Fishman took us, Grade Six, to attend it.

At this memorial assembly, Mr. Fishman spoke about Achad Ha'am. He began with the usual words: "There is a Moses in every generation". He continued by saying that Achad Ha'am's spirit is immortal and it will influence Jewry in all future generations and at all times.

During the existence of the school there were numerous teachers. We list them according to the beginning of their tenure in our school.

Mrs. **Dvora Bley**– taught lower grades in 1922/1923
Mrs. **Malka Alper**– taught Hebrew, history and Tanach in 1923/1924 (now teaches in Tel Aviv)
Mrs. **Yentl Cayman** – taught lower grades in 1923/24–1924/25
Mr. **Zev Tchernitsky** – taught science in 1923/24–1924–25 (now an officer in IDF)
Mr. **Moshe Fishman**– principal 1923/24–1926/27 (He is in Israel)
Mr. **Zalman Ariel–Leibovitz**– taught science, Hebrew and Tanach in 1924/25
Mr. **Haim Hochberg, z"l**– taught Hebrew in 1924/25–1928/29
Mr. **Sternberg**– taught Polish in 1924–1926
Mrs. **Bella Peletz**– taught the preparatory class in 1924/25–1926/27
Mrs. **Bina Friedman, z"l**– taught Polish in 1925/26–1038–39
Mr. **Yaakov Kobrinsky**–taught Hebrew, Tanach, arithmetic, geography in 1925/26–1932/33 (He is in Israel)
Mr. **Shimon Feinstein, z"l**– taught Hebrew, Tanach, arithmetic, singing in 1923/24–1938/39
Mrs. **Hinda Segal**– taught in 1925/26–1934/35 (She is in Israel)
Mr. **Moliar**– taught Hebrew and Tanach in 1929/30
Mrs. **Tsippa Margulis**– taught in 1930/31
Mr. **Baruch Avivi (Voliver)** – taught Hebrew and Tanach in 1930/31 (He is in Israel)
Mr. **Aaron Rosenstein**– taught Hebrew, Tanach and arithmetic in1931/32–1938/39

[Page 144]

Mr. **Zeidentseig**– taught art and handicrafts in1926/27–1928/29
Mrs. **Genia Leyer**– taught Polish in 1928/29
Mrs. **Bracha Hayot, z"l**– taught in the preparatory class in 1927/28–1931/32
Mr. **Goutwort**– principal in 1933/34–1938/39

This list does not include substitute teachers and kindergarten teachers.

Tarbut Hebrew Gymnasia

The gymnasia was founded in 1921. It was during the time of the consolidation of Volyn and the beginning of the newly established Kingdom of Poland.

Yiddishkeit was sensitive in its national element and was livelier than in other parts of Poland. It was capable of determining its own spiritual route.

This healthy national spirit made it possible to anticipate what would be happening to Jewry in the near future. This Jewry was searching for internal anchors to save it in dire times. The Tarbut organization was based on these sentiments.

The Organization for Education and Culture–Tarbut – began in Kiev in 1917. This was the year of the Balfour declaration and the chance for Russian Jews to take part in the rebuilding of the Land of Israel.

The Jews of Volyn joined this movement to build its own cultural and independent life. There was an urgent need to do it because there was now a threat of assimilation.

This is how the Hebrew high school was founded in Rovno and soon afterwards in Kovel. It was an important cultural center in Volyn.

In 1921, two years after the opening of the Kovel branch, Mr. Asher Frankfurt proposed the establishment of a Hebrew high gymnasia. The proposal was accepted and the school year opened with three grades and two preparatory classes. Every year another grade was added until in 1926/27 a senior class was established. The first graduating class of the high school was produced.

For 17 years, that is from 1921 to 1938 there were 11 graduating classes and the total number of graduates was 159.

[Page 145]

The following table shows the development of the school:

Number of students in 1921–1938

Year	No. of classes	No. of students
1921/22	5	200
1922/23	6	273
1923/24	6	264
1924/25	6	250
1925/26	7	260
1926/27	8	266
1927/28	8	276
1928/29	8	269
1929/30	8	230
1930/31	9	223
1931/32	9	221
1932/33	8	194
1933/34	7	180
1934/35	6	166
1935/36	7	202
1936/37	6	207
1937/38	7	242

Teachers of the gymnasia

The High school was fortunate to have an excellent teaching staff. These teachers had a high pedagogic standing and an outstanding education. Each one of them is worthy of a lengthy discussion because they are the remnants of the splendid and praised group of teachers in the Tarbut schools in Poland. The gymnasia teachers were scholars and had deep knowledge of their subjects. What can be done? Time did its bit and the spiritual image of these teachers is no longer available. It is difficult for me to describe them in full. I can only do it with anecdotes.

I well remember, especially, the figure of the teacher of Polish, the late Dr. Chiel. He was true to his name: Fear and trembling. When he entered the classroom, we were full of fear, without really needing to do so.

De. Chiel had the habit of standing at the blackboard until we would calm down. His reddish–brown hair stood out.

[Page 146]

Woe to anyone who did not notice this hair and did not rush to stand up.

Dr. Chiel was a good–looking man, like R. Yochanan. He had the charm of a complete personality. He was similar to the pioneers. His character was that of prominent personalities. As we sat at our desks we did not comprehend, yet, the substantive meaning of this outstanding soul. Dr. Chiel instituted a Spartan approach in the classroom and he demanded complete obedience from his students. However, when he opened his mouth and began to explain "Pan Tadeusz", we forgave his harshness. His lessons were times for deep thought. There was no one else in the high school who could explain material like him. He demanded much from us, but he also gave us a great deal. We had to memorize Pan Tadeusz. Woe to the student who missed or added a letter to the written text. We studied Pan Tadeusz in the winter of 1928 and it turned out to be a very important time in our lives. We gained a lot.

Dr. Chiel was quite independent. He had phenomenal knowledge. It was said that he knew the Iliad and the Odyssey by heart in the original Greek. He had an outstanding memory, but he was not influenced by others. He marched to his own drum. He used to tell us: "Man must have a spiritual spine of his own". He was a proud Jew who did not feel the weight of the Diaspora. He had been redeemed and he taught us to stand up straight and not to belittle ourselves in front of the non–Jews.

The principal, Asher Frankfurt, has been described a great deal and more can be added. I recall one image that I bring up because of its piquancy. Mr. Frankfurt's Hebrew was outstanding, but he was also knowledgeable in Polish. He could have had a contest with Mankiewicz… I remember that there was once a party in his honor and the representative of the government shouted: "Hurray for Mr. Principal". It is possible that for the sake of routine, Mr. Frankfurt replied: "It is not necessary! It is not necessary!"

Mr. Rotman–Netaneli's name is connected to an evening of Bartholomew that he prepared for us, poor Fifth grade students. It was the fault of the poet, the late Shaul Tchernichovsky. Definitely he was the one. In a Hebrew literature class, Mr. Rotman read "Legends of Spring" by Tchernichovsky. The beginning went well. Then we came to a phrase that scared us: "The weeds will dry; the cracks of the stem will fall". The beginning of the phrase made sense, but the ending? What do the words mean? What is the connection between them (in Hebrew)? I remembered a popular joke about the difference between "Proverbs" and "Job"? In Proverbs there is no connection between the verses and in "Job" there is no tie between the words. This is a magical Midrash! No connection between the words!

[Page 147]

Gymnasia teachers in the first years of its establishment

Seated, from right to left: Yosef Holder…Meir Reiss, Yaakov Netaneli–Rotman, principal Asher Frankfurt, Zalman Leibovitz–Ariel, Azriel Figelman, Yosef Avrech
Standing from right to left: Shimon Feinstein, Rachel Pip, Dr. Abba Shpruch–Poyzner

Mr. Rotman became enraged: "Nu, do you not know, my scholars? And you "Bava Vatra", (Mr. Rotman gave me this nickname because I used to sit on the last bench), what does the word "swaddle" mean? To help me out, one of the students got up and stated in a loud voice: Sir, there must be a typo here! There is no such word in the Hebrew language – "swaddle". That is all we needed… We are now grown up and we know, Thank God, that there really is such a word in Hebrew. We even know its meaning. However, for Heaven's sake!…

We behaved in a special way for our Hebrew teacher, L. Chazan. He was the only teacher who had written and published a book. We saw a genius in this author– a creative soul.

[Page 148]

Mr. Chazan had published, in Kovel, his novel "Redemption". He gave the manuscript to Shmuel Ingberg and the latter copied it in a clear, clean and beautiful handwriting. We envied him for having been chosen to copy the manuscript and thus also being the first reader of the book. Ingberg became very important in our eyes and we began to see him as the image of an author. We knew the phrase:" Get close to one anointed and benefit from it".

I owe a special debt of gratitude to Mr. Chazan as he awakened in me the desire to create the written word. A few years earlier, a student in the Fifth Grade, Yoske Dolgin, now Yosef Aricha, began to publish his articles in "The Star" of Luvoshitsky. Yoske became known as the best goalkeeper among all the soccer teams in town. When he stood in the goal crease, no one was able to score a goal. We were so surprised when his first book, "Food and Vision" arrived. There was only one copy and it belonged to Mrs. Freilichman. She guarded it as if it were a jewel. She only allowed us to look at it. We were jealous of Yoske because one of us had merited to become one of the muses.

How was he inspired? Perhaps there was a sign from God that whispered to hm: Go into literature. The same whisper probably also told him:" Why do you need soccer? Turn to stories and legends". By the way, our parents viewed soccer as something prohibited. There was a field behind the high school building where we played soccer during recess or before classes began. There was always some Jew who came to the field and when we told him we were playing soccer he would groan and moan and say: Oy, it hurts your mother!" It is possible that Yoske said to himself: "I can't beat this Jew" …

I was not fortunate to be a student of Dr. Reuven Ben–Shem (Feldsheve). He appeared in our town like a comet. He appeared and disappeared. He arrived fresh and happy, like a young Dionysus who left his band of Gods having fun on Mt. Olympus. He came to Volyn and taught the youth of Kovel to laugh, to stand up erect and to be interested in life and creativity. He came to establish a new way of life. He brought us new existence.

In spite of the fact that he was like Dionysus, he was a true representative of Eretz Israel. This is the Diaspora, but anywhere, I, Ben Shem, tread it is a part of our holy land.

He walked straight and he was full of national Jewish pride. The residents of our town saw in him a new kind of Jew, a part of an evolving epoch in Judaism. He came having earned a doctorate in philosophy. He was well educated in the classics and he was the epitome of a scholar– young in age, but deep in knowledge.

[Page 149]

Fifth Form, Tarbut Gymnasia 1928

First Row from top standing from right to left: Yerachmiel Virnik, Shmuel Gilberg (Gilboa), Eliezer Leoni (Tsuperfein), Mordechai Melamed, Zvi Wohl, Tsuker, David Bromberg, Moshe Goodis, Haim Fried
Second row: Moshe Lerner, Miriam Goldstein (Volk), Rivka Ber, Hinda Bratt (Segal), Shoshana Cooperberg, Sara Plashtets, Sara Karsh, Sara Finkelstein (Bromberg), Sheindel Kleinerman, Yerachmiel Rovner
Third Row, seated: Guralnik, Hava Volvoler, Israel Movshovits, home room teacher Dr. Ida Tsvigel–Fisher, Tuvia Weisbrot, Zissel Rudman
Seated on the floor: Haim Lifshitz, Haim Hizhik, Ossya Eventchuk

    The greatness of the beautiful personality of our teacher was evidenced before I went to him to ask him to become one of the builders of the Kovel Memorial Book. He replied in a positive manner, but he asked for a two months delay. Two months later the excellent article was ready. Dr. Ben–Shem looked at me with very sorrowful eyes and confessed: "During these two months I struggled with memories of the town– I was really sick. When I remember Kovel and everything that happened to it and its Jews, I am completely broken. My article was written not in ink, but with the blood in my heart".

    Here are the names of the teachers according to the times they served in the high school:

Mr. **Zalman Ariel–Leibovitz**– taught Jewish studies in 1921–26 with a stop of two years. (He is in Israel, where he serves as principal of Bialik School in Tel Aviv.

[Page 150]

Mr. **Shimon Feinstein**– graduate of the Peterburg Conservatory– taught singing from 1921 (he is a victim of the Holocaust)
Mr. **Eliezer (Lussya) Hodorov**– taught physical education from the establishment of the high school until 1925. He is now in Israel. A well–known and talented ship captain, he was famous for his heroic deeds which honor us as well as him.
Mr. **I. Feldman (Pladi)** – taught art in 1921–22. He is now in Israel and is a well known and veteran artist.

Mr. **Yosef Avrech**, graduate of the Odessa Yeshiva founded by Prof. Kh. Tchernovits (young rabbi) and a student of Dr. Sh. Tcharna. He was born in Kovel and taught Tanach and history from 1921 on–until he was killed in the Holocaust.
Dr. **Abraham Durtchin, z"l**. He obtained a doctorate in chemistry from Berlin University– taught mathematics in 1921–22. He visited Israel.
Mrs. **Pip**, graduate of Lvov University. She had an excellent religious background and taught Polish literature in 1923–28. A victim of the Holocaust.
Attorney **Yosef Holder**, born in Kalush, taught German language and general history in 1923–27. A victim of the Holocaust.
Mr. **Zeidentseig**, born in Poland– taught art in 1924–25.
Engineer **Meir Reiss, z"l**, born in Rovno, brother–in–law of Z. Ariel–Leibovitz, graduate of Advanced Technical School in Lieges (Belgium)– taught, mainly, in the high school of Clara Davidovna. His subjects were Mathematics and Physics which he also taught in the Hebrew gymnasia in 1924. He died in 1939 in Slonim while escaping the Nazis.
Mr. **Azriel Figelman**, graduate of the Advanced School of Commerce in Kiev– taught Mathematics in 1921–28.
Dr. **Abba Shpruch–Poyzner (Pevsner)**. He was born in Brody (eastern Galicia) and taught physical education in 1921–23. He graduated from medical school in Italy and practiced for many years as a respected doctor in Florence. He escaped before the Holocaust and was saved by the French underground. He is now practicing medicine in Israel.
Mr. **Yaakov Netaneli–Rotman**. He was a graduate of Lvov University. Taught Jewish studies and science in 1922–29. He is now in Israel and is the principal of Sokolov–Laor High School in Jaffa.
Mr. **I. Israelevsky**– taught only one year in the high school–1922. He was a specialist in the lower grades. Immigrated to the United States.

[Page 151]

The first graduating class of the Hebrew High School, 1927

[Page 152]

Mr. **L. Chazan** – taught Jewish studies in 1925–32. He is in Israel. He is a writer and teaches at a high school in Rehovot.
Dr. **Reuven Ben–Shem (Feldsheve)**, graduated in Philosophy and Psychology from the University of Vienna. He is an ordained rabbi and taught Russian language and history in 1925. He is in Israel and is the principal of Sokolov–Laor high school in Jaffa
Dr. **Ida Tsvigel–Fisher**, graduate of Lvov University– taught Latin, Physics and Chemistry from 1926. A victim of the Holocaust.
Dr. **I. Chiel**, doctor of Philosophy– taught Polish language and Latin in 1925–29. He became a well–known attorney in Vilna. He was a victim of the Holocaust.
Mrs. **B. Kasher–Erlich**, graduate of Lvov University– taught German language and history in 1927. A victim of the Holocaust.
Mr. **I. Reshel**– taught art and arithmetic in 1927. Made Aliyah in 1951 and died a year later. Published children's textbooks.

Mr. **Michael Gruber (Giladi)** – taught Jewish studies in 1929–31. He is a teacher at Bialik school in Tel Aviv.
Mrs. **Hadassah Shprung**– taught geography, science and biology. She is in Israel.
Mr. **Sh. Rubinstein**– taught Hebrew language and Tanach.
Mr. **I. Ginsburg**– taught Jewish studies.
Mr. **I. Kowalski**– taught mathematics
Mr. **Mordechai Leyer**, had a diploma in philology and history from Krakow University– taught history in 1938–39. He was a victim of the Holocaust .
Mr. **Moshe Rosenfeld**, diploma from Vilna university– taught mathematics and logic in pre–WWII years.
Mrs. **M. Hager**, diploma from Krakow university– taught science and geography in the last years of the existence of the high school.
Mr. **David Erlich**, diploma in philology from Krakow university and – taught Polish language in pre–WWII years.
Mr. **Aaron Pines**, diploma in History from Warsaw University and another diploma from the Institute of Jewish Learning in Warsaw– taught Jewish studies in pre–WWII years.
Mrs. **Zinger–Brihel**, diploma from Lvov University– taught geography and handicrafts in pre–WWII years.

[Page 153]

Mr. **P. Schechter**– diploma from Lvov University– taught handicrafts in pre–WWII years.
Mr. **I. Kleinberg**, diploma in philology from Krakow University– taught English and German languages in pre–WWII years.

These teachers, together with the venerated principal, Mr. Asher Frankfurt, z"l, made the school into one of the best educational institutions in Volyn and in Poland.

The gymnasia was also well–known for its two libraries– Hebrew and Polish. In an educational institution which had as its aim to give its students a Hebrew and a general education, the high school paid much attention to the acquisition of teaching tools. In particular, much was focused on the improvement and expansion of the two libraries. In addition to reading books, there was also a considerable number of science books and other texts to serve the students.

In order to expand the Hebrew library and to interest the students in its contents, Mr. Frankfurt, the principal, organized "Book Month". During that time the students collected hundreds of important and interesting books, especially scholarly editions from Russia.

There were changes in higher circles in Poland as well as the designation of high schools as preparatory institutions for university, the libraries were geared for scientific study. Many of the appropriate books were transferred to a special laboratory, under the supervision of the teachers of these subjects.

The number of volumes in Hebrew reached 2500, while the number of Polish ones was over 2000. In addition, 420 manuals for teachers were purchased.

[Page 154]

Building the Bialik Gymnasia

We all remember that the Gymnasia was located in the house of Verba, z"l, on the river bank. It was one of the old buildings in the new town. The building was in danger of collapsing and the authorities demanded its evacuation. It was one of the reasons that propelled Mr. Frankfurt to begin the process of building a modern, improved edifice for the Gymnasia. This took place in 1934 when a committee was struck: Moshe Perl, Yitzhak Gitlis, Menachem Reisisher, Israel Finkelstein, Yosef Shochet, Leib Fish, Mordechai Leyer, Yaakov Kuptchik, Aaron Frantz, Zvi Pugatch, Israel Prozhansky, Efraim Tenenbaum, Aaron Melamed, Zev Tsurif and the principals: Yaakov Kobrinsky and Kh. Goutwort. In addition, the following joined as overseers: Yaakov Burk, Moshe Pugatch and Dr. M. Tsichnovits– still with us.

That year Mr. Frankfurt visited Eretz Israel to collect funds towards the construction from among his students and admirers.

On 28.10.1935 a thank–you letter was sent by M. Weisbrot in which the following was included:" It is our holy task to thank you in the name of all our friends and in the name of the 1000 students of the school for your active assistance for the benefit of the building.

Dear friends, we began building not with pleasure, but with the knowledge that we had no choice. The authorities forced us to do it and we had no other way… We still require a lot of money to complete the construction. You, our dear comrades in Eretz Israel, have helped us in this task. We are certain that you will continue to do it for the benefit of the building".

Frankfurt struggled a great deal until he saw the building standing up. The secretary of the Gymnasia, Mr. Yaakov Kuptchik, wrote the following: "Almost every annual general meeting of "Tarbut" would end with the resolution: We are going to construct a building for our educational institutions. Once there was even a special committee selected consisting of our most active members… Time went on. The apartment where the Gymnasia was housed was becoming more dilapidated from month to month and from year to year. The authorities began to press us to remove the school from this ancient building. A committee formed by the government to investigate the location discovered that it was in great danger of collapsing.

[Page 155]

Principal Mr. Asher Frankfurt with his former students during his 1935 visit to Eretz Israel
He was collecting funds for the construction of the Bialik Gymnasia

[Page 156]

This was the time when the idea to finally begin construction of the school began to germinate in Mr. Frankfurt's mind. It was to be a special building following all pedagogical and health rules– strong and spacious.

The three of us–A. Frankfurt, M. Perl and myself sat down together and we prepared information for a selected group. This was in order to form a building committee. Mr. Frankfurt described the plan– which plot of land was required, what must be built and how much it would cost… A question was posed: Mr. Frankfurt, where are we going to find the money for this project? How much can we expect from members of the Kovel community?

Another person, who had not heard the question, came into the room. He was asked how much he would pledge for the construction and he replied: three hundred zlotys. This reply melted the fear in our hearts. It was decided: we are going to build!

"We have to buy the lot", but there is no money. It was a winter night and we left late at night and suddenly:" You know, I am buying the lot today!" I was surprised, but I did not say anything. The next day, Mr. Frankfurt told me:" I got a loan of three hundred zlotys yesterday and I put down a deposit on the lot".

Summer came and after much discussion, the building plan was approved by the authorities. A foundation had to be built. We needed cement and sand, but, most of all–money. We really did not have any money because everything collected during the winter was used to pay for the lot. No matter, thankfully, there were still some wealthy members of the community who had not been approached yet. It was necessary to do it, but who will be sent? Mr. Frankfurt grabbed one of the members of the committee and began to go from house to house and people reacted positively.

Money was needed for bricks, plaster, metal, payment to the workers and Mr. Frankfurt went to Eretz Israel. There he had many former students whom he could approach.

Great effort was made to put up walls for the ground floor and then work stopped…Winter came and the windows– without glass panes– protruded like blind people's eyes. When spring came, the foundation was flooded and the walls were covered in moss. We despaired.

Summer is here and we need lumber, but we have no money. What to do? Mr. Frankfurt went somewhere and obtained four thousand zlotys. The walls were bought and work began again. It was a miracle that the building was covered with a roof before the cold returned. The remaining winter months served as vacation time. The plan was to complete the building during the summer and to open the Gymnasia in the fall of 1937.

[Page 157]

The construction took three years. The cornerstone on Yuridica Street was placed on 16 Tammuz 1934. The celebration upon completion was on Aleph Kislev 1937. There were many participants in the festivities which included a grand parade.

When the cornerstone was placed the following special scroll was read:

"Blessed are you, our God that has brought us to this day.

Today is Friday, the 16th day of Tammuz, 1934, 1864 years since the destruction of our second temple, thirty–seven years since Dr. Binyamin Zev, ben Yaakov, Herzl convened the First Zionist Congress, seventeen years since the Balfour Declaration, 12 years since the League of Nations announced our national home, 16 years since the establishment of Poland by Dr. Ignaz Mosteshitsky and Governor Yozef Pilsudski, during the presidency of the Zionist movement of Nahum Sokolov. On this day the cornerstone was placed for this school, Gymnasia Tarbut in Kovel, Volyn. This was accomplished by the friends of the Hebrew schools, the authorities and all the volunteers.

In the year 5697 since creation, in the ninth month, the month of Kislev, the school was inaugurated, with great happiness, in the presence of its founders and representatives of the government, as well as Friends of Hebrew School and representatives of other institutes in the Kovel.

[Page 158]

The building stretched over an area of 325 m sq. on a lot of 3200 m.sq. It had three storeys with a staircase in front. The structure had 22 rooms and halls. Of these, 8 halls were divided for classes, but one was a gymnasium, three were laboratories, an office, a staff room, principal's office, medical room, cloakrooms and a library.

At the laying of the cornerstone for the gymnasia building, the inspector from the Kovel area said that the completion of the construction will give Mr. Frankfurt a beautiful graduation diploma. The completion of the building was much more than a graduation diploma. It was a brilliant success for Mr. Frankfurt, z"l. The dream of his life was achieved. He reached the heights of his educational and public life. He was only forty–nine years old at the time. The gymnasia had existed for 17 years in a precarious position– waiting for a disaster to happen. Now he was given wonderful tools and the gymnasia became the high ground to which all students aspired.

Mr. Frankfurt, z"l, reached the height of popularity. A committee has been formed to celebrate his fiftieth birthday in 1938. Its members are Moshe Perl, M. Leyer, Yosef Avrech, M. Rosenfeld and Yaakov Kuptchik, z"l.

A congratulatory letter was sent to him by "Tarbut" of Poland, "Tarbut" of Kovel, teaching staff of the gymnasia, the committee of the Society of Friends of Hebrew Schools in Kovel and graduates. Among other remarks, the following was said: "You are the one who founded the gymnasia and you led us to fight for its existence, development and success. The institute was erected in spite of the tremendous struggle and times of despair. You encouraged us all. The building is wonderful and is temple for the education of our youth.

Our cultural life is difficult. We still have a further goal and there are many obstacles in our way. World events proved that the ideals of redemption are our only anchor in the stormy sea, the sea of exile. There are so many threats trying to obliterate us. You understood this, dear Mr. Principal, seventeen years ago when you began this holy task of national education. You undertook the correct road for our culture: total revival of the Hebrew language and its spirit– a complete Hebrew education without any shortcuts".

[Page 159]

Contribution of the Gymnasia in the rebuilding of Eretz Israel

It is well known in general and Jewish history that small towns, or even villages, became famous due to the sages and scholars that had settled there.

Zionist and Hebrew Kovel received its spiritual strength from the Hebrew Gymnasia. It was a miniature "Yavneh". Our town became known throughout Poland as a Hebrew and Zionist town. Due to this fame there were many outstanding teachers who were well educated and they contributed much to the spiritual and cultural development of the town. These teachers did not only teach their students, but they were involved in public life throughout the town.

The Gymnasia, was, first and foremost, the fortress of the Zionist and Hebrew movements in town. It was a wonderful nursery where young people were nurtured and they were the ones who carried, on their shoulders, the dream of the revival of the Hebrew language and the rebuilding of Eretz Israel. This is where the strike force was honed and it went out to conquer the Jewish youth and to bring to them Zionist ideas.

Almost all the outstanding counsellors and leaders in the Zionist and pioneering youth movements in town were graduates of the Hebrew Gymnasia. These graduates were the spokesmen of Hechalutz, Hechalutz Hatsair and Hashomer Hatsair. They also were the debaters with those who opposed these ideas. If you met a young man or woman on the street speaking fluent Hebrew and dreaming of making Aliyah, you knew that they were the results of the education in the Hebrew Gymnasia. This Gymnasia which was a temple on the banks of the Turia River.

It seems to me that our teacher and rabbi, Yaakov Rotman–Netaneli, who lives with us here in Israel, defined best the essence of our Gymnasia. He said that his duties in the Gymnasia were not only to teach, but he saw himself also as an ambassador. His role was to encourage the youth of Kovel to make Aliyah. This is true because the Gymnasia was like an embassy whose aim was to prepare the Jewish youth for Aliya.

Indeed, the Gymnasia did wonders. The graduates of the Gymnasia did not only stand out in Kovel, but also here in Israel. Among them are teachers, kindergarten teachers, writers, important functionaries and public figures.

[Page 160]

Talmud-Torah

by Yaakov Teitleker

Translated by Ala Gamulka

On a winter evening in 1899, in the dark alleys of the "town", passers-by are wading through deep snow puddles using their flares. They are hurrying home to escape the terrible cold that is getting worse as the night descends. The windows of the low, shaky houses are reflected into the dark of night. They look like frozen eyes covered in frost. The thickets are extended. Here and there is heard the squeaking of the store doors being shut by their owners. They feel no more customers will come and they want to escape the cold and the inactivity. They seek the warmth of their families.

At the same time, the students of Talmud Torah on the market street of the "town" are sitting at a long table studying their Gmara. Near them sits Rabbi Reuven, the teacher. They repeat vigorously the sentence "An ox gored the cow". The Rabbi's white beard is spread on the table and tempts the students to perform tricks… Today is Thursday and they go over the weekly Mishna. They sit in groups of three close to the Rabbi. They vigorously move back and forth and recite together. They are louder than the Rabbi and their classmates. The latter, in the meantime, are playing with their buttons, shoving and pushing as is their custom.

Suddenly… what happened? Immediately, the oil lamps are extinguished. The students jump as if electrified and quickly run to the hallway. Their winter coats, hanging on hooks are grabbed and some fall and are trampled upon. Confusion, flight…" The Inspector!" "The Inspector"- is whispered about. The students and their teachers run to the door…

Truthfully, at the time, there was no permit for the Talmud Torah. It called itself "Jewish National School" and the inspector supervising the schools in the area forbade teaching in it. The leaders of the Talmud Torah had not exerted special efforts to make the proper repairs for an elementary school and among the few teachers there was no one capable of administering the secular studies. The Judaica teachers represented the backbone of the Talmud Torah. The leaders preferred to remain in the "underground" and to rely on God's will. As a result, there were many such alarms.

These alarms tired out the students as well as the teachers. Several years elapsed and progressive thinking did its deed. There was a a proper elementary school in the "sands" and this affected the thinking in the "town". The leaders finally invited a licenced teacher who could also administer the Talmud Torah in the open.

[Page 161]

Soon a teacher was brought from Rozhishets- Zusia Kanter. He was a qualified teacher and was recognized by the inspector. Thus, the Talmud Torah surfaced from the underground. Zusia Kanter was about forty years old then and he was energetic and exciting. It was not enough for him to be a symbolic seal of approval. He saw the low level of the Talmud Torah and he began to make improvements. The first "terrible" deed was to install a bell…It would ring on time and would teach the students what "early" and "late" meant. (This does not exist in the Torah, but was needed in the Talmud Torah). The leaders were totally against this innovation. The "Grabivitzer"- a famous rabbi who lived across the street from the Talmud Torah, saw it as a depravity. He was in a rage and he attacked the "non-Jew". He threatened to expel him for the town. The elderly chief leader, Meir the Gabbai, was prepared for a battle against this foreign reform. Meir would come twice a day to the Talmud Torah to prepare the students for communal prayers. He used to stress the "z" of "yizakhru" (no "s" sound!). The leader who was also the treasurer, Simcha Henich- one of the strongest personalities in town- threatened with a lawsuit. There were groups on both sides and they argued forcibly in the small synagogues. Finally, a truce was established. A parallel existence was instituted- secular studies in the morning and Judaic classes in the afternoon.

At that time there were six Judaic tutors. Sender Rosenzweig from Brisk was the head teacher of Gmara and its annotations. He was a large man with a prominent stomach (duly noticed by the students). He scared his pupils. When he resigned his replacement was Itzel Lioshtchik- a famous scholar and a well-known sermonizer in the synagogue in the "town". Another tutor was for beginners' Gmara was Reuven. He had a long white beard and was nervous and hot-tempered. The tutor of Torah and Rashi was Yitzhak-Leyzer- a gentle and even- tempered man. The Prophets teacher was Moshe-Yitzhak, a Lithuanian Jew, was welcoming and involved with his students. Mendel Dardaky- Hebrew language teacher- was a tall, skinny guy. He never changed his appearance. His other job was with the Hevra Kadisha where he taught and helped with burials. Both jobs did not provide him with enough income… There were three secular teachers. One was the principal, Zusia Kanter, who taught Russian language and arithmetic. Another was Henich Geller for Hebrew language and grammar. The third was Hershel Lekach for beginners reading and writing. Kanter and Geller were the first educated teachers for the Talmud Torah students. Geller's attitude to the students was a little too formal and "grammatical", but Kanter was beloved by them. He had a good psychological and educational approach and he knew how to endear himself to them with his friendly discussions, games, singing, playing the violin.

[Page 162]

He used to do art activities with the students during classes in spite of the attitude of the leaders who were opposed to it. There were about 200 children in the Talmud Torah. Tuition was free, except for one Rubel which the parents had to pay twice a year.

During World War I, the Germans entered Kovel in 1915 and they used the Talmud Torah building as a barn for their horses. Talmud Torah was then closed. When the Germans left at the end of the war, in 1919, it was not possible to used the ruined and burned out building as a school. Talmud Torah school began to wander among various rented buildings and synagogues in town. Finally, the town leaders, headed by Haim Gershonovitz, built a new building for the Talmud Torah on Listopdova Street (at the end of Karliova Buna in the section between the "town" and the "sands"). It was an appropriate building made of wood. Hershel Lekach, a former teacher at Talmud Torah, organized a new managing board headed by the teacher of Polish, Mrs. Brik (daughter of the government-sanctioned rabbi, the late Rabbi Brik). Teachers were hired (the majority had been on staff before) with the exception of Zusia Kanter himself. He had removed himself from Talmud Torah before the war. All necessary repairs and other arrangements were made as required at a religious elementary school. Still, permits were not given even to this renewed Talmud Torah. The Polish system of schools confiscated the building and the Talmud Torah returned to its former location. It was again necessary to use various synagogues in town. Finally, a group of merchants, headed by the generous Yudel Sofer (he was a leader at Talmud Torah), with the financial assistance of the Joint managed to erect a new building on the same lot where the original one had stood. Money from the Joint had begun to be used for different educational institutions in the Diaspora after the war.

The present Polish authorities left the religious Jewish school alone (they were not even interested in inspecting the teaching of the Polish language). In essence, the educational level of the school was not high and did not fit the progress of Hebrew teaching in town.

The fresh progressive forces of the general Jewish education concentrated on secular subjects. They left the national-religious side to the weak hands of the elderly leaders. The latter produced a non-education, antiquated and inappropriate. Poor children were their students. The Judaic tutors took over most of the school day and very little time was devoted to secular subjects such as: Hebrew language and literature, foreign language, mathematics… They were taught by non-professional teachers who did not follow the required curriculum. The head of these leaders was the same Simcha Henich- by now very old.

[Page 163]

He was happy with his honorary position- distributing pay to the tutors and teachers every Thursday in his home. The money came from the collector Pinhas who had done this since the founding of the Talmud Torah. The funds came from minimal membership fees and donations given by those praying in the synagogue. The tutors and teachers at the Talmud Torah never really earned a full salary.

The secular teachers in those days were: Yaakov Trager (also secretary of the board and executive director of the Talmud Torah), Lussya Hazan, Adolph Rosenzweig and I, the author of this article. The tutors were: Pinhas Weingarten- an ultra Orthodox Rabbi and hot-tempered, Sender Veiger, Yitzhak Reif (he was also the prayer leader at Prozhansky synagogue), Nissan Farber and Hershel Lekach (he became a tutor). Pinhas Weinfeld imbued his students with his deep knowledge and extensive learning, but Pinhas Weingarten- the chief tutor and acting principal of the Talmud Torah- taught unrelenting religion and he conducted common prayers among the student body. He influenced them to follow a true religious life with all the rules. The fortress of Judaism established the power and the "little Jews" stood guard…

In 1939, after the quick war between the Germans and the Poles which ended in the total defeat of the latter, the Bolsheviks entered Kovel. All Hebrew schools, including Talmud Torah, were closed. Teachers were fired. Instead, the Bolsheviks established, in the same buildings, Yiddish schools. Polish inspection no longer existed. The administration of these schools was assigned to Kh. Tabachnik (Mirsky)- a veteran Communist and a former Yiddish teacher. He had a strong ambition to elevate School No.5 (i.e. former Talmud Torah) above the others since the students were poor-proletariats. He quickly assigned the school's principalship to the Yiddish teacher Aaron Shinitzky. This was a talented, certified pedagogue. He had been principal of the Yiddish school on Kremlitzka street in Warsaw and had escaped to Kovel when the Nazis came. He was accompanied by the teacher Leah Dimant- a well-known Communist and a good teacher. To assist them, Tabachnik hired some former teachers that he could trust that they were not bourgeois. These were Naymark from the Puvshekhni school, Liova Gelman and myself.

It was as if a magic wand had been used to change dark grey school to one decorated with pictures and art.

[Page 164]

The art was done by the students who were quickly trained to do it by the artist and teacher Shinitzky. New furniture, equipment and learning materials were brought. They were removed, by order of the assistant to Inspector Tabachnik, from wealthier schools. School No. 5 now had a rich library, artistic studio, exhibitions of art work done by the students. This was the first time in their lives that they were doing art. The singsong of repletion of the Gmara and the inspirational lectures by Rabbi Pinhas, delivered every hour, were now replaced with happy modern songs. In place of the angry faces of the tutors with their ready straps there were now warm smiles and gentle touches of well- dressed teachers. They had never seen this before- not even in their dreams. On the days when the students paraded throughout the town, School No.5 was the leader. The students waved red revolutionary flags. The assemblies, conversations, games social contests in the school and against others, the presentations and the frequent celebrations- all left their mark…

In addition to the experienced teaching methods in the school there were also contributions by other educators- some as part of their job and others as volunteers. One of the frequent visitors was the Communist educator Dimant. He saw it as his duty to give the "Proletariat" of the school the right approach and to teach them the newest songs. This was to deepen, grow and aggrandize the "free" appreciation of the students. He wanted to eradicate the old, dark tenets of their faith still in their hearts. His favorite song that he strove to inculcate in the hearts of the students-which he sang every Shabbat at recess- was the song about the bravery of the Jews of Birobidzhan. These Jews tilled the land with their horses- even on Shabbat! He repeated the refrain with great enthusiasm and special dedication…

It is amazing that the veteran students of Rabbi Pinhas who had been educated in the Torah way and followed religious rules vigorously, now appeared as actors in anti-religious plays prepared by their new teachers. They were still in the same building of the Talmud Torah and now they showed talent as mockers of rabbis, Judaism Torah and Talmud.

[Page 165]

It is true that the influence of practical education, where teachers know how to conduct it properly can be great. However, success did not remain long even with this progressive education. On June 22, 1941 the Germans attacked their pact partners. The new teachers escaped to save themselves. The Nazis did not know the difference between religious, national and secular education. Everyone was exterminated…

Jewish Educational Institutions

by Dr. Mordechai Leiberson

Translated by Ala Gamulka

In our town there were two elementary schools: a. Herzliah School on Pomnikova Street and b. School named after Dr. Klomel, z"l, on Briska street. I was a student in Herzliah. At one time, the school was located on Mitzkivitcha street, across from the main post office. Later it was moved to the building of the Hebrew high school Tarbut. It stood on the banks of the river Turia on Warshavska street. Eventually, the school was given a new beautiful building on Pomnikova street– the house belonging to Mr. Fried, of sainted memory.

One of the first principals was Mr. Fishman (now in Israel). Later it was the teacher Yaakov Kobrinsky who administered the school until 1935. When he became principal of the Klomel School, Kobrinsky was replaced by the teacher Gottfried, z"l, – until the school was closed in 1939, when the war broke out.

Principal Kobrinsky managed to elevate the school to a high level, thanks to his organizational skills and limitless devotion. He was certified as a mathematics and physics teacher from a Russian university and he taught mathematics, science and geography.

There were sixteen graduation cycles from Herzliah. It was an institution that educated and directed Jewish youth. It inculcated Zionist ideals and carried, with pride, the national emblem. Many of us who are in Israel are graduates of this school that was once called Herzliah.

In memory of the teacher Haim Hochberg

Haim Hochberg, z"l, taught Hebrew, Tanach and History. He died young, after a serious illness, at the age of 35. He was a fine man. I see him in my memory– tall as a tree, dark complexion, a scholar and a prince of a man. He was bright and knowledgeable with a good sense of humor– an excellent psychologist.

[Page 166]
Haim Hochberg rescued many a student from being labelled "unsuccessful". He was able to show him the road to success. His classes in Hebrew, Hebrew grammar, Tanach and Jewish History were exemplary of high pedagogical ability. It was a great privilege for all of us to be among his students. He was the homeroom teacher of our class in levels C and D. He then became ill and did not recover.

[Page 167]

Teacher Hochberg died in Nissan 1930. On the day of his funeral he was accompanied by the students from all levels and their parents to his resting place. This is how, in a sudden and dramatic fashion, was cut down a magnificent and rich personality in the Jewish education field.

Twenty–six years have passed since then, but his aristocratic image still stands in front of us, his students and admirers. We were enthralled by our teacher and educator. He was a magnificent personality, tireless and always encouraging us to work and succeed.

I recall that when he returned to school, after he seemed to have recuperated, he said: "My dear students, believe me that my doctor forbade me from getting out of bed, but I cannot live without you. I find encouragement in you and I trust that I can overcome my illness". He often emphasized that when he rose in the morning, he was racked with pain in his joints. Eventually, the terrible disease took him away when he was still young.

1931/32 graduates of Herzliah School

Standing right to left: Avraham Waks(in Israel), Avraham Gutman (exterminated in the Holocaust in Kovel 1934), Hana Zeidel (in United States),Teleroit (in Israel), Shoshana Khininzon (killed in Holocaust in Kovel), Yehoshua Toler (in United States), unknown, teacher Hinda Segal (in Israel)– homeroom teacher of Level One, Hak Isaac (died in Holocaust)
Seated from tight to left: Hayot, z"l, (died in Israel), Rosenstein, z"l, Hebrew and Tanach teacher (killed in Holocaust), Blanca Kasher – teacher of German (killed in Holocaust), Principal Yaakov Kobrinsky– teacher of mathematics, science and geography, Bina Friedman-Levin– teacher of Polish and general history (killed in Holocaust), Shimon Feinstein, z"l, – teacher of music and art, a talented organizer of choirs in Hebrew schools and Tarbut (killed in Holocaust)
Seated in first row from right to left: Avraham Kreiss (in United States), Sarah Rotenberg, z"l, (killed in Holocaust), Mania Bork, z"l, daughter of the editor of "The Voice of Kovel", Yaakov Bork, z"l, (killed in Holocaust), Bat Sheva Gendler, z"l, (killed in Holocaust), Zehava Steinberg, z"l, (killed in Holocaust, Hannah Perl–daughter of community leader Moshe Perl, z"l, (in Israel), Ben Zion Schechter (in United States)
Seated in Row B, from right to left: Meir Nimirovsky, z"l, and Avraham Pilkreitz, z"l, (both killed in the Holocaust)

The Hebrew High School Tarbut

The jewel in the crown of Jewish Hebrew schools in Kovel was the Tarbut Hebrew High School– founded in 1921. From its beginning, its principal was Asher Frankfurt, z"l, a respected pedagogue and an excellent administrator. In addition to his role as principal he also taught Algebra, Geometry and Trigonometry. He visited classrooms regularly and was interested in all subjects. He always cared to maintain the high level of education of his students.

The High School became known as an institution of high level and great standing– not only in town, but also throughout Poland. Frankfurt was behind the push to erect a new building for the school. It was done in 1937. The building had two storeys and was broad and beautifully planned. The classrooms were spacious, sunlit and airy. There were gyms, laboratories, a large library and study rooms. The furniture was modern and appropriate for required hygiene.

The principal worked hard to collect the large sums needed for the new building. He wandered far and wide in other parts of Europe and he even arrived in Eretz Israel. He returned encouraged and happy that his dream was realised. The official opening of the school became a great party and a tribute to the "father" of the High School.

The first day of September 1939 arrived and the WWII broke out.

[Page 168]

Class of 1936/37– Sixth level in 1935

Standing from right to left: Mordechai Leiberson (in Israel), Ita Reichstol, z"l, Hannah Zeidel (in United States), Tamar Finkelstein, z"l, Yehoshua Frankfurt, (nephew of Frankfurt z"l, (in Israel), Dr. Tsvigel, z"l, –teacher of Physics and chemistry, Hannah Perl (in Israel), Shoshana Khininzon, z"l, Esther Kuptchik, z"l, daughter of the school secretary Yaakov Kuptchik, z"l), Mania Perlmutter, z"l, Esther Bass, z"l

Seated in first row, right to left: Teacher Dr. Kutchinsky, z"l, (teacher of Polish), Mordechai Leyer, z"l, (teacher of Latin, Greek and Roman history), Blanca Kasher, z"l, principal Asher Frankfurt, z"l, Yosef Avrech, z"l, (teacher of Hebrew, Judaism and Jewish history), Hadassah Shprung (teacher of geography, science and biology) (in Israel), Michael Gruber (teacher of Hebrew – in Israel), Gutman, z"l, (teacher of general history and Polish)

Seated in second row, from right to left: Liberman, z"l, Shoshana Shochet, z"l, Yenta Tessler, z"l, Leah Mammut, z"l, Niura Landau, z"l, Sarah Rotenberg, z"l

The school was closed from the beginning of the Soviet regime until the Russo–German war broke out on June 21, 1941. During the Soviet times the school moved to the building of the former Moshtchitsky school and became High School number 10. The languages of instruction were Yiddish, Russian and Ukrainian. Most of the previous teaching staff stayed. It was a difficult adjustment period. Principal Frankfurt and the other teacher suffered greatly until they could follow the new instructions. There were many times when I met them on the streets and I saw that their love of teaching was no longer visible. They seemed depressed and inhibited.

[Page 169]

Founding of the Primary Schools and the Hebrew Gymnasia

by A.M. Weisbrot

Translated by Ala Gamulka

The Zionist organizations in town did not only work directly for the different funds and propaganda. They understood that Zionism and the Hebrew language were essential to the Jewish world and they concerned themselves with establishing the Hebrew language, in the people, as an expression of existence and revival.

It is for this purpose that the boards of the General Zionists and the Zeirei Zion convened and decided to elect a joint committee. Its task would be to establish a Hebrew School where the town children would be educated in the spirit of Hebrew culture.

Representing the General Zionists were: Gitlis, teacher Avrech, Bork, Finkelstein, Goldstein, Yustman and Zukerman.

[Page 170]

Zeirei Zion members were: A.M. Weisbrot, Schwartzblat, Lublinsky, Saltzman, Polishuk, Shapiro, etc.

Tarbut Committee in Kovel

Seated right to left: Yosef Milstein, A.M. Weisbrot, Yitzhak Gitlis, Tsippa Roiter, Moshe Fishman, Moshe Dodiuk
Standing right to left: Asher Frankfurt, Yaakov Klonitsky, Bernstein, Korman, Goldstein, Shalom Rabiner, Haim Ber

We rented the top floor of Werba's house, on Lutske Street (Warshavska). It stood on the banks of the Turia river. In 1919 we established there the primary school called Herzliah. The first principal was Mr. Manievits. The second principal was Mr. Ariel (Leibovitz). He was succeeded, for several years, by Mr. M. Fishman. Among the teachers I remember these names: Durtchin, Feinstein, the sisters Pipovna, Shpruch. Berkovska. Bley, Avrech, etc.

The main aim of the school was to establish the education of Jewish children on the Hebrew language and so to bring them closer to the redemption of our people. The school was maintained by a low tuition. Poor people were exempt from paying. The budget was balanced with the help of the Joint. Our representatives had great influence there.

The school was also the location for most meetings of the Zionist groups. There were also some evening parties held there and they brought in an income used solely for the school. It is important to emphasize that the ladies of these groups were most helpful.

Once the school was established it was essential to also found a Hebrew library. We collected many books from our members and we had several activities to enrich the library. Mr. Erlich donated all his Hebrew books to the school library.

When the Bolsheviks entered town in 1920, an order was given to close the Hebrew school and the library books were confiscated.

Dr. Israelit, head of the General Zionists in town and A.M. Weisbrot, representing Zeirei Zion complained to the local authorities. They also communicated with the secretary of the Communist Party of Ukraine asking: "If the Hebrew language is not alive and there should not be a school dedicated to teaching it, why is the library to be blamed?". The secretary accepted this reasoning and she ordered the books be returned. When the Bolsheviks left town, the school was reopened. It began to flourish again and its activities were broadened.

The establishing of Herzliah school proved that the idea of teaching the Hebrew language had merit. The school was too small to accommodate the hordes of students who wished to be admitted. The Jewish population in town grew and the demand for Hebrew education broadened.

We realised that another Hebrew school was needed. It became the school named after the late Dr. Klomel.

[Page 171]

Dr. Klomel, z"l, had served as the chairman of the Zionist organization of Poland and head of Tarbut. The naming of the school after him was an expression of the value of the personality Dr. Klomel. He had been instrumental in helping to establish the school. The principal was Yaakov Kobrinsky (in Israel).

Towards the end of 1924 a third Hebrew school was established. It was named after Prof. Friedlander, z"l. The Zeirei Zion committee founded it and it was located on Mitzkivitcha street, across from the post office.

The establishment of the Tarbut School

The primary schools were the source of Jewish education, but after graduation, the students were stranded in mid–stream. The thought occurred about what to do next and how to ensure the continuity of Jewish education. It was decided to open a Hebrew high school. The permit to open would only be given to an academic with an advanced university degree.

At that time, Asher Frankfurt had just completed his studies and had returned to Kovel. He became the first principal of the Hebrew Gymnasia. It was opened in 1921. The school became a centre of culture in town. This was due, mainly, to the addition of outstanding teachers with a high academic background. Among them stood out: Avrech, Dr. Khayal, Dr. Tsvigel, Figelman, and, still with us in Israel, Leibovitz, Khazan and Rotman–Netaneli.

This high school had a considerable influence on the Jewish youth in town. Many of them were educated in the school. Even those who had studied in Polish schools abandoned them and came to learn the Hebrew language and its culture. There were even students from nearby villages and even from further away.

The students of the school also belonged to various youth movements and they brought new blood to the established Zionist movements. These students were the leaders of the Scouts, Hechalutz, Hashomer Hatzair, Hechalutz Hatzair and Gordonia.

The influence of the school was so great that other educational institutions– Polish ones– e.g. Academy of Klara Erlich, were forced to include Hebrew language and Jewish studies in their curriculum.

The school grew from year to year until the building became too small. Mr. Frankfurt, the moving spirit of the school, had a new idea– to relocate the school in its own building.

[Page 172]

He wanted to erect a new building which would become the palace for Hebrew culture. For that purpose, Mr. Frankfurt came to Eretz Israel and was fortunate to obtain large donations from his students and friends. Indeed, a magnificent building was built, the Hebrew Gymnasia named after our poet, H.N. Bialik, z"l. Until the Nazis entered town, the gymnasia became the outstanding educational institution in town.

These four schools (the three primary schools and the Hebrew gymnasia) had, as students, the majority of the Jewish youth in town. I addition to the teachers listed earlier there were several young teachers who performed their tasks with reverence and enthusiasm. They were worshipped by their students. The following should be mentioned: Zev Tchernitsky, Malka Alpert, Devorah Bley, Meriminsky, Hochberg, z"l. These educational institutions were the cultural center in town. The best leaders of the Zionist parties were there. The best plans for enlarging the Zionist influence in town came from there.

It is well–known that there were other towns where Hebrew schools and Zionism existed. There was, however, nothing like Kovel. In Kovel, Jewish education reached heights that were unheard of in the Jewish population of Poland.

Kovel was considered in Poland as one of the most Zionist towns. It perhaps can be said that Kovel was a relatively small city, but it was in second place, after Lodz, when it came to collecting for Keren Hayesod.

Hundreds, or even thousands, of the best Jewish youth of Kovel made Aliyah. They were instrumental in building the state. This was due to the Hebrew education they had received. These educational institutions were the nursery in which the Zionist dream grew and succeeded.

Herzliah School and Tarbut Gymnasia

by Tzvi Tannenbaum

Translated by Ala Gamulka

The year was 1919– a year of upheaval in Poland. The country had not yet recovered from the thundering canons of the Germans, Russians and Poles. Governments changed and there was a feeling of instability. In this stormy time was born the idea of founding a school dedicated to the Hebrew language. The initiative came from the General Zionists in town and those who brought it to fruition were the teachers Manievits, Lipsker, Avrech, Feinstein, Durtchin and Poritsker, may they rest in peace.

[Page 173]

The establishment of Herzliah School brightened all corners of town. The Jews of Kovel were proud of this educational institution. The foundation of Hebrew education and culture were based there and it was certain that only good will come of it.

The school was merely the first step. Two years later, in 1921, all hopes were achieved with the founding of the beautiful Hebrew Gymnasia. Its principal was the sainted Asher Frankfurt. The Gymnasia was famous throughout surrounding towns and villages. Many students streamed towards it in order to acquire a Hebrew education. I recall that at a meeting in the village of Kamin, I was surprised by the beautiful Hebrew language used by the youth walking on its streets. I immediately understood that I should not be surprised since I had met such youth in the building of the Hebrew Gymnasia in Kovel.

In this wonderful laboratory the Hebrew movement grew. Many important Zionist activities took place there. The graduates came out wishing for Aliyah, life on a kibbutz or on a cooperative moshav.

Almost all those who made Aliyah were educated in this school. Many youth organizations originated there as well. These were the Scouts headed by A. Hodorov, Hashomer Hatzair, Hechalutz and Hechalutz Hatzair. They were all founded by students who had received a Hebrew education.

Students of Level 5 of Tarbut Gymnasia and their teachers in the year 1925

[Page 174]

May the founders be remembered with pride. Their hard work was quite successful. They managed to educate a generation of Jewish youth that was knowledgeable and was full of love for its homeland. These young people publicized the value of Jewish education everywhere. One cannot forget the Lag Baomer parade, Hanukah, Tu B'shvat and Purim parties. Beautiful Hebrew singing was heard from this building the house of Werba near the bridge. It was an island of the spirit of Eretz Israel in the foreign and strange sea. How excited we were to accompany our comrades who made Aliyah. It was a celebration for all of us. We reaped what we had sowed in years of hard labor. Our constant prayer was: "We will meet again in our Holy Land". Indeed, many of us were so fortunate. However, many others, sadly, did not so merit. These lines are a testimony and a headstone to the hundreds and thousands of young people who were killed before their time and who did not fulfill their life's dream.

About the Kindergartens of Kovel

by Chaya Hotman (Becker)

Translated by Ala Gamulka

Let my lot be with you

(H.N. Bialik)

As the Tarbut school grew and developed the need was felt to open a Kindergarten. There were two reasons for it: first, to instill spoken Hebrew in children at a young age and, secondly, to sow a field to feed the Hebrew schools.

Kindergarten teachers were invited from the capital of Poland- Warsaw. However, they could only arrive at the end of June, when they finished their studies at their Kindergarten teachers institute- Tarbut- in Warsaw.

When spring came, children were registered and it was necessary to look after them immediately past Passover. It was in the hands of the principal, Manievitch. I was invited to look after these children until their teachers arrived.

Teacher Feinstein, z" l, taught singing. He taught me various songs and games. The next day I would teach these songs and games to the children.

Finally, kindergarten teacher Sheft came and helped me out. In those days it was not a real kindergarten. It was simply a preparatory class and it was nicknamed "House of Shelter".

A true kindergarten, organized and well-appointed, was established with the arrival of the kindergarten teacher Hava Sehr-Werba. It was she who founded a serious kindergarten. It was outstanding in its inner organization and esthetic appearance. It stood on a high pedagogical level.

[Page 175]

The kindergarten founded by Tarbut
Standing on the left is teacher Haya Becker-Hotman

In 1934 I returned to Kovel from my work in small towns and until my Aliyah, in 1936, I worked as a teacher in the Tarbut kindergarten. I knew to value and recognize the hard work of the Tarbut leadership. It was headed by I. Gitlis and M. Perl. They were imbued with understanding a child's spirit and soul. It is thanks to them that the kindergarten was established

In addition to the Tarbut kindergarten there was, in town, a private one under the principalship of Esther Gutenboim. It, too, provided a Hebrew education to children. There was also the kindergarten of the Taz group, led by Sonia Margalit.

[Page 176]

The Hebrew Kindergarten of Kovel

by Hava Sehr-Werba

Translated by Ala Gamulka

The Hebrew education movement in Poland was established as a result of the work of educators, Zionist leaders and other important figures. These could be found in every town and village. They were the ones who were first to establish Hebrew educational institutions in Jewish communities. It was only after their number had grown that the Tarbut movement took over their running.

The Hebrew kindergarten was founded many years before the elementary school. In some towns it was the opposite- elementary and high schools before kindergarten. It usually was realised that it was necessary to establish a Hebrew kindergarten as the first phase in Hebrew education.

When the new Poland was established, the authorities were intent on instilling the knowledge of Polish language and culture. The network of government Polish schools was broadened. Jewish parents believed their children's future lay in graduation from such schools and they registered them in Polish kindergartens. They wanted their children to have the proper accent. Hebrew educational institutions had to overcome great struggles in order to compete with the Polish schools.

In this reality, a Hebrew kindergarten was opened within the elementary school. It was after Passover, before the summer. It was thought that young children would have difficulty getting out of the house during the harsh winter months. It was important to have these children with their age group in good weather.

The kindergarten was established in a room close to the school's entrance. The sight of the young children, well-dressed and sporting ribbons in their hair, the low furniture and many colorful objects- made the school students curious. They continuously opened the front door in order to have a glimpse at the kindergarten room. This is how hundreds of eyes looked every morning and their smiles were wide and welcoming.

The kindergarten children belonged to teachers, Zionist leaders and their relatives and other families that were influenced by the Hebrew movement in Kovel. Among them were those who spoke Russian or had been influenced by Polish culture, but they followed their national instincts and made sure to give their children a Hebrew education.

Some parents brought their children from a great distance, from the old town and from the sands. Distance did not frighten them because they were enthusiastic about Hebrew education.

[Page 177]

Even the parents would greet the teacher by saying Shalom. There was so much hope and dreams in this greeting!

The central office of Tarbut considered Kovel as a Hebrew town. This becomes obvious in the letter I received from them. The Union of teachers in Warsaw praised Kovel: "Take the position in this town. It is a lively place. There is a Hebrew school, as Hebrew high school, a Zionist atmosphere. You can contribute by opening an organized Hebrew kindergarten".

[Page 179]

The Jewish-Polish *Gymnasia*

by Dr. Yaacov Hasis

Translated by Amy Samin

In 1917, one of the young women of Kovel, a teacher, returned to the city from Russia. Her name was Klara Davidovna-Erlich. Working together with a veteran teacher named Shebtzov, who was the principal of the Russian *gymnasia* before the First World War, that year she opened a *gymnasia* in which the languages of instruction were Russian and Ukrainian. The *gymnasia* was opened on Karoliova Boneh Street, where the state *gymnasia* for girls was once located.

Aside from Klara, all of the teachers were Christians, and a number of Christian students, boys and girls, also studied there. One of the first teachers, Mrs. Miller, who taught German, is worth mentioning. She was a musician by profession, and when the Bolsheviks entered the city she was active in the field of music. Gabriel Nikiporovich taught painting and technical drawing, Iben Vasilivich taught mathematics, Serafima Victorovna Ositskia taught French (she was the only anti-Semite amongst the teachers. She was the daughter of Polkovnik, a Russian from the era of Nicholas), Yevgenya Nicholivna – history, Lisenko taught the Ukrainian language, and Nicholai Piodorovich – physics.

When the Polish government was established it became necessary to abandon the Russian language, and in 1921 the *gymnasia* stopped being "Russian-Jewish" and became "Polish-Jewish." This change brought about the need for adjustments in the teaching staff, because neither Klara nor the rest of the teachers knew the Polish language. Furthermore, not a single teacher in Kovel could be found who had a Polish education. With no other choice, Klara brought in teachers from Galicia, who spoke Polish fluently. Those teachers saw it as their duty to promote Polish culture in the school.

The first teacher to arrive was Dr. Flack, a mathematician by profession. He also served as the principal of the *gymnasia*, because the authorities deprived Klara of the right to hold that position because she did not speak Polish.

[Page 180]

Mr. Horvitz, a science teacher, also arrived with Dr. Flack. He was one of the most talented and notable teachers for a considerable period of time, and he left an impression on many of the children of Kovel.

A German teacher also arrived, whose name I cannot recall; the Latin teacher Turnheim, Crome – Polish literature, Dr. Mazelas – the Hebrew, religious studies and history teacher. A. Ratt, – German language, Dr. Shafroch – physical education, M. Zeidenzeig – drawing, M. Reis – physics and mathematics, the principal Klara Erlich taught science, and Dr. Ziskind may his blood be avenged – served as the school's physician.

They were joined by a Galician who came to the city with the Austrian army, settled there and married a Kovel girl. His name was Fesler. He taught general history. He was a talented educator, magnanimous and very well loved in Kovel. Later he settled in Robna and worked as an attorney.

Until 1927 the *gymnasia* was not recognized by the authorities, and they refused to grant it any rights. This meant that the graduates of the *gymnasia* found the doors of the universities in Poland closed to them, and anyone who dreamed of obtaining higher education would leave the *gymnasia* by the sixth or seventh grade and go to Brisk or Vilna. The *gymnasia* in those cities were recognized by the government. In fact, there was a recognized Polish *gymnasia* in Kovel with full rights, but there prevailed there the infamous "numerus clausus" [methods used to limit the number of students], and only a few Jewish students were accepted there.

Various cultural activities developed in the *gymnasia*. There were various groups such as the drama club, a club about the geography of the Holy Land, a literature club, a football [soccer] team called Lagia, along with an academic journal which was published in three languages – Polish, Hebrew, and Yiddish – very precisely edited.

In 1927 the *gymnasia* was granted rights by the government, and many of those who had left in earlier years returned in order to receive their diplomas, which would allow them to continue their studies.

The first class to receive a diploma with full rights graduated from the *gymnasia* in 1928.

A common expression in the city was: the Hebrew *gymnasia* creates pioneers, and Klara's *gymnasia* creates educated, knowledgeable people. There is a little bit of truth in the saying, because a few of the students of the Jewish-Polish *gymnasia* studied medicine in the universities of France, Prague and Italy, and became known as important doctors in the city. I will mention their names: Tania Neimdack finished his studies at Warsaw College and worked as a physician in Kovel; Moshe Wisberg pursued his studies abroad, returned to the city and worked as a doctor; Grisha Verba studied medicine in Prague and Yosef Melamed also studied medicine in Prague and later in Italy, and then worked in Kovel as a surgeon. During the war he worked as the head of the surgery department in a military hospital in Russia.

[Page 181]

Graduates of the Jewish-Polish gymnasia in 1926

[Page 182]

Two other figures in the *gymnasia* worth noting are: Eliezar Hodorov, organizer of the Tzofim [scouts] in Kovel and who is currently one of the outstanding captains in the state [Israel], and Ruth Deshbeski of blessed memory, who studied veterinary medicine, an unusual profession amongst Jews in general, and especially Jewish women. During the war she went to Asia where she worked as a veterinarian, where her reputation preceded her on the steppes of Kazakhstan. She would ride on horseback in order to make her rounds amongst the communes and farms in the area. She became a living legend among the Kazakhstani people in the region.

The *gymnasia* prepared an entire generation of free-thinking intellectuals and professionals. When the war broke out, Mrs. Klara Erlich left the city and went to Russia to live with her sister in Moscow. The *gymnasia* building became a pile of rubble and no sign of it remains.

[Page 183]

Class 6, 1926 – 1927

Back Row, from right to left - Moshe Gelman, Yeshayahu Skolnik, Mika Gelman, Esther Sass, Bennick Petrakovski, Selah Mendel, Moshe Gelman, Meirom (Meir) Rosenblatt, Eli-Yitzhak Verbe.
Second Row – Velvel Lipshitz, Nina Ladrahandler, Chaike Glazer, Shapira…Damav, Roizya (Ruth) Deshbeski, Esther Flott, Chaike Erlich, Brunia Beronzpat.
Third row – Nunia Oppelind, Grisha Shemstein, Yisrael Geller, Satran, Rosa Bonn, teacher Dr. Fesler, Jania Burstein, Yisrael Fuchs, Yagodnik, Leah Pogtash, Stinberg.
Seated on the ground – Sheindel Roisen, Regina Friedman, Y. Rosensveig, Yoske Gurtenstein, Tzippa Bayerach, Hina Asiok, Yagodnik.

[Page 184]

The Poet Kalman Liss

by L. Olitzky (Warsaw)

Translated by Ala Gamulka

People of Thoughts and Predictions

There was a certain man from Ramataim-Zofim: Rav Hanin said a man who descends from people who stood at the height of the world"
Megillah, 14

(Notes)

During the years following WWI, I lived in my hometown -Trisk, Volyn. From time to time I amused myself by visiting the capital, Kovel. I went to see my school friend, Moshe Perl.

It was a time when Jewish culture was growing, in Volyn, also. The larger towns had Tarbut high schools, but the smaller ones had Jewish peoples' schools. Hebrew and Yiddish libraries were established, named after our classic writers. Drama clubs and other clubs were formed with the cooperation of Yivo in Vilna. In the larger towns, the publication of periodicals and weekly newspapers was begun.

Volyn Province had the ambition to follow the capital of Poland- Warsaw. Kovel had a Tarbut high school, Hebrew and Yiddish elementary schools. In general, it was a Zionist town and there was also a weekly Zionist publication. My village, Trisk, was only 18 kilometers away. Kovel had its militant Jewish youth, outstanding Jewish schools, a library, a good drama club. It represented the Jewish fortress of Volyn.

[Page 185]

Once I went to Kovel to give a review, in a Hebrew-Yiddish publication, of a local production. I was caught in a dilemma. I did not have anything good to say and I did not feel like giving a bad review.

There was a poem in the presentation called "Little Beast". It appealed to my critical eyes with its simplicity and muted language. Something in it felt true. The song filled my head and I was deaf to the rest.

Soon afterwards, I again came to Kovel. A young, working class man came to see me. He was wearing a gray military cap. He took it off and was red with embarrassment. Under his messy hair I saw a pair of eyes filled with happiness:

G-g-ood m-o-rning! - he stammered. Are you Leibel Olitzky?

[Page 186]

I am Kalman Liss. You liked, I heard, my Little Beast. I want to show you…

…who is this stutterer? – I was not disposed to listen to him. What Little Beast? Ah!...
I was involved with my own problems and I was not really pleased. Just because I like Little Beast, I would now be subjected to this "country pastor", like a flock of geese or a compulsive cow. I was uncomfortable and I took him outside the house.
-Let us sit down here.
He did not do it. He was unhappy with the "test".
-Hum. I will recite a few poems…I have many…

- I don't have much time… What does it mean that you will recite?

I will recite- he says stammering still. His eyes were filled with delight. – I know my poems by heart.

He then began to envelop me with his poems to the tune of "Ashrei" of religious Jews of yesteryear. I, a man with poor memory, wondered about his and complimented him. I thought I would thus get away from giving my opinion about the poems. They did not leave any impression on me. He insisted on hearing my thoughts.
-I must say that I still prefer your Little Beast. But, continue to write…
He said good-bye and left with a glowing face. It meant that he would now truly devote himself to his work.

I did not see him again for a long time. He did not come to Kovel, but he stayed with his grandfather in the village of Frovol. I later learned that he was studying in Vilna at the teachers' seminary run by Dr. Charna. When he graduated, he took a teaching job in a shtetl in Volyn. When he left there, he came to Trisk to see me. In spite of his stammer, he showed himself to be a friendly guy, involved with people.

Kalman Liss, z"l

[Page 187]

He immediately got to know the teachers and leaders of the Jewish Peoples' school. He befriended the students. He brought poems he, himself, had created and written. The Jewish youth were quite taken by him.

-We should hire him as a teacher in our school.
Within a few months he made himself ridiculous by his correspondence with someone in the weekly Kovel publication. It was about the cultural activity in the village where he was working. He did not forget to recall, with a provincial self-pride, that he when he went there, he stopped in Trisk to visit the writer L.O.…
-A country bumpkin! - said the so-called "sophisticated" people of Trisk about him. "He plans to be a poet! It is not enough for him to be a teacher."
As if overnight, Kalman Liss, in whom young blood, energy and spiritual powers of creation were active, overcame his Little Beast and his correspondence. He produced beautiful poetry in the journals of Warsaw.

He had already lived in Warsaw where he co-edited a journal for young people. He soon began to work successfully in the "Tsentus" of Otvotsk. We heard that he had an excellent approach to developmentally challenged children that were attending the school.

Whenever he came to Kovel for the High Holidays to visit his mother and sister, he stopped in Trisk to see me. He did not only visit me, but also the school. The school population was thrilled with him. He became a child again among the children.

He was already, even then, wearing the cape of an important poet. The young poet was even quite gracious towards the town and me, the elderly writer- still living in a rural place. He told me, indirectly:

-Don't take it to heart that you live here. In Warsaw, we speak of you…
He immediately would start to speak of his own affairs.

[Page 188]

He spoke proudly and enthusiastically about his wife. She is extremely intelligent, smart and a connoisseur of poetry. She also stems from an honorable family- the Lubavitch Schneersons.

A few years later I moved to Warsaw. However, neither one of us looked for rapprochement. Perhaps we had a mutual suspicion of each other. As a rule, we did not meet too often. I worked in a school and I kept myself far from literary circles. After he was married, he lived in Otvotsk and he only came to Warsaw on social business. He was a member of the "red" group of writers while I had the impression, perhaps a false one, that he did not approve of me because I was working in a Bund school, even though I was impartial.

Nevertheless, when we once both came to Kovel for Pessach, we, as colleagues, invited each other to our homes. His mother, a slim, gray-haired, pleasant-faced woman, said: it pleases us, my son and I, the in-laws of the famous Schneersons. We drank a glass of wine, but we did not get any closer. In Warsaw, we remained strangers. He never invited me to his house in Otvotsk. Not even when I was there for the summer. I did not think highly of him then.

We again found ourselves on foreign soil- on the river of Krinitz. He introduced me to his wife. She seemed, and actually was, older than him (he was her second husband). She was a nice woman with red hair. Her face was reddish-white and full of freckles. She was not a beauty. However, her stature, fine attitude and her manner of speaking showed her aristocratic and intelligent background. Did she, the "red" one bring him to the "red" group of writers?

Their mutual attitude confirmed the belief of their friends that he was under her intelligent and smart influence. Even his poetry was guided by her. She knew literature well.

[Page 189]

She directed the rich flowing stream of his creativity so it would not flood empty areas.

His material good fortune had already come to him. He was well loved. His movements were controlled and his face was earnest. All this did not fit in with his white linen shirt embroidered with a Ukrainian colorful pattern. However, it really emphasized that this was a Volhynian poet of proletariat stock. His little pipe, always sticking out of his mouth, emitted smoke which obscured his face and made everything worse. It drew the attention of passers-by – here goes a poet!

Nevertheless, his face, crowned with his blond mop of hair stood in contrast to that of his wife with her red hair. It looked like the moon, near the sun, receiving light from it. He always seemed to look at his wife's eyes and mouth in a subdued manner. Well, what? She came from Lubavitchers and he- from a small village called Frovol.

When people spoke of Kalman Liss, about the good in him, they always remembered it. If they had complaints about him, they would often forget to remember.

The Communist party in Poland was dissolved by an order from the authorities. Kalman Liss, the vehement combatant within the "red" writers' group, left his comrades. Was this not a "miracle from heaven?" However, his friends only blamed him for this and not his wife. A teachers' strike was organized in "Tsentus". He did not join the strikers and he was declared a strike-breaker. No one faulted his wife for his behavior.

On the first day of WWII, the Germans bombarded the "Tsentus" and killed teachers and children. Kalman Liss was badly wounded. He was taken to a hospital in Warsaw. He remained there until the city fell. He was then brought back to Otvotsk. Before I escaped from there to the Soviet side, I went to say goodbye to him.

[Page 190]

He was improving by then. He smiled happily at his beautiful child, sleeping in his bed. It was rumored that, he, too, as soon as he felt better, would need to escape. Not one of us had done it. He spoke with excitement of the destruction of Warsaw:

-No…One cannot imagine it if one did not witness it with his own eyes…
His mother and sister in Kovel waited for him. Why was he not coming there as were thousands of refugees? Kalman Liss did not return.

One does not speak badly of the dead. I believe, still, that those holy ones who died in the ghetto are absolved of all their sins. They are all placed on the list of martyrs. We will remember them for generations to come.

In our list of holy poets, I see the star of the Volhynian poet, Kalman Liss.

Dear Kalman! A poet from my homeland, Volyn! You went to the slaughter with your dozens of handicapped children. No good angel was saved. Your own child in your arms. The sun shone on you and flooded you with light. The sky, even then, was full of clouds. Kalman, every step purified you. Even if there were marks on your conscience, the sun lit them up. Together with the pure souls of your students you were called to the highest spheres. Your blood-stained body remained holy together with their blameless bodies. The letters of your works fluttered like a wreath around your poet's head.

May your holy memory remain as a remembrance of our people.

[Page 191]

Kalman Ben-Zion Liss

by Esther Liss-Chaim

Translated by Ala Gamulka

Kalman Liss was born in Kovel in January 1901. He was the third child of his parents Yaacov and Rosia. They had four children. The father died young and the oldest brother, Zvi, had to earn a living and take care of the family. Zvi died of the Spanish flu and the mother remained alone with three children. She needed to have an income. This was a clever and energetic woman and together with her oldest daughter, Clara, she managed to educate her offspring. Clara, after her marriage to Halt, became well-known in Yiddish theatre circles in Kovel as a good singer.

Kalman studied at the famous Polish-Jewish high school of Klara Davidovna-Erlich. He was a diligent student and began writing poems at a young age. After some time, his works were published in the Yiddish press. Later he translated poetry to Yiddish from Russian and Polish. These were works by Pushkin, Lermontov, Mitzkewicz and others.

After he completed his high school studies, he wanted to pursue Agronomy and was accepted at the University of Grenoble. However, due to financial need he was unable to pursue his dream. He was forced to change direction and to study something that wold provide him with local employment. It would also allow him to become independent. He studied at the Teachers' Seminary in Vilna and was quite successful. For several years he taught in small towns, such as Kissilin, near Lutsk. He used his free time to write poetry. It was common to see him with paper and pencil. He wrote many poems during this period. He was a happy and friendly person, but he was absent-minded and was nicknamed "The absent-minded professor".

Those close to him did not understand his literary activities. Only his mother felt it and, as he himself emphasised, she gave him advice and was his best critic. He always loved nature, freedom and children and these were often subjects of his creations. He did not remain long as a teacher in small towns because the job did not give him satisfaction. He entered advanced studies in Psychology and the education of Deaf-Mute children, in Warsaw. He did well on entrance exams.

In this institute, at that time directed by the well-known psychologist Dr. Grigorovska, he obtained an excellent education and soon was appointed as director of Tsentus- a Jewish institute for the education of mentally handicapped and deaf-mute children. It had been created by the Joint. He excelled at his position and was well-loved by his students. He married Sarah Rubinstein, of the famous Rubinstein-Hornstein family.

[Page 192]

Sarah, too, was a professor. They lived in Otvotsk and had a son, Yaacov. When Sarah gave birth to her second son, she died. Soon the child, too, died. This terrible blow had a terrible influence on Kalman. He found comfort in creating literary works-poems and books intended for youth. He was well-received. He loved his home town of Kovel and Volyn and he mentioned them in many of his works.

In 1939, two months before the beginning of WWII. He was invited to London to attend a conference of Jewish poets. From there he was to continue to the United States. However, due to the precarious conditions, he felt he could not leave his job. He stayed and the first bomb that fell on Otvotsk hit the school. He was critically injured in his leg. Even after the leg healed, he was still in pain. During the German occupation he hid at he home of the janitor of the school. However, he was denounced to the Germans. He had tried to hide his son with some non-Jews, but he, too, was denounced. The child was killed by them. Kalman did not want to escape and abandon his students and he stayed until the last minute. He died a hero fulfilling his job. The murderers who had annihilated the Jews of Poland, killed a young, productive person who had contributed so much to Yiddish literature.

[Page 193]

Kovl (Kovel)

by Kalman Liss

Translated by Gloria Berkenstat Freund

I want to tell everyone
I do not want to be ashamed in front of anyone
To say something from my heart
All the old, dear names.

Of my Kovl - Volyner city
With the small alleys
Where my childhood blossomed
Fresh as a flower, as in spring - valleys…

Lutsker Street of my birth,
Dear, kind ribbon
Covered with a small group of low houses,
If you recall, do you remember?

Your low huts
With entry booths on the street corners,
Like dreams in the dusk
Like the dreams at dawn…

Here as last night, I think last night
Let it be as it was,
Three, two small houses on the "Lutsker"
And the rest maples, lilacs. At the very beginning of the highway
Small mountains of stones, press [road building] machines,
At the sides, small ditches
And the water trickles in the ditches.

[Page 194]

Do not ask where, not when, from where
Who needs to ask ditches?
Everyone knows, to the "Torya" [River]
Streams storm after the rain.

And the old beloved bridge
With its wooden railings
How many dreams were dreamed there
Resting on its wooden beams!

Alas, the Torya, dear Torya,
Drawn out as a serpent,
Your small ripples, the clear ones
Still reflect in my eyes!

Your shores very soft
Incized into meadows
Keep drawing
In one dream, remembering…

In the summer, in the extreme heat,
After half a day in *kheder* [religious primary school],
A goodbye to my mother
And a fig [thumb one's nose] to the dark bathhouse attendants.

Who needs seats and who needs brooms
To be suffocated by steam?[1]
Clean, in water, let there be reeds
But fresh … the heart quickens…"

On *Shabbosim* [Sabbaths] and holidays…
Torya, Torya, they took leave!
I still carry enough love, praise
In my heart for your roads.

[Page 195]

But let me run now
As you let them, your thoughts free -
I am a child again, and I am drawn
To the place of the carousel:

To the wooden church, the round one
With the seats in half circles,
I have a *tsenerl* [a 10-piece coin] - a wonder
I shall be shown there.

Let the magician again draw
Ribbons from a cap,
Perhaps, I will, as before,
Also imitate a trick today?

And the sand, the heaped
Yellow hill, with the tall cross;
Do the knights all still lie there?
Does the crowd all quiver for them?

Do the bandora players still sing and narrate
Everything with a groan.
That Poland once struggled
Here in 1863?[2]

And the lyre player, the grey one there,
Hair fluttering, white doves,
Draws still all the same sadness,
Sings still all the same praises.

> I will tell everyone,
> I will not be ashamed in front of anyone,
> I will say something to myself
> Take all of the old love…

Translator's Notes:

1. The poet is describing the bathhouse in which bathers sat on seats in steam heat and beat their bodies with bundles of twigs dipped in cold water to increase the absorption of steam into the body.
2. A reference to the January 1863 Polish Uprising against the Tsarist regime controlling Poland.

[Page 198]

Yona Rosenfeld

by Yohanan Twerski

Translated by Ala Gamulka

I first saw him, in Kovel, when I was a youth. (My grandfather, the Rabbi from Trisk, established his "court" there). I clearly recall his gait. A writer…the soul is nourished by blood, but it is the entire being of man as man and of a people as people. He was one of the first writers I met.

"My first creations", he speaks about himself in the collection of his writings. In volume one, "there were ordinary descriptions of my life. Later, I turned to other topics and more complicated situations."

In one of his first psychological stories he describes a young man whose hand was amputated in the hospital. "It was only a month ago…he says in deep sorrow…that he and others were equal physically and now he is detached from everything. It seems to him that other human beings are distant from him and are strangers". No, it's not only his imagination. His fiancée's little brother, whom he loves, checks his empty sleeve constantly. "uncle Meir, where is your hand?". His bride becomes quite hysterical. Is she ashamed or disgusted?

Yona Rosenfeld himself saw, in his lifetime, how man can harm another one.

[Page 199]

In his autobiographical book "All Alone", he describes various events from his youth.

He was no longer a child, but he had not grown as tall as others in his age group. This made him very sensitive. His brother sent him, as an apprentice, to an engraver. His boss made him do many unpaid tasks. The boy was a slave and he became jealous of a puppy. Everyone loved the puppy, especially the daughter of his boss. The boy was never called by his first name, but was always "hey, you". At night the women of the household assembled in the kitchen. There was only a thin partition between the kitchen and the hallway where he slept. The women did what they wanted and did not lower their voices, in modesty. It was as if he were not even a male or a human being. On Shabbat and holidays he did not have clean and proper clothes. The lady of the house gave him her old shoes (male shoes were too big). When he met a young woman he felt that she would notice the women's shoes he wore. This really bothered him. In addition, he was to accompany the daughters to market and to carry the shopping bag. He could not have been more ashamed– men are to do women's work!

The young man was excited and in his anger he poisoned the puppy. This is how the writer spent his youth. It was an atmosphere in which "man is poisoned". It is like a snake that is crazed, but cannot bite his enemy.

Here, in Kovel, life was good for him. He had a small, white room. A girlfriend with a loving, gentle voice. Yona Rosenfeld had a better life than he had had in Warsaw and even, later, in New York

There–says one of his protagonists– you meet geniuses everywhere. I said to myself– even if you are wrong, like all your friends, even if you are truly a genius, you would be despondent if these worthless people think themselves to be smarter than you…what is the use of genius, if others think of themselves to be geniuses, but they really are not?

Rosenfeld's young wife brings tea. He turns to me, thrusting his forehead and bowing his shoulders.

–So, you are a grandson of the Trisker? Did you notice? In the animal kingdom there are no insults. Animals attack each other and they intend to kill or defend. Man sets upon his fellow man in anger. His intention is to insult. This is how our ancestors did it. They demanded payment for insults. Your grandfather wishes to return evil back to goodness? What? It seems to me that not everything is owed just as it is not entitled.

[Page 200]

B

In the summer of 1937 we moved to Brighton Beach in New York. From our windows we could see the ocean sparkling blue. The sand, early in the morning, would be shiny and cold. It became hot. People streamed in. They seemed to all look alike, sweaty and tired. Dozens of people were on the beach. There were Italian and Jewish women. Their bodies did not show that they spared themselves any food. Young men with suntanned faces and muscular bodies. Young women sporting sunglasses…. There was modesty and brashness, shame and fierceness. The good and the bad. The senses were wanting and satisfied. Some want to enjoy themselves and jump into turbulent surfs. Others play ball in the water. They shriek like babies and splash. A few only dip their toes and leave. People lie, almost dead in the heat, on colorful towels spread on the sand. Others turn their back to the sun as if they wished to be baked.

The beach looked like an altar to sun and water when we stood at the windows of our apartment. It was summer 1937 and Hitler's shadow was spreading and growing. Here there were no worries, only happy times.

Yes. Here it is easier to ignore world problems since they are only possibilities at this time. However, when those close to us are suffering, we need to pay attention. "Happiness is limited", once wrote Rosenfeld. "Great happiness can cause obstruction of the heart. A terrible catastrophe can bring a sharpening of ideas". Is it true that only great suffering is needed? That eventful summer Yona Rosenfeld suffered terribly. He was ill with cancer. He soon died. However, that summer he was still our neighbor. His apartment was in our complex, El Mirassol.

Whenever one enters the room of someone very ill, one feels that it is very cold there, in contrast to the heat outside. Rosenfeld used to sit at the edge of his wide bed. It seemed as if he were reclining.

Look! Guests! It is a holiday when guests come and when guests come it is a holiday. He looks straight into my eyes and says" I am now a pile of bones! A weightless body".

Like a lover who does recognize his beloved after her death– this is what he fears. No one will recognize him after he dies. Rosenfeld was always tiny and he begrudged it. However, now he was even smaller. He was almost unrecognizable. Listening to him one feels that he wants, but does not want others to agree with him

[Page 201]

"In difficult times", he once wrote, "people become childish. They require warmth".

–No, Rosenfeld, what are you saying? You will recover!

A slight smile appeared on his face.

–Sometimes, man does not lie, but he also does not tell the truth.

I sensed that when one enters a sick room in happiness, one does alleviate his pain. Is there more happiness possible as when a healthy person visits a dying one? I remind Rosenfeld of his work and his face changes.

–Am I working? Of course! When one wishes to marry a woman, but doesn't, one gets boils on his face. This is what happens to talent that is stopped. A creator needs to create. Woe to the writer who does not produce. No, we must not divorce the pen. One must continue to work and to create. If not, one would express literary thoughts by deluding oneself. Don't be crazy…Have you noticed how much wisdom lies in our subconscious? With all our present knowledge and that of another thousand years, we will not reach its depth. Yes. I still work.

I remember that Rosenfeld's stories are archived by the editor of the Forwards. He is angry at Rosenfeld. For hours and hours one can hear the typewriter in Rosenfeld's room. Out of pride, not to anger anyone and perhaps as a last effort, he is involved in writing his new novel.

–Yes. I work a lot. The doctor said my heart and lungs are healthy. I used to walk along the boardwalk twice a day. I even swam in the ocean. It is good to leave the noisy crowds. A quarter of a mile out, it is the sound of the waves that one hears, not the "bouncing bell". It reminds you how great is the sea and how small is man. Don't go too far! Lately, I did not go far from shore, but I still went into the water on a daily basis. People wondered about me – he is sick and he dips in the ocean? If most people did not wash their faces, they would say: look at the sick one – he washes his face! You should know that I used to regularly swim in the ocean, summer and winter. Such a pleasure! The water cuts the body like a knife. One minute equals an hour in the summer…yes, my heart is healthy…but my back…from a difficult childhood. Maybe…question mark!

Is everything a question mark? A moment of silence. Through the window we hear broken sounds – laughter, singing, shouts and declarations. The waves are splashing the pier. There is a beginning and a continuity.

[Page 202]

–Rosenfeld, what is the subject of your new novel?

His stare deepens, as if he were trying what is beyond his vision.

–I always have difficulty choosing the subject – he replies in his Volyn Yiddish.

–It is more difficult than the actual writing. That I do easily from the inside. The topic comes mainly from meeting people. Truly, I remember events when I was less than three years old. However, you spend most of your life, at least your younger years, in a shop. I was in a small Godforsaken town up to my Bar Mitzvah. You see a few people living a gray life. Did you ever feel the damp emptiness emanating from kitchens of the poor because so little cooking happens there and also the lack of air. Your young days are filled with days that are all the same. Yes, when you experience this life, you cannot, I believe, go deeply into your subjects. At first I used to describe ordinary lives. Later, I went into more complicated subjects. Sometimes I could not even get out of them. In any case…since I do not have a great choice of characters, I must write about various situations that my characters encounter. Thus a character stops being just a character. Truthfully, there really is no such a situation. The middle of the pillow sinks under Rosenfeld's head and folds are created around him. What I mean, is that the character exists, but he remains the same as long as there is no change in his situation. We find even the biggest heroes in difficult situations and the wisest people without a solution.

Mrs. Rosenfeld, his "delicate and tiny" wife, approaches his bed, her face "pale and babyish"– this is how he described her – and wants to spread his blanket over him.

–No, Hayale, I will do it myself. By myself. I must do what I can as long as I am able to do so. If people fuss over me, I will feel that I am really sick. What, the doctor? I don't like doctors. I remember one who had a drink with me and as soon as he said "lechaim", the word became "to death"! What do the doctors know?

Does he really believe this or does he just want to believe in miracles? Perhaps– who knows– the doctors misdiagnosed? …He is unable to eat much, but he must have something every couple of hours it can be a glass of milk with biscuits or warm potatoes. This eases somewhat his deep pain. He shoves his bare feet into sandals and goes down.

[Page 203]

He prepares his meal by himself. He sits on a chair in his sandals and blue and white pajamas. A pillow supports his back. He says to the women:

Please forgive me. A sick person is like a child. No one needs to be righteous with him.

The hot potatoes, full of starch, emit a steam.

–This is a life saving food! …The potatoes remind him of distant days, his childhood in Volyn, in Kovel…a simple and eternal odor emanates from them. It is also the scent of mushrooms. He wipes his mouth with a napkin. And the smells of the ocean. It is a healing and rejuvenating smell. It is for eternity!

It is obvious: he is more broad minded. Does he feel something in his heart?

Do you know, a guest or a host that does not speak, is one of the worst things.– A short recess– sometimes I say to myself that man cannot be hard headed up to his death. How can one stand a person who has no sense of humor? Humor is the second thread in a gray cloth. An artist cannot be one–sided. Take Chekhov, for example, of all the writers in the world – actually I should not judge…I only know Russian literature…Out of all the Russian writers, Chekhov is the one closest to my heart. He is deep, humorous and tragic. That is, the lives of his tragic heroes reach the absurd, and the absurd becomes a tragedy. How wise he is! Dostoyevsky is more monotonous in his choice of subjects and heroes. I mean, their morbidity…Maupassant– I read him in Russian– most of his topics deal with relations between men and women. Most of his stories are just anecdotes. He looks into man's soul, but not too deeply. However, Chekhov…there is no topic in life that his sharp eye does not see! When we go deeper in life, we manage to sail away, at least from their outer veneer. As for our own writers, I was most taken by David Bergelson. He is talented and he is able to criticize life quite acutely in his writings.

Rosenfeld returns to his bed.

–Do you know that all people know how to write and to tell a story. Everyone is interested in the lives of others. However, now, we are much tuned into ourselves and we don't see other people. Stupidest and cruelty are actually the same thing!

In the picture of Rosenfeld, painted by Manievitch, he now resembles Shalom Aleichem. A very complicated Shalom Aleichem.

[Page 204]

C

The early morning hours are good in Brighton. The noise of the city is still far away. The sand, trampled on yesterday by hordes of people and filled with their garbage, now is plowed and is full of sea shells. As you walk on the beach, covered in a cape, perhaps it is still damp, your towel draped on your shoulders, you smile at strangers passing by. You smile, not just to be polite, but because you are happy and proud that you were among the first ones.

Loneliness is felt in Yona Rosenfeld's room. It is the loneliness that a dying person feels among thousands of people. He will have an operation shortly. He stretches on his bed.

–In addition, he whispers, the pain does not go away. There is much sadness in this pain!

It is very hot now outside. The heat is like an anesthetic for the senses. However, this room, it seems, seems cooler. The telephone rings on the other side of the wall. A voice is heard saying "hello". Rosenfeld lifts his head.

–They want news.

–Why do you say this, Rosenfeld? People are interested in your welfare.

–No. They want news!…they want something spicier and sharper. Did you hear, when Dr. Koralnik died, one of his friends phoned us. An educated woman . Did you hear the news? And now…

In the doorway we see I.I.Singer, his bald head gray as a rock. His face clean shaven. How different are these two friends! One completely open and the other always hiding. Singer is a realist and likes the world as it exists. Of course, he also knows the power of mystery and pretense in the soul. (Somehow he does not get caught in it). This is why he wants to uproot any delusion from the beginning. Rosenfeld was more open , (he, too, like any person, guards his deepest, last secret). Singer, it seems, wants to be an observer, but he is overlooked. He is an honest and warm person, according to those close to him. His heart is open, but his mind doubts everything.

–Nu, Yona? – he sits down as a trusted friend.

The conversation immediately becomes an argument. For some reason I sometimes want to catch Singer's meaning. Perhaps I just want to show him that although I am young, I am not idle in front of this successful and famous writer. How our points of view differ almost about everything. Rosenfeld listens with alertness. He begins to speak.

[Page 205]

Most of what he says seems to be in parentheses. You don't know what is more important. He suddenly smiles at his guests.

–Look now. You are listening to my words in unnatural silence. It is if I am no longer here! – he stops– sometimes you are told about this one and that one and you don't know who he is. You imagine because it must be important. He is deathly ill.

Singer leaves. His car, parked outside the building, roars and joins the other cars. Rosenfeld whispers:

–Do you know. I now see people in two groups– the sick and the healthy. Compared to the two groups I find myself outside the circle. There are people who make me think about things I do not know are in my head. When they leave, I still don't know that I know what I don't know that I know.

When he is alert, Rosenfeld is very interesting.

D

Even in the streets close to the ocean the air is strange. The sun will soon set, earlier than usual. Will there be a storm? Dozens of people are using straws to drink from cool bottles. Their mouths are dry. Shoes of many people are strewn on the beach. Women are coming to the ocean and young fathers are pushing strollers. Young women wearing makeup and men with thick cigars. People are walking and others are driving, comfortable in their seats.

Rosenfeld faces the window. Tomorrow he will have his surgery. It is doubtful that it will save him. Still, when in difficult times, one clings to hope.

–Do you know– he says suddenly– my stomach is full of stones and metal. When the sun sets, street lights are lit and you cannot see the darkness. You no longer feel the magic of summer nights nor its silence. On moonlit nights…it is so noisy you don't sense the moon! Maybe it's for the best. Night and silence. I think– perhaps you will laugh– that the two combine as one. As a result we have corruption. Look at human beings –don't they all have a tendency to be sad? What is the purpose? We are still not accustomed to night and the power of darkness. Tell me, please, why does night always bring a worsening of a person's condition? Do you know, in my childhood,

[Page 206]

On Friday nights, the candles burned almost to the end. Now, the darkness is so sweet. You can taste a thousand different flavors in the darkness. On weekdays, babies were afraid of the dark, but not now!

He suddenly feels that I am sucking on an unlit pipe (especially now, as in all times of stress, it is difficult to refrain from smoking, but one must not do so in a sick room.)

–You are "smoking" an unlit pipe? – how amusing! One person is showing off a thick cigar to show he is an important doctor; another – to show he is a respected businessman! How short–sighted people are! Such nonsense…such mystery!

Rosenfeld bites his lower lip due to his pain. A moment of quiet. There are sounds and light in the doorway. Here it is semi–darkness. Rosenfeld curls his mouth and, it seems, is speaking to a third person, on the side. His voice is very weak.

–Do you know, it is a mistake to think that man needs a reason to kill himself. Everything depends on the person. One – maybe he is predestined to do it– would kill himself after a short time of suffering. Another will overcome all obstacles, even if they are difficult and lengthy. I am certain of one thing– in the whole world there is no one who has never thought about it even once– about suicide! Few people really do it. It is possible that even they want to change their minds at the last minute. They are in a magical circle– both life and death are too difficult for them. One is worse than the other. I have thought much about death, maybe even more than others have. Most people travel on a river with perfect trust, without fear. But I…I never felt trust even in my lack of trust…By the way, do you know that the acme in love affairs borders on death? Exactly now…it is not a philosophical calm, but numbness. Terrible physical suffering can confuse you. Total withdrawal from life is no longer frightening…Do you know that perhaps one is more afraid of death when one sees the moment has come. But I am not dismayed.

The room is quiet. There is a shadow on the wall, nothing real.

–I don't know what is the reason, but most people die at night. I will probably die at night. At the beginning of the day I feel so fresh, as if I am reborn!

[Page 207]

–Rosenfeld, you will be lucky and work many more years!

–Yes, maybe… I don't want to die. The pains are quite unbearable. However, not wanting to live and wishing to die, are they not the same!

E

It is a bright morning. On the horizon one can see a large ship. On the beach there are awnings that resemble colorful mushrooms.

In Rosenfeld's house there are people who speak in low voices. Rosenfeld prepares himself to go to the hospital. Has he prepped his soul for his destiny?

It is time to go. He looks at the mirror on the wall.

–Do you know –he once said– over the years a person changes his purpose, but, still, there is something specific I used from birth to death. It is no wonder– when compared to eternity, our life is quite short. There is not enough time to change everything!

He leaves the mirror and his Adam's apple moves up and down.

–Should I go first or last?

He looks around him– is he saying goodbye to his home? I knew: in Rosenfeld's eyes a mezuzah is not necessary, but perhaps he would have been happy to have one on his door frame.

He enters first into the elevator. The iron cage descends into the well with screeching of the cables.

* * *

His illness was postponed for a few years. "I am now working on a second autobiography ". He wrote to me. "I should have written it first because I speak about myself during early childhood. It was a beautiful time". Near his end he turned back to the beginning. He never completed his book.

He died not at night, but at dawn. It seemed to him that he had been reborn.

[Page 208]

Yosef Avrekh

by Yaacov Teitelkar

Translated by Amy Samin

A memorial tribute to the Hebrew teacher of the Tarbut Hebrew Gymnasia of Kovel

Yosef Avrekh was born in Kovel in 1892 to devout and pious parents. His father, Ben-Zion the *shochet* [ritual slaughterer], possessed an upright bearing and a majestic appearance, and was one of the most experienced and respected *shochatim* in the city, and his mother Pasil the *shochetanit* was the daughter of a pious and good family, purely righteous and self-denying, and who knew all the writings of the sages of blessed memory by heart, and prayed the deliberately whispered prayer three times a day just like a man. Even as a young child "Yoske" the *shochet*'s son, displayed lofty talents and a deep longing for study and scientific knowledge. Sensitive, impulsive, and full of movement,

Yoske was a standout amongst his friends and classmates in the *heder* [small religious school] in the neighborhood of the "city" ("Stat") - the place where there stood the cramped house squeezed in amongst the crowded wooden houses of the neighborhood - and he was the accepted leader of the group of boys, the conductor of games and amusements, and the instigator of youthful pranks. However, his thoughts were not only of games. While still a boy he was not satisfied with his studies in the *heder*, nor by the stories of children's literature, which to him were unsatisfying. He searched for "external" books, books that were substantive and would reveal to him the mysteries of the world before which he stood, wondering and silent, to know the meaning of the great vision of the bush that burned but was not consumed… he sought, and he found them. He took a risk and snuck them into the attic, where concealed from prying eyes he would devour them, completely engrossed with all of his being.

[Page 209]

Refined and purified after a disappearance of several days, he was "discovered" by his friends, who gathered together in a group one night with the starry sky spread out over their heads and the pale moon looking down on them with "the eyes of Yaacov our father", watching between the wide passageways and the far off distances. And in a mysterious whisper he revealed his hidden "secret" to them, after making them swear a sacred oath to keep the secret and never, G-d forbid, reveal it to anyone: Do you see those stars? They are not stars at all, they are worlds, just like our world… and that moon's eyes are not eyes. Those are wells in her soil - the soil of the moon… and the heavens - Shh! No one should hear… That is not the heavens, it is a cavity, an empty space of air.

Through reading a great many children's books, newspapers, and magazines for adults, Yoske acquired a vast knowledge of the Hebrew language, and he initiated the idea of resuscitating spoken Hebrew in the everyday life of society; and he implemented the idea in a consistently vigorous manner, showering his friends with spoken Hebrew wherever they went. With all of his soul and all of his might, he believed in the Zionist idea and the enchanting personality of Herzl captured his heart, and he prophesized while dreaming and while awake, and he included the subject at every opportunity in conversations with his friends.

In 1904, when the unfortunate news of Herzl's death was received, Yoske gathered his friends in the street and gave them a comprehensive speech about Herzl. At the end of his speech, he lifted his right hand and solemnly swore: "if I forget Jerusalem, may my right hand lose its cunning…" and that pledge came to be.

Yoske's mother Pasil the *shochetanit*, a housewife and owner of a shop in the marketplace of the city, an ink manufacturer, was constantly busy at home and in her shop - she often needed the assistance of Yoske. One day, she suggested to him that he go to the mill in the city where they ground grain into flour for sale. Yoske jumped at the idea, happy at the opportunity for a tour of the windmill with its mysterious, enormous wooden sails… With great curiosity and hurried inquisitiveness he left nothing untouched or undiscovered at the mill. He looked at the grindstones, at the upper stone and the lower, wondering about the rotation of the wheels and the straps wrapped around them, making their continuous way. He became enthusiastic about their movement and caressed them; he was caught up and suspended from them… The mill was stopped. Yoske came home from the hospital after about two weeks, with his right hand lost to him.

From then on, there was a fundamental apposition in his life. His parents began to think about practical matters. Yoske agreed to be sent to study for four years in a renowned yeshiva in Odessa in whose management a number of the great authors of the generation participated, including Mendele and Bialik. After four years Yoske returned home from Odessa a well-versed Torah scholar. After only a few days he went into teaching. He founded the first elementary school in Kovel and took one of the most important positions in the cultural and spiritual life of the city in general, and of the Zionist movement in Kovel specifically.

[Page 210]

He stood at the forefront of the instigators for the Tarbut movement next to Asher Frankfurt, and became a Judaic studies teacher in the *gymnasia*, educating the young generation of dedicated pioneers about their people, Zionism and how to actualize their nationalist ideals - his lifelong dream since childhood - until the outbreak of the war.

Yosef Avrekh was a lofty person, refined, meticulous and noble. He was a deep person, with a profoundly realistic outlook on life, viewing the world from a lofty vantage point, influenced by prophetic justice. A dreamer with his eyes wide open… A philosopher whose chief philosophy and view was the problem of the people of the world, the eternal abuse of the people of Israel, the deprived, downtrodden and supplanted by the nations of the world. He recognized and valued life. He respected nature and its charms. He appreciated and noticed the supremacy and the splendor in its revelation and what was hidden inside. He longed to find solutions to its mystery in all particulars, the purposefulness of creation which he never ceased pondering. He loved life, and was involved in it with every fiber of his being. He was impressed and enthusiastic about the zephyr, the sounds of silence, the enchantment of the scenery and the refreshing green carpet of the fields outside of the city, where he would walk every morning, taking in the essence of the day. The texture of the pale blue of the Turia River, where he would swim at the crack of dawn and would express his feelings and thoughts in conversation and wax enthusiastic about the creation of the world and everything in it.

Yosef Avrekh at the time of his studies in the Odessa yeshiva.
Avrekh is sitting third from the left in the second row (from the top down).
In the third row, fifth from the right sits the poet H. N. Bialik of blessed memory.

[Page 211]

With the outbreak of the Soviet-German war, when Hitler announced his well-known declaration to destroy all of the Jews of Europe, which announcement was broadcast on the radio, that same hour Yosef Avrekh ran around his room like a wounded lion, shouting: "Who does this crazy, arrogant idiot think he is?! The world - abandoned, with no justice and no judge?! The world will allow him to destroy all the Jews of Europe?! It will never happen! He must fall, and he will fall!"

In 1942 the Nazis crowded all of the Jews of Kovel into the field of the city in order to kill them in the village of Bachba, 6 kilometers from the city along the Brisk road, in graves that had already been dug. Who could have guessed and who would have said how deep and how fatal were the hellish torments of those about to be slaughtered, and who can describe the suffering of Yosef Avrekh, when he saw so clearly that: the world has been abandoned, that there is no justice and no judge! No one did anything to stop the murderous conspiracy against an entire people, of a magnitude and structure the likes of which had never before been seen in history! Or the volcanic tempest in his heart that burst its bounds and became a desperate cry of a plundered people in the light of day, for nothing. Weak and feeble, in everyday life, frightened and shaking before the violent rulers; this time Yosef Avrekh rose up from among the rows of thousands of Jews being led to massacre, with courage and mental strength beyond one's comprehension, and raising his voice and his only hand, intrepidly - as was told by eyewitnesses - approaching the murderous Germans, he filled their ears with his wrath, spitting bile and contempt in their faces and predicting their inevitable defeat on the crucial day soon to come!

His single remaining hand was instantly amputated by the sword of the murderer. He was shot where he stood. He fell in battle. Wallowing in his own blood, he gave out one last battle cry: "The people of Israel live! Death and vengeance to the criminal Nazis!" In his service to his people, in his dedication of all of his might in life, and in his demonstration of the existence of the people in the face of the enemy's sword, and being answered by the sword on his head as a rebuke, he died a hero's death, the self-sacrifice of a proud and brave-hearted Jew, a hero protecting the honor of his people.

May his soul be bound up in the bonds of everlasting life.

May his soul be bound up in the bonds of the sacred and pure heroes, and may his memory never be forgotten!

From the Writings of Yosef Avrekh

Translated by Amy Samin

The *Massorah* [notations regarding the exact traditional text of the bible] explain to us the origins of the name Gilad, the important region on the eastern side of the Jordan River, which was frequently a rock in the dispute between the Hebrew tribes on the eastern side of the Jordan and the Moabs and the Amons from the south, and the Arameans from the north.

[Page 212]

It comes from the words: *Gal-Ed*, in other words, the heap of stones will stand forever between the children of Yaacov and the children of Lavan (Genesis 31:48); in other words, the pile of stones (and those scattered in abundance on the heap) must mark the eternal boundary between the Arameans (children of Lavan) and the Jewish tribes on the eastern side of the Jordan River. The writing thus emphasizes that what was done is a fact, because the eastern side of the Jordan was a permanent settlement of the tribes of the children of Israel and that other elders of the Israelites and of the Arameans already determined the borders.

* * * * *

The eastern side of the Jordan River - this was an ancient inheritance for the Israelites, the cradle of their cherished homeland, before they occupied the land of Canaan.

* * * * *

The song of Bil'am, who turned from one who curses to one who blesses; the marvelous song that says "How goodly are thy tents, Yaacov" and "It is a people that shall dwell alone and not be reckoned among the nations" (Exodus 23, 24) portions of the eastern side of the Jordan River and its background, the hatred, the powerlessness and fear of the Moabites before the tribes of Israel.

* * * * *

At the beginning of the book you will find the name of the eastern side of the Jordan: "These are the words which Moses spoke to all Israel on the other side of the Jordan" etc. (Deuteronomy 1:1). Soon after, you find another mention: "Beyond the Jordan, in the land of Moab, Moshe began to declare this Torah" etc. (Deuteronomy 1:5).

* * * * *

The eastern side of the Jordan plays an important role in the influence of prophetic culture in the creation of poetry and the concept of the unity of faith, the people, and the land. It is clear to me that at the present moment, when evil peoples are calling for the destruction of our lives, not just as a group but as people, the annexation of the eastern side of the Jordan to the area of the homeland is an ideal, not the reality. But it is important for us that we do not, in our consciousness, diminish the value of the eastern side of the Jordan to the rest of the country, that we do not despair of it, and so - one day we will dwell there.

(From his articles: "The Hebrew Irredenta and Reflection in the Tanakh" Printed in "Kovetz HaYovel" in honor of the principal of the *Gymnasia* and the editor of the *Tarbut* magazine in Kovel, Mr. Asher Frankfort, on the occasion of his 50th birthday (1888 - 1938) and in honor of the 17th anniversary of the founding of the *Gymnasia* (1921 - 1938). The journal appeared in 1938, edited by Yosef Avrekh, may G-d avenge his blood).

[Page 213]

Kalman Gutenboim, z"l

by Yitzhak Ogen

Translated by Ala Gamulka

I first met Kalman Gutenboim in Vilna in the month of Elul, 1936. I had long wished to meet this man as there were many stories about his life within our family circle. He lived in Kovel and was married there to my aunt, my father's sister- the daughter of Rabbi Nitzberg, z" l. The rabbi was known for his book "Demeshek Eliezer". I recall a visit from my late grandfather in our house in Vilna. During one of his conversations with my father the name of Kalman Gutenboim came up.

Kalman Gutenboim and his wife Ida, daughter of Rabbi Nitzberg

The elderly rabbi, a scholar who was famous for his few words- spoke with enthusiasm about his wonderful son-in-law (after several years of knowing him- they lived in the same apartment). He told us about Kalman's monkish way of life, his deep diligence as well as his outstanding character. The elderly rabbi spoke with enthusiasm and reverence. Some time later I read books written by Gutenboim- one about Schopenhauer (a deep and yet popular analysis). I also tried to read his book about Einstein's Theory of Relativity. These and his later books- The novels "Strangers" and "Mystery"- awakened my desire to meet the author, a member of our family. This only happened in 1936.

That summer I went to Vilna- after spending a few years in Eretz Israel- to visit my parents. Kalman Gutenboim had moved from Kovel to Vilna.

[Page 214]

Our meeting was quite hearty. There was something in him that captured my heart. His exterior appearance was not particularly attractive. He was a tired man with some ailments. However, after a short conversation I realized that he was weary from the work he did day and night. He was constantly doing research and studying. He was an introvert and modest. I succeeded in obtaining his trust. The quiet man became a non-stop talker and I absorbed his words.

We strolled through the streets of Vilna- the poor streets in the Jewish section. They touched our hearts with their bareness. We sailed along to the suburbs, to the parks and" Spire mountain". This is where Mikhel wrote his works and where Ma'ane wrote "My soul's wish". In front of us, on one side, was the Vilila and on the other, the Vilika river. Here, in this distant and lonely place (the Christian residents only visited on special occasions while the Jews avoided attacks by bullies), we sat for hours and discussed philosophy. He found me to be receptive to his thoughts. Usually, he was on his own and did not find a listening ear. Truthfully, he was liked by the Jewish intelligentsia who wrote in Yiddish (he was publishing articles in Der Tag (the day), edited by Zalman Raizin. However, he was not a member of a specific group. Unlike most of the Yiddish writers, he was a Zionist. Secretly, his heart dreamed of Eretz Israel. He wanted to work there, but he was auto-didactic and there was no one who could recommend him. At that time, he was invited to give a series of lectures in Russia (his books about Schopenhauer and Einstein had reached Russia and had made an impression- or perhaps someone in the family had intervened…). However, he could not accept the Communists and he knew that he would not be able to give his opinions freely in Russia. He would not give up on freedom of thought. I still remember his ideas on materialism and Marxism. No, he was not a person who should lecture in Russia. In addition, the long trip was daunting. There was much work to be done and his head was full of plans. In one conversation he told me that he was writing his autobiography, about his original philosophy. He figured he needed ten more years to complete the task.

As often happens with bright people, his conversation flowed easily. His words were simple, but deep. It is only after several years that I appreciated the beauty of its contents. He was comfortable in the world of human thought. His torch lit the way in the darkness. A circle of light hung on him and led him forward. I stood inside his circle and it seems to me that I see the man as he was lit up. I saw that he never wavered in his origins and roots. Man's suffering was his outlet- before and after his ideas. This lonely man, away from the crowd, was a wonder in my eyes.

[Page 215]

In those days he told me about his contacts with the great thinkers of our generation. I saw his aloofness in a different light. He could read and write in Russian, English, French and German and he had friendly relations with many scholars. In connection with his book on Einstein, he corresponded with him. He also was in touch with Michelson, the famous physicist and others. I cannot forgive myself for the sin I committed. I encouraged him to give me the letters he received, or at least some of them so I could bring them to Hebrew University. It would be Dr. Shvedron who would receive them. The shadow of the Satan from Germany was felt in Poland. Gutenboim agreed and we had decided that I would come to his house to choose the letters. I was busy with all kinds of happenings in Vilna, my home city and I was easily impressed. I postponed my visit to him. When I came to say good-bye to Kalman Gutenboim, a hasty parting, it was agreed that he would send me the letters. Although I felt the importance of these letters, I did not expect him to take time away from his work to send them to me. My heart is heavy and full of sorrow. Everything was lost and nothing remained.

Writings of Kalman Gutenboim: (Bibliography)

1. Arthur Schopenhauer- his life and philosophy. Published by A. Gitlin, Warsaw, 1922
2. Special and General Relativity Theory. Published by A. Gitlin, Warsaw 1923
3. Strangers- a novel. A. Gitlin, Warsaw.
4. Mystery- novel. Warsaw, 1924

[Page 216]

Prominence

In honor of the Fiftieth Anniversary of the Birth of Mr. Asher Frankfort, may God avenge his blood

by Yosef Avrech

Translated by Amy Samin

Principal of the Hebrew Gymnasia,
Mr. Asher Frankfort,
may God avenge his blood

[Page 217]

As a student of the school established by *Mefitzei Hahaskalah* in Russia in the first decade of the twentieth century, who intended to assimilate at the time when many were fleeing from the *heder* and the *yeshiva* to *Skalah* and enlightenment, it was difficult to imagine that the young man, Frankfort, a *Skalah* protégé, would serve up - along with the *Tanakh* and the Hebrew language - various delicacies from Karilov, Pushkin, Larmontov and others, going against the stream and making an inverse flight from the *Maskil El Dal* school to the *yeshivas* in Kovel and Brisk. And about two years later, to the Russian school in Kovel and later to the trade school and to the small *gymnasia* in Brisk. Afterward he graduated from the institute for commercial science in Kiev, in order to later establish a Hebrew *gymnasia* and become the guardian of its physical and spiritual development.

And when Frankfort left, crowned with the degree of bachelor of commercial science and economics, the World War was in progress. He tried to make use of his education obtained in the institute and did commercial clerical work. He was made a senior clerk in a large contracting office in the field of bridge and road construction.

Later, he also worked in commerce. In spite of that, he did not neglect the most important kind of public work of that time. He became a member of the aid committee for Jews impacted by the war. Later he joined the aid committee for the victims of the Ukrainian pogroms during the time of the Russian Revolution.

The entrance of the Poles into Kiev made it possible for him to return to the city of his birth as a repatriate, not just in its simplest meaning, but a spiritual repatriate to Hebrew culture in his former homeland. Soon after his return, he began his efforts to establish the Hebrew *gymnasia*.

He made a daring leap, causing amazement in the eyes of his acquaintances and friends. The *alrightniks* among them were astounded: respectable, profitable businessmen had been assembled, was Frankfort planning to open a religious school for girls? Even more, they were amazed by his lobbying efforts among the curators and ministers: a *gymnasia* where the language of instruction was to be Hebrew? It was indeed a wondrous riddle, whose solution would be extremely difficult.

And where would they find textbooks in the various subjects written in the Hebrew language? "How can a language that has been frozen and lifeless for hundreds of years serve for all of the concepts and expressions of these times? How strange!" People suggested that he open a *gymnasia* where the language of instruction would be Polish. But he, Frankfort, answered them with the words that Rabbi Yohanan ben Zakai said to Vespasian: "Give me Yavneh and its sages."

And in the offices of the curators and the ministers, they were amazed. But the great miracle of the rebirth of Poland, which had been lively and filled the being of every Pole - served as a backdrop for he who explained to them the vision the revival of our culture, and that vision its place in the hearts of those who could make a difference. The idea of the culture was put into practice, giving it flesh and blood, like in Rovna, Bialystok and Vilna, so the *gymnasia* in Kovel was founded.

[Page 218]

Of all of the awful problems the principal had to solve, the worst of all was the question of the sources of income for the institution. The accepted assumption was that an educational institution with the idealistic goal of changing values must rely on the means of the *Tarbut* company and be supported by them and by other public funds. Frankfort, however, solved the problem in an entirely different manner. The *gymnasia* was funded by tuition fees paid by the parents.

However, occasionally it had legal and moral support and, occasionally, also material help from the center. But the institution did not depend on the expectation of help from the center, if he had it would soon have the same destiny as Frishman, and would go bankrupt and perish.

Kovel was not a well-to-do city, not by its population and not by its finances, and there were more high school level educational institutions than were warranted. The paradox of Frankfort's activities was that the institution which logically should have depended on outside help, had a life of its own and paid taxes to the center.

The vitality of *Tarbut* institutions served as a typical sign of their right to exist, and the solid ground upon which the idea of *Tarbut* was based. But along with that it served to prove the administrative strength and talent of the *gymnasia's* founder and principal.

The days of crisis came, which even now have not completely passed, and poverty also came knocking on the doors of the institution. The faces of the teachers and their families bore witness to those lean years. But in spite of everything they were steadfast.

… Thus he carried on, continuing his work up until the new Olympian leap - the construction of the building. First the building: the authorities would not allow the institution to carry on in its old building, which it was feared might collapse. On the other hand, it would be difficult to find another location in which the rent would not consume all of the operating income. Therefore, a new building must be constructed.

And if you say: the institution doesn't have enough money to clear its debts and the rent from previous years, how would it be possible to think about such a thing as constructing a new building? Some would say, that is why we must build, since the institution does not have the funds to pay large amounts in rent year after year.

It would seem that the answer is both paradoxical and lacking in logic: an enchanted circle without any opening. And here you discover the greatness of the man we are honoring. That idea, which garnered him supporters in the meetings of the go-getters of *Tarbut*, and with the community leader M. Pearl, to whom it seemed a nice hallucination lacking any basis in reality, took on an actual shape under the initiative of Frankfort.

What hidden strength bubbled and flowed within him. Vigor overflowed his banks like a lava flow from a volcano, spreading out and inflaming everything in its path.

[Page 219]

Thus his strength ignited a tremendous bonfire of achievement and creativity. All of the members of the group of excellent businessmen were amazed at the shrewd combinations and transactions of the man we are honoring: purchasing and clearing the land, and making a down payment for the hauling of the building materials. They were enchanted by his marvelous ingenuity, like an eagle's flight, the tremendous initiative of "seven miles in one step" of A. Frankfort.

The derisive smiles and laughter in the mustaches disappeared. Where was the paradox? Everything was so real, so logical and sensible. The businessmen were electrified, and girded their strength for the gathering of subscriptions and contributions (financial, materials, and building blocks) for the building project.

And the results - the grand laying of the cornerstone before a large audience, and all mouths that had been filled with claims that his boasts of a tremendous initiative were unrealistic, and who had said that it would be worthwhile to see how and when the building would actually be completed, were suddenly empty. One of the official guests at the occasion said this: "Now, this premise: Frankfort now stands at a miniature matriculation exam. He will take the full examination when construction is complete." In other words: "There is still a long way to go." And hand to hand, back to back, and above all the taskmaster - the honoree - with his piercing glance, demanding work and effort from the members like a taskmaster. When people started to relax their will and or become impatient, his raspy voice would echo secretly in the heart and the brain: "Get up and work! Get up and do!"

Only through ruses, juggling, and infusions - that is to say, of money - from the jugs to the well, I mean the budget of the institution, its salaries, the salaries of its personnel, loans, deferred payments, did the construction work continue and the walls rise up, tile by tile, and after the affair of the bricks, the affair of the beams and the joists, and after that the affair of the tin. It was expected of the *Tarbut* building. And only the eyes of the honoree, blazing with a sickly glow, and his focused face and his heart weakening inside of him, his eyes rolled slightly with the irrational element in his vigor, which was inexhaustible, from the painful affront to our culture, the great culture of an anguished nation which has no shelter; this culture, which was not inherited from the sacrifices and "did not win light in a windfall," but which was carved from its heart and its pain.

And the honoree dredged up strength from his personal pain and sorrow, if you do not do something big, the fruit of his work which he loved so well would be for nothing. The same personal insult, the same danger of disappointment that spurred on his initiative also spurred the act of construction until all was complete, and through to its decoration. The building was erected. Frankfort sat for the "full matriculation exam" and passed it.

(From the Jubilee File of the Fiftieth Anniversary of the birth of Asher Frankfort of blessed memory and in honor of the 17th Anniversary of the establishment of the gymnasia.)

[Page 220]

In Memory of Yosef Borak, Z" L

by Yaacov Kobrinsky

Translated by Ala Gamulka

There was no one else in Kovel like Yaacov Borak. He was a member of many committees. During the period between the two wars he was on the following committees: Tarbut, Taz, Ort, the orphanage, Gmilut Hasadim Fund, etc. He also belonged to the local branch of the General Zionists. Yaacov was a member of so many institutions not because he looked for honors, but because he was a man of the people. He had a deep understanding of the complicated labyrinth of our public and political lives.

It was complicated not due to ideology, but for practical reasons- makeup of the institutions, their financial arrangements, relations between the institutions, character of the leaders and "secrets from the inside". All these issues were clear to him. He was usually elected to the budgetary committees and also to those committees that granted inner funds. The latter were often forgotten by our brethren.

It was customary for him, and no one else, to publish the weekly "Voice of Kovel".

[Page 221]

The publication kept going for over 10 years. The "Voice of Kovel" served the Jewish community of Kovel very well. Yaacov Borak aspired to give the weekly publication a clear local tone. Every edition contained not more than one article of general interest. There were also recaps of news of the week. The rest was given over to interests of Kovel and vicinity, municipal issues, the community and the various institutions, youth organizations. There were also reports about accidents and robberies. Occasionally, works by local authors and poets were included (Kalman Liss, Moshe Weinstein, Olitzky and others).

He managed to draw the attention of writers from among the local Jewish intelligentsia. They provided literary material, without being paid. Of course, being a stubborn man, he exacted from every person respect for the publication. I recall that a visiting troupe came to present some plays in Kovel. The impresario wanted to change the accepted custom and refused to give Borak a press pass.

"I don't need your review"- claimed the latter. Borak simply replied: "I am not coming to the play to write a review, but I still must be in the theatre. Otherwise, the public in attendance will boo every performance. If one of your actors will fall off the stage and break an elbow- I, as a journalist, must write about it in the local weekly publication or to inform the Warsaw newspaper". (Yaacov Borak was also a reporter for "Moment")

Yaacov Borak did not ally the "Voice of Kovel" with any political party- officially or financially. However, because it was so independent, the publication spoke for the Zionist organization. It announced all its many activities. He never wavered from the Zionist and national route. At times, this attitude caused serious financial losses. At one time, people representing the B.B.O.R (a group of non-affiliated people who cooperated with the government- followers of Pilsudski), offered Borak some compensation for providing them space in the publication. He refused and used a diplomatic excuse to do so.

In the last years before WWII, when the Jewish community had an inkling that a terrible event was to come, the "Voice of Kovel" pushed Aliyah. The publication remained true to its purpose up to the day the war broke out. Our public life then was silenced.

He was unable to get out in time and he was murdered by the killers together with our saintly brethren.

[Page 222]

About the *Kovel Voice* and Its Editor
(Passing Thoughts)

by S. Bama

Translated by Amy Samin

In the dim mists of time the prominent and upright figure of the editor of the *Kovel Voice* comes to life: his gaunt face, his bespectacled eyes, and his pointed nose gave him an ascetic appearance: his somewhat fragmented speech, his coarse, deep, cutting voice seemingly fashioned to convince you with its internal logic. His long legs bore him, a busy public figure, to every public gathering. As a faithful Zionist, he preferred national interest to inter-factional conspiracies. He didn't take anyone into account, and he criticized those who deserved it with his honed and witty pen.

* * *

"A public figure": indeed he showed up everywhere he was expected to be, and everywhere he was not. He succeeded in gathering around himself a faithful group of workers who were altruistically devoted with all their hearts and souls to the newspaper. His "agents" could be found at all public activities, both general and Jewish. With his long sharp nose he sniffed out and found the right people for the city council or the *starostwo* (eldership) on the one hand, and the community council on the other.

* * *

He brought the very best of the "intelligentsia" of the city to the newspaper and still wasn't satisfied. He was in contact with well-known authors, and got their permission to reprint in his paper the best writings of the journalists from the general-Jewish papers, and every week he provided the city's residents with articles of both passing and enduring content.

* * *

He was an autodidact, but he was able to adopt modern ways of expression. More than once people were amazed at the phenomenon of a man of broad scope who was indeed active in the province, was involved in general political and public-Jewish life, and who remarked on every public event worthy of acknowledgement, both large and small.

* * *

His writing was simple and to the point, he knew every hidden wrinkle of the spoken language, and wove it into his written words. His written expressions were logical, detailed,

[Page 223]

comprehensive and convincing. It did not lack an iota of modernism on the one hand, and on the other was based on the popular and juicy *gleichvertel* (witticism). His articles achieved his goal: to stroke or caress those who deserved it, and to strike or injure those who deserved it.

* * *

The *Kovel Voice* had a general character, but everyone knew that it was a Zionist newspaper. Among the provincial newspapers in the region, it was the most notable and had the highest level of writing and journalists. And more than once it was quoted by the general-Jewish newspaper in Warsaw, the capital. And when political competitors appeared - such as the Bund - and wanted to muddy the city of Kovel's Zionist character, the *Kovel Voice* rose up with a fighting spirit and national pride, and in the end was victorious.

* * *

"Well then, Mr. S.B.," someone said to me, following my participation in the big memorial service for Herzl that was held in the Great Synagogue. "Perhaps you could honor our newspaper with the fruits of your pen?" You couldn't refuse the pleasant tone of Ben-

Avinoam - such was his accepted nickname - and in the next Friday edition there appeared an article entitled "*Bein ha-Metzarim*" ("Between the Straits"), which was given pride of place.

* * *

It is the Friday before you make *aliyah* (immigrate) to *Eretz Yisrael*. The printing machine is spewing out the newspaper's last galley proofs. The fresh-inked letters dirty the hands of the editor as he fixes his glance on the greetings for the immigrant. Tears roll down his cheeks and fall onto the soft, fibrous paper of the newspaper. "Send your list from there and I will be comforted by it," he says, and from his mouth escape words with many meanings: "Who knows when I will have the opportunity to make aliyah to *Eretz Yisrael*?" He always gave the lists from *Eretz Yisrael* a place at the top of the paper, though he never did have the chance to go there himself.

* * *

When you go to *Eretz Yisrael* and stand on Mt. Scopus in the journalism department of the Hebrew University, and page through the annuals of the *Kovel Voice* which are in the archives there, you are able to stand at a geographical distance and see the value of the newspaper and the position that it had in Jewish-general life. And if Jewish Kovel will continue to live on in the Jewish consciousness, the *Kovel Voice* and its editor will have played no small part in that.

[Page 224]

The Art of Theater in Our City

by Yaacov Teitelkar

Translated by Ala Gamulka

The story of the "Jewish Drama Group" in Kovel

During the Russian rule, up to WWI, it was absolutely forbidden to perform on stage in Yiddish in Kovel. Occasionally, troupes came from Warsaw, Vilna and other places. They, too, tried to get around the regulations by pretending to perform in "German". Truthfully, most of the plays performed in those days were written in "Deutcherisch"– Hebrew script with Germanic sounds and Yiddish words.

These plays were attended mostly by the wealthier people and the Russian–Jewish intelligentsia. The masses were less interested in them.

The development of Yiddish theater in Kovel began at the start of WWI, when it was conquered by the Germans. The Jews had reasonable freedom in conducting public cultural programs in their language. One of the main reasons for the growth of the "Jewish Drama Group" in Kovel was the special economic situation in which the residents found themselves. At the time the town was filled with Jewish refugees from nearby villages. The war had reached them and the widows and orphans required immediate assistance. The residents of Kovel undertook this help so the needy people would not succumb to their dire situation. This is when the Peoples' Kitchen was founded by the town leaders. They were headed by the well–known, generous wife of Dr. Feinstein. She worked tirelessly for the good of the poor– materially and spiritually.

The usual sources of collecting funds among the population were insufficient. Those in charge had to find other sources of income. Therefore, in 1917, before and after the Balfour Declaration, the first signs of Zionist seeds emerged in Kovel. Thus, among the members of the intelligentsia that were followers of Mrs. Feinstein, the idea was born to form a Jewish Drama group. It would perform in pure Yiddish, with high performance standards, but it would also provide an income to be used for the needy refugees in Kovel.

[Page 225]

The Jewish Drama Group of Kovel
10th Anniversary 1917–1927

[Page 226]

The founders of the "Jewish Drama Group" were: the talented director Vannin, Moshe Pugatch, and chairman Moshe Kogan. They were theater lovers and were quite talented. Moshe Pugatch came from among the Zionist youth and Kogan was a product of the popular–nationalists of Kovel. They both brought experience and specific theatrical points of view which they had acquired in their travels in America. This was where Jewish literature and theater were blooming in those days. They both had the same purpose– to develop theatrical taste among the people. The selections they chose were from the best European and Jewish repertoire as well as plays by Gordon and Goldfaden. They presented plays three or four times a year, but they were very serious and dedicated.

The roles were presented artistically and were well–rehearsed. Every performance, beautifully directed by Pugatch, was a highlight in the life of the population of Kovel. The plays were received enthusiastically and respectfully. It seemed that the seeds of the "Jewish Drama Group" were sown on the fertile soil of the talented youths of Kovel. Soon, there was a full staff of outstanding theatrical forces around the Group.

The traditional Jewish attitude to "theater" as a Purim Play and the actors as "Comedians" with a bad reputation, changed. The eternal struggle between fathers and sons about modernity also subsided. During the first years of its existence, the "Jewish Drama Group" served as a bridge between the audiences of Kovel and the various visiting troupes (The Vilners from Warsaw and Vilna, Turkov's Vict group). The latter appeared often in the best Jewish dramatic productions. When they arrived in Kovel, they would immediately contact the "Jewish Drama Group" and perform in their theater. Thus, they received advice, help and technical support and contact with the theater–going population of Kovel. The top goal of the "Jewish Drama Group" was to foster artistic theatrical tastes in the masses. They concentrated on all parts of the population in town. The Russian–Jewish intelligentsia had been nurtured within Russian culture and was usually distant from Jewish language and culture and looked at it as broken "jargon". The intelligentsia was given the opportunity to have classical literature recognized. Many of its members joined as actors and others enjoyed the performances. The audience was the beneficiary. There were plays by Borokhin, Brandes, Madam Kivok and others. The "plain folks" were represented by the chairman Kogan, a beloved comedian, Khalat, Grempler, Rosen and others.

[Page 227]

The national–Zionists were– founder of the group Moshe Pugatch, Shevka Frishberg, Haya Liss, Aaron Melamed and his sister Yocheved, Hannah Kopelberg, Shalom Klonitsky and others. Even the "religious" leaders who were against their offspring participating in "theater" gave in and joined the modern trend. Their representatives were: the Friedman brothers, Teacher Naimark, Segal, etc.

This is how the" Jewish Drama Group" became an important, all–party, neutral vehicle. It drew many young people, as well as lovers of popular theater and culture. Every section ignored its particular points of view for the good of the others. This is how the "Jewish Drama Group" became beloved by all residents of Kovel.

However, in time, there were new influences in the economic life of the Jews in the new Poland. They also touched the daily life of the Jews. The Polish government had a strict Anti–Semitic policy and thus the Jews of Kovel suffered economically. There was poverty and great need. It was necessary to develop more practical ways and to cut down on culture. There were also other reasons. Some people married and became involved in their family and business. Others left for far away places and there were those who did not approve of the change in values. Members left the group and were replaced by new ones who did not see things in the same way. Pugatch left and was replaced by a local actor who had settled in Kovel –Torren. He was an accomplished performer who directed as well. However, he did not continue the custom of having the audience get used to the art. He was more interested in adapting the plays to the spectators. There were very few left of the original group and there was a decline.

Torren tried to draw to the group new members from working youths and simply theater lovers. He appealed to the surrounding villages with great success. The secretary, Khalat, knew how to approach community leaders for donations and together they were able to keep the group going until the last days before the Holocaust.

[Page 228]

The Habimah– Studio
(founded by Shalom Klonitsky)

The need for Habimah and its genesis

If the Jewish drama group in Kovel was born due to economic need, i.e. in order to serve as an additional source of social assistance, then the Habimah–Studio of Sh. Klonitsky was a unique Hebrew cultural phenomenon.

It was in the second half of the thirties that the Hebrew cultural movement in Kovel was in full bloom. The two elementary schools and the Tarbut Hebrew high school were thriving and growing. The pioneering movements (Hashomer Hatzair, Hechalutz Hatzair, Union of Working Eretz Israel) expanded and together they created a base and a strong background for more cultural activities. There was an opportunity for the Hebrew language to permeate social–cultural life in Kovel. However, these activities were limited to the educational institutions and the centers of the movements. Their influence was not evident outside their walls. Thus, the main purpose of Tarbut was not visible: the renewal and mastery of the Hebrew language in the Diaspora and the preparation for life in the homeland.

There were many among the teachers and Tarbut leaders in Kovel who recognized, understood and appreciated the value of theatre in the dissemination of language and culture, especially Hebrew language. Up to then the language was considered to be purely that of the book. However, the teacher, Shalom Klonitsky was the only one who dared to present this proposal: to deepen the knowledge of the language in cultural Hebrew life by forming a public Hebrew theatre stage available to all. Sh. Klonitsky was a member of Tarbut, a veteran Zionist and a talented actor. He belonged to the Jewish Drama group and had esthetic and artistic theatrical viewpoints. He had learned this through experience and by reading theatrical literature. He had intuition and original inspiration. It was natural that to the main purpose– cultural growth– there was also added a secondary one. It was to create a Hebrew stage that was artistic and would satisfy, in an esthetic fashion, all those seeking culture and art. This idea was germinating in Sh. K. for many years and he was prepared to dedicate all his strength and pride to achieving it.

Connection

As is usually the case with all new ideas and dreams, there are many who look at them, but few who are willing to make an effort to achieve them. It is important to emphasize that Sh. K. did not find listening ears among the leaders and committee members of Tarbut.

[Page 229]

They listened with understanding and recognition, but they were unable to offer their help with technical and material items needed. They even admitted to this on their own… They had many excuses such as financial deficit and pushed him away. They told him to come back. The vice mayor, Moshe Perl, (who was not yet the chairman of Tarbut), was the only one to do his utmost for the good of Habimah. He arranged for official permission from the administration.

Overcoming difficulties and the first trial

Sh. K. was not one to be stopped by the difficulties and barriers on the way. He did not retire to his corner. Sh. K. decided to found Habimah on his own, no matter what.

Sh. K. found actors among the youth, graduates of the Hebrew high school, the pioneering young people and teachers. These people were inexperienced amateurs and thus, Sh. K. chose literary classic Yiddish fragments, mostly from Peretz. He edited them and adjusted them according to the abilities of his actors. The first performance was entitled "Decree from Heaven". At the last moment, Tarbut removed its sponsorship and Sh. K. was forced to cancel the already printed announcements. He had to find other ways to accomplish his plan. It was on Erev Pessach of 1928 which was close to the twelfth yahrzeit of the death of Peretz. Sh. K. decided to use the opportunity and call his presentation "A Peretz Evening". It was easy to receive a permit from the authorities. Sh. K. then was obliged to change the content of the presentation. He included the accepted characters of Peretz: the prophet, pharisaic, etc. They were given special treatment and individual attention by the actors. Sh. K. himself was a generous social leader as a member of the educational committee of the Orphanage, he obtained a permit in its name. The Tarbut committee had revoked its sponsorship by being indifferent and narrow–minded.

Preparations were made and new publicity was done. Invitations were sent. On 8.4.28, second day of Hol HaMoed Pessach, there was a horde of unexpected guests. The hall of Talmud Torah, 3 Listopdova Street, was completely full.

Sh. K. intended, with this first presentation, to show an original Jewish way that he wanted to give Habimah. It was different from other amateur groups. He wanted an innovation.

[Page 230]

Truth be told that with this excellent, talented presentation which integrated movement, music and lighting effects, Sh. K. totally surprised the audience. They, in turn, applauded and showed their appreciation. The trial was successful and the victory was complete.

Masada

Sh. K. was flush with success and encouragement and he decided to enlarge the Habimah Studio. For its premier production "Masada" was chosen. Many of those among the Tarbut leaders who were previously hesitant or indifferent, changed their negative attitude to the dream of the Habimah in Hebrew. New forces joined the effort. Sh. K.'s new right hand was the talented young artist A. Reiner. He, too, had the dream of Hebrew art and theatre that were to be part of the cultural life in town. He found an opportunity to devote himself to this dream and to find undiscovered talents. In addition, the music teacher Feinstein and the pianist Luba Avrech also joined the Habimah Studio. They contributed from a musical point of view. The talented dancer, graduate of the orphanage, Sarka Tchizshik (Harpia) brought the wonders of original artistic dance movements.

The second presentation was the then actual poem "Masada" by Yitzhak Lamdan. However, in order to write a complete script, Sh. K. needed special preparation. The young actors were inexperienced on stage and required special attention– individually and as a cast. The material in Masada had to be rewritten as a play in the spirit of Habimah. It was essential to have appropriate, moveable scenery for every act. Hassidic tunes were integrated into songs and music from Eretz Israel. Choreography was created. Every detail had to be done cooperatively to have an artistic, excellent presentation. This task, undertaken by Sh. K. himself, took a long time. It was only at the end of 1930 that the play was presented. Everything was ready. Only approval of Tarbut was missing. Again, Sh. K. turned to the

Tarbut committee and again he was met with apathy and hesitation– lack of funds and vision. Again, Sh. K. needed the help of the Orphanage. He was given the necessary technical help, a place for rehearsals and its talented graduates to participate.

[Page 231]

Epilogue from "Masada" by Lamdan

On 20.3.31, the theatre hall of Kino–Meisky (Express) was not only completely filled, but a new phenomenon could be seen. Hundreds of people who were unable to obtain tickets pushed the front doors of the theatre to such an extent that the Polish police was called upon to restore order… There were also representatives of the Polish intelligentsia (invited by Moshe Perl) and members of the city authorities. The presentation was quite successful and left a deep impression on the varied and large audience. There was a review by a critic in the local paper. He was a member of the Yiddish intelligentsia– distant from Hebrew culture– and was considered to be anti–Zionist.

Here are the words published in the Voice of Kovel (Emet–Stanlik): "In other nations, those who live normal political and cultural lives, this play would be a great holiday. It would be an energetic holiday and an artistic achievement". "We saw, in front of us, a fortress of culture, knowledge and culture. We saw "Masada"! In this play was felt, quite prominently, the theatrical importance of beloved, enthusiastic and heroic Masada. This is a real fortress in the cultural life in our midst!"

[Page 232]

Here is an opinion, in the same edition, by a representative of the Hebrew teachers and a member of Tarbut– I. Kobrinsky:

"The play by the amateur group Habimah was an encouraging phenomenon in our poor cultural life. This exceptional presentation was a triumph of stubbornness of one person– Shalom Klonitsky. For many years, he had the dream of establishing an artistic Hebrew theatre." "Over the years, those near and far, clipped his wings. However, his hopes were stronger than the doubters! On the evening of the performance of Masada, his dream was fulfilled". "Immediately, at the start of the play, it was obvious that it was prepared with great understanding and talent. The sets were artistic and were most suitable to the content. It can be said that such scenery is not seen in other amateur productions". "We cannot stop ourselves from commenting here on the "hidden talent"– the young artist Reiner. A great part of the success of the play belongs to him". "The audience thoroughly enjoyed themselves. The core of every dramatic presentation– integration of various artistic ventures as one whole entity– was perfectly executed. The acting, dancing (Harpia), music (excellent, by L. Avrech), the scenery!". "The audience applauded shouting Wonderful! Excellent!". Hurray– Klonitsky! The Habimah party was a true Hebrew celebration!"

The people of Kovel begged for additional performances and Masada was presented again a month later, on 5.4.31, during Hol HaMoed Pessach. There were some technical innovations and this performance was even more successful than the first one

Development of Habimah–Studio and its continuation

After the presentation of Masada, Habimah studio became a permanent fixture. Top leaders of Tarbut, mainly Moshe Perl, began to seek a permit from the authorities. There was sound financial backing and the studio was a legal, independent entity within Tarbut. A permit was finally obtained, with the help of the well–known community leader, editor of News of Kovel– Yaakov Borak. It became a separate group.

The name Habimah was chosen by Sh. K. to ease the request from the authorities. In those days, the Polish government was suspicious of any cultural amateur groups. They thought it was a screen for revolutionary ideas. However, the name Habimah was well–known to the authorities as a Hebrew theatre. The word "Studio" was added to differentiate it from the original Habimah in Eretz Israel.

Soon Habimah became famous in the area and in nearby towns.

[Page 233]

Sara Tchizshik (Harpia) in the role of the bereaved in "Anthemia" by Andreyev

There were requests from Rovno, Lutsk and Ludomir for the group to perform in their towns. However, this did not take place. Habimah Studio could not undertake the financial responsibility for such ventures. The Tarbut center in Rovno did not appreciate the value of this cultural presentation by Habimah and it did not help them to achieve this trip.

[Page 234]

Anthemia

After Masada, Habimah studio prepared a third play– Anthemia by Leonid Andreyev. As in previous plays and for other technical reasons such as: slowness of the translation by the author I. P. Tsitronel from Ludomir, it took a long time, over a year, between Masada and Anthemia.

The presentation of Anthemia on 18.5.32 at the Kino Meisky, was very successful. There were 40 members of the cast. The dream of Hebrew theater in Kovel was achieved. Habimah Studio became entrenched as part of the Hebrew cultural life in Kovel and surrounding areas. Every performance became a celebration in town. Habimah studio allowed itself to perform not only on Sabbath nights, but on week days as well. These presentations, too, became celebrations.

Habimah Studio was blooming and growing. Plans were being made for a fourth play - "Shabtai Zvi" and perhaps others. However, the reality of living in the diaspora– temporary and uncertain– changed these plans. The theater hall became a fallen Succah of David… The pioneering youth had been the mainstay of the theater group. Now they were all planning to make Aliyah and were preparing themselves.

Klonitsky himself received a certificate for Aliyah in 1934. Most of the pioneers made Aliyah and Klonitsky joined them. When Sh. K. left the shining existence of Habimah in the cultural life of Kovel disappeared. No one undertook to continue the effort.

The Mission of the Habimah Studio in Kovel and its Goal

by S. Kalonimus

Translated by Ala Gamulka

The Habimah Studio in Kovel, in its short 3 years, managed to draw a crowd of admirers that was interested and followed with love and friendship its blooming and growth.

The attitude of the leaders of Tarbut changed completely after Masada and Anthemia were presented. At first, these leaders had the attitude of "let the children play". There was criticism, demands and requests, but they were all done upon reflection and for the good of the studio. Everyone had his own opinion. Now, after the summer holidays, as I am going back to work, I wish to analyse these demands and to understand the purpose and ways of Habimah.

Firstly, we must note that the studio is nationalistic–Hebrew. Let us not fool ourselves in thinking that the studio only presents plays for the dissemination of the language itself. In the plays there is propaganda for the language, but that is not its only goal.

[Page 235]

The mission of Habimah is to show the Hebrew crowd nationalistic artistry. There are plays which reflect the life of the Jewish nation in different eras. The life of individuals and that of the community are shown with all their ups and downs, hopes and yearnings. It is essential to throw a light on the differences between young and old generations and to touch upon all the problems in our world. It is to be done in an artistic–theatrical method.

There is no rule telling us that we must look for material for our repertoire only in the original Hebrew, as some would demand. Not everything written in Hebrew can be performed on stage, even if written by a Jew. For example, the play "Shabtai Zvi", by Zholovsky, was superior to anything written by our own authors. He, the Pole, was able to remove the mystic curtain engulfing this tragic hero. He discovered for us the highs and lows of his soul. This material is perfect for a play, especially in Hebrew! There are many dramas written in Hebrew or Yiddish which deal with proper Jewish heroes, but they are only an imitation.

There are well–known dramas of I. Gordon who wished to bring the beauty of Japhet in the tents of Shem. It was a poor imitation because it was against artistic laws. Art is international, but the form was national. Difficulties common to many peoples are shown in a different way within every nation. This is why we must have only these plays that are close to our hearts and that discuss problems of our world. This is why the Hebrew studio must present plays which deal with universal issues, even if they come from the outside.

For example, a non–Jew will look at the Jewish Shylock in a different way than a would a Jew. The difference is great and it has value for us. It is possible to use material from other languages as long as the issues are meaningful for us. A good example is Anthemia by Andreyev. It is a Russian work that was written when the folk was persecuted by the Tsar. It is a cry against the heavy load that the enslaved Russian people are carrying. In spite of the fact that the main protagonist in this drama is a Jew called David, it is the deep sorrow of the people that is emphasised. The Habimah Studio, when it presented Anthemia, used the material to show the pain and suffering of the Jews in the Diaspora with David as our Job.

[Page 236]

It also shows the minimal value of man in front of the forces of nature.

In general, the studio must follow the teaching of Rabbi Meir: "I found a pomegranate which I ate, but I threw away its peel". When it comes to the way the play is presented on stage by Habimah, symbolically and mystically, there is no rule. Even if the play was mystic and symbolic, it does not mean that Habimah is only to put on such plays.

The directors of Habimah considers the human content and the condition it is in at present. Material conditions are not always convenient.

Those who think that the goal of Habimah is to amuse those who are bored at home and that the repertoire must be funny comedies, songs and dances are mistaken.

Habimah is an artistic venture and its goal is to elevate the audience and not to bring it down. The size of the audience is not important, but its quality is. If there are any complaints. There should only be from Habimah to the Hebrew intelligentsia, the teachers and principals who sit without lifting a finger. Their indifference is a sin and a crime. Help us create the right atmosphere and then Habimah will become an important cultural– artistic entity that is highly valued in our town.

It is acceptable to criticize a seedling that is trying to grow, but there must be a willingness to collaborate.

(From the yearbook of the Union of Jewish Academicians in Kovel, September 1932, year 2, no. 2)

[Page 239]

Torah and Hasidism

Images of Torah Scholars

(Personalities chosen from among those praying at the Kommertchesky synagogue)

by Yekhezkel Goldberg

Translated by Ala Gamulka

The Scholar, Rabbi Eliezer Nitzberg, z" l

Rabbi Nitzberg, z" l, was the lion among those praying at the synagogue. He was the town rabbi and a great scholar. He was well-versed in Talmud and its interpretations. He always continued learning. When he stood at the lectern, he either read a religious book or he created new interpretations of the Torah. Every evening he used to come for prayers at the synagogue. In spite of the fact that the place was well-lit, he still used a candle.

Rabbi Nitzberg, z" l, wrote the book "Yad Eliezer" (the hand of Eliezer), published in Warsaw in 1931. It included explanations of the Shulchan Aruch. He also wrote "Divrei Eliezer" (the words of Eliezer), published in Vilna in 1911. These were new interpretations of the Shulchan Aruch. Another book by him was "Demeshek Eliezer" (from Eliezer's home) which was of high quality and full of wisdom.

[Page 250]

In the forward to Yad Eliezer, the scholar writes: "I will mention the good deeds of God and I will praise his goodness. I was fortunate, through his goodness, to be in this place of Torah to this day. I was able to bring new interpretations to the Torah. Our sages said: God has only four corners of Halacha. I am grateful for my part in it. I am fortunate to be in this house of learning and I hope to continue to do so as long as I am alive. The Maharsha said: fortunate is the person who came here holding a Talmud. Scholars were also called writers. I am now publishing Yad Eliezer. This is the second part and I expect that everyone who reads my book will find something useful in it. It is especially pertinent to those who teach.

Now I wish to thank God, with all my heart, that he has kept me going to this day. I pray that my writing will be well-received among the scholars. I thank him for the past success and I pray for the future. Please, God, continue to help me as you have in the past. Keep me strong so I can learn and teach and interpret the Torah. May you give me more years to continue my work so I can publish again. May he continue to lead me and not allow me to fail. We should all be lucky enough to continue to worship God and to follow the teaching of the Torah. May God always be part of our being and may we continue to do good deeds. This is also a wish for our descendants. Amen. So be it".

Rabbi Nitzberg, z" l, died in 1935. In "Moment" of 30 January 1935 the following obituary appeared: "After much suffering, the rabbi of the congregation, Rabbi Eliezer Nitzberg, z" l, died. He was well-known in the Torah world by his publications- Demeshek Eliezer. He was born in Prozhny in 1849. At the age of 35 he wrote his first book -Demeshek Eliezer. The book was well-received among scholars. Divrei Eliezer and Torat Eliezer followed.

These books brought him to a high level of authority in the educational world. In 1911 he came to Kovel to serve as the town rabbi. He was liked and appreciated by the residents.

Rabbi Nitzberg was 86 when he died. All Jewish houses of commerce closed for his funeral. All the Jews participated. There were also rabbis from surrounding areas.

[Page 241]

Rabbi Yehuda Reider, z" l

Rabbi Yehuda was a prominent scholar, well-versed in the Mishna. He was tall and had been a businessman in earlier times. When he aged, he left his daily work and devoted himself, day and night, to studying in the house of learning. He was constantly involved in studying Torah. He recognized those who studied like him and he befriended those interested in doing so. He became a father to the youth who were sitting and studying in the house of learning. He used to say to them: study, my dear ones, with love. The Torah is a source of consolation in old age. Look and see: if the gates of the Talmud were closed to me- how would I spend the rest of my life?

On winter nights Rabbi Yehuda used to leave the house of learning at six o'clock and would return there at midnight. He continued studying until daybreak. None of this made him arrogant. He treated every person with respect and so he was well-liked and accepted by everyone.

Rabbi Pinhas (Hacohen)Weinfeld, z" l

The townspeople gave him a nickname. They called him Rabbi Pinhas Hotzels. He had vast and varied knowledge. He knew secular literature as well as he knew holy books. He had a keen mind and was highly cultured. He was well-versed in modern Hebrew literature, but he was also a solid mathematician. He was known in town as an experience bookkeeper.

He had a restless mind and was always searching and questioning. As soon as he put on his tallit, he would go to the book case to look at various books. He was an expert on Ibn-Ezra. It is well-known to all those who have read Ibn Ezra that there are some unclear and secret passages. Rabbi Pinhas could solve these issues due to the depth of his knowledge. In spite of his brilliance in all matters of Torah and his deep knowledge of Mishna, he was still a simple man.

Rabbi Yosef Shapira, z" l

Rabbi Yosef was a short, skinny man. He looked like a ordinary man, but he was one of the Torah greats. This small body contained amazing fountains of Torah. He was one of the greatest scholars in town. He was a stickler for accuracy in Talmud and especially in Rashi. He lived on income from his students. Some of his pupils were Yossel Shochet, son of Rabbi Velvel, z" l and the author of this article. He was an excellent pedagogue. He knew how to present complicated questions and bring them down to the student's level.

[Page 242]

He would explain the material in a simple and easy to understand language. Thus, no doubt remained and the complicated became easy. When his answers were similar to those of the previous interpreters, we suspected him of ignoring a specific sentence: "One who brings an item in the name of the one who said it- brings redemption to the world". Rabbi Yosef would say: when a person goes along a straight path and does not deviate, he meets other people… This laconic answer showed a view of the world that truth belongs to everyone. Anyone seeking it with a full heart will reach it in his own way.

Rabbi Zeev (Vevetzi) Erlich, z"l

Rabbi Nachman of Breslev said in a different place: "Everyone says there is this world and the next world. We believe there is a world to come. It is possible there is also this world in some universe. It may be hell. Everyone is always suffering. Perhaps there is no world of now, at all". These words can be said about Rabbi Vevetzi, z" l. He did not know what this world was because he was always deeply involved in the world of divine emanation, the heavenly world. He was one the most enthusiastic followers of the Rabbi from Boyne, a descendant of the Rabbi of Rizhin. He knew all of Mishna by heart. As dawn would rise, he hurried to the synagogue to begin his memorizing of various parts of the Mishna. He earned his livelihood as a tax collector for the hospital and later he worked in the Home for the Aged.

Rabbi Shmulik, z"l

Rabbi Shmulik was one of the first readers of Tzfira in town. As a veteran reader, he received as a prize, History of the Jews by Gratz in a Hebrew translation. He knew several languages and did much charitable work. He collected funds for the needy and always welcomed guests to his home. The poor knew he had a good heart and would come to his home early in the morning. They knew he would not send away a hungry person. He would arrange meals for the poor in different homes in town. If someone remained without a placement, he would take them to his own home. When there were several poor people who were not invited by anyone, Rabbi Shmulik would lock the doors f the synagogue. He would not allow anyone to leave until everyone was placed.

There were some poor people who were embarrassed to eat at a stranger's home. Rabbi Shmulik brought them to the restaurant owned by Schwartzblat and the wealthier residents paid for their meals. When the Association for Help for the Needy was founded- Beit Lechem- Rabbi Shmulik, Baruch-Hirsh Gelman and Avrech, z" l, were its leaders.

Rabbi Shmulik earned his living by teaching in various private homes.

[Page 243]

Havatzelet Heder
From right to left: Seated are the teachers: Aryeh Veverik, Shmuel Goldberg, Noah Steinberg

In these homes he also received funds to distribute among the needy. Rabbi Shmulik always spoke of the generosity of Mrs. Roza Gasco.

Although he was busy with teaching until late in the evening, he always immersed himself in the needs of the people. He invested much effort in deepening religious education. He was the first to establish a Heder called Havatzelet, with a permit from the inspector. In this Heder were taught religious subjects, Hebrew and Polish. Anyone who completed studies in this Heder was accepted into the third level of the high school. He himself taught religious subjects; Bible was taught by a Cantor from Matseyev; math- Gershon Yagodnik; Polish and geography- Leibish Veverik.

[Page 244]

From the Way of Life

Friday nights

On Friday nights, after the meal, people would go to the house of learning to study "Orach Haim" (Way of life) – an interpretation of the Torah. It was snowing outside and the cold was unbearable. Jews sat in the house of learning and enjoyed themselves by studying. Among those who participated were: Moshe Shochet, Yitzhak Verba, Elyhau Verba, Pinhas Berg, Shmuel Goldberg, Leibel Shinkar and Baruch-Hirsh Gelman, z" l. They would study until midnight. Their saying was: The weekly portions of the winter are covered in furs". When they finished a portion, they would yell three times: "they will rejoice" with great happiness and they went home with the holiness of the Sabbath shining on their faces.

The Psalm Reciters

In the house of learning there was a group of Psalm Reciters. It was headed by Akiva Turskevitch and Zev Contract, z" l. These were hard-working men who after a long week would meet early on Shabbat morning to recite Psalms together. Afterwards, Rabbi Moshe Yagodnik, z" l, would study the weekly portion with them. It was their only spiritual experience. Some of them progressed in their studies and could learn the weekly portion by themselves using different interpreters.

Third Meal

The Third Meal was served on two separate tables. Those who studied sat at one table, while the second table was occupied by ordinary working men. The actual food was supplied by Rabbi Yitzhak Verba, z" l. He would prepare a plaited challah (out of 12 braids – for the 12 tribes). There were also small challahs, slices of fish. There was enough food for 30-40 people. However, the spiritual food was special. Firstly, the chants, from the depth of their hearts- Yedid Nefesh, Bni Heikhalsa Dkhasifin, Ra'ava D'ra'ava, Al mistater b'shafrir khevyon- all sung with warmth and happiness. Afterwards one of those assembled would tell a Hassidic fable about one of the great righteous people. He would whisper and everyone paid attention, their mouths gaping, to every word said. It was twilight, but no candles were lit. There was utter silence in the house of learning. It was so quiet that the buzzing of the flies could be heard. The story teller continued so as to lengthen Shabbat and rest time. It is well-known that hell rests on Shabbat and the souls of the dead have a respite from their pains.

[Page 245]

If someone tried to hurry up the Third Meal so the evening prayers could be done, he would be told: "Let your father rest in the Garden of Eden". They would do Grace after the meal and then the evening prayers. This was followed by Havdalah to show the end of the holy day and the return to regular week. Faces of people changed and their clothes were different. It was now necessary to wait another week.

The table of the ordinary working men was long and there were dozens of Jews along it. These were hard-working people, all week, who needed to earn a living for themselves and their families. However, when they sat at this table, their backs were straightened, their frowns disappeared. Their faces were lighter and they looked like royalty. They all sang the Shabbat chants with excitement and enthusiasm. Rabbi Moshe Yagodnik, z" l, would speak to them and they listened to his words with baited breath. This was their spiritual food for the rest of the grey, difficult week. In contrast to the students, these people hurried to the end of the meal, blessed quickly, prayed the evening prayers. They now remembered their heavy load of earning a living and providing for their families. The beauty of Shabbat left them and their faces darkened anew.

The praying group in the Rizhiner Shtiebel

[Page 246]

The Center for Torah Study Named for Shlomo Projenski, z"l

by Rabbi Shmuel-Yosef Werba

Translated by Ala Gamulka

This Center for Torah Study was one of the oldest in town. Even in 1910 I found it to be ancient. Forty-five years ago I was elected Gabbai of this synagogue and I initiated the construction of a second floor on this old house. It now looked more modern.

The town rabbi in those days was the scholar, Rabbi Moshe Zackheim, z" l from Pinsk. Rabbi Moshele Zackheim was a gifted man, one of the greatest scholars of his generation.

Part of his job description was to pray in the great synagogue, but, from time to time, he would come to us. He loved our Center for Torah study and its occupants.

One time, Rabbi Zackheim, z" L, approached me and Piny, son of Shlomo Projenski, with a special request: he asked us to invite a scribe to write, on parchment, Prophets and the third part of the Bible. The purpose was to be able to read the Haftara of the weekly portion from the parchment. As a rule, only the five books of the Torah are written on parchment.

We satisfied the Rabbi's request and we invited Yudel the Scribe to do it. He inscribed the two sections on parchment.

When this holy work was finished, we invited, on Shabbat, Rabbi Zackheim and we honored him by asking him to chant the Haftara.

I recall many Shabbat and Holy days in the synagogue. In front of my eyes jumps an image of celebrating Simchat Beit Hashoeva (procession to and from the well). The members would celebrate it with great splendor. In our town, there was an observant Jew, a craftsman, called Motel Toker. Since I was the Gabbai of the synagogue I invited him to come. He brought 50 bottles of liquor which he pored into a large vat and boiled it in honey. Before the Hakafot (circling with the Torah), all the members would assemble in my house and drink this special drink. Motel Toker prepared it with great expertise. Afterwards, the Gabbai would be ushered into the synagogue with song and dance. We invited the other rabbis in town for the Hakafot.

There was a special fund for assisting the poor in the synagogue. Among the members there was one man called Yeshayah-Leib. When he was younger, he used to supervise the paving of the roads. He had a daughter ready for marriage, but he was a poor man and could not give her a dowry.

One winter day when I was walking to town, I entered the synagogue and I found Yeshayah-Leib sitting behind the oven and reciting Psalms. "How many times did you recite Psalms today?"- I asked. The man did not reply, but he began sobbing. "Why should I tell you my bitter story. You cannot help me. My daughter is already thirty years old. I found a decent groom for her and I promised him 300 Rubles as a dowry.

[Page 247]

Now the man came to me and threatened that if I do not immediately give him the money, he will cancel the engagement. Where do I go? I do not have even enough money to serve the groom a decent meal".

I calmed down Yeshayah-Leib and I told him: "Go home and tell your wife to prepare a sumptuous meal. Invite the groom and tonight you will write the betrothal document". Yeshayah-Leib looked at me wondering what I was talking about. However, he did as he was told, put on his coat and went home.

I went to Kovka Bokser. When he looked at my face, he saw immediately what I wanted. He said to me: "Why are you here? You scoundrel." I told him: "Lend me 100 rubels for six months". He hesitated at first, but his daughter-in-law Tsiupa Bokser told him: "If you refuse to lend 100 Rubels, give, at least 50 in cash". From there I went to Shlomo Klorglon and there I received 100 Rubels. Next to me were two other men who helped me. We gave the money to Velvel Tsoref. He invested it in the stock market and in the evening, he brought me 400 Rubels, not just 300.

We came to the synagogue and we sent the sexton to bring us 8 bottles of liquor and cakes. We invited the rabbi and we all went to the house of Yeshayah-Leib. We wished him Mazal Tov and we arranged the betrothal document as required. Yeshayah-Leib gave the groom the dowry and he even had 100 additional Rubels to pay for the wedding.

There is one member in our synagogue that I wish to discuss. His name is associated with a special project. He is the one who built the orphanage in town with his own money. I am speaking of the lawyer, Yaakov Appelbaum, z" l. Before I describe the construction, I must mention, from a cloudy memory, the "rebellion" that the members of the synagogue conducted against lawyer Appelbaum. This is how it happened: our synagogue was named (among us) for Shlomo Projenski, but for the authorities it was called Kupechesky Synagogue. The opening of the synagogue required a special permit and, as a lawyer, Appelbaum undertook the permit in his own name. He was the actual owner of the synagogue.

We rebelled against this ownership and we decided to call for a general meeting of all the members. We hoped to be able to approach the authorities for a change of name.

I still have the minutes of this meeting and I quote:

[Page 248]

Minutes of the general meeting of the members of the Kupechesky synagogue named after Avraham-Shlomo- Projenski, z" l held on Hoshana Raba, 1928.

Agenda:

The transfer of the synagogue and all it owns to the members.
Decisions:
After many arguments and explanations, it was decided:

    a. To choose a special committee, with official powers, to conduct discussions with the members who, until now, had private rights in the synagogue. Their rights were about administration and religious matters. The committee will deal with matters within the community, but, if unsuccessful, will turn to the authorities.
    b. The following members were elected to the committee: Rabbi Shlomo Klorglon, Rabbi Shmuel Yossel Werba, Rabbi Yekutiel Weitz, Rabbi Avraham Woff, Rabbi Zvi Bokser, Rabbi Israel Reichstol, Rabbi Yosef Milstein and Rabbi Kofky Bokser.

The rebellion was successful and as of 1928 the Center for Torah Studies was owned by its members.

Lawyer Appelbaum had a daughter in Trisk and she used to visit from time to time. Once I joined her from Trisk. On the way I said to her: "There are many orphans in Kovel. They grow up uneducated and there is no one who takes them in to their homes. Your father has been blessed and he should build, with his own money, an orphanage in Kovel ". He had not reacted to my words, but his daughter, Masha, liked the idea.

On Shabbat we presented Appelbaum with the facts. During the reading of the Torah I asked the cantor to recite a special prayer for Appelbaum because he had decided to build the orphanage. Indeed, Appelbaum built a beautiful orphanage – at a great cost. On Shabbat and Holy days, he would eat with the orphans. He invited two of them to live in his house and they were apprenticed to tailors.

His daughter also helped with the orphans. She used to bring them to the synagogue at Yizkor (Memorial) time so they could pray for the souls of their parents.

[Page 249]

The Great Synagogue, Its Cantors and Poets

by Yitzhak Waldman

Translated by Ala Gamulka

The Great Synagogue was well-built. It was a place where all the members would assemble to hear the singing and the praying.

The Great Synagogue was like a mother that protects its young in regards to the many small centers of learning around it. The latter admired this special place of Jewish spirit.

I was formed in the Rizhiner center for Torah studies. I spent many days and nights there. I listened to amazing tunes and to great stories about special sainted people.

I remember well the Melaveh Malka on Saturday nights. There was so much awe and beauty at those times. We used to assemble after Havdalah and sit and speak of the righteous people, of the Rabbi of Rizhin, of the Tzadik from Sadigura. We would sing Hassidic tunes with great devoutness.

[Page 250]

This is how the members enjoyed a world that was all good, a world of gentility and beauty- until midnight.

There was a difference between the Rizhiner center for Torah studies and the Great Synagogue. I found out that the Great Synagogue was built by famous artisans who were brought in especially from Odessa and other locations in Russia. The elegant Ark! No one had ever seen one like it in any other centers for Torah studies in the area. The Ark shone with its white brightness and the gilt on it was outstanding. A special aura was observed on the Bima (lectern) which stood in the middle. The cantor with his choir would stand on it and their voices penetrated everywhere.

The Jews of Kovel truly loved the Great Synagogue. Old and young, men and women, came in droves to enjoy the wonderful tunes. It became crowded especially when Cantor Arahle Feintuch and his choir were leading the prayers. His music was beloved by the members and they would sing with him.

Arahle Feintuch followed compositions by Nissan Belzer and Zeidel Rovner. These were exceptional tunes in the Jewish musical world. Many of his singers settled in town and participated in the choir.

The choir of the Great Synagogue

I do not know the reason Arahle Feintuch did not last long in the Great Synagogue and left town.

Arahle Feintuch was liked by the members not only for his music, but also because of his soloist, the wonderful baritone, Leib Glambotsky. Who among us does not remember Glambotsky? It was an unforgettable experience to listen to his amazing voice. He energized all of us and touched our souls. However, the expression: "All who are beloved by the Gods die Young" was true for him. He died young after a difficult illness.

After Arahle Feintuch's departure a cantor came from Budapest- Teichtel. He had a pleasant lyrical voice and the leaders of the synagogue tried to convince him to stay.

Cantor Teichtel arrived in town close to the High Holidays and he immediately began to search for young boys to audition. He soon organized a magnificent choir. He also turned to Herzliah High School and Mr. Feinstein, z"l, recommended several boys with good voices.

Rehearsals took place in a small side room. The leaders of the synagogue, Asher Schwartz, Yosef Tsal and Yossel Krasnolsky would appear there every evening.

The choir performed on the Shabbat before the new month. Cantor Teichtel composed great tunes.

[Page 251]

He also conducted the choir. He recognized me as a soloist and honored me with the singing of "Kvodo Male Olam". The crowd enjoyed my singing. I continued with other solo performances.

Cantor Teichtel, too, did not last long in the Great Synagogue. We were left again without a cantor.

We then began using our own people. Among the members of the choir there were several with beautiful voices who also had a musical education. Among those who stood out is Meir Diner, a dramatic tenor. He tried to replace the cantor and continued to sing with the choir. It was now conducted by Yosef Khalat, the famous baritone. Khalat had difficulty following in the footsteps of Arahle Feintuch, but he had learned much from him. Khalat continued in the tradition of Arahle. He had been truly popular among the members.

Khalat was brought to Kovel, when he was still a young child by, Cantor Arahle. He grew up there and his talents were nurtured. He was employed as a secretary to Rabbi Brik and later to Rabbi Nahum-Moshele, z" l. Khalat had dramatic talents and he was one of the founders of the theatre in Kovel. He was one of its best actors. When he appeared on stage the crowd would hail him. He was beloved by the audiences. Many of us surely remember his role as Hotzmach in "The Witch" by Goldfaden.

Khalat was quite successful and was fortunate to find a talented partner, the writer Ahertchik Melamed, z" l. The latter helped in conducting.

Ahertchik knew solfege and played several instruments. He also could write musical notes. He composed, from memory, the notes to the tunes of Arahle Feintuch. It felt like the original.

Among the choir singers also stood out baritone Ephraim Vidra and lyrical tenor Murik. Among the outstanding young boys were Gershon Yagodnik, Moshe Kharat, Yekhezkel Seltzer. Some people would say that, I, too, was one of them.

The choir acquired a reputation in the surrounding towns. It performed, on Shabbat, in Ludomir, Lutsk and Rovno. It appeared with Cantor Zingerman, a dramatic tenor. He had a strong voice and he used the tunes and compositions of Lewandowsky, Sulzer and other modern composers.

For the first time, we performed with Cantor Zingerman in Rovno on the High Holidays. The choir was housed in a hotel for a whole month. The conductor was Yosef Khalat and the choir achieved great success.

[Page 252]

When the choir returned to Kovel, after the High Holidays, we found out that the Polish government had informed Zingerman that, as a Russian citizen, he would have to leave Rovno.

The leaders of the Great Synagogue approached the authorities to allow Zingerman to settle in Kovel. Their request was received in a positive manner and Zingerman was hired as the cantor of the synagogue. He was quite successful in many special prayers and his followers were enthusiastic about him.

Zingerman, too, did not stay in Kovel. He moved to the United States. The members could not accept the "empty space" and used to bring, from time to time, cantors for auditions. One of them was Tzipris who conquered the crowd with his Hassidic melodies.

He was followed by Wexler who brought a large choir from Lublin. Among this group was the bass Mendel Hoff. He reminded us of the baritone Leib Glambotsky who was missed by the members.

Cantor Wexler invited Ahertchik Melamed to conduct the Lublin choir. That is how we discovered Ahertchik. He had talents as a conductor, composer and excellent organizer of the choir of the Great Synagogue.

The Elder of Neskhiz and His Descendants

by Eliezer Leoni

Donated by David Kimmel

Note: The Elder of Neskhiz was R. Mordekhai Shpira (Shapiro), 1748-1800, son of R. Dov Ber of Tultchin. His thoughts on the Torah, festivals, and many topics about day-to-day life are collected in **Rishpei Aish** ("Sparks of Fire"). The Neskhiz Dynasty survived into the twentieth century and included rabbis named Shapiro, Katzenellenbogen, Perlov, and Padova.
The Elder of Neskhiz – or, as he was called by his hasidim, the Moharam (an acronym for *moreinu verabbeinu harav rav Mordekhai*, "Our Teacher and Rabbi, Rabbi Mordekhai") – is associated with one of the miracle stories of the city [of Kovel].

Before he left Kovel [for Neskhiz], the legend tells, the Elder of Neskhiz blessed it so that it would not be subject to fires and would remain safe from adversity and disasters. And indeed, "as the *tzadik* decreed, so did the Holy One, blessed be He, fulfill it." Until the destruction of the city by the Nazis, it suffered less than did other cities. During the First World War, although rioters attacked the Jews in the area, they did not come to Kovel. The Jews of the city saw in this the ongoing [influence of the] blessing of the *tzadik*.

However, for reasons hidden and concealed from our understanding, the Side of Evil gained in strength. In the upper worlds, the blessing of the Elder was no longer honored and the city was destroyed.

The city was characterized by the Torah and hasidism of the dynasty of Trisk, which began with the Elder of Neskhiz. The first rabbi of Trisk dynasty to settle in the city [of Kovel] was Rabbi Yaakov Leibnyu, son of the great [R. Avraham,] Magid of Trisk [and] author of *Magen Avraham*. The Magid of Trisk's father-in-law was Rabbi Yaakov Leibnyu, son of the Moharam. The Magid named his son Yaakov Leibnyu after his father-in-law.

[Page 253]

As we said, the genesis of the dynastic line of Rabbi Yaakov Leibnyu began with the Moharam, who was the Chief Rabbi of Kovel in the second half of the eighteenth century, and who would sign [documents with the expression], "the insignificant Mordekhai who dwells in the holy community of Kavle [Kovel]."

The Moharam was born in 5508 (1748) and was a contemporary of Rabbi Nakhum of Chernobil, who was the grandfather of the Magid of Trisk.

Rabbi Mordekhai, [the Moharam,] was a grandson of Rabbi Isaiah of Kroke (Krakow), who served as judge (*av beis din*) of Kovel. Beyond that, the family tree of the Moharam reached back to the prince Abarbanel. And it is known that Abarbanel's family line reached back to King David.

When he was in Kovel, the Moharam lived in great poverty. Hasidic legend tells that his wife, Reiza, was urged by her family to gain a divorce from her husband, because he was so involved in serving the Creator that he did not apply himself to supporting his family.

Once in the winter, as the Moharam was learning at night in their cold room, the rebbetzin sat in her bed amongst the pillows and blankets because of the cold, doing her work, when she suddenly she saw sparks of fire appear on [the Moharam's] forehead. A great awe fell upon the rebbetzin and she realized that this was a sign from heaven [telling her] not to complain against her fate.

The Torah genius, the Moharam, had three sons.

The oldest was the brilliant Rabbi Yosef of Ustila, who was judge in Hrubieszow and Ustila.

His second son was the brilliant Rabbi Yaakov Aryeh (Leibnyu), who was called "the rabbi of Kovli [Kovel]." His hasidim called him "the holy genius, the heavenly lion, our master and rabbi, Rabbi Leibel of Kovli [Kovel]." Yaakov Aryeh was the grandfather of Yaakov Leibnyu, son of the Magid of Trisk, [as mentioned above].

Rabbi Yaakov Aryeh, "the rabbi of Kovli [Kovel]," had two sons and two daughters.

One son was Rabbi Israel of Stabichov and the other was Rabbi Levi Yitzkhak of Kamin.

One daughter, Gitele, was the wife of Rabbi Menakhem Manish Margolios, son of the brilliant Rabbi Khaim Mordekhai Margolios, author of *Shaarei Teshuvah*.

The other [daughter,] Rikele, was the wife of the great Magid of Trisk, Rabbi Avraham, author of *Magen Avraham*.

The Magid of Trisk was the son of Rabbi Mordekhai of Chernobil, who [in turn was the] son of Rabbi Nakhum of Chernobil.

The Magid [of Trisk] was born in 5566 (1806) and passed away on 2 Tammuz 5649 (1889).

Legend tells again that [family members] wished to separate the couple, the Magid of Trisk and his wife Rikele, the daughter of the *tzadik* of Kovel. When Rabbi Mordekhai of Chernobil, [the father of the Magid of Trisk,] learned about this, he said, "Is it possible to separate those who cling to each other – which is to say, me and my in-law, the rabbi of Kovel, [R. Yaakov Aryeh Leibnyu], there being between us a very strong love, so that the days of the lives of both of us depend upon this?"

Indeed, both *tzadikim* passed away in the same year, 5597 (1837).

[Page 254]

Rabbi Mordekhai of Chernobil passed away on the 35th day of the *omer*-counting of that year and the *tzadik* of Kovel [R. Yaakov Aryeh Leibnyu] on the 27th of Elul.

The Moharam's third son was Rabbi Yitzkhak of Neskhiz, of whom his father said that he [the Moharam] had taken his [son's] soul and all of the "drops" [of its soul] from an extraordinarily high, very exalted place, and that every day another angel would come from the Garden of Eden to teach him in his childhood.

The Moharam was great in hasidism. Rabbi Uri of Strelisk, author of *Imrei Kodesh*, and the *tzadik*, [R. Kalonymus Kalman Epstein,] author of the *Meor Veshemesh*, both learned the ways of hasidism and serving God from the Moharam – one of them for seven years in a row and the other for three years in a row.

Indeed it is told that the *tzadik* of Lublin, [R. Yaakov Yitzkhak, the Seer (the *Khozeh*),] asked in heaven who the leader of the generation is, and he received the answer, "Rabbi Mordekhai, son of Gitel [the Moharam]."

[R. Avraham Yehoshua Heshel,] the rabbi of Apt, spent time with the holy [Seer] of Lublin. The holy [Seer] asked him if he knew the *tzadik* of Kovel, Rabbi Mordekhai, [the Moharam].

The rabbi of Apt answered, "I do not know him."

The holy [Seer] of Lublin answered him, "The Moharam can raise a soul to its root."

The rabbi of Apt decided to travel to Neskhiz, where the Moharam lived after he left Kovel. However, [the rabbi of Apt] did not merit to meet [the Moharam], because the Moharam was summoned to the heavenly yeshiva [and passed away] before the rabbi of Apt came to him.

The students of the Moharam wrote down various words of wisdom that he said.

He once told his son Yaakov Aryeh [Leibnyu], the "rabbi of Kovli [Kovel]," "My son, my son, a leader of the generation must have a great qualification. If within a fifty mile (literally *parsah*) radius of a *tzadik* a woman is having trouble giving birth, if he does not literally feel her sufferings and birth-pangs and does not suffer together with her, what right does he have to call himself a leader of the generation?"

And the Moharam said, furthermore, "To say that nothing is done in the world without my knowledge is possibly overstating matters. But for a radius of five hundred square miles around me, nothing is done in heaven against my will."

The Moharam used to say that every place that a Jewish *tzadik* stays is the Land of Israel. He found support for this in the words of the early authorities that a person who learns Talmud is like a person who lives in the Land of Israel. Mar Bar Rav Ashi was in Bavel when he edited the Talmud. He sat between two mountains and caused four clouds to come and surround him, and then he caused the air of the Land of Israel to come there – and then he edited the Talmud. So too [any] *tzadik* has it within his power to cause the air of the Land of Israel to come and surround him.

The Moharam's rebbe was R. Yekhiel Mikhl of Zlotshev, who was one of the students of R. Dov Ber, the Magid of Mezritch [a successor of the Baal Shem Tov].

Once, when the Moharam was in Mezritch, he went in to look for his rebbe, the Magid of Zlotshev.*[Page 255]*

One of the renowned students of the Magid of Mezritch asked him, "Whom are you looking for?"

The Moharam answered, "I am seeking my rebbe."

He asked him, "Who is your rebbe?"

He answered him, "My rebbe is the Magid of Zlotshev."

This student of R. Dov Ber answered him, "Both you and your rebbe need a rebbe."

The Moharam was wounded by this laconic remark and decided to avenge the insult to his rabbi.

The Magid of Mezritch had the custom of learning particular subjects with individual students. With this student, he would learn Kabalah after midnight. That night, when [the student] sat before [the Magid of Mezritch] to learn, the Magid saw that his student did not understand the learning, and he asked him, "Why is it that today you do not understand anything that you are learning?"

[The student] told of his conversation with the Moharam.

The Magid told him, "Go and appease him."

The student went to appease the Moharam. The Moharam said [to him,] "I can forgive my own honor but I cannot forgive the honor of my rabbi. And now know that all of the [spiritual] levels that you had until now have been taken away from you. Now go and toil anew in serving God, and regain what you had [previously] attained."

The Moharam passed away on 8 Nisan 5560 (1800). After he passed away, hasidic legend tells, he was called from the Garden of Eden to hear the greeting of the Sabbath in the supernal palace, on the highest of levels.

The Moharam saw an old man [who remained] sitting. He asked him why he was not summoned too, and [the old man] replied that this was a punishment because he had not donned a white garment in honor of the Sabbath.

The Moharam said to [an agent of] the heavenly court that since this old man deserved no other punishment than this, he [the Moharam] did not want to enter the supernal palace in the Garden of Eden until that old man was also allowed in.

The heavenly agent went [back to the heavenly judges] and asked [them what to do,] and he was given the reply that he must do the will of the Moharam. And [so the Moharam] came together with that old man to the supernal palace.

[Page 259]

The Zionist Movement and Zionist Youth Movements

Dawn of the Zionist Movement in Town

by Eliezer Leoni

Translated by Ala Gamulka

There are very few towns and villages in Poland where the Zionist movement was as deeply entrenched as in Kovel. Zionist ideals pierced the depths of all social layers in towns. People with opposing ideas united in the realm of Zionist activity.

A good description of the beginnings of the Zionist movement in town can be found in "Hamelits" from 1896: "Various classes and parties united with love and in peace for the sake of the Zionist ideas. The movement to settle Eretz Israel has been entrenched, for the past few years, among the chosen few. However, lately, the rest of the residents have also been taken by the dream with one voice.

Zionist Council 1918

Seated, right to left: Sarah Blumenfeld–Tslavitch, Mendel Kossovsky, Brukhin, Heinich Geller, Burstein, Moshe Davidiuk, Barukh Reiter
Standing, right to left: Avraham Erlich, Berel Roizen, Ida Nitsberg–Gutenboym, Yosef Avrech…

[Page 260]

Dr. M. Feinstein and other honorable people – fully devoted to their love of Zion and Jerusalem – managed to disseminate these ideas in an excellent fashion. Their hard work brought, after Passover, the establishment of "Agudat Zion" and many members joined and donated generously. The new group was involved in teaching Hebrew language and literature to the youth, distributing good literature among the populace. It also presented subjects such as Jewish history and the words of the wise sages.

It was most pleasant to see people from all movements, differing in their thoughts and habits, doctors, scholars and Hassidim, join together for conversation and advice. They were all unified in any matter in the Jewish world".

The first meeting of "Hovevei Zion" took place on a Shabbat in 1894. The meeting was held in the Talmud Torah on Ludomir Street. The courtyard was filled with Jews wearing long kapotas. It is interesting to note the speeches at this meeting were half in Hebrew and half in Yiddish.

The synagogue, in the house of Yudell Schechter on Lutske Street, also served as the clubhouse for the General Zionists. The Zionist committee and the Zionist library were also located there. Among the founders of the library – who also collected the books – were Isser Miller. Eliyahu Burk, Mikhel Roizen, Yerucham Lublinsky and the son of the late Moshe Gonik. I do not need to emphasize that these cultural leaders spoke Hebrew among themselves. These were the first to establish the base for the revival of the Hebrew language among the town residents.

At the Zionist synagogue the following were listed among the founders of the Zionist movement in town: Alter Gevirtsman, Dr. Feinstein, Mikhel Feinstein, Berish Ziskind, Ben Zion Mersik, Yonah Meisels, Berl Tsuker, Dr. Perlman, Dr. Lifshitz, Gershon Goldstein, Avraham Sheinboim and Heinich Geller, z"l.

At the beginning, the Zionist movement was only known to a few, but it soon became a popular calling. The movement educated the masses by teaching them Hebrew language and Jewish values.

The educated youth in the Zionist movement volunteered to give "Shabbat classes" to the workers. On this day of rest, they taught a chapter of Tanach and Jewish history. At the end of Shabbat, they continued with arithmetic and various sciences. The curriculum followed the Zionist programme.

These young volunteers hung posters in the Houses of Learning. The posters invited the workers to participate in the Shabbat classes. Many heeded the calling. On 16 Elul 1899, the first class took place.

[Page 261] [Page 262]

The experiment worked well. Many people filled the classrooms of the Talmud Torah where the lessons were held.

Among the first Zionists the figure of the teacher and educator Heinich Geller, z"l, stands out. The contribution by Geller to the history of the town is unmatched. Geller was a regular columnist in Hamelits and Hatsfira. His description of the life of the town is a first–class historical document relating to the end of the 19th century and the beginning of the 20th.

Geller was born in 1866 in Berestechke. His father was the teacher Zanvil Geller. At the age of 10 he travelled to his relatives in Lutsk where he studied at the yeshiva. In his spare time, he perfected his knowledge of Hebrew, Russian and German. At the age of 16 he began to write poems and articles in Hebrew. He occupied an important position among the Zionist leaders in Lutsk.

In 1882 he started to travel among the towns and villages of Volyn in order to organize the Zionist movement. He was imprisoned, for these activities, by the Russian authorities. In 1890 he married Frida Kibuk and settled in Kovel.

At the beginning he dealt in commerce and later he was a clerk in the City Hall of Kovel. In 1894 he left business and chose the teaching profession. He remained in it for the rest of his life.

In 1905, he opened, with other scholars, a Hebrew school with free tuition. In 1906 he had a coffee house, in his home, called Jaffa. It was actually a meeting place for members of the Zionist council. He was imprisoned once more by the authorities, but prison did not scare him away. As soon as he was freed he continued his activities in order to strengthen the Zionist movement in town.

Jewish National Fund Committee in Kovel–1929
A memento for the vice president of J.N.F in Kovel,
Mrs. Eventchuk on your saying goodbye

Right to left: Mrs. P. Prager, wife of Moshe Perl, Mr. H. Grinberg, Mrs. Eventchuk, Mrs. Milstein, Mrs. Gilberg

His unstoppable devotion to the broadening of the Zionist movement in town and to teaching the Hebrew language –over dozens of years–caused his health to deteriorate. He died of pneumonia on 11 Nissan 1926. He was sixty years old.

The Zionist movement in town was popular with the working class. The figure of the "Special emissary" arose from among this group. This was a person who dedicated his entire life to the entrenching of the Zionist ideals in town. It was someone who worked day and night to attract more souls to Zionism and who convinced the assimilated to return. It was a person who distributed Zionist literature and who gave speeches in all the Houses of Learning about his topic. This type of person was imbued with ideas of revival from a young age.

This type of man of the people, an emissary of Zionism at the beginning of the movement in our town is epitomized by Eliezer–Meir Miller, z"l. He worked in the construction of chimneys in wealthy homes.

[Page 263]

However, after a hard day's work, he carried packages of Zionist leaflets and he hurried to distribute them among the Jewish youth and the working class.

His death created a heavy mourning pall in town. In Hatsfira of 24 Kislev 1902, Geller published a lengthy eulogy about the deceased. In it we read how involved he was in the dissemination of the Zionist dream. Geller writes:" Last Sabbath eve we lost one of the most faithful Zionists. Eliezer–Meir Miller was an honest and straight–forward man. His death has brought a heavy loss to Kol Zion. He was an energetic comrade who was dedicated to the Zionist ideals with his whole being and did more than possible for the movement.

The deceased was a poor man, but his influence on his generation was great. They were craftsmen, like him. He was educated and knowledgeable in Zionist literature, but he was a noble man who brought many simple people into the Zionist fold. He sometimes, on his own, bought books extoling the Zionist ideals and he worked hard to disseminate them among his acquaintances. He did this not for glory, but because Zion and Jerusalem were in his soul constantly.

The deceased barely made a living, but he was still among the first to contribute "shekels" and he also bought bonds. His great love of Zion can be described in this fact: When he learned that the bank was open for business he rushed to the Kol Zion committee house to share his happiness. He wrote in the guest book about his proposition to celebrate the opening of the bank in one of the coming days of Hanukah with a large crowd. He was only forty when he died".

It has been stated earlier that the Zionist movement in town united people with opposing points of view. It should be noted also that the most ardent Zionist was the town rabbi at the beginning of the 20th century, the celebrated Rabbi Moshe Zackheim, z"l.

Rabbi Zackheim was born in Czernowitz. His father was Rabbi Mordechai Zackheim. At an early age he was known for his depth of knowledge of the Talmud and its interpreters. He married the granddaughter of the Gaon of Vilna, from Shkalov. She died young. He started out in business, but he was not too successful. The Jewish community of Kovel invited him to become its chief rabbi. In 1887 he was sent a contract and he came to Kovel in 1888. Rabbi Zackheim left many pieces of writing about innovations in Halacha and legends. There were also many interpretations of Talmudic and Kabbalistic literature.

[Page 264]

Rabbi Zackheim stood out in his personal attributes, his wisdom and his great diligence on behalf of the community and its charitable institutions. He was a true Zionist still from the beginning of the development of the movement in the eighties. He was a member of the organization Kol Zion to his dying day.

Pinhas Dashevsky

Among the leading Zionist figures in town in that era was a very interesting person. For a period of time Pinhas Dashevsky, a student at the Polytechnic institute in Kiev, was front and centre in the news in the Jewish and non–Jewish world.

In the winter of 1902 Dashevsky came to Kovel and was a private tutor. It is not known what made this young man of 22 to come such a distance. It is rumored that love was the motivation. A few years later Dashevsky married Anna Shenker– one of the two sisters who headed the girls' school.

When Dashevsky arrived in town he discovered a very active Zionist movement. There was a Zionist club called "Jewish Teahouse". It was a front for widespread Zionist activities. Dashevsky became chairman of the club and appeared as a speaker at many functions.

Dashevsky was born in the village of Korostishov, Kiev Region. His father was a military doctor. At first, he was an assimilationist, but soon he was intrigued by the Zionist ideals. He was one of the founders of a student Zionist group which was based on social–Zionist thought, It was called "The Revival" and its aim was to bring the national ideals to the Jewish masses.

[Page 265]

These were the days of the slaughter in Kishinev– spring 1903. Prior to the pogrom there were the incendiary speeches of Pavel Krushevan, the editor of the anti–Semitic newspapers Znamia (Standard) and Bessarabyets (Bessarabian).

Dashevsky could not accept the slaughter. Although he was in Kovel, he planned to murder the one responsible for it – Krushevan.

Once when he visited the late Meir Entin he was highly agitated and seemed to be struggling hard. Dashevsky asked Entin: Can you imagine a Jew would murder Krushevan? Entin tried to change the subject and said: Why should we sacrifice a Jew? Krushevan is not such an important and famous personality.

Dashevsky was angered by this reply and did not continue the discussion. He suddenly disappeared from town. A few days later there were headlines in the Russian, and the Jewish, newspapers–Hatsofeh, Hatsfira– announcing that a young Jew called Pinhas Dashevsky had tried to kill Krushevan.

Dashevsky had armed himself with a pistol and a Finnish knife in case his hand would slip and he would murder an innocent person. He chose the knife and thrust it in Krushevan's neck. He then immediately notified the policeman who was standing guard. Krushevan was only lightly injured. On 17.6.1903 Dashevsky was in court. The well–known attorneys, P.G. Mironov and A. Gruzberg undertook his defence– pro bono.

Dashevsky appeared in court looking noble. He announced that he was a Jew and a loyal Zionist and the asked the judge to call him by his Hebrew name – Pinhas, and not Piotr. In his defence speech Dashevsky emphasized that his wish to murder Krushevan came to him when he was living in Kovel.

Dashevsky was sentenced to five years of hard labor and the loss of his rights. The story created much excitement among the youth in town and it caused a general awakening for the need for self–defence. The late historian Dubnov wrote about Dashevsky: "He became a saintly hero among holy victims who accept their sentence. After that, the heroes who used self–defence in the pogroms were imbued with his spirit".

His sentence was shortened by a pardon from the Tsar and he was able to finish his studies as a chemical engineer.

When he was freed from prison, Dashevsky returned to Kovel and married Anna Shenker. They had a daughter called Ruth (Rosia). She was quite talented and studied in the gymnasia of Klara Erlich.

[Page 266]

She then trained as a veterinarian.

In 1910 Dashevsky travelled to Eretz Israel with a group of Students and professors from Kiev. There he went to Rehovot and he met his old friend Meri Entin. In their conversation he spoke of his time in prison and that he was not treated badly.

Dashevsky returned to Russia. The Soviet authorities employed him in various technical institutes. Eventually, he was no longer favored and he was arrested in 1933. In June 1934 he died in a Soviet prison after eight months there. He had been ill.

The first people to make Aliyah to Eretz Israel

The Zionist organization in town did not content itself with Zionist education only. It called for a personal contribution– to make Aliyah and to settle in Eretz Israel.

This was in the days of the 6th Zionist Congress when Uganda was proposed as a refuge.

In Kovel there were some who were for Uganda, but they were in the minority. Those who swore "If I forget thee Jerusalem, may my right–hand wither" decided to achieve their dream of settling the land.

In 1903 the first two pilgrims from Kovel went to Eretz Israel: Meir Entin and Dov Weinstein. They travelled to Odessa where they met Lilienblum and Droyanov and received proper information from them.

When they arrived in Eretz Israel they settled in Rehovot. They chose this settlement due to the articles by Moshe Smilensky in Hatsofeh. These articles spoke about the private initiatives in Rehovot. First, they worked at Menucha Veavoda (Rest and work)– the company that founded Rehovot. After some time, Weinstein left Rehovot and moved to Segera and eventually Menchemya. He died during WWI after he had been tortured by hard labor at the hands of the Turkish regime. Meir Entin died of old age on 14 Adar 1956.

Some time later Baruch Pantorin made Aliyah with his wife Masha (sister of Dov Weinstein). They settled in Menchemya. This settlement was attacked many times by the Arabs, but the Pantorin family never left it.

Pantorin loved the people of Kovel and he always tried to arrange jobs for those who made Aliyah from there.

The first pioneers mention the name of Baruch Pantorin with great respect and love because he looked after them as a father does for his children.

Pantorin died in 1925 and was buried in Menchemya.

[Page 267]

Zionist Activity Before the Balfour Declaration

by Avraham–Meir Weisbrot

Translated by Ala Gamulka

Before WWI Zionist activity in town was quite limited. Those most active were: Gitlis and Finkelstein. Dr. Feinstein also belonged to that group and he was even a delegate to one of the Zionist Congresses.

Aside from teaching Hebrew and having programs for Jewish National Fund, there was not much influence exerted by the Zionist movement on public life. It was not a movement of thousands. Its representatives were few. They were mostly wealthy or members of the intelligentsia.

Public activities had a philanthropic character and were evident in four important institutions. These were:

Educational institution "Maskil Al Dal"– for poor children. It was a secular school with little Jewish studies. Its principal was Mr. Yudkovitz, a renowned pedagogue, specially brought from Chernigov. However, he fell ill and died at the age of 34.

The first library in town was established in those days. It had books in various languages. It was founded was Mr. Erlich who donated his private library to it.

Philanthropic activity did not confine itself to spiritual work only. It also assisted with material needs.

Committee of Zeirei Zion and the first pioneers of Kovel

Seated right to left: Asher Lublinsky, unknown, Avraham-Meir Weisbrot, Tzvik, Yosef Tzvik, Haim-David Bernstein
Standing from right to left: Shlomo Saltzman, Gershom Melamed, Bork

[Page 268]

Among the activities helping in a material way, we must mention especially "The Peoples' Kitchen". It was founded by Michael Kaditz who was chairman and Mrs. Tsippa Roiter. The kitchen was intended for laborers and other needy people. From time to time balls and plays would be arranged with income being earmarked for maintenance of the kitchen.

A fourth public institution we must mention, in particular, was the establishment of the Jewish Municipal Hospital. The leading spirit behind this institution was Mr. Klorgloz. He was assisted by several personalities, including lawyer Appelbaum.

All activities took place during the times of the Tsar.

In 1917, with the Germans occupying the town, there was a great change in public activities. It now encompassed many parts of life. The Germans drafted almost everyone to work. The men were in labor camps and construction of houses for the Germans while the women were mostly employed in laundries.

The almost unbearable work conditions caused the laborers in the camps to have an uprising. They congregated in Prozhansky's synagogue for a protest assembly. It was then decided to turn to the German authorities and the Jewish mayor, Mr. Mendel Kossovsky, with a demand to limit to eight the daily work hours, to distribute work in a judicial manner and to pay with food.

A committee was elected which included A.M. Weisbrot and Mr. Klonitsky. They came to the German army commander and Jewish mayor Mr. Mendel Kossovsky and presented the demands of the camp laborers. The committee was promised that the laborers would now be treated with dignity and justice. Truly, the promises were fulfilled. There was now order and a special department was created to register the laborers. Its secretary was Mr. Yaakov Bork.

First steps in organizing the Zionist movement

The Zionist movement in town grew from a few members to a popular group after the Balfour Declaration. A public meeting was held in the large hall of the workers' kitchen in order to explain the purpose of the Zionist movement. This meeting was also attended by the camp laborers whose representatives had demanded several activities for their protection.

After a lengthy and lively discussion, it was decided to establish the Zionist organization and to include all factions. It is well known that only in a joint effort would they be successful in founding the organization.

A committee was elected. Its members were: Yaakov Bork, chairman, A.M. Weisbrot, vice chairman, Gitlis, Yustman, Finkelstein, Goldstein, Schwartzblat, Shimon Eisen and a student by the name of Rosenzweig– just arrived from Russia.

[Page 269]

The committee took upon itself the task of organizing the public activities in town and to attract many to Zionism.

The committee rented a few rooms near the workers' kitchen. This served as the first Zionist club. Important work was developed there and every Shabbat there were lectures and discussions on Zionist topics. Hundreds of members were registered– mainly young people. Their activities stood out in the cultural field and in collecting funds for Jewish National Fund.

The Zionist activities were successful. In those days, when there were revolutions in Russia and Germany, there were many left-leaning groups that popped up in town. They felt it was time for their ideas to influence the public.

I remember a large meeting– 500 people– called by most of the public organizations then existing in town.

The Zionist organization was also represented. The chairperson of the meeting was Dr. Moshe Kaditz, leader of the leftists. The leftists threatened those assembled with their speeches and people were depressed. Soon, one of the Zionist speakers, in plain language, put down the heated rhetoric of the leftists. He told them that even if grass will grow on their cheeks, a forced, authoritarian situation will not come to town. The speaker asked those assembled to follow the Zionist movement since that was the only solution to the social and national problems of many Jews. He disputed the leftist contention that liberty can be obtained by terror and extermination and he proved that their ideas were hanging by a thread and were based on a weak premise. His words calmed those assembled and they carried the speaker on their shoulders.

At this time the Zionist movement in town grew and blossomed. Many members joined and a clubhouse was opened. There was broad popular–cultural activity. The clubhouse became a center for Jewish life in town. Many cultural and educational institutions were established as a result.

Division in the Zionist organization

As previously stated, the Zionist organization included all factions in the movement. However, eventually, the many heated discussions in the clubhouse became quite ideological. A division according to world views was in the offing. Most of the youth were members of Zeirei Zion and it became the main part of the Zionist movement in town. Some time later, in 1921, an offshoot of Zeirei Zion, was established after the Prague Conference. It was the Union group. Still, there were joint programmes in cultural, educational and Aliyah fields.

[Page 270]

The leaders of Zeirei Zion were: A.M. Weisbrot, chairperson, Saltzman– secretary. Members of the board were: Bernstein, Lublinsky, Melamed, K. Bork, Dov Polishuk, z"l, Schwartzblat, z"l. The Union was headed by, among others: Zvi Shapira– chairperson, Volvoler and Puritsky.

In 1920, the fourth Zionist Congress took place in Warsaw. The delegates came from various factions within the Zionist movement. For the first time, the following 4 delegates were chosen to represent our town: – Yaakov Bork and Rabiner– General Zionists, A.M.

Weisbrot and Marus Hodorov (now a physician in Russia)– from Zeirei Zion. At this conference Zeirei Zion became a party by itself and it established its own central institutions.

The Eretz Israel office

The Eretz Israel office was one the important institutions in Zionist circles. All Zionist parties in town participated in it. At one time, its secretary was Dov Polishuk.

This institution undertook the job of organizing Aliyah and to help every person, either with information or with material assistance.

During the time of escape from Russia there were members of Dror in town– Berdichevsky, Bankover, Poliushko, Ben–Dori, z"l, Minkovsky, and others. They, together with other pioneers staying in town on their way to Eretz Israel, found a warm atmosphere in the Ertz Israel office.

I remember that these people felt at home in Kowel. The Zionist atmosphere characterized the town and this made it easier for them as they traveled.

The Eretz Israel office also looked after youth that wished to make Aliyah and helped them in every way possible. It was instrumental in encouraging many to make Aliyah.

Participation in the helplessness of Zionism within the Joint

Our activities did not remain only in acquiring membership to the Zionist ideals. We also participated in various institutions in town. We must stress our work in institutions of the Joint. It was one of the main groups that saved poor Jews from the shame of hunger. There are not enough words to describe the great assistance provided by the Joint to the Kitchen for the Hungry, provision of food for children and approving budgets to maintain schools and hospitals. Special mention should be made of the struggles between the helpless Hebrew movement, guarding the budgets of the schools, and the Bundists.

[Page 271]

Seated from right to left: Haim–David Bernstein, Israel Prozhansky, Michael Feinstein, Avraham–Meir Weisbrot, fifth is unknown, Yaakov Bork, Langer
Standing from right to left: Shayev, Dov Soibel, Haim Greenberg, Muqrin

The latter group was headed Mr. Bilov. He was actually a secret Communist. This was discovered when the Bolsheviks came to town.

Thanks to the Zionist activities, the Joint provided more funds for Tarbut School. Heading the Joint in town and in the area were: A.M. Weisbrot, Simcha Heinich, Gitlis, Lublinsky, Bernstein, etc.

The Joint was the main factor in the establishment of the school named after Prof. Friedlander, z"l, on Mitzkivitcha Street. Its organizers were active members of Zeirei Zion.

Prof. Friedlander was born in Kovel and had served as vice chairman of Joint worldwide. He was murdered together with Rabbi Cantor, z"l on the border of Poland and Russia. They were on an important mission to Russia.

Zeirei Zion wanted to commemorate Prof. Friedlander by founding a school named for him.

[Page 272]

The Joint responded to our request by contributing to this school. This was in spite of the fact that it had stopped subsidizing Hebrew schools at that point. The school continued to be supported by the Joint for some time longer than other institutions. This was thanks to the fact that we were fortunate to have the widow of Prof. Friedlander on our side. Mrs. Lilian Friedlander was living in Eretz Israel by then, but she was keenly interested in the school. The Joint also supported the founding of the Folks Bank. It eventually was included in network of popular banks in Poland. The bank was very important in helping craftsmen, grocers and owners of small businesses. This aid allowed them to maintain their work and they earned a decent living. For several years, the bank was headed by Haim Greenberg. Others involved in running the bank were, among others, Sheynkar, A.M. Weisbrot, Glass, Gitlis and Moshe Perl. When Greenberg left, he was succeeded by Moshe Perl. He remained in that position until the Nazis entered town.

Cultural activities of the Zionist Organizations

The Zionist and non–Zionist organizations had general cultural activities in order to have people join their point of view. These activities were assemblies, parties, balls, etc. However, the organizations really competed among themselves by inviting well–known and important people from the outside. These people described to the audiences the problems facing the Jewish world in Poland and elsewhere.

Three of these General Zionists, hungrily received by the Jews of Kovel, were Dr. Yehoshua Gotlieb, z"l, Yosef Haptman, z"l, and may he have a long life, Yitzhak Greenbaum. The General Zionist movement in Poland was divided into two streams: "Al Hamishmar" (on guard) and "Et livnot" (time to build). Greenbaum was the leader of the Al Hamishmar party and Gotlieb and Haptman led Et Livnot. The Zionist movement was influenced by Greenbaum as he was the actual leader of the Polish Jews. His appearances in town became important events. Many people came to hear him speak since they saw him as someone who would be making Aliyah.

Greenbaum had a charming personality, but Dr. Gotlieb was an excellent speaker. He was known as an outstanding orator. Even those who did not agree with his point of view, still followed Dr. Gotlieb because of his rhetoric and his beautiful language skills.

Yosef Haptman, z"l, was an esthete, with a beautiful soul. He came to town many times. Each one of his literary speeches became a cultural event in town. He was a journalist and a brilliant writer.

[Page 273]

Avraham Levinson, z"l, was one of the best–known representatives of the Union. He was a star on the stage of Jewish public life in Poland.

He was one of the young Jewish members of the Polish parliament. Immersed in literature and culture, he spoke well. Every one of his appearances was a pleasure for all. He could speak about lofty subjects in simple language that was understood by everyone.

The best–known representative of Zeirei Zion was Israel Ritov. He was an important and popular speaker in Poland. He understood his audience and he knew how to excite his listeners to turn to Zionism.

The workers party had Zvi Rosenstein, Malkin, Koltun (he became leader of the Communist Party in Israel), emissaries from Eretz Israel– Rashish (now mayor of Petach Tikvah), Yehuda Almog, Yitzhak Tabankin, Duvdevani, Zerubbabel, etc.

Folks Bank Committee

A special event was the appearances by Zeev Jabotinsky, z"l, in our town. His speeches were attended by his followers and those who were against him.

Jabotinsky was listened to with pleasure even by those who were far removed from him ideologically. They argued with him, if possible, but they all valued his great talent– his ability to explain.

[Page 274]

There were also appearances in town by those opposing Zionism, especially at election time. The most outstanding among them was Haim Rassner, z"l, head of the craftsmen union in Poland. Even the Zionist crowd found him interesting. We had bitter, difficult debates with him. We argued with him with and without permission. We often interupted meetings where Rassner was speaking. It was not just for the sake of interruption, but it was an important struggle for the souls of the Jews of Poland. It was a holy war. An ideological struggle between two philosophies: Zionism and its opponents.

The religious crowd had as one of the leaders of Mizrahi– Rabbi Brod. He was a representative of his district to the Polish parliament. He was accepted by many other factions who listened to him even if they did not always agree with him.

Our lives were enhanced by these colorful leaders, the opportunity given to the Jewish community in Kovel to hear opposing views and the dialectic struggle between different world concepts. It made it easier for individuals to choose their path in life. It is really because of free choice and understanding that most people followed Zionism.

An unforgettable event was the first appearance of the emissary of Keren Hayesod– poet Leib Yafeh.

[Page 275]

Everyone came to hear him. Leib knew how to draw even those who were not so generous. He excited people and he awoke in them their national spirit. Their hearts were opened and they donated to Keren Hayesod hundreds of dollars. Kovel managed to collect, for Keren Hayesod, large amounts. The total was second to that of Lodz only. It was well–known within the Zionist crowd in the country that Lodz led in total funds, but Kovel was always second.

There were also authors and poets who visited: Ansky, Tchernichovsky, Segalovitz. Mastboim and Kolbek. Nearly every theatre group from Warsaw or Vilna came to town and discovered an audience craving artistic endeavors. From time to time, there were traveling theatres such as those of Ida Kaminska and Sigmund Turkov. We should especially note the performance of the world– famous cantor Sirota.

Members of Zeirei Zion in Kovel in 1926

All these performances shed a beautiful light on the gray life, the everyday world of the Jews of Kovel. They struggled hard to maintain their existence. The desire to be free, to establish a state and to make Aliyah, to be like other peoples, rooted in land and in labor– these were healing and brought some sweetness to their drab lives. It gave them hope and encouragement.

Anyone who visited our town, be it from central offices or as emissaries from Eretz Israel, was warmly received. When they left town they confessed that here there was a Jewish community that would give everything for the building of our land and that was prepared for great sacrifices in order to create free, proud, upright Jews.

The Poaley Zion Movement in Kovel

by Aharon Werba

Translated by Ala Gamulka

The history of the Jewish workers parties in Kovel is, probably, similar to that of such movements in Russia., Ukraine and Poland. The socialist-Zionist workers movement in our town held an important place in our public life. Perhaps it must be stated that it was even more than just important. I was active in its ranks for a short time. I had been part of the workers movement of Eretz Israel in Hechalutz and Dror. I will give a short account of this party in Kovel.

Our town did not have much heavy industry. There were no large factories. There probably would not have been workers there as there were in other towns in Ukraine and Poland. Still, the town served as a large centre in the district and it provided services to a population of tens of thousands. Hundreds of laborers were involved in specifically Jewish occupations: tailoring, sewing, shoemaking, baking and blacksmithing.

[Page 276]

There were also those who constructed wagons that were used for transportation of people and goods. (There were no motorized vehicles in town or nearby). The socialist parties were active among these laborers- also the Bund and the Communists. It was only later that the Poaley Zion party became active.

In spite of pursuits and harassment by the police, there were professional unions of bakers, needle workers and office clerks. The Bund was controlling these groups and there was also considerable Communist influence. As of 1926, Poaley Zion became important.

The spiritual force in these professional unions was Batya Mendel. She was a dynamic activist and full of energy. She came from a bourgeois family and she lived in her brother's house. He owned a stationery store. She earned a living by sewing. Batya was the chairperson and secretary of almost every professional union. She was also active in the cultural field among the laborers. When Poaley Zion was instrumental in establishing a Yiddish language school, Batya joined the school committee and helped with advice and in deeds. She continued this work as long as the school existed.

Poaley Zion occupied a place of honor within the workers movement thanks to some active members. It originated many cultural and professional programs. Its influence was not only on workers. Soon after its founding, the movement managed to participate in municipal elections. It succeeded in obtaining places in city hall. The leader and founder of Poaley Zion in town, Meir Reiz, z" l, served for several years as a member of the steering committee. If I remember correctly, it was the first time that the workers group, thanks to Poaley Zion, had its own representative in city hall.

I recall that the Poaley Zion movement began its activities with the arrival in town, in 1925-26, of Meir Reiz. He was an engineer by profession and he was invited to serve as a teacher of mathematics and physics in the Tarbut Gymnasia and in the school of Klara Erlich. This respectable position of a teacher was not enough for comrade Reiz. He was not like the rest of the teachers in Klara's school. Most of them came from Galicia and spoke Polish. They were content with the status of a "professor" and they were believers in the governing authority. Comrade Reiz was a member of a socialist-Zionist movement and in spite of the danger of losing his job as a teacher in a Polish gymnasium he strove to establish a branch in town.

Soon he was joined by a group of young men and women and Poaley Zion became important in our town. Reiz was a man of the people, highly cultured and friendly.

[Page 277]

His personality drew a group of young writers, among them Kalman Liss. He was s sensitive young man, cultured, involved in his surroundings and a lover of Volyn. He used to sing about it: "My Volyn is simply freezing". This is how one of his poems about Volyn begins. Moshe Grinstein, z" l, another young dreamer, was secretary of the Tarbut Gymnasia. He was imbued with sadness as evident in his poems and works. Leib Olitzky, a young author, very talented, was known in the world of Yiddish literature for his creations. These three were close to Meir Reiz and with his encouragement and influence they became involved in disseminating culture among the people. Until the establishment of Poaley Zion, there was no cultural activity in Kovel, in Yiddish. It was a town with many residents. It is unnecessary to state that there were no schools in which the language of instruction was Yiddish.

Kovel was a Zionist town. The Zionist movements left their imprint on our town. There were strong, large Zionist youth movements and they drew the majority of the young people among us. There was an extensive system of educational institutions- Hebrew language- serving students from kindergarten to high school. There were thousands of students in these schools. There were also Polish schools that were intended for Jewish children. The Polish government was interested in spreading the language over these formerly Ukrainian areas and it subsidized these schools. It also supervised closely the quality of teaching. In this atmosphere, Meir Reiz stood out. It was mainly due to the subjects he taught and his tremendous knowledge that he was able to keep his position as a teacher in the Polish-Hebrew high school. (In the end, he was fired, at the insistence of the director, for his public activities).

In this nationalistic and Zionistic atmosphere on one side and Polish assimilation on the other, Meir Reiz began his activities in Poaley Zion in Kovel.

At the beginning, the movement was small, but at the end it was very successful. At first, the public doubted the ability of the few leaders who invaded the area that was held as a monopoly by the Zionist movement in town. Other movements did not even try to enter the cultural and educational fields. Perhaps this was due to the few members they had or because they did not expect to succeed. It is a fact that when Poaley Zion was organized, it began its activities in Yiddish. Yiddish authors were invited by the movement to visit town. Among them were Peretz Markish, Moshe Kolbek (close to Poaley Zion at the time) and others. Hundreds attended their lectures. New readers, from Kovel, were added to the ranks of the Workers parties' publications.

The Zionist parties, even those connected to the Zionist workers party, were not able to enter the workers' groups. Their members came from among the merchants and owners.

[Page 278]

The same was true for the youth movements. They also came from the same ranks. It was only with the establishment of Poaley Zion that contact was made between the workers and Zionism. The movement was heard at meetings and its voice was joined to those of the veteran parties already existing in town. It was accepted that there could not be a meeting of workers without a representative of Poaley Zion.

The movement "dared" to participate in municipal elections and it was quite successful. In the Kovel city hall there were Jewish representatives and even the vice-mayor was a Jew. This was due to the fact that the majority of residents in Kovel were Jews. These representatives belonged to Zionist groups or were simply Jews. The novelty was the election of a representative of Poaley Zion. He was even elected to the executive committee.

The jewel in the crown of the activities of comrade Reiz and the movement was the establishment of the school in which Yiddish was taught.

There were Yiddish schools in Volyn even earlier. In 1921 representatives of Volyn participated in the first conference of Yiddish schools held in Warsaw. The Central Yiddish Schools Organization was founded. Poaley Zion had a strong delegation at this conference. However, the Polish government was uneasy about these schools. It believed they would produce a generation of revolutionary socialists. It thus made things difficult. It closed the schools in Volyn. The residents there were mainly Ukrainian and they desired independence. The government wished to deepen the influence of Polish. It hoped to Polonize the Jews. The Yiddish schools in Ukraine did not please the government since they were opposite to its aims. It was easier to close the schools. Most of them did not have proper permits and the majority of teachers were unlicensed. These were good excuses for the closure of the schools. The education department in Warsaw cancelled the permit of "School and Education" of Poaley Zion because religion was not taught there. It took much effort to undo this edict.

All the various authorities did not care for these schools and made their lives miserable. In this hostile environment, be it the government or the more prosperous Jewish community (they saw the Yiddish school as overdoing it)- all prevented the establishment of a Yiddish school in Kovel.

The people active in Poaley Zion cared about and loved Yiddish. The question of teachers was solved by the fact that several well-educated people took upon themselves the task of becoming teachers in this school. They did not even care if their salaries were reasonable and paid on time. An outstanding effort was made to collect funds to pay for an appropriate location- one that would be accepted by the authorities so they would issue a permit. Finally, after much work, the Yiddish school in Kovel was opened.

[Page 279]

I do not remember how many students there were in the school during its existence. I am certain there were more than 100 in its first year. This was not insignificant. The school brought to the movement many popular activists and some of the best youths. The high school graduates served as teachers and counselors. I believe that Dr. Ziskind was very helpful. He was a beloved, even-tempered man. Also, the sons of the rabbis, more modern in their thinking, gave a hand to this project. Krause, the son of the Rabbi -called the Grabivitzer- served as secretary. Mrs Gutenboim, daughter of Rabbi Nitzberg, z"l, an educated woman who maintained a large library in town, taught in the school. Her husband, Kalman Gutenboim, a philosopher and a scientist, also helped in the success of the school. It was rumored in town that he understood Einstein's theories.

In 1927 I was recalled to Warsaw to work in the Central office of the movement. Even though I left my town, I still continued to follow whatever was happening there. In time, there were changes. Due to pressure by the authorities, comrade Reiz had to leave his teaching in the high school. Other staff members moved to different towns. Some went to bigger cities and some just left. However, the original seed took and was fruitful for several years. Names of members who helped so much with the movement are not listed here simply because I no longer remember them. Unfortunately, I had nothing in writing since it did not exist. Many hard-working members have remained anonymous.

This article should serve as a memorial to good and loyal people who were swept in the storms of war. It is also an encouragement to those who are still alive here and elsewhere. Their hearts are with us.

[Page 280]

From the Dawn of the Hechalutz in Kovel

by Shlomo Heri, Moshe Weisbrot & Shamai Frankpovitch

Translated by Ala Gamulka

The first seed of Hechalutz in town was sown in 1918. The founders were a group of daring people who did not like the existing situation and wished for a new one. They wanted something imbued with the achieving, hard-working aura of Eretz Israel. Their names are: 1. Shlomo Heri, 2. Moshe Weisbrot, 3. Shamai Frankpovitch, 4. Mendel Kaptchuk, 5. Berel Soibel, 6. Yekutiel Kopelberg, (served as first secretary) 7. Mordechai Fishbein, 8. Rivka Weisbrot, 9. Shtcharbeta, 10. Shaike Melamed.

In those days there already existed in town a club of Zeirei Zion. The leaders of Zeirei Zion wanted the Hechalutz to join under their banner, but this was unanimously refused. The first founders met and sent an emissary to Warsaw in order to receive instructions for starting the chapter.

Right at the beginning the members of Hechalutz decided to establish, in town, training facilities. There was a proposal to found an agricultural farm in Kovel. However, it was not possible to do it for various reasons. Instead, a carpentry shop was opened. A hall was rented from Monish Roizen. Since Hechalutz did not have a permit, a tag day was organized for the benefit of the Home for the elderly. However, all income was designated for the carpentry shop.

There was a collection of crates in town and the carpentry shop looked real. There were orders from the High School of Klara Davidovna and from the School of Measurers. The first closet was purchased by A. M. Weisbrot for his wedding day.

In order to publicize Hechalutz, everything was done in the open. If Moshe Weisbrot, son of Rabbi Israel Lubliner, appears in the streets as a laborer and is not afraid of what people will say- then Hechalutz is real. The children of the town leaders wished to live as workers in Eretz Israel.

It is difficult to understand, but we must remember that there were homes in town where parents sat Shiva for a son or daughter who went out for training or joined Hechalutz. This shows how much effort was involved to appear in public in work clothes, as a true laborer.

The clubhouse of Hechalutz was located in the carpentry shop. It was the office as well as the place for meetings. The first conference of Hechalutz took place in Warsaw in 1921. The Kovel representative was Shlomo Heri.

The carpentry shop did not last long. In its place it was decided to establish a locksmith shop.

[Page 281]

In order to finance the locksmith shop there was an evening in the Odeon Theatre on Shabbat, April 1, 1922. The artist G. Orlov was invited and he presented a comedy in 4 acts: "A bridegroom must have bedbugs and needs to speak German". Orlov played the bridegroom. Those in charge of the evening were Batya Armernik and Shamai Frankpovitz. The proceeds from the play were used to establish the locksmith shop. It lasted one year.

In 1921 the first members of Hechalutz made Aliyah. They were: Moshe Weisbrot and Yeshayahu Gibor. A special evening was organized in their honor and all political parties were represented.

The evening took place on the eve of Simchat Torah. The next night, at the end of the holiday, almost the entire town went to say good-bye to these two pioneers. They paved the way for the hundreds of pioneers, from our town, who followed and made Aliyah.

When the veteran members made Aliyah, the activities of Hechalutz lessened and it was almost eliminated.

In 1923, a new Hechalutz was founded.

The first pioneers to make Aliyah
Seated from right to left: Pinhas Tzvik, Moshe Weisbrot
Standing: Yehuda Melamed, Gershon Beit-Halachmi (Weisbrot)

[Page 282]

The Halutz in Kovel

by Aharon Werba

Translated by Ala Gamulka

Kovel played an essential part in the pioneering movement in the twenties. Our Halutzim were important in town and village, kibbutz and moshav, public work, workshop and office, cooperative production and service– in all branches of labor and productivity in Eretz Israel.

The Halutz movement in Kovel began to blossom at the end of WWI when there was an emergence of the Zionist hope for a new life. There was immigration of Polish Jews to Eretz Israel.

The town was close to the Russian border and it became a transit station for members of Halutz and Dror arriving from Russia. Some were just passing through, but others remained for a long time. Since they had a Zionist background, they were able to integrate in the movement and to help make it grow and develop. Some even were the leaders.

The Hayot family, a Zionist one, settled then in town. It contributed greatly to the growth of Halutz in Kovel. Huma Hayot represented Hehalutz Hatzair in all of Poland. Other contributors were A. Bialopolsky, z" l, and I. Bankover.

The Dror members were active and dedicated and were successful. Many young people from local Zionist groups and even unorganized youth joined Halutz. Dozens were organized into preparatory kibbutzim in order to make Aliyah.

Even at the beginning of its existence, the young group held an honorable place in the public institutions and organizations in town. Their opinions were accepted in the Eretz Israel office. Up to then the office had consisted of representatives of Zeirei Zion and General Zionists. The Halutz member became the secretary and his task was to divide the few certificates that came to Kovel. Also, a Halutz member was the secretary of HIAS.

The main purpose of Halutz was to prepare members for Aliyah. A field outside of town was dedicated to that. The young pioneers transformed it into a vegetable garden. There were also groups that accepted physical labor, such as cutting down trees in different homes in town. There was no commune in town, but the members spent many hours together.

[Page 283]

This was a novelty. It was the first time, in our town, that wealthier people met with working folks. The latter earned their living by doing physical labor. Halutz consisted of the wealthy, the poor and the middle class.

At the beginning, pioneering groups in Volyn were self–organized. However, as the movement grew in the province, the central office in Warsaw took over direction. This is how Volyn became a center of Halutz.

Halutz Executive committee in Kovel
17.xi.1927

[Page 284]

The first conference of Halutz in Volyn took place in Kovel in 1924. The hall of the office of Eretz Israel was too small to contain the many delegates. The center was represented by P. Rashish (today mayor of Petach Tikvah), Moshe Shapiro, z" l, who was in Poland at the time as an emissary of the Histadrut and A. Berdichevsky (today in Yagur).

The conference gave a good push to many activities. The members of the executive elected at the conference were: Batya Bendersky (Eitchies), z" l, comrade Dobromil (now Dovrat) and the writer of this article. They traveled throughout Volyn to strengthen the organization and to establish new locations.

The provincial map was covered with a large network of preparatory kibbutzim, quarries, lumber yards, tar factories. In the forest of Volyn there were hundreds of pioneers living a communal life in difficult conditions. They had to overcome many pitfalls, but they did so and were fortunate to make Aliyah. The pioneers of Kovel played a substantial part in these communes.

Seated, from right to left: Haike Fried, Aryeh Tchlin, Levi Schwartz, Yeshaya–Leib Ber
Standing: Eli Mendel, Mordechai Erlich, Pessach Levenberg

Then the "Mecca" of the preparatory kibbutzim of Poland was established– Kibbutz Klosova. The large preparatory kibbutzim in Rokitno, Rafalovka and Dombrovitza were important. It is too bad that the historians of Halutz did not mention the fact. Kibbutz Kolosova became better known and overshadowed the others.

Kibbutz Klosova was founded in 1924 by a group of pioneers coming from towns nearby. If I remember correctly, comrade Simcha Finkelstein (today Simcha Even–Zohar) was one of the founders of this kibbutz. In time the kibbutz became an emblem of the pioneering movement in Poland. When comrade Even–Zohar made Aliyah, the main influencers in this kibbutz were from Kovel. The author of this article was elected secretary of the kibbutz, but there were others from Kovel who ran Klosova. Practical operations of the kibbutz were done by members from Kovel– Liova Gelman, B. Levin and others. It was an active group with great energy and dedication that led all activities of the kibbutz.

Hand in hand with the hard labor in the quarries– something the teenagers and students were not accustomed to – there was an extensive cultural Zionist and general activity.

In Grochov the preparation was for agriculture, but Klosova was known as a preparatory location for construction workers. The friendly atmosphere generated by the intelligentsia of Kovel helped new members to integrate and to overcome any difficulties.

[Page 285]

Many members of Klosova from Kovel are with us in Israel. They continue their busy lives. Others are scattered across the world and we hear from them from time to time. The values acquired by these members in the Halutz movement in Kovel stand them in good stead in their lives here an in other lands.

Executive committee of Halutz in 1933

Standing, from right to left: Mendel Erlich, Kremer, Baruch Toib. Shalom Klonitsky, Hava Fried
Seated: Michael Gonik, David Ovental, Moshe Gitlis, Moshe Roizen, Yaakov Beker

[Page 286]

The First Training Division in Kovel

by Yitzhak Margalit

Translated by Ala Gamulka

When the central office of Hechalutz decided that members were to go on to the next step, that of fulfillment and life of labor, our hearts were aching. We were asking: how do we do it? It is not simple for people of ideas to become the proletariat. We had to change our lives in radical fashion. In addition, our parents saw us as a lost cause.

It is not surprising that there were many struggles for us until we went to work. To be exact, we became proletarians only a third or fourth of the time. We were still Hebrew high school students. We used to get up at the crack of dawn, in total darkness. We worked until 8 o'clock and then we began our studies. We worked in the large sawmill in town as well at the brick factory of Segal.

This group of trail blazers became the nucleus of the Halutz kibbutz in Kovel.

Prior to this upheaval, there was a hidden and simpler one. We were still members of Hashomer Hatzair. Our branch was struggling to survive as there was not enough money. We sought a way to help and to overcome this problem.

In the yard of Avraham Gozen there were piles of lumber. We decided to become lumberjacks and to dedicate all the money earned to saving the branch.

We worked for several days and we cut down all the trees. However, there were 8 large tree trunks left. We, the high school students, were too weak to cut them to pieces. We came to Gozen and asked him for our pay. He was stubborn and declared that until we finished the entire job, we will not see a penny.

We were desperate. Our hard work was going down the drain. What would become of our branch?

We used our "Jewish brains" and came up with a solution: Gozen's house stood on Optitchna Street on the river bank. We decided to push the remaining tree trunks into the river and thus to get rid of them. We formed a chain from the barn to the stairs leading to the river and handed over the trunks. The current pulled them away from sight. We then came Gozen and told him: we finished the job and cut down all the trees.

[Page 287]

He believed us and paid our wages, thinking he had won.

First meeting of those from Kovel who made Aliyah. Pessach 4.4.31

The end justifies the means…

I wish to tell you of another invention by the "Jewish brain". The gates of Eretz Israel were barred. In training were veteran members who were in dire straits– they were ill. Some had a heart condition or pneumonia or Bronchitis.

Aliyah was quite selective. The doctors from the Eretz Israel office were very strict. We knew these members would not pass the medical test. It bothered us because we knew that if they could not make Aliyah, Hechalutz would suffer a moral loss.

One day, comrade Levy came from the office of the Klosova kibbutz. As a representative of Hechalutz, he revealed a secret. On the following day were expected Dr. Horowitz and Dr. Mundlek from the Eretz Israel office. They would be examining all candidates. Levy suggested that I should welcome them and take care of them. All efforts were to be made to allow candidates who are not physically fit to be certified for Aliyah.

In the morning we went to the train station to greet them. We settled them in the Varsil Hotel and tried hard to make their stay as pleasant as possible. Levy suggested that I serve as their secretary and they agreed.

The doctors began their task. They gave me the appropriate forms and explained to me the different categories. Positive– means a sick candidate and negative means a healthy one. It was agreed that I was to act as the "Deaf angel". In other words, if the doctors said "Positive" I would write it as negative due to my poor hearing.

The doctors did not suspect those approved and signed the forms I had filled out. In this fashion we were able to send many members to Eretz Israel.

We had dinner together in Varsil cafi and they said they were pleased with the great welcome and the productive job we had accomplished.

It is possible that, at the time, it was not a very nice thing to do, but the terrible events that followed cleansed the sin. In this way we were able to save hundreds of members from Kovel from the claws of the Nazi Satan.

[Page 288]

About The Halutz During Its Low Point
(Between the Third and Fourth Aliyot)

by David Perlmutter

Translated by Ala Gamulka

As time went by, the pioneering movement acquired organizational frameworks to achieve its goals.

At the beginning there were fluctuations. Pride and shame alternated. The first years of pride after the Balfour Declaration had passed. In Eretz Israel there was a breakdown and some people returned to Kovel. 1923 was a low year for Zionism and for the Halutz movement.

The number of branches of Hechalutz in Poland was lower. There were very few of them. Only the true believers and the stubborn ones remained.

The branch in Kovel almost did not exist. We were few. We did not have a hall and not even a branch. We were a group of friends with a common dream. The central office of Hechalutz tried to encourage the movement. It suggested to change the day of remembering Tel Hai to a special day and to draw from the strength of Joseph Trumpeldor. We were few, but we believed our task to be a commandment. I still remember that special evening. We did not have a hall so we met in the room of one of the members at the outskirts of town.

A small lamp lit the room, those assembled and the small picture of Joseph Trumpeldor standing on the table. We read from the Halutz brochure that had been published for 11 Adar 1923. We discussed the situation, the future of our generation and our part in it.

Somewhere in town there were many people going to various fun places. Modern dances, such as the Tango, captured the hearts of the young and they danced until dawn. It was as if they could breathe the air of the Galilee and feel the struggle of the day and the land. They believed the breakdown would pass and more people would come. For various reasons, the breakdown passed and many people came. The Fourth Aliyah began.

[Page 290]

The Scouts Organization in Kovel

by Eliezer (Lusia) Hodorov

Translated by Ala Gamulka

In November, 1918, I came from Chernigov to Kovel. It was after I had lived through two revolutions in Russia- March and October.

As a scout I was heavily influenced by these revolutions. Until the first one, our nationality did not stand out and we were considered as General Scouts, international, so to speak. We were Russians, Ukrainians or Poles. When the revolution broke out, we organized a group of Jewish scouts. The Sokol Sports organization in Chernigov, led by Czech athletes, was the foundation for Maccabi- a Jewish sports club.

I was active in Scouts and in Maccabi. I spent days training. I always thought about Kovel and I decided to introduce scouting to its young people.

When I arrived in Kovel I found a new reality. The town had been conquered by the Germans during the previous three years. The Russian language was unknown to the younger generation. Soon after I returned, I organized the Scouts in town. The first group was part of a Russian high school. It grew and became a branch. It was the first nucleus and from it sprang a nationalistic-Hebrew youth movement. The Scouts movement became a national movement and it appealed to many in Kovel and in the rest of Volyn.

When the German army abandoned town, it left a large warehouse of backpacks, camping equipment, tents and blankets. I received money from the Scouts organization to purchase all of this. I also found materials for the sewing of the scouts' uniforms. These uniforms became very important in the life of the youth in town.

It was the first time that Jewish youth appeared in uniform. When we came as organized groups, as a unit, we captured the hearts of the Jews.

Not once did I see tears in the eyes of elderly Jews when we passed through town in lines, wearing our uniforms and playing drums and trumpets. We made the Jews of Kovel very happy.

Our main goal was to work for the good of the people and to prepare for Aliyah.

The Poles took over in 1919. When they came, I immediately approached the town commander and I soon received permission to continue our activities.

[Page 291] [Page 292]

The authorities would not interfere. Within two years after the organization of the Scouts, there were, in Kovel, about 400 scouts (male and female). My loyal helpers in the establishment of this movement were Bella Sher, Dusia Vertzel and, later -Israel Geyer and Raya Levy.

The students of the gymnasiums and the Hebrew high schools were the main component in the tremendous growth of the Scouts movement. The movement was people- oriented and did not only consist of students and leaders. The gates were open for youths from all parts of the community. Many were working youths- barbers, tailors, shoemakers, grocery clerks, watchmakers, etc.

This was the first time in the history of the Jewish community of Kovel that barriers between poor and rich, worker and aristocrat, fell. There was no differentiation between them. They were all equal not only in their uniforms, but also in their values.

The leadership of the Scouts Organization

*From right to left: Shvalba (carrying the flag), Bronzaft, Zunia Vertzel,
Lusia Hodorov, Pinhas Toib, Aharon Levy (Sharboim), Israel Pantorin
The ladies: Bella Sher, Rachel Pantorin, Rachel Fisher, Lana Cass*

It was a democratic movement which taught that personal characteristics, not origins or trade, were what established personal values. Anyone who showed talent and ability was given the opportunity, by the Scouts movement, to reach the heights of its leadership. Social standing was unimportant. This was a new idea in the Jewish community of Kovel.

When I began to develop physical activities within the Scouts movement, I was invited by the principals of the Jewish schools to teach there. This is how I became the first teacher of physical education. It was a first in the history of the town.

The curriculum included Swedish and Czech exercises, as well as sports, trips, games, etc. The scouting program was well received and expanded throughout the town. It served as a transition from life in the Diaspora to that of Eretz Israel. The working youths were prepared for work and leisure. Several Scouting units were organized- all ages were represented. There was feverish activity in all areas interesting to the young people. The war years had put a brake on the energy of the youths and now it was again functioning like a strong flood.

There were also classes for Hebrew language, history and geography, groups for Czech physical education, soccer, dancing, staging and gymnastics. Lectures were offered on various topics. Keren Kayemet and Keren Hayesod had explanatory sessions and prepared the youths to work on their behalf. As well, there were training groups designated for pioneering work in the fields.

The sports activities grew in scope and included new parts: sailing, swimming, skating races in the winter. In addition, everything connected to setting up and dismantling camp was introduced.

[Page 293]

I must emphasize that the youth of Kovel, and the rest of Volyn, stood out in their honesty and goodness. These are traits that cannot be found just anywhere.

As mentioned above, the first Scouts unit was established in the Russian high school. Activities took place at recess between classes only. The language used was Russian, but, during exercises, I gave instructions in Hebrew. The principal called me many times and asked me to use a language he understood, i.e. Russian. He would then be able to include non-Jewish students.

When the Hebrew high school was opened, all activities were centered in their building. I wrote a play based on the life of the scouts. It was "My dear nation, do not worry! We are with you!' The play was presented in the school and was quite successful. Hundreds of people came to see it. It had a great influence on the parents and friends of the scouts. When the play was over, all the teachers were invited to a discussion over a glass of tea. The fact that the tea was served in cups caused laughter. There was a lively give and take and the goal was achieved.

Every day, after classes were finished in the schools, we met for long hours- deep into the night. The physical and spiritual education progressed in giant steps. On holidays, and even on Shabbat, in the summer, we went to the forest. There, we set up camps- sometimes for the entire summer. Life in the forest, in a threatening atmosphere, required much courage. The scouts were truly brave.

In 1920 I was approached by nearby towns and I was asked to come and organize Scouts organizations. Representatives came from Vladimir-Volynsk, Brest-Litovsk, Kremenitz and Rovno. The story of our scouts even reached Bialystok and Vilna.

I began in Vladimir-Volynsk. I traveled there with Israel Geyer, one of our active members. We were both dressed in uniform

While we were in Vladimir-Volynsk, a delegation arrived from Ustile and asked us to organize there, too. We went there by horse and buggy. We were to stay in a beautiful home of wealthy people. Two hours later, army representatives invited us to join them. When we arrived, 7 police officers surrounded us with their rifles pointing at us.

It must be mentioned that, at that time, we were illegals. The Polish authorities forbade us from performing any activity thinking that it would be easy to substitute rifles for sticks. All our material was written in Russian. In Russian, the word Scout means "Young spy".

The written prohibition about the Scouts movement was kept by me in a bag with many pockets.

[Page 294]

They checked the bag, but did not find the written prohibition. I took it out under the table and I ate it. It was not easy to swallow.

One of the military police officers threatened that on the following day he would shoot us. However, he first wanted to check with his Russian-speaking assistant who knew all about the Scouts.

When the assistant came the following day, he burst out laughing. He told us that he had been a scout and he told the police officers to return us to Kovel.

For three to four years I organized branches in thirty towns and cities. The number of scouts under my supervision came to 3,500.

Training farms were organized to prepare pioneers for Aliyah. In 1924 I began my own preparation and I made Aliyah in 1925.

In my lifetime I was able to meet young Jews in many parts of the world. I never found any that could compare to the youth of Volyn. Even during the Shoah, they held their heads high and walked to the killing fields.

[Page 294]

History of the Scouts Movement In Kovel

by Eliyahu Mendel

Translated by Ala Gamulka

When WWI was over, the Hodorov family, with its 4 children returned to our town. Among them was Lusia, the third in line, who was around 13 years old.'His great energy and exceptional organizational talents made him seem much older.

We were children and the war had left its mark on us.'We became "militarists" and we played at "war".'For that reason, when Lusia called for us to come and enrol in the Scouts movement, a semi–military group, it was the right time.'The first to join were students of the Vineberg High School.'I was among them.'We hurried to Lusia's house on Briska Street to join.

The first meetings took place in a large room in the Hodorov house.'We sat on the floor, near the walls that were decorated with military symbols: tents, ropes, bottles, sticks, etc.'We then heard, for the first time, about Baden–Powell and the tenets of scouting.'We held our breath as we listened to stories about the war between the British and the Boers, when Baden–Powell stood out with his brave feats near the city Mafikeng in South Africa.

The movement grew and expanded from one day to the other and there was not enough room for us.

[Page 295]

The Scouting organization in its first years

[Page 296]

In those days the Russian high school, with Shevtsov as its principal, still existed.'Most of the students were Jewish.'We received permission to use its large hall for our meetings.

At the beginning, the movement did not yet have a Hebrew name.'We had strange terminology for orders and commands.'They changed frequently.'The leadership was called "Mifkada" (headquarters in Hebrew) and was headed by Lusia. Other members were Zunia Vertzel, Misha Habakin, Yossi Segal, Geyer, Perlmutter, Gasco, Galperin, I. Schechter.

Our knowledge of Eretz Israel and Zionism was limited.'However, thanks to the scouting movement we began to have a Zionist approach.'There were no Zionist movements in Kovel yet at that time.'The Scouting movement left its mark in us.

We began to search for a Hebrew name.'The literal meaning of Scout is spy.'We were afraid of the reaction of the authorities who could arrest us as spies.'At the same time the Scouting movement was taking root in Poland and other towns in Volyn.'There the Hebrew word was Tzofim.'Lusia accepted this term and we stopped being scouts.'We called ourselves The Organization of Hebrew Tzofim.

In the 1920s, new winds were blowing.'The Bolshevist forces began to invade Poland.'The soldiers of Bodoni quickly conquered Kovel.'A new "Messiah" appeared in town.'A large section of the youth were its followers.'The Scouting movement changed.'Some of the veteran leaders went to work in other locations.'However, the changes did not last long.'In the fifth week of the conquest by the Bolsheviks we met in the Festival of Zelig Roiter.'We expressed sorrow for our misconceptions and we avowed openly that we were wrong.'During this evening, Lusia and other leaders cried aloud.'When we posed for a picture, we joined two pieces of cloth, one white and one blue.'They symbolised the national flag.'We swore allegiance to Zionism and to Eretz Israel.

In the seventh week the Bolshevik invasion was stopped and events moved swiftly.'The war was over.'Much of Volyn was under Polish rule.'New and fresh forces came onto Jewish public life.' The youth stood at a crossroads and looked for direction.'The Scouts movement came out of its spiritual breakdown and was stronger than before.'There were attack by the Bulbuvtzis and Jewish blood was flowing.'In our childish beliefs we realized that there was no place for us in the Diaspora.'Our road led to Zion.'Lusia helped a lot by electrifying us with his speeches about Zionism and Eretz Israel.

[Page 297]

We came under the full influence of the Zionist movement in town.'It even gave us space in the Zionist club.

Inside the Zionist movement there were many changes.'Life did not stop.'New groups were formed and others disbanded.

These changes were also evident in the Scouting movement.'Some of our leaders posed the following question:'Since now there is Hashomer Hatzair in Poland, should we not join it?'It did not take long and some of our members, led by Yonah Perlmutter, formed their own group and called it Hashomer Hatzair.'A competition followed between the two youth movements (there were no other youth movements in Kovel).'From an ideological point of view the two were quite similar.

The only difference between the Hashomer Hatzair (yonovtzi) and the Scouts (Lusovtzi) was that the former had many working young people while the latter consisted mainly of students.'The former held their sticks like rifles while the latter had them under their arms, as do scouts all over the world.

The competition was fierce and it was a difficult fight among brothers. The Zionist leaders tried to make peace between them, but they were unsuccessful.

The Angel of Death interfered and put out the fire in his own way: the father of Yonah, the leader, died.'Yonah now had to earn a living and look after his family.'He did not have time for Hashomer Hatzair.'The members dispersed.

This was not the end of the story.'As our knowledge of Zionism deepened, the Scouting movement was not enough for us.'Many active members wondered: why do we not join Hashomer Hatzair, a national organization?'Hashomer Hatzair had a great influence among the youth.'Our leader, Lusia, objected vehemently.'He was too independent and too impulsive and could not follow instructions from above.

We then turned to Izia Boim.'He was due to graduate from the Russian high school and was a serious fellow.'We chose him as our leader and we contacted the central office in Warsaw.'We thus became part of the world–wide organization of Hashomer Hatzair.

Lusia Hodorov did not give in and he found a place for himself in other towns and cities in Volyn.'In order to bring his movement closer to Eretz Israel, he changed its name to Brit Trumpeldor.'He had many followers among the youth in Lutsk, Rovno, Dubno and Brisk.'

[Page 298]

Hodorov chose an executive committee.'However, when he made Aliyah, the movement petered out.

I want everyone to know that one must not confuse Brit Trumpeldor of Lusia with the one that is part of the Revisionist movement.'They are similar in name only, but not in their ideas.'Lusia was a veteran member and was active in the Histadrut in Israel.'The labor movement was his life's purpose still in the beginning of his Zionist activities.

[Page 298]

Hashomer Hatzair

by Aharon Levy, Mordechai Blorie

Translated by Ala Gamulka

We, the members of Hashomer Hatzair, remember with excitement the rich youthful period when we were part of it.'Some of us are in kibbutzim of the movement and others are not.

The branch of Hashomer Hatzair in Kovel, all through its existence, was a'place of growth, like a limb on a blooming tree.'It represented the workers of Eretz Israel.'Just as the limb is fed by the tree, which influences it and helps it to grow, so the Hashomer branch always was able to elevate the pioneering movement while it was fed by it.

We can assess the influence the movement had on each one of us and the loyalty we felt to it by repeating the phrase: "Shomer once, always a Shomer!"'There was an integration of values that had a refreshing effect on various youth groups in town.'The students were attached to Hebrew culture, while the workers and the poor youth were under the influence of this blessed cause.'Our movement led us on the road to personal and social development, to standing upright and to mixing in society.'Perhaps the movement was not well understood by other Jews and sometimes there was a difference between understanding and opposition.'There was much effort invested in getting recognition as a movement with essential values.

The branch of Hashomer Hatzair in Kovel was established at the time that the general movement became part of Volyn Province.'This was in the early 1920s.'There was never an official sanction by the Polish authorities and we always depended on the fact that our application was lying in a drawer of the area commander.

[Page 299]

"Reporting" by Hashomer Hatzair

[Page 300]

Years later the branch was under the protection of Hechalutz.'It did have official permission.

The first to be taught were physical education, scouting and soccer games.'As the first members matured, there was enthusiasm for social and ideological integration.'Everyone was inspired to become a pioneer.

Members of Hashomer made Aliyah and were insistent on integrating into the work force– even though there was opposition from farmers.'Each person had to struggle to become a laborer and to continue to have work.'All this made those still in Kovel eager to make Aliyah and to be productive members of the proletariat.

In 1925 there was amalgamation with the Trumpeldor Scouts which led to a growth in numbers.'The additional members were ripe for activities.'The location of the club was 5 Fabritzana Street.'It was a side street not far from the main street.'Every member, while passing on the main street, would find the time to check the club even when there were no scheduled activities.'The club was subsidised, with great difficulty, by the monthly fee paid by–" elders", "scouts" and the "young lions"– ten years old and under.'Some of these fees were dedicated to the movement.'When the funds were insufficient, the adults would contribute to cover the deficit.'They wanted to make sure the club would not fail.'There was also an extensive library in the club.

In 1926 there were new, promising additions.'These were the students of Tarbut high school.'It was a spontaneous movement of students who spoke Hebrew.'The club immediately received a Hebrew hue.'Group conversations and meetings were held in Hebrew.'The high school students brought in a valuable educational background.'The movement to Hashomer Hatzair did not pass without difficulties.'There was opposition to it.'The struggle for recognition became more serious and it continued for many years.'Hashomer Hatzair was seen as a competitor to the educational institutions and not as a complement to Jewish learning.'Even after the separation, when many of our members left and abandoned the Zionist movement and loyalty to the workers of Eretz Israel, the attitude did not change.'The only institution that continued friendly and cooperative relations was Jewish National Fund.'It was possible to work for this cause by donating, from an educational point of view.

[Page 301]

Mishmar HaEmek group

[Page 302]

The organizational activities were expressed in the various levels–according to age.'There were also learning opportunities for adults, a class for principals.'There were also provincial and country–wide gatherings where there was an opportunity for people to meet for the first time.'These were people who would eventually build and work on a kibbutz.'It was followed by the cooperative settlements in our homeland.'There were summer sessions for the youth as well as for leaders.'Those who attended were the ones who showed independence.'We also began a new program– winter moshava– held during the break from school.'It was intended to bring in new people.'These were children who attended Polish schools.'We feared that they would be candidates for assimilation and would remain strangers to Hebrew culture and love of Zion.'This activity was successful and it became the main purpose of our branch for several years.'It also set an example for branches in other locations.

The movement saw self–fulfilment as a main goal.'Each person saw himself or herself as if they were already participating in the rebuilding of the land.'Each one had as a purpose life on a kibbutz and as the solution for all struggles that befell every young Jew.'However, not all of them saw themselves as being able to reach self–fulfilment.'Some of the seniors reconsidered their path.'A plant in the field cannot absorb all the water it is given and the latter returns to its source.'In the same way, some of the seniors did not advance forward.'Those remaining were a small in number, but they were serious and enthusiastic and planned their move to the preparatory kibbutzim.

There was a Depression in Eretz Israel and some people came back.'The branch was then in the hands of a loyal group of leaders.'They knew how to dedicate themselves to educational and internal activities.'These young people did not give up.'At the outskirts of the camp there were a few who gave up the national dream.

In 1929, Eretz Israel was open to Aliyah of pioneers.'Several groups were organized as nuclei for kibbutzim.'Our branch did its best.'We cannot forget the festive meetings that came one after the other.'It was the awarding of the symbols of the movement to the graduates.'The graduates were accompanied to the preparatory kibbutz.'Everything was crowned with singing and admiration for those making Aliyah and joining their groups in Eretz Israel.'In 1929–31, most of the graduates made Aliyah.'It was the time of the 1929 events and the gates of the country were closed.'They were then reopened.'Between the closing and the reopening, many graduates managed to infiltrate and make Aliyah.

[Page 303]

For a while, the activities slowed down, but not for long.'The individual examples of those who were successful in making Aliyah and joining their kibbutz soon brought new recruits.

The years 1933–34 were full of growth within the Hashomer movement in Poland, in general and in Kovel, in particular.'There were 700 members in our town.'The hall on Fabritzana was too small and could not contain all the enthusiastic young people.'They were searching for a purpose in their lives within the Hashomer, scout and Hebrew movements.'The youth came from Tarbut, Herzliah and Klomel schools and they brought an obvious Hebrew atmosphere.'In addition, working youth and students from non–Hebrew schools also joined.'In those years, the movement had a great influence in the Hebrew schools.'They were helped by teachers who saw the value of the movement and its connection to Eretz Israel.'We finally were successful.'The Hebrew teacher realised that there was a cooperative connection between him and Hashomer Hatzair.'These were full partners in preparing their students for their future in Eretz Israel.

There were many new activities planned by the branch.'When the Festival of Pessach came, the children immediately talked of their desire to go to the moshavot– in nature.'They were normally far away from fields and forests.'Our movement tried hard to bring them closer.'Every year, dozens of these "desert children" from the various groups went to the villages and the forests.'Some played or danced or went on hikes, while others discovered agricultural labor.'In these moshavot the atmosphere of kibbutz and Eretz Israel was cultivated.'The villages of Lublinitz, Horodlitz and others became, with time, something very close to their hearts. It was likened to a bridge for continuity.'The winter sessions were also well developed.

One of the main activities was the acquisition of Hebrew language and culture.'The wall posters of the different groups were published quite often.'For a while, the local "Voice of Kovel" published a page in Hebrew prepared by members of Hashomer Hatzair.'There were Hebrew language sessions and the Popular University was famous.'It had weekly lectures on various scientific topics.'We were fortunate in having the best teachers in town as presenters.'In addition, there were evenings of singing in public and choirs.

[Page 304]

The branch leaders were also able to serve the Jewish public that was tired from working hard all year.'They came to see performances of the branch in town streets.'The members of the branch went into the Jewish quarters and were able to encourage them.'On Lag Baomer, all the streets were full of happy and enthusiastic young Jews, parading and singing.'Another important day was Purim.'On that day, Hashomer Hatzair organized groups soliciting donations for Jewish National Fund. They went to homes dressed in costume– always a theme connected to Eretz Israel.'They would sing and present the blue box.'At the end they would meet at the home of the elderly teacher Mr. Prozhansky where they danced and danced.

There were other evenings, full of mystery.'We feted those who completed their training and were, somehow, going on Aliyah B.

The years 1936–1937 were slow.'The economic situation was dire and there was a stop to Aliyah.'There were less members and a lack of leaders.'The branch was smaller.'This was common to all youth movements in town.'Even then, we maintained our status as number one when it came to members and to our work for Jewish National Fund.'It was difficult to hold activities.'It was only a special effort by friends of the movement that permitted us to pay our rent to maintain our club.

In 1938–39, there was illegal immigration to Eretz Israel.'A new chapter was written in the history of our branch.'We had more members, especially from among the working youth, from public schools and from the employed intelligentsia.'They, too, wore the gray shirt of Hashomer Hatzair.'The reason for this increase in numbers was based on the political situation in Poland.'The constant Anti–Semitic atmosphere caused the youth to see that there was only one solution–Aliyah.'Again, as in all times of awakening, our movement was active in Tarbut high school.'During this period, we, created, together with Hechalutz Hatzair, a club for students within the school.'We had assistance from Yitzhak Zukerman, a future leader of the Warsaw ghetto.'It was a productive cooperative effort which brought outstanding young people into our movement.

In addition to educational gains, there were also pioneering ones.'There were more people going to preparatory kibbutzim and on Aliyah.'At that time was founded Kibbutz Hakovesh in Bialystok.'Its members were planning Aliyah in the near future.'At Hashomer Hatzair plans were being made to celebrate 50 years of its existence.'However, the war broke out.'There was much panic. The danger of the Nazi conqueror was imminent.'Everyone understood what was happening.'Suddenly, the Red Army entered town and liberated everyone.'The local Jews received the Red Army with open arms.'It is essential to discuss the work of Hashomer Hatzair at that time.

[Page 305]

Choir of Hashomer Hatzair in 1937

[Page 306]

    Kovel was an important crossroad between East and West and it became, from the beginning, an obvious transit station. Thousands of refugees, mostly Jews, were moving eastward. Our movement had a useful role. Our members came to help. The seniors and the younger members went to the entrance to town, wearing their uniforms, to assist all hungry and thirsty Jews. The clubhouse became a refuge. Some of the leaders of the Bund, Dr Erlich and Alter, spent a few days there. It was said that they were not pleased when they saw wall decorations with themes of Eretz Israel. They wondered: "How did this come here?" Our members organized kitchens. An elderly man, Nehemiah Ber, should be remembered for his support of the youths performing their first social work.

    At that time, the members of Hechalutz and the first leadership of Hashomer Hatzair used Kovel as their center of operations. There was an atmosphere of cooperation and the motto was to stay together with the people and, at the same time, remain true to the dream of Aliyah. It is symbolic that these young people were entrusted with the universal flag of Hashomer Hatzair. Shmuel Breslau, one of the future leaders of the Warsaw ghetto, brought it on his wounded body. We accepted it for secret hiding in a dark cellar. We swore to each other that we would take care of the flag and we would bring it out of hiding at the right time.

    Indeed, we were fortunate to bring the flag to Eretz Israel, through Russia and Vilna, so that it would again fly in front of our youth.

    We were troubled. We recognized the authorities, but we would not give up the idea that we would not reach our country. Our happiness was mixed with sorrow. We decided to maintain loyalty to Eretz Israel, to the Hebrew language. Even the emotional calling of Alter Katzizna, then in Kovel, to convince the Hashomer youth to forget and to make do, did not make a difference. We were prepared for what came next.

    We organized groups for learning Hebrew language, Jewish history and listening to broadcasts from Eretz Israel.

    While we were preparing for what comes next, we heard that there was a chance for Aliyah: in Vilna, which was then given back to Lithuania. Most of the graduates looked north. On roads that were not really roads, in temperatures of –40 degrees, in constant danger and fear of imprisonment, they managed to reach Vilna.

    When the Nazis conquered Kovel, the Scouts remained. They were entrusted with the future of the club, to look after the interests of the Shomrim in our town. We heard, through letters and emissaries, that they remained loyal to the cause.

[Page 307]

    A few days before we made Aliyah, we heard about the strong stand of many members, especially Shoshana Perl Sheinbaum, and others.

    We discovered that, in Kovel also, there was a group of fighting Hechalutz which consisted of Shomrim and Halutzim who were there during that difficult time. Kovel served as an important transit station for emissaries– Hantche, Frumka, Tussia and others, who were moving eastward. The proof for this is the writing on the wall of the synagogue. The group of Halutzim going to their death demanded revenge. Signed: Sheindel Schwartz, Leah Fish, et al.

    After the war, those who survived, in Russia, in the forests, in Vilna or in the Red Army, went to Eretz Israel. They were illegal immigrants and soon integrated in the life of the country. Many Hashomer Hatzair members from Kovel are now in Mishmar HaEmek, Beit Zera, Shaar Hagolan, Ruchama, Amir, Merhavia and other kibbutzim. They all remember those days in the Hashomer Hatzair branch in Kovel at 5 Fabritzana Street.

[Page 307]

Some Thoughts on the Hashomer Hatzair Club

by Mordechai Melamed

Translated by Ala Gamulka

There was no other choice for the youth– only our movement.'It is true that there were some young people who laughed at our dreams and called us "Golden youth".'They were not serious and were not interested in world events, only in having a good time.'The majority of young people felt the need for belonging to the movement.

Who really were the young people who came to the movement?'They belonged to the parts of the community that were used to spending their time in synagogue.'When things changed and the Shtiebel was no longer interesting, they were bored.'At first, they came to the club out of curiosity and to be amused.'Eventually, they became more serious.'They began to understand that the movement was a way of life and a world view.

These people also began to come to Hashomer Hatzair.'The movement received them with open arms.'It knew its role.'This was an educational movement and it was certain that the raw material would become Jews loyal to their nation and homeland.'They would fight for social justice.

It was claimed that Hashomer Hatzair was a movement catering to youth from better homes: intelligent students, and that it was not for the ordinary youths, that it would not understand the working young people.'It is true that most of the members were students, but they originated from the same homes as those who joined Hechalutz Haoved.'They considered themselves to be more proletarian.

[Page 308]

It is also true that Hashomer Hatzair appreciated scholarly people since they were needed to educate the new groups that were joining the movement.

Hashomer Hatzair was able to integrate the educated with the uneducated.'The former gave of themselves willingly and the latter happily accepted.

The movement followed its own Ten Commandments.'Fulfillment of goals was more important than the personal wishes of anyone who was still studying.'Some could not cope and had to leave the movement.'If they did not succeed, the movement itself abandoned them.

The Kovel branch also went through some changes.'At first, there was a group of fellows who belonged to the Scouts, founded by Lusia Hodorov.'They were mostly students.'They then left the Scouts and established the branch.'The Scouting movement had an important position with its activities.'I remember well the "Order Exercise", the "Ties", "Alpha Beta Morse", "Summer moshava" and simple hikes.'Zionist–socialist teaching and activities was also part of the program.'Scouting was mainly done with the youngest group– Young Lions.'The next group–Scouts–were educated in pioneering and Zionism–socialism.'They were taught the meaning of a kibbutz.'They learned about the new life in Eretz Israel and Jewish history, but they still had to understand life in exile.'Scouts had to be well–informed about all these topics.'They learned about it by reading books, in conversations and group activities.'The leader was the head of the group.'When the Scouts knew everything, they were ready to move on to the "Seniors".'They then received a badge saying "Be strong".'At the age of 18, Scouts made the move and went to the preparatory training kibbutz.'They were finally beginning to fulfill everything they had learned and for which they had prepared themselves all this time.

There was an ongoing argument between the Zionist movements and the non–Zionists.'The latter saw us as young people having fun, far away from the gray life.'I remember one evening when I appeared as the emissary of the branch and welcomed a new professional union that had formed in our town.'When I descended from the stage after my speech, I was approached by a detective from the Polish police.'He wrote down my name and address.'Then, a few friends, who were non–Zionists came over and said: "We did not know that you know what to do.'From now on we will change our minds about your movement".

It is true that we were young people having fun.'It is normal for the very young, but this was not fun for fun's sake, laughter for the sake of laughter.

[Page 309]

Hashomer Hatzair branch in 1932–33

[Page 310]

It was what pulled the youths to our branch.'While having fun, the leader knew how to produce cultural and ideological activities.'He knew how to have the youths acquire the seriousness of the movement.'For that reason, there was a library which had materials that involved the youths in issues being discussed.'In addition to literary, historical–nationalistic material there was also a wall newspaper where everyone could express their opinions.

The" literary trial" that was performed also added to the thoughts of the youths.'It is superfluous to mention that the group conversations were the main vehicle for indoctrinating the Shomer tenets.'I remember how we would sit during these conversations.'Everyone participated with an opinion.'These were serious and deep and went on for a long time.'At the end, everyone got up, danced a Hora and let off steam.'Then we sang the anthem of the branch: "We are singing and making Aliyah".

I remember the beautiful hikes.'One that is etched in my memory had a bit of "resurrecting the dead".'It was a great summer day, a Friday afternoon.'We went from Kovel to Matseyev and we arrived in their branch in the early evening. We met the locals as they were having great fun dancing.'We joined them.'Suddenly, a wind began and the skies were filled with black clouds.'It began to pour.'When the rain stopped everyone went to their homes.'We went with one of the Matseyev members to sleep in his barn.'We reached another barn, not far from the designated one.'It was raining non–stop.'We entered and lay down on the hay.'We suddenly heard banging on door accompanied by screams: Fire! Fire! It is burning!'We hurriedly got up in pitch dark.'We made it to the door and saw, not far away, that the barn we had not reached due to the pouring rain, was on fire.'It was hit by lightening and the fire ignited.'We instintinctively ran there and we shivered as we watched the flames.'We were up late the following day.'We had a festive meal.'We still were able to laugh, but we all felt the great miracle.

On Sunday morning we left Matseyev early, walking and being jolly.'Suddenly our friends from Kovel appeared.'They almost fainted when they saw us.'They were coming to our funeral because they had heard from an emissary from Matseyev that fellows from Hashomer Hatzair had burned in the barn.'All the eulogies were not needed.

It was a beautiful, productive time when the Tarbut students began to come, in crowds, to the club.'It was the time of "Ben Sham".'He was a new teacher who came to Kovel and mesmerised the youths.'Under his influence there were many students who joined the club.'Teachers were also interested.

[Page 311]

The new recruits fueled the activities.'The old forces were tired.'The Seniors were good at speaking, but they were unable to fulfill.'They felt uncomfortable and began to distance themselves from the club.'Some of the Seniors joined Poalei Zion or the Communists.'In their place, new forces joined and invigorated the club.

The new stream of enthusiastic students saved the situation.'At the same time, young people who were not studying also joined the club.'They had either completed the Heder or were in Polish schools.'They came to a plowed field and found a new way to live.'This is where the new generation was formed.'It was prepared for its role in the nation and the homeland.'It was ready to march with certainty towards the next day– when the sun will shine in their new land.'It was a fearless generation, full of national pride.'They knew how to fight for their people and their country.

From the Seniors Group to the Hashomer Hatzair Club

by David Perlmutter

Translated by Ala Gamulka

When WWI ended and the refugees returned from far away places, the idea of scouting was brought to Jewish Kovel.

The pride of scouting continued for several years– until the early 1930s.'Since it did not have a pioneering basis, the movement deteriorated due to infighting.

In the low years of 1923–24, there really was no youth movement worthy of its name.'The Zionist movements only functioned at election time or at Aliyah periods.'There were always some adherents who continued the actual work for rebuilding Eretz Israel.

The Jewish youth liked to dance.'The needs of the people were many.'The charitable institutions used the dancing fad and planned many parties.'There was dancing until morning.

The youth were also into the Shimmy and tango.'Special outfits, appropriate tie, shiny shoes, some money in their pockets– these promised a night of fun.

The Seniors did not accept this attitude.

One by one, they came from different social and cultural backgrounds, but they did come.

[Page 312]

They would hear a discussion of a Peretz story or they would judge Raskolnikov (of Dostoyevsky).'They would study geography of Palestine and would look for a purpose for cooperative living.

It was the hatred of the minutiae of daily life, of the petit–bourgeois atmosphere in town, that brought them to this point.

This was the group of Seniors– 10 young men and two young women.

They loved to discuss, to go on hikes and the togetherness.'They were not really seniors…

We were few in number and our activities were temporary.'We joined every Zionist program and anything that had an advanced public feature.'We loved the world and the universal revolution was close to our hearts.'We enjoyed Russian literature that began to reach us.'However, our eyes and hearts looked forward to the Jordan, to Eretz Israel.'This is how we saw the world and communal living.

Our activities were "Question parties" or literary trials.'We managed to attract a loving crowd that was ready to follow all our requests.'We had many functions for Jewish National Fund and similar causes.

One day we discovered that the General Zionists were opening a club and we went into negotiations to join them.

After we promised to behave, they gave us a small room– it was the stage for the adjoining hall.

On this stage, behind a green curtain, we did our work until we took over the house, the yard and the street.

5 Fabritzana

The club had two rooms.'The sign outside said that this was the hall of the Zionists in Kovel.'Inside there were newspapers on tables, various games and a canteen for the visitors.' At first, there were some Zionists who came every evening to spend time reading, playing and drinking tea.'On those evenings we would hide behind the curtain where we talked, argued or listened to a lecture.

The topics were: beautiful literature, sociology, current events. The serious arguments were among the youths who were called Seniors, for some reason.'Soon, the Zionists stopped coming to the club and we had more joiners.'Our parties attracted many young people, as well as children.'The educational movement was established.

[Page 313] [Page 314]

In those days, the universal movement of Hashomer Hatzair was also growing.'Contact was made with Eretz Israel and emissaries came to visit.'The pioneering basis became the cornerstone of our world view.'In the club there was strong nucleus of pioneering–nationalistic youths.'The purpose of self–fulfilment and educational activity was its motto.

Others left.

5 Fabritzana became the center of Hashomer Hatzair.'It was important in the life of the youths and of the town.

We reached the elementary school students and we formed the first educational groups.'Our success was evident when the students of the Hebrew high school joined us.

There was a good group of counselors and the club grew.'It became an important part in the life of the youths as well as in the Jewish community of Kovel.

Many of our townsmen are in Eretz Israel and they well remember 5 Fabritzana.'They remember with thanks the day they entered this house.

Hashomer Hatzair Club with the poet Shaul Tchernichovsky, z"l on his visit to Kovel

[Page 314]

Hachalutz Hatzair

by Aryeh Rabiner

Translated by Ala Gamulka

I was a student in the third or fourth level of Tarbut high school.'Suddenly, something similar to an electric current passed through town.'It was a current that pulled us.'It was called Pioneers.'We really did not know what it was.'We had heard rumors of pioneers in Eretz Israel, but now we were connected, conquered and infected. We seemed obsessed and we referred to ourselves as Little Pioneers.'(I don' t really recall if we did it ourselves or if we had help).'If there were big Pioneers, why should there not be little ones?…

We organized ourselves in secret, in the underground.'There were three reasons: fear of our parents, fear of punishment by our teachers and the last, the most conservative one, fear of other children.'We did not want them to find out our secret and tattle.'Woe to us if that had happened.

The Hashomer Hatzair club preceded us.'There were some children who were secretly members of that movement.'However, there few in our school.

We began to met in secret– either on a hike, so to speak or a Bar Mitzvah party.'One day, someone arrived from the big city and organized us as true members of Hechalutz Hatzair.'I believe it was Huma Hayot who was then a member of Dror and is now living in Yagur.

[Page 315]

Dina Zatz, z"l, with her apprentices

How strange!'Young Pioneers with their insignia: hammer, anvil and seven stars.'An attractive and interesting insignia.

This was only the beginning.'Our underground activities did not last long because we were unable to do it.'We wanted to show ourselves in the club, in the library, on the way to the club, in arguments with our so–called adversaries.

It seems that during that time, when there were living pioneers visiting– emissaries from Eretz Israel who arrived in Kovel – we were so interested that we were drawn completely to the cause.'We gave our hearts and all our time to the dream of return to Eretz Israel and to its rebuilding by the pioneering settlers.'We worshipped the idea of life on a kibbutz.'The kibbutz, the Hebrew commune, became our symbol, our example, our daily wish to be there with the pioneers who are already achieving the dream.'No one will forget the first parade on Lag Baomer when we walked for the first time with our green flag (a sign of youth then).'We stepped with might, straight, happy and proud of the insignia on our shirt flaps.'We wore hats with a green ribbon.

[Page 316]

This was a demonstration of an awakening youth, ready to give of itself for a better future for its nation strewn in various exiles.

Our hearts beat wildly whenever a new song was brought from the pioneers in Eretz Israel.'We trembled as we listened to songs sung by the conquerors of the swamps in the Jezreel Valley and the pavers of the roads in the north of the country. Every word was learned well.'It can be said that every word strengthened our young hearts.'We were happy to learn another song, another word that the Pioneers of Ein Harod were singing.

Whenever an emissary came, we swallowed his words and drank in everything that came out of his mouth.'We kissed every sound coming from his lips.'Every emissary, even the ugliest one, seemed handsome in our eyes.'To us, he was endearing and romantic like "The Nights of Canaan" that we sang then.'For us, they were personal examples of the great life being developed in our country– the country we were hoping to reach.

I remember this story:'an emissary from Eretz Israel was lecturing to a large crowd.'He was warm and he took off his short jacket.'We noticed that his shirt was torn.'We, the pioneers, saw in it the simplicity of life, but someone in the crowd (probably one of the adversaries of Hechalutz) shouted "Change your torn and patched shirt ".'We, the youth, saw this as sacrilegious and we moved towards the person shouting and we were ready to pounce on him.'We did not change our minds and when we went outside, we waited for the shouter.'I believe he was slapped a few times…

I brought this story to prove and to remember how enchanted we were.'It was so important to us to bring anything that came from our Eretz Israel.

The youthful period passed fairly quickly.'Most of us went to the preparatory kibbutz.'Those who pretended to be a year older managed to do it earlier and others went at the right age.

In our town, Kovel, life was ebullient.

The Hechalutz Hatzair club received many members.'They came, they learned, they danced, they sang they went to summer camps, to camps for leaders, to conferences and meetings.'They then went to preparatory kibbutzim and from there they made Aliyah.'This word attracted us.'Is there an artist who can describe Aliyah of pioneers from Kovel?

Every wagon driver, policeman or boatman in Kovel seemed to celebrate with us the evening when the Pioneers were saying goodbye prior to their Aliyah.'Perhaps they were happy to get rid of some Jews or they were infected with our enthusiasm.'They accompanied the pioneers to the train station singing loudly.'Who did not come to the train station?'Young and old–even though it was midnight.

[Page 317]

Hechalutz Hatzair in Poland– Kovel branch – 3.II.1934

[Page 318]

They filled all entrances to the station.'Did anyone pay to go the station pier?

I remember that, once, the ticket seller was drawn into the crowd and he danced with the pioneers and the Hassidic parents who came to say goodbye to their children making Aliyah, in spite of their wishes.

Where did we hear "Let us be strong", "Hatikvah" and "Pioneer, make Aliyah", if not at the train station in our town, Kovel?'Most of Kovel was asleep, but the pioneers were calling "Shalom, Shalom".'The echoes of Shalom announced a new period for our people.'They left sadness in the hearts of the younger pioneers who were accompanying their older brothers.

The few non–Jews who were with us at the station were confused and a little afraid of the crowds around them.'Some said: "It must be some Rabbi who is leaving or coming to the Jews".

Who can forget the "Box Evening" in the branch?'Who can forget the questions and answers of those long evenings during the Kovel winters?

Who can forget the immense cold in the hall of Hechalutz at 55 Lutske Street?'In spite of the cold, the hall was filled with life.'We learned, sang and danced.

Who will not remember the small room near the stage?'It was the office that was always filled with dozens of young members who were begging, crying and asking to go earlier to the preparatory kibbutz.'There were also many young women (over 20) who wished to join Hechalutz Hatzair.'Usually, only those under 17 were accepted.

Who would not be touched by the memorial evenings for Gordon, Borochov, Brenner, Trumpeldor that were so emotional?

Who would not remember, with love, the tiny library that served hundreds of pioneers?'Who would not hold, in his heart, the warmth of those special evenings, drinking tea and eating latkes?'We would stay late after a party and speak from our hearts and listen to one another.'Very strong ties were formed between the members and this friendship continues, I believe, till today.

These parties were special.'They were meetings of friends for discussions and closeness.

These summer evenings, when we sat outside on the stairs, we envied the members of Hashomer Hatzair.'We did not have money and we were thrown out by the owner of the club.'We stood outside and we would not move.'We looked at the darkened windows of our club and we cried in our helplessness.'Our cash box was empty and we could not afford to pay the rent…

[Page 319] [Page 320]

A friend, an adult, came forward and paid some of our debt.'The club, again was full of brightness and happiness.'Young people hoping for a better future returned…

When we speak of Hechalutz Hatzair, we see in front of us the image of our "mother"– Dina Zatz, z"l.

She was an exceptional phenomenon within the Hebrew pioneering background in Kovel at its inception.'Dina was a refined and humble person, full of light and warmth.'She stood out among her contemporaries, her pioneering friends, in that she never lost her youthful enthusiasm.'She also knew how to influence others– big and small.

It seemed like she ignored the term "adult".'It was just a word for her.'She called everyone– "kids".'These were her "kids" … She was always on the move, full of life and infecting others with her enthusiasm. She never rested and was totally devoted to the young pioneering movement.'She became its loyal mother and looked after her young apprentices.

Pioneering Kovel cannot be described without Dina and Dina cannot be imagined without pioneering Kovel, its activities, parties, clubs, conferences, summer camps and preparatory kibbutzim.'Her "kids" were an essential part of it.

Group of Hechalutz Hatzair in Zelini in 1930

We recall the shed–house that stood at the end of a side street, empty of homes.'Here, in this shack, she taught the children the first pioneering songs and she inspired them to love the new idea of working Eretz Israel.'All the strong songs came from the work of Dina with her young recruits. It seemed as if due to their excited voices and their songs, the side streets were liberated from their emptiness.

The boys and girls enjoyed being with the simple, straight–forward Dina.'They embraced her with their true beliefs and she gave them her motherly, deepfelt love.'She caressed them warmly.'Many of them did not have this in their homes.

The Hechalutz Hatzair club had Dina– who came from a plain home.'She was able to draw the boys and girls from poor homes and she insisted on keeping the honor of the pioneer.

She taught Hebrew, lectured, counseled and explained.'She sang and prepared programs with which she was successful.

[Page 321]

Dina was the moving spirit who encouraged the Hechalutz Hatzair movement.

She established a home in Eretz Israel where she was married.'Her ardent hope was fulfilled when she gave birth to her own daughter.'No one could rival her.'Suddenly, a catastrophe.'Dina became ill and was unable to heal.'She could not take care of her child and she soon died.

Dina, who was so motherly all her life, finally became a mother.'She died without benefiting from the joy of family life.'She had influenced so many others during her life.'When her daughter was born, she, herself, was taken away from this world.'She was still full of love and good intentions to help others.'The cruel destiny stole her away from us.'She went with those who do not return while she was still young.'Her daughter was orphaned and Dina never heard the word "Ima"– she who had worked so hard for the good of the "kids".

May her memory be a blessing and may she forever remain in our hearts!

Hechalutz Hatzair in Kovel

[Page 322]

In Kovel there were mother youth and Zionist organizations: Beitar Youth- well known in town; Revisionist-Zionist party; Haoved; Hamizrah party; Gordonia; Freiheit(freedom) and Religious Hashomer.

Unfortunately, we did not obtain any material about these movements and organizations. Their work for Zionism, rebirth of Hebrew and preparation of youth for Aliyah was exemplary. This will not be forgotten. Their memories are bound in the eternal ones of the Jews of Kovel.

[Page 325]

Institutions, Movements and Organizations

Municipal Institutions

by A.M. Weisbrot

Translated by Ala Gamulka

Prior to WWI, town council members were elected by property owners. For that reason, most of those elected were Christians, in spite of the fact that they constituted a minority of the population. The Jewish population, a majority, was represented by wealthy Jews who were approved by the authorities.

During the German-Austrian conquest, Mr. Mendel Kossovsky, z" l, was elected as mayor. He did his best to help the Jews of the town, but his authority was limited. The real power was in the hands of the Germans. Still, the mayor succeeded in canceling some harsh decrees by the Germans, towards the Jews.

The Germans had some respect for religious representatives. Rabbi Yitzhak Shaul Krauza, z" l, endangered his life many times when he brought requests and demands for the good of the Jews. One time the Germans announced a decree which the Rabbi was unable to cancel. He walked out of the office of the town commander and slammed the door. It was said that the Rabbi would be arrested because of this action. However, the Germans looked into the matter, weighed the pros and cons and, in the end, decided not to arrest him.

When the Poles entered town and took over, they appointed Mr. Mordechai Verba, z" l, as vice-mayor. He did not dabble in politics and was a wealthy man. In public life, he prayed for the good of the government. He always strove not to irritate the authorities, but, still, the Jews were able to, through him, bring up their concerns. Often, the Jews were successful.

Towards the end of 1925, democratic (more or less) municipal elections were announced. There was active participation in the elections of all parties. By then I was already in Eretz Israel. I heard that the number of Jewish council members was considerable. Thus, the authorities were obliged to allow the Jews to be part of administrative decisions. Mr. Moshe Perl, z" l, head of the Zionist Union at that time, was one of those elected as a member of town council.

During the time of Mr. Perl's activity, there was a change in the administration of the town council. The authorities began to listen to the demands of the Jews. There was considerable support for institutions and schools. The influence of the Jews on the town administration was apparent.

In subsequent elections, the Jews again had good representation in the town council. Mr. Perl did his best to help the Jews- whatever he could salvage from a group consisting of known Anti-Semites (followers of Pilsudski).

The town council, a general municipal institution, took care of all residents. In addition, there was the Jewish community council. Polish law allowed it special rights in dealing with purely Jewish matters.

[Page 326]

The first head of the Jewish community was Mr. Mendel. In those days the members of the executive committee were mainly wealthy members of the synagogues.

It was only in a later period that the members of the committee were elected democratically. The power was then handed to the Zionist groups. They constituted the majority of the Jewish population of Kovel. When it came to electing the chairman of the executive committee of the community, it was evident that a Zionist would be the one. Indeed, Mr. Moshe Perl, z" l, was the chairman. The secretary was Mr. Moshe Pugatch, z" l. When the Zionists joined the committee, this institution became Jewish-Zionist in atmosphere and there were many special activities in that vein.

On the Taz Institution in Kovel

by Sonia Margalit

Translated by Ala Gamulka

I remember well the activities of the Taz from 1928. I began, then, to work as its secretary. At that time the institution had great difficulties. There was a large deficit. The various departments of Taz did not work continuously. Fortunately, at the time, many of the town leaders joined in the effort of helping the institution develop. They had much influence among their acquaintances and soon the results were quite positive.

The lively moving spirit of Taz then was Dr. Kerner (in Israel today). He was a gentle person and he felt the difficulties of the Jewish children of Kovel who needed to be cared for according to their needs.

Until 1929 there was a semi-camp in Kovel. It was an open field where the children spent their time and were fed until the afternoon. These were the first steps, but it was not enough.

The first regular summer camp was arranged by the new leadership. It was in a pine forest in Horodlitz, 7 k"m from town, in private homes of farmers. It was a simple arrangement, but it was supervised by the committee with great devotion. The happy laughter and shouts of joy of the children, liberated from the narrow, filthy home in the slums, filled the village and echoed far away. The children came from Matseyev, Ludomir, Krutka, Shkolna, Mishtchanska, etc.

In order to emphasize the need and importance of the Taz activities, the following examples can be given:

[Page 327]

Executive Committee of Taz in Kovel

[Page 328]

In order to recognize the children, to know their conditions and to decide on their urgent needs, it was necessary to visit their homes throughout the year. Those visiting were Sara Havkin, daughter of the respected Erlich family (they passed their beautiful two-story house when they walked to "town"). The sister of the director of the Jewish-Polish high school Klara Erlich, saw her work as that of a responsible person. Her devotion did not depend on anyone. In her mind, all the children were important and all needed to go to summer camp. They paid the minimum – 3 zloty per month. She was quite enthusiastic and sentimental and did not think of the budget… I had the opportunity, several times, of joining her on her visits. In one home on Matseyev, far from the center of town, the father was a carpenter and he traveled weekdays in the villages. The mother sold fruit in the market and had to rise at dawn. There were four young children in a small, narrow room. In all parts of the room, even under the beds, there were piles of fruit. In the corner there was a crib with a baby in it. It seemed as if he wore black because there were swarms of flies around him. It was fortunate that the baby was wrapped in muslin rags and that deterred the flies from eating him alive.

In a second house, in the basement of Mrs. Kartoflie, lived a tutor. He taught seven children. They were all skinny, pale and hungry, lacking sunlight and air. Among them was one who was mentally challenged. In contrast to his sad friends, he laughed non-stop- a wild laughter. This tutor also was hired to learn Mishna when wealthy people died. He refused help of any kind. He always smiled and said: "Thank God! Things should not be worse."

There are many such memories that remain. Taz received children from these homes and the children, under Taz, enjoyed special care. They were given good nourishment, clothing, medical help, etc. The tots who attended the kindergarten run by Taz constituted another group. They were children of craftsmen and small businessmen. These parents were unable to send their children to summer camps.

The administration of Taz, encouraged by Dr. Kerner, decided to erect a building for the summer camp of Taz in Horodlitz. At that time, the administration was in the hands of Dr. Kerner (still with us), attorney Felix, Dr. Shemshtein, V. Pen, Yoel Hayat, Yehiel Shtein, Lipa Hayat, Yosef Weis, Shmuel Milshtein, Leibel Shteinman, Mrs. Sara Havkin, Dr. Shatz, dentist Dr. Baruch, Shlomo Shamash, Melamed (Stoliar), etc. They all were convinced it was a difficult task, but they were determined to do all they could.

[Page 329]

I recall the first outing to Horodlitz together with contractor Haim Forshteler (he, too, contributed to the building fund by agreeing to receive his payments in installments over several years). Dr. Kerner wanted a building surrounded by sunlight. The contractor said it was impossible. Dr. Kerner spread his arms and said: "This is how you will build it! It does not matter how it looks from the outside. There must be sunlight and air for the children". When the children were sent the first time to the new building, Dr. Kerner and his wife (she was active in the women's auxiliary) walked on Shabbat evening in order to spend the night with the children and to check on the amount of sunlight and air.

The craftsmen of Kovel were helpful, as best they could, in the construction of the building. They invested much love and toil in it. They gave extra hours of their own free will, not to receive a reward. Unfortunately, I do not remember the names of all of them, especially the carpenters. Yehiel Shtein, a barber, worked not far from Taz. He would often make his customers wait while he did a good deed for a poor woman or a child. Lipa Hayat was a stern Jew. However, for the good of Taz he would often neglect his business. Shmuel Milshtein, Yosef Weis, Shteinman were all members of the Bund and were committed, heart and soul, to Taz. Most of the work of Taz was organized in the barbershop of Shteinman and in the workshop of Weis. They were all lovable, generous and admirable. They were aware of the needs of the poor in town and were ready, at any time, to save a Jewish soul in Kovel. Shteinman was also a town councillor and he did a great deal there for the benefit of his poor brethren. The tailor V. Pen, a respected Jew, aristocratic in looks, Yoel Hayat, Shlomo Shamash- they took time from their hard work to do good. The Jewish doctors and dentist- all added to the institution called Taz.

For several years, the Taz members worked in great harmony, until Dr. Kerner and his family left Kovel. There was a crisis in the activities of Taz. The headquarters became smaller and smaller until they were housed in two small rooms in the apartment of Gershonovitz. The furnaces were heated by seeds donated by the Zuperfein brothers with some additional oil. Matters reached a point where Dr. Volman, chief secretary of Taz in Warsaw decided to visit Kovel. He was a busy man and was seen using two telephones at the same time, but he had a special place in his heart for the wonderful work done in the Kovel Taz. After Dr. Volman came (he is now in the United States), the activities increased to a new height. Important and energetic people and some who had not participated before were approached. A special importance in the new activities of Taz was the addition of Dr. Ziskind, z"l.

[Page 330]

He was one of the original founders. A most productive and bright period in the history of the institution followed. It was the Ziskind period. Unfortunately, it did not last long. New administration members were: Dr. Ziskind, Dr. Tsachnovitz, Dr. Shemshtein, Klara Davidovna-Erlich, Dr. Lechel, Moshe Perl, attorney V. Pomerantz, V. Pen, Yoel Hayat, Mrs. Baruch, Sh. Milshtein, Sh. Shamash, Mrs. Sara Havkin, Mrs. Kobrinsky, Meir Kritz, Mrs. S. Kleiner, N. Olshetsky, Dr. Vidra, dentist Eisenberg. Dr. Ziskind was elected chairman. He took his work at Taz seriously. The clerks at Taz used to come to work at 8:30 am, but Dr. Ziskind was already there from

8:00 am. Dr. Ziskind also approached all the involved women in town and influenced them to organize themselves around the Taz activities. His wife was well-versed in all his public work and she, too, devoted herself to the work at Taz. She led her friends.

Dr. Ziskind, z" l, was energetic and full of good ideas. He did not accept defeat. All his practical suggestions were received by the majority. He once almost lost his life. I must tell the story.

The first thing that the Taz administration thought was important was the enlargement and renovation of the building in Horodlitz. It was planned to use the money obtained from town hall with the help of two members- Moshe Perl and attorney Pomerantz, z" l. There was also a general collection that brought good results. Everyone, even those who did not benefit from Taz activities, contributed as best they could. However, the total amount was still not enough. The dining hall of the building had a roof that was not plastered.

In June, at the opening of the summer camp, Dr. Horodlitz went to check the new building. It was a hot day and Dr. Ziskind was worried that the children would suffer from the heat in the dining room. He was so worried that he forgot to go to the hospital where his patients were waiting. He tried to find a solution.

He consulted other members of Taz on the telephone and he became even more excited. He returned home and fainted. For about an hour he did not come to. After this he spent many weeks in bed. His doctors forbade him to speak about Taz matters or to meet people who would remind him of Taz.

When he recuperated, he, of course, returned to his Taz activities. The work progressed. Bricks were obtained for large sums of money. The number of breakfasts in schools was increased.

[Page 331]

Children in the Horodlitz Colony

[Page 332]

Meals were served in the Talmud Torah. That year, the General Meeting of Taz was attended by the intelligentsia of the town as well as all small businessmen and craftsmen. Jewish Kovel had never seen such a meeting.

The nursery and kindergarten in town were also enlarged. It almost had the look of a governmental institution. Taz looked after children in the main. It was as if a magic wand was waved. Breakfast food was wrapped in white paper and was distributed by the teachers to the children during recess. Clothing was available before the holidays. Nuts and sweets were wrapped in colorful paper and this became a festive occasion. The tables were decorated with flowers and there was good order and cleanliness everywhere. The children felt like members of a large family. Dr. Pomerantz came in direct contact with the work of Taz. He was a sentimental man and was keenly interested in the children. One child who was presented as a very sickly one was taken by Fania, Mrs. Pomerantz, to her home. He became like a son to her. She took him to movies and other places. He enjoyed life with her.

It is impossible to remember everyone. Especially when one recalls that these enthusiastic and kind leaders of public life are no longer alive. Let those few that I did remember be an eternal memory for all those who were acquaintances and friends.

Finally, I wish to give details about the Women's Auxiliary that included: Mrs. Sara Havkin, Dina Ziskind, Golda Perl, Bluma Schwartz, Fania Pomerantz, Busha Gendler, Grinberg, Markiter, Tania Kutzin, Mrs. Dr. Shatz, Sonia Kleiner, Dr. Eisenberg's wife, and , still with us, Mrs. Kobrinsky (in Israel), Mrs. Darabaner- I met her after the war- and Mrs. Dr. Tsachnovitz.

[Page 333]

The Orphanage

by Yaacov Teitelkar

Translated by Ala Gamulka

Before WWI, Jewish life in Kovel was normal and the number of orphans was reasonable. The issue of orphans was not a problem, at all. The residents of Kovel were not disturbed by the need to feed the orphans. The orphans did not feel that they were carrying a heavy load. They felt comfortable with the care given to them by everyone. It reminds one of the story, by Shalom Aleichem, "Motel Feisi, son of Hune" which reflects honestly life in a Jewish shtetl during that period. The orphans were under good influence, charitable deeds and the exaggerated worries expressed by everyone. They would say: "Life is good. I am an orphan!" Neighbors and other residents saw it as their duty to bring an orphan home to be with the family and to provide him/her with a warm atmosphere and education as they did for their own children.

The situation changed after WWI. The bloody war, the pogroms and the killing of Jews in the towns and villages of Volyn, decimated and destroyed many families. There was a trail of mourning and orphaning. There was a great increase in the number of orphans from the villages around Kovel who came to town for shelter. This was a heavy burden. The people of Kovel themselves were in dire straits. The economic life of Kovel during the war was ruined. It was difficult to care for the orphans on an individual basis as there were so many of them and there was a lack of funds within Kovel. Hurriedly, the Folks Kitchen was established by the Assistance Committee organized in town by representatives of the various synagogues. The committee distributed aid received from the Joint to all those who needed it.

One of the most active women in the Folks Kitchen was Reitze Levin. She was one of the first to recognize the great need of the poor orphans. They had nothing more than the meal given to them in the Folks Kitchen. She, by herself, arranged for some of the orphans to be taken in by families. They needed a home, humanitarian conditions and for someone to look after them.

[Page 334]

(They were called Children of Reitze at all times). The number of orphans that streamed in from surrounding villages grew constantly and there were not enough private homes to accommodate them. There was no other solution, but, Reitze and others, decided to organize an orphanage. It was to be a place of shelter and rest, special and permanent.

Reitze Levin headed the effort by Mrs. Tsachnovitz, Misha Armernik, Shimon Eisen, Klara Erlich, Mrs. Havkin, Batya Armernik, Dr. Shemshtein, Dr. Tsachnovitz, Dr. Vitman, Gurin and Yaakov Borak. In 1918, the first apartment was rented in the shacks of Antin, on Lutske Street and it became the location of the first orphanage in Kovel. The committee members began to do earnest, organized work. They made sure that the poor orphans were bathed, dressed in nice, clean clothes, were fed, were calm and had spacious rooms. The basic needs were financed by assistance from the Joint. It had quickly served the Jewish communities that had been impoverished and nearly destroyed by WWI. An important department of the Joint was the one that dealt with help to orphans of war and pogrom.

In the summer of 1920, there was stop to the independent activities of the committee when Kovel saw the arrival of the Bolsheviks. Although they had various projects, they did care for the abandoned and orphaned children. They opened a Yiddish school (on Lutske Street in an Antin shack) and they provided space to these children in it. The well–known pedagogue, Bilov, was the principal. The teachers, male and female, were: Sarah Blumenfeld (now in Israel), Klara Segal, Sonia Danziger, Sonia Rubinstein, Sonia Liublinska, Hershel Nitzberg (son of Rabbi Nitzberg). The house mother was Sara Havkin. The orphans received an education, good care and were fed (paid for by the Joint). This arrangement did not last long as the Bolsheviks fled from the Poles in the summer (on the eve of Rosh Hashana). Life in Kovel, including that of the orphans, returned to its former routine. There was much work as there were close to 500 orphans under the responsibility of the committee. There were 195 boys and 290 girls (of those there were 160 full orphans and 325 with one parent still alive). The full orphans were billeted thus: 75 in the orphanage, 55 with relatives and 30 in private homes. The relatives and the private people received clothing and food for the orphans, in addition to a decent payment for their work. The orphans who still had one parent were given food and clothing in their homes. The committee also paid full tuition in the town schools where the orphans studied.

[Page 335]

Establishing a cornerstone for the orphanage named for the late lawyer Appelbaum

[Page 336]

Full tuition paid for these orphans was a substantial donation for the maintenance of the Hebrew schools. The Polish authorities did not fully subsidize them.

The value of the orphanage was high. Many saw it as a redemption. It is interesting to note that many mothers of semi–orphans who did not need the orphanage and even just ordinary mothers worried about the future of their children. They came to the committee to ask for advice. They were not turned away and the committee found a way to send the children to various youth institutions in other countries. This is how the children were able to build an independent life for themselves. There were several missions: 2 went to Eretz Israel, 19 to Argentina, 12 to Africa, 28 to Canada, 13 to England, 11 to the United States, 4 to relatives– for a total of 109.

A secondary curiosity. In spite of the great efforts of the committee to look after the orphans who required their help, the number of orphans in the orphanage grew. This was a suspicious matter and an investigation ensued. It tuned out that there were about twenty "orphans" who had both parents and who "infiltrated" the list. The parents were worried about their children and were jealous of the orphans who were receiving good care and an excellent education and were prepared for a positive independent future. This is why these parents were ready to commit this sin and to deny their own existence…

According to regulations of the Joint, these children were to be dismissed, but the committee decided otherwise. The committee undertook to continue to support these "orphans" in various ways. It considered the situation and decided that these were unusual circumstances.

The orphanage continued to develop. There was help from responsible and settled community leaders: Michael Roizen, Mr. Shapira, Michael Rosenblatt, Mina Tolier (in Israel now), Shalom Klonitsky and others. The work of the committee expanded. Soon the Kovel orphanage became a central facility. All other orphanages came under its jurisdiction.

During this great time of pride and growth of the institution, surprising news came from the Joint. It was obliged to stop its activities in subsidizing orphanages and the committee would have to do it on its own.

[Page 337]

The orphanage building, named for Dr. Yaakov Appelbaum

The committee now had to carry a heavy load. In addition to its direct subsidy, the Joint now was beginning to cut down its basic support– 25% at a time. This "retreat" of the Joint was well thought out in advance and its aim was to make the orphanages be self–sufficient.

[Page 338]

In 1923 the Joint completely withdrew and the Orphanage committee in Kovel had to face the facts.

The situation of the orphanage was difficult and dire, but the committee did not give up. The recognition that they were responsible for a large number of poor, miserable and lonely orphans pushed them to continue the work in a larger and more independent manner. Their efforts multiplied. All those who looked after the orphanage were seen by Kovel residents as a big family called orphanage with strong ties. The secretary of the committee, Asher Erlich, a bookkeeper by profession, was also an excellent counselor to the orphans. He looked after all their needs, material and spiritual. Although his political views were far left, he was well liked and appreciated by the committee. They were mostly all Zionists. They completely trusted him. It was natural for Reize Levin to be seen as the mother of the orphanage. She had given up her private life and was totally devoted to the institution. She spent days and nights there. No one was surprised that Mina Tolier– then the treasurer of the orphanage–used her own funds to pay the milkman and the grocer because the cash register was empty. Shalom Klonitsky invested all his strength in educating the orphans and in leading them in artistic endeavors. He was also the representative of the children in the school where he had sent them. He was always involved in activities for their benefit. It was not surprising that his own parents complained that he was rarely home. Fasha Leiner, an aristocratic and delicate woman (granddaughter of the Rabbi from Radzin), came to the orphanage as house mother and a counselor (she replaced Sarah Blumenfeld). She gave her warm motherly heart to the young orphans. No one was surprised when she refused to remarry after the death of her husband. She had found her purpose in the family of the orphanage.

Thanks to the dedication of these loyal people, there were always activities for the good of the orphanage. They were usually successful. The committee always felt that they were not abandoned and that the entire population was behind them. This encouraged them to try even harder. An important contribution was made by the Kovel Relief Ladies Club in the United States. They sent considerable amounts of money from time to time. They also sent 100 gold coins every month for bread.

[Page 339]

Committee of the Orphanage with the orphans

[Page 340]

In addition, they arranged for the purchase of two dairy cows so the children would drink milk. Thanks to the help from all sides, there was almost no sense of loss because of the Joint withdrawal. The orphanage remained open for new orphans who would arrive.

In 1925 the conditions of the orphanage worsened. Expenses were high and new efforts were required. It was decided to include Lawyer Yaakov Appelbaum in the enterprise. The elderly Appelbaum was still full of energy and he accepted the call to become Chairman of the Board. He was excited about his contribution and he dedicated himself to the task, ready for any sacrifice. He decided to perpetuate his work for the orphanage. He was an experienced community leader and he knew that if the orphanage had to move often to new locations, paying extra costs, it would not be possible. Failure would be the result in spite of all efforts. He wanted to prevent this from happening and he bought a lot with an old building, without the knowledge and agreement of other board members. He decided to raze the building and to build, in its place, a proper orphanage. He knew the difficulties ahead and that is why he was careful not to present his plan openly. He did not want it to be refused. After some struggle, he decided to pay for the building out of his own pocket in order to fulfill his dream.

In 1929, the old building was taken down and the construction of the new one began. By the end of that year, the orphans returned from summer camp to a magnificent, spacious new edifice, erected by their "grandfather", Yaakov Appelbaum.

In 1930, Appelbaum had a new idea: to create a day camp for the orphans in the village of Horodlitz. Since he no longer had extra funds, he asked for assistance from the orphanage board. There was much deliberation, struggling and aggravation until Appelbaum succeeded in the fulfillment of his idea. Finally, with the help of the central office in Rovno, a summer camp was arranged for the orphanage. Not only orphans enjoyed the camp, but also children of poor, sick and needy parents. There was enough food for dozens of children and they returned from summer camp healthy, wearing new clothes and shoes.

In time, because there were always new orphans added, as well as their growing up, the orphanage was obliged to establish a semi–boarding facility. This was urgently requested by poor, wretched parents for their offspring who came back from school hungry.

[Page 341]

These children were semi–boarders, were fed well and did their homework under the supervision of a licensed teacher. They stayed there till evening when they returned home to sleep.

All the orphans who finished their studies were placed by the orphanage in various shops to learn trades. Those orphans who showed exceptional talents were given the opportunity to go to the high schools in town. When the training was completed (until 1938 at least 368 orphans took part), special parties were given in their honor. They were then to take their first steps independently towards their future as useful citizens.

Many of these orphans who grew up in the orphanage and were trained by them managed to occupy important positions within society and remained in Kovel. Their emotional bond with the orphanage continued. They always enjoyed visiting the orphanage to see their teachers and counselors. Those who made Aliyah were given money for travel expenses as well as clothing and other needs– just like those who had families.

In 1938, the orphanage celebrated its 25th anniversary. A special edition of an internal newspaper called "Our 25th anniversary newspaper" was issued. Those who prepared it were: Rabbi Moshe Nahum Tversky, Rabbi Efraim Kirszner, Rabbi Moshe Bratt, Rabbi Moshe Asher Landa, Rabbi Yaakov Yankelevich, A. Baruchin, Miriam Lerner, Asher Erlich and the author of this article. In this newspaper was described the huge painstaking work done by community leaders to achieve their goal. They speak of the importance, value and role of the institution from a social, national and religious point of view. The difficult circumstances of the present are also discussed and there is a plea to the population of Kovel to help in maintaining the orphanage in the future.

In the fall of 1939, when the war between the Germans and the Poles ended, the Bolsheviks again entered Kovel. The shining period of the orphanage ended. The Bolsheviks quickly caused a socialist revolution in Kovel. All educational and public institutions were under Communist control and changed completely. Soon the orphanage suffered its fate. All the children who had studied in Hebrew schools in Kovel were transferred to Yiddish schools run by the Bolsheviks. In addition, the Polish orphanage was annexed to the Jewish one. The original, nationalistic–popular look of the orphanage was erased under the new authorities.

[Page 342]

The Ort School

by Baruch Bork

Translated by Ala Gamulka

One of the important and beautiful institutions in Kovel was the ORT school. It educated a working and productive youth. The ORT school was founded in the 1920s with the active initiative of several community leaders from among the trades people. They were headed by Avraham Glass.

The school was located in a private, rented apartment and had several departments. The first principal was the teacher Azriel Figelman, z"l.

All the needed equipment was provided by the ORT center in Warsaw. The school had a good reputation and this caused much interest among the Jewish youths in Kovel and surroundings. The school developed and continued to succeed. Graduates found work in local shops. Many of them eventually worked for themselves. Exhibitions of the creations of ORT school received much recognition among the people of Kovel. The school was especially famous for its decent and artistic work. The tailoring section, directed by Mrs. Hayat and Mrs. Fogelson, was well–known and was always busy with orders.

The ongoing budget of the school was mainly covered by the central office and by tuition paid by the students, income from sales of works, donations, etc. The financial situation was never satisfactory. There were many crisis occasions. The teachers never received their full pay and there was also a group of volunteer leaders, headed by Dr. Sokolovsky. This is how the school could continue its existence. From time to time there were campaigns for funds for the school and the citizens of Kovel were generous. In addition, the students, together with the Drama Club of Kovel, presented plays. Any income went to the school. There were also flower days which brought in some funds. In general, there was a need for a devoted group of friends who would help in the activities of Dr. Sokolovsky–loved by all. Occasionally, representatives of the central office came to help with various projects for the good of the school. All these activities allowed ORT to disseminate trades learning and education among the poor sections of the Jewish population of Kovel. There were also special courses in sewing for women. They had an excellent reputation. Many ORT graduates are now living in Israel and work in their trades. Among the ORT leaders in the last years were: Dr. Sokolovsky, Asher Frankfurt (principal of Tarbut school in Kovel), Avraham Glaz, Yehiel Stein, Israel Gortenstein, Shlomo Shames, wife of Dr. Tsichnovits, wife of Dr. Vitman, wife of Dr. Eisenberg (dentist), Pinie Sheinboim, Volf Penn, Yankel Schwartz, Yitzhak Sheynkar and Shieke Friedman.

[Page 343]

A group of ORT female students with their teacher Ts. Yucht

The one who contributed the most to the existence of ORT school was the important community leader– a tradesman– Avraham Glaz. He did not bother much with his shop and so deprived his family of income. Day and night, he continued his demands from his colleagues to help out. He traveled to Berlin to the National conference of ORT in order to obtain something for his special project– ORT school. He is now in Poland. It is incumbent upon us to give him the hearty thanks in the name of hundreds of ORT graduates who had a decent life because of his efforts, devotion and volunteering for the institution.

[Page 344]

Medical Institutions and the Physicians of Kovel

by Dr. Mordechai Leiberson

Translated by Amy Samin

The city of Kovel with its 32,000 inhabitants had 25 physicians, of whom 14 were Jewish. The work of the doctors was centered around the city's hospitals. One was the governmental Simikovi Hospital and the second the Jewish Hospital on Behalf of the Jewish Community. The director of the latter was Dr. Weitman. The budget which supported the hospital was partially based on support from the municipality but the majority of the support came from the community. This hospital had an average of 60 beds. In the city there were also a number of clinics run by municipal organizations as well as a few run by the community. The Taz association organized a large polyclinic which served the Jewish public in the medical field and in its daily needs. In this field, the work of the Jewish doctor at Taz was on a volunteer basis. The treatments and medical assistance in this organization were enjoyed mainly by the simple folk of the Jewish community. From the time of its founding until the destruction of the clinic in 1939, the heads of this institution were the famous doctors of the city, including: Dr. Feinstein z"l, Dr. Zisskind, and Dr. Appelboim. In the day to day medical care, they were joined by doctors each according to his profession and specialization:

Dr. Schatz, internal medicine; Dr. Vidra Yosef, internal medicine, gynecology, and obstetrics; Dr. Nymark, internal medicine; Dr. Lekal, ear, nose, and throat; Dr. Zisskind, pediatrics. Administrative work was handled by Sonia Margulis. In addition to all of the clinical medical work the management also did vital prophylactic work in the field, providing vaccinations against all kinds of seasonal infectious diseases such as smallpox and typhus, as well as detection of the disease tuberculosis. In the summer, Taz organized camps for the schoolchildren from the poorer strata of the Jews in the community. These were the famous colonies of Horodlatz, the summer resort next to Kovel. The operation of those summer camps was in the hands of the doctors: Dr. Zisskind, Dr. Schatz, Dr. Vidra, and Dr. Tzichnovitz. A good diet, the fresh air of the pine forests, sunshine, water, and sports were the factors that immunized and strengthened the children before their return to the city for their renewed studies. One of the most senior physicians of the city was Dr. Feinstein. He dealt in general internal medicine, and was very well liked and respected in the city. He was a figure who inspired respect, with his imposing figure and a smile always spread over his face, which drew to him all who came to him for counsel and medical assistance. He passed away at a ripe old age. He was one of the doctors of the old Russian–Jewish school, which has disappeared and is no more.

Dr. Tzichnovitz, a doctor of general internal medicine, was involved in public affairs and was an activist, and spent much of his time dealing in public health matters. He was the school physician at the Jewish schools and the Hebrew *Gymnasia*. His lectures on personal and public hygiene, and hygiene of the student were very interesting.

[Page 345]

For years he preached on cleanliness of the body, nutrition, proper attire according to the season, sports – in short "a healthy soul in a healthy body." He gave of his time and energy to work for Taz, organizing summer camps for the children of the city who needed it. He survived the Holocaust and lives in Russia with his family. He was an ardent Zionist, and I am certain that his heart and his longing are given to our country.

Dr. Zisskind Petya z"l was a pediatrician and also dealt in internal medicine. He was a serious doctor who was devoted to his patients, and also a public activist. He was among the managers of Taz for many years and even the severe heart disease that afflicted him only temporarily stopped him from the treatment and care of the health of Jewish children, whether they were in Taz or not. He was murdered during the Holocaust. His younger daughter Sofka lives in Israel, and the other, Freya, lives in France.

Dr. Vidra Yosef z"l practiced internal medicine, gynecology, and obstetrics. He was a popular doctor in town and was devoted to his patients. He served the public and gave of his knowledge and ability to those in need of medical help in Taz and also worked at the Jewish school. He and his family were murdered in the Holocaust.

Dr. Weitman's specialty was dermatology. For years he was the manager of the Jewish hospital and he also devoted his time to public medical work in Taz. His family was murdered in the Holocaust. According to reliable reports, he survived and is in Russia.

Dr. Shomstein z"l specialized in internal medicine. He arrived in Kovel during the 1930's and immediately endeared himself to all levels of society in the town. He was an excellent physician and a good diagnostician. He and his family were murdered during the Holocaust.

Dr. Schatz z"l practiced general and internal medicine. He gave of his time and energy to public medical work in Taz. He and his family were killed in the Holocaust.

Dr. Lekal was an ear, nose, and throat doctor, an excellent specialist and surgeon. He was one of the assistants to the famous Professor Noiman of Vienna. He worked in Taz. He was murdered during the Holocaust.

Dr. Nymark z"l, who practiced general and internal medicine, was one of the younger doctors of the city. He quickly became endeared to everyone, and was considered a serious and devoted physician. In Taz, he worked as an internist. He and his family were murdered during the Holocaust.

Dr. Hassim (in Israel) is an expert in diseases of the lungs – tuberculosis. He practices in this field in Israel and through his serious knowledge in this field is helping to eradicate the disease among the Jews living in Israel.

Dr. Ratnovsky–Ratniv Pioter, a surgeon, who worked with Dr. Retaisky, the manager of Simikovi Hospital, and with Dr. Yaborovsky in the Jewish Hospital. He worked in Taz as a surgeon. Today he lives in Russia where he serves as the chief surgeon in a military hospital.

[Page 346]

Dr. Weisberg, a general internal medicine physician, was one of the younger doctors. His wife, who was of the Burstein family, was a teacher at the Klara Ehrlich *Gymnasia* in 1938–39, and later at High School No. 10 during the days of the Soviets. She was murdered during the Holocaust.

Dr. Varba Gershon (Grisha) is an ophthalmologist (oculist) and today is the manager of the municipal polyclinic in Kovel. One of the younger doctors. He completed his studies in Czechia. He is a graduate of the *Tarbut Gymnasia*. He is the son of the attorney and activist Leon (Leib) Varba z"l. He has not been allowed to leave Russia despite his wishes.

Dr. Geller z"l was a graduate of the Jewish–Polish *gymnasia*, and practiced general internal medicine. He completed his studies in Czechia. In Kovel he worked in the Jewish hospital for a number of years. He was murdered during the Holocaust.

Dr. Melamed Yosef z"l, also a graduate of the Jewish–Polish *gymnasia*, was a surgeon. In the days of the Soviets he worked in the hospital and in a clinic. He was murdered in the Holocaust.

Dr. Weinstein Binyamin is a graduate of the Jewish–Polish *gymnasia* who finished his medical studies in Italy. He lives in Tel Aviv and practices internal medicine.

Dr. Marmelstein Yosef (Yozik) is a graduate of the Slovetski Government Gymnasia. He began his medical studies in Warsaw and completed them in Lvov, during the Soviet days of 1939. He is an internist, and today lives in Australia. He survived the Holocaust as a doctor in the Partisans.

Dr. Eisenberg z"l was a dentist. He was quite well–known in the city. He and his family were murdered in Kovel. His only son lives in Israel. He graduated from the Technion University in Haifa and works as an engineer.

(Mrs.) Dr. Kotzin z"l was also a well–known dentist in the city. She was murdered in the Holocaust.

Dr. Kotzin z"l was a famous dentist. He was a Zionist and public activist. He was cut down in the prime of his life.

We also recall the well–known figure of the medical assistant – feldscher[1] – Reb Motink z"l, who was the permanent assistant of the famous Dr. Schatz. He was murdered in the Holocaust.

Baskin, one of the first medical assistants in the city, also owned a pharmacy and was very well–liked in town.

Magister Shtillerman, a pharmacist with *Leinat HaTzedek*. He ran the pharmacy with dedication and loyalty. He was murdered in the Holocaust.

Kramer Avraham was the husband of the teacher Grau. He worked in the pharmacy of Praj Movesky.

Magister Erlich z"l was a pharmacist with Friedlander. She was the sister of Klara Erlich, the principal of the *gymnasia*. She was murdered in the Holocaust.

[Page 347]

We recall the memory of the ranks of the Jewish nurses, who anonymously and with unfailing devotion, brought relief and medicine to the patients at all hours of the day and night. I do not remember their names.

In the days of the Soviets, from 1 September 1939 the public medical institutions of the Jewish community were closed. The Jewish hospital became Municipal Hospital No. 2. The Taz was shut down. *Leinat HaTzedek* also closed, and the pharmacy was destroyed. The doctors went to work for the government.

Translator's Note:

1. a health care professional who provides various medical services

The Founding of Bikur Cholim and the New Hospital

by Eliezer Leoni

Translated by Amy Samin

Prior to discussing the hospital, we must pay tribute to an exceptional person, a great doctor, one of the directors of Bikur Cholim– Dr. Mordechai Kolkin, z"l. Dr. Kolkin was the first Jewish doctor in town. He died young, at the age of thirty– three. The townspeople remember, no doubt, that when they went to the new cemetery, they could see, not far away, Dr. Kolin's gravestone. Next to it was that of his three–year–old son.

There were many legends told about Dr. Kolkin. He stood out in his qualities and in his good deeds for needy patients. He never asked for payment from one of them. In addition– he supported needy patients with his own funds. It was common to discover that when Dr. Kolkin left the home of a poor patient, his family would find money under his pillow. He was well–off and he did not wish to embarrass the poor family by giving them money directly.

The elders of town tell the story that, once, when he was in his wagon on his way to one of the patients, the horse was moving lazily and was barely able to stand erect. Dr. Kolkin shouted at the Jewish driver because he was anxious to get to the sick patient who was in danger. The driver replied: "yes, dear doctor. I know you are in a hurry to reach your patients, but I can't do anything. My horse is sick and I do not have the money to buy another one, a better one". "How many rubels do you need to buy another horse?" asked Dr. Kolkin. "Fifteen"– replied the driver. "Will this be enough?"– asked again the doctor. "It will suffice"– replied the driver.

Dr. Kolkin took fifteen rubels from his pocket and added fifteen more. He said: "With the additional money, you can prepare for Shabbat and you and your family can eat well".

[Page 348]

Dr. Kolkin died on 16 February 1892, at the age of thirty–three. On the day of his funeral, all stores were closed, even those of the non–Jews. The Rabbi ended his eulogy with these words: "Go out now, angels of peace. Carry him on your shoulders. May his soul, in the Garden of Eden, be bound with the living. He was honest and charitable and his good deeds will be repaid double".

Bikur Cholim was founded in 1882. Its directors were: Dr. Kolkin, Dr. Feinstein and B. Rabinerzon. When the permit was obtained in1891, the institution began to do more activities. From year to year, the state of the institution ameliorated and it served the purpose for which the townspeople had established it.

In order to understand the breadth of medical help that the hospital offered to the Jews of Kovel, we can study the annual report of the hospital from 1900. In that year, there were 209 patients: 89 men, 74 women and 46 children. In addition to those hospitalized, there were also visits by 920 patients. They were able to recuperate at home. There were 235 men, 245 women and 390 children. Many received free medications from the pharmacy in the hospital.

In 1895, the administration of the hospital realized that it was lagging in scientific research. There was a need for a new, modern hospital, equipped with up–to–date gear. The administration approached the Minister of the Interior to assign 10 000 rubels, from the meat tax, towards the construction of the new hospital.

These efforts were fruitful and in 1898 the required permit was received. The lot for the construction had been prepared earlier in one of the suburbs. It was a large space, surrounded by greenery. As soon as the permit was given, the construction began. It took close to three years. The building was magnificent and well–suited to medical and hygienic requirements. It contained 16 large rooms, 16 beds, a pharmacy, doctors' room, a bath house, laundry and other necessary offices. The expenses came up to 12 575 rubels.

The building of the hospital and its enlargement were possible thanks to a donation given by a saintly person. Near town, there lived a wealthy man called Melishkevitz. His father was the treasurer of the federal archives in Kovel. When he died, he left his son all his wealth. Melishkevitz visited the hospital and was impressed by its beauty and comforts. In recognition, he donated, on the spot, 4 000 rubles. He also announced he was ready to give more, if needed. This donation helped to make the building even better and to build lodgings for the guards and the medic. They also added an ice cellar.

On 14 May 1901 the official opening of the new Jewish hospital took place. It was an elegant celebration. At 2:00 pm a large crowd gathered.

[Page 349]

Among the people there were some non–Jewish guests: army generals, municipal clerks and doctors, the mayor and his friends– all beautifully dressed. The cantor and his choir sang "Song for house dedication". They were followed, on stage, by Rabbi Brik. He led a short prayer in honor of the dedication and then spoke, in Russian. He explained to those assembled the meaning of the commandment "Bikur Cholim" (Visiting the sick). Our religious leaders in the past had always considered it to be one of the most important commandments. Those performing this commandment earn their place in heaven.

At the end of his speech, the Rabbi thanked the directors Prozhansky, Brandeis and Rabinerzon, all the people who took part in the erection of the building and all those who donated beds and other household goods to the hospital. He especially praised Dr. Feinstein, the head doctor in the hospital.

The Lives of Kovel's Laborers

by Mordechai Hinizon

Translated by Amy Samin

I would like to commemorate the city's trade unions and activists of the city.

At the head of the Woodworkers Union stood Michel Hinizon, Lederman, Colodner, and others. At the head of the Bakers Union were Zeelig Burstein, Friedman, Kagan, and so on. The Needleworkers Union – Batya Mendel, Rahel Masir, Chayat, and others. The Construction Workers Union was led by Kagan, Melamed, and others. The Leatherworkers – Goldener and others.

I further recall the Evening Classes company, led by David Mailer, Zela Kaploshnik, Dr. Reis, and others.

Alongside the professional associations, there existed a Workers' Library, which was used as a meeting place by the workers during their leisure hours, after work. On Saturdays, the library management would arrange question–and–answer receptions attended by the local working intelligentsia and by guests from outside. Among those from Kovel who participated were, mainly, Weintraub, Waxman, Feigelman the teacher, and others.

There was also a dramatic association, which put on theatrical plays in Yiddish which aroused great interest in all of the workers of the city.

The workers were represented in the municipality by Yagodnik, Steinman, and Dr. Reis z"l. However, fascist Poland looked askance at the rising power of the trade unions and began to constrict their movements.

When the trade unions decided to celebrate the first of May together in 1928 and appealed to the *starosta*[1] for a permit to do so, it was denied. However, the workers paid no notice and gathered in large numbers near the trade union building.

[Page 350]

Then the Polish police arrived and began to forcibly disperse the crowd. The crowd spontaneously organized itself into a procession and began moving towards Warszawska Street. However, a massive response came from the police, both on foot and mounted on horseback; they began raining murderous blows on the protestors. Several activists were arrested and imprisoned for 10 months. In March of 1929 the trial was held, which ruled to release them, however that same evening more arrests took place, and many of the workers and the working intelligentsia were jailed. The Woodworkers Union was disbanded and the Workers' Library was closed and its contents confiscated.

Translator's Note:

1. A government official

The Clubhouse Named For Y.L. Peretz

A. Doari (Potchter)

Translated by Ala Gamulka

The clubhouse served as a meeting place for middle and working classes. The main attraction was the library which had 2 000 volumes in four languages: Yiddish, Russian, Polish and Hebrew.

The organizers were: Meir Reis, Dobrovdka, Weintraub, Yoske Yeruchamovitz and Fania Schwartzberg. The first librarian was Margolian. He was followed by Potchter and Fania Yeruchamovitz.

The clubhouse served as a meeting place for those who were unable to study in high school and higher, but were interested in learning science, literature, singing and music. There was no political or party affiliation. It was simply cultural. The youths were seized by the idea and dedicated all their strength and energy for the good of the clubhouse. They came in the evenings, after work, to spend time together and to hear lectures on artistic and literary topics, given by various speakers.

Music held an important place in the life of the clubhouse. There was an orchestra of 20 people. It was organized by Mr. Broshek who played the violin. Others were Arlichgerecht, Fimes, Potchter, Moshe Weinstein, Aharon Friedman and Fidelman.

The orchestra had prepared a concert to be performed in front of the public. However, for some reason, it did not happen. There were internal concerts and all income was reserved for the maintenance of the clubhouse and the library.

It is not for nothing that the clubhouse was named for the great, popular writer.

[Page 351]

Founding executive of the Clubhouse named for Y. L. Peretz in Kovel

Peretz wrote stories for the people and the library was intended for workers– laborers, clerks and teachers. All these people would gather in the clubhouse to read a newspaper, play chess and discuss world events.

[Page 352]

Righteous Lodging

Yaakov Teitelkar

Translated by Ala Gamulka

There were various popular–traditional institutions of charity in Kovel. They were "Bikur Cholim", "Residence for the elderly", "Fund for the Needy", etc. "Righteous Lodging" held an important place among these institutions. This charitable institution was similar to "Kupat Cholim" and was meant, first and foremost, to look after the poor of our town.

The name "Righteous Lodging" literally means– house where charity will lodge. In general, this description suits all the philanthropic institutions of the Diaspora existence. It indicates the original purpose of this institution, i.e., charitable lodging, in the homes of its members, of lonely, segregated and sick people. These people had no family. It was important to do it and especially in times of epidemics and calamity which sometimes affected the entire population of Kovel. There was a need for volunteers who could offer help immediately.

The basis of "Righteous Lodging", like the other institutions, refers to the earlier times of the Jewish Diaspora. Then, social help was done by individual families, when the villages had a stable life, one large family. People looked after each other in a good way.

In the meantime, the population of the town and the village grew and blossomed. Culture, education and an organized society could be seen through the spiritual ghetto wherever there were Jews. In time, everything changed and modern educational institutions were created. Charitable institutions also changed and wore a new façade. Leaders with advanced views took over and placed the institutions on a proper public standing.

One of the first leaders who undertook the job of organizing "Righteous Lodging" was the famous, modest philanthropist of Kovel– Yosef Shochat. He dedicated himself to the institution and gave it all his energy and his might. This is in the full sense of these words. He did much for the advancement of the institution. Instead of the traditional treasurers, a modern committee was elected. The committee included: representatives of the religious Jews, the best from synagogues and shtiebels, Zionists, merchants and trades people, political parties and various organizations. An apartment was rented. It included an organized pharmacy (in the house of Pickholtz–Goldberg near the bridge). The pharmacist was Zalman Shtilerman. His medical service was helpful and important to the poor and even the middle class.

[Page 353]

The duties of the institution branched out, spread out and expanded. The traditional aim of "Righteous Lodging" was for volunteer–members to host the sick, poor and needy in their homes. Now, with the approval of the committee, Rabbis and other organizations, there was an additional task of distributing medications and therapeutic instruments, medical appointments (doctors were cooperative), assistance with obtaining admission to the hospital, visiting nurses in homes of the sick, etc.

Shlomo Tolier, z"l

"Righteous Lodging", as other charitable institutions, depended on pledges and donations for their existence. These were done in synagogues and Shtiebels– donations from collection on the eve of Yom Kippur, from the community budget, monthly fees paid by members (collected by the veteran treasurer "Voptsi"), and sums given by community leaders. However, all these funds could not cover the perpetual deficit of a charitable institution due its constant needs, great expenditures and small income.

[Page 354]

Soon the unpredictable years of WWI came and the town was flooded with refugees from nearby fronts. The economic and health situations worsened, the deficit was great and medical needs could not be looked after. The "Righteous Lodging", as other institutions, underwent a big crisis and it was ready to dissolve.

When the war ended, the desolation in the public institutions was huge. Towards the end of 1919, the Poles entered town. There was a change in authority as well as new ways of life and the work grew exponentially. The Poles investigated and found that the apartment of "Righteous Lodging" was inadequate for a pharmacy. Due to the economic breakdown, there were many internal arguments between the committee and the pharmacist. Yossel Shochat– a straightforward man, resigned from the presidency. "Righteous Lodging" was orphaned and was waiting for redemption… and here he came– in the image of the energetic town leader– Shlomo Tolier, z" l.

Shlomo Tolier came to Kovel from Bilitskrov (Russia) in 1919. He was an energetic businessman. He was a partner in the electrical station and owned a factory manufacturing nails. He found time to dedicate himself to the turmoil of public life in town. Most of all, he was involved in "Righteous Lodging" and expanded all his energy to the rehabilitation of this institution. In 1921, he took over, from Yosef Shochat, the running of the institution. He immediately undertook to reorganize the committee and to bring in new recruits. The new committee consisted of: Shlomo Tolier (president), Michael Rosenblatt (vice president), Mika Gasco (secretary), Leib Fish, Leibel Frishberg, Yehiel Eibshitz, Moshe Schwartzblat, Volf Gonik, Mordechai Mokrin, Avraham Glaz, Avraham Geller, Liova Stock, Shteinbach, Shlomo Schnitzer.

His second task was to rent a new, appropriate apartment for the pharmacy, as required by the authorities. It was in the house of Tsippa Roiter on Warshavska Street. Soon he addressed the need for an economic grounding for the institution by increasing the number of members, raising monthly fees, organizing parties and concerts by famous cantors (Sirota and Koussevitzky). They were brought especially to Kovel. There were also flower tag days. There were also constant struggles with the Polish magistrate for additional funds for "Righteous Lodging". There was improvement in the set–up of the institution and its accomplishing its duties. All this was due to his efforts. He managed to elevate the institution, to advertise it in the community and to create a strong basis which would guarantee its existence and development.

This successful situation in "Righteous Lodging" continued for 13 years. His 10th anniversary was celebrated in 1923. He was recognized for excellence with a special plaque commemorating his activities for "Righteous Lodging".

[Page 355]

In 1933 he left Kovel (the Polish authorities confiscated his electrical station). He went, with his four brothers, to Lublin. They opened a factory there. He was replaced by Michael Rosenblatt. Even after his departure from Kovel, Shlomo Tolier was still important. His influence was still evident. "Righteous Lodging" was put on the right road by him and it continued to develop and succeed. It became well–known in all parts of the population and many poor or sick or needy people found a place there. They were supplied with all their needs. Then came the satanic world sinner, Hitler, may his name be erased, and he overturned everything. All the patients and the doctors, the receivers and the givers– those who perform public service in good faith– may their memory be a blessing for generations!

Institutions, Groups and Gathering Places
(Streams and moods of some of the Jewish youth in Kovel)

Meir Rosenblatt (Paris)

Translated by Ala Gamulka

The 1930s– Polish anti–Semitism– were tough times for the Jews. They struggled daily for their existence. On the other hand, it was a period of the deepening of national identity. Among the Jewish youths of Kovel there was a change of values– a thirst for cultural values.

The students of the Jewish–Polish high school, headed by Klara Erlich, met with other Jewish students from the Polish high school. They also connected with the students of Tarbut high school. The latter met with Hassidic young people.

In this special atmosphere, several unusual youth organizations were created in Kovel.

The Zionist, non–party youth organization in Kovel

There were dozens of Jewish youth, who identified as nationalists, but were unable, for various reasons, to join the existing Zionist youth organizations in Kovel. Senior students and graduates of the high schools had debates about joining one organization or another.

[Page 356]

Someone made a suggestion: "why don't we create a Zionist, unaffiliated youth group?"

Talk became deed and in 1930 a different organization: "The Zionist unaffiliated youth organization in Kovel". Kovel had groups of all colors of the rainbow up to then.

The organizing meeting was held in the Beit Am hall on Senkevitcha Street. There were about twenty to thirty young people. Representing Tarbut high school were: Yitzhak Guberman, Penina Goltsblat, Yerachmiel Goldsmidt and others. From the high school of Klara Erlich came– Velvel (Zeev) Lifshitz, Liova (Aryeh) Reiner, the author of this article and their friends.

The program aims of the movement were: activity for the Funds, research into the history of Zionism, geography of Eretz Israel, deeper study of Hebrew culture, etc.

Yitzhak Guberman was elected chairman of this new movement. Together with the chosen committee, he began to develop a broad and many–faceted program. The home of the movement became Beit Am. It was offered by the Kovel Zionist organization.

Unfortunately, the days of this new youth movement did not last. There was a great struggle within the various Zionist youth movements to entice these unaffiliated young people. Several of the leaders of the new group went in different directions. Others just left. The movement collapsed. However, the fact that had even existed was typical of the train of thought of some of the Jewish youths in Kovel.

Yiddish Clubs

The students of the Jewish–Polish high school had a very shallow and limited knowledge of Jewish culture. They wished to learn more after school hours.

As proof of this need, a group of students organized a club for the study of Jewish literature. Meetings were held in the warm and welcoming home of the Gelman family on Fabritchna Street. The hosts– Moshke and Meike Gelman, may they rest in peace– welcomed their fellow students.

In addition to the high school students, there were Hertz Levin, Liova Gelman and Aaron Werba who recited the works of the leaders of Jewish literature.

We worked hard on analyzing "Mipi Ha'am" (from the people) by Peretz. We would read a story, ask questions and awaken ideas. There was an interesting and substantive exchange that usually ended with a discussion of the cultural, social and present problems.

[Page 357]

Literature and History Clubs

The students of Klara Erlich were energetic and active. They did not stop at Jewish literature since they were also interested in general Jewish topics– history, Tanach, Jewish life, history of Zionism and the pioneering movement.

They were joined the few students from the Polish high school. They, too, were hungry for Hebrew culture.

The lively leader in these clubs was, for a long time, Russia–Ruth Djeshevsky. She had studied in the Polish high school. One day she left it and transferred to the Jewish–Polish high school.

She was the daughter of Pinhas Djeshevsky, z"l, who was known around the world as the person who attacked the persecutor of Jews, Pavel Krushevan. The latter had been responsible for the Kishinev pogrom. She, obviously, had inherited a fiery and stormy temperament from her father. Her uncle was Avraham Sheynkar, a well–known Zionist in Kovel. This is where she learned about the first Zionist congresses.

She was sensitive, educated and talented in literature and other cultural subjects. She was swept up by the cultural values of the Jewish renewal movement.

The meetings took place at least once a week. Sometimes they were held in the home of Russia Djeshevsky and other times in different houses.

The students of the Jewish–Polish high school who attended were Tsippa Beirach, Velvel Lifshitz, Reiner, Rosenblatt and others. Those from the Polish high school were: Fania Osiuk, Fira Khazanov–Ziskind, Fania Forshteler, Regina Roiter, etc. The only representative of Mirenitche School was Srulik Burstein.

The lecturers were mostly students of the Hebrew high school. Frimer spoke about the majesty of the Jew who praises his superior, as described by Mendele. Tuvia Weisbrot discussed the "Exodus from Egypt" as the earliest socialist movement in history. Yerachmiel Goldsmidt recited "Auto emancipation" by Pinsker.

Questions were posed, opinions given and there was excitement and argument. The youths searched for solutions to current, burning issues. Over all, Jewish topics were of utmost interest.

The discussions in these wonderful clubs went on for hours. Late at night, after the meetings were over, the quiet streets of Kovel still echoed with the discussions.

These clubs were not run by teachers or leaders. They were autonomous creations.

[Page 358]

They were an integral part of the Jewish youth scene in Kovel. They became essential to many of the young people.

Ohel Shem

The House of Learning of the rabbi from Trisk had, several times a week, Hassidic young men who came after work to study Gmara. Here is Yochanan (Yochanantchik) Tversky– smiling, but with a penetrating look. He was the son of the town rabbi– Nahum–Moshele. There is the silent Fishel Gitlis, son of Yeshayahu the Scribe; another is likable Leibel Tabakhandler, son of the Lubavitcher Hassid Rabbi Avraham–Nachman; there is serious Asher Kleinerman. Others are the young boys, gifted children and grandchildren of the ritual slaughterers of Kovel.

On the other side appear several graduates of the Hebrew high school and the Jewish–Polish high school. They were knowledgeable in Tanach, Hebrew literature and Jewish History, but they wanted to enrich their knowledge in original sources. They were Yitzhak Klonitsky– friendly and round, lovable Yitzhak Guberman, happy and talented Israel Steingarten, Liova (Aryeh) Reiner– always involved in artistic endeavors, Meir Rosenblatt and others.

Unseen threads connect the first group with the second. The two groups sensed that one can complement the other.

This is how the special, outstanding Ohel Shem was formed.

The young people met several times a week– sometimes in the House of Learning of the rabbi from Trisk –located in the outskirts of town– and other times on the "sands" of the little House of Learning of "Righteous Lodging".

The Hassidic enthusiasm merged with the scientific method. Deep beliefs joined dreams of culture and development. Leibel Tabakhandler studied Gmara. Everyone was seriously studying Tanach, Rambam and discussing Jewish values. They went deep into Jewish philosophy and human experience.

The club grows and draws new faces. Effervescent Mates Krazhner, leader of the Zeirei Mizrachi of Kovel; gentle Hershel Bakun; Yehiel Goldberg who is always busy with his own problems; Berl Landver, son of the Rabbi; the brothers Melamed, the saddlers who live in "town" and the three Bochover brothers.

They study seriously until late at night. They get closer and become friends.

[Page 359]

Members of Ohel Shem
Standing right to left: Mates Krazhner, Hershel Bakun, Yitzhak Klonitsky, (unknown fourth)
Seated right to left: Hershel Avrech, Yeshayahu Avrech, Meri Rosenblatt, Goldschmid

A party is organized in the Trisk House of Learning. There are speeches and Hassidic dancing.

When the studying is over, everyone goes home late at night. The "town" people go in one direction while the "sand" residents go in the other direction.

* *

Young people from different social strata, with varying degrees of culture and learning– managed to unite in clubs and groups, in friendship. They yearned for Jewish content, Jewish thought and they were interested in sources. They dreamed of a world of honesty and justice.

Most of them were killed in the name of God. May their memory be a blessing!

[Page 360]

The Orphanage From Within

M. Olitzky (United States)

(Translated from Yiddish to Hebrew by E. Leoni)

Translated by Ala Gamulka

I spent five years of my life in Kovel. Usually, these childhood years are the happiest times in one's life. Unfortunately, for me, these were bleak and gloomy years. Being an orphan and living in a foreign place were heavy burdens. I was shy and sensitive from birth and the atmosphere in the orphanage depressed me. I was obliged to accept my bitter fate and to face reality. I constantly thought how I could escape from this place and these thoughts added to my feelings of depression and sadness.

I felt tormented every time I came to the orphanage for the noon meal or to obtain a loaf of bread. I was comforted by the fact that I did not have to sleep there with all the other children. I was staying in a private home; sometimes alone and other times with more children of Reitze.

The orphanage building was not fully completed and it stood in a corner of town near the municipal prison. The short lane emerging from Mitzkivitcha Street was covered in snow in the winter. In autumn our legs were mired in clay and slime. The orphans walked on by holding on to the rickety fence.

The lane dissolved into a large square near the prison. There were two walls– the red one of the orphanage and the white one of the prison. They both inspired gloom. Passers–by would lower their gaze so as not to be suspected of looking up at the tiny windows. They were all in disrepair.

The depressed mood did not ameliorate when one entered into the rooms of the orphanage. The building had not been completed yet. The walls showed helplessness and desolation. There were long wooden tables where the children sat. Occasionally, there were white tablecloths. In front of the kitchen door there were many hungry children waiting impatiently for their "daily bread". The three meals of the day were monotonous: in the morning and in the evening–bread with jam or fat and a semi–sweetened tea; at noon there was soup with black bread. Sometimes there were a few pieces of meat. The bread was not rationed, but there was really not enough in the meal to satisfy hunger. Small children and sick ones were given milk. On Shabbat there were slices of challah.

I did not usually eat with the other children. I had special privileges because I lived far from the orphanage. I avoided the other children and I went closer to the table. I was embarrassed by the large piece of meat I was given on a plate because the other children looked at me with their hungry eyes. I also tried not to bump into Mr. Appelbaum.

[Page 361]

Old man Appelbaum built the orphanage with his own money. He also continued to give material help. He did not want to accept me. It is possible the reason for this was the difficult economic situation or my "old" age– I was 14. The "old man" was respected, but he really was not the boss. The true bosses were Reitze Levin and Erlich. They were on my side to be accepted into the institution.

Reitze Levin, or as she was called simply Reitze, sank her whole being into working for the orphans. She had started as a young girl. She came from the dynasty of Sarah Ben Tovim and dedicated her days and nights to these poor orphans. In daytime she would roam the town to find homes, work and money. Often, she would collect Challot for Shabbat. In the evenings she looked after the children and their clothing. She went to sleep late at night at her parents' house. It was a long way and she was received angrily at home. She sacrificed her personal life. She gave up on having children and did not marry Erlich. The entire town was expecting them to marry and everyone was anxious to wish them Mazal Tov. For the good of the children, she found them private homes. She hoped it would be easier for them to succeed and become independent. These were the children of Reitze.

I never knew the first name of Erlich. He was short and a little stocky, but his face radiated goodness. He always carried a thick walking stick with which he was able to "cross the Jordan" It paved his way in the mud and slime as he went to work in the orphanage. Officially, he was the secretary and bookkeeper, but he was really "everything". All the problems of the orphanage were thrown on his shoulders and he took care of them.

There were many good people who tried their best, but it was not enough to satisfy dozens of children. Sadness was always visible on their faces. It was rare to hear a child laugh. I don't need to add that they did not sing.

In my lowly opinion, this situation was not decreed from above. The educational side was inadequate. The absence of experienced and knowledgeable teachers was obvious. They would have enriched the lives of the children and made them happier. Pasha, the official teacher, was bothered by administrative duties. She made sure the children received food on time, that linens were clean and clothing was, more or less, not torn. She often had to search for bread for their meals. She, too, was not pleased with the situation. She often complained that she had to perform duties that she was not happy to do.

[Page 362]

She could not do more. Her love for the children was boundless. As she passed hurriedly through the building, she often hugged the children.

For the children these hugs were not enough. As a result, they became serious quite early. They began to think about studying and a trade. They wished to become independent and to leave the orphanage. Their dream was to grow up and become one of the children of Reitze. The latter lived in private homes and not every one knew that they were orphans.

Erlich also knew and understood that the educational part was inadequate. He planned many assemblies or celebrations, but they never came to fruition. He had other problems to worry about.

I slept over in the orphanage on some nights. The bedrooms were on the second floor. They were long rooms with iron beds covered in blankets. Before bedtime Pasha would light small red lamps. In this gloomy light, the rooms looked even darker.

The first night I went to the bedroom, I was shocked by the red light and I stopped at the door. In the dim red light, I noticed a few children crouching on their beds. Others stood at the windows and looked at the bright moonlit skies. Their sad faces were lit and they were all deep in a heavy and depressing muteness.

I lay on my bed, in my clothes, until late at night. I did not close my eyes. I felt the loneliness of the orphans and I understood my situation.

On that night I wrote my poem. A few years later it was published in "Literary Pages".

Children

Where should I go with my smile, since
Children also have the serious faces
Of grown ups?
In daytime they stand with their faces looking down
They are in foreign places.
At night they look out through the window pane
Their eyes reflect tiny moons
Like large tears of milk.
They dream of a mother's bosom which had not nursed them
How good it must be
A piece of bread spread with butter,
Like a ripple moon.
Where should I go with my smile
When even children are serious?

[Page 363]

The Founding of the Ort School and its Development

Avraham Glaz (Poland)

Translated by Ala Gamulka

Towards the end of 1922 there was a meeting at the courtyard of lawyer Appelbaum. The artisans' association was there. Many people came to the meeting and a committee was chosen. However, no one agreed to be the chairperson. I had no choice and I undertook the position.

In those days there was, in Kovel, a workshop for men's tailoring. There were eight or nine apprentices. Their teacher was Avraham Manis (he was called Avraham-Berl of Trisk). The workshop was on the outskirts of town, in the house of Avraham Sheynkar.

The next day, after my appointment of the chairman of ORT, I went to see how they were learning. When I entered, I saw the teacher teaching the boys Rosh Hashana prayers. He was also a cantor in the Brik synagogue. When I saw that the teacher had transformed the workshop into "opera", I decided to transfer the tailoring class to the center of town. I rented an apartment on Third of May Street, in the house of Asher the musician. The workshop was there now.

Six weeks later I went to visit my creation. Here, again, they were continuing to rehearse prayers of the High Holy Days. They were not even tired as there was no sign of tailoring work. I realized that this was useless. I called a meeting of the committee and said: I had hoped to create artisans, but here I see artists. We should disband this workshop and open another one for women's tailoring.

This is what happened: I sent a messenger to prepare a list of young girls who wish to learn sewing of women's clothing. He brought me a list of 30 such girls from the orphanage and 10 others from various places in town. When I had a list of 40 candidates, I began to look for a director.

[Page 364]

I got in touch with Vilna and they sent me a licensed director- Miss Fania Fishkes (later Mrs. Hayat). I rented a large, spacious hall on Mitzkivitcha Street. We received a permit and we began to do serious work. Thanks to Lieber Armernik who helped us to obtain the permit for the school, ORT was founded in 1923.

A year later, we opened another class. We brought another teacher, Miss Feigelson, who is now in Israel.

During that period of time, there was an event. There was a teacher by the name of Kopit in Kovel. He died suddenly and left a widow with two young daughters. The widow had no income and she went to Trisk to live with her son. He was a teacher there. One of the daughters, Esther Kopit, asked to be accepted as a student in ORT. I accepted her and her mother used to bring her twice a week. I asked the orphanage to accept the girl so she could acquire a trade. I was given a negative answer with the excuse that the orphanage does not accept semi-orphans.

It so happened that an orphan from the orphanage, a young gir,l wanted to be accepted at ORT. The chairman of the orphanage himself, Mr. Appelbaum, came to me and asked me to take her in the middle of the school year.

I said: Appelbaum, my friend, I will accept her on the condition that the orphanage accepts Esther Kopit. He agreed. Esther Kopit is now living in Israel.

In 1924 the economic condition of ORT was dire. We were instructed by ORT headquarters in Warsaw that we had to sustain the school on our own or to close it. ORT was now independent of the Joint, but had no funds. I called a meeting of the committee. Some members were in favor of closing the school, but I was of the opinion that we had to do our utmost to continue. Some members resigned from the committee. With great difficulty, we continued our work and we did not pay attention to the fact that some ORT schools, in other cities, were closed.

It did not take long and the central office in Warsaw sent us 20% of the budget. After much begging, the amount went up to 50%. We collected the rest from internal sources. This was the way we were able to put the school back on its feet. It grew and broadened. In 1925 we opened a third class, directed by Mia Tchuch-Volvoshes.

In 1926 I was sent, from Kovel, to the second world conference of ORT in Berlin.

[Page 365]

In 1928, or so, Dr. Sokolovsky, a dentist, was elected chairman of ORT. Pinhas Sheinbaum and I served as vice-chairmen.

After Dr. Sokolovsky died, the principal of the Hebrew high school, Asher Frankfurt served as chairman. This is how the school existed until WWII broke out. When the soviets were in Kovel, we still received, for 8 months, funds to cover our budget. Afterwards, I received a letter telling me to close the school because it was "unusual". I gave Miss Mandel, the secretary of the orphanage, the entire inventory. The workshop continued there. Haya Margolis was the teacher.

The Carpenters Association

Hertz Levin

Translated by Ala Gamulka

On the corner of Old Lutsk Train Station Street, there were two little houses. On the tables would lie a few Yiddish newspapers, and some pictures of Yiddish writers hung on the wall.

Every evening one would find young fellows leafing the newspapers or reading a book using the colorless electric lighting.

Officially, this is the Carpenters Association. Truthfully, it is the meeting place of the workers revolutionary youths.

Every Shabbat, when our parents went to synagogue, the young workers went here to discuss current issues.

This is where they rejected the old world, the small bourgeois, disabled existence. In short, the order that must disappear and be replaced by the creative workers and the future, fair world.

The leader was Mendel, a carpenter for many years. He was a tenacious, caustic man with clear, intelligent eyes. He worked hard from a young age with his father. He did not have a good education, but he had a healthy, practical outlook on life.

For Mendel, all problems were simple and clear. He conducted various secret actions with obvious authority. He commanded with military discipline.

[Page 366]

At every theoretical discussion, he felt his lack of background. He needed a base, a proper education.

He appealed to the progressive youths, the sympathisers. Every week there were lectures about Jewish writers or a literary discussion or a collection evening.

I remember the discussions about Matke the thief and Buntche Shweig, the recitations of the works of Peretz, Mendele the book seller, Peretz Markish, Kolbek and others. I can still see the earnest faces of workers who presented various, mainly political–economic questions at the collection evenings.

Every theme was studied seriously and deeply and every issue was well handled. I must admit that the discussions were on a high academic level.

Following is a short list of the participants from the workers university. They were all killed by the Germans murderers:

Moshe Kuperberg

A simple proletariat, always unhappy man. He read books all week and on Shabbat he scanned the "Literary Newspaper". He had great romantic dreams and many ideas. None of these were ever realized.

Ephraim Dobrovdka

He once studied in a Yeshiva and was knowledgeable in Jewish literature. He looked for a purpose in the modern world, but he could never really detach himself from the Yeshiva atmosphere.

Moshke Weintraub

The opposite of Dobrovdka. Cosmopolitan with poor background in Jewish literature in general and a follower of Marxism.

A European with progressive ideas, always sporting an ironic smile. He had a mop of messy hair. He was a typical anarchist.

He could discuss, all day, economic issues and he would not allow anyone else to speak. He never agreed with anyone else, not with other members, not with leaders of western politics, not with the systems of the East.

[Page 367]

If anyone ever tried to argue with him, in a private conversation, he would interrupt, using sarcasm: "your brain is too small to understand me…" A minute later he would smile and resume his monologue.

Kalman Liss

He was a tumultuous, isolated person who described, in simple language, Jewish people– the hard–working Jews of the villages in the wide Ukrainian fields. Kalman Liss, my childhood friend, from Heder days until my departure from Kovel.

He began writing at a young age and he always had in his bag a few new poems which he was ready to recite – to gauge the reaction of his friends. Not a day passed that Kalman would not find me on Levitzker Street and forcefully dragged me to his home.

"Mother", he would yell, "Make a glass of tea for Hertz. In the meantime, I will read him my latest piece".

His simple ways, good–nature and naivete made him a bit comical.

No one is a prophet in his hometown. Kovel did not give him a career of a writer. He later accomplished it in Warsaw.

In Vilna, where I studied with Kalman in the Hebrew Teachers Seminary, we went together to the cemetery. There was a monument there of a Jewish writer who was killed at a young age by the Poles in 1919. The monument had an eagle with imposing wings, but one of them was cut off while in flight.

The bird was killed.

Kalman, with tears in his eyes, signed his name on the monument. A few minutes later, he said courageously:

"You will see. My birds will take me very, very far".

Kalman's life was finished in a similar way. He deserves the same monument.

Yeruchomovitch

He had a pale, tortured face with some white hair on his head. A sick, elderly man. He spent years in prison and was used to that life. He could not handle freedom

[Page 368]

–How do you plan to arrange your life, Yeruchomovitch?

–I have no plans to make. I will probably come back here, with the moles.

He was not wrong.

It is difficult for me to describe a few other members. It was the circle of people who helped in the cultural growth of the Kovel proletariat, the people's university.

* * *

At the beginning of 1928 I left for Paris. Seven months later, almost all the members of the club, including Moshke Weintraub, were arrested.

* * *

Two years later, the same members were paraded through the streets of Kovel to announce that they were sentenced to 8 years.

* * *

Six years later I received a letter in Paris from Mendel, from the central prison in Galicia.

He proudly suffered his difficult fate. There was no sign of bitterness. He wanted to know what was happening in the wide world– closed to him.

[Page 368]

The Home for the Aged in Kovel

Meir Rosenblatt (Paris)

Translated by Ala Gamulka

Whenever a Jew recited Psalms and reached the phrase "Do not abandon us in our old age" (Psalms 71; 9), he would heave a sigh. The fear of being alone in old age, without assistance or subsidy, subject to a bitter and cruel fate – created sadness and unhappiness in his heart.

Previous generations of Jews respected and admired the elderly. Our ancient literature always praised them. It equated old age with intelligence and life experience.

[Page 369]

Our sages said: "The elderly, our bright people, as long as they get older, their intelligence settles on them". Also "Construction of children is a contradiction and the contradiction of the elderly is constructive".

Kovel existed on the eternal values of Judaism. It stood out in its devotion to and care of the elderly. It did not want them to feel alone and solitary, but to make their last years more pleasant.

The Home for the Elderly was founded in Kovel after WWI. There were two buildings- one for men and one for women. The houses stood on Pomnikova Street, on the corner of Fabritchna.

I remember the following as among those who did this holy work: Batya Armernik, Michel Roizen and Michel Rosenblatt. The image of Batya Armernik is well etched in my memory. She was the second wife of Berel Armernik, z" l. Batya dedicated her life to the Home for the Aged. She knew nothing else- only caring for the poor old man who had to leave his home and come to the Home for the Aged. She worked hard to make sure these elderly people were not lonely. She visited them several times a day and always brought special food to make the elderly happy. In spite of the fact that she was wealthy, she did not really enjoy life. She did not wear fancy clothes, nor did she have jewelry. She was dressed modestly and simply, which showed her great soul. She was a person who always cared for others.

Batya Armernik raised two war orphans- the Friedman siblings. She also brought up a third child. She said he would be her "Kaddish".

The elderly continued their lives until they died, surrounded by devotion, love and caring.

This was the life inside the Home for the Aged, until the big change in the life of the Jews of Kovel when the Soviets entered.

When the Red Army entered, there was a definite change in the way all charitable institutions functioned in town. In the first weeks under Soviet rule, the fate of the Home for the Aged was not clear. However, the devoted town leader Michel Rosenblatt worked energetically to help the elderly and not to abandon them. He knocked on the doors of various government office, brought food from the cooperatives and searched for underwear and clothing.

Soon, the Home for the Aged came under the auspices of the general social insurance and Michel Rosenblatt was named director.

His main worry was that the Home for the Aged should not lose its Jewish function and that the elderly should live in an atmosphere that represented their values.

[Page 370]

When treif meat was given from the Food ministry, he replaced it with kosher meat. Before Pessach he made sure that the elderly people were provided with Matzoth and would have a proper Seder.

In the last months before the Russo-German war, the Home for the Elderly was moved to a central Home for the Aged in a village near Kovel. Michel Rosenblatt stayed in town and, with great sadness, said good-bye to his "babies"- the elderly of Kovel.

[Page 373]

On the Eve of the Holocaust

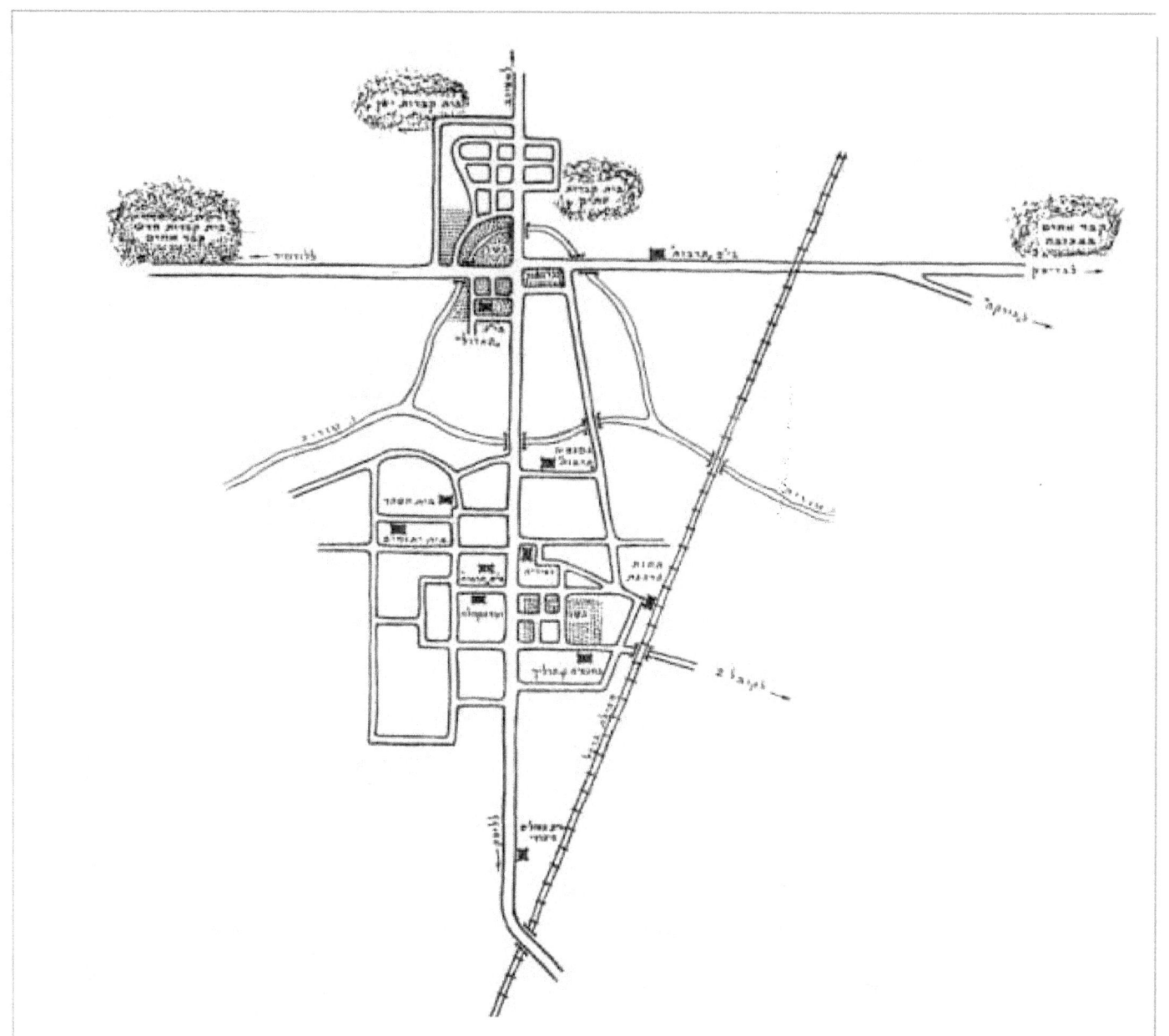

A Sketch of the City of Kovel

[Page 374]

The Last Meeting

by Baruch Avivi

Translated by Ala Gamulka

My little hometown! How you enraptured me at all times, at all of my life stations, from childhood to this day?

I saw towns in Poland even more beautiful and larger, but you are most beautiful of all; I knew that there were long and wide streets in those other towns, tall and magnificent houses, blossoming gardens and shiny asphalt roads…

Your small streets, old wooden houses, stone covered roads and the sands in long trails are dearer to me.

I still see the narrow lanes snaking along the length and the breadth of the town, the wooden bridge connecting the "city" with the "sands", the Turia River streaming slowly. In its clear waters can been seen bodies of many children. We are all children of dear Kovel.

With youthful tremor I remember the Great Synagogue, the Houses of Learning, the Shtiblach of the Stolin and Trisk Hassidim, the Rabbi's "courtyard", the Hebrew primary schools and the High School– the pride of our town. They are all etched in my heart and I will never forget them.

Does the small house on Matseyev Street, built by my father, in good days, still stand? It was on the crossroads of four streets– Brisker, Trisker, Matseyever and Lutsker.

The many years that have passed have not dimmed your image. Every corner in town, from the beautiful train station to the distant "Gorky"– are all dear to me, then and now…

I was away from you, my hometown, in Vilna, Warsaw and Tel Aviv, but I never forgot you. I would return to you in my dreams and when awake.

How could I forget the good and innocent Jews, the dear children I educated to love Eretz Israel, my childhood friends who did not merit to reach the shores of our country?

I remember my last visit with great sorrow and pain. It was just before WWII. One could smell fires and fears grew of what would happen.

[Page 375]

My heart predicted evil events. Old men and youth walked as if they were shadows on the empty streets. One could detect great fear in their eyes.

The quick goodbyes in the train station where fathers and mothers, brothers and sisters, relatives and friends stood close together. There were unpleasant –looking soldiers there, as well. I was offered hands for shaking and looks filled with love and blessings.

Suddenly, my late mother could be heard shouting: "Son, when will we meet again?"

She and the other people accompanying me did not know, neither did I, that this was our last meeting. We would never see each other again…

Kovel – My Home[1]

by Meir

Translated by Gloria Berkenstat Freund

Kovel, the city of my childhood, the city of my young dreams, was absorbed gradually in my memory.

Here the country road began that led from Lutsk, ascended up the hilly "viaduct" and descended to Lutska Street, ran through the comfortable life of the Jews and municipal hospitals; here was Cuperfein's oil press and here was Armarnik's mill – set out over Fabryczne, Koleyove and 3rd of May Streets [that] became smaller among the dozens of shops on both sides of the street and ended in its sandy part near the Turya [River], dropped into the city across the bridge, meandered farther through Warszawer Street, diverged in Ludmirer [Street] where the Kovel Jews would be led to their eternal rest, turned onto Brisker [Street], faraway to Gorki and disappeared in the distant gardens and orchards of Maciever [Street].

[Page 376]

Here were your residents, several small industrialists, more merchants, [people from] various professions – doctors, lawyers, teachers, technicians, hundreds and thousands of retailers, artisans, workers, dear Jews who toiled all year long.

Kovel of the struggle for an income, for daily bread; in a fight with Polish anti–Semitism, of the limits of a precarious economic situation.

The city of merchants' associations, of retailers' unions, of artisans' associations, of a people's bank, of a merchants' bank, of the interest–free loan fund; of widespread social work that itself supported dozens of organizations and institutions like an experienced state system:

Of *Linas haTzedak* [society for the homeless], where poor Jews received help from doctors and the necessary medicines without cost; of *Beis Yesoymim* [home for orphans], where small babies were raised; of *Moyshev Skeynim* [old–age home], where the old people lived out their lives in dignity; of *Bikur Khoylim* [society to provide lodging for the needy and visitors to the sick], of the Jewish hospital, of *Hakhnoses Kale* [society to assist poor brides], of *Gemiles Khesed* [interest free loan society], of *Maos Khitim* [help for the poor to celebrate Passover]; of the *ORT* [*Obschestvo Remeslenovo i. Zemledelcheskovo Trouda* – Society for Trades and Agricultural Labor] school where young girls learned a trade; of *TOZ* [*Towarzystwo Ochrony Zdrowia Ludności Żydowskiej* – Society for Safeguarding the Health of the Jewish Population] and its summer residences where hundreds of malnourished Jewish children were healed in fresh air.

The city of diverse educational systems, in which all communal [political and religious] leanings were reflected:

Of the first kindergartens, of the increased number of public schools, of the Herzlia and Dr. Klumel school; of the *Tarbut gymnazie* [secular Zionist secondary school] and of the Polish–Jewish middle school; of the [elementary] school of *Tsysho* [Central Yiddish School Organization – secular socialist Yiddish schools]; of the large *Talmud Torah* [free school for poor boys], of the dozens of khederim [small religious elementary schoolrooms], of the *Yeshivus* [religious secondary schools];

Of People's Libraries, of Hebrew reading rooms, of the leftist Peretz Library, of literary courses and evening courses, of the dramatic societies, of the theater rehearsals of Khalat and Tarn; the choir, of the very talented Kalmen Lis' songs celebrating Volhynia; of Asher Frankfort, the untiring fighter for Hebrew culture; of the weekly newspapers; of the *Tanakh* [Torah, Prophets and Writings] circles and the Torah Society, where overworked Jews would find relief [studying] a page of the *Gemara*[Talmudic commentaries].

[Page 377]

The city of pious Jews, of the Trisker [rebbe's] court, of the large synagogue, of Pruszanski's house of prayer and the Komerczeske synagogue at the *Zamd* [the Sands – the newer part of Kovel]. Of the *shtiblekh* [one–room synagogues for specific groups such as Hasidic sects or occupations]: Trisker, Lubavitcher, Ruzhyner, Stepaner, Neshchizer; of Reb Welwele, of the old Grabowicer, of Nukhem–Moshele, of Efroim the religious judge, of Rabbi Lanke, of the heads of the *yeshivus* [secondary religious schools], of the Jewish *melamdim* [religious school teachers], of Reb Shmuelik Goldberg, of Yosl the *melamed*[teacher], of Reb Motle, of Reb Pinkhas, of Fidta and of Reb Nisl Farber.

The city of the Jewish civic club, of the Zionist community center, of the illegal meetings, of the communist youth; of the political effervescent life; of the widespread Zionist movement: of *Et Livnot* [This is the time to build], *El Hashomer* [On the Guard], *Mizrakhi* [religious Zionists], *Hitakhdut* [Zioinist Socialists], Revisionists, *Poalei–Zion* [labor Zionists], *Hahalutz* [Pioneers], *Hashomer Hatzair* [Young Guard – Socialist Zionist youth movement], *Tzairi Mizrakhi* [*Mizrakhi* Youth], Betar, *Hahalutz Hatzair* [Young Pioneers], *Freiheit* [Freedom].

The city of the first strikes, where the worker activist, Pesakh Szpringer, was led to jail in chains.

The city of Jewish folksiness, of Pesya the *katshkes* [raiser of ducks], Chava the *pipkes* [tobacco pipe], of "beautiful women," of the "tall Jewish woman," of Yosl the water–carrier, who sold simple water from the Turya [River], and "Warsaw" water [water from Warsaw] from the pump on Listopadower Street and which in Soviet Kovel immediately began to sell "Moscow" water; of Khil with his eternal yoke on his shoulders – "Well then, Khil, what day did the second day of Rosh Hashanah fall 10 years ago," – the city of the thin, stuttering Hershele with the typical appearance of a recluse – a goo–ood, a goo–ood, good night –.

[Page 378]

The city of the dear young Jews. Apprentices, employees, workers, of the Turya [River], in your water the young girls and men learned to swim, you did not move, lay a fathom deep; of *Lag B'Omer* [holiday usually occurring in May celebrated with excursions and bonfires] excursions, where hundreds and hundreds of young people walked through the streets with white and blue flags and spent the day in the surrounding woods; of the First of May demonstrations, where the young demonstrated their wishes for a better life, of the young sports organizations, *Makabi, Hashmonai, Bar Kokhba, Krima* with its football–gymnastics and other divisions.

The city of the youth circles for Yiddish literature, Jewish history; of *Ohel Shem*, where Hasidic young people in their last year at the middle school drew spiritual nourishment from the ancient wells; how hundreds of young people would disappear in the evening at the premises of *Hahalutz* and *Hashomer Hatzair* as well as Betar, *Tzairi Mizrakhi* and the Peretz Library.

And here, my small section of Lutsker Street, from Kaliyeva to Krulova Bane. On a summer night under the starry heaven, or in the frosty, dry winter evening, the Kovel young people occupied its kingdom. They strolled, taking up the entire width of the sidewalk. It was crowded, narrow, friendly. Here, one heard Yiddish, Hebrew, Polish, Russian. They spoke about the synagogue, about work, about politics, about love, about serious things. They bickered, they discussed. The air became full of a song, vigorous noise. Sometimes a couple separated, went apart [from the others], moved aside. The first innocent declarations of love were heard by the trees on Monopoliove Street and from Vulka [Street].

The city of the last years, just before the Second World War. Difficult economic conditions, intensified anti–Semitism, the hopeless situation of the majority of the young Jews, Kovel and the devil at the entry of the German beasts.

Kovel in the days of the Polish–Russian War – how you grew overnight, my city, how at once your streets became wide, thousands and thousands of Jewish refugees from deep in Poland flowed ceaselessly through them, escaping from the Nazi troops.

[Page 379]

How you accepted [the refugees] so fraternally, my home. Your Jews [accepted] them into your homes, gave them a place to sleep, brought them a meal, warmed them with words of consolation.

And thus, almost doubled [in size], you welcomed the Red Army, which brought them salvation from the Hitler beast.

Kovel in the years 1939–1941, the period of adapting to a new life, an economy built on a new foundation, total changes in the social–communal life.

Kovel in anxiety because of the new Hitler victories. The Soviet military went through the empty street toward the border. The 22nd of June 1941. The city was awakened by the first German bombs. War. The Trisker Rebbe blessed the Soviet tanks on Brisker Street.

The German troops entered your streets with force, Kovel, my city. The wild blood–thirsty beast already held you with its nails, my city.

– Escape, my brothers, hide, save your babies! –

Amalek had come again. Wild German murderers, wild blood–suckers, boundless bandits ruled over you and with them the Ukrainian murderers, your neighbors for 100 years, they defiled you, killed your children, drove them to work, looted Jewish possessions, locked [the Jews] in the ghetto, set their [annihilation] as their goal.

Kovel of the march of the martyrs. They drove your starved and defiled children through your streets, here at the Brisker highway, here in the village of Bachuv, here they had them undress, stood them near the prepared pits, here the volleys were heard. One after the other, dozens, hundreds, thousands fell. An entire city perished *al Kiddush haShem* [as martyrs]. The German murderers shot, the wild Ukrainian supplemented them with pitchforks.

[Page 380]

Kovel with its large synagogue that remained as a remembrance after the Holocaust, where many of the tortured Jews wrote their last words on its walls with their blood.

Kovel with its only large mass grave near Bachuv where, immediately after the war, the dear hands of several of your devoted children fenced in and erected a wooden *matzevah* [headstone].

But Kovel, my city, you have not yet perished.

Among the many millions [of people] in New York, in noisy Paris, in Buenos Aires and in distant Australia, you still live, my home. At memorial evenings, in a yahrzeit [memorial] candle, in a deep moan, in memories that are handed down to children, Kovel, my city, you continue to come into our memories.

More than anywhere, you live in Israel, where your children are building a home for themselves; where they will be able to live without terror or fear, as free, proud people and Jews.

You Live Forever, Kovel, My City

Footnote:

1. We have placed the article by our fellow townsman, Meir Ben–Michael from Paris, in this section as this is a summarized account of what we lost when our town was destroyed.

[Page 381]

My Trip to Kovel in 1939[1]

by Dr. Y. Glicksman

Translated by Sara Mages

The journey to Kovel in those days - October 1939 - wasn't the easiest thing to do.

In theory, there was a rail service. But in reality, no one knew when the train would leave. Those who wished to travel - walked slowly to the train station and waited for several hours. Sometimes they waited for a day and sometimes - for an entire day. Rovno's train station - as in other cities that were occupied by the Soviet army - was besieged, day and night, by thousands of people. Masses of people lay on the filthy floor of the train station and shivered with cold.

It was a large population of refugees, most of them Jews, who were uprooted from their homes and wandered from place to place. They, their children and their wives, couldn't find a place to rest in. No one cared for them. The hunger sucked the marrow of their bones and diseases spread

Finally I got to enter the train car. The train drags itself from Rovno to Kovel for 14 hours instead of two hours in normal times. The glass windows are broken, and despite the crowds and the congestion it is bitterly cold in the car. The car isn't lit at night and we're immersed in darkness.

Here our feet are stepping on Kovel's soil. The NKVD (the former G.P.U) seized the most magnificent building in Kovel. It wasn't easy to enter this building, and it was especially difficult to get an audience with the city's officer. Various officials interrogated me for the purpose of my visit.

The next day, at dawn, I reported by the prison's gate with a food parcel for Victor Alter. I saw a long line of mournful sobbing women. These were the wives, sisters, and old mother of Jewish, Polish and Ukrainian prisoners.

[Page 382]

All of them held baskets and packages and waited, in the cold and in the rain, for the time of "delivery."

I was lucky that I came on "delivery" day. However, the people who stood at the prison's gate told me that there was no assurance in the matter. Sometimes, after many hours of standing in line, they scatter those who wait and don't accept their packages.

At times - so I was told by the waiting women - they do accept the package, but a shortly after the prison guard returns it to inform you that the prisoner was not there.

Then, terrible thoughts start to haunt you: maybe the prisoner is dead? It's being told in the city that night after night corpses are taken out secretly from the prison. However, it's possible, that they "just" took the prisoner to another prison. Or, maybe they sent him to a concentration camp? Who knows? The family will never know.

Very quickly I tasted the flavor of the Soviet prison in Kovel. It was a small empty room in the basement of the NKVD building. It was bitterly cold in this dungeon. For two days I lay on the cold floor in a state of semi-consciousness. I couldn't sleep in the cell because a light bulb, which was lit day and night, was hanging over my head. The light bulb was strong, about 250-300 watt, and blinded my eyes. The bright light stabbed my eyes and caused them great pain. I felt like they placed me next to a spotlight.

The only window in the cell was covered with a thick screen, and a beam of light painfully penetrated inside. Therefore, I wasn't able to distinguish between day and night.

I wasn't given food for two consecutive days, and furthermore, I wasn't even given a drop of water to wet my throat or wash my hands. No one was interested in my fate. No one asked me for my wish. Dead silence reined around.

On the third night, at dawn, an NKVD officer entered the cell and started to scream: Pack your bags! Get dressed fast!

He took me out. It was four o'clock in the morning. At that time the police was very active in Kovel. The streets were still as if life was taken from them. Six soldiers armed with rifles that their bayonets pointed upwards surrounded me.

Finally we arrived to the prison. They put me on the third floor in room number 33. It was a very large room, intended for several dozen prisoners. However, I was in it alone. All the glass windows were broken and the winds raged in the room undisturbed.

To my delight, there were a few crumbled and worn strew mattresses in the room. The lightest touch raised plumes of dust. The mattresses were very dirty and full of fleas. I made a "king's bed" from these mattresses.

[Page 383]

In spite of that I couldn't undress because the cold was unbearable and ate my bones. Rain and snow blew through the windows.

I must comment that the regime that prevailed in the Soviet prison in Kovel wasn't typical to Soviet prisons in other locations. The regime was much more severe in other Soviet prisons.

Translator's Note:

1. During the Soviet occupation many Jewish and Polish socialist's leaders concentrated in Kovel. They fled eastward in the hope that the Soviet authorities will welcome them. In this manner, Victor Alter - the well known leader of the "Bund," and Miteshislav Mustek - the leader of the Polish railway workers and a member of the Polish Sejm for many years, arrived to Kovel. An important consultation of Jewish and Polish socialist's leaders was held in Kovel a few days after the city was occupied by the Soviets. A memorandum, which was written in this meeting, was given to the Soviet mayor. A wave of arrests came in response to the memorandum. Alter was arrested on 26 September, 1939.
Dr. Y. Glicksman, the brother of Victor Alter, describes his journey to Kovel to visit his brother who was incarcerated in the Soviet prison in Kovel. His words, which are given with a few omissions, were taken from the book "Henrik Ehrlich and Victor Alter," which was published in 1951 by "Unzer tsayt," New York.

"*Anusim*" on the Eve of the Holocaust

by Yaacov Kobrinski

Translated by Sara Mages

The school year 1940-41 in the "Vocational High School No. 3." This school replaced the school named after Dr. Klumel, and its language of instruction was Yiddish. We - I, who was given the task to continue as the school's principal, and the teachers: Genia Liar, Ester Pomerantz-Shalita, Baruch Toyeb and Aharon Rosenstein of blessed memory, and may he live long, Yakov Shalita, who lives with us in Israel - were a group of modern "*Anusim*" [1] within the walls of this school. The rest of the teachers were new, "party" members, and despite the fact they were good honest people and were friendly to us - there was an atmosphere of "keep your tongue." It was better to be quiet about the recent past. Besides that, we were sure that special duties were also given to a number of students from the higher classes and to a number of parents - and this required us to be very careful and caused alienation.

And here, two weeks before Yom Kippur 5702 [1941], the superintendent, Moshe Tabachnik, appeared at our school every day. He was very interested to know, if we properly managed the propaganda that the students should come to school on Yom Kippur (on Saturdays the studies were like in other schools). He also hinted that it will be a test to the teachers' educational skills… I felt, that the students were excited and confused, and waited for an unofficial hint from me. We knew well the feelings of the others without saying a word. Two days before the holy day, I released myself from my administrative duties, and participated in the games during the big break. Between the games and the small talk about this and that, the student received a hint that they should come to school, but they won't be forced to write or eat. My dear holy sheep didn't fail me. The teachers stood the test, and the lessons were designed so there was no need to write. But, there's no rule without exception. Rabbi Moshe Teverski zt"l came to my house a few days before Yom Kippur and asked me with tears: "How is it possible that my son, a fifth grade student, will desecrate the sanctity of the day?" And my advice was: "As of today your son is sick with dysentery, and I promise him a certificate of illness from the school's doctor for a week."

[Page 384]

Etched in my memory is the graduation party on Saturday night 14 June, 1941. We sat at a social gathering, the lovely and pleasant - the students of the sixth and seventh grades with their parents, delegates from other classes, and almost every faculty member. There were, of course, also representatives of the authorities who gave routine speeches. A seventh grader blessed in moving words, and handed me the class' gift - an elegant volume of Shalom Aleichem's children stories, which was published in Yiddish by the Soviets in Kiev.

My turn came to speak. In this occasion I didn't want to appear before my acquaintances and friends from the past with routine words. On the other hand, I wasn't allowed to appear before my superiors as "political unconscious." Therefore, after a few heartfelt words about our life together at school, I said that we need to be grateful to the regime, the person who represents it, and the precious treasure that he had given us - peace! "Put before your eyes what's happening across the border, just 50 kilometres from here, and you'll understand how lucky we are!"

I confess: that at that time my mouth and my heart weren't a hundred percent equal, because I was very worried about the future. What we feared the most, come to us, the dreadful journey eastward of the German soldiers, may their names be blotted, started exactly seven days after this party. Except for half a dozen, or maybe up to ten of those who attended that party - no one survived.

May their souls be bound in the bond of everlasting life.

Translator's Note:

1. *Anusim* - "forced ones" - persons compelled by overwhelming pressure, whether by physical threats, psychological stress, or economic sanctions, to abjure Judaism and adopt a different faith.

Jewish Life in Kovel Under The Soviet Rule

by Yehoshua Frankfurt

Translated by Sara Mages

The Soviet occupation brought a big change in the Jewish street in Kovel. It wasn't the character that was known to us from the years before the war. There was an atmosphere of depression. Many Jews were forced to close their stores and their workshops, and sat, almost, idle.

The new regime brought in its wake a total change of values. People moved about gloomy and anxious, wondering and looking forward. They knew that they had to look for new sources of income, but they weren't ready for it in any way, especially, mentally.

[Page 385]

However, this wasn't the only change that took place in the Jewish street. It wasn't the economic insecurity that burdened the hearts of our brothers in the city. What depressed their spirits the most was the political insecurity and the denial of freedom of speech.

The new regime, and with it the first wave of arrests, quickly made it clear that it was necessary to learn the theory of silence. They had to remove from their talks on current events many topics that were close to their hearts. And the most important thing: they could no longer trust their "closest friends," because, this time, the words of our prophet: "Those who destroy you and those who lay you waste shall go forth from you…" were fulfilled. There were informers, who, for so called "ideological reasons," saw themselves as emissaries, and brought words of slander to the attention of the new rulers.

The voice of most of the Jewish community fell silent. The public life, which pulsed in various forms, has been paralyzed. Most of the Jewish youth, who was educated in the national spirit either in the network of Hebrew schools or in the Zionist youth movements, was sentenced to a double decree: On one hand they weren't allowed to speak Hebrew and had to break away from the realization of the Zionist vision, and on the other hand, they had to recognize Yiddish as their national language, and to integrate into a new way of life, which was foreign to their spirit and belief. This youth wandered gloomy and disappointed.

It should be noted, that not everyone accepted the new situation. There were those who met secretly to refresh their Hebrew and talk about forgotten times, and there were also those who weren't satisfied with these secret meetings. They left their homes and fled through unknown roads to Lita and Romania, in order to emigrate from there to Israel.

This was, in general terms, the face of the Jewish street at the end of 1939. At that time, the Soviet authorities decided to include the local population in the elections to the "Supreme Soviet." The Soviets decided - as it became clear later - to try to pull to their side the most important local people, famous people, that their influence was also known outside their place of residence.

The goal was twofold: First, to prove to the outside world that the residents of "Western Ukraine" saw the Soviets as "liberators" not "invaders." Second, to show the local residents, that even their former leaders support and cooperate with the new regime. They also had another trend: to show, that the Soviet regime wasn't only based on communists, but also by people who had other views in the past, people, who officially ceased their affiliation with their former political party, and now are called "nonpartisan."

As fate would have it, the choice in Kovel fell on Asher Frankfurt z"l. For some reasons, the Soviet authorities decided that he was the suitable man for the "Supreme Soviet."

The story began in the deepest secrecy. One night, some time before the preparations for the elections, a man dressed in the NKVD [1] uniform appeared at Asher Frankfurt's home at midnight, and invited him to join him.

[Page 386]

It's easy to imagine the reaction of Frankfurt and his family members. They stood frightened and alarmed, and asked the "man in uniform" what he had to take for the road. Are they arresting him, does he have a warrant for his arrest or for the entire family, etc…However, they failed to get a hint from him about the purpose of his visit. His only answer was: I was ordered to bring you to a certain place, and that's all. When Frankfurt z"l asked to take a bundle of cloths with him, the "man in uniform" said that they should hurry and there's no need to take anything.

A small elegant Soviet style passenger car, one of the few that appeared in the city at that time, was waiting outside. Later we found out that the car belonged to the secretary of the Communist Party in the region.

The car stopped next to the NKVD building. Frankfurt z"l was brought to a room in which three people sat. Of them, only one was known to him personally. He was the secretary of the local Communist Party. His wife served as a "*politruk*" [political commissar] in the United Jewish High School.

Frankfurt z"l was surprise that the reception was somewhat warm. The officials' serious "tone" disappeared immediately, and he was invited to sit with a kind smile. They asked for his forgiveness that they troubled him at night. Tell us about yourself - one of them turned to him. "What I should tell you?" asked Frankfurt z"l. They answered: "Tell us the story of your life." Amazed and full of hesitation Frankfurt started to tell them the story of his life. After the first few sentences, one of the men remarked, that even the "high ranking officials" in Moscow would be proud of his pure Russian. Indeed, this wasn't an exaggerated compliment, since in addition to his religious education he was also educated on the knees of the Russian culture, and he spoke this language during his many years of studies in Kiev and Odessa.

His story lasted for two hours, and before he finished the three men rose to their feet and thanked him for his words. They immediately informed him that he would be invited to another meeting, but he shouldn't tell anyone about this meeting.

The reason for this meeting hadn't been told to him, and when he saw that the meeting was shrouded in secrecy, he realized that he had to be patient, and wait until they reveled its meaning to him.

The elegant car was waiting outside. To Frankfurt's surprise, the "man in uniform" saluted him, opened the car door, and invited him to enter. The family was happy that he was brought back home.

[Page 387]

The next day he went to his work as a school principal. At that time the authorities consolidated the two Jewish high schools the city - the Hebrew High School and Klara Erlich's high school - into one high school whose teaching language was Yiddish. As stated, Asher Frankfurt z"l was nominated as the principal of the united high school, and Mrs. Klara Erlich was appointed as his deputy. In theory, this was the official management, but in fact, the decisive opinion on fundamental issues was given to the "politruk," the wife of the secretary of Communist Party in the city. Officially, her role at school was to guide in matters of sports and military training, and she also organized the activities of the *Komsonol* [2] among the high school students. In fact, the "*politruk*" acted as the institution's "mistress." Her attitude to the teachers and the management was the attitude of a master towards his servants. She tried to emphasize her power, loved to explain the basics of the Soviet education, and the primacy of the Soviet educational methods.

The morning after the mysterious meeting, the "*politruk*" welcomed Frankfurt z"l as before. She didn't give him a clue, even though she knew something. However, there was a high degree of respect in her attitude towards him. Suddenly, she began to listen seriously to his words, to answer with Amen to each word that he had spoken, and consulted with him about the arrangements that she was going to regulate. And lo and behold: previously, she served as a consultant and master - suddenly, she became docile and was willing to take advice and guidance.

Several days later, in the middle of the night, there was another knock on Frankfurt's door. The "man in uniform" appeared, and in a faint voice invited him to come with him. Again, he was brought to the NKVD building. The same "trio" sat and asked him to continue his story. He was asked a few questions, mainly about his past activities. It was difficult for him to distinguish the responses to his answers, because the light in the room was directed at him, while the three men, who sat across the table, were almost immersed in the shade.

Two hours later, they stood up, thanked him for his story, reminded him to maintain the confidentiality of the meeting, and that he would be invited for the third time.

In those days, the attitude of the "*politruk*" towards the principal improved. It became more dignified and more flattering. She started to show interest in his health, was worried about his comfort, and reacted badly when he was interrupted. She arrived to school early, greeted him with a smile, and left the building only after he left. The tension in Frankfurt's heart increased. In addition to the "trio" other people, who usually didn't present themselves, also attended the next meetings. Their faces weren't familiar to Frankfurt z"l, and made an impression that they were men of power from elsewhere. Frankfurt z"l was forced to retell his life story a number of times. At the end of his words he was asked a several questions, they praised him and parted from him.

In one of these meetings they questioned him at length with two questions:

[Page 388]

The first - why he founded the Hebrew High School, and the second - under what circumstances did he make the agreement with the Ukrainian minority in the region before the elections to the Polish Siejm [3]. There was a hint in it to the well known case in the Polish Jewry about the "Minority Treaty," which was arranged by Yitzhak Gruenbaum. Its aim, among others, was to increase the number of minority delegates in the Polish Siejm.

Asher Frankfurt z"l conducted the negotiations with the Ukrainians in the Wolyn district. He was known to the Ukrainians as one of the opponents of the Polish regime, and the Polish desire to dominate Wolyn. This point was extremely important for the "trio." They dwelled upon it many times, and kept on asking him if it was true that he didn't approve the Polish regime in Wolyn. In addition to that, they showed an "understanding" for his answer about the founding of the Hebrew High School. His explanation was that as a national Jew, he saw the need to establish a Hebrew High School which will educate the young generation in the national spirit, train it for his immigration to Israel, and prevent its assimilation. Later also told them, that despite difficulties and obstacles that the Polish authorities set up, he continued to struggle for the existence of the Hebrew High School. He didn't give up even when his school wasn't given state rights, when at the same time, the second high school in the city, that its language of instruction was Polish, received these rights.

Frankfurt's story, on how at one time, before the elections to the Siejm, he was offered to place his candidacy in the B.B.W.R [4] list, the Sanation's [5] list under the leadership of Colonel Koc, the assistant and advisor of Marshal Rydz-Śmigły, in order to attract Jewish votes in favor of the ruling party. He was promised that in addition to providing a place in the Polish Siejm, he will receive rights and recognition for the high school, or the post of the director of the government's high school in the city whose director was Mr. Gura.

However, he had been told explicitly, that if he didn't agree to the proposal, the high school will be closed, or he would be dismissed from his post as director.

In response to his refusal to support the "Sanation," Frankfurt z"l was suspended from his position as the school's principal for a period of time. He was forced to pass a test in the Polish language at the University of Vilna. He was reconfirmed by the authorities as the school's principal only under the pressure of various public factors.

These words found an attentive ear and were accepted by the Soviet "interviewers."

One night Asher Frankfurt z"l was called again to the secret meeting, and in the presence of a number people (among them the regional Communist Party secretary, and a representative of the government from Kiev), he was told that it was decided to present his candidacy for the upcoming elections to the "Supreme Soviet," meaning, as a candidate of the "nonpartisan" who was recommended by the Communist Party.

[Page 389]

He doesn't need to deny his past affiliation with the Zionist organization, but, he should declare in public meetings that he sees the Soviet regime and the Soviet system of government, the right solution for the nations of the Soviet Union, including the Jewish nation. Frankfurt z"l tried to say, that the matter wouldn't be well received because he's known by many as an ardent Zionist. Also, personally, he doesn't find himself worthy and suited for this supreme notable job. The answer to his words was short and sharp: comrade, your candidacy has been approved by Comrade Khrushchev (at that time, Khrushchev served as the secretary of the Communist Party in Ukraine, and was its leader).

The answer blocked the way to all sorts of questions and additional inquiries. To the amazement of those present, Frankfurt z"l asked to give him time to think about his answer. They couldn't understand how a man dares to ponder a decision from high above. He promised to give his answer on the next day.

The next meeting was attended by the "trio" and the representative from Kiev. Again, Frankfurt pleaded before them that the public wouldn't approve it, and besides that, his frail health prevents him from accepting this honorable and responsible role. Their answer was that the matter has been decided and it was impossible to change it. The meetings of the "Supreme Soviet" are being held twice a year, and a special rail car will be made available to transfer him and his family to Moscow for the meetings. Also, he will not have to worry about the school. A special office will be arranged for him in the city, and he will receive representatives from the entire region during a few office hours. He was promised that they'll take care of his needs, and it won't be difficult to fulfill all of his wishes in regards to his duties.

From now, everyone started to treat him with great respect. He was invited to parties with representatives who came from other locations. "Visitors," accompanied by the local "party" secretary, came to the high school to meet Frankfurt z"l. They treated him with politeness, whereas the local "party" secretary and his wife, the "*politruk*," literally worshiped him.

At that time, the Soviet authorities started to hold preliminary meetings in the workplaces to select the candidates for the "Supreme Soviet." In one day, meetings were held in the railway workers chamber and in the liberal professions (teachers, clerks etc.) chamber. The meeting of the railway workers went well. Frankfurt's candidacy was presented by the chairman (a member of the Communist Party from the outside). He read Frankfurt's biography without mentioning, even in one word, his Zionists activities. He praised Frankfurt's resistance and struggle against the Polish government and his good relation and close ties with the Ukrainian people.

It wasn't the same at the meeting of the intelligentsia. This meeting was turbulent.

[Page 390]

The chairman of the meeting was shocked when panic broke out in the hall when he announced, on behalf of the Communist Party, his support for the candidacy of Frankfurt z"l.

Many of the Jewish and Ukrainian communists in the city participated in this meeting. During the Polish rule, they were political prisoners for many years, and couldn't accept the fact that the Communist Party will present the candidacy of an ardent Zionist to the "Supreme Soviet," even on the behalf of the "nonpartisan".

Veteran communists came on the stage - to the chairman's embarrassment - and expressed their vigorous opposition to the proposed candidate. However, there were also those (surely few in number) who immediately understood the situation, and started to praise the candidate and found him fit.

Suddenly, a former political prisoner got up and opened his statement on behalf of his friends, the political prisoners. While he was talking, the chairman emitted the following sentence: "You claim that you appear on behalf of a group of communists, however, we don't know, yet, what kind of communists you are." It was a meaningful warning.

During his speech, the speaker called in the direction of Frankfurt z"l, who was sitting on the stage next to the chairman, to declare in public whether he completely renounce his Zionist past, and sees a grave mistake in his political views in the past.

Frankfurt interjected and replied immediately, that he doesn't deny his past activities, and he's not willing to see them as a mistake.

Panic rose again in the hall. The chairman, who wasn't ready for such a sequence of events, loudly announced the postponement of the meeting.

Intensive debates started in the government circles. One day, Frankfurt z"l was rushed (this time it was during the day and not at night) to the secretary's office who informed him, that the Communist Party reevaluated the situation, decided to grant his request, and will not present his candidacy to the "Supreme Soviet." From then on, he could continue to serve as the principal of the Jewish High School.

A heavy stone was lifted from Frankfurt's heart. He remained in his position until the Nazi invasion. It's interesting to note, that with the outbreak of the war with the Germans, the Soviets offered Frankfurt z"l to leave the city in a special train that was intended to evacuate the government institutions in the city and the region.

Frankfurt z"l didn't accept the offer because of his poor health (he suffered from angina pectoris), but he advised everyone he knew to leave the city and not to stay with the Germans.

Translator's Notes:

1. NKVD - The People's Commissariat for Internal Affairs.
2. Komsonol - the youth division of the Communist Party.
3. Siejm - the lower house of the Polish parliament.
4. B.B.W.R - *Bezpartyjny Blok Współpracy z Rzadem* - Nonpartisan Bloc for Cooperation with the Government.
5. Sanation - Sanacja in Polish - A Polish political movement.

[Page 391]

Under Soviet rule, in captivity and return to Kovel

by Monia Galperin

Translated by Sara Mages

For a certain period the city was in a state of interregnum – between two successive regimes. There was no rule in Kovel. The Polish Army was destroyed, defeated, the fighting subsided and it was quiet on the war front. In the race between Germany and Russia we didn't know which of them will enter the city first. Those, who saw in their astrology that the Germans might enter the city, were horrified. They packed their belongings and got ready to escape to Russia.

A day or two later, a squadron of planes appeared in the city's skies, and when they flew low we clearly saw that they were Soviet planes. A wave of joy passed over the city's Jews, but our joy wasn't complete because the Germans were already in Luboml.

At four in the afternoon we received a notice that we've nothing to fear because the Soviet tanks will arrive to the city's gates within a few hours. There was no end to our joy. Many of the city's youth left for Hulova to welcome the Soviet Army. The first tanks, on which our youth sat and sang with joy, arrived to the city at five in the afternoon.

The Russians came from the direction of Lutsk. Trucks, full of Russian soldiers, traveled on both sides of the road from the viaduct on Lutska Street to Brisk Street. The city's Jews welcomed the soldiers of the Red Army with enthusiasm that is hard to describe in words. The city rejoiced all night.

The first act of the Red Army was the opening of the prisons. Political and criminal prisoners were released. The political prisoners, who were arrested for the crime of Communism, took the power in their hands. We saw then a strange picture – office managers sat in their offices in prison uniform because they haven't had the time to prepare their official uniform. Many of Kovel's Jews, who sat in jail during the Polish period because of their affiliation with the Communist Party – enlisted to the police after their release.

In the early days the administration was very flawed and the city greatly suffered from lack of sources of income. However, the situation slowly improved and all the healthy men and women were called to work. The professionals were given jobs in the cooperatives and the non-professionals were given jobs in various offices. Each had to identify himself with a work card. Those who didn't have this card – were given the evil eye.

A short time later the Soviet authorities gave an order that everyone must be counted and get a Soviet identity card. The city's Jews received the order willingly and reported to the census in an organized manner.

[Page 392]

At that time there were many refugees from Poland in the city who didn't want to get a Soviet citizenship. The authorities let them be and didn't take revenge on them.

Half a year later, notices were posted in the city that those, who want to return to Poland, need to register in a specific location and special railcars will take them to their place of residence.

At that time, a rumor spread in the city that the Jews who live on the German side of Poland, especially in Lublin, engage in various businesses and live well. For that reason many of the Jewish refugees registered for the departure from the city because, as we know, the Russians banned trade.

At the end of the census the Russians collected, in one night, all the trucks in the city. They came to the homes of those who participated in the census, put them in the trucks and sent them by train to Russia.

Life went on in the city until 1941. One Saturday night, when all of us were in the cinema, we were shocked by the news that a war broke out between Russia and Germany. On Monday morning the city, and the surrounding area, were bombed. It was the real proof that war broke out even though all of us believed that it would happen later.

Most of the young men were recruited to the Red Army. The Soviets placed a train with a lot of cars in the train station to transport the residents to Russia. Many filled the cars and waited for the engine to arrive. But two days later, when the long–awaited engine didn't arrive, the Germans bombed the train, the train station and the city itself. Many lost their patience and returned to the city, but those, who had strong nerves and stayed on the train, were rewarded with an engine who took them to the interior of Russia and thanks to that they survived.

I was recruited to the Soviet Army and worked, with others from Kovel, as an electrician in Gorki. The German bombardment intensified from day to day and Gorki was also bombed. We realized that we were in great danger and decided to escape from the city in a car. We arrived to Kamen–Kashirskiy, from there to Sarna and advanced eastward. The road was difficult and dangerous and we were bombed all the time until we arrived to Poltava.

In Poltava an order caught up with us that those, who came from the Ukraine, would be release from the Red Army and must proceed on foot to the depths of Russia.

And so began the terrible days of wanderings, without a home, without a shelter, without heat, without food and water. The front line wasn't known to us and when we arrived to Pirtin we were captured by the German. The Toker brothers, Eli Schnitzer, Petkovsky and others, whose name I don't remember, were captured with me.

The Germans sorted us out and separated us from the non–Jews. The barbarians undressed us, took our clothes and gave us rags to wear. They took our shoes and we walked barefooted.

[Page 393]

The prisoner camp contained about 15.000 men. There was only one well and we had to stand in line all day to get a glass of water. The non–Jews received flour and potatoes every other day. The Jews didn't even get that. The Germans, who advanced to the front, looked at us as strange creatures because they were sure that a single Jew wasn't left in the world. The situation was uncontrollable. Each of them abused us and beat the living daylights out of us with their rifle butts.

One day they arranged us in groups of 12 men. Each group was given two kilo of bread. We divided the bread among us and a march of 45 kilometers to the west began. An order was given that we should walk in straight lines and everyone who will stray from the line – would be responsible for his death. We were tired, broken and exhausted, and it's clear that we weren't able to comply with the command. Eli Schnitzer was the first to stray from the line and was shot on the spot, in front of us. He, may he rest in peace, remained lying on the road and we weren't able to bring him to a Jewish grave.

From Pirtin we came to the town of Boryspil. When we arrived two German officers came towards us. Each held two drawn pistols in their hands and they started to "harvest" us. It was a terrible massacre and only 50 survived out of a group of 150 men.

It was in the months of September–October. Snow and torrential rain fell and it was terribly cold. The non–Jewish prisoners were placed in a barn and we were abandoned outside. We stood for about two hours exposed to the intense frost. Those, who have not yet reached the point of exhaustion, started to dig a pit with their hands. We went down to the narrow and dark pit, one on top of the other, and so we lay all night.

In the morning we continued to march down Via Dolorosa – in the road of suffering and torture until we arrived to Vasilkov airport. The barbarians didn't end their acts of murder and extermination, and when we got there only thirty men were left.

We stayed in Vasilkov Camp for a week without food and water. The hunger and the thirst were terrible. When I saw that all hope was lost and I was going to die of starvation, I took a gamble and jumped over the fence to the Ukrainian prisoner camp. I was lucky that no one realized that I was among them. The next day I saw from a distance how the Ukrainians attacked our young men, undressed them, left them naked and stole all they had.

In this situation, it's not surprising that our young men literally begged the Germans to shot them. More than that: when they saw a man falling from the murderers' bullets, they envied him and said: Look please and also see. How lucky is this man! But the Germans, may their names and memory be blotted out, pretended to be "righteous" and said: *Gott behüte!* – Germans don't shoot humans.

[Page 394]

Germans don't do such repulsive acts with their hands. The murderers knew that they have someone to rely on because the Ukrainians will carry out the murders in no less "talent" than them.

Boryspil was the last stop for the Jewish prisoners. All the Jews were eliminated there. From here on, only the camps of Ukrainians prisoners kept moving forward. Ten thousand men marched in each convoy and I, the lucky one, was one of them. The convoy moved in the direction of Kiev.

For the first time I felt sort of a "pleasure" in walking. What was the pleasure? The convoys of Jewish prisoners were escorted by mounted Germans and the unfortunate had to adjust their steps to galloping of the horses. Those, who lagged running behind the horse, were hit on the head with rifle butts and pickaxes' handles. The Ukrainian convoys were escorted by Germans who walked along them. For that reason I said that I felt kind of pleasure walking.

At night we arrived to a place near Kiev. We were brought to a large identification field. My eyes were blinded by the big bonfire. The woodpile reached the height of a two story building. I was told that they were only looking for Jews. We lined up in rows of five men. They brought each row closer to the big fire, took a good look at the prisoner's eyes – and those suspected of being a Jew – were taken out of the row and shot on the spot. Those, who were only wounded, were thrown to the field and their screams were horrifying.

We were only given a slice of bread and soup. The bread was moldy and it was impossible to eat it and the soup was foul water. We arrived to a train station and they loaded us on the cars. Two hundred men crowded in each car. The density was terrible and many suffocated on the way. Fortunately, I stood next to a window and somehow enjoyed some air. Many jumped out of the cars, but they were shot by the Germans. There were those who managed to escape. We arrived to Shepetovka. I decided to escape, no matter what. I took advantage of the chaos that arouse during the unloading of the prisoners – and escaped to the forest. I ran like a hunted animal through fields, swamps, pits and virgin forests until I arrived, after a great deal of wanderings, to Kovel.

I came from Lutska Street and passed by the viaduct. I entered the first Jewish house that I came across and asked what was happening in the city. I was told that a ghetto hasn't been established yet and the Jews still live in their homes. I arrived to our house on Ludimir Street and the members of my family were frightened when they saw me because I looked different. I was injured, dressed in rags and my bones protruded from hunger. I didn't feel the change in me. After a month of illness I started to think about a job.

[Page 395]

The director of the department of labor in the Judenrat was Moshe Perel z"l. When he learned about my return he sent someone to call me for a private matter.

I went to him. He invited me to his room. He talked to me very kindly and coaxed me to get a supervisor electrician job in the new barracks that were being built behind the new cemetery on Ludimir Street. In those days there was a lack of certified electricians in the city. Aharon Zimmerman, the only certified electrician, was exhausted from all the work.

The Germans didn't accept the excuse that there was a shortage of electricians. They appeared in the Judenrat, created havoc, broke furniture, beat the members of the Judenrat and shouted: "give us electricians!" Moshe Perel was very happy when I accepted the job at the barracks. When I went to work on Ludimir Road I didn't see single Jew. Each time I walked by the cemetery I stopped and peeked inside. There was a lot of neglect. The Ukrainians cut off the trees and when they fell they broke the stones. I looked at this destruction from afar, but I couldn't help. I remember that one day the wife of Leib the undertaker came towards me shouting loudly: "who gives permission to the hooligans to defile and desecrate Jewish holy places." She asked me to "influence" the Ukrainians not to desecrate the cemetery. I approached the gate. Not even single tree was left in the cemetery and the stones were cracked and broken.

A short time later I got a job at the Municipal Electric Company and worked there until the establishment of the ghetto. One day, an order was issued that all the professionals must obtain a work certificate and concentrate in the ghetto in the "sand dunes." I went to the Community Council (the Judenrat) to get the certificate but I couldn't find it. There was disorder this area. There were those who had two certificates and those – who had none. There was a lot a pressure to get a work certificate and the members of the Judenrat were powerless to satisfy the all the demand. Having no choice, they closed the office and left. A lot of disgruntled people broke doors and windows, burst inside and grabbed the certificates. The thirst for life was so great that the owners of the certificates imagined that it was a barrier against disaster, kind of an alliance with the Angel of Death.

I stayed with my brother who lived at the house of Yehazkel Perelmuter z"l on Listopadova Street. Yitzchak Boxer z"l, one of the leaders of the Judenrat, lived with my brother. When I got there I found Boxer as he was making himself a lot of cigarettes. I asked him the reason for it, and he "innocently" told me that the "*Gebietskommissar*" called the members of the Judenrat for an urgent night meeting that would probably last till morning. The poor man didn't know that he was summoned to "Heaven." This was the final road for him and for all the Jews of Kovel…

[Page 396]

The Refugees' Kitchen

by Zalman Poran (Prossman)

Translated by Sara Mages

September 1939. The great bloody erupted, thousands of refugees streamed eastward and many of them arrived in Kovel. All the rainbow colors of Polish Jewry "decorated" the city's streets.

The first to notice this horror of humans, uprooted and hunted like wild animals, was Reb Nehemiah Ber, may *Hashem* avenge his blood.

He puts aside his business, why should he have a wife, why should he have children. With great enthusiasm he begins to organize the relief work for the masses of refugees. He confiscates the building of "Talmud Torah," installs a soup kitchen, gathers foodstuff from the silo and the winery – from the rich, the municipality and also from the Christian residents.

R' Nehemiah Ber and his grandson, hy"d

Our respectable Jews with the city's rabbi, R' Nachum Moshe'le, at the lead, move heaven and earth: Is it possible? Have you heard such a thing? A non–kosher kitchen! They feed the Jews carcasses and *treif* [non–kosher food]. Reb Nehemiah, who wasn't afraid of these words of rebuke, calmly answered: On the contrary, please, open a kosher kitchen and I'll close my non–kosher kitchen. However, as long as there is no other kitchen – I'll not close my kitchen. When it comes to saving life, I'm sure that God would forgive me.

R' Nehemiah's house takes the form of a train station. Various refugees run around there day and night: simple Jews, rabbis, authors, public activists from Greater Poland and even nuns.

[Page 397]

Everyone is seeking shelter at R' Nehemiah's house in the hope to revive their soul.

R' Nehemiah confiscates buildings by force and places refugees in them. He surprises his neighbor, Gitel Prosman, a widow with three orphans who lives in a narrow room, a very small room, and to this "palace" he stuffs eight refugees. The poor accepts it all with love and her lips mumble silently: R' Nehemiah knows what he's doing.

R' Moshe Schiffer is a laborer who lives in "Kovel Vtoroi," At midnight someone knocks on the door to his room. Who is knocking? – R' Nehemiah! He came to ask for the well being of a sick refugee who, as he was told, is bedridden for several days without food and medicine. R' Nehemiah carries in his bag a loaf of bread and a bottle of medicine. He must discover the whereabouts of the sick refugee and give him treatment and healing despite late hour and the grave dangers that lurk in the city's streets.

The Red Army captured Kovel. R' Nehemiah welcomes the Soviets with fanfare. Now salvation will come to all who suffer. However, soon came the disappointment, and again, the burden of social welfare rests on the shoulders of R' Nehemiah. Again, he provides help to the miserable and the hungry until the German murderers took his life.

I know, from reliable sources, that R' Nehemiah walked to the pit of death upright and with Jewish national pride.

Kindergartens in Kovel under the Soviet Regime

by Freida Rosenblatt–Buchwald (Paris)

Translated by Sara Mages

In 1939, when the Red Army entered Kovel, there was also a change in the field of education.

Three kindergartens were organized. Two – on the "dunes" [the area of the new city where the Jews lived], and one – in the city. Another kindergarten, of only one class, was established in the city a year later.

The large kindergarten, No. 1, which contained three classes, was managed by Sonia Margolis–Gelman. The teacher of Kindergarten No. 3 was Sugia Imberg. I forgot the name of the teacher of Kindergarten No. 4.

The education work in these kindergartens was conducted in Yiddish, but a respectable place was dedicated to the study of Russian songs and also for readings in the Russian language.

The fourth kindergarten, which was marked by the serial number 2, was managed by the writer of these lines and its language was Russian.

[Page 398]

This kindergarten was a mixture of different nationalities and outside the Jewish children it also contained Ukrainian, Polish and Russian children. The latter were children of Soviet citizens who came to the city with the Red Army.

The pedagogical and the administretive work were conducted under the supervision of the Municipal Department of Education ("Garana") which was directed by the supervisor, Ida Merzan (today in Poland), who was an expert in kindergarten affairs.

The tuition was very small. The parents paid according to their ability because each kindergarten was given a decent budget to meet its needs. The children stayed at school until six in the evening and received three meals a day. The kindergartens were well organized and the toddlers spent their time in a cultural atmosphere and under reasonable conditions.

Most of the pedagogical and technical staff in all the kindergartens was Jewish. The young teachers, who have completed their education, worked on their own and performed miracles in the education work during the two years of Soviet rule in Kovel.

The ruling spirit in all the kindergartens was Soviet–patriotic and the trend was to empty the kindergartens from their national Jewish content and give them the character of Russian schools. The Jewish cultural heritage, which was woven with great devotion by many generations of Kovel's Jews, faded right before our eyes

Apart from Sonia Margolis–Gelman, the director of Kindergarten No. 1, and the writer of these lines – all these young kindergarten teachers were killed by the German murderers.

I will light a memorial candle for my beloved and unforgettable friends who worked together with me until the last days of the Jews of Kovel: The warmhearted Meika Gelman who was always smiling; the lovely Rozek Lifshitz, wife of Moshe (Moske) Gelman; the talented Asia Atlas who was devoted to her work; the young and cheerful Neche Sass who didn't know what sadness was; the gentle Yenta Tesler who wanted to leave the city when the war broke out. When she came to see me before I left she told me with a sad face "it's difficult for me to leave my family"; Sima Imber, the beautiful and talented principal. I will also bring the memory of the elderly women from the technical staff: Mrs. Wilkomirski, Berger and others that unfortunately I forgot their names; the nurses Tania Kutzin and Heinech.

In the years 1939–41, I directed Kindergarten No. 1 which was located on Prison Street across from the orphanage. The kindergarten was housed in a beautiful building which was full of light and surrounded by a big flower garden. Sixty to eighty children attended this kindergarten.

[Page 399] [Page 400]

As stated, most of the children in this kindergarten were Jewish and the rest – the children of Soviet officials, and also Ukrainian and Polish children. All the work was conducted in Russian.

The children were divided into classes. Stasya, who was once the director of Maclerz–Szkolna [Polish Educational Society], worked in the toddlers' class. The second class was directed by Asia Atlas – a teacher of high professional level.

This kindergarten had an accountant, a storekeeper, a nurse, a doctor (who visited twice to three times a week) a technical staff, a cook, maids, and even a security guard who also worked as a gardener. The garden was full of flowers and the playground was the most favorite place for the children.

The work stood on a high educational level. The care for the child was felt in the daily work of the teachers and the technical staff. The children loved the kindergarten and willingly visited it. However, there was no a trace of Jewish education in it. Weekdays and holidays were dedicated to the introduction of Soviet patriotic spirit in the hearts of the young students.

In the picture we see the children of Kindergarten No. 2 during a large Soviet celebration in 1941. Here are Karteplie's grandchildren: Gita Guberman (daughter of the lawyer Yakov Guberman); Ruth (granddaughter of Yisrael Pruzansky); Sokna, her brother and her nephew – the children of the Porshtler brothers; Shapira's son; the daughter of Ester Murik, and the daughter of Riva Chasis. We also see the teacher Asia Atlas, the Berger friends, Schneider the music teacher and others.

As I was told, all these children, apart from a small group of Russian and Polish children, were murdered.

Shrinka Gvirtzman, the graceful daughter of Siake and Yasha Gvirtzman, left for Russia together with her mother but died of meningitis in far away Shakira before the end of the war.

The kindergarten children during a large Soviet celebration

In 1940, at the advice of the Soviet authorities, many Jewish families left for the depth of Russia. Some were hesitant to take their children to such distant places. They took them off the railcars at the last moment and gave them to their relatives "till the storm blows over". Two of them attended our kindergarten and perished together with all the children. One was the three year old daughter of Riva Chasis–Rubinstein and the second – six year old Ruth, daughter of Liza Pruzansky and granddaughter of Yisrael Pruzansky.

Ruth was very talented and sang and danced well. She's standing before me in her colorful Ukrainian custom and I look at her delicate face.

[Page 401]

She was the one who danced and sang in that Soviet ball. She welcomed the guests, greeted them in Russian, a language which was still new to her, and also gave a speech.

The audience was very moved by the performance of the little artist and the chief administrator took her in his arms and kissed her. Full of glamour, her face flushed, she escaped from his arms and like a pure cherub flew, in one jump, on the stage and continued to dance and sing. Dozens of Jewish toddlers, who were dressed in colorful clothes, sang and danced with her.

This was her "swan song" – her last dance.

The Crumbling of the Economic and Cultural Systems

by Leuba Galman-Goldberg

Translated by Sara Mages

When the war broke out I lived in Warsaw. I worked as a counselor at a summer colony of a large Jewish orphanage.

When Warsaw fell in October 1939 we brought the children back to the institution. Some were sent back to their relatives and those, who didn't have a relative or a savior, remained in the institution under the management's supervision and care.

On 25 November I returned to Kovel which has already been under Soviet rule. The main train station was decorated with pictures of the leaders of the revolution, Soviet government personal and many flags. Uniformed soldiers ran all over the place. However, there was also an unusual movement of masses of civilians, Jewish and non-Jewish refugees, who arrived to Kovel from Western Poland on their escape from the Nazis.

Immediately after my arrival to the city I noticed that all the shops and businesses were closed. The shopkeepers sold their entire stock and didn't receive new merchandise. The only stores, which were opened and sold various goods, were the government stores and long lines snaked by their doors. It was impossible to get anything without a line. Obviously, the grocery stores "won" the longest line.

The only place where it was still possible to buy something was the market. Women, whose husbands were exiled to Russia or were in captivity, and the refugees sold all sorts of things to revive their soul.

All life in the city had been transferred to new tracks.

Craftsmen, who previously worked separately, organized in cooperatives: sewing, shoemaking and hairdressing. In addition, the banks have changed their way of working.

There was no longer a question of current accounts, loans and investments. A large government bank was created from all the banks. Each institution had an approved budget and all the proceeds were given to the bank. All the previous bank employees continued to work at the government bank. Among them were: Moshe Perel, the kindhearted Rachel Fisher, Monik Goldberg, Fira Efrat and Aharon Sokolovsky, who excelled in their devotion to their work.

The various factories, meaning, the flourmills, tanneries and olive presses were nationalized and their owners were exiled to small towns around the city. Among the deportees was Yosel Shochat and others. Denziger and Zimerman were exiled to Siberia. The Siberian exile was also imposed on political activists who opposed communism in the past, such as the "*Bund*" activist Steinman.

However, not everyone had won the grand "prize" to reach Siberia. On the way, near Tambov, the Russians began to eliminate the deportation trains. Aharon Tsuperfain, hy"d, was killed on the spot and Noah was wounded. The guards thought that he was dead and left him there. When he woke up, he somehow managed to stay in a village near Tambov where he recovered from his wounds. He immigrated to Israel in 1950 and passed away in 1953. May his memory be blessed.

As stated, many refugees who tried to settle in the place "until the danger is past," gathered in Kovel. The city suffered from a terrible shortage of housing and it was necessary to house the refugees in synagogues and various public institutions.

There were also thousands of Ukrainian refugees in the city who arrived from the other side of the Bug River. According to an agreement between Germany and Russia, the Bug was set as a final border between the two countries.

Residents of rural villages, who were fascinated by the stories about the good life in the *kolkhozy*, loaded their belongings on their wagons and left to enjoy the wealth of the collective farms in Russia. However, the disappointment wasn't late in coming. They returned in masses and got stuck in Kovel.

To find a solution to the problem of unemployment and severe overcrowding, the authorities started to enlist people for work in Russia. They also announced the registration of those who wished to return to Poland.

Those, with a Communist outlook, registered to work in Russia. They wanted to help the "Socialist Homeland" in its desperate struggle against the Nazi monster. However, when they realized that this help was expressed in hard labor in mines with criminals - their enthusiasm faded and they returned to the city.

Different was the fate of those who expressed their wish to return to Poland to reunite with their families.

They never reach their destination. One night, they were collected, loaded on freight cars and exiled to Siberia. Despite their terrible living conditions most of them survived and a few even managed to immigrate to Israel.

Those, who remained in the city and received Soviet citizenship, gradually found a job and earned a living. A revolutionary change occurred in the occupation of the city's Jews. Suddenly, there were Jewish railway and factory workers. The educated received jobs in the various services - schools, hospitals and government offices.

With the entry of the Soviets, a number of Jewish Communists, refugees from Warsaw, established schools in our city. The Chief Inspector was an army officer and a former teacher. His deputy was Tabachnik-Mirsky, a native of our city. The comptroller of schools was Chaya Mendelson z"l, and the kindergartens - Ida Merzan.

All the schools were divided according to the origin of the students. The language of teaching at the Jewish schools was Yiddish, the Russian children were taught in Russian and the Ukrainian children studied in Ukrainian. I remember the impression that Talmud Torah had given me when I visited the school in the past. The big gray building, the yard empty from trees and greenery, the bearded teachers and the students that poverty and suffering were reflected from their eyes. But now, a different spirit hovered over the children. Singing emerged through the open windows. They were dressed in clean clothes and the girls were decorated with colorful ribbons.

The school teachers were: the talented principal, Aharon Shnitzky z"l, the principal of the Yiddish School of "Poalei Zion Left" in Warsaw (on Karmelicka Street); Lea Diamnt a teacher from Warsaw; Teitlker; Neumark z"l; myself and the nurse Mina Bidnick.

The students studied, drew, cut and paste pictures. Each class published a newspaper, danced and sang.

Also the image of the yard had changed.

The neglected yard turned into a vegetables garden. Each class had a number of beds that the children cultivated and guarded,

I remember the May Day procession. Our school received an award for a fine walk and there was no end to the children's delight.

Of course, all the religious holidays have been canceled and studies also took place on the Sabbath and on the holidays.

Our first celebration took place on New Year Eve 1939-40.

The Ministry of Education sent a Christmas tree to each school. The children decorated it in good taste and joy. The parents, Tabachnik the schools' supervisor, and soldiers attended this party. The children acted, sang and danced. The soldiers played the accordion.

It was strange to see the children of Talmud Torah dancing around the Christmas tree which is the symbol of Christianity.

I don't remember who initiated the unification of children from different nationalities, but the Ukrainian school on Meziov Street invited the students of the first grade to the party.

Military officers took an active part in all areas of life. They lectured at schools, kindergartens and in the parents' meetings. They told about the heroes of the revolution and the war in Finland. There wasn't a single party in the city without the presence of the representatives of the Red Army. They also invited the children to perform before the soldiers at the camps.

In our school, apart from the regular studies, there were also classes for working youth who hadn't finish elementary school, and classes for the illiterate. The teachers were sent, in turn, to rest-houses in Kiev, Kharkiv and Crimea. The children took field trips to Russia.

On each vacation the teachers took classes in sociology and Russian pedagogy. They also had to study the book "Kartki Course V.K.P.B" [*Vsesoyuznaya Kommunisticheskaya Partiya bol'shevikov*] by Stalin. From time to time, the teachers were invited to the "*politrukim*" [political commissars], the men of the Communist Party who tested their knowledge in the history of the Bolsheviks. Clerks and laborers had to study Stalin's book in all the institutions.

This activity was conducted with great energy until the outbreak of the war between Russia and Germany. In its wake, the Soviets were forced to evacuate the city. During the evacuation, the teachers tried to save the children in various ways. One successful experience was done by the teacher Zechindy whose husband worked in the municipality on behalf of the Soviets. She transferred the "*Komsomol*," the students of the Jewish Gymnasium, to Russia, and indeed, all of them survived and most of them are in Israel.

During the Soviet rule in the city, the Jewish youth was filled with faith in the lofty ideals of Communism. They dreamed of pursuing further education in the universities of Kiev and Kharkiv, and believed, wholeheartedly, in the omnipotent power of the Soviet Union. No one imagined that the Soviet troops would leave the city for a long time, too long for the children of Kovel and her Jews… They were proud of the rights that the Soviet regime had given to them after they have been abused by Polish rioters.

Therefore, the youth's world darkened when the Nazis entered the city. In an instant, the Nazis canceled and trampled all the rights that the Jews had acquired, and not only that, they also denied them the right to live. From pride and hope they've sunk into the abyss of despair.

Cry For Mourning

by Rabbi Yehuda, son of Kalonymus

Translated by Ala Gamulka

I call for mourning and lamentation
My tears will flow from my eyes
Day and night, they will not cease
I will weep and cover myself with ashes
I will lament and have others join me
All those who are embittered.
Silence and fugue will not happen.
Your eyes will be tearful and you will lament
Our weak arms will be upheld by sorrow.
Beat your palms in sadness
Ululate with your breaking heart.
You, the elderly and the senior.
Screams and groans are numerous
Moans and cries are heard
This is why you must wear sack clothes.

[Page 408]

Woe for this Beauty that is Rotting in the Earth

by Eliezer Leono-Tzufrifin

Translated by Jerrold Landau

If I were given the power, the power of the ancestors, to arise at night and sit on the ground to pour out my speech and shed tears over the destruction of Israel[1], over the hundreds of thousands of lads and elderly people, children and women, who were tortured by horrible torments and murdered with cruel deaths that the human conception cannot has no power to understand or portray.

- Dr. Yaakov Kletzkin

I am diving into the depths of the past. I remove myself from the place and the time, and place myself in a sweet illusion, in which everything stands atop its foundation. I walk in the streets of the city, perfuming myself with its aromas, listening to the sounds of the children playing, turning my ear to the chant of the *Gemara* bursting forth from the many *Beis Midrashes* of the city.

I walk through the fields, through the golden stalks, and dip myself in the cool waters of the Turya River. I meet acquaintances, friends, and engage in conversation with them.

But I awaken from my dream, and we are orphaned and bereaved. Our parental home was destroyed, and the parental homes throughout all of Kowel were destroyed. The sound of the frolicking children has ceased; the fiddles that played enchanting melodies have been silenced. A heap of bones, dismembered vertebrae, a pile of skulls – these are the terrible and frightening remains of our dear ones.

Now I look at the images of the natives of Kowel, as they shine forth from the pages of the book, enveloped in a sublime, awesome ether – and I cannot not sufficiently feed my eyes of their endearing faces.

It is possible that we did not appreciate the beauty of their form, the sublimity of their essence, their human greatness, while they were alive. Now, however, it is as if the veil has been removed, and they are filled with luster, exuding light, glory, and greatness.

With holiness and fear, with trembling of great awe, I behold their faces. How wonderful are they! I sense in their presence something holy and sublime that purifies the soul. The natives of Kowel! You were very pleasant to us. The paths of your lives were wonderful, and the period of your destruction and disappearance was terrible.

Who could have said and who could have thought that this would be the end of our beautiful dear ones, pure in heart, and upright in their ways. What sin did you transgress? Who did you oppress, who did you steal from, who did you kill, that this became your fate?

[Page 409]

I immerse my eyes in the splendor of your faces, and certainly see that you do not seem at all as natives of the Diaspora. Your faces are immersed in sunlight. Glory and pride radiates from you.

How did the gold become dull?[2] Youth of Kowel, where are you? Our hearts were full or pride when you walked together in the outskirts of Kowel. You were the pride and hope of us all. Our eyes wept tears of joy: Behold, a Messiah has arisen for Israel! Your heads were full of the morning dew. Song came forth from your essence as the song of the morning stars.

Youth of Kowel! You knew the great travesties about which the future generations talk. As you went to annihilation, there is agony and bitter mourning for all of us. Even the heaps of your graves weep bitterly.

I recall you and lament, as I weep day and night. You fell, oh children of Kowel, in the beauty of your prime, as pure, clear cherubs. Now, the impure ones have overturned the dust of your graves, as their murderous hands search through your skulls – perhaps a gold tooth remains there.

How could we have thought and how could we have imagined, at the time the iniquitous ones pillaged our cubs and the bloody ones desecrated the graves of our eagles? To us, the bereft ones, there is no greater anguish than the anguish of the desecration of your graves.

Would that we have the chance to supplicate over your remains and gather your fingers and toes, which the murderers tossed over the fields. We would kiss every lump and clod of earth, for they are holy to us. We cover your holy, pure bones in a *tallis* [prayer shawl] made of tears.

We will not forget this atrocity, nor allow it to be forgotten! With an iron and led pen, we have etched your deep torment in the rock of history.

There are not sufficient tears in the source of our tears to weep over the great, terrible destruction. Honor has been removed! The crown of our head has been taken away. Our stature is diminished and bent. Our eyes gaze through the air of the world, and the heart shouts out a bitter outcry, the sound of which reverberates from one end of the world to the other: Why have we been wronged in a way that no other generation in our history has been wronged?

We do not research that which is hidden from us, and we do not interpret that which is too mysterious for us, for the matters are hidden and concealed. Therefore, we, the bereaved and bereft natives of the community of Kowel, have come to beg forgiveness from our holy martyrs. If we have sinned against you, let the pages of this book atone for our sins.

[Page 410]

It is an ancient belief that only the upper soul ascends to the heavens, whereas the "spirit of the bones" – the lower soul, remains bound and cleaves to the bones of the deceased until the advent of the Messiah. This spirit is attached to your bones, our dear deceased, moves your lips with words of forgiveness and atonement.

Your memory is tied and bound in our hearts, and it will also never depart from the mouths of all coming generations. We know that you turned your glance to us in your final moments. You cried out, pleaded, and prayed that we will avenge your spilled blood. We hearkened to your cries, but we did not have the power to save. We have perpetuated your cry, and we have perpetuated your prayers. Let your voice ascend to the Throne of Glory, and the merciful and compassionate G-d shall open the gates of Heaven to you, conceal you under the protection of His wings, and may you attain your fulfilment at the End of Days.

Our comfort is that at the End of Days, when those who slumber in the earth awaken from their slumber to eternal life, and your bones will reknit together, our eyes will again behold the faces of our unforgettable dear ones, who went to their world with difficult, terrible tribulations that cannot be described by a human being.

Until then we have no comfort. No human language has yet been created for the words that would comfort and calm us. The shadows of our dear departed are stretched over the entire annal of our lives. Even as when laughter fills our mouths – our tears choke us.

As we remember you, our hearts drip blood. Were I able to have a discussion with the powers above, located on the other side of the screen of life, I would ask in a weeping voice: Why did you torture us such? Why was the crown removed and stolen from our heads? Why was fury poured out also on infants and sucklings? Is there an answer to this? G-d answered Job through the storm. Will an answer ever be given to the entire community of "Jobs?"

Translator's Footnotes:

1. A reference to the *Tikkun Chatzot* service. See https://en.wikipedia.org/wiki/Tikkun_Chatzot
2. Lamentations (*Eicha*) 4:1.

[Page 411]

Thus the City was Destroyed[1]

by Ben–Zion Sher

Translated by Amy Samin

(As told by an eyewitness)

"I am the man who has seen affliction by the rod of his wrath"
(Lamentations 3:1)

Chapter One

(From the entry of the Nazis to the city through the destruction of the first ghetto)

Recruiting, Supposedly, for Work

On the first day of the entrance of the Germans to the city, several Jews went out, including Leibush's son–in–law Pessiah Resilas and his sixteen year old son, into Trisk Street. They, and six other Jews, were immediately kidnapped and taken to Kovka Bukser courtyard. They were ordered to dig a pit and climb down inside. When they were lined up inside the pit – they were killed where they stood. Later, they came in the middle of the night and took away the lawyer, Goverman. He disappeared without a trace and none knew his fate.

The Germans began recruiting men and women for work. They also asked to recruit Rabbi Valula, may his blood be avenged, who was old and weak. The Trisk followers made an uproar that the rabbi not be taken for forced labor, collected three kilograms of gold, delivered the money into the hands of the "gevitas komissar", and thanks to this he was put into the Jewish hospital as a patient.

About 60 of us went to work in "Vyturio Kovel". Between the tracks was a canal, where people would throw broken glass, barbed wire, and scraps of tin. They ordered us to take off our shoes and dance barefoot on the broken glass. One of those with us was the butcher Isaac Hochman, husband of Rivka Aidless. Rivulets of blood trickled down his legs, and we lifted him in our arms.

On the third Shabbat after the Germans' arrival, trucks appeared in Macheib Street and Lutzka Street and gathered about 20 people. They told them they were being sent to work.

[Page 412]

However, when we saw that they were also loading all sorts of weaklings, disabled people, the elderly, and the sick into the cars, our hearts shuddered and we were engulfed in a cloud: Are they really sending them to work?

The next day, a goy came from Bychawa to buy a horse. Trembling with fear, he told us that the day before trucks filled with Jews had arrived in Bychawa, where they were ordered to dig a large hole. The Jews were thrown into the hole, and cries of "Shma Yisrael, Adonai Elohainu Adonai Echad" [Hear O Israel, the Lord our God the Lord is one.] rent the heavens. Then it went quiet, as all of the Jews were shot and covered with dirt.

At first we didn't believe his story, but when we saw that the goy was trembling and terrified, we started to believe him and were torn apart by these tidings of Job.

Before the killing, they told the unfortunates to write letters to their families, saying they were near Kobryn, alive and well, eating and drinking, wanting for nothing. After a month, six weeks at the most, they would return to their homes.

The poor families, in their innocence, believed what was written in the letters. Wives waited for their husbands, sisters waited for their brothers, brides waited for their grooms, and children waited for their fathers. But when six weeks had passed, and two months had gone by, and people saw no signs of life – the unfortunate families ran to the community council, to learn when, finally, they would return. A messenger from the community came with the happy news, that tomorrow all of the people who had been taken away to work would return.

The next day, all of the women and children went out, walking all the way to the village of Zamshany (between Ratne and Kovel). They waited a day, then two, and not a single person appeared. Then the women understood the depth of their disaster; that, in fact, they had no one for whom to wait, that their husbands would never return, that they had been widowed and their children orphaned

The Burning of the Torah Scrolls

About a month after the Germans arrived, a few German policemen came to the community council and demanded 20 men for work. They took the workers to the great synagogue. There they were told to go to every house of study in the city and remove the Torah scrolls and lay them down next to the great synagogue. Anyone who left even a single Torah scroll in the ark would be shot on the spot.

From the great synagogue we removed 32 Torah scrolls. Inside the synagogue there was the carpenters' house of study – we took out five Torah scrolls from there, as well. We took Torah scrolls from the Ruzhyner, Trisker, Karliner, Kotzker, and Naskizer synagogues, from the large house of study, and from the tailors' house of study. Altogether, we collected about 200 Torah scrolls.

Being in the Trisker synagogue, I took a Torah scroll and hid it in a closet near the seat belonging to Mordechai Hari of blessed memory. The Germans searched the house of study and never found the hiding place of the Torah scroll .

[Page 413]

They told us to lay the Torah scrolls down next to the carpenters' synagogue and to arrange them in stacks, four scrolls in each column and arranged one on top of the other. The Germans provided us with gasoline and ordered us to burn the Torah scrolls. The scrolls burned, the letters vanished in the air, and the wind scattered the ashes in every direction.

When I arrived, after a while, from the ghetto on the Sands to the ghetto in the city, I went to the Trisker synagogue and found the Torah scroll there. I left it with a goy, an acquaintance of mine, named Pliushk.

Three years later, when I returned to the city, I went to Pliushk and found the Torah scroll – minus its ornaments and decorations, and with a few sections cut out. When I was in Lodz I added all of the missing sections. That Torah scroll has remained in my possession to this day.

In the Shadow of the Gallows

I had a partner, the butcher Moshe Feldman of blessed memory. On the eve of Passover Manthei [Translator's Note: the police commissar], may his bones be crushed, entered Feldman's barn on Michkabitza Street and found a piece of sochatin there, stiff leather, which had sat there for many years. Manthei was looking for an excuse to blame Feldman, who slaughtered cows, preparing them for the Jews to eat for the Passover holiday. He immediately ordered his arrest. The next day, the first day of Passover, six Germans came and took him out of jail, leading him to the tavern owned by Gedaliah and Lazer Soinuich, may their blood be avenged.

The gallows and the noose had been ready since the night before, and underneath them stood three crates. Feldman, who was a sturdy fellow, wouldn't let them put his head into the noose and showed great heroism. He kicked the hangman in the leg, and gnashed his teeth in the faces of the killers, knocked them to the ground, and the Germans couldn't hang him. So they called for reinforcements, Ukrainian murderers. After a hard and desperate struggle, the murderers succeeded in overpowering him, put the noose around his neck, knocked away the crates from under his feet, and Feldman hung there.

But a miracle happened: the rope came loose, and Feldman remained alive, standing on his feet, and swooped down on the hangman like a wounded lion. The Germans hung him again, and again the rope came loose. Gradually Feldman lost his strength, and when they hung him for the third time, the rope remained intact, and Feldman breathed his last after a prolonged death rattle.

At night, when we returned from working in Gorky, we found Feldman hanging, and over his heart a tin sign that said "Hung for slaughtering cows in order to prepare meat for the Jews for the Passover holiday…

[Page 414]

His body may not be removed from the rope for three days, so that the Jews will hear and see and sin no more."

Feldman continued to hang there for the first day of Passover. Through the efforts of his brothers and community representatives, Manthei was persuaded that it would be fitting to remove his body from the rope on the second day.

His brothers, Hane Feldman and Joseph Feldman, whose knees were shaking from grief and sorrow, asked me to lower their dead brother from the rope and to bestow upon him the final kindness. They had an apprentice, who worked with them in the slaughterhouse, named Avrasha. I told the young fellow: "Come and help me." The young man begged me, saying "Ben–Zion, have mercy on me. I can't do it, my hands are shaking."

I went to the yard of Gedaliah Soinuich. I took a ladder and found a sharp knife, and I went to cut the rope. I saw a frightful sight: Feldman's head was all swollen, blue, his tongue hanging out, and the rope had dug deeply into the flesh of his neck.

We brought him for burial in the new cemetery. We found an available spot next to the grave of his father Zvi Feldman of blessed memory, and there he was buried. The rabbi Nahum Moshele, may his blood be avenged, told us that Feldman must be buried in his clothes, because he was holy.

The burial took place on the night of the second Seder. All of the Jews of the city, including those who had matzah and wine, did not hold the Seder. No one ate, no one drank, everyone cried and mourned, because they saw Feldman as a communal sacrifice.

Manthei's Acts of Cruelty

Manthei would not eat breakfast until he had killed three Jews. At five in the morning he would start his motorcycle and set off in search of prey. The very rattle of the motorcycle brought the fear of death.

One Friday we worked on Horodlatz Road. When we returned from work, we sat near the house of the road engineer and waited for the employees who worked in the slaughterhouse. From far off we could hear the rattle that heralded the approach of Manthei. We took cover in a canal, and saw Manthei riding along armed with an automatic weapon. After him came three trucks full of Jews with shovels in their hands. Among them, I recognized Leibel Lushik and Aharon Shczupak. We thought in our hearts: what do Jews have to do in the cemetery on the night of the Sabbath?

Next to the gate of the cemetery, the murderer ordered them to get out of the cars. He opened the gate and put them inside. Then he lowered his automatic weapon and started firing on the Jews. The poor souls ran between the tombstones and fell. Within minutes he had killed all of the Jews who had arrived in the three trucks. We were afraid to go home, and remained near the engineer's house all night.

[Page 415]

The next day I climbed up on the engineer's barn and I saw the horrific atrocity: all of the Jews had been left lying over the tombstones, dead.

Establishment of the Ghettos

About a year after the Germans arrived in town, the Ukrainians whispered in the ear of the *Gebietskommissar* asking what was the point of having ghettos in all of the towns in the Volhynia, and yet Kovel was being given favorable treatment?

Two ghettos were established in the city. One was in the city, and the other on the "Sands". In the first they gathered all of the merchants and owners of free professions, women, children, old people, the handicapped, and the sick. In the second they concentrated all of the workers of various professions. Between the two ghettos there rose up a sort of Chinese wall, and there was no communication between the two. The command threatened with death any worker who crossed into the ghetto in the city, and any merchant who crossed into the ghetto on the Sands.

Together with the refugees who had fled from their own communities nearby, there were at that time about 24,000 Jews. The ghetto in the city held about 10,500 people, and in the ghetto on the Sands there were concentrated about 13,500 people.

On the night the ghetto was established, Fishel Roitenberg went to his Polish neighbor, to hear the news from him. He told him that heavy clouds were piling up over the heads of the Jews in the city. Policemen were arriving from Naskij, Matzyeb, Holoba, and from all over. Terrible slaughter was imminent. He must flee from the city lest he and all the Jews be killed.

Fishel, may his blood be avenged, came to me and told me of this. I had a Polish neighbor, who had told me at the time that if, God forbid, something happened, he would give my children shelter in his home.

At two o'clock in the morning, I woke my children from their slumber, dressed them, and took them to the home of my neighbor. To my great amazement and dismay, the Pole renounced me and refused to open the door. After my tears and pleas melted his insensitive heart, he listened to my insistent pleading and told me that I must send my children out with the cows, and he would send his children out with his cows. The children would spend time together, and the murderers would not notice them. I did as he said.

In the morning I went out to check on the wellbeing of the children. I was stopped by a police squad of about one hundred men. They didn't touch me, but they informed me that in about half an hour I must be inside the ghetto. I could bring with me the clothes I was wearing, and my children. By the time I found my children, the extension they had given me had passed. In my house sat one of my neighbors, a Polish woman, with whom I had deposited all of my property. I wanted to take some garments for my children, but she would not allow me to enter the house.

I went out into the street, which was deserted. The city was like a graveyard. I went to Hane Feldman's house, which was inside the ghetto, to find a corner for myself and my children. The house was full to bursting.

[Page 416]

Everyone stood crowded together. No one even dreamed about a place to sit. From there I went to Beryl Zweiter, but I didn't find a place there, either. With no other choice, my children and I stayed in a cowshed.

In time, I found a place to stay with Avraham Matisis, whose house bordered the Dolgonos church on Trisk Street. Many of us remembered the priest of that church. Who could have guessed that this priest, who was considered a friend of the Jews, possessed a soul that was diabolical, dark, satanic, and murderous.

I remember: On Sunday, which was a day of rest for us in the ghetto, I saw a gathering of villagers from Dolgonos, Lubliniec, Kalinovka, and Kortelesy. These masses streamed into the courtyard of the church. The priest climbed up on a tree and gave a hate–filled speech, which I give here word for word: "Darling people," the priest said in a loud voice, "dear people! We must give the Nazi kingdom our last crust of bread, the last cow, the last egg, the last drop of milk! We must give our sons and our daughters to the Nazis, that they may do all of the hard work, because woe to us, all of us, if the bandit comes here, the mustachioed Kolhoznik [*i.e. communist*]." The priest continued, "Dear people, darling people! I ask you and I warn you: do not give a single crust of bread to a Jew! Do not give him a drop of water! Do not give him shelter! Anyone who knows the hiding place of a Jew, find the Jew and deliver him to the Germans. There must not remain even a trace of a Jew, we must obliterate the Jews from the face of the earth! Only when the last Jew has ceased to exist will we win the war." All of the villagers applauded, kissed the feet of the "Holy Father", came together and swore, and rejoiced in the coming obliteration of the Jews in the area.

The Vast Slaughter in Brisk Square

On the seventeenth of Sivan in 1942, at five o'clock in the morning, the gate to the ghetto opened and Moshe Perl, Leibel Bass, the butcher from Lodz (who served as the police commander), and Shalom Erlich came out and approached us. "Jews, everyone go out to the Brisk Square – those who are found there, we guarantee their lives. But anyone who hides in a basement or an attic – the hand of the killers will be upon him, and his blood will not be on our heads."

I told my wife, may her blood be avenged, "If the community leaders promise, no misfortune will befall us. Let's go out to the square and be with the large community of Jews." Unbeknownst to us, the killers had misled our community leaders.

We went out. I saw a huge crowd of about 10,000 people.

Suddenly, Kasner (the *Gebietskommissar*) and Manthei, his right hand man, appeared. They stood in the center of the market, looking at the multitudes of Jews, and none of us could have guessed at what was about to happen

[Page 417]

to us. We were sure that the promises made by Kasner to the community leaders that we were to be sent to work, were firm and valid.

However, soon all of our dreams were dashed. Suddenly there swooped down on the square about 4,000 armed Ukrainians. We were surrounded. We saw clearly that a great slaughter was imminent.

In the great crowd was the rabbi Nahum Moshele, may his blood be avenged, the son in law of reb Yaacov Leibenow, may his righteous memory be blessed, who never ceased studying Torah. He asked permission to say a few words to the Jews of the city in the final moments before dying. In a voice choked with tears the rabbi said: "Dear Jews, I see before my eyes a terrible slaughter, the likes of which our people have never seen. An outpouring of blood is about to drown us. Dozens of generations of mankind to Noah, and dozens of generations from Noah to Avraham. Every generation left behind a remnant of memory, and every son would pray for the elevation of the soul of his father. We are more wretched than all of the generations of Jews who came before us, for they are slaughtering all of us, our wives, our children, and our infants. No one will come to prostrate themselves on our graves, no one will say Kaddish for us, no one will hold memories of us in his heart. Our flame is extinguished; we will all descend, very soon, into the dark pit. Dear Jews, the world is so beautiful, the trees are blossoming, the birds are reciting poetry, and we must descend into the pit. Our people thirsts for life. Our rabbi Moshe, peace be upon him, when his sentence was pronounced, asked the Master of the Universe, that he be laid to rest like the grass–eating beasts of the field, or like the bird floating in the four directions of the world." Lord, look from your holy dwelling place and see – who have you harmed, upon who have you vented your rage. We have sinned, our sons have committed a crime, but these angels, these infants, these pure angels, these babies, what sin have they committed that your wrath be spilled upon them? What is their crime; that they must rot in the pit?"

"Jews, we are approaching martyrdom. Let us be united as one person. Let us go to our deaths with gladdened hearts. This horrible moment shall pass, and the merciful Lord above us will give our souls repose under His wings."

After him the teacher Yosef Avrech, may his blood be avenged, spoke. He looked at his many students, who had gathered around him, and said, "This wonderful youth, how much energy was invested in nurturing and educating them! We built a house of study, a splendid Hebrew gymnasia, and now everything is about to go up in flames. Lord of the nations, do not cover up our blood, do not smother our cries. Let our moans and prayers ring out in the vacuum. I feel deep sorrow when I see this glorious man, these precious ones, thirsting for life, wrapped in their vision of redemption, wellsprings of Torah and wisdom gurgling in them – my heart breaks to see you being led like sheep to the slaughter."

Turning to Manthei, he said, "The people of Israel fight with all the force of the universe. Their memory is lost, but they will live forever. Many killers rose against us, and we saw our downfall, yet we will also see your downfall.

[Page 418]

Don't imagine in your soul that you will win the war. I tell you, your defeat will soon come. It's a shame, such a shame, that we will not see your downfall."

When Avrech finished speaking, Manthei took out a large pistol, pointed the muzzle at Avrech's head and shot him, and his brains spilled to the ground.

When they saw Avrech fall to the ground, wallowing in his own blood, panic ensued. People started running about wildly. Dreadful shouts were heard, and everyone began running towards the Ukrainian police. The order to fire was given. When they saw the many who had fallen from the bullets of the killers, they prostrated themselves on the ground. Many trucks arrived, and they forced the people into them and took them to Bychawa.

A bullet hit me next to my ear, a lot of blood flowed from the wound, and I fell to the ground, unconscious. I lay there from 6 until midnight. I opened my eyes and did not see a single person. Live people I did not see, but I saw many dead people. The corpses of the dead were scattered all over the square. Those were the days of grid, dry days of summer heat, and woodworm – all kinds of creeping insects sucking the blood of animals – sat on the corpses, which were showing signs of decay. Ukrainian policemen came, pushing wheelbarrows. They collected with shovels the puddles of blood into the wheelbarrows, dug a hole in the center of the square, and buried all of the dear and copious blood that had been spilled.

Later an order was given to collect all of the corpses and pile them into three stacks. Altogether, 277 people were slain. Two Ukrainians approached me thinking I was dead, one grabbed my legs and the other my arms, and they tossed me into a pile of dead bodies.

The Ukrainian policemen left, and once again silence reigned. I sat up on the bodies, and suddenly I heard the sound of weeping coming from the second pile of the dead. I got up, approached the spot and saw a young girl with an injury to her leg. I recognized her. It was Baba Rojter, may her blood be avenged.

The wound was bleeding, and the infection pained her. She begged me to help her stop the pain. I didn't have a bandage to put on her injury, and I tried to quiet her. I told her to control her pain, because the Ukrainians would hear her cries and return to kill her. "Let's wait until morning, perhaps help will come." I left her, and went back to sit on the pile of the dead with sorrow in my heart and thoughts of mourning in my brain, from whence will come my help?

With the sunrise came 100 Jews from the other ghetto in two vehicles. They were accompanied by six Germans. They had been sent to rinse away the blood and bury the bodies. The Germans left to enter the ghetto in order to plunder the homes of the Jews, taking wine and all sorts of foodstuffs, and ordering Motke Weiner, who served as an overseer of that group of Jews, not to dare to touch any of the dead in their absence.

In the other ghetto they knew nothing of the eradication of the first ghetto. When they saw the dead lying before them they wept piteously, pulling out their hair and striking their faces with heartrending cries.

[Page 419]

This one recognized his father among the dead, that one his mother, another his sister, yet another recognized his wife, and another his small son, and they began mourning the horrifying lamentations: "Oy for what has happened to our parents and our children! Dear fathers and mothers, how they have orphaned us! How we grieve for you! Oy for the radiance that has been turned to darkness!" One looked at his dead son, embracing him and clasping him to his heart, crying bitter tears: "My dear son, my son, my dear son, would that I had died beneath you! How the light has gone out from your eyes!"

When the Germans entered the ghetto, I rose up from the pile of the dead and stood on my feet. Motke Weiner helped me out of my bloodstained coat and threw it onto the dead and with his spittle scrubbed away the thick layer of blood that covered my face.

The Germans returned from the ghetto, bottles of wine in their hands, and ordered the people to load the dead into vehicles. Motke Weiner supervised that unhappy "work" and ordered me to carry the dead. In the pile of the dead I found Isaiah–Leib Freedman (the brother of Yodel Sofer) and Ariyeh Landoi, may their blood be avenged, with shrouds under their armpits. The shrouds were red with blood and stuck to their clothing. The unfortunates had thought they would receive a proper burial in a Jewish grave and made sure to bring shrouds.

We approached the pile where Baba Rojter lay. I wrote a note, for I could not speak after the shock I had received, "Go slowly gentlemen, for here lies a living person." They lay her above the dead so she would not choke. The girl lay there silently, not a sound came from her mouth. Her legs were swollen.

They opened the gates of the ghetto, and we traveled along Trisk Street in the direction of the cemetery. We entered the cemetery, and saw there Russian prisoners digging a pit next to the purification room near the tents of the righteous. We dropped the dead into the pit and prepared to fill it. I said to Motke Weiner: "What has become of the girl? Have we buried a living person with our own hands?" Motke replied: "She is lost anyway. We will tell one of the Germans about it, perhaps a miracle will happen and he will let her live."

The Germans approached us and asked why we were hesitating to fill in the pit. We answered them: "This is what happened." One of the Germans pulled out a gun and shot Baba in the head, then shot her again, and the poor girl fell into the pit. "Now you can fill in the pit," said the German with satisfaction in having succeeded in solving the complex problem.

To my happiness, the Germans did not count the people. They were sure that I was in the documents, that I was on the list of the one hundred, and thus I was able to return with them to the second ghetto.

[Page 420]

The Bitter End of Rav Valulah, May his blood be avenged

Before I move on to describe the second ghetto, I must recount my meeting with Rav Valulah of blessed memory before his death, because in terms of chronology, Rav Valulah was among those from the first ghetto who were slaughtered.

One day I appealed to the community council to arrange work for me near the Jewish hospital *Bikur HaHolim*, because I longed to meet the rebbe.

As will be told later, we were forced to shave our heads, and it was forbidden to wear a hat during working hours. I took a handkerchief, tied four knots in it, covered my head with it, and went into the rebbe's room.

The rebbe sat disconsolate on the bed, wearing a white robe. He had a yarmulke on his head and tears pooled in his eyes.

The rebbe was very surprised – why was my head shaved and why was I covered with a handkerchief? I didn't want to make the rebbe sad, so I deceived him as to the bitter reality, and replied that we worked very hard and I did not have a summer hat to hand, so I wrapped my head with a handkerchief. The rebbe didn't believe me; he could feel that the situation was growing worse. I tried to console him. The situation had improved, I said. The portions of food were better, and we hoped that Hashem had not left us.

But the rebbe was not convinced: the situation was worsening. The rebbe felt that this would be our last meeting, and who knew whether we would have another. This time, he even denied me the blessing he was accustomed to giving me: that I would reach the ghetto safely and no evil befall me. But in this silent meeting, he seemed very sad, very depressed, and he parted from me with coldness.

I continued to take an interest in his fate. The goyim told us that they saw with their own eyes six Germans taking the rebbe to the jail. We didn't believe their story; we believed they were trying to torment us, nothing more.

Again I asked the community council to send me to work near the Jewish hospital, because I wanted to know the truth. I went to the hospital, but did not find the rebbe. There were Polish nurses working there, and they told me things as they were: six Germans entered and asked "Where is the man of God? Where is the holy Jew?" They replied that he was in such and such room. The Germans dressed the rebbe and took him away, with him dragging his feet.

While I was living the life of a partisan in the forests, two people appeared with their hands bound. They told me they had escaped from the jail, where the Germans were killing all of the prisoners. The weak and the elderly they had thrown into the deep pit of the lavatory.

When the Germans were defeated and the Russians entered the city, they removed 300 corpses from the pit, which was 70 meters deep.

[Page 421]

The corpses were disintegrating, and they wrapped them in blankets. The goyim said that among the corpses they saw a human corpse adorned with a beard. According to their understanding and estimation, it was Rav Valulah, may his blood be avenged.

The corpses were taken to an unknown place. And until today the resting place of the Rav Valulah, may his blood be avenged, is unknown.

Chapter Two

Life in the Second Ghetto

Oh that my words were now written; oh that they were inscribed in a book!
Job 19:23

For the Babes and Sucklings

As I have told, the second ghetto was made up only of workers and professionals. I stayed with Leibel Bebchuk, who enjoyed freedom of movement because the Germans considered him an expert in laying asphalt. Bebchuk tried to arrange work on my behalf on Horodlatz Street. And why was that? On that road there were farmers I was acquainted with, who would occasionally throw a loaf of bread or a bottle of milk to me.

The children, whose fathers for some reason did not work, did not get any bread, and it was expected that they would starve to death. I had a small bottle, one tenth of a liter, which I filled with milk and soft bread crumbs. I hid the bottle inside my sleeve. When we returned to the ghetto the policemen would only check us in the chest area, so I was sure they would not discover the bottle's hiding place.

The mothers would add ten parts water and dry bread crumbs to that milk, put the pap into a handkerchief, and the babies would suck it like wine. From that small bottle twelve mothers would feed their children. The babies recovered thanks to this food, looked good, and smiles even began to light up their faces.

The Abuse of Corpses

Once I walked from Horodlatz Street to the ghetto. I passed Kantorska Street and came across a murdered boy. I took a good look at him and I saw that it was the 18 year old son of Leibel Bebchuk.

With great effort we managed to bury him. The community council sent me and Fischel Roitenberg with a stretcher.

[Page 422]

We approached Kantorska Street and collected the precious blood in a bag. We put the deceased on the stretcher and brought him to the cemetery.

At the cemetery a horrifying picture was revealed to us: local farmers had vandalized the grave of the 277 who had been gathered in the Brisker Square. Bodies had been flung from the pit and stripped of their clothing, rings had been removed from fingers and watches stolen, gold teeth had been pulled, and the corpses had been abused. The dead were scattered about, some inside the pit, and some in a large area surrounding the pit.

I entered the purification room and found Esther Stefek there in a state near death. No one knew how she had gotten there. She lay there naked, opened her eyes and closed them, unable to speak. I could hear her sighs, and for a moment I listened to her death throes. The heart was as a fossil, and even the living saw themselves as dead.

Terrible Working Conditions

We smuggled food into the ghetto in various ways. I had an acquaintance, a goy, in the village Karsyn. When I would bring the dead for burial, he would prepare milk, flour, slices of bread, and potatoes for me. I would fold these riches into the stretcher I carried the way a soldier carries his rifle, and thus I entered the ghetto unmolested.

With us in the ghetto was Moshe Pressper, may his blood be avenged, who had two daughters. Those daughters, may their souls rest in Heaven, paid with their lives for bringing food into the ghetto. They had Christian friends from their school days with whom they were still in contact.

The girls would bribe the policeman with gold coins, and this payment would allow them to leave the ghetto for a short while, and they would take milk and bread from their Polish friends for the starving Jews of the ghetto. Once, the mother and the two girls were caught near the Amernick mill and were killed on the spot.

Thus the Germans learned that the Jews were smuggling food into the ghetto. They decided therefore to give us distinctive marks, so they would recognize us, even from far away. The women were ordered to pull back their hair in a ponytail, and the men were ordered to shave their heads and to go about bareheaded. It was clearly stated in the announcement that anyone found to have a hat in his pocket would be killed on the spot. The situation worsened every day.

It was during Tammuz [June/July] and the heat was unbearable. The sun beat down on the shaven head. Due to this torture of hell, the skull swelled. The head was purple like a watermelon, and eyes bulged out of their sockets. These unfortunates lost their human spirit and became monsters. Facial features were so greatly changed that I didn't recognize my own neighbor. Moreover: wives could barely recognize their husbands. No medical assistance was offered, and many – a great many – died in great agony.

[Page 423]

Desecrating the Dead

In the first days of the ghetto's existence, they didn't delay the burial of the dead. The Germans allowed the dead to be removed from the ghetto, and taken for burial. Later, an order was given that the dead could not be buried individually. When a person died, they waited until five more had died before burying him. Only when six people had died would we be given a cart to transport them for burial.

One Sunday Ben–Zion the butcher, may his blood be avenged, the father of the teacher Yosef Avrech, may his blood be avenged, died. On the same day, two small children also died. Sunday came to an end, Monday passed – and there were no further deaths. The bodies began to decay, but they wouldn't allow us to bury them. On Tuesday, a young man died. On Wednesday an older man died. We had only five dead. Where could we get a sixth body? We went to the community council, and said, 'We are suffocating from the stench of the dead.' Our entreaties did not help: we were not allowed to bury the dead.

I went to remove Ben–Zion the butcher from his room. I took a hold of his legs, and the flesh fell from them and remained in my hands. I fainted. When I awoke from the syncope, I asked them to give me a blanket. I wrapped Ben Zion, may his blood be avenged, in it and thus we placed him in the cart. We set off to bury the dead accompanied by two policemen.

We returned to the ghetto from the cemetery and as we passed the gate we saw Manthei, Kasner and their secretary. Next to them was a small auto, and they ordered us to put all of our money into it. I had only 11 pfennig in my pocket. They didn't pay attention, and allowed me to enter the ghetto.

Among us was Yaacov–Yitzhak Kishkarnik, who worked in the slaughterhouse. He had a decent amount of money which he kept in the rubber boots he wore. The secretary ordered him to remove the boots and found the bundle of money. Next they approached the son of Kartaflia the tailor, who had a glass shop next to the bridge over the Sands. They found a decent bundle of money on him, as well. Kasner pulled out his Nagant [a revolver] and killed them on the spot.

In the morning I was sent, with a few other Jews, to take the two who had been killed for burial. They allowed us to bury them without waiting until another four dead bodies had accumulated, because they fell outside the walls of the ghetto.

I was shocked, and even today it is difficult for me to avoid the difficult impression: the wives of those who had been killed did not even come out to see their husbands who had been killed, they didn't come to say farewell, they didn't shed a tear, because theirhad hardened, they had lost their minds, they daydreamed while awake and did not comprehend what had happened.

We Return to the First Ghetto

On the 20th of the month of Av the community representatives announced that permission had been given to move to the empty houses in the first ghetto, and everyone must register.

[Page 424]

I lived with Avraham Gunik, may his blood be avenged. The Germans employed him as a cattle assessor, and saw him as a "useful" Jew. When the poor unfortunates were taken from Brisker Square with Gunik among them, to be destroyed in Bychawa, Manthei asked: Where is Gunik? When he was told that Gunik was in Bychawa, he rushed off like a crazy man on his motorcycle to the place of destruction, and removed Gunik, literally, from the pit. Gunik's wife and son he was unable to save, for they had already been destroyed.

Gunik said to me, 'Since you know the city so well, choose a suitable house and we'll move in there together.' I told him: 'There was a tailor with us, Kalman of Trisk, who lived next to the house of Shia Bar Bakar, opposite the *Talmud Torah*. The house is clean and has been renovated.' Gunik went and registered the house in his name.

On the 25th of Av the order was given to move immediately into the first ghetto. All of us were equipped with a few garments, two suits and, under the armpit, a pair of shoes. We set out late at night. We reached the ghetto and found the houses empty. The furniture was brought to the great synagogue, and the clothing to the school named for Moshkitski. Every day they sent groups of sixty people to sort the many garments, which filled the building from the foundation to the rafters.

The son of Yitzhak Roitenberg, may his blood be avenged, a lad of 17, recognized a tie from home and hid it in his pocket. They checked his possessions and found the tie. The unfortunate youth was hanged on the spot, from the wall of the school. They hung a sign on him on which was written: "Hanged for stealing clothing." Only after three days had passed did they cut him down from the noose.

Since there was no furniture to be found, we lay down on the floor and went off every day to work.

Erecting Bunkers

Opinion was divided amongst us: some said that the workers and professionals would stay alive, and others said that it would be a complete slaughter, and we would all be obliterated. The second opinion won, and we began to prepare for what would come.

There were some excellent professionals in the ghetto – carpenters, blacksmiths, builders – and they began to build bunkers under the sidewalks and the streets, and secret hiding places in attics. At night we would hear the muffled sound of hammering.

One night, Avraham Gunik said to me: "Do you hear the sounds of work?" Gunik's son–in–law served in the police force, and from him we knew of the big plan of the preparation and installation of the bunkers. He told us: "Don't be under any illusions. The situation is dire, the Germans are planning to wipe out the last remaining vestiges of the Jews of the city."

We called one of the carpenters, to explain to us why they were building bunkers.

[Page 425]

His advice was to build a secondary–wall, a double wall, connected to the oven, and people would enter the space through the opening of the oven. He also advised us to hide the part that was removed between the first and second walls, and to cover the opening with planks, so that if – God forbid – our hiding place was discovered we could quickly flee to the attic.

It seemed to us a good idea. The carpenter took down some planks from the *Talmud Torah* and from the House of Study of the followers of Stephan, and built the wall. He covered it in plaster and the wall became an integral part of the room, and did not rouse any suspicion.

According to the capacity, we could hide only 12 people. But with cramming and squeezing, 18 people would fit.

On the 6th of Elul we went into the space behind the wall. The ghetto was in turmoil. We heard shouts and terrifying howls. They were forcing people into vehicles. Manthei knew about the bunkers and he decided to destroy them, once and for all.

Children played a very tragic role in the discovery of the bunkers. More than once a child burst into tears and endangered the lives of all. The bunker–dwellers would attack the parents of the child: "Because of your children we will all go to hell." The poor parents, with no other choice, were forced to send their children out of the bunker.

When Manthei saw Jewish children wandering about, he understood that the parents must be somewhere close by, and in that way he would locate the bunker and take those hidden inside out to be killed.

We stood in the hiding place for twelve days, with no food or water. During that time, Manthei emptied almost the entire ghetto under the ground. Once he seized 300 people and took them to the great synagogue, and from there to their destruction.

Manthei and his band of murderers sniffed around our hiding place. The head thief stamped his foot and said: "There are Jews hiding here!" The smell of sweat coming through the wall of our hiding place worked against us. From the smell, the murderer assumed there were living people in the place. The killers cut away the floor, turned the entire house upside down – and didn't find a thing. And so the day passed safely. The next day, they came back. "There are Jews here!" Manthei shouted in a hysterical voice. They began destroying the walls. They ripped out one wall – and were unsuccessful. But when they broke into the wall of our hiding place, one plank fell and we were exposed.

"Get out!" the murderers shouted. I kept my composure, and when the first people left the hiding place, I jumped up and with my head I moved the boards that covered the exit opening and climbed up to the attic. Avraham Gunik, his son–in–law, Yosef Zin, the carpenter, and Berel, son of Haim Trisker, came with me.

Since the killers had already checked and rummaged about in every corner of the attic and didn't find anyone, they didn't check there again. After they had gotten all of the people out of the hiding place, they left.

[Page 426]

The Tragic Event

Avraham Gunik, may his blood be avenged, suffered from asthma. We saw that there was a mere step between him and death by strangulation. He told us, if he drank at least two teaspoons of water he would be able to restrain his cough and he would catch his breath.

I risked my life and, at night, left the attic and entered the house of Shia Bar Bakar. I found a tub full of laundry there. I found two kettles in the kitchen, and I squeezed the water from the laundry into them. It was full of soap, lime, and lice. I went back to the attic with the two kettles filled with water.

In the attic we found a small cover to a kettle, which could hold two teaspoons of water. We all agreed that each of us would drink two teaspoons of water in the morning and two in the evening, and that Avraham Gunik would drink whenever he had a coughing fit.

Yossel Zin downed two spoons of water and started to cry. We asked him: "Why are you crying?" He answered: "This thirst is torturing me. Let me drink two more spoons, and I won't drink in the evening." Avraham Gunik said: "His crying could bring down a holocaust on us. Let him drink and calm down."

We lay up in that attic for ten days. No one bothered us. We took two shingles off of the roof, and through the opening we saw that they were putting people into the great synagogue, and in the evening leading them in the direction of the cemetery. In addition, we saw groups of children whose parents had sent them out of the bunkers, wandering about. The Ukrainian policemen gathered them up and also put them into the synagogue.

Over time, the beard of one of those who was with us in the attic grew. He said that the hair of his beard bothered him, and that he thought he would go down into his house and bring back a barber's razor. We begged him not to do such a thing, because he would be putting all of our lives in danger.

He didn't agree to our pleas, instead insisting on doing what he wished. To our misfortune, as he was descending he tripped and fell to the floor with a great deal of noise. The Ukrainian policemen standing outside heard the noise, came inside, brought all of us down from the attic and took us to the great synagogue.

[Page 427]

Chapter 3

The Horrors in the Great Synagogue

That the generation to come might know them, the children which should be born, who should arise and declare them to their children.
Psalms 78:6

The Last Farewell to Life

Next to the great synagogue stood a force of Ukrainian policemen, who checked us and emptied our pockets. When we entered – we found all sorts of people, women, children and infants. We were ordered to squat with our heads down and between our legs. Anyone who raised his head could expect a bullet from the murderers. Only mothers who held infants in their arms were allowed, with no other choice, to sit upright, because the murderers were not interested in committing mass murder inside the walls of the synagogue. For the same reason, they allowed the children to wander and stroll about. Children of the city, my heart goes out to you! Who will give validity to your sorrow and grief! Oy, the lamentation that will be said for your great sorrow. Blood dripped from my heart when I saw the tears spilling from your eyes.

The children wandered through the hall of the synagogue with bowed heads, looking at the people who had been brought low, and crying bitterly: 'No, that's not my father!' Later, they approached a group of women, looked into their lowered faces and cried loudly, 'No, that's not my mother!'

At 11 o'clock in the morning Manthei arrived, and ordered us to get up and gather into one corner. He counted the people and wrote the number in his notebook. He separated out 35 men, who looked healthy, and put them in a different corner. A vehicle came and collected them, then set off in the direction of the cemetery. Manthei accompanied them. When they arrived, they were ordered to dig a pit. The pit was three meters deep. Its length and width were determined based on the number of victims gathered in the synagogue that day.

The death of that group was "easy". When they finished digging, Manthei ordered them to face the pit, then he killed each and every one of them with a shot to the brain with his Nagant. When we arrived at the cemetery in the late afternoon, we found them dead inside the pit.

At 5 o'clock in the evening, six trucks arrived at the synagogue. Manthei entered accompanied by policemen and ordered us to get up and get into the vehicles.

[Page 428]

Everyone knew that the end was near and his days were over, and the unfortunates instinctively approached the walls of the synagogue and wrote their first names and their surnames, and that on this date they became martyrs. And if someone remained alive, he should avenge the blood that was shed.

I approached the wall to write my name. Avraham Gunik called to me, 'Write my name, also, because my legs are paralyzed and I cannot move.'

I told him: 'Izzy, your son–in–law, will write your name.' Izzy said to me: 'I only write in Polish, and I want my name to be written in Hebrew letters and in Hebrew writing.'

I approached the wall and wrote: 'On such and such day we shall become martyrs. If there remains a trace of the Jews of Kovel, remember us and avenge our blood that has been spilled.'

I must mention that Manthei did not disturb us while we were writing, although when there was a pause in the writing the Ukrainian policemen lost their patience and with the butts of their rifles began to pry us away from the walls: "Enough, you bloody Jews! The trucks are waiting," they shouted.

Avraham Gunik, may his blood be avenged, could not stand on his feet. I took his right hand, and his son–in–law took his left, and we led him out of the synagogue. He begged us, while weeping bitterly, to put him on the first truck, for he wanted to die quickly. He and his son–in–law got into the third truck, and I boarded the last one.

Each vehicle was accompanied by 16 armed policemen. The trucked headed in the direction of Trisk Street. As they passed over the river, the victims threw their jewelry out into the water. Along the way I saw people jumping out of the trucks. The policemen allowed them to jump, but as each victim left the vehicle, he was immediately shot in the head.

The vehicles stopped near the cemetery, which was surrounded by many policemen. The victims entered and gathered near the purification room. They were told to undress and throw the clothing into the purification room.

Everyone undressed together – men, women, even children and six month old babies. When the people from the first vehicle had undressed, they were led to the pit. Entire families went together to the slaughter, even brides with their grooms. The children clutched their parents. A ten year old boy wrapped tightly around his father's thigh, and the small children and babies were held in their mothers' arms.

The extermination was carried out thus: two boards were stretched over the pit. They told the unfortunates to stand on them facing the pit. Three murders stood behind them, dressed in white and with their faces masked, their hands covered in white mittens and holding automatic weapons.

They aimed the muzzle at the brain of the victim, so that the bullet wouldn't miss its target, although the kill shot hit the heart, the earlobe, and other places. When the parents fell into the pit, their children were pulled in after them, and most of them died of suffocation.

[Page 429]

While they eliminated the people from the first vehicle, those from the second vehicle were ordered to undress and approach the pit, where they were eliminated. And thus the horror was repeated over and over, until the end of the last victim.

Not a single word came from the mouths of the victims. Their hearts were fossilized. They did not weep and they did not sob. Husband did not speak to wife, and groom did not speak to the bride who stood to his right.

I approached the pit, which was filled to the rim with the dead. As I stood on the plank, I saw Yisrael Ishiner, who had been shot in the heart, and he was twisting over the pile of the dead, the entire length of the pit. This atrocious sight made my head spin, and I fainted and fell into the pit.

The last of the victims were killed, and the pit was not covered with dirt for it had passed the edge. I lay there unconscious until 11:30 that night. Suddenly I realized that I was alive, but I didn't know if I had been hurt. I tried to move, but the dead lying on me were pressing on me and suffocating me. Only my head was above the dead bodies.

With the last of my strength I freed one hand, and then the second. The blood of the dead was still warm, and it flowed from my hands. I wiped the blood from one hand. I believed I had been wounded, but lo and behold my hand was uninjured. I tried to free my head – but in vain. There lay upon me a woman whose hair was tangled with mine.

During the night the wind blew, clotting the blood that had been spilled, a kind of stew, on a thick night, and it was difficult for me to separate my head from hers. I started to rip out her hair.

[Page 430]

After a great deal of labor, I succeeded in freeing my head. I propped my hand on the dead and with inhuman force I freed the rest of my body and climbed up.

From my body flowed streams of the blood of our dear dead. I stood next to the pit and saw it rising and falling, rising and falling. The moans of the suffocating people were horrible. Six hours after the *actztia*, the victims were still fighting with Mr. Death.

The new cemetery
Here our dear ones, who left the great synagogue, were destroyed

Putting Me Back in the Great Synagogue

The first question that tormented me was: what now? Where shall I go? I was naked as the day I was born, with only underwear covering my skin. The cold overcame me. Goosebumps gripped me at the sound of the groans of the suffocating.

I left the cemetery, desolated and completely covered in blood, alone in the dark of night. Behind me – the groans of my brothers and sisters, the great Jewish community of Kovel, and before me – the fear of the darkness, the fear of extinction, the fear of loneliness, and the fear of the great devastation.

As I stood by the gates of the cemetery, an inkling of an idea came to me: I knew a farmer named Hoder from the Karsyn village, who had bought a small house not far from the cemetery. Hoder had a white horse. He worked for me, bringing the calves to the train station, and he made good money.

I said in my heart, I'll approach Hoder, maybe he'll save me, because I had saved him by giving him an advance on his salary so he could buy things he especially needed.

Hoder had a large dog, scary and threatening. Although since the dog knew me, I thought to myself, maybe he won't attack me.

I approached the gate. The dog began to bark ferociously. I thought to myself, the dog is barking and Hoder will come out towards me. The door opened, and there to my annoyance were four policemen, who approached me. Two of them were from Kovel. One of them, named Elioshik, lived on Shelkatchka Street, and the other was named Kandratovich, and he lived on Kantorska Street. The other two were from the village of Bitnia.

They asked me: "Where did you come from?" I replied: "I came out of the pit of death. I fell in still alive, and I got out. My appearance testifies to that." They asked me: "What do you want?" I replied: "My request is, take me back to the pit, the place where my brothers and sisters are buried. Shoot me in the head and let my blood mingle with theirs."

They replied: "That we will not do." I added a plea: "If you don't want to go to the trouble, call for Hoder to take me into his yard and kill me. Hoder has a white horse that can carry my body to the cemetery. No matter, never mind. Hoder can carry me in his arms for burial. I deserve that."

[Page 431]

The policemen responded: "That we also will not do." Those two policemen knew me well, and apparently, out of a misguided sense of conscience, they couldn't bring themselves to kill me with their own hands. And so they said: "We will show you mercy and take you back to the great synagogue."

I told them: "This is not mercy you are showing me, for you are doing me a great wrong. Why prolong my death throes? In any case, tomorrow they will execute me. Better I should die today, and not tomorrow."

Kandratovich lost his temper and hit me hard with the butt of his rifle, and told the two policemen from Bitnia to take me to the great synagogue.

I Persuade Zydel to Avenge our Spilled Blood

When those gathered in the great synagogue saw a naked man covered with blood, they were consumed with horror. Even the Ukrainian policemen stared at me in amazement. On the pulpit was a large pile of the coats of the slaughtered. I shook from cold – the chattering of my teeth could be heard from far away. I thought in my heart, who will give me a coat and warm me? The son of Moshe Hijick sat next to the pulpit. Putting himself in danger, he took a coat from the pile and threw it to me.

The synagogue was in darkness. Next to the clock, on the western side, there stood a lantern that gave off a faint, melancholy light. The people hinted to me that they wanted to know what had happened to me – but we were not allowed to speak.

The night passed, a night of horror and terror. In the morning they brought children, whose parents had been removed from the bunkers, and they brought a group of about 70 people down from the attic of the synagogue of the tailors.

Suddenly we were startled by the sound of gunshots. In the synagogue was Sarah Erlich, who was seven months pregnant. They brought her, together with her husband Yosef. In the synagogue, they separated them. She lifted her head – she wanted to see her husband in the final moments of her life. The murderers shot her in the belly, and her bowels spilled out. She rolled and writhed in her suffering from the pulpit to the stairs. They took her out and put her in Rabbi Goldshmid's house, opposite.

At about nine o'clock, they brought a group of people, and among them were Zydel and Moshe Shach, along with their wives. Zydel and his friend looked sturdy and clean–shaven. They had hidden in the dairy farm of Sarah Erlich, and had been found there.

Zydel saw that I was covered in blood, and asked me to explain. I told him what had happened, and added that at five o'clock Manthei would come and count the people, and then we would all be taken out and slaughtered. And since he looked healthy and sturdy, he would surely be forced to dig the pit and would be killed while digging. "Anyway we are going to be killed, and it is irrelevant whether we are killed now or at five o'clock.

[Page 432]

So I'm asking you, in the name of all of our brothers who have been put to death and those who will be led to the massacre today, and those who will be led tomorrow and the day after until the last memory of the Jews of Kovel becomes extinct – I ask of you, at the moment Manthei enters and begins to count those gathered here, throw yourself at him and with your teeth tear out his throat. So the world will see what the Jews of Kovel did to the Minister of Massacres. So that the world will see, and know, that the Jews of our city were not slaughtered like sheep."

As they sat with their heads down, Zydel and Moshe Shach indicated to me that when the bandits came in they would throw a few coats on him and confuse him. I said: "I will throw my coat, and I will risk my life and take two more coats down from the pulpit. When Manthei asks me the reason, I will say I returned naked from the cemetery and I am cold."

At 11:00 in the morning Manthei arrived. "Get up and gather in one place," yelled the murderer. Zero hour had arrived, and we couldn't miss even a moment.

However, when Zydel saw Manthei, he became discouraged, his face paled, and he ran off to the side.

Manthei counted the people, and took Zydel and his companions off to dig the pit. Zydel walked off in quiet surrender, like a sheep being led to the slaughter.

The Orphan's *Kaddish*

At five o'clock, the vehicles came to take us to the cemetery. Once again those gathered approached the walls, writing their names and the date they became martyrs.

As I went outside, my eyes fell upon an act of cruelty which, each time I recall it, my slumber is devoured. Policemen wandered about, holding in their hands planks studded their entire length with nails 20 cm [nearly 8"] and longer. I saw a woman who could barely walk, with a baby in her arms. With one hand she held her baby, three months old, and with the other hand she struggled to climb into the vehicle. One of the killers approached her and struck her in the back with the plank with the long nails. When he pulled it out of her body, her liver and lungs fell out onto the ground. He grabbed the baby and beat him against the pavement; his head was thrown one way and his tiny body was thrown the other way. The killer threw the brutalized bodies of the mother and her baby into the vehicle.

This time I boarded the fifth vehicle, and not the last one, for I was in a hurry to die.

There was in our town a Jew called Moshe the Old Butcher. He had a son named Zalman who was married to a woman named Devorah, the daughter of Old Trek. Zalman, his wife, their two sons and their daughter sat with me in the vehicle.

He sat there pale and silent. Suddenly, he jumped from the vehicle. Immediately, gunshots were heard, and Zalman was left lying dead next to the daughter of Yehoshua Kovritz.

[Page 433]

When Devorah saw her husband lying dead in the ditch, she took her two sons and brought them near to me, saying: "Their father is dead, say *Kaddish* with them for the elevation of his soul." With copious tears, I said *Kaddish* with the children. They recited the *Kaddish* like grown men. All of those being taken to die in that vehicle sobbed brokenheartedly, repeating the words: "May his great name be blessed forever and ever" with the devotion and eagerness of those about to die in the name of the Lord. The recitation of the *Kaddish* continued until we reached the gates of the cemetery.

I am Returned Once Again to the Great Synagogue

When we reached the cemetery, the gates opened, the people were removed from the first, second, third, and fourth trucks, and then – "Stop!" They didn't remove any more people. The guards were surprised, and didn't understand what was happening.

Soon we learned the secret: at two o'clock they had brought two truckloads of Jews from Bitby, Lyubytiv, and Poane, killed them, and threw them into the pit. Since the capacity of the pit was only six truckloads, it turned out that they had "taken" our places and the pit was overflowing.

With no other choice, it was decided to return us to the synagogue. When we arrived, those gathered there were seized with joy. If people were returned from the cemetery, it was a sign that salvation was coming. At last God was showing His mercy to the Jewish people.

To my great sorrow – I disillusioned them. I told them how things really were, that salvation had not yet come, that the wings of the angel of death were still spread over us, and that the devil still held the knife in his hands and he would paint it with our blood until the last drop of our blood was shed.

The Desecration of Our Daughters' Honor

Once again I shed tears over our children. The coming of dawn brought a new group of children, whose parents had taken them out of the bunkers. The children looked pale, tired, hungry – for 14 days no food had crossed their lips. In one of the corners was piled the feces of children who had tarried here and were then taken out and executed. The wretched children burrowed in the feces of their lost friends, put them into their mouths and began to vomit. The heart breaks with such sorrow, for it was not in our power to save them and bring back their spirits. The Ukrainian guards watched the children, writhing convulsively with hunger – and laughter filled their mouths.

At seven thirty in the morning, some guards entered – chose 10 pretty girls aged 15–16 and good looking, and told them they had been chosen for work, washing windows and floors. They took them to the house of Rabbi Goldshmid, across the street, where they defiled them. From all the torture they suffered, they had no strength left to stand on their feet and we had to carry them back to the synagogue.

[Page 434]

Those wretched girls sat, sobbing softly. In their eyes, all the well–springs of sorrow and grief had overflowed. Alas, that I saw them so! Why did God not extinguish my sight? In my heart, in the language of silence, I wept a bitter lament: 'what sin did you ever commit, that you should be so abused?' I began to revile God. I, Ben–Zion, a God–fearing Jew, turned accusingly to the Creator of the Universe: 'Why did you vent your rage on these cherubs, why did you spill your wrath on these tender flowers, on these gentle girls? No one will prostrate himself on their graves, no one will remember them, no one will recall them, no one will plant a flower on their fresh graves, for no marker will be left for them. Shall we live by your sword?'

The Horrors I Beheld in the Synagogue

I had scarcely lamented the desecration of our girls' honor, when I was shocked by new horrors: a man with a threatening appearance was thrown into the synagogue. He looked like he was insane, unkempt, with eyes that gleamed and blazed and bulged out from their sockets. I looked at him, and murmured: 'Is that him or not?' I strained my eyes and looked into that threatening face. 'Yes, it is him. It's Asher Frankfurt, may his blood be avenged, the principal of the Hebrew Gymnasia.' Frankfurt was brought in with his wife and son. They had hidden in the attic of the Naskizer house of study. The killers found their hiding place, took them out and brought them to the synagogue.

The woman sat with the young man, though Frankfurt refused to sit. We were sure the guards would kill him with a bullet. But to their eyes, he was just a man who shook his head from side to side – they thought him insane and didn't harm him. In the evening, they took him along with all those gathered and killed them in the cemetery.

I had not yet recovered from the shock of Frankfurt when along came another new horror: I saw a man brought in who ran to the *bima* in panic, and began spitting fragments of tongue, throat and gums while blood flowed from his mouth without ceasing. I looked at him, and it was Nahum, the son–in–law of Shmuel Zeletz, may his blood be avenged. After him came running Heike his wife, pulling out her hair. They separated her from her husband and forced her to sit together with everyone.

Although the woman sat some distance from me, I implied that she tell me why her husband was spitting blood. Despite the danger, Heike told me: they had hidden in the attic of the home of Lazer Kaditch, together with their three year old daughter. Their daughter burst out crying, endangering their lives and those of the others hiding with them. Her husband lost his mind, and went down into his house and brought back a barber's razor. He grabbed the child by her arm, slaughtered her with the razor and threw her out of the attic to the ground. The child, of course, was crushed – her small body became like stew of meat, blood and crushed bones.

[Page 435]

When his sanity returned and he took an accounting of what he had done to his small daughter, he again went down into the house and drank sulfuric acid, which immediately began to burn his mouth, tongue, and throat. He began to produce terrifying screams: "Shoot me! Fire is burning inside me!" Because of the pain, he left the hiding place and went downstairs. The police found him and brought him to the synagogue. When Heike saw that they were taking her husband, she got up and went after him.

The poor fellow lay on the *bima*, then deliberately got up so that the guards would kill him. But, infuriatingly, they did not harm him, for they wanted to prolong his death throes. Terrible were his moans, and those of his wife, who had pulled out all of her hair, leaving not a single strand on her head.

We were sure that when Manthei came at 11 o'clock to count the people, he would be killed and put out of his misery. Although he came, counted the people, and took 35 with him to dig the pit, he did not harm Nahum. It became apparent that Nahum would die before they came to take him out of the synagogue.

At 10 o'clock in the morning, six guards entered. They selected 8 people, including myself. They took us out of the synagogue and led us behind the municipal bathhouse. The area was filled with tall shrubs. The guards told us: "Many corpses are rotting here in this place. Get them out of here." They stood off to the side, their rifles pointed at us, and warned us: "Anyone who tries to escape will be killed on the spot."

We walked between the shrubs and started searching. We came upon many corpses, though it was difficult to get close to them. They were crumbling and covered with swarms upon swarms of flies. My work partner was a young man from Brisk named Wolf. The Germans had a dugout of peat on Meichev Street behind the house of Pelek Peidel, may his blood be avenged, and this young man served as the manager of that dugout. We found the body of a woman. We lifted her, and the body fell to pieces. We pulled her by her hair, and the hair came away in our hands. Wolf was squeamish, and began to vomit.

Another work pair carried a dead body with the flesh falling away from it, the internal organs spilled out. In spite of that, they carried it over and threw it into the wagon. We couldn't pick up the dead bodies. I lifted him, but Wolf turned his head away and didn't move from his place.

The guards saw what happened, pointed their rifles at poor Wolf and warned him: "If you don't pick up the body – soon you will be just like him." I asked Wolf to gather all of his strength and pick up the body. But the young man told me: "What difference does it make if they kill me now or a few hours from now? Better they should kill me at this moment." The guards told me to come out of the bushes. When I stood next to them, they shot the young man and he fell next to the corpse of the woman.

[Page 436]

They gave me a different partner. We picked up the woman in our hands. Along the way her organs were left behind. We threw her into the wagon, in which there were already three bodies. We did not recognize the faces of the dead. The eyes had come out of their sockets, and in their place were swarms. The whole body was rotten and crawling with worms. When we had lifted the bodies onto the wagon, we returned to the synagogue.

Chapter 4
My Flight from the Synagogue and My Rescue "How is the gold become dim!"
Lamentations 4:1

The First Echoes from the Outside World

When I returned to the synagogue, I saw that the guards were bringing in an entire family: husband and wife, a small boy, and a girl of about 17. I recognized the man, although I had not seen him in the ghetto. Apparently he had paid a great deal of money to one of his Polish acquaintances to obtain Aryan certificates for the entire family, and they had been living all this time as Poles. But to his misfortune, a dispute broke out between the wives of two Polish neighbors, and the other went and reported on them to the police, and he and his family were brought to the synagogue.

I told him of the things that had happened to me, and that I was about to be sent to my death for the third time. I said to him: "All the time that you went about freely, you probably read a newspaper and have some knowledge of what is going on out there in the world. He replied thus: "If can you hold on another 3 – 4 days, I am sure we will be saved." I asked: "On what do you base that?" He replied: "On the night of Shabbat the Soviets bombed 'Vyturio Kovel' From there they have drawn the conclusion that there will be a decisive turn in the course of the war. If the Soviet pilots go deeper and they reach Kovel – the conclusion is that the Germans are about to be completely defeated. Tradition has been in our hands since the days of the evil Haman, the scourge of the Jews: '…before who thou hast begun to fall, thou shalt not prevail against him, but shalt surely fall before him.' [Translator's note: Esther 6:13] In my opinion, Ben–Zion, if you survive the next few days, my faith is great that you will remain alive."

I said to him: "And what can we do? When people jump out of the vehicles, they shoot and kill them on the spot."

[Page 437]

How did I Escape from the Great Synagogue?

The things I heard from my neighbor got me thinking. Perhaps, in truth, my hope was not lost? Perhaps there is a path to rescue? Maybe it is not G–d's will that I be among those who fall into the pit?

While I sat deep in thought, the trucks were approaching. They had come to take us on our final journey. "Get up!" Manthei screamed. I approached the wall and wrote my name for the third time. Manthei showed patience. Let the Jews write to their hearts' content. But the Ukrainian policemen removed us with the butts of their rifles: "That's enough, you bloody Yids! Stop dirtying the walls!"

I turned my head and saw three Jews approaching the Holy Ark and hiding under the stairs. I said: "I'll try my luck." I approached the stairs and begged: "Jews, let me in." They replied: "The place is narrow and can only hold 4 people." I answered: "It is not my intention to bring disaster upon you. I will go to the slaughter, together with all of my brothers." There was a young man there named Shtuper. He told me: "I have been lying here for 8 nights. Tonight my soul will leave me. Anyway, I'm dying, and what's the difference if I die here or in the pit – I will get out, and you get in under me." He got out and I took his place. Among the three people who were with me was the son–in–law of Chava Erlich and an old man, a grain merchant named Aharon. I do not remember the name of the third. They said: "He has slept in this hiding place for 4 nights, and that one for 6 nights." I said to them: "And what will be the end? What is the point of laying here if there is to be no rescue?" They replied: "When they have taken all of the people out of the synagogue and they bring in no others after them, the guard will be removed from the synagogue, and then it will be possible to take advantage of the opportunity, and jump out via the window. But the problem is, they take out and then immediately bring in new victims, and we are still yearning for that opportunity. Maybe G–d will be merciful, and tonight they won't bring new victims, or they will bring them late at night – we'll take advantage of the darkness – and run away. Let's shake hands on it that each one of us will go in a different direction, so that we won't all be caught together."

The people were taken out, no new ones were brought in, and the guards left the synagogue. We said that if by seven o'clock the hall was still empty – we could move. But, to our misfortune, new victims were brought in from the bunkers. We left the hiding place and mixed in among the people. The next day, we decided: tonight we will hide under the stairs, and if we don't succeed in escaping – we will get into the trucks and be taken to the slaughter along with everyone else.

The hall emptied. It was six o'clock – and there was no one there. Zero hour was approaching – seven o'clock. I said: "We won't miss the opportunity. We'll get up and run!" I left the hiding place and stood up on a bench along the eastern wall. I opened a window, stuck out my head, and saw that the place was very high.

[Page 438]

I said: "If we jump, we will all be crushed. My advice is that we take 10 coats from the *bima*, throw them outside, and if we fall – we will fall on a soft surface and there will be no danger to our lives." My suggestion seemed right to them. Yoska, the son–in–law of Chava Erlich, climbed onto the pulpit, and from the pulpit to the window – and jumped out. I jumped out after him. With Reb Aharon there was a problem. He was an old man, clumsy, and when he climbed on the pulpit it began to squeak. The guards who stood outside heard noise from inside, and went in to investigate the matter.

Reb Aharon was able to run away, although his head was hit hard on the wall of the synagogue, and he lost a lot of blood. The guards were making up their minds whether to shoot him to death, and in the end decided not to waste the bullet since, anyway, he was going to die. I hid beneath the floor of the Ryzhin synagogue, and from there I heard the sighs and moans of Reb Aharon, may his blood be avenged.

The Great Tragedy of Three Small Orphans

I lay under the Ryzhin house of study until midnight. Silence prevailed. The voices of the guards fell silent. I left the hiding place and entered the bushes; I reached the home of Hane Feldman, may his blood be avenged, which was behind the bathhouse.

For what reason did I go, of all places, to the Feldman house? On my first day in the synagogue, I saw the names of Hane Feldman, his sister, his brother, Yosef, and the wife of Moshe Feldman – written on the wall. I understood that the house was empty. I went into the bedroom – there were about 20 beds there. I jumped from bed to bed and reached the last one. I lifted a blanket and covered myself. I thought in my heart: 'I will enjoy a good night's sleep before I die.' While I was laying there and contemplating my soul, some guards entered the house with Ukrainian girls. I was sure they were chasing me and had found my footprints. But it soon became clear that this was not their purpose. They had come for robbery and looting. They opened the closets and filled their sacks with all the goods and wealth to be found in the Feldman house, then ran off.

At dawn I fell asleep. I was sure that during the day the policemen would not bother me, because Manthei was on patrol during the day, and he was sure to put to death any policeman who robbed a Jewish house without his knowledge and permission.

When I awoke, I sensed according to the position of the sun that it was about ten o'clock. I lifted my head and looked at the Trisker Bridge and saw my Polish and Ukrainian neighbors walking at their pleasure and no one harmed them. My heart stirred within me, and I turned complaints to G–d: 'By what right do they move about freely and enjoy the sunshine, while I am pursued like an animal? Why?' I shouted in a loud voice. I was still yelling and pouring out my heart, when there I saw standing before my eyes a figure out of the valley of the ghosts. She was filthy with mud, grimy with ash, and black as pitch.

[Page 439]

The figure spoke to me in Yiddish: "Don't you know me? You were at my wedding. I am the sister of Yankel Zalman, the butcher. The bride of Forshteller of Monopoliova Street."

She began to tell me: "Seventy people hid in a bunker, among them the good and beneficent Dr. Shatz. Seven days ago the killers came and took everyone, and I stayed alone with my two children and the son of my sister in law." I asked her: "Where is the hiding place?" She replied: "Under the foundation." I wanted to enter and see the children, but the entrance was so narrow that I could not pass.

I went up to the attic, removed two shingles, and saw all of the Jews who had been kidnapped and taken to the synagogue.

The woman calmed down a bit, climbed up to the attic and said: "In the bunker are scattered lots of dollars and gold that the poor unfortunates left behind. We'll take a basket, gather the money, and take it to the police. Maybe they will have mercy on us and take us out of the ghetto."

I asked her: "And the children, what will become of them?" She replied: "I'll leave them." I told her: "Without the children, I will not go."

I asked her to show me the children. The oldest was eight, the second five, and the girl six and a half. The woman left the attic, brought the children out, and told me: "Come and see them." When I saw the children I started crying and pulling the hair from my head. Woe to the eyes that saw such a sight! The children lay on the floor, for they couldn't stand on their feet. From lying in the mud and mildew, the muscles of their legs had cramped, their legs were crooked, the bones of their bodies were sticking out, and they looked like living skeletons.

The woman said that starvation had wreaked havoc on their bodies. If we could have gotten some food and fed them, they would get back their strength and be able to stand.

In the home of Hane Feldman, may his blood be avenged, there stood a half barrel of beef fat, and I also found some potatoes, millet, and lentils. In my heart, I thought: "If we feed the children 2 or 3 times a day, maybe we can get them back on their feet."

In the house I found many Primus stoves, fuel, and matches. I peeled some potatoes and grated them into thin pieces. The Primus wouldn't start, and I couldn't find a needle to clean the eye, so I poured fuel onto the top ring of the Primus and in that way I cooked the potatoes. Of course they stayed as hard as they had been, though the fat melted and was soaked up by the potatoes. I put the 'casserole' onto a plate and brought it to the woman. After a few minutes she returned and her face was beaming with joy: "My children's souls have revived. They licked the plate clean."

After four days of healing, I told the woman I wanted to see the children. When I saw them – my heart fell.

[Page 440]

Their condition had worsened. I lifted the boy, and he fell down. Lift, and fall. "Uncle, let us lie down, we haven't the strength to stand on our feet," the children begged me.

I understood that I must leave the woman with the children – and get away from there. I left the attic, gathered pliers, a hammer, and scissors. I got up at midnight and escaped from the house.

I walked along the river towards the Monopol. It took me over two hours to cut through the wires of the fence, which were so dense that a fly could barely get through. I wanted to get out – but I couldn't, because my clothes got caught in the sharp wires. I was afraid the dawn was coming. Every moment could be fatal. I undressed and left my clothes on the other side of the fence. With no other choice and completely naked, I entered the river. My conscience troubled me for leaving the woman and the children behind, and I hoped I would drown in the river. Although the water was shallow, I heard that under the Monopol there was a deep hole that would, every year, swallow up a couple of human victims. I looked for the hole, but in vain. The dawn broke, and I spent the whole day in the water. At night I heard the droning of the Soviet planes that bombed 'Vyturio Kovel'.

Life in the Dark Pit

For two days I hid in the woods in Dolgonos. I feared that the farmers who came to the woods would find me and turn me over to the killers. I moved from my place and walked in the dark of night until I reached Ruzhin. That night I heard people speaking Yiddish. I followed the voices and found four young men, aged 18 – 19. Two of them were the sons of Moshe Belker, who lived next to Yodil Sofer. The other two were from the Sands, and I do not remember their names.

The youths knew that I had acquaintances among the farmers, and told me: "If we could get hold of half a loaf of bread, we could hang on for a month." I pitied these young men, whose bellies were swollen from drinking water and their only heart's desire was to eat a slice of bread before they died.

A kilometer and a half away lived an acquaintance of mine named Yaacov, whom I had done many favors. We crawled on our bellies until we reached his house. The youths remained outside, and I went inside alone. I had a bag belted at my waist. When the farmer saw me and recognized me, he began to hit his head and asked after my wife and our four children. I told him it wasn't the right time for such stories. "Bring me a slice of bread and I will leave here." The farmer told his daughter in law to pack bread, cheese, butter, and clothes into a bundle. Suddenly my friend and redeemer looked out the window and his face went pale.

[Page 441]

He told me: "You'll get no bread from me, for they are watching me. Nazi "law" states that whoever gives a slice of bread to a Jew – he and his whole family will be killed. I am willing to lie in a pit with you, but my daughter in law and her children, what sin have they committed?" He began to weep. I told him: "That's just an excuse. Just say that you refuse to feed me a piece of bread." The farmer took up a large, sharp knife and said: "Take the knife, cut off my arm, and rub your body with my blood and it will warm you."

I saw that the situation was very bad and I left the house the way I had come. The youths who had waited outside confirmed the farmer's words, for they had seen the shadow of a man pass by the front of the house.

We lay down to sleep. Since I was naked, I lay between the young men so they would warm me. Then our greatest fear came to be: the commandant of the village, Varmachok, walked 8 kilometers on foot to Koshri, reporting to the Germans that Jews were hiding in the grove. In the morning, the commandant arrived in a wagon accompanied by 10 Germans.

I do not know if it was coincidence or fate – in the morning I parted ways with the youths, and lay down alone under a shrub that was about 15 meters from the shrub under which the youths were hiding. The Germans approached the shrub, found the young men clinging closely to one another. There was one shot; the bullet went through the back of one and into the heart of the second, killing them both. The other two youths began running, and they were shot as well. Since they had been told that three Jews were hiding, and they had found four, they were sure that their "mission" was completed, and did not go on to search the other shrubs.

In the morning, some non–Jewish children from the village came, dug a pit, and threw the murdered youths inside of it.

Once again I was left isolated and alone in the world. I went on my way. I reached Kalbachek and entered the pit under the mosque. I stayed there for 25 days. I returned to the Dolgonos woods, dug a hole with my fingers, covered it with twigs, and made that my home. I lived in that hole for a year and two months, and I subsisted like a beast of the field. Ukrainians wandered around, recounting stories of the killings still going on in the city, and my ears absorbed every word of the horrendous tales.

After a year and two months had gone by, I said in my heart "I must leave this hole, for no matter what – anyway I will not prolong my days here. Once, when I left my hole, from far off I saw one of my Polish acquaintances chopping a tree in the grove. It turned out he was the head of a company of partisans that meted out punishment on the Germans. I joined the partisans – and this was my salvation.

Footnote:

1. For many nights I sat with Ben-Zion and wrote down his testimony, and I spent quite some time on the arrangement and wording to give them a proper Hebrew appearance. I put a lot of effort into this work, because I was convinced that this testimony was unique. This is an authentic historic report, written by a man who with his flesh and his own eyes witnessed all of the horrors of the extermination of the Jews of Kovel. With this testimony, the Kovel Yizkor Book exceeds local boundaries and becomes a universal Jewish document, so that even those not of our city will read these shocking words with bated breath. A. Leoni

[Page 442]

The Entrance of the Germans into the City

by Dora Rophe-Goodis

Translated by Ala Gamulka

The Germans entered town on Friday, 27.6.41. Prior to their entrance there was heavy bombing on three sides: Matseyev Street, Brisk Street and Trisk Street.

The city was on fire. It began in the flour mill belonging to Armernik and spread from there over the entire area.

People searched for refuge and many of them found it in the Big Catholic Church.

The bombing continued all day. By Saturday morning the entire town had been conquered by the Germans. Two German officers entered the church and announced that the town is in their hands. They demanded from those gathered there to go back to their homes. Life will return to normal and no one will be hurt.

I went outside and I saw a frightening sight: the entire area, from Fabritchna Street to the Christian cemetery, burning intensely.

[Page 443]

The streets were filled with the German army. We saw the Germans catching Jews- supposedly for work. It was an omen for things to come.

I went with my late father to our laundry on Warshavska Street. When we arrived, we saw Germans taking Jews for labor. We slipped away from there and we hid in our store. There was a Christian neighbor in the courtyard and she denounced us. We heard loud banging on the door.

The Germans ordered me to work in the tobacco factory on Lutske Street. I was told to take a pail and a rag. In the factory I found many young Jewish girls who were also forced to work. I began to wash the floor and the windows. I was freed a few hours later and I returned home.

A few days later the Germans hung large posters on the streets. They announced that the Jews were to bring to the Command office radios, jewellery and other valuables. In addition, every Jew was to wear a white ribbon with a large blue star of David in it.

During the first weeks of the German conquest, life was, more or less, normal. Here and there, there were some frightening incidents. However, we did not see them as symptoms of the coming Holocaust. We believed we would be spared.

Our belief was strengthened when the Germans announced, innocently, that they would not interfere in our daily lives. The Jews were to elect a Judenrat — an Executive Committee- to organize our existence.

The following were elected to this committee: Vilik Pomerantz, chair, Shlomo Mandel, Itzel Bokser, Moshe Perl, Boris Levin and Yehuda Fried. Anna Lerner served as secretary.

Our serenity did not last. Our skies were darkened with heavy clouds. There were no pleasant rains, but instead there were bloody and tearful floods that were meant to exterminate us from this world.

Soon SS units arrived in town and the brutality began. Any Jew found on the street was whipped and his beard was torn off.

The SS units used to announce a curfew on a specific area and then they burst into the homes. They pretended to take the men for work, but none returned. Our non-Jewish neighbors told us that they saw many Jewish bodies lying on the streets, but, at first, we did not believe them. After several weeks, when our Jews did not return, we began to understand that these terrible stories were true, unfortunately.

This is how life continued from July 1941 to May 1942. During Passover 1942, we baked matzos and conducted a Seder. Our tears choked us and there was a true meaning to the sentence:

[Page 444]

"This year we are slaves, but next year we will be free". We believed the sun would emerge through the heavy dark clouds and we would come out from darkness to light.

On the first day of Passover, in the morning, we went outside and witnessed a horrible sight: the butcher Feldman was hanging in the center of town at the corner of Brisk, Matseyev and Krutka Streets.

This hanging dispersed all the delusions which had been part of our belief. When we looked at Feldman's thrust tongue and his weeping eyes we saw the frightening ending that awaited us.

After Passover, there were rumors that a ghetto is being planned for our town. We knew that, in other towns, there were already ghettos and that our turn was coming.

The members of the Judenrat hurried to the High Commissioner's office, but they were unsuccessful in obtaining any information from him. He calmed them down and told them not to pay attention to unfounded rumors. However, talk and reality did not coincide. Soon an order came out telling the Jews to exchange their white ribbon for a yellow patch. The patch to be worn in front and the ribbon on the back.

What we dreaded did happen. On 21.5.42, at 4 am, the Germans announced the formation of two ghettos. The first – the "Sand ghetto"- covered the street between Kolyova, Listopdova, Zheromaskigo and Stara Kolyova. The second- the "Downtown ghetto"- was in the area to the left of the Turia bridge- between the Trisk Street, Matseyev Street and the Brisk Street bridges.

In the first ghetto were gathered all those who were able to work and they were given appropriate passes while in the second one were found the old, the sick and the children. Those in the second ghetto knew what their end would be.

The Germans announced a time limit of 10 minutes. In those short minutes people were to leave their homes and move to the ghetto. They took what they could and the rest was stolen by the Germans and the Ukrainians. The murderers had a great deal of loot- everything the Jews had accumulated with hard work.

There was a wall erected between the two ghettos. We, in the first ghetto, knew nothing of what was happening in the second one. However, a Jewish militia man would go from clerk to clerk and inform us about the dire events, each one worse than the previous one.

One night we heard shooting that continued until noon. When it stopped, a Jewish policeman arrived looking petrified. He suddenly burst out in crazy laughter. When he calmed down, he told us a story that horrified us: during the night there was an order given in the ghetto for everyone to take a few items to prepare for work.

[Page 445]

However, when he saw that those being prepared for work were elderly or women or children, it was clear that these unfortunate people were being taken to their deaths. Some managed to hide in cellars and attics, but those caught were killed on the spot.

These poor souls were gathered in the big marketplace. There was commotion and yelling. The children were crying together with their mothers. The air shook with these sounds.

I recall a terrifying picture: in Prazhmovsky's pharmacy there was a pharmacist called Granovsky. He resided in the house of Gelman. During the upheaval in the marketplace, both he and his wife were killed. Their little girl, only three years old, did not know what happened to her parents and she ran around crying: "Mama! Papa! Where are you?" Shlomo Mandel took the child and tried to comfort her. An SS officer passed by and asked the child: why are your crying? Mandel replied: her parents are lost and she is trying to find them. At that moment the officer pulled out his pistol and as he was saying — don't cry, my child — he shot right into her mouth.

The lost souls were forcibly placed on trucks and were driven to the train station. From there they were taken by freight train to the village of Bakhava.

In this village there was a valley formed by the digging of sand for construction. They brought our people to this valley and ordered them to undress. They were all shot to death. Nearby there was a detention camp for Russian prisoners. The Germans ordered these prisoners to cover the bodies with earth. Some non-Jewish eye witnesses spoke of the earth that was moving with the death tremors of those buried there- they had been buried alive. These movements continued for many hours. The people struggled and tried to escape until they died. This "action" continued for three days and 10 000 people were put to death. It was done by SS troops assisted by blood-thirsty Ukrainians. Around this valley of death, the Germans hung a sign saying: Danger! Mines! Do not approach!

When Kovel was liberated in 1944, I returned. We were a small group of survivors who came to pay respect to our fallen brothers and sisters.

Everything was confusing. We could not find our way to the village, but some Ukrainians we met on the road directed us to the mass grave. We began to dig and after one meter we found bodies. Some bodies were only covered with 10 cm.

The men said Kaddish in memory of their relatives and all other members of the Jewish community of Kovel. There was great sadness. The community had been eradicated.

We collected some money and paid for a wire fence around the mass grave. We cried and cried. What else could we do?

[Page 446]

As an Aryan in the Kovel Ghetto

by Ephrain Fishman

Translated by Selwyn Rose

After an exhausting and fear–filled escape I arrived in Kovel one day in February 1942. My disguise as an Aryan had succeeded and I had to find suitable lodging somewhere in the town. I approached the lawyer, Werber, whose address I knew and told him I was a Jew in disguise and sought his help in finding a place. He introduced me as the son of a Polish acquaintance from Równe to a Polish lawyer who helped me to arrange accommodation with the Powel Czun family living at 61 Monopolowa Street.

Every evening this Pole, as I saw while I was there, placed a parcel of sandwiches on his patio that disappeared by morning. I noticed all the time he was very careful when he did this. I followed up on his actions and discovered that Jewish people were coming, snatching the parcels and leaving the place quickly. From then on I too added part of my food. The activity didn't go on for long because after two weeks the Jews stopped coming to take the food – possibly they either escaped from the town to the forests or had perished.

Like all Polish and Ukrainian residents, I visited the labor office to get a work permit and ration card. The head of the office was a man called Wanski and according to rumors was a *Volksdeutsche*[1] from Poznan, the owner of a factory of knitwear. He controlled man–power in the Kovel area and demands for workers came through him and he would pass on the demand for the daily quota of workers needed to the *Judenrat*[2].

Because I spoke a number of languages I was employed as a translator in a German construction company, executing various works for the rail system. The manager of the Kovel branch of the railroad was a German named Lutz, together with an engineer called Dehring – both from Germany. Within the framework undertaken by the company, both Jews and non–Jews were employed. The conditions enjoyed by both groups of workers were different – the Christians received a fixed wage with the addition of a daily loaf of bread and the Jews received a minimal wage with no additions. It should be mentioned that there was an internal "arrangement" – the Christians forwent their bread because they had enough of their own and they passed their ration to the Jews.

One day, when the bread was being distributed, a Kovel Jewish man called Paletsky made a comment [in Yiddish] "He is an uncouth Pole" and a second Jew, Goldstein, answered "He should die an uncouth death!" In order not to endanger myself by a slip of the tongue like that, I found it advisable to talk to Paletsky and took him aside and told him to be careful not to talk too much – that there were Poles "who understood everything and even 'the walls have ears'".

[Page 447]

He opened his eyes wide and it was clear he understood. From then on our relationship was normal. When I had the opportunity I told him what had happened to the Jewish communities of Równe and Lutsk telling him also of the various programs the Germans had for the workers of the factories. He asked me about escaping to the forest and obtaining papers as an Aryan.

On more than one occasion they hanged Jewish workers in the factory for failing to report to work, as a threat to the Jewish population. One day the manager, Lutz, came to the office glowing and full of joy he told the staff about the bodies of Jews he had seen swinging to and fro on gallows. It was from his story that I learned about the Jews being hanged for smuggling food into the ghetto or not turning up for work.

The corpses, that were left hanging for a couple of days, were removed by permission only after payment of a heavy sum and taken for a Jewish burial.

The situation of Kovel's Jews worsened when a new chief of police by the name of Kassner, owner of a large dog arrived. The popular rumor in town claimed that the dog could identify Jews by smell. The rumor caused waves among the Jews who were gripped with fear whenever they came within sight of the animal. The fear was sensed, apparently by the dog and he would attack them while his blood–thirsty master would shoot the unfortunate victim as a "*coup de grace*". He was a sadist by nature. He could not dine until he had killed or tortured someone.

On the first of May 1942 at 8 o'clock in the morning, when all the Jewish workers assembled at the railroad station ready to go to work by truck, the factory manager, Lutz, appeared and organized them into ranks of three and after giving the order to stand to attention, began a derogatory speech haranguing the Jews accusing them of exploiting the status of the workers, commanding them to end the assembly by singing the "*Hatikva*". The singing of "*Hatikva*" under those circumstances was so vigorous and enthusiastic that those present felt it expressing the hope that the suffering of the persecuted people, even on the verge of despair, was accompanied by a spark of faith that Israel will endure and triumph.

I managed to visit the ghetto several times meeting with Riter who was the *Judenrat* member responsible for work schedules. I advised some of the Jews to escape because the same fate as Równe's Jews awaited them. The following day, early in the morning, sporadic shooting and the explosions of hand–grenades were heard from the direction of the market in the old town. That same morning I was taken back to my home by Ukrainian guards because of a general curfew. Neighbors who lived in the old town spoke of a bitter struggle among the young Jews who had barricaded themselves in the cellars of their shops and the synagogue, and the Ukrainian police.

[Page 448]

About five Ukrainians, at least, were brought out of the ghetto with smashed skulls. After some time we found some comments in Yiddish, Polish and Hebrew on the walls of the houses calling for vengeance against the murderers. The search for Jews in hiding continued for another few days and at the end of the week there were still a few individual Jews being taken to police establishments by Ukrainian police.

I heard the details of the fate of a couple of young Jewesses from the mouth of a German and a Ukrainian. Riva Freidman, a laboratory technician could have saved herself from liquidation because she had a card marked as "Required Jewess" but she refused to leave her mother and sister Regina in spite of the insistence a German who worked with her in the same institute and she was taken together with the other Jews.

Regarding the eventual fate of the attorney from Równe, a member of the *Judenrat*, I know the following details: He was transferred with his family to the ghetto in the new part of town. He was mobilized with another 50 people of standing in the town, for the burial of the dead. When the work was finished they were ordered to dig their own graves and thus they ended their lives. Their families remained alive for the time being in the ghetto. On that day of liquidation Ukrainian police moved through the town and marked all the Jewish homes. Notices were put up in town warning that anyone found looting Jewish property – would be shot. For several weeks collections were carried out and all the belongings sorted out in special store–rooms. Part of the items were allotted to the Municipality, part to the Ukrainian institutions or the needy families among the population who had applied for assistance and part, especially jewelry and expensive clothing, was sent by rail in special wagons to Germany (I witnessed with my own eyes these transports).

At the end of 1942 there were more than 10 young Jews in Kovel from other towns that lived with Ukrainian or Polish families. They all held papers as Aryans. There was an underground connection between them and occasionally they managed to wink at each other in the street as encouragement. Occasionally they helped each other look for emergency shelter or different lodging. Among these youngsters were a brother and sister Jochet(?) from Lutsk. They forged their papers by changing one letter of the family name to Jiost(?).

In my presence they acted as strangers to each other. He worked as an electrical engineer and she as a RÖntgen technician with Doctor Jaborovski – may his name and memory be erased. Dr. Jaborovski suspected her as being Jewish from the first moment she arrived to work with him. During her first days he pestered her with penetrating questions. With the liquidation of the ghetto he told her unequivocally that he would ask for a police investigation of her origins. She escaped to Równe. Her brother was also compelled to escape after the liquidation because the Gestapo was tracking him.

I was informed that he had been arrested in Równe and imprisoned. At the time of the revolt of the prisoners in 1943 – he escaped,

One morning I woke up to the sound of shooting and explosions. I made my way to work because my absence could have awakened suspicions about me but I was returned when only about half–way (on the corner of Monopolowa Street and Warschawski Street) because that part of town had been declared under curfew.

[Page 449]

The firing continued for a couple of hours until noon. That action against the Jews was accepted with complete passiveness by the Christian population and was considered to be of "moderate proportions." "Only" only about 10,000 had been taken to the lime–pits. The Christians related afterwards that the pits had been prepared a week previously. There were some Jewish people who also bore witness to that. A few days before the liquidation I spoke with some Jews who worked with me at the railroad station. I offered Goldstein some money but he refused it because he knew that his days were numbered. I advised them to escape to the forest but they didn't seem interested in the idea because they had heard from escapees that the Christian partisans weren't willing to accept Jews – especially after the Ukrainian police joined the partisans and sowed anti–Semitism among the ranks of the partisans.

I would like to mention some good things and bad things concerning a few individual Poles and Ukrainians. Among the residents of Kovel 2 was a Polish detective, a *Volksdeutsche* about 22 years old whose function was to penetrate different circles and discern the origins and intentions of suspicious people who arrive in town. He was furnished by the Germans with special documents and plenty of money. He spread the money and also supplies otherwise unobtainable to everyone who gave him information about the Jews. His name was Artomonov. According to the rumor I heard that at the time of the German retreat he escaped to Poland and was seen in the vicinity of Krakow.

The engineer Czerniak and the engineer Czun lived in the Monopol district and worked in the Municipality. They would inform the *Judenrat* about orders and instructions that they received from the German administration about new decrees that were about to come into force so that the *Judenrat* would know of all sorts of operations that were about to occur before the event.

Trapolowski was a Pole who lived in Kovel 2. His son was mobilized and served in the Russian army falling in the first days of the war leaving the father with his two daughters, Yanka and Dora. The elder daughter was a clerk in the Labor Department and directed workers to different institutions according to the requests that came in. Because everyone had to go through her, she received personal details from every worker, she knew every Jew that appeared with an Aryan name and ignored the fact. She would help them to penetrate into Polish companies. She invited me also to their home and introduced me into the circle of young Poles. When the ghetto was liquidated she transferred me to the branch–office of the Labor Department in Maniewicze (Monevitch). The Ukrainian partisans saw her as a representative of the government and one dark night they kidnapped her and the following morning she was found cut into pieces.

(Abstract edited by T. Weissbrot)

Translator's Footnotes:

    1. *Volksdeutsche* – a designation instituted during the Nazi regime defining people of German extraction living in foreign countries, as Germans, irrespective of their present nationality.
    2. *Judenrat* – a Jewish council forced upon Jewish communities under Nazi rule, answerable to the Nazi authorities for controlling the Jewish population in the ghettos and (mainly) supplying forced labor.

In the Jaws of Death

by Asher Peres

Translated by Selwyn Rose

Rumors arrived in the ghetto that a terrible slaughter was imminent and approaching. I went to the gates of the ghetto to see if I could get some more information. The people were gripped by fear and panic, pushing and being pushed, crushed and disorganized towards the gate, sweeping towards the Ukrainian guard and outside the ghetto boundaries.

I exploited that moment's opportunity and fled for my life. I had an acquaintance who owned a bakery situated facing the town's cinema on Mitskevycha Street. I made my way there and to my relief I found my brother there, now together with me in Israel.

We hid in our friend's house for about a week but he couldn't hide us longer because the Germans took possession of the bakery for their own use. One night I left with my brother, alone, abandoned and without knowing where we should go. We got to Macziew Street, crossed the bridge and found shelter in the cellar of an abandoned house. With the dawn we decided to lie low all day and by night to escape to the forest.

Suddenly a Christian woman came in and began to fill a sack with items belonging to the Jews who had abandoned the house. When she saw us she pretended that she sympathized with our plight and began to clasp her hands and promised to bring us bread and milk.

We didn't deceive ourselves regarding this "righteous soul"; we realized our situation was serious but with no alternative we stayed there because escape during daylight would be like just giving ourselves into the hands of the murderers who lay in wait for Jewish blood at every step of the way.

After about an hour a Ukrainian policeman came with his brother, a detective. The policeman was an acquaintance of mine and I was sure he had come to save us and take us to a safe shelter. To my great astonishment he began to threaten us that if we didn't give him gold and jewelry – we'll be killed on the spot. We gave him everything we had. He stripped us of all our clothes, beat us up severely and took us to the Great Synagogue. On the way he warned us not to tell the Germans that he robbed us of the gold, if we did – he'll rip us to shreds.

We arrived at the synagogue at 10 o'clock in the morning. We saw a long line of men and women standing in front of a barrier and next to them an SS officer wearing white gloves. Next to the officer was a bucket full of gold rings. Everyone who went in was obliged to throw a ring into the bucket. Whoever didn't have a ring on the finger – was severely beaten. When it was my turn I was forced to tell the truth that the Ukrainian policeman had taken it all from me - my silver, the gold, dollars and even my shoes. The SS officer didn't touch me but in fact attacked the Ukrainian policeman with blows that caused the blood to flow.

[Page 450]

I am recording just the tip of the iceberg for the unhappy residents of my town and also for the sake the next generations, of the enormous threat that surrounded me from the very first moment that my feet entered the synagogue: in one corner sat a Jewish man, a pile of bones, his lips moving ceaselessly: "I have waited for Thy salvation O Lord." Rosh Hashanah was imminent – O, Lord, eradicate the evil decree of Thy judgment, have mercy upon us, inscribe us in the book of life.

While the man was still pleading for mercy in walked a Ukrainian policeman leading a number of small children aged about one year and above.

The Ukrainian policemen – may their name be obliterated — played out a gruesome scene: they tossed the children in the air, as one would toss a ball and on falling the pure little angels were torn to shreds turning into a mixture of blood, ripped flesh and broken bones. All this was performed before the eyes of the horrified mothers.

One of the mothers recognized her child and like a crazed animal she fell upon the Ukrainian trying to save the fruit of her womb from his defiling hands. The murderer kicked her in the chest and sliced the baby into two and threw the two halves of the body at the fainting woman.

After about 7 days in the synagogue the order was given to mobilize 10 men for labor. I was among them and I was ordered to clean the house belonging to Menahem Reissesher(?).

When I returned to the synagogue I found many people missing. They told me that the healthy men had been taken away to the cemetery and there they were given shovels and ordered to dig a trench. When the work was finished they shot all of them in the grave they had dug for themselves.

My brother burst out crying and told me that in half an hour the murderers will return and take all of us to be slaughtered. I felt the blood drain from my face but I didn't panic. In that hour of dire peril I noticed a small opening beneath the *Bema*[1] of the synagogue. I pushed my brother in there and then tried to get in myself but the area was blocked by the bodies of two women who had been strangled. I pushed them to one side and managed to force my way in.

After about an hour some SS men came with Ukrainian policemen. The vehicles moved up close to the doors of the synagogue and the police lined up in two rows and began to force the miserable people out. From my small opening I looked out at how our dear loved ones went on their last journey. The Ukrainians snatched the smallest children who had been left without their mothers and fathers and smashed their heads on the sides of the trucks. The head came off this one, that one's neck was broken and that one died like a chicken being slaughtered. Thus in agonies such as this our little cherubs went on their way heavenwards.

The synagogue emptied out as they were all taken to their death and the Ukrainian police guard alone remained.

[Page 451]

We began to creep out cautiously from our hiding place to find the policemen asleep near the stairway. We took advantage of the moment and jumped out of the window. The police opened fire on us but we were not hit.

The town was in darkness and my brother and I continued towards our house. It had been destroyed and plundered. We went into the Karlini synagogue. The floor was broken up and we hid in the cellar. We lay there under the floor the whole day. We looked out of cracks in the building and saw Ukrainians coming with carts and wagons, stealing and destroying everything.

At night we left our hiding place and made our way towards the barbed wire fence of the ghetto with the idea of escaping. The barbed wire was very tangled but after a super-human effort we managed to break through. We suffered for months from the injuries we got from the rusty barbed wire.

When we got out we ran to the Golubchek(?) farm. When we got there it was dark and we went into the cow-shed and climbed up into the hay-loft staying there for a few days. Golubchek came every so often to give hay to the horse - but he didn't discover us.

Our situation was desperate. Hunger seemed almost to kill us and we expected to die of hunger. It was already twelve days since we had eaten even the smallest morsel and had no water, our throats were parched and speech was difficult to the point of enforced silence.

When Golubchek came in to feed and water the horse we went down from our hiding-place disclosing our presence to him. Seeing us he became a little fearful and started crossing himself. He saw us as if risen from the dead – specters from the valley of the ghosts because he had been told we had long been taken out for execution.

Golubchek brought us bread and sweet tea and warned us against anyone in the house knowing of our presence because his son-in-law was a rabid Jew-hater and was likely to inform the Germans that we were here.

We stayed in the hay-loft for about half the winter. We were almost naked. We covered ourselves with a thin blanket under the tin roof that itself produced intense cold. Strong winds blew and the cold seemed almost to kill us.

Our good fortune ended when Golubchek's son-in-law chanced on one occasion to come up into the loft. When he discovered us he let out a loud shout that because of us he and all his family would be killed by the Germans. Golubchek intervened and found a way to save us. There were two Jewish men hiding in the Zelena forest who were in touch with Golubchek who gave them bread and other food supplies. He had a talk with them and told them about us being in his hay-loft and one night one of them came to take us away. I went alone while my brother stayed. With great difficulty I managed to stand on my feet and dragged myself after my rescuer. We walked the whole night over rough ground until we arrived at the Zelena forest. On arriving there I discovered the Steinkrok(?) family – the cinema owners.

Our first act was to dig ourselves a trench for shelter in the forest. The digging took us a a whole week we were so broken and exhausted.

[Page 452]

We lay down there the entire night. In the morning we heard the sound of shooting. We escaped deeper into the forest and no one discovered our tracks. I occasionally went to Golubchek together with Steinkrok and we brought back life-supporting supplies of food and water. We brought sacks full of bread, I took my brother with me and we returned to the forest. The pathways were very poor and not well marked and we made a mistake. We sank into deep mud and were a step away from death by sinking in. All night long we trudged along unknown paths and only with the dawn did we find our hiding place. When we arrived we found Steinkrock's wife and his son crying bitterly in the belief we had been executed.

The following day I went on my own to the place where the second Jewish family was staying, hiding in a Christian house in Zelena. They told me not to lose heart because salvation would soon come.

On my way back I ran into a group of Polish partisans armed with pitch-forks. They shouted at me to stop and asked me where I had come from. I answered I was on my way home after visiting a Polish acquaintance. The partisans decided not to kill me for the time being. They intended to capture all the Jews hiding in the forest and kill them all together. On the way they found Steinkrock and his family, my brother and the two Jews. They beat them cruelly and ordered them to report that night to a certain house in Zelena. I told them not to obey because I felt something was not right and didn't bode well but they didn't listen. When they arrived at the house the Polish partisans killed them.

I and my brother went in another direction. We went to a house in Zelena and the house-wife, Drokova hid us in a bunker in the cow-shed. We stayed there for a couple of days. Afterwards we walked until we arrived at Kivertsi. Fierce battles were being fought all over the area between the Russian and German armies but the Russians gained the upper-hand. With the liberation of the area by the Red Army we were released as well and we were saved from the clutches of death.

Translator's Footnote: – the raised platform in the synagogue from where many of the prayers are led and the Torah recited.

[Page 453]

I Lived With Mentey
(As told by an eye witness)

by Aharon Weiner

Translated by Ala Gamulka

During the time he lived in Kovel, Mentey walked around with fears that, sooner or later, he would be tasked with the building of ovens meant for the Jews of New York. He fully believed that the Nazi conquests would reach across the ocean. The Fuhrer would rule over the entire world including all the seas. The United States would be overcome and be defeated and he, Mentey, would be invited to establish Majdanek and Auschwitz in Greater New York.

[Page 454]

This murderer thought along the lines of global destruction — a total annihilation of world Jewry. He openly stated that the Earth cannot stand both Nazi Germany and the international Jewish capital. Hitler could not be certain of his conquests as long as the Jewish community of the United States was still in existence.

When I arrived in Kovel, there were no Jews there any more. It was after Bakhava, after the elimination of the two ghettos and after the last Jew brought to the Great Synagogue was massacred. Here and there one could find remnants of the fertile Jewish community of Kovel. There were 6 Jews, in the open, who worked for Mentey. I believe that the number who were hidden by their Polish friends was not more than that.

I once told Mentey: Do you not see that there are no Jews remaining in town? Why do you care if these six will stay alive? He replied: You, Jew, have to understand. You see six Jews only, but I see five million Jews in the United States. They are our enemy as they declared a war of elimination on us. If not for them, there would not have been a World War.

I lived with this animal for many months. Daily I looked at his murderous face. Every day I had to listen to his curses and abuse and I saw the great sacrifice of innocent victims that he performed in his courtyard.

My road of suffering that brought me from Neskhiz to Kovel, to the house of this killer was as follows: when Mentey murdered the Jews of Kovel, there were no craftsmen left in town. The area commanding officer, Shpitura, heard that in Nesekhizh there were a few shoemakers. He demanded that they be brought to him and he would open a shoemaking shop. This is how I came to Kovel to the house of the late Appelbaum. This is where the offices were located.

Mentey had 3 Jewish shoe makers. One night the three escaped. Mentey had the police search for them, but they could not be found. When he heard that there was a Jewish shoemaker working for the area commander he sent a Ukrainian policeman to bring me to him. The policeman told me to come with him. He brought me to Monopoliova Street and we stopped at a beautiful house. Inside was housed a school of Ukrainian policemen, headed by Mentey.

I entered and I saw a character pulling up his pants nervously. He looked at me with suspicious eyes and said: "You are the shoemaker! Come with me". He brought me to a room and said: You will work here! I had three Jews and they escaped. I hope you will not run away.

In the room I found a woman. Her father was a hatmaker and his shop was near the bridge. I asked her: How did you get here? She told me that she had been hidden by Germans, but they were afraid to be caught and decided to kill her.

[Page 453]

She was brought to Brisk Street where she was shot, but she was only lightly injured. She went to the doctor and asked him to bandage her. When the doctor discovered that she was Jewish he immediately notified Mentey. After much torture she admitted that she had been hidden by Germans and she was jailed.

Mentey caught the Germans who had hidden her and sentenced them to five years in prison. He left her, for the time being, alive. The prison inspector had recommended her as an excellent dressmaker. This was her good fortune.

Suddenly I saw a young girl in Mentey's house. I did not know who she was.

[Page 456]

I asked her name and she told me she was Bina Roiter, the daughter of Asher Roiter. She had hidden in a house where Germans resided. The Germans lived downstairs and she was in the attic. When the Germans would go out she would come out of her hiding place to collect food scraps from the tables. This is how she sustained herself. However, she felt she had to escape from the house because in the long run someone would discover her. She had saved some gold coins and she decided to give them to Mentey in the hope that he would let her live. He received her, did not hurt her and made her his telephone secretary.

Once Mentey said to me: "These cursed Jews are tormenting me. They do not let me sleep at night. It seems to me that there is at least one Jew still alive." He was afraid that his loyal helpers, the Ukrainian policemen did not execute the precise job on behalf of the purity of Aryan race. He was certain that the most dangerous enemies of the Reich are still in the town. You see, how can I sleep if my enemies are around me?

What did the murderer do? He found a young Ukrainian boy. He fed him with the best food and gave him a large salary. His task was to search everywhere for Jews. This young boy, may his name and memory be forever erased, was an excellent worker. The next day he brought Itzik the builder with his wife and children. Itzik had hidden for many days in a cellar. When he was brought to Mentey he was crawling. He was bent from the mud and dampness in which they had lived. They separated him from his wife and children. They brought a bit of food to revive him, but he kept some of it for his wife and children. The poor man did not know that they had already been killed.

A Jew named Wolf Kipper who was hanged in Kovel in 1942

Mentey used to murder the miserable souls in his courtyard. There was a broken automobile standing there and this is where he placed the one to be killed. The courtyard looked like an abattoir. When I looked through the window I saw human bodies thrown together with dead cats and dogs. Mentey did not want to even use a cart to take out only one or two bodies. It was only when he had several such bodies that he would order their removal for burial.

On 11 Kislev of 1942 35 Jews were brought from to Neskhiz to Kovel- for extermination. Among them were my children. I begged Mentey to allow me to say goodbye, to look at them and hug them. I wanted to give them a last kiss, but he would not listen to my begging. "They have to be killed immediately" – was his shrill command. "There is no place for Jews in this world!". Still, he softened a little and brought me my oldest daughter. When my daughter saw me, she began to tear her hair out and hit her head on the ground. She screamed with inhuman sounds: "Father, save your daughter. They are going to kill me".

[Page 457]

I begged Mentey, with tears rolling down my face: "If you cannot spare all my children, at least leave me this child".

The murderer looked at me and said with stoic calmness: "You must understand that it is impossible to do so. I do not have a place for your daughter. There is no place at all for Jews in the world".

They were all brought to the cemetery and killed there. When Mentey returned from his "action" he came to me and said: "I did you a favor because you are useful to me. I chose a good and easy death for your children and the other Jews." "What do you mean by easy?" I asked. The murderer replies: "Usually we beat the Jews to death and we finish it off by shooting. This time I took pity and I did not allow the policemen to torture them. Not only that, but I personally shot them. I am a good shot and I managed it with bullet. I am certain your children did not even feel anything".

The murderer said what he said and then he ordered me to collect the shoes that were removed from the dead. "Now fit these shoes to the feet of the policemen, their sons and daughters." Among the pile of shoes I found my oldest daughter's dress. I wrapped it around me the way one does with a tallit and I sobbed out loud.

Mentey did not interfere and he let me cry. When I finally stopped I went into the courtyard. It was a cold winter day — one of the coldest. The Ukrainian boy brought new victims. I saw a Jew shivering with the cold with his feet covered in rags. His little daughter stood next to him completely frozen. I asked him: "Where are you from?" The miserable man replied that he was from Liubomol. "I was caught and now I am waiting for death". The next day I was shaken by a worse calamity. I saw a Ukrainian policeman escorting a woman carrying a baby with another child following her. As the woman came to Mentey he grabbed the baby from her arms and threw it angrily down. When the killer saw that the baby was still alive, he picked him up and tore him in half. He then threw him on the pile of dead cats and dogs. The following day I saw the poor mother lying dead with the bodies of her children next to her. Near them lay the saintly man from Liubomol with his daughter. The mother's blood flowed together with that of her children as did the blood of the father with his child.

Three days after Purim in 1943, an unusual event took place. All the Ukrainian policemen headed by Shpitura rebelled against Mentey and fled into the forest. At night, Roiter's daughter came to tell me that something terrible was happening. A rebellion? We got up and saw an unbelievable sight: all the Ukrainian policemen stood armed. They broke the furniture with their guns, destroyed documents, burned pictures of the Fuhrer. They approached the German who was lying on his bed and shot him. They were searching for Mentey. Lucky for the murderer that he was sleeping that night in the command headquarters.

[Page 458]

If they had found him they would have cut him into pieces. The policemen destroyed everything and ran away.

In the morning, at dawn, we heard shots. Mentey returned and when he saw that the building was ruined and the policemen had disappeared, he began to behave abominably. He killed a Polish priest who happened to be in his way and he also killed two Jewish construction workers.

We lay in the attic and we did not know what to do: should we surrender to him or should we wait for the right moment to escape? Roiter's daughter went downstairs and informed us that Mentey had returned and was looking for us. We had no choice and we came downstairs. He looked at us and said that he was going to Lieutenant Rapp, the head of the police, to ask him what to do with us. We were certain that he would give the order to immediately kill us. We waited for death. Mentey came back and told us that since we came back of our own good will, Rapp had instructed him to keep us alive.

In our hearts we resolved to escape no matter what as soon as the right occasion presented itself. Since the Ukrainian policemen had gone the building was left unguarded. Mentey was afraid to sleep there and went to Rapp at night. We were alone in the building and we even had the keys.

As we were trying to decide how to escape, ten trucks approached the building. They were filled with German policemen. The Germans were surprised to see us: What? You are Jews? There are still some left of this cursed race? They pointed their guns at us and were prepared to shoot. Mentey interfered in and told the policemen: "Don't touch them. These are my workers." A few days later all the Germans left the building and again we were alone. I told Roiter: we must run away now. If not, our end was near. She replied that she would not run away since she had nowhere to go.

Mentey used to come back to the building at 7 in the morning. We arose at 5 am and we wrote a good-bye letter to Mentey. We asked his forgiveness for the fact that we were leaving him. We had no work now and we would return when there would be more work. We placed the letter on his desk and we left. One of my Ukrainian friends told me later the when Mentey read the letter he was so angry that he went mad. Roiter's daughter did not join us. When the murderer saw her, he shot many bullets towards her. He only stopped his madness when he saw that her body was like a sieve because of all the bullet holes.

[Page 459]

The Gleanings of Genocide

by Aharon Weiner
(As told by an eye witness)

Translated by Ala Gamulka

Soon after the Germans entered town, they, so to speak, established a civilian government. It was headed by special departments of the police (Sonderabteilung). Representatives of the Jewish community were invited to speak to the German authorities. They were, Mendel, Perl and Dr. Pomeranz.

The three were told to choose a committee (Judenrat). Its purpose was to conduct a census of the population. The first committee was housed in the Jewish Community building on Koshtsiuska Street.

Even in the first weeks the Jews were ordered to give to the authorities their radios, foreign currency, jewelry, cash, bicycles, sewing machines and furs. There were long lines-several kilometers- of citizens bringing theses items. Some waited several days until they were able to give over their belongings.

After that, an order was given to the Jewish Community to provide workers for the Germans. Every household was told to send one worker. Anyone who refused had to hire someone in his place. They were allotted 120 grams of bread daily. The work was difficult and exhausting: they had to harvest potatoes from the fields, load wagons with coal, cut down trees and pack up goods for the front.

The women did housework- cleaning rooms, laundry and other sanitary jobs. They were also employed in factories, saw mills and flour mills. Only Jews were obliged to do this kind of work. The non-Jews were exempt. The Jews also had to hang a yellow star on their doors and shutters. The Germans had, as soon as they entered, ordered the wearing of a blue Magen David on a white background. This rule involved adults as well as children. It was followed by not allowing Christians to meet Jews. As the sun set, curfew followed. It was not permissible to leave the house. Anyone who wanted to sneak into his neighbor's house was in great danger.

***

At the beginning, Kovel had a High Commissioner who did not cause too many problems for the Jews. He accepted bribes and presents and he did not bother or kill the Jews. Highly observant Jews saw in this the results of the blessing of the Righteous from Nesekhizh. He had once blessed the town that it would not know any suffering. However, the calm days did not last long. Someone denounced him to The German authorities saying that the Commissioner was too kind to the Jews and that he had forgotten why he was sent to Kovel.

[Page 460]

He was replaced by a human beast, a sadist, a murderer called Kassner. He came, so to speak, as a simple worker and headed a group of them. He was cunning and managed to befriend the Jewish workers. He questioned them about the relationship of the High Commissioner with the Jews. He wanted to know if the Commissioner was good to the Jews and did not bother them. The poor innocent workers replied that the High commissioner was a good, kind man and that he allowed the Jews to feel calm.

Kassner informed the central command and the High Commissioner was immediately removed from his position. He was sent to trial and the town was handed over to the bloody Kassner.

While the High Commissioner was in his position, Dr. Pomeranz had contact with him. As soon as he was fired, Dr. Pomeranz was arrested and no one knew what happened to him. Certainly, his end must have been the same as that of other Jews in town.

***

As soon as the town was given over to the murderer Kassner, the situation changed completely. We felt that a great calamity was coming. And it was so. One evening Kassner appeared in the ghetto and waited for the workers. He did not come alone, of course, but with his murderous cohorts. They surrounded the ghetto. Kassner stood at the gate and checked the belongings of the men and women in case they smuggled money or food into the ghetto. Twenty people were caught with food. He immediately ordered them all to go down on their knees. Men, women and children congregated to see how this would end.

Kassner slowly pushed up his sleeves and had a murderous grin on his face. He pulled out his pistol and shot one of the kneeling people.

When the first victim fell, Krakover arose and ran away. He somehow was energized by inhuman forces, jumped over the fence and continued to run. Germans who were there caught him and stabbed him with their knives. He continued to run, but he was trapped. Kassner ordered him to be brought back to where he had been on his knees and then he shot him dead. All the people in the ghetto stood and watched this horrible event. Even his wife, his children and his parents were among the spectators. Kassner then arranged for the removal of the bodies, the cleaning of the sidewalk of blood and the erasure of this murderous deed.

Whenever Kassner drove his motorcycle on the street, there was great fear. Young children would jump from the windows into trenches in order to hide.

[Page 461]

One day Arthur Schultz came to the ghetto (owner of the billiard room in Kovel). He was regarded as a "friend" of the Jews and no one suspected he was sent by the Gestapo. He was interested in hearing how the Jews lived in the ghetto. He asked who had arms and who intended to join the partisans. He promised to do all he could to save the Jews from the jaws of death. A few days later Schultz appeared in the ghetto wearing an S.S. uniform. He was once walking on Monopoliova Street and saw Mania Armernik. He killed her on the spot.

***

One day, the wife of Prof. Reuven Erlich was walking with her son and daughter from Tishovsky Street. She had been informed that she was required to go to work. As she neared Brisk Square, the Ukrainians began to shoot in the air. It seemed like a game, supposedly. The women and children were frightened and began to run. The Ukrainians then shot them. The bullet hit the boy and went through his body into the mother. Both were killed. The poor little girl was left alone and began to run. She reached her uncle's house- Dr. Whiteman on Koshtsiuska Street. I, her aunt, Soibel-Whiteman, Raya Bokser (wife of Izsak Erlich), Gitel Ravenko (Burk) and Shoshana Schneider were working there. The child looked so awful that even the Germans had pity on her. It was a heart-wrenching sight. I will never forget her desperate shouts:" I am not a Jew!" "I am not a Jew!' "Don't kill me!" "Let me live!" We managed to calm her down with great difficulty. However, her fate was sealed as she was killed with the elimination of the ghetto.

[Page 462]

Thanks to a Righteous Woman in Sodom

by Sarah Bronshteyn-Gevertzman

Translated by Ala Gamulka

It was 27 July, 1942. After the first "actzion" the Kovel ghetto was in anticipation of its final elimination. On that day I managed to escape from the ghetto with a group of Jewish workers and I went to my apartment on Monopoliova Street. This is where my neighbor, Elsa Kamitova was living.

I begged her to help me because there was no one else to ask. She did not hesitate and did not ask for any reimbursement. She gave me documents belonging to her relative.

Coincidentally, or perhaps not so coincidentally, her mother-in-law, Karolina Kamitova was visiting from Holova together with her husband Mikolai. He placed a kerchief on my eye to make it look as if I were ill. He brought me in his wagon to their farm near Holova.

The Jews of Holova were still free. I settled in the house of the Kamitova family pretending to be a relative -Wanda from Kovel. On September 2, 1942, after the first "actzion" in Holova, four Jews came to us. They dug a trench and we all sat in it. Grandma Kamitova brought us food, water and even clothes.

A few days later the other people left to go to their acquaintances and I was left alone. Until November 11, 1942 I stayed in the Grandmother's house in the daytime and at night I returned to my "catacomb", i.e., the trench.

On 15 November of that year an order was given to cleanse Holova of Jews. The last few Jews were thus eliminated. It was very dangerous to remain in the Grandmother's house because the Ukrainian police roamed the streets in search of Jews. There were even times when Polish families were slaughtered because they had hidden Jews.

The family opposed my hiding in the house, but Grandmother Kamitova did not want to abandon me. She brought me to a field, far from the house and covered me with hay. I lived in this field for a week. At night Grandma would bring me food. She would crawl to me so that no one would see her.

[Page 463]

Grandma Karolina Kamitova

The dear and gentle grandmother who risked her life to save mine. "You should love thy neighbor as you love yourself". Daily and hourly, she showed deep religious belief, was simple, was devoted heart and soul and made certain not only to save me, but also to make my life better.

When the family was sure that I had left the village. Grandma brought me back to the trench. I "lived" in it all winter and spring of 1943. I never left my "home". Around 3:00 am Kamitova would bring me food through a small opening.

When the police of Holova left and ran away to the forests, making life easier, Grandma told her family about me. I returned to their house and I hid in an attic. Others hidden by this family were Dora Katz (now Dr. Devorah Drutman-Katz – here in Israel) and Rachel and Pinie Bunis who live in the United States.

Grandma also helped other Jewish families with food or clothing. She did all of this not to earn a medal, but out of humanitarian caring and love of others.

[Page 464]

In the Maw of the Lion

by Rivka Shtern-Goldshteyn

Translated by Ala Gamulka

When the war between Russia and Germany broke out, I was in Lutsk, in the Pedagogic Institute. One day, the town was overcome by a barrage of explosions that descended upon us on a clear day.

I rushed to return home because I heard that there were many bodies lying on the side of the roads. The way was not clear and I feared that I would be stuck in Lutsk.

The teachers tried to calm me down by telling me that these were only manoeuvres and that the bombs were not real. Everything would be peaceful again in a few days. I listened to this talk and I filled my knapsack with books in the hope that I would stay quietly in my father's house in Kovel. I could prepare my assignments in the meantime.

In Kovel the devil had not yet started its work and the streets were calm as before a storm. However, there was no doubt that the murderers would come to town in a matter of days or even hours.

I had studied in the Moshtchitsky School in Kovel and there I heard from the History teacher there were periods in human life when Mars, the God of War, "waves his weapons". At that time, terrible blood baths occur. It was clear to me that we were going through such a time and that we would all be annihilated.

However, especially in this angry time when the entire country was a killing field, we felt the desire to live as the animals in the fields, the birds in the skies, in the lakes, on a lonely rock in the sea- but to remain alive. I told my father, z" l, to let us escape from Kovel where the Nazi killer was on the doorstep. I had a sister in Persefa and we went to her. We spoke Polish and no one suspected we were Jewish.

In Persefa there were only five Jewish families and the Germans did not bother them. They shared information. These were elderly Germans, not the Gestapo, who had served in WWI. They promised to help us.

Unfortunately, they were not able to help. One fine day the Gestapo appeared and took us to Rozhishets where there was a ghetto for Jews from the surrounding area.

I stayed in the ghetto, with my family, for two weeks. An event occurred which helped to save my life: Between Kovel and Rozhishets there was a settlement called Brishtseh. Germans inhabited it. When Volyn Province was taken over by the Soviets, all the German residents were evacuated to Siberia. Their homes were occupied by Poles who had lived on the banks of the Bug River. They grew beets in the fields and needed workers

[Page 465]

One day, a representative of the Gestapo came to Rozhishets and demanded from the committee to send 200 young, healthy women to work in the beet fields of Brishtseh. I was advised to be included and I did go. These young women were among the best Jewish youths of Poland. Most of the girls were not girls from Rozhishets, but refugees from other parts of the country.

We walked about 10-12 km. They placed us in a large hall and spread hay on the floor to serve as beds. A hut was erected near the hall and a large vat was put in. This was to be our kitchen. We received 150 grams of bread and 30 grams uncooked oats per day. We worked in the fields from 6 am to 6pm, eating this meagre allotment. The Ukrainian murderers would whip the slower girls who could barely stand up. At 12 noon they brought us in for lunch. Since there was not enough time to boil the oats, three girls were left in the kitchen to prepare the food. I was one of them.

In time, we managed to develop good relations with the manager of the farm- a Pole. We told him not to treat us like animals of burden because we were school girls. The manager took pity on us and promised us, in the name of the Triad, that he would not only treat us with respect, but that he would also try to save us.

One Friday in August 1942, at dawn, we saw a young Jewish boy running towards us with his last breath. He told us that during the night all the Jews of Rozhishets were taken to deep hole, but he had managed to escape.

We hid him in a safe place and we went to speak to the manager. With tears in our eyes we begged him to save us from the death trap. He calmed us down by saying there was no truth to the rumors. He thought he would know about this happening if it was really so.

As we were arguing with him, we saw in the distance swirls of dust growing stronger and closer. We also heard the sounds of hoofs. Very quickly, a large contingent of Ukrainian police officers appeared. They were riding wild horses. We told the manager that they came to take us. The good man hid us in the barn and instructed us not to go our until he returned.

The Ukrainians police officers spread in the fields and battered the Jewish girls with their guns. They took them to Rozhishets. On the way they passed a large, thick forest. Many girls were able to escape and to hide in the bushes. Some were shot as they were getting away. Only half were brought to Rozhishets.

[Page 466]

Not far from the manager's house there was a large fenced area for cows as well as a milking station. The manager knew the guard of that area, Boyko, and at night he took us there in secret. The guard was a good man and he took us to his house, 2 km from the fenced area. We hid in his barn almost the entire winter. The good man would bring us food and water.

Once the guard came to tell us, tearfully, that he could no longer hide us because the villagers were whispering that he was keeping Jews. He took us back to the milking station and we hid under the roof. It was a cold winter and one night there was a snow storm. It caused the straw roof to fly away. There was only a little straw left and it barely hid us from passers-by. We were subject to the elements. One Sunday, two young locals were approaching. We heard one of them say: I heard there are young Jewish girls hiding here. The second one replied: It cannot be that in this terrible storm someone is still alive. Let us at least look in all the nooks and crannies. If you are right, we will do with them whatever we want. We listened to the conversation and our hearts stopped. We were certain our end was near.

The local boy went upstairs and looked here and there. He did not find us. His friend was angry with him and said: this is how you check, you donkey-head? Take a rake and poke away with it. If it is covered in blood when you remove it, this will be a sign that living people are here.

The murderer listened to the instructions and went up to the attic with a rake. Fortunately, the rake only poked my boot and not any other part of my body. This is how we were saved from the evil man.

The Germans ordered all residents to move to the village of Rokinia since in Brishtseh they were resettling Folksdeutch. Our situation was dire. The guard told us that he could not take us because he was afraid for his own life. He said we should simply join the caravan and mix among the people. We arrived in Rokinia and we hid in the first barn we found. The guard promised to bring us food in the evening. Five days passed by and he did not appear.

When all hope was lost, we went out and gathered some snow to satisfy our thirst and break our hunger.

Finally, the guard came and told us he could not hide us in his house because his Antisemitic neighbor would inform about us to the police. He advised us to go to the fields, dig a hole in a haystack and hide there.

In the meantime, my girlfriend left me and went to search the for her nanny's house. She had worked for her parents for many years. I was left all alone in this menacing world. Everywhere someone was looking to kill me. In the middle of the night I went to the haystack. Dogs attacked me.

[Page 467]

They almost tore me to pieces. I was afraid to say anything because I did not want to be overheard. I fell into a hole as I was running. It was January 1943.

I tried very hard to create an opening in the haystack to be able to hide my entire body. I finally fell asleep with my head hanging out of the haystack. In the morning, the guard came and was surprised to see me still alive because I was visible. He brought me bread and a bottle of milk. He told me that at night there are groups of Ukrainian police officers circulating there. It must have been "Christ" that saved me because I am holy. For that reason, he must guard and save me.

I will never forget what this man, this non-Jew did for me. If there is a God in heaven, he must allow Boyko into heaven among other good people.

This is what happened: During the time of the Soviets, there was, in Rokinia, a young Russian girl from Kiev, 17 years old, who was a teacher. Her name was Evgeniya Botovits. When the Red Army retreated, she escaped and left all her documents behind.

Boyko found out about the documents and he scoured the entire village to find them. He put his life in danger for doing it. When I received the birth certificate of this young woman, I became Evgeniya Botovits.

Now, my dear girl, said Boyko, everything is open to you. No one will touch you. He wrapped a scarf around me- one that the local girls would wear and I became one of them. I walked aimlessly on the roads. I planned on returning to Persefa, but I had to pass a bridge guarded by German police. I came to the village of Michaelovka and I knocked on the door of one of the farmers. I asked if anyone needed a shepherd for the cows.

I was employed on one of the farms, but my skinny body was my undoing. The Ukrainians who worked with me suspected that something was wrong with me. They joked and said I was either a princess or I was sick. Finally, they said I must be Jewish.

One evening, a messenger came from the farm to inform me that the manager wanted to see me. The manager was known as a hard man. He was a Folksdeutch. I felt in my heart that the end was near. I was prepared for a certain death.

The manager asked me who and what I was. I replied that I was Russian, born in Kiev where my parents still resided. I showed him all the documents. My name is Evgeniya Botovits. He said, in a sarcastic tone: the voice is that of a Soviet girl, but I am certain you are one of those who are not allowed to be around here. The hint was quite clear.

[Page 468]

The manager continued: I will give you a letter to my elderly mother who lives in the village of Demitrovka. She is looking for a maid and you will remain there.

I came to his elderly mother and the woman was surprised that her son sent her a maid. She did not need any help. However, since her son sent me, she could not fire me without any reason and she would send me to her neighbor.

That is what happened: I worked for the neighbor and I milked 8 cows daily. I worked in the fields, I baked bread. I became a professional farm worker.

One day I went to the barn to take hay for the horses and I saw a Jew hiding there. I calmed him down and told him that, I, too, was Jewish and that I would take care of his food. When my boss found out that a Jew was hiding on his premises, he threatened him with a pistol and told to leave immediately.

Two weeks later the Jew reappeared and told me that this time he did not come to hide, but he came to save me. He was hiding in a house of Seventh Day Adventists and he heard that everyone knew that I was Jewish. I was to leave the village because I was in danger.

I went to the neighbor and told him I wanted to work somewhere else and perhaps he knew of an opening. He told me his daughter was married to a German and she needed a maid. He took me to his daughter's house. On the way I recognized the road. When I reached the village, I realised that I had returned to Brishtseh. I had escaped from there.

I was liked by the Soltis and I worked for him. Once time, when the harvest was finished, he made a party and he invited all the important villagers. Among them was the German commander. It was in July 1943. My employer put on a white dress on me and I served the guests. At the end of the party, the commander informed Soltis that he wanted me to work for him because his maid was stealing.

The commander lived in a large palace. The village school was also located there. Behind it was a prison heavily guarded by the army. I was truly in the maw of the lion. My job was to clean the rooms, work in the kitchen and to bring food to the pigs.

It was vacation time in the school and I was temporarily housed in the room usually occupied by the teacher. He had gone to spend his vacation with his parents. When I entered the room, I became very frightened. On the wall there was a picture of the teacher. I had studied with him in Lutsk. I knew that when the teacher would return, he would inform my employer who and what I was. How would I escape death?

[Page 469]

I did not lose my cool. The commander received many Germans from Lutsk and I told them I was afraid to stay there because of the partisans in the area. They listened to me and took me to Lutsk. These Germans provided food to the German army. I was employed as a secretary.

I worked for them until January 1944. That is when the Red Army saved me from the maws of the lion.

[Pages 469-471]

My Escape from the Ghetto

by Lola Friedman-Ingber

Translated by Iddo Amit

Donated by Phil Friedman

The Germans were drafting Jewish girls for different labour projects. I was taken to work at the train station. There, I got to meet one of the Righteous Among the Nations, a Baptist by fate, Mr. Berilko[1]. The entire family were Baptists and were secretly visiting the Ghetto.

When I was banished from my labour, because I refused to do menial[2] work, the Berilkos suggested that I hide at their house until the matter subsided. Indeed, I hid with them for a whole month.

During one of the nights, Mr Berilko told me about the horrors happening at the Ghetto. The Germans were running wild, shooting indiscriminately, and forcefully dragging Jews to hard labour.

The Berilkos were worried that one of the Nazis would show up at their doorstep and catch me. Then, we will be all doomed. Therefore, they suggested that I return to the Ghetto and gave me a clear promise that they would prepare "Aryan" papers for me.

I simply cannot describe what I saw that night in the Ghetto. I was shocked and terrified. I saw them frantically digging bunkers – to escape from death. But no one was fooling themselves, they knew that death is close, certain, and help is beyond reach.

It is a wonder to me, and will always be a wonder that I was strong enough to watch these horrors. To hear the cries of those walking to their deaths and not to be petrified. People were falling into each other's arms, hugging, saying their farewells in cries that reached the heavens. They asked for forgiveness, said the Viduy prayer together out loud. Mothers were parting with their new-borns held in their arms. Brothers split from brothers, a man from his wife, a groom from his bride, teachers from students. The entire Ghetto was flowing with the stream of tears from the miserable and lost.

At dawn, the Ukrainian police stormed into the Ghetto, mercilessly murdering every bystander. Whoever could, ran into the bunker. A group of 20 men and women hid in our bunker, which was only 2 1/2 metres long and 1 ½ wide.

While sitting underground, we heard terrible cries. Those were the death cries of people, being dragged to the death camps.

This horror took two whole days. After that, it was quiet. The Ukrainians were looking for hiding places. When we heard the sounds of hammers our hearts nearly stopped. The murderers found the bunker next to ours and destroyed its inhabitants with the rage of preying animals.

We sat in the bunker for six weeks without going to the surface. When we learned that the Ukrainians were no longer conducting their nightly searches, we surfaced, to look for food in houses and in other bunkers. We received information about the fate of the Ghetto and the other bunkers. We learned that the Gubermans, who were all in one bunker, took poison during one of the nights.

In addition, they told us that the Germans had told doctors and other professional men that they were willing to let them live, but them alone, without their wives or children. Dr. Zyskind ZL[3] rejected the offer discussed. He would not buy his life back by paying with the life of his family.

We had a few moments of happiness in the bunker. It will sound strange to you, because where would this happiness come from? However, there were – when we heard the echoes of Soviet bombers, when we heard the thunder of the bombs carrying through the air. We regarded the bomber as our angels of salvation. SHFOCH CHAMATCHA[4] our lips formed without sound. The day of destruction of our murderers will soon come. The time for vengeance for the rivers of spilt blood will come. If there is a God in the heavens, he will dip his arrows in the blood of the unholy. The shovels will turn red with the blood of the damned, as our hands turned red from the blood of our pure children, and the blood for the poor mothers, who were shielding their babies with their bare hands.

I'm sitting in the bunker and thinking dreary thoughts. Has my day finally come? I am so young, and yet my feet are nearing their grave. Will they lead me tomorrow to the gallows for my final descent?

The life in the bunker is unbearable. There is no food and no water. We dig with our palms into the dry soil, to find moist dirt with which we can wet our lips. The moss is delicious for us. It calms us down, sooth us and quenches our thirst.

Our nerves are on end. We have taken the decision to get out of the bunker, no matter what. We are facing our doom no matter what we do. What would be the point of prolonging our dying?

The Ghetto is surrounded with a wooden fence from all sides. Above it, a barb wire. On the riverside, there are only barb wires. A wire cutter was our only weapon. We decided to cut the wires, cross the river and escape.

We waited for a dark, rainy night. But as if to spite us, the nights were clear and bright. One dark night, we left the bunker and were faced with a horrific sight: the Ghetto was deserted. Destroyed. The silence was heavy. The doors were broken, the houses stood in ruins – there was anxiety in the air.

We crawled towards the shovels and waited for the guards to leave. When we started cutting the wires, some gunshots were heard, aimed at us. Fortunately, they missed us. For safety, we lingered for two hours. We crossed the river at its shallowest point and found shelter at one of the ruins in Ludimir Street. We were torn, tired and hungry. The next morning, we unfortunately discovered that the ruins were being used as a play area for Ukrainian kids. When they saw us, the threatened to reveal our hiding place to the Ukrainian police. We had one guy with us who knew the kids, and he calmed them down.

I started walking to the Berilkos. It was 8AM. I dressed up as a Christian girl and put a sweater around my face, as if my teeth were aching and I was headed to the dentist.

The road was very dangerous. I had to cross the entire Ghetto and be careful of the Ukrainian police. I managed to safely reach the Berlikos on Lutzke Street, and their happiness knew no bounds. They were sure I had been executed.

The papers were ready. The Berlikos gave me a train ticket to Kiev, where they had relatives. I changed my clothes and went out to catch the train. The situation outside was still very delicate. Mrs. Berliko walked me to the train leaving for Kiev. I said my goodbyes to this wonderful woman, found my seat on the train car, and I was saved.

Translator's Footnotes:

1. Originally ברילקו, I am not sure about spelling here.
2. Contemptible work? I assume it means something to do with the lavatory.
3. The late Dr Zyskind – literally "blessed his memory."
4. A sentence from the Passover Hagada. I'm not sure how to properly translate it. Literally, "pour your rage on the gentiles."

[Page 472]

I Struggled With Death…

by Sima Pantorin-Reichstol

Translated by Ala Gamulka

Several days before the final and total elimination of the second ghetto in town- beginning on July 22, 1942- I arrived in the German "cantine". It was located in the house of Dr. Vitman. I had worked there as a laborer and I found the gate locked. My heart was pounding and I feared the worst… I had no choice but to return to the ghetto. There I found my family members who had been moved from the first ghetto in the "sands". They were upset and depressed, crowded together, afraid and waiting with despair for the tragic end to all the holy ones. The latter were awaiting their preordained fate. We tried to find a solution to our predicament and, like many other inhabitants of the ghetto, we decided to build a bunker under the house. We were hoping to escape immediate extermination. Perhaps, who knows? Perhaps G-d will take pity on us…

In the meantime, I joined the laborers who had been transferred from the first ghetto. We dug out potatoes in the fields across from Monopoliova Street. That day, when I was in the fields, a young woman with her younger brother approached me and begged me to give them some potatoes as hunger had truly seized them. I realized, from her speech and her looks that she was Russian. I wondered about her and I asked how they came to be here. She explained that she was in the Labor Camp staffed by Russians. They had been brought to Germany to work and were sent back with those who were unable to work and who were to be exterminated. She wanted to run away from here as she did not wish to die with the Jews…

Our bunker (in the house of Jezembecher), was ready and was well camouflaged. We: my husband Leibel Stock, our ten-year old daughter, Hela, my mother, Pessel, my brothers: Shmuel Reichstol, his wife and their two children; David Reichstol, his wife and daughter, Dr. Vidra's wife and another 20 people. We went down into our underground "residence" and we lived there in constant fear knowing we were unable to stop the terrible fate that awaited all of us.

Above our heads we heard the footsteps and the unruly yelling of the Germans and their helpers- the Ukrainian police. They had come to exterminate the ghetto completely. It was dangerous to go outside to obtain bread and water. Sometimes it was impossible. My brother Shmuel's young boy became quite ill and was dying. He begged for water, but there was none in the bunker- not even enough to wet his lips. I could not stand the suffering of this child and I decided to find water for him, no matter what would happen to me. I got up, took the pail and stole in the dark towards the wire fences. The fences designated the borders of the ghetto. I pumped water from the well and I tried to go back. At that moment an armed policeman loomed in my path.

[Page 473]

I saw certain death facing me. My heart stopped. My will to live was very strong. At that moment I remembered meeting the Russian woman in the fields. A great idea popped into my head. "Leave me alone"- it was not my usual voice- "I am Russian. I lost my way from the Russian labor camp and now I am trying to get back. I don't want to die here". The policeman, who must have been Russian, stared at me and lowered his gun. "Fine, if you are Russian, the road is open to you. I can't help you right now because the camp is surrounded by the Germans. Run away and hide and tomorrow come back here. I may be able to help you." He watched to see which way I would go to hide. I did not know if I could trust him. Perhaps he was just misleading me. I was confused, but I knew I could not go back to the bunker and expose my dear family and friends.

I began to run and a little further I found a destroyed house. I went inside and hid under the sagging boards. I lay there for a night and a day holding my breath. Through the cracks I could see the Germans and the Ukrainians running like wild animals with their guns drawn. They were searching for bunkers and planning to exterminate anyone they found there. The houses had been broken into and the belongings of the Jews had been stolen.

My hunger was really bothering me. I thought to myself: in any case, I am doomed to die. Let me try my luck. In the dark of night, I came out of my hiding place and I came closer to the area where I had pumped water the previous day. With inhuman strength I began to dig with my fingers under the wire fence until I was able to make a hole. I pushed my head through it and I somehow managed to drag the rest of my body. My dress was torn and my entire body was hurt and cut from head to toe. However, I did not feel any pain. I was simply petrified when I saw the same policeman marching with his drawn gun. To my great surprise I discovered that he was sincere. He recognized me and allowed me to escape.

I began to run with any strength I still possessed towards Monopoliova Street- along the columns-. Fortunately, I did not meet anyone until I reached the small wood near the Polish section. There I found a pile of straw. I put my head in it and I fell into a deep sleep. I woke up in the dark of night in the middle of a scary nightmare: My late father came and pushed me off the pile of straw…

I regained my strength and wiped the blood of my injuries. In the morning I arrived in the home of my Polish friend Lussya. We had worked together in the cantine and I had left some of my clothes with her before we went into the ghetto. In them I had hidden my savings. When she saw me, she glared at me and said: "You, too, are alive?" She pretended to feel my sorrow and threw to me one of her simple dresses (this actually helped me to save myself). She quickly locked me in and she left the house.

[Page 474]

I saw through her evil scheme. I immediately climbed to the attic and I hid among the discarded pieces. Soon the Ukrainian policemen arrived. However, when they found the front door locked, they believed the neighbors who asserted that there was no one inside and that the "conniving" Polish woman had led them astray.

When Lussya returned home she was again surprised that I was still alive. I chose the right moment and I escaped from the house. I went to the Kushar area dressed as one of them.

In the Kushar area I roamed the streets and many of the residents, mainly Poles, believed the story I told them. (Even I began to believe it…). I was a deserter from the Russian labor camp. They would give me bread in exchange for work in their homes. However, the Ukrainians mostly looked at me with evil and examining eyes. They would whisper: "Perhaps she is a jewess?" Another would add more remarks and the rumors would change from ear to ear. It did not take long for the Police commander to come and arrest me. He questioned me about my name, my family, where from I came from… He threatened me that if he would not find my name in the list of Russian labor camp workers he would cut me into pieces. I stood my ground in spite of the threats and beatings during the inquiry. They kept me in jail for two days. When I was freed, I had to crawl on all fours. My successful improvisation and my strong stand finally convinced the murderous commander. He gave me a note saying that "Anastasia Ivanovna Kavali" from the Russian labor camp was allowed to remain in the village. I was offered a job in the home of Roman Semeniuk. He and his wife were elderly and needed workers on their farm. I began a new life. I learned and was able to do all jobs related to the farm. I milked the cows when the milk would freeze and I was bare-footed in the snow… (My bosses had figured that I did not need shoes…). I carried the milk in jugs to town (12 k"m away)- together with the other young women and I sold the milk in homes. When I went to the house of Prozhmuvsky, the pharmacist, (we had left some of our belongings there), his daughter recognized me and was kind enough not to denounce me to the authorities. She paid me with items that we had left with her. I brought the item to my employers and they thought very highly of me.

This life continued until the spring of 1943. I worked very hard. Even the near past seemed distant and clouded over… Sometimes I thought I was really the Soviet Anastasia. However, the war was swirling around me and there was great danger at every step.

[Page 475]

My instincts did not allow me to believe I was safe. The dim hope that I would make it to the end of the war and still find someone alive in my family gave me the will and the strength to suffer in silence and to manage my bitter fate.

In the summer of 1943, the Russians advanced to Kovel and there were fierce battles. The front changed constantly and there was great tension. At the same time the Ukrainians wanted autonomy and they revolted against their German lords. There were battles between Bulbuvtzis and the Germans and, at the same time there were massacres of Russians and the wives of the Russian officers. Again, I was in danger from the Ukrainians as a Russian. One of my Russian acquaintances in the village offered me a secret job with the Ukrainian partisans in the forests near Kovel. I remembered everything I had gone through and what I had seen in the ghetto. My heart was full of revenge. After some hesitation, I accepted the spying role for the partisans. I used my daily visits in town as a milkmaid. I gathered all possible information and I gave it to the partisans. The Ukrainians began to suspect me and one of them began to follow me and to bother me. I informed the partisans of this event. They did not hesitate and one night they came to his room and killed him.

All the village people, the neighbors, came to the house of the victim and paid their condolences. They crossed themselves and cried. I, too, tried to come and I even crossed myself. However, I could not cry…This was noticed by others…

The following day two Gestapo men came- an officer and a soldier and they began to question me. The officer decided that I should be killed, but the soldier was against it. He did not think that there was enough proof as to my guilt. The officer took out his pistol and aimed at my heart…

This was the second time I faced certain death. At that moment a strange thing happened: the soldier pushed the officer's armed hand and the pistol fell down. They began to fight. My employers intervened and they were able to make peace. Roman Semeniuk, my employer, brought drinks. I avoided death again.

However, the suspicion of my cooperation with the partisans did its deed and the Bulbuvtzis declared, in secret, a death sentence on me. My elderly employer who really liked me while I was in his house, was afraid of my fate. He quickly prepared a hiding place under the standing grain in his field. I spent two months lying there and the old man provided me with bread and water. The spot was tight, suffocating and damp. I had enough and I decided to leave my hiding place.

[Page 476]

Two days later a couple of Bulbuvtzis arrived and took me out. They stood me next to the wall of the barn, lit cigarettes and asked me in an evil tone: "How do I want to kill you, with a pistol or a gun?" This was the third time I faced certain death. I did not believe that I would escape this time. I truly did not want to see death. I waited for the right moment when they- so confident- looked to the side and I jumped with all my might to the back of the barn. I began to run. I was certain they would shoot me and kill me and my troubles will come to an end. However, fate intervened. When I began to run, I immediately fell into a deep cache of potatoes. I landed inside the straw covering the potatoes. I could not be seen. I heard shots above my head. My tormentors went in the other direction. I stayed in that cache until night fell and it was quiet. I climbed out and left the village. I ran non-stop until I reached the forest. There I found the commander of the partisans and I begged him to let me join their unit. However, the commander convinced me that I was more useful to them on the outside than inside. He furnished me with a deck of cards and sent me to the various villages as a fortune teller. I began to wander among the villages again. I told fortunes and I found information for the partisans. When I reached the village, I discovered that the Germans had surrounded the forest and eliminated most of the partisans.

On July 22, 1944 the Russians came. I left the village and returned to town. It is difficult to describe my feelings when I saw the complete destruction of the town. There were only some piles of stones where the houses had stood. They looked like gravestones. There was so much ruin and no people…I wandered among the remnants of the ghetto. I looked for a sign of my family. I found nothing. My strength left me. The strong will to live that had kept me going until now dissipated. I believed that I had no reason to stay alive.

At the same time refugees arrived in Kowel. Among them were Shieke Goldstein and Pinhas Pantorin. Their friendship helped. I remembered my brothers in Russia. I was offered a job and thus I returned to normal human life.

* * *

The tragic death of Ruth (Rusia) Dashevsky z" l

I heard about the tragic death of Ruth (Rusia) Dashevsky from Pinhas Pantorin. She had escaped to the Soviet Union at the beginning of the war. She worked as a veterinarian in central Asia. In 1944 Pinhas met her in Alma Ata. They spent three days together. Rusia told him of her wish to return to Kowel. Pinhas was then on his way back and he promised to help her. When I heard about it, I immediately wrote her a letter describing the horrible destruction. Rusia was not scared by m descriptions and she replied that in spite of everything she truly wished to return. She wanted to live in Kowel even among the ruins. I contacted the mayor and he offered her a job as a veterinarian. In November 1944, a woman came to my house and told me that Rusia and her mother had arrived in Kowel and were on a freight train.

Pinhas harnessed his horses and we drove to welcome them. When we arrived at the train, we saw a horrible scene. Rusia was lying in the wagon on a straw mat. She was very skinny, filthy and burning with fever. She could not even speak. Her mother was sitting next to her and told me that Rusia had contacted Typhus on the road. They wanted to hospitalize her in Kiev and she refused. She wanted to be back in Kowel. We immediately contacted the authorities and asked for her to be admitted to the hospital. Perhaps we could still save her. Rusia went to the hospital in Liuvitov.

When she was taken down from the train and placed on the cart, she opened her eyes. After a serious attempt she said: "Sima, Petya, why are you trying so hard? Everything is lost. It is too late. I am dying. Where are you taking me? "These were the last words of Rusia. She died the next day in the hospital in Liuvitov. She was buried there.

When I arrived at the hospital with Pinhas to find out about her condition, we found out from the doctor, to our great sorrow, that she had died and had been buried. Rusia had a ring and her mother gave me her ring as a memento. I would thus remember my dear friend until my dying days.

[Page 478]

How was I saved from Destruction?

by Miriam Goldstein

Translated by Selwyn Rose

Brukhovychi, not far from Holoby, in a small house, surrounded by cherry-trees that seemed from a distance to bury the entire estate – four Jewish children were hidden: me, Leah Katz, her brother and their cousin, a little girl of three, Bilha.

It was difficult to understand why the old Polish couple – Jakob and his wife Kaczyna endangered themselves and hid us for two years in their home. He, a strict Catholic, believed perhaps that the four sinful souls had been sent to him by Heaven in order to convert them to the covenant of Jesus. His wife Kaczyna had mixed feelings: worldliness, mysticism, faith and superstition were all mixed-up together inside her. Perhaps she was bewitched by the money that we offered her for our safety would give her the possibility of freeing herself of her internal pressures or perhaps it was the support and respect that she acquired for the Jews that she had served as a maid or home-help before the war. She saw saving the children of the Jews as an act of heroism and believed it would bring her a reward. She often repeated that it was desirable to save more Jewish souls and her favorite expression was: "I'm likely to go to the gallows for one – why not for twenty!" How her reward would come to her, she didn't know, neither did we. One thing we all believed during these terrible days of hunger, cold and fear, that eventually it will come to an end. But when?... It was spring 1943. We were hidden in a ramshackle structure that served as a barn, silo, cow-shed and pig-sty. The roof was rickety and the pillars supported both the walls and the roof.

In one of the corners of the barn, where the cows stood, we dug a trench and covered it with hay and dung. The trench had been made with such precision that even the experienced Ukrainian murderers were unable to detect it. (By the way – we prepared other trenches for ourselves in the farm-yard just in case we should ever need them). A spring day… Daylight outside, quiet, trees are budding. The serenity of spring penetrated our own beings and awakened within us a feeling of nostalgia and the hope for freedom, for a tranquil normal life. Perhaps this spring will bring us redemption? The circumstances seem to indicate that during this period the search for Jews in order to execute them has somewhat relaxed. Hitler's wild animals performed their work well. The important thing was that no one saw us and no one informed on us to the Germans and Ukrainians. The Ukrainian murderers wandered around about us like dogs and never missed the opportunity to enjoy murdering a Jew. We were standing along the side of the barn looking out through the chinks and were happy to see people in front of us although at that same moment we forgot that more than one of this people could easily be our killers. At that moment there appeared in the field ahead of us, at about 30 meters away, 4 or 5 Ukrainians armed with rifles loaded and ready to fire.

[Page 479]

Like lightning. frightened and petrified, we scampered into our trench from where we could hear their shouts: "Ha!! Jews' shoes; where are the Jews?" We heard their boots passing to-and-fro above us running around, climbing on the roof, standing almost next to us, we actually heard their breathing…the noise and confusion continued. The dog barked incessantly. Suddenly everything stopped and went deathly still and quiet…what can have happened? It is hard to describe what we felt then. We understood that these were likely our last moments… we clung to each other and held our breath. I cannot know exactly what my brother's feelings were but I, even at the moment of greatest danger, if only a wisp or handful of hay separated us – I held stubbornly to the thought: "I must survive." I had learned by heart the words: "The Lord will give strength to His people; the Lord will bless His people with peace!" Other prayers I knew not. Neither did my little cousin Bilha but she learned from me these same words and repeated them in times of danger.

We didn't move from our hiding-place, and waited…How long we sat there, threatened with death, in our damp trench, along with frogs and other vermin it is hard to say. For us it seemed like forever. We were certain that they had taken the old Polish couple somewhere. Perhaps shot them on the spot…

Suddenly the silence was broken by the dog barking. This time it was not a threatening bark like the previous one but more of a murmur of satisfaction suggesting a person known to him. (In the time that we had been on the farm, we had learned to distinguish between the dog's different barks). We felt that something had happened in the yard… "Thank G-d, they've gone." Suddenly we heard the happy voice of Galyankova. With her special sense of humor she told us what had happened: When the Ukrainian hooligans entered the animal enclosure they immediately sensed that there were people there. They found a pair of shoes on the ground (we mostly went bare-foot), a few bowls and spoons that had been forgotten. In fact they were searching for a Jewish man who was wearing a belt with a money-belt who had escaped from them. They were saying in the neighborhood that he was hiding-out at the Galyanovka farm. Kaczyna was unfazed. She found a reasonable explanation for every situation. "All the items belong to my daughter-in-law and her children who are afraid to stay in their house because it is near to the Germans." The truth was that the Poles were afraid of the Ukrainian hooligans and most of them had left their farms and gone to live in Holoby.

The situation then was terrible for us as well as for our saviors. The hooligans demanded from the Galyanovka family to bring out the Jews they were hiding or their blood would be on their won heads. Galyanovka understood that even if she surrendered us it wouldn't save them and she stubbornly insisted that it was not possible that she would hide Jews because she was so poor that she didn't have enough to feed themselves. The hooligans turned the house upside down but found nothing. Then they commanded the old man Jakob to dig a grave for himself. That broke their spirit. Jakob took a shovel in his trembling hands and began begging the murderers to allow him to go into the house and get his Missal – he wanted to pray before he died. That saved them. The murderers saw it as proof of the honesty of the old couple and released them. Before they went the hooligan promised the couple that if the Jew, who wasn't there now, was later found there, all of them will be killed.

After all that we had to leave Brukhovychi. We wandered around from place to place around the village of Nowyzishel(?). Hungry, exhausted, hunted and desperate, expecting every minute to be killed…When it was winter we returned to the old Polish couple and there we stayed until Kovel was liberated by the Red Army in March 1944. Thus were we saved from death.

[Page 483]

Kovel in Its Destruction

Glorified and Sanctified

bt Yaacov Teitleker

Translated by Ala Gamulka

Glorified and Sanctified Be God's Great Name… Glorified and Sanctified, in martyrdom, may be the names of the multitude of our brothers and sisters, fathers and mothers, sons and daughters, the elderly and the babies, our relatives and friends who were murdered and slaughtered, strangled and burned, tortured and raped- no longer with us- by profane Nazi villains. They were innocents who had done no wrong… throughout the world which He has created according to his will.

This world was created by God and we do not understand it. Wild beasts of the forest and of the human race tore, with their teeth and sharp nails, our dear goslings. We lost them forever.

May he establish his kingdom, bring redemption and Messiah…

They did not merit to see, with their own eyes, the Return to Zion, the beginning of redemption and the establishment of our state. This is what they had hoped for, prayed morning and night for and were killed for today.

Speedily and soon… Their dream, our dream has been realised in full in our time as they were eliminated from earth.

In your lifetime and during your days and within the life of the entire house of Israel… the cruel and horrible fate of our exile caused us to pay such a steep price for our historic rights. In the peaceful lifetime of those who were taken from us – six million souls were exterminated from the mournful house of Israel.

May there be abundant peace from heaven…

Lie in peace wherever you are and may your souls be lifted by the divine presence with other pure and saintly ones. They were sacrificed on the altar of the nation and they will be included in the eternal life of Israel.

He who creates peace in his celestial heights… and includes peace in the heavens- he will give us strength and courage and he will envelop us with serenity. We have suffered immensely and our hearts are hurting. We must delve deeply into the story of the Holocaust and teach future generations. They must know and remember what the Amaleks had done to our generation. This must not be forgotten! It must be remembered forever!

[Page 484]

The Bells Rang

by Pinhas Drori

Translated by Ala Gamulka

The bells rang, my hope did not reply…
In a parade of dead people, she marches…
My nation is also part of this parade. Its flags are the injuries.
He always walks
And returns…

The bells rang and announced victory-
Shadows listened to the sighs of the bell.
The bells rang forgotten sounds
Blood poured on the flowers.

The bells rang and the canon stopped.
In the abyss and the deep mire, forgotten man
Arose and searched for the celebration
In the eyes of his brother who was killed yesterday.

The bells rang: for whom and why?
Will love come down to the valley of hate
Will it come at dawn to welcome the day with light?

The bells rang for me, too,
They thundered.
Waves and waves of despair came over me
I remember you, mother, at night
And I cried in the dark corner

As the bells rang.

[Page 485]

Writings on the Wall

by Shlomo Perlmutter

Translated by Ala Gamulka

Our beloved, 20 000 Jews of Kovel, men, women and children, left behind a mass grave in the village of Bakhava near our town. Also, there were thousands of writings on the walls of the Great synagogue which served as the last collection place before they were exterminated. There are also some stories…

I was able to copy some of the writings and they are listed here. Some additional facts: towards the end of summer in 1944, a few months before the area was liberated by the Red Army, I managed to come to the town which only had about six Jews. This was no longer Kovel, our hometown always full of life, as we had known it. The towers of the destroyed customs house were lying on the ground. I immediately understood the extent of damage and ruin. I came off the tracks on Kolyova Street- it was partially destroyed. I made my way among the broken-down houses and reached the center of town. My heart was full of strange feelings.

Seeing the upheaval and the emptiness caused me to feel revenge. I was pleased that not only our beloved had suffered, but the Polish and Ukrainian residents had lost their homes as well.

In the "Sands" I did not see one living person. There were abandoned houses, burned bricks, broken pieces of furniture. The grass growing on the side of the road dimmed its color.

The Orphaned Great Synagogue

[Page 486]

The storm here must have been horrible and the quiet that followed was awful.

Near the temporary wooden bridge that connected the "sands" with the "town", I looked at the ruins of the ghetto, across from the Great Synagogue that was still standing and up to the cemetery…

Here I met the first survivors who took me to their homes. The only Jewish home in Kovel where about six mourners and orphans from the town and its surroundings were living.

Afterwards we went to the synagogue which our beloved had turned, before their death, into a holy of holies. Hundreds and thousands of writings were etched on its white walls. Scores of Hebrew and foreign letters were drawn on them. Letters written in pencil, ordinary and unsharpened, in colored pencils, with pen and ink and some even scratched with finger nails. These were written by merchants, high school students, housewives, scholars and Hassidim, pioneers and the assimilated. They all wrote and they all wished to have their memory preserved.

Among the many writings done by our beloved during their last moments of life, stood out an odd one that was done in an unintelligible language on the East wall near the Holy Ark. Its composer had obviously spent much effort to do it with his finger nails in the hard wall. It shouted out of terrible pain and was noticed immediately. The composer worked hard to write it as high as possible and I had difficulty copying it. It said:" Here live the dead ones. Their blood cries for help in their sentence to death". I looked at this several times and when I finally understood, I was unable to take my eyes off it. There were dried blood stains near the writing. Even after several years the stains did not fade and this left in me an even deeper appreciation of the terrible events that had taken place here.

Scores of souls were felt and they filled the deserted room. They pressed for a trial. I became one with these souls and I listened to their whispers…

I sat in the synagogue for many hours. I walked from wall to wall, from one memorial to another. A great dread came upon me when I attempted to copy the writings.

I was able to copy only some of the writings. I believed that I would still return a few times and I would be able to complete the job. However, we soon were told that the walls of the synagogue had been painted over and this is how the writings disappeared forever. These writings had been left to us by our dearly beloved.

[Page 487]

Notes in Hebrew by Our Loved Ones

Translated by Amy Samin

To those who come after us!

Remember these young souls:

Soroleh Y.
Kagan P.
Gibnet Y.

*

Zamir Yehoshua ben Moshe
15.9.1942

*

Remind those who come after us!
In another hour the pure blood of our people's youth will be spilled,
Blood as clean as the waters of the Sea of Galilee.
We demand vengeance! Cruel vengeance!

Yehuda Shechter

*

In eternal memory
The souls that fell in vain at the hands of the German murderers.

Ziskind Simcha, 18
Ziskind Miriam, 50

*

Frieda Stillerman daughter of
Yitzhak Marder 15.9.1942

*

In blood and fire Judah fell, in blood and fire Judah will arise. The Eternal One of Israel will not lie. 19.9.1942

Miriam Roizen

*

Earth, don't cover our blood,
Heavens, take our vengeance.

We are going to a cruel death together with all of Kovel at the hands of the cruel murderers.

Thursday, 14 Elul
Bluma, Ya'acov, David and Yehuda

[Page 488]

Sheindel Schwartz 27.8.1942.
David Eisenberg.
Leah Fish Pioneer Group.
Rahel Fogelman.

*

Toybitsh Hannah.
Toybitsh Baba 16.9.
Frishberg, Chaya, Berl.

*

Kasil Weiner
Chaya Frishberg, remnants of the Shomrim Group

*

I am twenty years old. Oy, the world around us is so beautiful. Why are they taking sending me down the drain; all that I am craves life. Have my final moments come? Vengeance! Avenge me, whoever reads my final wish.

(unsigned)

Notes in Yiddish by Our Loved Ones

Translated by Gloria Berkenstat Freund

Bloyweis Alter, 5.9.42 [September 5, 1942], died.

*

I was with Ratien; he asked me to come in a few days. Thus they caught me. Ymunache caught me.

S. Melnicer

*

Revenge!
Kanan Fayga at the murderer's hand.
Came from outside the ghetto.

[Page 489]

Yankl Giwant is here. Berl, too. We all fell into the hands of the murderers on Wednesday. 3.9.1942 [September 3, 1942]

*

Berl fell *Shabbos* the 5th of September.
His death was easy.

*

Dear parents, brother and sister!
I greet you. I am with Fayga Kanan. She is alone. We go to a more beautiful world, bravely.

Monday – 7.9.1942
[September 7, 1942]
Yankl – Fayga.

*

Alas, we wanted to live   Henikh

*

Nota

Fayga   Leah

Families
Taub
Perished
6.10.1942 [October 10, 1942]

Moshe

Perhaps   Peysi
                                                                You live – take revenge

*

Alas, I waited for you with Yankl for two days… The entire time I was with your brother, as with you. So good together. Motele, my heart! We leave the beautiful world. The blood should not be silent. We go to a Jewish state.

I kiss you. The entire family.

Fayga

[Page 490]

Chaya Rabiner Monday at night. Forgive me. I did not want to cause you pain. I could not do anything else.

*

Rusman Zakhariah Thursday the 2nd

*

Yehoshaya (Shaye) Frydman was director of the People's Kitchen. Perished Wednesday 24.8.1942 [August 24, 1942]. My son, Leibl, perished two months earlier. Also Uncle Yerukhem and Chana Finklsztajn and Malka perished.

Yehoshaya Frydman

May this be a *matzevah* [headstone]; perhaps my son will read this!

*

Kapczyk Mendl, Shimkha with his wife and children. 25.8.1942 [August 8, 1942]

*

Shlomo Granicz's son-in-law, Liberman was in the synagogue with his wife and child three o'clock at night. 25.8.1942 [August 25, 1942].

*

I, Yerukhem *ben* [son of] Reb Shlomo Ludmirer was here for five days in Tishrei [September or October], 1942. I ask you to say *Kaddish* [prayer for the dead], if no relatives remain.

*

Generation Druker!

I, Ahron Druker, of Krakow, found my death.

*

Forgive me!

Mama, you should know that I was caught when I went for water. If you are here remember your daughter, Yente Soyfer, who perished 14.9.1942 [September 14, 1942].

[Page 491]

I, Fayge Szwarc, was here in the synagogue for five days in Tishrei (September or October), 1942.

*

Yakov Lewertob perished 6.9.1942 (September 6, 1942).

*

Yakov Geler lost 9 Elul [22 August] 1942.

*

Cantor of the *Beis haMedrash*, Pruszanski, Shlomo *bar* [son of] Chaim-Moshe, son of Gitele, here in the synagogue. His wife, may her soul be bound up in the bond of everlasting life, 6 days in Elul 5702 [19 August 1942].

*

We wait here for death – Avraham *ben* [son of] Shmuel Rajcsztal, with his wife and child and Bila and her child 24.8.1942 [August 24, 1942].

*

So many dreadful scenes,
So many cruel pictures,
So much pain – without any word of protest!
Only tears - - -
No hand raised.
No clenched fist.
Only calls to God!

Leibl Sosne
22.8.1942 [August 22, 1942]

*

Josef and Gitl Rapaport 27.8.1942 [August 27, 1942].

*

We sit in the synagogue and wait for death.
Pesakh and Ester Tasgal
23 days in Elul

[Page 492]

In the course of 10 days, thousands of Jews were led out of the synagogue to slaughter – small and large, young and old; but the most terrible thing is this, that they went without a word of protest, like calves.

May the future generations remember this shameful death and -- disgrace.

*

Ben-Tzion Szer went to his death for nothing.
27.8.1942 [August 27, 1942]

*

B"H [*Borukh Hashem* – Blessed is God, meaning Thank God]
Chaim *bar* [son of] Shlomo Szwarc

*

Bar Chana
Bar Zelig
Ephraim Segal
Gitl Segal

*

Liebl Sasne!
They know that everyone was murdered. Now I go with my wife and children to death. Be healthy!

Your brother, Avraham

*

Dear Sister, who perhaps was saved and you will find yourself in the synagogue; read these, my last words. I find myself now in the synagogue before my death. Be lucky here and survive the bloody war; remember your sister.

Polye Fidlman

*

Sunday, I, Eidl Fiszbejn, was here.

*

Goldsztajn, Bet Sheva
Goldsztajn, Avraham
Goldsztajn, Borukh Leib (Butsye)
Goldsztajn, Mariam
    Perished on 28.8.1942 (September 28, 1942)

Yehoshayke! Take revenge for the blood of those who perished.

Brayndl and Avraham-Yitzhak Kazak were here on the 27th of Elul, 1942 [9 September].

[Page 493]

Notes in Polish by Our Loved Ones

Translated by Amy Samin

Roza, daughter of Hinoch died in a tragic manner. I fought, I wanted to live – in spite of the futility. My heart, my heart, goes out to my Liniosinka, for her sake I wanted to live, if only to see her. My sorrow is great.

*

[Page 494]

Dearest Andziulu! In just a few more moments we will be departing, my brother and I, for our eternal death. Should someone from our family remain alive – may they avenge our spilled blood.

*

Liuba Rozenszveig has ended his years on 30.8.1942. Avenge our blood!

*

Farewell, my beautiful world, in the last hour of my life. Your friend, Chana Avrech.

*

Perl Kleiner and her brother Yosef take their leave from everyone. 12.9.1942

*

Ehrlich, Rahel died in a tragic manner on 6.10.1942. For twenty days I suffered because I wanted to see my brother Shalom. It is hard for me to leave this world, but that is our destiny.

Ehrlich

*

I am going to the eternal silence. Sonia Melnicer.

*

The Sheva Goldstein family died a tragic death at the hands of the Hitlerists 12.9.1942.

*

[Page 495]

Yosef Apelboim! 12.9.1942 God, avenge us!

*

I will write one last time before my death. I don't know if any of the Jews will remain alive. Alas, I will not be the happy one.

*

Moszko and Tunik take their leave of everyone. 15.9.1942 The last Mohicans of the Barzilai and Tojbiczów families.

*

Bilah Grojser and her family were imprisoned and slaughtered 14.9.1942

*

I will rest in the common grave of the tortured with my best friends Sonia and Kuba Rojter, the easier for our common misfortune. 27.8 1942

*

The pure Jewish blood, may it drown all the Germans. Vengeance! Vengeance! May they be struck by lightning!

Yisrael Wajnsztejn

*

The Lencz family was killed 23.8.1942 and I write this in the last moments before they take us out to be killed.

*

Niura Rajber-Landau will die today. I so badly wanted to live! 23.8.1942

*

[Page 496]

Silence,
The murderers are coming.
Silence prevails in the world.
Listen to the sound of the hearts dreaming with all their might.
Listen to the sound of the hearts ceasing to beat.
Lord, let us take You in Your eternity
The murderers will pay, pay with their blood!!
How can I rejoice – if I am already in the grave?
But I wanted to be alive.
Their children will cut down the last to remain…
Another hour…another moment. . . . . .
I bid farewell to my beautiful world
Before I was able to know you…

Tania Arbeiter and all of her family. 23.8.1942

*

Pola Wydra. 23.8.1942

*

Innocent blood has been spilled. Golda Wajnsztejn 23.8.1942

*

Rahel, Belka, and Sonia Blucher died a tragic death. They met the fate of all the Jews: loss of life. 15.9.1942

*

[Page 497]

Ania Bokser and her mother Dusia,
Moshe Dunawiecki and his wife. 15.9.1942

*

Bora Rozenwald and his wife Lema were killed. 19.8.1942

*

Killed: Zelik, Fenia, Eliahu Rozenwald of Brisk, on the Bug River. 20.8.1942

*

Gedaliah! Avenge our innocent blood! Beba Milsztejn 23.8.1942

*

My dear Monik (Poliszuk)! Avenge the blood of your father, your brother, and your sister, who fell into the hands of the murderers. Remember! This must be your mission in life.

Fania - Feibel

*

Berensztejn, Yankel
Berensztejn, Hania
Berensztejn, Tema
Fell at the hands of the Germans.

*

The Fishbein family died with Pollack on 29.8.1942 Riva, Bela, Yisrael and Rahel.

*

[Page 498]

Avigdor Balter was imprisoned on 13.9.1942

*

Moshe, 45; Bela, 46; Manya, 13; Sza leave this world and everyone in it.

*

My dear sisters! We are not dying as others do, for our death comes at the hands of barbarians. We saved ourselves until 6.9.1942, more we were not able to do, for we were betrayed. Avenge our blood. Pray for us. Gittel Segal, born 1922, Ethel Segal, born 1924. Farewell. The fate of our parents is unknown to us. 7.9.1942

*

Here live the dead, crying out from their graves for justice. Benjamin Piteta

*

Adolph Rozencwaig 30.8.1942

*

Dear Yosef! Avenge us! – Dora, Amik, and Ziva Segal 12.11.1942

*

Fania Tannenboim and her children, Sioma and Pepa 12.11.1942

*

[Page 499]

Remember What Amalek Did to Thee

by Pinhas Pantorin

Translated by Ala Gamulka

On July 7, 1944, I heard the announcement on the radio, long awaited by me, that Kovel had been liberated by the Red Army on that day.

On the day I received the news I was in central Asia, in a hospital where I was lying, seriously injured in battle.

It is difficult to say that the news stirred up my heart since I knew that all the Jews were buried in a common grave. However, I still was energized and I decided to travel to Kovel, the town of my birth.

I did not lose a minute and I immediately contacted the local authorities. As a medal-winning officer I was given a responsible position in Kovel.

I arrived, on a military train, the first Jew, to the burned town. It was on July 22, 1944.

For three years I dreamed and wished for this moment of returning home. However, the waiting and hope were in nought. My eyes saw something so horrible that it is difficult to describe it.

Reciting the Kaddish at the common grave

This was a town of the dead where killings had taken place. A town without any people still alive and without any houses, roads or sidewalks. Everywhere one looked one only saw fallen ruins, piles of stones and bricks.

The "town" had no remnant of street signs. There were ditches and defence positions. It was full of mines and there were signs "Danger! Mines!" everywhere.

I participated in many battles from Kiev to Stalingrad and back to Krakow. On the way I saw many ruined towns, but the destruction of Kovel was worse than that of Stalingrad.

Kovel was surrounded by the Red Army for three and a half months, but Hitler's henchmen had turned the town into an important defence location and they fought there to the end.

My first steps were directed to my home on Fabritchna Street, Number 4. Miraculously, the house still stood. From afar I saw that someone was living there. To my great sorrow, it was not my wife and son, but Polish peasants. I chased them out with a pistol in my hand.

From there I went to the cemetery on Ludomir Street to pay respects to my late father.

As I approached the cemetery, I met several peasants who warned me not to go inside since the entire area was mined.

During battles I was often in danger and I ignored the warnings. I went inside. I did not care if I remained alive or if I would die in an explosion.

The gate and the fence were dismantled. Inside the cemetery there was not even one tombstone standing. Everything was in ruins and the stones had disappeared.

I spent a long time in this holy place. It was as if I were speaking to the dead whose tombstones had been vandalized. I asked: why were you quiet? Why did you not take revenge on those who had done the destruction? Of course, these questions were quite rhetorical.

Some time later I found some of the tombstones in the yards of peasants. They were used as part of a sidewalk.

When I left the cemetery I found, on the right, near the gate, a common grave where the members of the "Jewish Police" and some of the Judenrat had been buried. It was estimated there were about 200 bodies there.

This is how my life began again in the ruined town. This was the town where I spent my childhood and where I grew up.

There were about 250 people in Kovel at the time. They were all Christians. Many of them, when they found out I was coming, left in the middle of the night. They were afraid of my revenge.

As much as possible, I tried to avenge the blood of our holy ones. Their cries of "Revenge!" echoed in my ears constantly. Their suffering was in front of my eyes.

I collected much evidence to accuse the Nazi helpers and I handed it in. They were mostly eliminated, according to my instructions.

I also participated in actions against nationalist Ukrainians- Benderovtzis. Even in 1944 they were a force to contend with in our area. The Benderovtzis were loyal assistants to the Germans. We had serious battles against them, with the help of Soviet units. We were in danger many times.

We found most of the common graves and we decided to put a fence around the two big cemeteries in Bakhava. The Soviet authorities helped us to obtain the necessary wood and wire. We collected some money among the Jews still in Kovel and we built the fence around the graves of our beloved.

In November 1944, while the fighting with the Germans was still on, we completed our task. The big cemetery was fenced in and a memorial stone was erected. The 40 Jews then living in Kovel, took part in the ceremony.

We very carefully collected the bones and heads strewn in the area.

In front of the common grave in Bakhava

We covered them with sand that was saturated with blood. It was red. Even the grass roots were red. In some places the sand was mixed with holy blood.

We recited Kaddish and after we prayed "El Maaleh Rachamim", we stood near the graves where our dear parents, wives, brothers, sisters and children had been buried.

We stood for a long time and we thought about the cruel deeds of the murderers.

I call upon all Jews, wherever they are:

Remember what the Nazi Amalek did to us!

[Page 502]

What I Saw and Heard During the City's Liberation

by Dr. Yakov Hasis

Translated by Amy Samin

The Terrifying Destruction

The fate of man is a strange thing. When I left Kovel for Moscow on the 16th of June 1941 to attend a conference for experts in the subject of lung diseases, I didn't give it much thought. My parting from my family and friends was that of someone who is going away for only ten days, with no special excitement. I would even say everything was completely normal. There was no perception of the impending Holocaust.

In 1943, when I was on the Kazakhstani prairie, it came to my attention that something dreadful was happening in the German-occupied areas. I read a great deal about the torture of the occupied population, about cold-blooded murder, about the flowing of rivers of blood, but I did not know, then, that the Jewish people had fallen into the hands of the beasts of Hitler, and were facing total annihilation.

With the advance of the Red Army, and with the liberation of the Volhynia region, my excitement grew. I believed that the authorities would remember me, and that one day I would receive a message to return to the liberated area, to the place to which I was tied with my broken, but hopeful, heartstrings.

The order was not long in coming. It arrived in April of 1944. I received a telegram from "*Galbesnofer*" (*galbani sanitarni otadil*) of the Ministry of Transportation's health services, telling me to set out for Rovno, which had been liberated from the Nazi occupation, and take part in establishing a health care institution in the field of tuberculosis.

In March of 1945 I set out once again, on a long and dangerous journey, but I knew that it was to my home I was going.

In Rovno I was overworked. I was the only professional doctor in the area, and I worked from 8 in the morning until 11 at night. There were many tuberculosis patients to be found there, mostly villagers, and in a neglected state.

[Page 503]

The question as to why they would neglect themselves instead of receiving appropriate medical treatment was answered with this horrifying reply: "Because the doctors were slaughtered." (As we know, most of the doctors in that region were Jews.)

In Rovno I met with a group of Jews, made up of just a few people, survivors who had remained alive because they fled to the forests and joined the partisans. A few had found a hiding place with peasants in the area. But those were only isolated instances. Most of them were sent to their deaths by the Nazis.

In Rovno I learned that in Manievich there were a number of sons of Kovel who had survived the great slaughter. I traveled there and found Bella Flaumenbaum and her small daughter, Shalom Donitch, and others. They described the great tragedy – the destruction of the first and second ghettoes. We didn't sleep a wink. All night long I listened to the description of the destruction of our town, of how our precious people were tortured, shot, and massacred. Full of worry and grief, I returned the next day to my work.

On the 8th of August my supervisor at work came to me and asked if I was of a mind to accompany him on the first train to Kovel, which had just been liberated.

I accepted willingly. We traveled by train, which consisted of an engine and only one car, and we reached Vatoroy Kovel.

Up to Holova, the road had been paved, because it had been in the hands of the Russians for a number of months. But as we approached Kovel, the road was littered with trenches, the killed, and minefields.

We reached the railway workshops, which had been completely destroyed. We walked along the paths, and everywhere we went we were warned not to veer off to the sides, because the whole area was sown with mines.

The whole area was covered with tall weeds. It was obvious that no one had set foot here in a very long time. The paths of Kovel were in mourning. As we walked along, we did not meet a single living soul. We reached the train station, which had once been bustling with life and had become a pile of ruins. The entire surrounding area was also destroyed. Via Satara Vakzalna Road we entered the center of town, which was also completely covered in weeds. I reached our house on Starzchika Street. The house was undamaged, but all of the furniture had been stolen. The house was empty – not a stick of furniture and not a single person was there. Next to the house I saw a trench. The Rubenstein houses opposite ours had been destroyed. Only the Finkelstein house remained whole. The few houses that remained resembled graves, because all who had once dwelled there had been wiped out.

I glanced at a group of Russian soldiers, who with the help of Nazi prisoners cleared the area of the landmines. I found small comfort in the sight of exploding mines, which pulverized the murderers.

I felt suffocated. I was appalled at the destruction and the emptiness. The language of man is too meager to relate all that my eyes beheld. I could not endure the grief that was in my heart, and after a few hours I returned to Rovno.

[Page 504]

The Horrors of Annihilation

After a few weeks, I returned to Kovel. I had been told that a few Jews had returned to the town – some from Russia and some from nearby hiding places. I met, among others, Pinchas Fantorine and Sima Reischtol. From them I learned of the annihilation, and of the places where the massacres took place. We traveled to the new cemetery, the place where they wiped out the last remaining remnants of the Jews of the city, who had survived the two big *aktions* [actions].

We saw knolls of earth. When we asked, "What is the meaning of these mounds of dirt?" they explained to us: "The groups of unfortunates who were brought to this place of death dug ditches with their own hands. Each group stood at the edge of the ditch, while behind them stood Ukrainians, Poles, and Nazis armed with submachine guns, who cut down every last one. Immediately after the murder of the first group, a second group was brought whose task it was to cover up the dead from the first group and to dig a ditch for themselves. Peasants from the area told us that many hours after the ditches had been covered in earth, they could hear the moans of the wounded struggling with the angel of death.

From there we went to Bachba to the largest mass grave. The place was deserted, except for the shepherds who grazed their sheep. We informed the peasants of the area not to dare to graze their sheep on the mass grave, or we would take revenge on them.

The Heroic Stand of the Teacher Yosef Avrech, may his blood be avenged

While I was in the city, I heard that Dr. Zavitska, a Polish woman about 50 years of age and who had been a known anti-Semite, had survived. I was told that she wished to see me.

I discovered her address, and we met. She was gravely ill, and a short time afterwards she died from a malignant tumor. In a voice choked with tears, she told me – as an eyewitness – of the annihilation. She described the involvement of the Ukrainians in the mass murder, and told me of the disgraceful role Dr. Yaborovski played in the slaughter.

But she wanted, in particular, to mention the greatness and heroism of the unfortunates in their last moments of life. Engraved in her memory was the appearance, full of Jewish national pride and remarkable courage, of the teacher, Yosef Avrech, may his blood be avenged. That Jew, said Dr. Zavitska, revealed supreme, exalted, and heroic spiritual strength and raised the morals of the Jews to new heights that daunted the hangmen. This tormented Jew, an amputee, whose prosthetic arm the murders had removed, walked proudly upright to his death.

According to her testimony, the Jews of the city walked proudly, adorned with a halo of courage, towards death.

[Page 505]

In this majestic parade towards annihilation, the eternal values of Judaism and the ethics of the people of Israel were revealed.

The Horrific Actions of Dr. Yaborovski, may he rot in hell

Dr. Yaborovski was considered, so to speak, to be a friend of the Jews. He was the only non-Jewish doctor to work in the Jewish hospital. However, "friend" in his case had the meaning: "God protect me from my friends"…When permission was given to the destroyer, the monster lying dormant deep within his Jesuit soul awoke.

His "fine actions" were described to me by Dr. Zavitska as these: since he was considered a friend, many Jews entrusted him with their wealth, in gold, money, and jewelry - until the fury should pass.

When the fighting ended and the city was liberated from the hands of the impure, a few of the depositors approached Dr. Yaborovski and asked that he return the valuables they had left in his care. But he ignored their claims and did not return anything to them. More than that, he heaped derision and scorn upon the Jews, abused them with curses and insults, and told the Jewish doctors, his colleagues: "For generations you ate our flesh, and sucked our blood like leeches. Now your time has come. Now an end is put to your vile people."

Dr. Yaborovski openly justified the Nazis' acts of annihilation.

Meetings with Kovel Doctors in Russia

At various times and occasions, I had the opportunity to meet with the Jewish doctors of our city, those who took their chances and were able to escape before the arrival of the Nazis, and thus were saved from the Holocaust.

Dr. Weitman: He was a senior physician, a specialist in dermatology. He worked in the Jewish hospital and was one of its managers. He lived in a private, two-story house, which stood next to the jail.

During the war, I met with him for the first time in Kiev, in 1941. It was in the morning, after the heavy bombing of the Darnytsia railway station in Kiev. Dr. Weitman had been drafted into the Russian Army and on his journey with the other draftees the convoy was bombed, claiming many victims.

When I met him, he was very upset. He had had a long night of wandering. Seizing the opportunity, I struck up a brief conversation with him. He didn't have much time, because he was hurrying to his unit, from which he had become separated.

In late 1944 I met him for a second time when I was in Rovno. On his way west, Dr. Weitman arrived in that city with his unit, and when he learned from the Jews he happened upon along his way that I was in Rovno, he asked to speak with me.

[Page 506]

It was one of my saddest duties to tell him of the devastation of Kovel, of the complete destruction of his house, and of his family - not a single one of whom had survived. As he listened, the doctor cried bitter tears like a small child. This meeting was also brief, for he was forced to head out to the front with his unit.

At our parting, I revealed to him that I was of a mind to cross the border and immigrate to the Land of Israel. Dr. Weitman was thrilled and grateful for this revelation, and said that he also wished to do the same even though it wasn't exactly the simplest thing to manage since he was afraid to desert the Russian Army.

I have not seen him since then. I heard that he had gone with his unit to the front in the direction of Czechoslovakia.

Dr. Chachnovich: He was a senior doctor in Kovel, a cultured man who was involved with people and active in public life. He was a specialist in internal medicine and pediatrics.

In 1941 I learned that he and his wife had left the city with the Russian Army, before the Nazis had arrived. They decided to leave Kovel because their only daughter had gone to relatives in the city of Rostov, in Russia. As far as I know, Dr. Chachnovich is still alive, and spent the war years living in Siberia.

Dr. Yosef Melamed: He was a young doctor, who completed his studies in 1937. He was drafted into the Russian Army and left Kovel before the onset of hostilities, leaving behind a wife and son.

In the Russian Army, he specialized as a surgeon and was appointed chief surgeon in the military hospital. In 1944, while I was in Rovno, Dr. Melamed and his hospital arrived in that city. We met and were together for a few months, until he received orders to move west with the hospital, following the advance of the Russian Army. I know that he remained alive and is working as a doctor in the Soviet Union.

Dr. Pinchas (Patia) Retnovisky: He was a young doctor. He was also certified as a doctor in 1937. When war broke out between Russia and Germany, he left the city with the Russian Army. At the beginning of 1945, he arrived in Rovno on his way to Kovel. He came to see me. All night long we talked about the city and its residents, about the mutual friends we had, and about their horrific end. I told him of my plan to move west and immigrate to the Land of Israel. He decided to remain in Russia. After some time he traveled to Kovel, to see with his own eyes the horrible destruction. Later, he returned to his unit which was camped in Belorussia and I never heard anything more of him.

I also heard of other young doctors from Kovel who were drafted into the Russian Army and were saved, including Dr. Grisha Varba and Dr. Weisberg.

[Page 507]

From the Scene of Destruction

by Dr. Mordechai Leiberson

Translated by Amy Samin

I left the city on 25 June 1941, a few days before the Nazi thugs invaded. The war broke out on the morning of 22 June 1941. An air of soul-deep depression enveloped all of the residents of the city, especially the Jewish ones.

Job-like tidings had already reached us from the Polish-German side of the occupation, on the other side of the Bug River, and the news sowed feelings of fear and embarrassment. However, although the Jews of the city sensed what was in store for them, they still did not muster the strength to rise up and flee for their lives, but instead looked ahead with fatalistic belief to what would come.

Only a few, some two to three hundred Jews, youth and younger people up to about 40 years of age, many of them bachelors, left the city and headed toward Russia, to the heart of an unknown land, with the hope surging within them that with the cessation of the fighting, and the passing of the rage, they would return to the city and find their families alive and well.

But things evolved in a completely different manner, and that which we did not dare to think of, rose up and became a horrific fact. The Holocaust had come. In 1942 – the year of the total destruction of the children of Israel, Poland and all of Europe kneeled and moaned under the boot of the Hitlerite beast.

And in the summer of 1942 the axe fell upon the sacred community of Kovel. Not a single survivor or a single remnant of our brothers and sisters remains there.

On 1 May 1945 I returned to Kovel and found our town completely destroyed. In April of 1945 I had been on my way from Moscow to Poland as a conscript of the Polish army, which was organizing in the area of Poland which had been liberated. My role was medical officer with a rank of lieutenant in the Polish Air Force.

When I arrived in Brisk-Litovsk, I deviated from the army's marching orders, because I longed to see our town. After a long and tiring journey, due to disruptions in the railway lines, I arrived at the central station of Kovel at three o'clock in the morning on the first of May, 1945. The train station once famous for its architectural beauty had been completely destroyed, and in its place stood miserable wooden huts.

At six o'clock in the morning I went down, gingerly, into the city. It is difficult to express in words what my eyes beheld. The city gave the impression of a large cemetery, although here and there appeared the form of a man. Ninety percent of the houses had been destroyed. Fierce fighting had raged in the city, and it had changed hands several times. It is easy to imagine what had been done to her by the aerial bombing and the shelling from canons on both sides.

[Page 508]

It was natural that my guiding instinct led me to my former home, the house I had lived in for 20 years, where I was raised and grew up, and where I spent the years of my childhood and adolescence. With my heart pounding and trembling deep in my soul, I approached Listopadova Street and searched for number 94, the number of our house. I did not find a single remnant of it, nor of any other houses, nearby or farther away. Rows of tumbled rocks and mounds of bricks on both sides of the street – this was the dismal picture of a street that had always been teeming with Jewish life - happy and cheerful, busy and worried.

Across from our house once lived the head of the community, Reb Shlomo Mendel of blessed memory, he and his large extended family. There remained not a single trace of his house, either, the life which had resided there extinguished. I continued on my way, glancing around me. Here once stood the bakery and home of Aharon Zilberstein of blessed memory. Now nothing remains of the house. This gloomy picture returned again and again the entire length of the street, until coming to the intersection of Listopadova and Toshovski Streets. I noted the ruins of the homes of the families Pomerantz, Goldover, Guttman, Yehezkel "Biliner", Freisant, Freed, and others.

I barely recognized Toshovski Street: mounds of rubble and ruin. Here once lived the Gasko, Pomerantz, Melamed, Gevirtz and many, many other families.

At the intersection of Jeromsky – Pilsudski – Poniatovsky Streets there was a public park square; within stood a stone monument with a Red Star at the top. In the center was a square of white marble engraved with the names of the officers and soldiers of the Red Army who fell in the city's liberation from the Nazis. On the first line was engraved the name of Colonel Margolit of Odessa, and next to that the names of several Jews who also fell in the liberation of the city.

I stood at attention and paid my last respects to those heroes of Israel, who fell in a foreign land defending the honor of the people of Israel, wherever they may be.

Across from that public park stood the ruins of the homes of the well-known, righteous families of the city: the Polishok brothers, Aharon Gitlis, the Projnesky family, Hershel Melamed, Ziskind (owner of the Sheert soap business), the Avraham Gonick family, Ashkenazi, and others.

I turned in the direction of Jeromsky Street – once called Folksall. At this street corner, which once was bordered by Nova-Kolioba Street, stood the ruins of the interior of the Trisk synagogue (der Trisker Shtiebel). Although the house was intact, on the inside all was plundered and destroyed. I had prayed in this synagogue with my parents, and all of the Jews in the area had prayed there, both on holy days and on weekdays. The habitual cantor was the head of the community, Reb Shlomo Mendel of blessed memory, here also prayed the judge of Kovel, Rabbi Moshe Asher; the man who blew the shofar during the High Holy Days was the ritual slaughterer, Reb Avraham Gevirtz of blessed memory. I entered the synagogue. The holy ark – looted and destroyed. The bookcases – ransacked and burnt. On the floor, there were rolled up pages from the holy books, though I did not find any pieces of parchment from the Torah scrolls. The yard was deserted and gloomy.

[Page 509]

On Nova-Kolioba Street I saw a few intact houses. The famous seminary had been destroyed, unlike the bathhouse next to it. I turned at the intersection of Warszawska, Lotska, Pomnikova, and Nova-Kolioba Streets. Here was once the hub of the city, and now – a cemetery. A few of the stone buildings remained, but of those which had been made of wood, not a vestige remained. The office buildings were destroyed and derelict; those that had remained in one piece were closed and locked with seven bolts. There was nothing left of the business center. At the intersection of Nova-Kolioba and Lotska Streets once stood the bookshop and stationery shop belonging to the Plott brothers of blessed memory. Near that was the commodities trading house of Leib Fish of blessed memory. A little further on – the Sheintop restaurant. At the intersection of Nova-Kolioba and Warszawska there had once been a shop selling musical instruments that had belonged to the Polishuk brothers of blessed memory, the restaurant of Kagan of blessed memory, the paint shop belonging to the Goldstein brothers of blessed memory (one of their brothers, the engineer Goldstein, was a graduate of the Tarbut Gymnasia in the Holy Land). Opposite was the photography studio belonging to the Sosnie brothers, the laundry of Rupa of blessed memory, and more. Further on, the business belonging to Mottel Lander of blessed memory, and a row of textile houses such as the one belonging to Moshe Gandler of blessed memory and others, the shoe stores once owned by Opoliner and Erlich of blessed memory, and the haberdashery (notions) of Gabi, Heri, and Goldman of blessed memory.

The municipality building on Warszawska Street remains intact, as does Friedlander's pharmacy. On Michkabitz Street the Meisky cinema is still whole, and on the day I visited the city a film was showing. Opposite, the house of the community leader, Reb Moshe Perl of blessed memory, was in ruins, as were the houses of the rest of the Jewish families on that street.

The post office had been destroyed, and the Russians had opened a temporary post office in the home of the Roitenberg family of blessed memory. The home of Yisrael Reichstol was in ruins. Dr. Weitman's home remained whole, although not a single member of the family was left.

On Michkabitz Street I met the one and only remaining family in the entire city. It was a widow and her two children. Her husband had been murdered in the forest by the Ukrainians. This woman was of the Bernholtz family, and her origins were in Kopiezow. She was one of the survivors of the forests.

On Pomnikova Street, where once had stood the Herzliya School, were mounds of debris. I moved on to the other central section of the city, along Lotska Street and to the intersection of Paberichena-Westro- Kolioba Streets. The same day, I met there Pinchas (Peta) Pantorin. He had come from Lvov to see the city. Their house had remained intact, as had the home of the Gelmans. Once, the Gelman courtyard had been the base for a chapter of *Hashomer Hazair*. How much life there was in that courtyard! How many hopes were spun there! That courtyard had bustled with the lives of wonderful Jewish youth, and now there was only desolation, destruction, and the silence of death. Indeed it was difficult, extremely difficult, this meeting with this horrible reality.

[Page 510]

Along Lotska Street the homes of Amarnik, Dr. Neimark, Avish, Veiger, and Zuperpin of blessed memory stood in ruins. The flour mill was partially demolished, and the branch of *Hehalutz* was destroyed. That place also reminded me of days past. For many years I belonged to that branch of *Hehalutz*. Here the finest Jewish youth of the city wove their dreams. Some of them were able to immigrate to the Holy Land and saw the fulfillment of their dreams, but most of them were buried forever in the huge common grave of the Jews of the city, in the pits of the village near the city.

I turned towards "downtown" along what was once Warszawska Street. At the intersection of Warszawska and Karoloba Bonah Streets most of the houses were completely destroyed, with two or three exceptions. On the corner, the homes of Geller and Perlmutter of blessed memory. Soviets were living there. The home of the late Dr. Zeskind had remained intact. The state *gymnasia* was in ruins, as was the high school for surveyors.

For me and for others of our city, that school was etched in our memories as a nest of anti-Semitic hooligans. It was from there that all of the rioters came during the disturbances that struck the city in the summer of 1929. That school was notoriously shameful, and so I "grieved" very little for the building and its occupants.

I reached the bridge over the Turia River. The concrete bridge had been destroyed. Next to it downstream was a miserable little wooden bridge, and the river itself had run dry – its waters diluted and with almost no trace remaining. The *Tarbut Gymnasia* building, once housed in the home of Varba of blessed memory, was a mound of debris.

The new and magnificent home of the *Tarbut Gymnasia* on Yoridika Street, which had been built in 1935, the place where I studied for many years, where I received both my Hebrew and my general education, had collapsed and was covered with rubble.

On the other bank of the Turia River there was considerably less destruction. On both sides of Warszawska Street there stood empty shops and businesses.

Those businesses had once belonged to respectable families who were part of the legend of the city up until the last moment of their lives, which were cut short with terrible cruelty, the likes of which had never been seen in any period, at any time, in human history.

In the home of the former miller, Zuckerman of blessed memory, I found a few Jewish youths, survivors of the Holocaust. They had been partisans. They came from the surrounding towns: Trisk, Retno, Kopichov, Macheib, and Malnitza. I fell into conversation with one of them. He had fled from the murder pit. His neck and skull were scarred from the bullets that had been fired at him. Through some miracle he remained alive, and in the night he fled for his life into the forest. They lingered in the city temporarily, for they were preparing to move on to Poland, and from there to Eretz Yisrael, but a problem with the appropriate documents had delayed them.

[Page 511]

From there – I went on to the great synagogue which had stood at the hub of that part of the city. It had remained intact, but everything inside had been stolen. The beautiful ark of the Covenant, which had been the glory of the Jewish community, had been smashed – all that remained were a few scraps of wooden openwork which were at too great a height for the hands of the unclean murderers to reach. The pulpit at the center of the synagogue had been destroyed. The bookcases, the pews, and the other furniture had all been stolen. As an eternal memorial, the names of hundreds remained on the walls of that holy place. They were the surnames of the martyrs of our community, which had been wiped off the face of the earth in 1942 – the surnames of our brothers and sisters, the flesh of our flesh and the bone of our bone – written in pencil, and in ink, and in their righteous blood. There were hundreds upon hundreds of the names of our dear and beloved ones, who passed through the synagogue on their final journey to the cemetery, the place where they were murdered in cold blood by the German murderers and their various assistants.

That same day, in the evening, I left Kovel, which had become a great wasteland. I left, and never returned.

On the Rubble

by Moshe Goodis

Translated by Ala Gamulka

After four years of wandering through greater Russia and after I fought the Nazis, I was fortunate to visit our ruined town.

A long train, filled with Russian soldiers, I among them, neared our town. About twenty kilometers before we reached it, I was engulfed with love and longing for my place of birth.

Here is the town of Kibertza and there is the village of Fraspa. In the past I had many friends and acquaintances in these places. For a moment I amuse myself with the hope that perhaps someone is still alive. Maybe a witness has survived- one who saw the killings and the destruction and could tell us how it happened?

The train stops because the tracks are broken. I get out of the car. I want a rebirth. I recognize the station. I walk with other Russian soldiers on the sidewalk and I search the faces of the inquisitive locals. Suddenly- a Jewish face. A Jew is selling pencils. I think I know him, but it is difficult to identify him. He looks like a cadaver- skin and bones. He does not resemble a living person. I begin a conversation with him and ask him: "What miracle caused you to stay alive?" The living -dead replies in a gloomy voice: "I hid in a damp pile of straw for two years".

The whistle of the locomotive is heard and the train continues on its way. We arrive in Holova.

[Page 512]

Here, too, I get out of the car. I look for Jewish faces so I can ask how they survived. While I walk among the locals and ask them, another military train arrives in the station. A few minutes later, one of my friends from the car reaches me. He tells me, with baited breath, that a soldier wearing a Polish army uniform is running among the cars and yelling in a desperate voice: "Goodis! Goodis!". My heart is pounding. I hear a voice I recognize- my brother Yehuda! We fell on each other, crying and kissing.

After another hour of traveling, we meet again. This time in the ruins of Kovel. We took our rifles hoping we would run into the Ukrainian murderers so we could avenge the spilled blood.

We came into town through Stara-Kolyova Street. There was no other way. The extent of destruction of our town was evident from our first glance. It was far worse than other towns.

There was no trace left of the beautiful station. Kovel was a mountain of ruins. From Stara-Kolyova we reached the main street- Warshavska- and from there we continued towards the old town.

We stopped every few meters trying to guess whose house had stood here or there? Who once resided in this house that is left alone among the ruins?

In the old town, where the ghetto was located, there was not one house standing. Only the Great synagogue remained untouched- a witness to the great destruction. We went inside and here we saw a frightening scene. I will not forget it to my dying days. The four walls were covered with writing, in pencil, ink, nails and even blood. The notes were in Polish, Hebrew, Yiddish and Russian. These were the last words of our dear ones, a few hours before they were taken to the burial place. Parents wrote to their children, children wrote to their parents, brothers- to sisters, a husband to his wife and a wife to her husband, a groom to his bride and a bride to her groom.

The notes were written to family they hoped would still be alive. I knew hundreds of them, some were really close to me. I remember well the note written by my friend Moshe Lerner, z" l.

We left the synagogue in great despair and continued to Matsiovska street where had stood our house. We found the scorched earth, but where was the house? In the piles we found some of our belongings- linens, our father's short coat and even a rusted fork. If these items could speak, they would tell a horrid story. However, perhaps it was better that these items could not speak. Who knows – our hearts would have broken upon listening to the terrible tale?

As we were standing there, on the ruins, the two brothers, crying about the terrible events- a person came closer. A man wearing rags- half army uniform and half civilian clothes.

We held our riles in the ready since the person coming could be one of the Ukrainian murderers. Our surprise came quickly- it was our third brother- Avraham.

And so, in one day, after the destruction, three bothers found each other in the ruined town.

> To All Our Expatriated in Israel and Outside of it
> General Memorial Day for Our Dear Ones Is:
> 6 Elul

[Page 514]

In Memory of the Beitar Club in Kovel

by Yerachmiel Wirnik

Translated by Ala Gamulka

When was our last meeting?

Today, as I remember these words, I cannot forget my yearning. How distant are these days! However, the memory returns constantly and I see images of a house in my hometown. It is a quiet summer evening and people live in peace. They love each other and they are happy. An old man is sitting and telling them about days gone by. The eyes of the young people shine. They are thirsty for more, yearning and hoping. Suddenly! Suddenly a storm erupts and it destroys and ruins. How distant are these days!

***

When we are tired after our long trek, we throw away our wanderer's stick, loosen our belt and sit at the edge of the path. We look back, from that day, at the difficult road we had traveled. We do not know what our future will be, but we remember the past. Our bodies cannot retrace our steps, but our memories sustain us. We remember the days that have passed. The body continues on its way, but a body without memory is like a moonless night, like a light bulb without electricity.

The body and the memory are on a crossroad. The direction is unclear. The body continues as its fortune would dictate– it is unknown. Memory is like a live fire, hovering over the steps visible on the road taken. All mementos are grouped together and they return to the tired body. Memories, like a buzzing bee, tell what has happened.

Fortune is kind, but it cannot return to its youth. This is why it allows youthful memories to return.

From that day on I like to tell what memories whisper to me.

***

When did I last see them?

Warsaw, August 1939. The new leadership of Beitar, headed by Menachem Begin, is eager to begin its work. My role is that of editor of the weekly Beitar publication "The State" and director of the cultural department. Work is proceeding at a feverish pace. However, Aliyah was most advanced in preparation.

[Page 515]

Committee of the Revisionist Zionists in Kovel

Thousands are streaming to our homeland in the Aliyah channels organized by the Jabotinsky movement. This is the first time in the history of Zionism that the locked gates of Mandate Eretz Israel are opened. Hordes of young Jews arrive on the shores of the homeland– without certificates from the High Commissioner to Palestine, but they are armed with holy belief and readiness for sacrifice.

Suddenly – a new turning point. When the Molotov–Ribbentrop pact was signed, there were new fears in Poland. Depression came to the office of Beitar on 24 Tverda Street. Information came from the Romanian border that the last transport of Olim was stopped in Sniatin. Over one thousand people were hoping for redemption, but instead were stopped.

On September 1, the sun set in the middle of the day. Hitler's killers attacked Poland. Warsaw was bombed from the air. Our hearts were heavy.

Begin tried to continue his work –planning programs. Yosef Klerman sat at the printing house and prepared a new edition of "Our World". "The State" was published and was distributed. However, from hour to hour worries escalated. The hordes of Nazis reminded the citizens of Poland that their time was imminent.

Begin prepared an agenda for emergencies. There were some Beitar emissaries from Eretz Israel who were in Warsaw and they would be in charge after local workers are drafted.

[Page 516]

In the meantime, we sat in our offices and tried to continue our activities.

On the fifth day of the war, Uri Tzvi Grinberg burst into our office. "Why are you sitting here?"– he yelled– "Leave immediately, Poland is lost!" He pointed to the map of Poland being attacked from all sides. "It is not a question of weeks, but of days" – shouted Tzvi. "Get out, get out, now!"

***

On the seventh day we Warsaw as it was bombarded. It was the first time in my life that I saw the last train in a city in dire straits. I had seen such pictures in the movies, but actual pictures were more accurate than a film. We scattered on all roads. Some on foot and others in cars; some in carts and others on the train. Begin went to Brisk, Nathan Yellin–Mor to Grodno, Klerman to Sosnowitz, Dr. Israel Shayev to Vilna– I, together with Berl Geyer, continued in the direction of our hometown, Kovel. There, our families waited for us with trepidation. On the way, Geyer disappeared. The train was bombed heavily from above and it did not move again.

I reached Kovel after a tiring voyage, a dangerous trip with a horse and buggy. It was the second day of Rosh Hashana. The buggy entered town as the shofar was sounding in the houses of worship. "Tekiah", "Shvarim", "Truah". Between shofar soundings one could hear the voice of those praying: "Hayom harat Olam" (Today the decision is made) . Never before had I understood the meaning of that phrase as I did at that moment.

In my father's house (my mother was no longer living) I found familiar people. Here were Muska Stein, Shraga Khaitin, Yosef Klerman, Israel Shayev. In short, I found in my house most of the officers of Beitar, the Revisionist Party and "Brit Hakhayal" (Covenant of the soldier). We had all gone in different directions, but we all returned to Kovel. All other roads had been taken over by the Nazis.

***

This was the last time I saw them. It was also the last time I saw my blood relatives– my father, brother and sister as well as my kin in spirit– the Beitar representatives in Kovel. They had come to receive advice and guidance on how to reach Eretz Israel. Among them were Pinhas Kopelberg, Greenblatt, Gutman (they managed, after much difficulty, to reach Israel). Also, there were many who fell on the way and their burial place is unknown.

[Page 517] [Page 518]

Kovel was–in area– the largest city in Volyn. However, this fact did not give it the chance to serve as its capital. The honor was given to Lutsk. There, the authorities of the province were centered and all instructions emanated from it. When it came to the geographic distribution of Beitar, things were different. The Kovel detachment was one of the best organized not only in Volyn, but in all of Poland. It did not take long for the leadership in Warsaw to designate Kovel as the center for Volyn. This is where the national leadership was established and various departments were centered there. The leaders of the Kovel detachment also served on the national committee. Often, the head of the detachment was also the head of the area. Among the members of Beitar and the Revisionist party that carried important positions the following should be mentioned: Shabtai Shikhman, Yaakov Yundof, Yosef Ne'eman, Pinhas Pantorin, Pinhas Kopelberg (all in Israel); Shmuel Zin, Yosef Gelman, Yitzhak Zimering, Yosef Shapira, Yosef Avrech, Nathan Zukerman, Gelfand, Vineberg, Krause and many others who were exterminated by the Nazi murderers and were buried in a common grave.

It is with thanks to them and many other anonymous ones that the Jabotinsky movement grew and developed in Kovel. The movement building served as their home. Here, between four walls, decorated with Zionist slogans, they spent most days and nights. Here were educated the members of the "generation of the brilliant one and the cruel one". Thus, were created dreamers, fighters and builders.

Very, very few of them managed to come to us. Most of them were killed in gas chambers of the Nazi murderers. They are no longer with us. Still, they walk among us always. On dark nights, when we are alone, they burst the many walls and appear in front of our eyes. They want us to know they are still with us.

May their memory be blessed for eternity!

***

When the book was completed, we received the article written by out fellow townsman, Yerachmiel Wirnik. Actually, the article should be in another section, but we felt it was better to include it here or else it would not be available.

The Editor

Central School for Olim, Outstanding performers and Counsellors in Kovel– Feb–March 1934

***

[Page 519]

Deep Pits, Red Clay

by Sh. Halkin

Translated from Yiddish to Hebrew by I. Teitleker

Translated by Ala Gamulka

Deep pits, red clay-
I once had a home.
In the spring - beautiful flowers bloomed
In the fall – wandering birds screeched.
In the winter- bright snow shone.
Now- robbery,
Bereavement, loss, destruction are rampant.

My house has been destroyed
It is invaded on all sides
Its entrances are broken
By the murderers, the killers

The villains, the oppressors
Slayers of mothers and children
Without any mercy.

Deep trenches, full of blood-
I once had a home.

Empty fields- without anything growing,
The ditches are filling up.
The soil is becoming redder.
The dead are now its backbone.
These ditches- my house is in there.
There are lying my strangled brothers,
Their limbs are broken,
They are shot like rabbits
In the houses and in the pits.

The trenches are deep and full of blood-
I once had a home.

Good times will still come
On the wings of fate and recompense
The wounds will heal and there will be restoration
Our sons will grow up in peace
Our sons will grow up in happiness.
They will visit the graves of our dear ones
They will come to the bloody trenches.
Our pain will never disappear!

Deep trenches, filled with blood
I once had a home.

[Page 521]

They Fell on Guard Duty

Devorah Baran
(God will avenge her blood)

Translated by Ala Gamulka

She was born in Kovel. Her father was a manufacturer, a religious Zionist. She was educated in the Tarbut school and later in ORT. She joined "Hechalutz Hatzair" during her school days. In 1938 she went to preparatory kibbutz Borochov in Lodz. She worked there as a seamstress. When it was closed during the war, she joined a group of six members who stayed in Lodz to watch over the embers of the kibbutz and the movement. Central office moved her to Warsaw and later to the agricultural wing of Hechalutz in Tcherniakov. She was one of the most responsible members when it came to her work. She joined a fighting unit of Dror and battled in the "central ghetto" as part of the Hanoch Gutman unit. She died at the age of 23, her gun in her hand, in the battle of the ghetto. This was on May 3, 1943.

(From the book "Destruction and Uprising of the Jews of Warsaw" by Melech Neistat)

Remembering

There were several fighting units in the bunker. One day, it was suddenly attacked by the Germans. They knew that, inside, there were Jewish fighters and they shouted from the outside:" Get out!" The situation was dire. However, Hanoch Gutman did not lose his cool. He ordered Devorah Baran, a loyal member of our movement, to go our first. He thought the Germans would not shoot her. The Germans were overcome by her beauty and her daring. In one moment, she killed some of them with a grenade that she threw at them. The others ran away, scared. On the next day, the Germans returned and attacked the bunker. They lobbed grenades and ten members, Devorah Baran among them, lost their lives.

(Related by Tzvia Lobatkin in the book "Story of the Ghetto Fighters", page 191)

[Page 522]

Luba Lederhandler
(God will avenge her blood)

Translated by Ala Gamulka

Luba was the daughter of Tuvia Lederhandler. She graduated, with excellence, from high school and was preparing to make Aliyah.

When the Germans conquered Kovel, Luba stayed in town. The Jews were imprisoned in two ghettos, but she managed to escape and hid in the forests around Kovel, with the partisans. She pretended to be a Christian and served as liaison between various Ukrainian units.

She managed to evade the murderers until July 1944. She lived, as a Christian, with her three friends on Monopoliova Street. She continued her partisan activities and was in touch with the Jewish ones in the Kovel forests.

Two weeks before the Russians conquered the town, Kovel was bombed by them. The house Luba and her friends lived in was heavily blasted and they had to leave.

A vicious Pole recognized her as a Jew and denounced her to the Gestapo. The four young women were shot right then and there and their bodies were thrown into the Turia River.

Luba was 23 when she was murdered.

(From Pinkas Kovel, published in Argentina)

[Page 523]

Leah Fish
(God will avenge her blood)

Translated by Ala Gamulka

She was born in Chorochov, Volyn in 1918. Her parents were religious Zionists. She was an excellent student in a Polish school and had private tutors for Hebrew. She joined Hechalutz Hatzair and organized its branch in her hometown. At the age of 18 she went to the preparatory kibbutz in Grochov. She became a counselor. Several times she decided to make Aliyah, but she listened to her friends at work and in the movement and stayed. In addition to her work in the movement, she also studied on her own.

When the Germans came, she was sent to Vilna and from there to Kovno to work in the Lithuanian branch. She dutifully fulfilled her mission. She even learned new languages. There was still a chance to make Aliyah, but the central office again stopped her. In spite of her deep longing for Eretz Israel, she obeyed. She wandered in the different villages and brought the idea of Eretz Israel to the many young people.

When Lithuania was annexed by Russia, the Zionist movement had to go underground. She traveled to Moscow and went to various offices to obtain a permit for Aliyah. She returned to Vilna and her last letter from there was received in Eretz Israel. Reading her letter, it was obvious that she was heartbroken about not being able to make Aliyah. When it was decided to move sections of the central office to Volyn, she moved from Vilna to Lvov and then to Kovel. The news about her great work was only known in a roundabout way. Her name was mentioned constantly among the active members. Volyn Province was her last place to be active. Members who visited Kovel after it was liberated from the Nazis, found in the synagogue, four names etched in the wall. They knew they were going to die. She was among them.

(from the book "Destruction and Uprising of the Jews of Warsaw" by Melech Neistat)

[Page 524]

Sheindel Schwartz
(God will avenge her blood)

Translated by Ala Gamulka

She was born in Kovel to wealthy, Zionist, progressive parents. They made sure she had a proper general as well as Zionist–Hebrew, education. She studied in Tarbut High School in Kovel and was one of the most capable students. She was active in several clubs in school. This was a quiet, friendly, modest, pleasant person, helpful to weaker students without standing out. She was well–liked by students and teachers and was modestly dressed– almost as if neglected. She was pretty, aristocratic and attracted others with her happy look, her black eyes and her blond curls. She never put on airs. Her face reflected softness, goodness and intelligence. In 1937, when in the seventh grade of the high school, she joined Hechalutz Hatzair in town. There was much opposition to this at home, as her family wanted her to join one of the movements within the school. Hechalutz Hatzair had members who were mostly from poor and working families. She was one of the organizers of Hechalutz Hatzair in her class and she dedicated herself with enthusiasm to all activities. She studied, organized trips, counseled and taught others. Her whole life was intertwined in these activities. When she joined the movement, she wanted to leave school and to go to a preparatory kibbutz. Her parents were against it and she completed her studies with excellent results. On June 11, 1938, two days after her final exams, she went, happily, to the preparatory kibbutz in Grochov. She had difficulty adjusting, from a physical point of view, to the new, communal life. She overcame it and worked in the chicken coop. she spoke lovingly about her chicks. She also participated in the world conference of Hechalutz that took three months. When the Grochov kibbutz received a group of refugees from Germany, she was chosen as one of the counselors. She did her job faithfully and well. She used to read, voraciously, the newspapers from Eretz Israel and listened intently to the emissaries. Her time in the preparatory kibbutz was spent happily and in anticipation of her Aliyah.

On September 1, 1939, Grochov was bombed by the Germans. Still, out of 250 members, not one wanted to leave. They continued their work in the barn, the coop and the fields. Quiet, gentle Sheindel knew how to encourage and strengthen others. She was involved in everything and with everyone. When the central office planned to leave and members were to follow together, she was among those in charge and to organize.

[Page 525]

The walk to Kovel took ten days, on roads bombed by the Germans. They walked at night and hid in the daytime in the forests. They were hungry, their shoes wore out and their feet were injured. She withstood all difficulties and propped others. It was only when she was alone that she burst out crying. These trying days strengthened her and made her into an adult.

In Kovel, the movement had to decide on its next steps during the Holocaust. Emissaries were sent to the Romanian border and members returned to Warsaw to prepare for the underground movement. Groups went to Vilna in Lithuania, hoping to make Aliyah from there. She was the liaison and had to bring messages from the movement, in these dark days, to all parts of Volyn and Bialystok. This was a difficult and dangerous job. To make things easier she registered as a student in the university in Lvov. She had to reach distant villages, to find members of the movement and to encourage them, to organize them and to lead them. She was only able to meet with other members every three months.

In the beginning of 1941, there was a seminar for the active members of the Lithuanian branch, in underground Vilna. She had to sneak through the border and she arrived to give a report on her experiences in the underground in Poland. The people she addressed were preparing to do these activities in Lithuania. In Vilna she said good–bye to members making Aliyah. She was not bitter about not being one of them. "There is no other way"– she explained to the members. She had to be part of organizing the movement in the underground. She was only worried that her friends in Eretz Israel would forget her. During these activities, she was arrested by the Soviets and spent time in prison, in Lutsk, with Yitzhak (Odok) Golobner.

She escaped when Lutsk was conquered by the Germans and she continued her activities in the underground, even during the Nazi regime. It was difficult to maintain contact with other parts– rural Poland. Not much was heard about her activities, but it as known that she had a difficult task. She continued to go from place to place, to bring material. In a Hechalutz letter from Poland of 15 November, 1943, her name is listed among the organizers who fell in Volyn. She was 23 years old.

Members who visited Kovel after it was liberated from the Germans, found, in the synagogue, partially left standing, writings on the wall. Among them, in Hebrew, in a special frame: "Good–bye from the members of Hechalutz who are going to die. We remained loyal to our ideals to the end. Avenge our spilled blood!" Signed– four names: Sheindel Schwartz from Kovel, Leah Fish from Chorochov, Rachel Fogelman from Lachovitz and David Eisenberg from Warsaw.

(From the book "Destruction and Uprising of the Jews of Warsaw by Melech Neistat)

[Page 526]

Yechiel Sheinbaum
(God will avenge his blood)

Translated by Ala Gamulka

Yechiel Sheinbaum was born on December 2, 1914 in Odessa. When he was two years old, his parents, father Pinchas and mother Zlata moved from Odessa to Kovel. There were three children: he, Yechiel, and two sisters. One of them, Orah, is in Kibbutz Yagur, Israel. Yechiel studied in the Tarbut high school and joined Dror (Freedom) in Kovel. He was 16 when he ran away to the preparatory kibbutz in Klosov. His poor physical condition could not withstand the difficult work and he became ill. His father and sister came to take him back home, but he stubbornly refused to leave.

When his time came to serve in the army, he studied diligently the theory of defence and battle and reached the rank of officer. From the army he returned to kibbutz Kovel and he traveled throughout Volyn and Congress Poland. He was organizing branches of Dror in different places. In 1938, he participated in the conference on unification of Dror and Hechalutz Hatzair. In 1938–39 Yechiel lived in Kibbutz Borochov in Lodz. He tried to make Aliyah many times. However, the central committee did not allow it as he was needed for the organizing and educating of the movement. In 1939 Yechiel smuggled members from Poland, conquered by the Nazis, through Volyn, to Vilna. Together with other members he established the Dror branch and dedicated himself, with love, to the education of the children. In 1940, when most of the members of Shachriah Kibbutz were leaving Vilna, the central office decided that Yechiel must stay in place in order to help the remaining members in their work. Then the war broke out. Yechiel continues meeting the members in the Shachriah farm in Volakompa and the Zakrat forest.

[Page 527]

He began to think about becoming a partisan. On September 6, 1941, when we were all exiled into the ghetto, Yechiel said to me: "We must leave today for the forest".

However, I asked him to join the other Jews going to the ghetto, since we did not have any weapons and we had no contact with the partisans.

We were chased away from Vivolska Street, our home, through Novgorod Street. Suddenly, Yechiel began to sing a pioneering song. Everyone looked at him and think him to be madâ€¦ He started to speak to the walking Jews by saying: "Jews, look, understand what is happening to us! Don't believe in miracles!"

11August 1943. After the Kovno–Punary massacre, Yechiel worked feverishly. He convened pioneers to him and he organized them. He was like a commander of a battalion.

On September 1, 1943, at 5:00 am, the Germans suddenly attacked the ghetto. Yechiel was called to action. He gave orders with the quickness and experience of an outstanding military man. He organized groups and brought weapons from cellars and attics. The ghetto was dying. Many Jews, in family groups, were walking to the gate of the ghetto, to the Germans. Others went into hiding.

Yechiel saw all of this. His wife, kneeling beside him related: "He was feverish, his hands were trembling– still he did not give the order to shoot. He was enraged and spoke about Eretz Israel: "If we get out alive today, we will leave tonight for the forest. We cannot wait any longer".

The Germans completed their task and ran to the street. When Yechiel saw them, he began to fire. He stood erect near the window and was shooting like a madman. The Germans returned automatic fire. A bullet hit Yechiel's neck and stream of blood hit his wife. She had just enough time to close his eyes and to escape. The Germans again attacked the fort, now missing its leader, ransacked the house and blew it up.

Later, when it was silent, when 6 000 of our Jews were gone, we found Yechiel's body. He was lying on a smoking pile of stones. His body was intact, but his yellow face showed the excitement and revenge.

We laid him in a casket and we carried him to the gate. The remainder of the fighters and the entire ghetto paid him their last respects.

(From the book "Jerusalem of Lithuania in Rebelion and during the Holocaust" by Dr. M.Dvorzhetsky, pages 394–398)

[Page 528]

From the Activities of the Kovel Expatriates Organization in Israel

by Tzvi Resnick

Translated by Ala Gamulka

An entire book can be written about the contribution Kovel expatriates made in all productive areas in our country: agriculture, construction, paving of roads, literature, art, education, defence, during the War of Independence, illegal immigration, struggle with the Mandate authorities, providing work, professional organization, cooperatives, public service, factories and workshops. There is almost no area free from the activities of our townspeople. Perhaps, one day, such a book will be written, and it must be done.

However, our present book is meant to commemorate, for eternity, our dearly departed and we cannot add the other content. We confine ourselves to the internal activities performed since the founding of our organization.

The organization was actually established as the first terrible news came about the annihilation of the Jews of our town. We all felt the need to get together and to offer help to the remaining embers who were saved from the horrible inferno. In the main, we wanted to preserve the memory of the town so it would not be lost.

Until 1951, there were several committees. They consisted of the following members: Asher Lublinsky, Mordechai Mokrin, Moshe Weisbrot, Zalman Tsin, Yaakov Kaminer, Eliezer Roitenberg, Shlomo Khari, lawyer Yitzhak Eisen, PIntsie Pantorin, Devorah Reichstol, Eli Mendel. May the memory of the following who are no longer with us be preserved: Baruch Tenenbaum, Meir Kaditz, Mendel Kotovsky and Pinchas Schwartz.

These members were the first pioneers of the organization which they formed from thin air. They were totally devoted and did their best to broaden and glorify the activities of the organization.

At the general meeting held on 10.11.51, a new committee was elected. It had mainly young and fresh participants. These were energetic people who were capable and willing to work. Among them were: Pinchas Drori (chairman), Moshe Gitlis (secretary), Moshe Weisbrot (treasurer), Bluma Shapiro, Shmuel Vikum, Mordechai Erlich, Tamar Kravitz, Pinchas Kopelberg, Pinchas Pantorin and Elyhau Mendel.

This committee must be recognized for several important achievements: the establishment of a fund for mutual aid, election of various committees, bringing in members from outside of Tel Aviv to the committee. They were Yosef Bronzaft (Haifa), Pintsie Pantorin (Jerusalem) and Mendel Kotovsky, z" l (Hedera). In addition, an audit committee was elected. Its members were: Zeev Gasco, Yitzhak Margalit and Dr. Avraham Gorali, who died young.

This committee commemorated itself with an important project– planting an orchard in memory of the martyrs of our town.

[Page 529] [Page 530]

Member Kuna Atlas, very active in this project writes:

" The idea existed already in 1954. Even before that, our brethren in Argentina donated a considerable sum for this purpose. However, it was not enough to start as more funds were required– 1000 pounds– in order to erect a monument in the orchard of martyrs of Kovel in the general forest of the martyrs of Poland.

We saw in this project an opportunity to show our desire to commemorate and never to forget the victims from our town. They were cruelly taken from us and were annihilated through no fault of their own.

We selected a committee that attracted active people. They visited the homes of our townspeople and received donations for trees to be planted, the number being equal to the number of family members who were killed in the Holocaust.

Orchard in the name of the Kovel martyrs

We budgeted a certain percentage of the donations to commemorate the unknowns who had no surviving family to remember them.

After a year, we came, on Holocaust and Bravery Day, to a planting ceremony and dedication of a sign in the name of the martyrs of Kovel.

Every year we visit, on that day, this symbolic cemetery to remember our dear ones who died sanctifying the name of God."

In August 1953 a new committee was elected: Elyhau Mendel, Bluma Shapiro, Mordechai Mokrin, Shamai Frankovitch, Kuna Atlas, Yekhezkel Goldberg, Shlomo Sirk and Tzvi Resnick. David Blitt also joined them. At the first meeting, Tzvi Resnick was elected secretary and Yekhezkel Goldberg– treasurer.

This committee completed the project of the orchard in the name of the martyrs of Kovel. The committee must be commended for the dedicated and fruitful work in this area. It was done with great energy. A monument was erected to the memory of the community of Kovel in the Saints Forest in the hills of Jerusalem.

On Friday, 25.6.54, a celebration took place In honor of the completion of the project and the visit of Mr. Zissia Werba from Uruguay. He donated $50 to the organization.

That year assistance was given to chronically ill patients and to the unemployed. Loans were awarded to the needy. We had an extensive correspondence with our brethren in Argentina about sending parcels to those who needed them. Preparations were also made for the annual meeting and memorial assembly, as was done every year.

At the annual meeting on 4.9.54 a new committee was elected: Bluma Shapiro, David Blitt, Luba Goldberg, Kuna Atlas, Tuvia Weisbrot, Avraham Vikum and Tzvi Resnick.

[Page 531]

The latter continued in his position of secretary and Luba Goldberg, as treasurer. The committee continued its regular work, i.e. assisting the needy and granting loans.

On Friday night, 7.5.55s a party in honor of the guests from Argentina: Mr. Haim Winter (chairman of the committee of our brethren in Argentina)– he donated 100 pounds for activities of the organization; Mr. Feldman who donated $25 and Mr. Balech, the editor of Pinkas Kovel that had been published in Argentina, in Yiddish.

After the party there was a discussion with Mr. Winter and, as a result, we were sent 20 copies of Pinkas Kovel. We sold each copy for 10 pounds.

At the annual meeting on 24.8.55, a new committee was elected: David Blitt, Bluma Shapiro, Pinchas Pantorin, Luba Goldberg, Avraham Vikum, Tuvia Fried, Tamar Kravitz and Tzvi Resnick. Luba Goldberg continued as treasurer and Tzvi Resnick as secretary. An audit committee was chosen– Mendel Turtchin, Shlomo Khari, Yitzhak Margalit and Bernstein.

At the end of the term of this committee the great project was begun– the publication of Sefer Kovel.

All previous committees dreamed of publishing the book. The idea never left their agenda. An editorial board for the book was elected and several active members were chosen to send letters and memos. The expatriates were asked to write down their memoirs – but nothing happened. The book was waiting for its redeemer. The committee managed to draft our town member, **Eliezer Leoni-Tzuperfein. He agreed to devote himself to the publication of the book. The choice of Mr. Leoni had an unbelievable success. Thanks to constant work, Mr. Leoni managed to obtain great material . as well as, give his own input and all this resulted in this book. Our towns folk took part and our destroyed town earned a memorial, as deserved.**

When the idea of the book came to fruition and the editor had a massive file, the committee was required to do the next step– collect necessary funds to accomplish this memorial project.

The first task was to have meetings where sections were read and people signed up with orders. In Haifa, there were three such meetings and they were quite successful.

In Jerusalem there was one meeting. The local committee undertook to publicize the book among our brethren in Jerusalem.

In Tel Aviv there was a meeting of active members in Sailors House. A large crowd attended and listened intently to the readings about the destruction of the town. They immediately paid 5 Shekels for the book.

[Page 532]

The second activity was a Purim party with all proceeds going towards the publication of the book. There were two such parties and the income served to provide sources for the funds needed. In addition, there was a flyer in Yiddish that was sent to our brethren in the United States. Mr. Meitze Levin was the first to contribute $25.

However, we received important help from another corner of the world– from France. They sent memoirs as well as money. Our townsman, Meir (Miron) Rosenblatt headed this task. He collected funds and created a good atmosphere around the book. The local expatriates from Kovel, in Paris, carried out their duties.

At the annual meeting of 13.8.56, a new committee was elected. Among its members were: David Blitt, Bluma Shapiro, Sima Pantorin, Luba Goldberg, Tuvia Fried, Leah Fidel, Noah Bein and Tzvi Resnick. The audit committee consisted of: Eliyahu Better, Yekhezkel Goldberg and Asher Lublinsky. Secretary– Tzvi Resnick; treasurer– Luba Goldberg.

This committee stepped up its efforts to obtain funds for publication. They visited townsfolk in their homes and signed them up.

An important contribution towards the publication was given by Mrs. Gutcha (nee Rubinstein) and her husband Boris Goldstein, from Honduras. They donated 50 pounds. Also, Sossel and Avraham Lichtchin from Mexico who gave $50 pounds.

The activities of the committees were multi–faceted. We never went off track from our main goal. It was to help survivors, the last remnants of beautiful Kovel. They arrived broken and without anything. We helped them with small loans and with finding jobs.

We must note the names of those members who helped the newcomers in finding jobs: Uri Alpert, Dr. Yaakov Khassim, Yitzhak Margalit, Masha Greenblatt and Baruch Avivi.

We must note that with the publication of the book, the work of the organization did not end. After we fulfilled our debts to our dear ones, we had to increase our help to those were alive, to help the newcomers and those old–timers who were needy.

Our dearly departed commanded us to love each other even more since so few of us remained alive. This heiitage forced us to make the organization even better.

In summation, we must remember those of our townsfolk who died in Eretz Israel or other countries and who did not merit to see "Sefer Kovel" with their own eyes. This was something they so wished to accomplish. In their lifetime they waited for the commemoration, in pictures and in words, of their beloved town. They imagined that thus they would merit to see comfort for the terrible suffering we had all gone through. Let us hope that these words will refresh their lips in their graves.

[Page 533]

Dr. Avraham Gorali, Z" L

Editorial Staff

Translated by Ala Gamulka

Among the active members of the organization whose names are etched in eternity and who looked after our people, the name of Dr. Avraham Gorali, z" l, stands out. He died young and was still full of energy and ready to work.

Dr. Gorali was always prepared to listen to the needs of the organization. He tried hard to help anyone who needed assistance. His heavy load of work as a lawyer did not interfere.

He was friendly and lovable. These were special traits that came from his love of mankind. He was always happy to help due to his kind heart. These traits were said about Avraham his whole life. Avraham chose to study law after he graduated from high school. He never used the fancy term "advocate". He attended the Hebrew high school and was imbued with a Zionist and pioneering spirit. He wanted to study the law in the broad sense of the word. After he completed his studies at the Vilna and Warsaw universities, he made Aliyah. He continued his studies as a research student at the Hebrew University in Jerusalem. He studied international law and received the title of PHD for his work on international relations. His thesis was entitled "The Jewish Minority Among the Nations". Prof. Gorman Bentwitch wrote a forward full of praise. The thesis was well received by others in the field.

From the beginning, Avraham Gorali was noted as an exceptional jurist. He had all the outstanding traits that could be found among Jewish jurists: a deep knowledge in the field of law, a sharp intellect and quick mind, an exceptional intelligence, a sense of justice and above all- a sensitive and warm heart. In addition, he had a sound feeling for the needs of the public and the nation. He soon had a good name in Jerusalem as an outstanding jurist and lawyer. Many sought his services- some were needy and without funds. He never dismissed them, but he undertook their issues and defended their rights pro bon and with great dedication. He was highly respected by judges as they accepted his arguments to be well-thought out and clear; short and interesting.

He joined the Hagana as soon as he made Aliyah. Most of his time was not spent on the law, but doing public and political work.

[Page 534]

The more he dedicated himself to political work, the more there was a demand on his time. He worked tirelessly in the field of public relations in the Jerusalem district. He especially dealt with liberating Hagana members who were arrested. The Mandate authorities pushed hard and there were many arrests for carrying weapons. There were more and more Hagana prisoners who were placed in various prisons, especially in Jerusalem. It was a tiring task, nerve-wracking for having to deal with stubborn British officials. Many Hagana members, old and young, were freed from prison and from the hands of the secret police, thanks to the courage and effectiveness of Avraham Gorali. He never tired of his work.

In addition to his legal work, public service and work for the Hagana, Avraham Gorali also developed a career as a journalist. He was a political commentator with a clear spirit and also an editor of legal journals. For several years (1936-39) he worked on the editorial board of Davar. He wrote articles and commentaries on political and international affairs. He fought for the legitimacy of the Jews in Eretz Israel. He was one of those who foresaw the establishment of the State of Israel when many had misgivings. Many of his commentaries were printed as leading articles in Davar and many were published anonymously as if written by the editorial board.

As time went on, he had too many commitments and he had to give up his journalism. He devoted himself to his legal work and he began to publish the rulings of various high courts in the country. These rulings were like legislation. He saw the future need for laws and regulations once the State would be established. Avraham Gorali founded and published the "Legal library". He did this work with great dedication, love and ability. He published his own legal books, as well. The "Legal library" was his personal project and in it he invested all his might. It was difficult work which consisted of juristic professional editing and also the use of proper language. Often new words had to be coined for special terms. (He also published some language research articles and participated in preparing professional terminology for the "New dictionary" of A. Even-Shoshan). There were 13 books in the "Legal library" and he wrote a forward for each one of them. These forward introductions were special in themselves. The best of the legal books that were published as part of the "legal library", edited by Avraham Gorali, touch on different aspects of the law. They are cornerstones in legal literature in Hebrew.

When the War of Independence began, Avraham Gorali was appointed head of the legal department of the Israel Defence Forces. He became the first chief prosecutor. He wrote the laws of military legal work of 1948.

[Page 535]

When the State was established, he became a member of the justice section. His main worries were law, justice and security of the state.

He was full of plans and hopes. One of his many programs, that he did not achieve, was the publication of a collection called "Justice in Hebrew and universal literatures". He had collected dozens of articles.

He was full of energy, plans and ideas. A kind man, full of good humor. He was taken in the middle of his life, before he turned 43. On his way to Beer Sheva, a road accident caused his death. He had lived a life of devotion to his people and to his country.

[Pages 487-498]

Kovel Necrology

Prepared by Bruce Drake

These are based on the notes left on the walls of the Great Synagogue by Jews waiting to be put to death.

Surname	Given Names	Other Surnames, Remarks	Page
ALTER	Bloyweis		488
APELBOIM	Yosef		495
ARBEITER	Tania	along with family	496
AVRECH	Chana		494
BALTER	Avigdor		498
BARZILAI	Moszko		495
BERENSZTEJN	Hania		497
BERENSZTEJN	Tema		497
BERENSZTEJN	Yankel		497
BLUCHER	Belka		496
BLUCHER	Rahel		496
BLUCHER	Sonia		496
BLUMA	David		487
BLUMA	Ya'acov		487
BLUMA	Yehuda		487
BOKSER	Ania	daughter of Dusia	497
BOKSER	Dusia	mother of Ania	497
DRUKER	Ahron		490
DUNAWIECKI	Moshe	and wife	496
EHRLICH	Rahel		494
EISENBERG	David		488
FIDLMAN	Polye		492
FISH	Leah		488

FISHBEIN	Bela		497
FISHBEIN	Rahel		497
FISHBEIN	Riva		497
FISHBEIN	Yisrael		497
FISZBEJN	Eidl		492
FOGELMAN	Rahel		488
FRISHBERG	Berl		488
FRISHBERG	Chaya		488
FRYDMAN	Yehoshaya		490
GELER	Yakov		491
GIWANT	Berl		489
GIWANT	Yankl		489
GOLDSTEIN	Sheva	along with family	494
GOLDSZTAJN	Avraham		492
GOLDSZTAJN	Bet Sheva		492
GOLDSZTAJN	Borukh Leib		492
GOLDSZTAJN	Mariam		492
GROJSER	Bilah	along with family	495
KANAN	Fayga		488
KAZAK	Avraham-Yitzhak		492
KAZAK	Brayndal		492
KLEINER	Perl	sister of Yosef	494
KLEINER	Yosef	brother of Perl	494
LANDAU	Niura	Rajber-Landau	495
LENCZ			495
LEWERTOB	Yakov		491
LUDMIRER	Yerukehm	son of Reb Shlomo Ludmirer	490
MENDL	Kapczyk		490
MENDL	Shimkha		490
MELNICER	Sonia		494
MILSZTEJN	Beba		497
PITETA	Benjamin		498
RABINER	Chaya		490

RAJCSZTAL	Avraham	Son of Shmuel Rajcsztal. With wife and child	491
RAPAPORT	Gitl		491
RAPAPORT	Josef		491
ROJTER	Kuba		495
ROJTER	Sonia		495
ROIZEN	Miriam		487
ROZENCWAIG	Adolph		498
ROZENWALD	Bora	husband of Lema	496
ROZENWALD	Eliahu		496
ROZENWALD	Fenia		497
ROZENWALD	Lema	wife of Bora	497
ROZENWALD	Zelik		497
ROZENSZVEIG	Liuba		494
SCHECTER	Yehuda		487
SCHWARTZ	Sheindel		488
SEGAL	Amik		498
SEGAL	Dora		498
SEGAL	Ephraim		492
SEGAL	Ethel		498
SEGAL	Gitl		492
SEGAL	Gittel		498
SEGAL	Ziva		498
SOSNE	Avraham		492
SOSNE	Leibl		491
SOYFER	Yente		490
STILLERMAN	Frieda	daughter of Yitzhak Marder	487
SZER	Ben-Tzion		492
SZWARC	Chaim	son of Shlomo	492
SZWARC	Fayge		491
TANNENBOIM	Fania	mother of Sioma and Pepa	498
TANNENBOIM	Sioma	daughter of Fania	498
TANNENBOIM	Pepa	daughter of Fania	491
TASGAL	Ester		491

TASGAL	Pesakh		491
TOJBICZOW	Tunik		495
TOYBITSH	Baba		488
TOYBITSH	Hannah		488
WAJNSZTEJN	Golda		496
WAJNSZTEJN	Yisrael		495
WEINER	Kasil		488
WYDRA	Pola		496
YEHOSHUA	Zamir	son of Moshe	487
ZAKHARIAH	Rusman		490
ZISKIND	Miriam		487
ZISKIND	Simcha		487

NAME INDEX

A

Abrahamowicz, 17
Aidless, 255
Akiba, 7
Almog, 170
Alper, 92
Alpert, 37, 109, 343
Alter, 162, 191, 236, 237, 306
Alter, 345
Amarnik, 326
Amernic, 69
Andreyev, 144, 145, 146
Antin, 207, 208
Apelboim, 313
Apelboim, 345
Appelbaum, 72, 153, 154, 167, 208, 209, 211, 224, 226, 284
Appelboim, 49, 64, 65, 213
Aramernik, 71
Arbeiter, 314
Arbeiter, 345
Aricha, 29, 38, 95
Ariel, 4, 31, 89, 92, 94, 96, 97, 108
Arlichgerecht, 217
Armernik, 72, 175, 207, 226, 230, 276, 288
Aronowicz, 17
Arsenieva, 38
Asher, 25, 31, 40, 50, 57, 62, 65, 83, 92, 94, 98, 99, 105, 106, 107, 108, 109, 129, 131, 134, 136, 155, 167, 210, 211, 212, 222, 226, 227, 234, 239, 240, 241, 271, 281, 284, 325, 340, 342
Ashkenazi, 14, 47, 52, 325
Asiok, 115
Atlas, 86, 248, 340, 341, 342
Avish, 326
Avivi, 4, 92, 232, 343
Avrech, 4, 41, 94, 97, 100, 106, 107, 108, 109, 134, 142, 143, 150, 161, 223, 259, 263, 312, 322, 330
Avrech, 345
Avrekh, 25, 32, 76, 128, 129, 130, 131
Axelrod, 69

B

Baden-Powell, 35, 42
Bakar, 264, 265
Bakhover, 72
Bakun, 223
Balech, 342
Balkovitz, 65
Balter, 316
Balter, 345
Bama, 138
Bankover, 169, 176
Baran, 334
Barrok, 66
Baruch, 4, 26, 37, 38, 66, 77, 92, 150, 151, 166, 179, 205, 212, 232, 238, 340, 343
Baruchin, 211
Barzilai, 313
Barzilai, 345
Bass, 106, 258
Batar, 62
Bayerach, 115
Bebchuk, 262
Becker, 38, 111
Begin, 329, 330
Bein, 4, 139, 342
Beirach, 222
Beit-Halachmi, 176
Beker, 179
Belker, 275
Belzer, 154
Ben Shmuel, 46
Ben Tovim, 224
Ben-Aharon, 10, 17
Ben-Avraham, 11, 17
Bendarsky, 53
Bendersky, 177
Ben–Dori, 169
Ben-Eliakim, 11
Ben-Haim, 10
Ben-Hazagag, 10, 17
Ben–Michael, 233, 236
Ben-Mordechai,, 10, 11
Ben-Shem, 32, 39, 42
Ben–Shem, 4
Ben–Shem, 95
Ben–Shem, 96
Ben–Shem, 97
Ben–Tardyon, 7
Ber, 96, 107, 156, 158, 159, 178, 191, 246
Berdichevsky, 169, 177
Berensztejn, 316
Berensztejn, 345
Berg, 151
Berger, 248
Berilkos, 293, 294
Berkovska, 108
Bernholtz, 326
Bernstein, 107, 167, 168, 169, 170, 342
Beronzpat, 115
Bershadsky, 51
Bess, 53
Better, 269, 272, 342
Bialik, 4, 41, 46, 53, 57, 96, 98, 99, 109, 111, 129, 130
Bialopolsky, 176

Bidnick, 251
Biliner, 325
Bilov, 170, 208
Bilubavitch, 53
Blech, 65
Bley, 92, 108, 109
Blitt, 4, 78, 341, 342
Blorie, 187
Bloyweis, 306, 345
Blucher, 315
Blucher, 345
Bluma, 345
Blumenfeld, 161, 208, 210
Blumfeld, 52
Bochover, 223
Bokser, 153, 276, 288, 315
Bokser, 345
Bonn, 115
Borak, 136, 137, 144, 207
Bork, 26, 50, 77, 105, 107, 167, 168, 169, 212
Borochov, 79, 199, 334, 339
Borokhin, 141
Botovits, 292
Boxer, 246
Boyko, 291, 292
Boymel, 83
Brandeis, 216
Brandes, 36, 141
Bratt, 96, 211
Brenner, 199
Breslau, 191
Breslev, 89, 150
Brihel, 98
Brik, 73, 83, 102, 156, 216, 226
Brod, 171
Bromberg, 96
Bronshteyn, 288
Bronzaft, 183, 340
Broshek, 217
Brukhin, 161
Buchwald, 247
Bunis, 289
Burk, 98, 162, 288
Burstein, 51, 115, 161, 214, 216, 222

C

Cantor, 37, 38, 151, 154, 155, 156, 170, 309
Cass, 183
Cayman, 92
Chachnovich, 323
Chaim, 119
Charna, 116
Chasis, 248, 249
Chazan, 95, 97
Chernitzski, 12
Chiel, 93, 94, 97
Colodner, 216
Contract, 151
Cooperberg, 96

Crome, 113
Crown-Chancellor Sajnesni Kriski, 10
Czun, 278, 280

D

Damav, 115
Danziger, 69, 70, 208
Darabaner, 207
Dardaky, 102
Dashbasky, 50
Dashevsky, 84, 164, 165, 166, 297
Davidiuk, 161
Davidova, 42
Davidovna, 36, 54, 97, 113, 119, 175, 205
Denziger, 250
Deshbeski, 114, 115
Diamnt, 251
Didrikh, 38
Dimant, 103
Djeshevsky, 221, 222
Doari, 217
Dobromil, 177
Dobrovdka, 217, 228
Dodier, 69
Dodiuk, 107
Dolgin, 38, 95
Dolitsky, 83
Dondik, 76, 77
Donitch, 321
Dostoyevsky, 53, 125, 194
Dovrat, 177
Dowzhinski, 67
Drake, 1, 345
Drori, 4, 301, 340
Droyanov, 166
Druker, 308, 309
Druker, 345
Drutman, 289
Dunawiecki, 315
Dunawiecki, 345
Dundik, 72
Durtchin, 97, 108, 109
Duvdevani, 170
Dvorzhetsky, 339

E

Efrat, 76, 83, 250
Efrati, 72
Ehrlich, 214, 237, 312
Ehrlich, 345
Eibshitz, 220
Einstein, 78, 132, 133, 174
Eisen, 51, 168, 207, 340
Eisenberg, 205, 207, 212, 214, 305, 338
Eisenberg, 345
Eismond, 26
Eismont, 49
Eitchies, 177
Elioshik, 268

Entin, 20, 21, 165, 166
Epels, 74
Epstein, 158
Erlich, 37, 38, 54, 65, 97, 108, 109, 113, 114, 115, 119, 150, 161, 165, 167, 173, 178, 179, 191, 204, 205, 207, 210, 211, 215, 220, 221, 224, 225, 240, 258, 269, 273, 288, 325, 340
Eventchuk, 96, 163
Even–Zohar, 178

F

Fantorine, 322
Farber, 103, 234
Feigelman, 217
Feigelson, 226
Feinstein, 32, 41, 49, 50, 55, 57, 70, 85, 92, 94, 96, 105, 108, 109, 111, 139, 142, 155, 161, 162, 166, 169, 213, 216
Feintuch, 154, 155, 156
Feisi, 207
Feldman, 96, 256, 257, 258, 273, 274, 277, 342
Feldsheve, 95, 97
Felix, 205
Fesler, 113, 115
Fidel, 4, 342
Fidelman, 217
Fidlman, 311
Fidlman, 345
Figelman, 94, 97, 108, 212
Fimes, 217
Finkelstein, 37, 38, 56, 96, 98, 106, 107, 166, 168, 178, 322
Finklsztajn, 308
Firogov, 52
Fish, 98, 191, 220, 305, 325, 336, 338
Fish, 345
Fishbein, 49, 175, 316
Fishbein, 346
Fisher, 96, 97, 183, 250
Fishkes, 226
Fishman, 4, 54, 55, 85, 89, 90, 91, 92, 104, 107, 108, 278
Fiszbejn, 311
Fiszbejn, 346
Flack, 113
Flanzman, 37, 38
Flaumenbaum, 321
Flederman, 4
Flott, 115
Fogelman, 305, 338
Fogelman, 346
Fogelson, 212
Forshteler, 205, 222
Frankel, 57
Frankfort, 25, 31, 32, 40, 50, 58, 77, 78, 131, 134, 135, 136, 234
Frankfurt, 58, 61, 83, 92, 94, 98, 99, 100, 105, 106, 107, 108, 109, 129, 212, 227, 239, 240, 241, 242, 271
Frankovitch, 341
Frankpovitch, 175
Frantz, 98
Franz–Josef, 69
Freed, 325

Freedman, 260
Freidman, 279
Freisant, 325
Frenrich, 52
Fried, 4, 96, 104, 178, 179, 276, 342
Friedlander, 108, 170, 215, 325
Friedman, 92, 105, 115, 141, 212, 216, 217, 230, 293
Friedrichson, 26
Frishberg, 141, 220, 305
Frishberg, 346
Frishbergs, 69
Frydman, 308
Frydman, 346
Fuchs, 115

G

Gabi, 325
Galman, 250
Galperin, 76, 186, 243
Gandler, 325
Gasco, 150, 186, 220, 340
Gasko, 325
Geler, 309
Geler, 346
Gelfand, 330
Geller, 20, 21, 52, 83, 102, 115, 161, 162, 164, 214, 220, 326
Gelman, 62, 63, 103, 115, 150, 151, 178, 221, 247, 248, 277, 326, 330
Gendler, 105, 207
Gershin, 53
Gershon, 77, 151, 156, 162, 176, 214
Gershoni, 37
Gershonovitz, 83, 102, 205
Gevertzman, 288
Gevirtsman, 162
Gevirtz, 325
Geyer, 182, 184, 186, 330
Gibnet, 304
Gibor, 175
Giladi, 98
Gilberg, 96, 163
Gilboa, 96
Ginsburg, 98
Gitlin, 133
Gitlis, 55, 98, 107, 112, 166, 168, 170, 179, 222, 325, 340
Gittlin, 53
Giwant, 306
Giwant, 346
Glambotsky, 155, 156
Glass, 170, 212
Glaz, 212, 213, 220, 226
Glazer, 115
Glicksman, 236, 237
Goldberg, 4, 61, 72, 73, 75, 76, 148, 150, 151, 219, 223, 234, 250, 341, 342
Goldfaden, 140, 156
Goldman, 325
Goldover, 325
Goldsblatt, 57

Goldschmid, 223
Goldschmidt, 72
Goldshmid, 269, 270
Goldshteyn, 290
Goldsmidt, 221, 222
Goldstein, 4, 56, 72, 74, 76, 96, 107, 162, 168, 278, 280, 297, 298, 313, 325, 343
Goldstein, 346
Goldsztajn, 311
Goldsztajn, 346
Golobner, 338
Goltsblat, 221
Golubchek, 282, 283
Goncharov, 53
Gonick, 325
Gonik, 162, 179, 220
Goodis, 96, 276, 327
Gorali, 4, 340, 343, 344
Gorberg, 67
Gordon, 41, 140, 145, 199
Goren, 74
Gortenstein, 212
Gotlieb, 170
Gottfried, 104
Goutwort, 92, 98
Goz, 38
Gozen, 179, 180
Grabowicer, 234
Granicz, 308
Granovsky, 277
Grau, 52, 215
Grayver, 79, 80
Grazovsky, 53
Greenbaum, 170
Greenberg, 4, 50, 169, 170
Greenblatt, 330, 343
Greenboim, 55, 62, 63
Greiber, 46, 49, 50
Grempler, 141
Grigorovska, 119
Grinberg, 163, 207, 330
Grinstein, 173
Grisha, 74, 114, 115, 214, 324
Grojser, 313
Grojser, 346
Gruber, 98, 106
Gruenbaum, 241
Guberman, 221, 222, 248
Gubermans, 294
Gunik, 263, 264, 265, 266, 267
Gura, 241
Guralnik, 96
Gurberg, 72
Gurfinkel, 83
Gurin, 207
Gurtenstein, 115
Gutcha, 343
Gutchia, 4
Gutenboim, 112, 132, 133, 174
Gutenboym, 161

Gutman, 105, 106, 330, 334
Guttenboim, 78
Guttman, 325
Gvirtzman, 248
Gzebmacher, 69

H

Hadrav, 35
Hager, 98
Hak, 105
Halkin, 331
Halt, 119
Hanasi, 76
Hanich, 49
Haptman, 170
Harpia, 142, 143, 144
Hasis, 113, 321
Hassim, 214
Havkin, 204, 205, 207, 208
Hayat, 205, 212, 226
Hayot, 92, 105, 176, 196
Hazan, 24, 32, 83, 103
Heft, 51
Heinech, 20, 21, 248
Heinich, 83, 161, 162, 170
Heller, 39
Henich, 102, 103
Heri, 175, 325
Herzl, 100, 129, 138
Heshel, 158
Hindes, 53
Hinizon, 216
Hite, 50
Hizhik, 96
Hochberg, 55, 87, 88, 89, 92, 104, 109
Hoder, 268
Hodorov, 35, 41, 42, 96, 110, 114, 169, 182, 183, 185, 186, 187, 192
Hoff, 156
Holder, 94, 97
Hornstein, 119
Horodlitz, 189, 204, 205, 206, 211
Horodsky, 47
Horowitz, 180
Horvitz, 113
Hotchles, 76
Hotman, 111
Hyeh, 76

I

Imber, 248
Ingber, 293
Ingberg, 95
Israelevsky, 97
Israelit, 108

J

Jabotinsky, 48, 62, 171, 329, 330

Jezembecher, 295
Josyfowicz, 16

K

Kaditch, 271
Kaditz, 167, 168, 340
Kagan, 216, 304, 325
Kalonimus, 145
Kaminer, 340
Kaminska, 171
Kaminski, 38
Kamitova, 288, 289
Kanan, 306, 307
Kanan, 346
Kandratovich, 268, 269
Kanter, 76, 102
Kapczyk, 308, 346
Kaploshnick, 34, 35
Kaploshnik, 216
Kaptchuk, 175
Karilov, 134
Karsh, 96
Kartaflia, 263
Kartoflie, 205
Kartoflik, 72
Kasher, 97, 105, 106
Kasner, 258, 259, 263
Kassner, 279, 287, 288
Kastelansky, 84
Kastelnesky, 49, 51
Katz, 289, 298
Katzizna, 191
Kavali, 296
Kazak, 311
Kazak, 346
Kelemet, 9
Kendal, 72
Kerner, 204, 205
Khaitin, 330
Khalat, 141, 155, 156, 234
Khari, 340, 342
Kharon, 71, 83
Khassim, 343
Khayal, 108
Khayat, 72
Khazanov, 222
Khininzon, 105, 106
Kibuk, 162
Kimmel, 156
King Jan Casimir, 12, 13, 46
King Sigismund Augustus, 8, 9, 10
King Sigismund I, 8
King Sigismund Iii, 11
King Władysław Iv, 16
King Władysław Iv, 13
Kipper, 285
Kirshner, 74
Kirszner, 211
Kirzhner, 72

Kishkarnik, 263
Kivok, 141
Kleinberg, 98
Kleiner, 205, 207, 312
Kleiner, 346
Kleinerman, 96, 222
Kleinman, 50
Klerman, 329, 330
Kletzkin, 253
Kloizner, 53
Klomel, 4, 23, 57, 104, 108, 189
Klonitsky, 4, 85, 107, 141, 143, 145, 167, 179, 209, 210, 222, 223
Klorglon, 153
Klorgloz, 167
Klumel, 234, 238
Kobrinski, 56, 238
Kobrinsky, 4, 89, 90, 92, 98, 104, 105, 108, 136, 143, 205, 207
Koc, 241
Kocherski, 12
Kogan, 140, 141
Kolbek, 171, 173, 227
Kolin, 215
Kolkin, 215, 216
Kolonymus, 4
Koltun, 170
Kopchick, 65
Kopelberg, 141, 175, 330, 340
Kopit, 226
Koralnik, 126
Korman, 107
Kosovski, 50
Kosovsky, 69, 70
Kossovsky, 161, 167, 203
Kotovsky, 340
Kotzin, 214
Kovalski, 13, 16
Kovichi, 26
Kovritz, 270
Kowalski, 98
Kowelski, 16
Krakover, 288
Kramer, 52, 215
Krasnolsky, 155
Krause, 174, 330
Krauza, 203
Kravitz, 340, 342
Krazhner, 223
Kreiss, 105
Kremer, 179
Krinsk, 52
Krinsky, 53
Kritz, 205
Krushevan, 165, 222
Kuperberg, 228
Kuptchik, 98, 99, 100, 106
Kuptshik, 77, 78
Kutchinsky, 106
Kutzin, 207, 248

Kuznits, 83
Kwartalny, 16, 18

L

Lachover, 4
Ladrahandler, 115
Lamdan, 142, 143
Landa, 211
Landau, 106, 252, 314, 346
Landau, 346
Lander, 325
Landoi, 260
Landver, 86, 223
Lange, 86
Langer, 169
Lanke, 234
Larmontov, 134
Lavi, 4
Lavrin, 9
Lechel, 205
Lederhandler, 335
Lederman, 216
Leib, 14, 16, 19, 41, 49, 72, 76, 98, 153, 155, 156, 171, 173, 178, 214, 220, 245, 260, 311, 325, 346
Leibenow, 259
Leiberman, 51
Leiberson, 104, 106, 213, 324
Leibnyu, 157, 158
Leibovitch, 4
Leibovitz, 40, 89, 92, 94, 96, 97, 108
Leiner, 210
Lekach, 52, 102, 103
Lekal, 213, 214
Lencz, 314
Lencz, 346
Leoni, 1, 4, 5, 17, 18, 82, 96, 156, 161, 215, 224, 275, 342
Leono, 252
Lermontov, 119
Lerner, 96, 211, 276, 328
Levenberg, 38, 178
Levin, 105, 178, 207, 210, 221, 224, 227, 276, 342
Levinson, 170
Levy, 180, 182, 183, 187
Lewandowsky, 156
Lewertob, 309
Lewertob, 346
Leyer, 92, 98, 100, 106
Liar, 238
Liberman, 83, 106, 308
Licht, 72
Lichtchin, 343
Lifshitz, 96, 162, 221, 222, 248
Lilienblum, 166
Lindenbaum, 74
Lioshtchik, 102
Lipshitz, 49, 50, 115
Lipsker, 109
Lipsky, 83
Lis, 234
Lisenko, 113
Liss, 115, 116, 117, 118, 119, 120, 137, 141, 173, 228
Liublinska, 208
Lobzovsky, 51
Lovoshitzki, 31
Lowny, 75, 77, 78
Lubliner, 175
Lublinsky, 107, 162, 167, 168, 170, 340, 342
Ludmirer, 233, 308, 346
Ludmirer, 346
Luitzki, 50
Lula, 44
Lushchik, 52
Lushik, 257
Lutz, 278, 279

M

M.G., 35
Ma'ze, 83
Mahler, 5, 8
Mailer, 216
Malkin, 170
Malkovski, 12, 13
Mammut, 106
Mandel, 227, 276, 277
Manievitch, 90, 111, 125
Manievits, 108, 109
Manis, 226
Mansovitch, 53
Manthei, 256, 257, 258, 259, 263, 264, 266, 269, 271, 272, 273
Mapo, 53
Marder, 305, 347
Margaliot, 5
Margalit, 19, 58, 112, 179, 204, 340, 342, 343
Margolian, 217
Margolios, 157
Margolis, 227, 247, 248
Margolit, 325
Margulis, 92, 213
Markish, 173, 227
Markiter, 207
Marmelstein, 214
Marx, 87
Masievich, 84
Masir, 216
Mastboim, 171
Matisis, 258
Matysowicz, 14
Mazelas, 113
Meisels, 162
Mekaveh, 38
Melamed, 51, 90, 96, 98, 114, 141, 156, 167, 168, 175, 176, 192, 205, 214, 216, 223, 323, 324, 325
Melnicer, 306, 313
Melnicer, 346
Mendel, 4, 20, 50, 53, 60, 62, 69, 70, 72, 102, 115, 156, 161, 167, 173, 175, 178, 179, 185, 203, 216, 227, 229, 287, 325, 340, 341, 342

Mendele, 129, 222, 227
Mendelstem, 53
Mendl, 346
Mentey, 283, 284, 285, 286
Meriminsky, 109
Mersik, 162
Merzan, 247, 251
Mesalonim, 52
Meshulam, 46
Mikhl, 158
Miller, 71, 72, 83, 113, 162, 164
Milshtein, 205
Milstein, 107, 153, 163
Milsztejn, 315
Milsztejn, 346
Minkovsky, 169
Mirsky, 103, 251
Misheli, 65
Mitzkewicz, 119
Mitzniv, 10
Mokrin, 220, 340, 341
Moliar, 92
Mor, 330
Morgenstern, 5
Moshkitski, 264
Mosteshitsky, 100
Motink, 214
Movshovits, 96
Mundlek, 180
Muqrin, 169
Murik, 156, 248
Mustek, 237

N

Naimark, 141
Nataneli, 31
Natan-Neta, 47
Naymark, 103
Ne'eman, 330
Neimark, 326
Neimdack, 114
Neistat, 334, 336, 338
Netaneli, 4, 40, 94, 97, 101, 108
Neumark, 251
Nicholivna, 113
Nikiporovich, 113
Nimirovsky, 105
Nissenboim, 50
Nitsberg, 161
Nitzberg, 132, 148, 149, 174, 208
Notie, 69
Nymark, 213, 214

O

Ogen, 132
Olitzky, 115, 116, 137, 173, 224
Olshetsky, 205
Opoliner, 325
Oppelind, 115

Orlov, 175
Ositskia, 113
Osiuk, 222
Ovental, 179

P

Paletsky, 278
Palva, 50
Pantorin, 166, 183, 295, 297, 317, 326, 330, 340, 342
Papa, 62, 277
Pearl, 56, 64, 135
Peletz, 92
Pen, 205
Penn, 212
Pentorin, 4
Perel, 245, 250
Perelmuter, 246
Peres, 281
Peretz, 47, 78, 85, 142, 173, 194, 217, 218, 221, 227, 234, 235
Perl, 47, 98, 99, 100, 105, 106, 112, 115, 142, 143, 144, 163, 170, 191, 203, 205, 206, 207, 258, 276, 287, 312, 325, 346
Perlman, 49, 50, 83, 162
Perlmutter, 52, 74, 106, 181, 186, 194, 302, 326
Petkovsky, 244
Petliora, 65
Petrakovski, 115
Petreyev, 82
Pevsner, 97
Pickholtz, 219
Pilkreitz, 105
Pilsudski, 39, 100, 137, 203, 325
Pines, 98
Pinsker, 47, 222
Piodorovich, 113
Pip, 41, 94, 97
Pipovna, 108
Pirogov, 47
Pismesky, 53
Piteta, 317
Piteta, 346
Pladi, 96
Plashtets, 96
Plekhanov, 86, 87
Pliushk, 256
Plott, 325
Pogrebinsky, 5
Pogtash, 115
Polishok, 325
Polishuk, 107, 168, 169, 325
Poliszuk, 316
Poliushko, 169
Polkovnik, 113
Pollack, 316
Pomerantz, 205, 206, 207, 238, 276, 325
Pomeranz, 52, 287
Poran, 246
Porer, 49
Poritsker, 109
Porshtler, 248

Potchter, 217
Poysner, 55
Poyzner, 94, 97
Prager, 163
Prejmovski, 26
Pressper, 262
Previn, 26, 77
Prince Kurbski, 8, 9
Projenski, 23, 76, 152, 153
Projneski, 49, 50
Projnesky, 325
Prosman, 247
Prozhansky, 98, 103, 167, 169, 190, 216
Pruszanski, 234, 309
Pruzansky, 248, 249
Pugatch, 98, 140, 141, 203
Puritsky, 168
Pushkin, 119, 134

Q

Queen Bona, 8, 9, 10

R

Rabainker, 69
Rabiner, 62, 79, 107, 168, 196, 308
Rabiner, 346
Rabinerzon, 216
Rabinowicz, 14, 18
Rabinrazon, 51, 69
Raizin, 133
Rajber, 314, 346
Rajcsztal, 309, 347
Rajcsztal, 347
Rambam, 5, 41, 222
Rapaport, 46, 310
Rapaport, 347
Rapp, 286
Rashish, 170, 177
Rassner, 171
Ratien, 306
Ratnovsky, 214
Ratt, 113
Reichstol, 106, 153, 295, 326, 340
Reider, 149
Reif, 103
Reiner, 142, 143, 221, 222
Reis, 113, 216, 217
Reischtol, 322
Reisisher, 98
Reiss, 94, 97
Reissesher, 282
Reiter, 161
Reiz, 173, 174
Reizel, 37
Reshel, 97
Resnick, 4, 340, 341, 342
Resnik, 4
Retnovisky, 324
Ritov, 170

Rogoff, 4
Roisen, 115
Roitenberg, 258, 262, 264, 326, 340
Roiter, 107, 167, 186, 220, 222, 284, 286
Roizen, 48, 83, 161, 162, 175, 179, 209, 230, 305
Roizen, 347
Rojter, 260, 314
Rojter, 347
Rophe, 276
Rosen, 141
Rosenblatt, 4, 115, 209, 220, 222, 223, 229, 230, 247, 342
Rosenfeld, 98, 100, 122, 123, 124, 125, 126, 127
Rosenstein, 92, 105, 170, 238
Rosensveig, 115
Rosenzweig, 102, 103, 168
Rotenberg, 105, 106
Rotman, 4, 94, 95, 97, 101, 108
Rovner, 85, 96, 154
Rozencwaig, 317
Rozencwaig, 347
Rozenszveig, 312
Rozenszveig, 347
Rozenwald, 315
Rozenwald, 347
Rozin, 52
Rubenstein, 4, 322
Rubinstein, 98, 119, 208, 249, 343
Rudman, 72, 96
Rupa, 325
Ruper, 69
Rusman, 308, 348
Rydz-Śmigły, 241

S

Saba, 39, 40, 64
Saltzman, 107, 167, 168
Samnovitch, 10
Sander, 52
Sanguszko, 8
Sasne, 311
Sass, 115, 248
Satran, 115
Schatz, 213, 214
Schechter, 98, 105, 162, 186
Schecter, 347
Schneersons, 117, 118
Schneider, 248, 288
Schnitzer, 220, 244
Schopenhauer, 132, 133
Schultz, 26, 288
Schwartz, 61, 155, 178, 191, 207, 212, 305, 337, 338, 340
Schwartz, 347
Schwartzberg, 217
Schwartzblat, 74, 107, 150, 168, 220
Seforim, 72
Segal, 37, 38, 72, 73, 92, 96, 105, 141, 179, 186, 208, 311, 316, 317
Segal, 347
Segalovitz, 171

Sehr, 111, 112
Seltzer, 156
Shach, 269
Shafroch, 55, 113
Shainin, 83
Shakespeare, 88
Shalita, 238
Shalom Aleichem, 85, 125, 207, 238
Shamash, 205
Shames, 212
Shapira, 19, 115, 149, 168, 209, 248, 330
Shapiro, 4, 107, 156, 177, 340, 341, 342
Sharboim, 183
Shatz, 205, 207, 274
Shayev, 169, 330
Shbedyuk, 38
Shczupak, 257
Shebtzov, 113
Shechter, 304
Sheert, 325
Sheifelt, 72
Sheinbaum, 191, 227, 338, 339
Sheinboim, 162, 212
Sheintop, 325
Shemshtein, 205, 207
Shemstein, 115
Sher, 182, 183, 255
Shershbeski, 52
Sheynkar, 170, 212, 222, 226
Shik, 49
Shikhman, 330
Shinitzky, 103
Shinkar, 84, 151
Shkolnik, 72
Shmoilovich, 9
Shmulik, 72, 150
Shneur, 20
Shnitzky, 251
Shochat, 64, 219, 220, 250
Shochet, 98, 106, 149, 151
Sholem Aleichem,, 57
Shomstein, 214
Shovelski, 26
Shpitura, 284, 286
Shpruch, 94, 97, 108
Shprung, 98, 106
Shtcharbeta, 175
Shtein, 205
Shteinbach, 220
Shteinman, 205
Shtern, 290
Shtilerman, 219
Shtuper, 273
Shvalba, 183
Shvedron, 133
Singer, 126
Sioma, 38, 317, 347
Sirk, 341
Sirota, 77, 171, 220
Skolnik, 115

Slotzker, 52
Smilensky, 166
Smolanskin, 53
Snervarovski, 26
Sofer, 90, 102, 260, 275
Soibel, 169, 175, 288
Soinuich, 256, 257
Soinyuch, 38
Sokolov, 4, 46, 88, 97, 100
Sokolovsky, 212, 227, 250
Soltis, 292
Soroleh, 304
Sosne, 310
Sosne, 347
Sosnie, 325
Soyfer, 347
Stalin, 252
Stefek, 262
Stein, 212, 330
Steinberg, 53, 90, 105, 150
Steingarten, 222
Steinkrok, 282, 283
Steinman, 217, 250
Sternberg, 92
Stillerman, 305
Stillerman, 347
Stinberg, 115
Stock, 31, 53, 220, 295
Stoliar, 205
Sulzer, 156
Sza, 316
Szer, 310
Szer, 347
Szklarzewicz, 10
Szkolnik, 16
Szoferfin, 75
Szpringer, 234
Szwarc, 309, 310
Szwarc, 347

T

Tabachnik, 103, 238, 251
Tabakhandler, 222
Tabankin, 170
Tabenkin, 61
Tannenbaum, 109
Tannenboim, 317
Tannenboim, 347
Tarn, 234
Tasgal, 310
Tasgal, 347, 348
Taub, 307
Tcharna, 97
Tchernichovsky, 94, 171, 196
Tchernishevskiy, 82
Tchernitsky, 88, 89, 92, 109
Tchernovits, 97
Tchizshik, 142, 144
Tchlin, 178

Teichtel, 155
Teitelkar, 22, 64, 128, 139, 207, 218
Teitleker, 4, 101, 301, 331
Teitlker, 251
Teleroit, 105
Tenenbaum, 98, 340
Tesler, 248
Tessler, 106
Teverski, 238
Toib, 37, 38, 179, 183
Tojbiczow, 348
Tojbiczów, 313
Toker, 152, 244
Toler, 105
Tolier, 209, 210, 219, 220
Toybitsh, 305
Toybitsh, 348
Trager, 103
Trapolowski, 280
Trojanówka, 60
Trotsky, 63, 70
Trumpeldor, 41, 181, 186, 187, 188, 199
Tsachnovitz, 205, 207
Tsal, 155
Tsichnovits, 98, 212
Tsin, 340
Tsitronel, 145
Tslavitch, 161
Tsoref, 153
Tsuker, 96, 162
Tsuperfain, 250
Tsuperfein, 4, 96
Tsurif, 98
Tsvigel, 96, 97, 106, 108
Turkanitch, 51
Turkov, 140, 171
Turnheim, 113
Turskevitch, 151
Turtchin, 342
Tversky, 211, 222
Twerski, 60, 122
Tzavik, 62
Tzeitlin, 53
Tzelvich, 52
Tzernitchki, 55
Tzichnovitz, 213
Tzipris, 156
Tzufrifin, 252
Tzupefein, 72
Tzur, 55, 57
Tzvik, 167, 176

U

Ungerfeld, 4
Ussiskin, 50

V

Vagsholl, 75
Valula, 63, 255
Valular, 51
Vannin, 140
Varba, 31, 214, 324, 326
Vasilivich, 113
Veiger, 103, 326
Veisbrott, 4
Verba, 4, 98, 114, 151, 203
Verbe, 115
Vertzel, 182, 183, 186
Vespasian, 135
Veverik, 150, 151
Vevetzi, 150
Vidra, 156, 205, 213, 295
Vikum, 340, 342
Vikus, 37, 38
Vineberg, 185, 330
Vinter, 4
Virnik, 96
Vitman, 207, 212, 295
Volk, 96
Volman, 205
Volvoler, 96, 168

W

Wajnsztejn, 314, 315
Wajnsztejn, 348
Waks, 105
Waldman, 38, 154
Wanski, 278
Waxman, 217
Weinberg, 52
Weiner, 260, 283, 287, 305
Weiner, 348
Weinfeld, 103, 149
Weinfer, 53
Weingarten, 103
Weinstein, 137, 166, 214, 217
Weintraub, 51, 73, 217, 228, 229
Weis, 205
Weisberg, 214, 324
Weisbrot, 96, 98, 107, 108, 166, 167, 168, 169, 170, 175, 176, 203, 222, 340, 342
Weissbrot, 280
Weitman, 213, 214, 323, 326
Weitz, 153
Welwele, 234
Werba, 108, 110, 111, 112, 152, 153, 172, 176, 221, 341
Werbe, 77
Wexler, 156
Whiteman, 288
Wilhelm Ii, 69
Wilkomirski, 248
Winfeld, 76
Winter, 100, 342
Wirnik, 328, 330
Wisberg, 114
Woff, 153
Wohl, 96
Wolfowicz, 14

Wydra, 315
Wydra, 348

Y

Yaborovski, 322, 323
Yaborovsky, 214
Yafeh, 171
Yaffe, 49
Yagodnik, 63, 115, 151, 156, 217
Yakovovich, 9
Yankelevich, 211
Yechimovitch, 10
Yellin, 330
Yeruchamovitz, 217
Yeruchomovitch, 229
Yohanan Ben Zakai, 135
Yosilov, 83
Yucht, 212
Yudkovitz, 83, 84, 167
Yundof, 330
Yustman, 107, 168

Z

Zackheim, 152, 164
Zafran, 38
Zagorodsky, 53
Zalichneko, 50
Zalman, 14, 20, 83, 89, 92, 94, 96, 133, 219, 246, 270, 274, 340
Zamir, 304, 348
Zatz, 197, 199
Zavitska, 322, 323
Zechindy, 252
Zeidel, 105, 106, 154
Zeidentseig, 92, 97
Zeidenzeig, 113
Zeletz, 271
Zerubbabel, 170
Zeskind, 326
Zev, 55, 56, 88, 92, 98, 100, 109, 151
Zidenzeig, 41
Zilberstein, 325
Zimering, 330
Zimerman, 250
Zin, 265, 330
Zinger, 98
Zingerman, 156
Ziskind, 113, 162, 174, 205, 206, 207, 222, 304, 325
Ziskind, 348
Zisskind, 213
Zokner, 69
Zopperfin, 1
Zuckerman, 326
Zukerman, 107, 190, 330
Zuperpin, 326
Zweiter, 258
Zyskind, 294

www.ingramcontent.com/pod-product-compliance
Lightning Source LLC
Chambersburg PA
CBHW082005150426
42814CB00005BA/232